THE WITNESSES

THIS EDITION has been prepared by members of the Washington Bureau of *The New York Times*, under the direction of Alvin Shuster and including Felix Belair, Jr., John W. Finney, John D. Pomfret, Nan Robertson, Eileen Shanahan and Fendall W. Yerxa.

THE WITNESSES

SELECTED AND EDITED FROM
THE WARREN COMMISSION'S HEARINGS BY
THE NEW YORK TIMES
WITH AN INTRODUCTION BY
ANTHONY LEWIS

McGRAW-HILL BOOK COMPANY

New York · London · Toronto

CONTENTS

III. THE ASSASSIN

IV. THE ASSASSIN'S KILLER

V. THE PRESIDENT'S SAFETY

INTRODUCTION

By Anthony Lewis

"All I remember is seeing my husband, he had this sort of quizzical look on his face, and his hand was up, it must have been his left hand . . . and then he . . . put his hand to his forehead and fell in my lap."

Those were the words of Jacqueline Kennedy to the Commission investigating the murder of her husband, the President of the United States. Their poignant simplicity recalls the first moment of shock for millions of Americans and others at the news of the assassination, and the following hours and days of grief—days that have not ended.

On Nov. 24, 1963, two days after John Kennedy's death in Dallas and a few hours after the murder of the man held as his assassin, Lee Harvey Oswald, James Reston wrote in the New York Times that "private anger and sorrow are not enough to redeem the events of the last few days." He suggested that the country's moral confusion over the assassination and its aftermath would be compounded if the evidence were kept secret. He asked whether "a Presidential or some other objective commission" could not carry out a full inquiry and make its findings public.

On Nov. 29 President Johnson appointed such a body; its formal title was the President's Commission on the Assassination of President John F. Kennedy. Mr. Johnson persuaded Chief Justice Earl Warren to overcome the strongest personal resolve against undertaking any extra-judicial duties and become its chairman. The President charged the Commission "to satisfy itself that the truth is known as far as it can be discovered, and to report its findings and conclusion to him, to the American people and to the world."

The Commission reported on Sept. 27, 1964. The Government Printing Office and private publishers printed the massive report and circulated it around the world. Then, on Nov. 23, a year and a day after the tragedy in Dallas, the Warren Commission took a further and most extraordinary step to inform the public. It published all the evidence that the seven commissioners and their staff had seen and heard.

There were 26 closely-printed volumes, 15 of testimony and 11 of exhibits, a total of more than 17,000 pages. Nothing was withheld except a few phrases omitted on the grounds of taste, and those were carefully indicated: a noteworthy example was the bracketed phrase in the middle of Mrs. Kennedy's testimony, "reference to wounds deleted." It was all there—the horror and the ironies, the majestic and the trivial, the witnesses great and small, reliable and suspect.

Publication of these supporting twenty-six volumes disclosed the remarkable character of the Warren Commission inquiry. Historians could remember no comparably painstaking effort to obtain all the facts immediately after a great national disaster. The Commission's questions to witnesses showed that it had attempted to proceed without preconceptions: the aim *was* "the truth . . . as far as it can be discovered." Men who had served briefly with Lee Harvey Oswald in the Marines, persons who saw him on a bus to Mexico City in September, 1963—the farthest reaches of relevance were explored. And all of the material was presented to the public quietly, without salesmanship.

The scope and completeness of the 26 volumes make them essential documents for the historian and for anyone seeking to appraise for himself the validity of the Warren Commission's central conclusion—that there was no conspiracy of right or left, that the assassination was the work of one unhappy man, Lee Oswald. At the same time, it must be recognized that relatively few persons will have access to the full set, or the time to read it. The purpose of this book, THE WITNESSES, is to present the highlights of the 26 volumes for the general reader.

It is the human drama implicit in the lawyers' questions and the witnesses' answers that will fascinate, even as it chills, most Americans and those abroad who cared about John Kennedy. There is, for example, one small exchange with Kenneth P. O'Donnell, President Kennedy's assistant and friend. He was saying that on the flight back from Dallas to Washington that evening he had sat and talked with Jacqueline Kennedy.

"What did you talk about?" asked a Commission counsel, Arlen Specter.

"We reminisced," Mr. O'Donnell said.

Mrs. Lyndon B. Johnson remembered those long moments in the returning airplane, too. She dictated her recollections into a tape recorder a week after the assassination, and a transcript was provided to the Commission. It is contained in full in this book.

"Mrs. Kennedy's dress was stained with blood," Mrs. Johnson said. "Her right glove was caked—that immaculate woman —it was caked with blood, her husband's blood. She always wore gloves like she was used to them. I never could. Somehow that was one of the most poignant sights—exquisitely dressed and caked in blood. I asked her if I couldn't get someone in to help her change, and she said, 'Oh, no. Perhaps later I'll ask Mary Gallagher, but not right now.' "

At this point one sentence that Mrs. Johnson dictated did not appear in the Commission volume. Some thought the Commission had taken it out; in fact Mrs. Johnson removed it before sending the transcript over, with the evident purpose of avoiding injury to Mrs. Kennedy. But understanding readers will find nothing unnatural or improper in the statement:

"And then with something—if you can say a person that gentle, that dignified, you can say had an element of fierceness —she said, 'I want them to see what they have done to Jack.' "

In this book, no one stands between the witnesses and the reader. The testimony is there as it was given—some calm and dignified, some agitated, some elevated in tone, some coarse or ungrammatical, much steeped in sorrow, some touched with humor. The witnesses range from President Johnson to Karen Bennett Carlin, who under the name "Little Lynn" was a striptease dancer in a Dallas nightclub. In the exhibits and in the testimony one catches glimpses of life on the highest levels of official Washington and on the lowest levels of our urbanized society. There are scenes in the Soviet Union and among Russian expatriates.

THE WITNESSES also gives an insight into the men on the Warren Commission and demonstrates the intensity and comprehensiveness of their working methods. Here is Chief Justice Warren, a friendly, grandfatherly figure to Lee Oswald's Russian-born widow, Marina Oswald, but a relentless questioner of other witnesses. The soft-spoken General Counsel of the Commission, J. Lee Rankin, is flanked by assistants who probe at the corners of the witnesses' testimony. Here in a wry excursion, is a powerful member of the United States Senate, Richard Brevard Russell of Georgia, questioning Marina Oswald about whether husbands beat their wives in the Soviet Union.

The organization of this book necessarily differs from that of the 26 Warren Commission volumes from which it was abstracted. Indeed, the Commission's volumes had no structure except an accidental one of chronology. In the first five volumes was printed the testimony of all those witnesses who appeared before the Warren Commission itself, in the order of their appearance. As it happened, the first witness, heard on Feb. 3, 1964, in Washington, was Marina Oswald. She was also the last, recalled to testify before a Commission hearing in Dallas on Sept. 6, 1964. Transcripts were prepared immediately and scrutinized by the Commission and its staff, which had divided the enormous job into different topics. It was at this stage that the chronological testimony was fitted into more logical categories for use in the Commission's report. Similarly, the next 10 volumes consist of sworn statements and examinations by Commission staff lawyers, rather than the Commission itself, also in chronological order. The 11 exhibit volumes consist of photographs and magazine articles and similar material again arranged in the order it was received.

In selecting the highlights for this book, the editors, following the pattern of the Commission, grouped material under five topics: First, the assassination itself, the circumstances from the planning of the trip to Dallas through the death of the President. Second, the arrest of Lee Oswald and his connections with the fatal shot. Third, the assassin—what brought Oswald to that moment in history. Fourth, the assassin's killer, the story of Jack Ruby. Fifth, the President's safety, the views of experts on why security failed and how it can be improved in future.

This book should be read with the following background of the Warren Commission's own conclusions in mind. The Commission was unanimous in finding that both Oswald and Ruby acted alone, that they had no connection with each other or with any conspiracy. Because legal proceedings against Ruby were not yet concluded, the Commission did not pass on his motives; it explored Oswald's microscopically but came up with no certain answers. It suggested that he had no rational purpose, no motive adequate "if judged by the standards of reasonable men." Rather, the Commission saw Oswald's last terrible act as the product of the entire 24 years of his life—a life "characterized by isolation, frustration and failure."

"Oswald was profoundly alienated from the world in which he lived," the Commission Report said. "He had very few, if any, close relationships with other people and he appeared to have had great difficulty in finding a meaningful place in the world. He was never satisfied with anything. When he was in the United States, he resented the capitalist system. When he was in the Soviet Union, he apparently resented the Communist Party members, who were accorded special privileges and who he thought were betraying communism, and he spoke well of the United States."

As factors that might have led Oswald to the assassination, the Commission listed "his deep-rooted resentment of all authority, which was expressed in a hostility toward every society in which he lived," his "urge to try to find a place in history" and his "avowed commitment to Marxism and communism, as he understood the terms." The report found that he had shot at former Maj. Gen. Edwin A. Walker in Dallas on

April 10, 1963, narrowly missing him, and cited this as evidence of his capacity for violence.

The Commission found that three shots were fired and that two struck President Kennedy. One hit him in the lower back of the neck but would probably not have been fatal. The other tore his skull open. From expert ballistics testimony the Commission concluded that the shots were fired from behind, above and to the right of the President's car—specifically, from the sixth-floor window of the School Book Depository at which a witness, Howard L. Brennan, saw Lee Oswald. Three cartridge cases were found inside that window, as was a 6.5 millimeter Mannlicher-Carcano rifle owned by Oswald. The cartridges and one whole bullet and two fragments recovered could only have been fired from that rifle, the Commission found, again on the basis of expert testimony; Lee Oswald's fingerprints or palmprint were found on the rifle, on a bag in which the Commission found he had brought it to work that day and on a carton next to the window. The report found that he had sufficient rifle ability to hit the target easily at the given distance, 177 to 266 feet, with a telescopic sight and the car moving steadily away from him in a straight line.

In assessing the protection of the President, the Commission was critical of both the Secret Service and the Federal Bureau of Investigation for not taking adequate preventive measures to identify potentially dangerous persons such as Oswald. At the same time, it recognized the great difficulty of the problem. It mentioned such past presidential assassins as Charles Guiteau (who shot Garfield) and Leon Czolgosz (who shot McKinley) and said each "was a failure in his work and in his relations with others, a victim of delusions and fancies which led to the conviction that society and its leaders had combined to thwart him." The Commission concluded that it would "require every available resource of our government to devise a practical system which has any reasonable possibility of revealing such malcontents."

Of Oswald, the report suggested that all his frustrations seemed to come to a climax in the last weeks of his life. His dream of glory in the Soviet Union had collapsed. His efforts to get to Cuba from Mexico had failed. He had a menial job, packing textbooks. His wife ridiculed his political views and complained about his sexual capacity.

"Oswald had an exaggerated sense of his own importance," the Commission said, "but he failed at almost everything he had ever tried to do."

All these themes can be traced in the portions of testimony and exhibits published in this book. Here is Marina Oswald's narrative of her difficult life with a rootless husband; here, on the other hand, are the comments from Dallas neighbors and friends indicating that Marina did not always make life so easy for her husband. Here is the first-hand agony of the motorcade in Dallas. Here also are the macabre incongruities that etch the central tragedy even more deeply.

There was the grim effort of some Dallas officials, still unidentified, to prevent the removal of President Kennedy's body from the hospital until an autopsy had been carried out and some papers signed. Mrs. Kennedy steadfastly refused to leave without the body, and President Johnson would not leave without her.

It was Mr. O'Donnell who bore the burden of this episode, and he was still agitated as he told the Commission about it. He described how he tried unsuccessfully to make the officials understand and then, finally, went ahead and began to wheel the casket through the hospital corridor. A man who seemed to have come from the coroner's office shouted loudly, "You can't do that—you can't leave here now," Mr. O'Donnell said in his testimony. He added coldly: "Nobody paid any attention to him." But even after reaching the plane with the body Mr. O'Donnell worried that some Dallas official would try to keep it from taking off. While President Johnson waited aboard for a judge to arrive so he could take the oath of office, Mr. O'Donnell posted guards at the airport gates and kept the plane's ramp raised to keep Dallas medical officers out.

As always in the turbulence of such an event, memories differ. Mrs. Kennedy and Governor Connally are certain that President Kennedy never said anything after the shots rang out. But Roy H. Kellerman of the Secret Service, who was in the front seat, firmly believes—and he remembers the Boston accent—that the President said, "My God, I am hit."

There are those, even after the Commission's extraordinary labors, who continue to have basic doubts about what happened in Dallas. Some skepticism is understandable; it is so hard to accept unreasoning providence as the author of such deeds. But beyond the mere skeptics there are those who have constructed elaborate conspiracy theories. It is impossible to prove a negative—to prove that there was no conspiracy. About all that can be said is that the Warren Commission went to great lengths to examine all such theories and unanimously found them without substance.

There is, for example, the testimony of Mark Lane, a New York lawyer who has lectured to paying audiences about his view that Oswald could not have been the assassin. The Commission invited him to lay before it all the evidence he had, but Mr. Lane repeatedly declined to testify about various matters. He invoked what he termed the lawyer-client privilege; he had briefly been counsel to Oswald's mother, Mrs. Marguerite Oswald. He also refused to disclose the name of an alleged informant who he said had told him of a meeting in Dallas among Ruby, a right-winger named Bernard Weisman and the Dallas policeman later killed by Oswald, J. D. Tippit. The Commission's examination of Mr. Lane went on and on, but in the end very little of it was relevant.

It is important to reiterate that no one should draw ultimate conclusions about the Warren Commission inquiry on the basis of the highlights provided here from the vast amount of material reviewed by the Commission. Where seven witnesses testified to Oswald's presence at the Tippit killing, only two can be quoted at any length in a book of this scope; where experts laboriously laid the foundation for their medical conclusions, only the most pertinent portions of their testimony are given here. In the 26 full volumes, anyone interested will find a completeness of detail much greater than is ever provided in a criminal trial under our accusatory system of justice.

What THE WITNESSES does provide is more than 300,000 words of the most significant testimony and exhibits, the flavor of the tragedy, a sense of the roads that led to Dallas on Nov. 22. One cannot escape the sensation of fate as one hears Kenneth O'Donnell telling what John Kennedy said to his wife that morning.

"He said that if anybody really wanted to shoot the President of the United States, it was not a very difficult job—all one had to do was get a high building some day with a telescopic rifle, and there was nothing anybody could do to defend against such an attempt on the President's life."

PRESIDENT'S COMMISSION
ON THE
ASSASSINATION OF PRESIDENT KENNEDY

CHIEF JUSTICE EARL WARREN, *Chairman*

SENATOR RICHARD B. RUSSELL　　REPRESENTATIVE GERALD R. FORD
SENATOR
JOHN SHERMAN COOPER　　MR. ALLEN W. DULLES
REPRESENTATIVE HALE BOGGS　　MR. JOHN J. MCCLOY

J. LEE RANKIN, *General Counsel*

Assistant Counsel

FRANCIS W. H. ADAMS　　ALBERT E. JENNER, JR.
JOSEPH A. BALL　　WESLEY J. LIEBELER
DAVID W. BELIN　　NORMAN REDLICH
WILLIAM T. COLEMAN, JR.　　W. DAVID SLAWSON
MELVIN ARON EISENBERG　　ARLEN SPECTER
BURT W. GRIFFIN　　SAMUEL A. STERN
LEON D. HUBERT, JR.　　HOWARD P. WILLENS*

Staff Members

PHILLIP BARSON
EDWARD A. CONROY
JOHN HART ELY
ALFRED GOLDBERG
MURRAY J. LAULICHT
ARTHUR MARMOR
RICHARD M. MOSK
JOHN J. O'BRIEN
STUART POLLAK
ALFREDDA SCOBEY
CHARLES N. SHAFFER, JR.

Biographical information on the Commissioners and the staff can be found in the Commission's *Report*.

---

*Mr. Willens also acted as liaison between the Commission and the Department of Justice.

I. The Assassination

MRS. JOHN F. KENNEDY

Mrs. Kennedy was questioned on June 5, 1964 at her home, 3017 N Street N.W., Washington, D.C. by J. Lee Rankin, general counsel of the Warren commission. Present were Chief Justice Earl Warren, chairman; and Robert F. Kennedy, Attorney General. The testimony lasted 10 minutes:

The Chairman. The Commission will be in order.

Mrs. Kennedy, the Commission would just like to have you say in your own words, in your own way, what happened at the time of the assassination of the President. Mr. Rankin will ask you a few questions, just from the time you left the airport until the time you started for the hospital. And we want it to be brief. We want it to be in your own words and want you to say anything that you feel is appropriate to that occasion.

Would you be sworn, please, Mrs. Kennedy?

Do you solemnly swear that the testimony you give before the Commission will be the truth, the whole truth, and nothing but the truth, so help you God?

A—* I do.

The Chairman. Would you be seated.

Mr. Rankin. State your name for the record.

A—Jacqueline Kennedy.

Mr. Rankin. And you are the widow of the former President Kennedy?

A—That is right.

Mr. Rankin. You live here in Washington?

A—Yes.

Mr. Rankin. Can you go back to the time that you came to Love Field on November 22 and describe what happened there after you landed in the plane?

A—We got off the plane. The then Vice President and Mrs. Johnson were there. They gave us flowers. And then the car was waiting, but there was a big crowd there, all yelling, with banners and everything. And we went to shake hands with them. It was a very hot day. And you went all along a long line. I tried to stay close to my husband and lots of times you get pushed away, you know, people leaning over and pulling your hand. They were very friendly.

And, finally, I don't know how we got back to the car. I think Congressman Thomas somehow was helping me. There was lots of confusion.

---

* Throughout this and the other testimonies in this edition, the witnesses' answers and other remarks are preceded by the symbol "A—".

1

Mr. Rankin. Then you did get into the car. And you sat on the left side of the car, did you, and your husband on your right?

A—Yes.

Mr. Rankin. And was Mrs. Connally——

A—In front of me.

Mr. Rankin. And Governor Connally to your right in the jump seat?

A—Yes.

Mr. Rankin. And Mrs. Connally was in the jump seat?

A—Yes.

Mr. Rankin. And then did you start off on the parade route?

A—Yes.

Mr. Rankin. And were there many people along the route that you waved to?

A—Yes. It was rather scattered going in.

Once there was a crowd of people with a sign saying something like "President Kennedy, please get out and shake our hands, our neighbors said you wouldn't."

Mr. Rankin. Did you?

A—And he stopped and got out. That was, you know, like a little suburb and there were not many crowds. But then the crowds got bigger as you went in.

Mr. Rankin. As you got into the main street of Dallas were there very large crowds on all the streets?

A—Yes.

Mr. Rankin. And you waved to them and proceeded down the street with the motorcade?

A—Yes. And in the motorcade, you know, I usually would be waving mostly to the left side and he was waving mostly to the right, which is one reason you are not looking at each other very much. And it was terribly hot. Just blinding all of us.

Mr. Rankin. Now, do you remember as you turned off of the main street onto Houston Street?

A—I don't know the name of the street.

Mr. Rankin. That is that one block before you get to the Depository Building.

A—Well, I remember whenever it was, Mrs. Connally said, "We will soon be there." We could see a tunnel in front of us. Everything was really slow then. And I remember thinking it would be so cool under that tunnel.

Mr. Rankin. And then do you remember as you turned off of Houston onto Elm right by the Depository Building?

A—Well, I don't know the names of the streets, but I suppose right by the Depository is what you are talking about?

Mr. Rankin. Yes; that is the street that sort of curves as you go down under the underpass.

A—Yes; well, that is when she said to President Kennedy, "You certainly can't say that the people of Dallas haven't given you a nice welcome."

2

Mr. Rankin. What did he say?

A—I think he said—I don't know if I remember it or I have read it, "No, you certainly can't," or something. And you know then the car was very slow and there weren't very many people around.

And then—do you want me to tell you what happened?

Mr. Rankin. Yes; if you would, please.

A—You know, there is always noise in a motorcade and there are always motorcycles besides us, a lot of them back-firing. So I was looking to the left. I guess there was a noise, but it didn't seem like any different noise really because there is so much noise, motorcycles and things. But then suddenly Governor Connally was yelling, "Oh, no, no, no."

Mr. Rankin. Did he turn toward you?

A—No; I was looking this way, to the left, and I heard these terrible noises. You know. And my husband never made any sound. So I turned to the right. And all I remember is seeing my husband, he had this sort of quizzical look on his face, and his hand was up, it must have been his left hand. And just as I turned and looked at him, I could see a piece of his skull and I remember it was flesh colored. I remember thinking he just looked as if he had a slight headache. And I just remember seeing that. No blood or anything.

And then he sort of did this [indicating], put his hand to his forehead and fell in my lap.

And then I just remember falling on him and saying, "Oh, no, no, no," I mean, "Oh, my God, they have shot my husband." And "I love you, Jack," I remember I was shouting. And just being down in the car with his head in my lap. And it just seemed an eternity.

You know, then, there were pictures later on of me climbing out the back. But I don't remember that at all.

Mr. Rankin. Do you remember Mr. Hill coming to try to help on the car?

A—I don't remember anything. I was just down like that.

And finally I remember a voice behind me, or something, and then I remember the people in the front seat, or somebody, finally knew something was wrong, and a voice yelling, which must have been Mr. Hill, "Get to the hospital," or maybe it was Mr. Kellerman, in the front seat. But someone yelling. I was just down and holding him. [Reference to wounds deleted.]

Mr. Rankin. Do you have any recollection of whether there were one or more shots?

A—Well, there must have been two because the one that made me turn around was Governor Connally yelling. And it used to confuse me because first I remembered there were three and I used to think my husband didn't make any sound when he was shot. And Governor Connally screamed. And then I read the other day that it was the same shot that hit them both.

3

But I used to think if I only had been looking to the right, I would have seen the first shot hit him, then I could have pulled him down, and then the second shot would not have hit him. But I heard Governor Connally yelling and that made me turn around, and as I turned to the right my husband was doing this [indicating with hand at neck]. He was receiving a bullet. And those are the only two I remember.

And I read there was a third shot. But I don't know.

Just those two.

Mr. Rankin. Do you have any recollection generally of the speed that you were going, not any precise amount.

A—We were really slowing turning the corner. And there were very few people.

Mr. Rankin. And did you stop at any time after the shots, or proceed about the same way?

A—I don't know, because—I don't think we stopped. But there was such confusion. And I was down in the car and everyone was yelling to get to the hospital and you could hear them on the radio, and then suddenly I remember a sensation of enormous speed, which must have been when we took off.

Mr. Rankin. And then from there you proceeded as rapidly as possible to the hospital, is that right?

A—Yes.

Mr. Rankin. Do you recall anyone saying anything else during the time of the shooting?

A—No; there weren't any words. There was just Governor Connally's. And then I suppose Mrs. Connally was sort of crying and covering her husband. But I don't remember any words.

And there was a big windshield between—you know—I think. Isn't there?

Mr. Rankin. Between the seats.

A—So you know, those poor men in the front, you couldn't hear them.

Mr. Rankin. Can you think of anything more?

The Chairman. No; I think not. I think that is the story and that is what we came for.

We thank you very much, Mrs. Kennedy.

Mr. Rankin. I would just like to ask if you recall Special Agent Kellerman saying anything to you as you came down the street after you turned that corner that you referred to.

A—You mean before the shots?

Mr. Rankin. Yes.

A—Well, I don't, because—you know, it is very hard for them to talk. But I do not remember, just as I don't recall climbing out on the back of the car.

Mr. Rankin. Yes. You have told us what you remember about the entire period as far as you can recall, have you?

A—Yes.

The Chairman. Thank you very much, Mrs. Kennedy.

LYNDON B. JOHNSON

The statement of President Johnson and covering letter:

THE WHITE HOUSE,
Washington, July 10, 1964

The Honorable EARL WARREN,
The Chief Justice of the United States,
Washington, D.C.

MY DEAR MR. CHIEF JUSTICE: I have attempted, in the enclosed statement, to set forth my recollection of the tragic events of November 22, 1963. I am conscious of the limitations of my narrative. I had no opportunity, in the difficult and critical days following the assassination of President Kennedy, to record my impressions. Recollection at this late date is necessarily incomplete.

However, I fully realize the great importance of your task, and I have endeavored, as best I can, to set forth the events and my impressions as they remain in my mind at this time. Although I fear that they will be of little specific use to you, I hope that they may be of some interest.

I hope that you and the members of your Commission, as well as the devoted members of the staff who have worked so long and diligently on this undertaking, will accept my thanks and good wishes.

Sincerely,

LYNDON B. JOHNSON.

[Enclosure.]

[Statement of the President, Lyndon Baines Johnson, concerning the events of November 22, 1963]

Friday morning, November 22, began with a reception in the Longhorn Room of the Hotel Texas, Fort Worth. President and Mrs. Kennedy and Mrs. Johnson and I had spent the night in that hotel. Then, President Kennedy and I went to a parking lot across from the hotel where a speaker's stand had been set up and we addressed a crowd that was gathered there. We then returned to the hotel and had breakfast.

After that, at about 10:30 a.m., we motored to the Fort Worth airfield. Mrs. Johnson and I then went aboard *Air Force II* for the trip to Dallas.

We arrived at Love Field in Dallas, as I remember, just shortly after 11:30 a.m.

Agents Youngblood and Johns and two other agents were with us.

We disembarked from the plane promptly after it came to a stop at Love Field. We were met by a committee of local officials and citizens. After greeting them, Mrs. Johnson and I, together with the special agents, walked over to the area where

President and Mrs. Kennedy would disembark. We were followed by the reception committee.

President Kennedy's plane arrived about 5 or 10 minutes after *Air Force II*. The President and Mrs. Kennedy disembarked and they greeted us and the people in the reception committee.

Then the President and Mrs. Kennedy walked along the fence, shaking hands with people in the crowd that had assembled. Mrs. Johnson and I followed along the fence, greeting people and shaking hands. This took 5 or 10 minutes, as I recall.

Mrs. Johnson, Senator Ralph Yarborough, and I then entered the car which had been provided for us in the motorcade. It was a Lincoln Continental convertible. I think that car was the fourth in the motorcade. We were the second car behind the President's automobile.

The driver of the car in which Mrs. Johnson and I were riding was Hurchel Jacks, who is a member of the Texas State Highway Patrol. Agent Youngblood was sitting next to him in the front seat.

I was sitting behind Agent Youngblood; Mrs. Johnson was next to me; and Senator Yarborough was on the left of the rear seat—that is, just behind the driver.

At first, as we left Love Field and proceeded through the less-populated areas, the crowds were thin. I recall, however, that Mrs. Johnson and I and Senator Yarborough commented upon the good spirit and obvious good wishes of the crowd. As we drove closer to town, the crowds became quite large.

We made several stops as a result of stops by the automobiles ahead of us. I did not get out of the car, but on occasion a few people broke from the crowd and ran over, and I shook hands with several people on these occasions.

The motorcade proceeded down Main Street and then turned right on Houston. It then turned into Elm, which is a block, I believe, beyond the intersection of Main and Houston. The crowd on Elm Street was smaller.

As the motorcade proceeded down Elm Street to the point where the assassination occurred, it was traveling at a speed which I should estimate at 12 or 15 miles an hour.

After we had proceeded a short way down Elm Street, I heard a sharp report. The crowd at this point had become somewhat spotty.

The Vice-Presidential car was then about three car lengths behind President Kennedy's car, with the Presidential followup car intervening.

I was startled by the sharp report or explosion, but I had no time to speculate as to its origin because Agent Youngblood turned in a flash, immediately after the first explosion, hitting me on the shoulder, and shouted to all of us in the back seat to get down. I was pushed down by Agent Youngblood. Al-

6

most in the same moment in which he hit or pushed me, he vaulted over the back seat and sat on me. I was bent over under the weight of Agent Youngblood's body, toward Mrs. Johnson and Senator Yarborough.

I remember attempting to turn my head to make sure that Mrs. Johnson had bent down. Both she and Senator Yarborough had crouched down at Agent Youngblood's command.

At some time in this sequence of events, I heard other explosions. It was impossible for me to tell the direction from which the explosions came.

I felt the automobile sharply accelerate, and in a moment or so Agent Youngblood released me. I ascertained that Mrs. Johnson and Senator Yarborough were all right. I heard Agent Youngblood speaking over his radio transmitter. I asked him what had happened. He said that he was not sure but that he had learned that the motorcade was going to the hospital.

I did not see anything that was going on in and around the President's automobile.

When we arrived at the hospital; Agent Youngblood told me to get out of the car, go into the building, not to stop, and to stay close to him and the other agents. When the car came to a stop, a cordon of agents formed around me, and we walked rapidly into the hospital and then we went into a room there.

Because of the method which Agent Youngblood directed for leaving the car and entering the hospital, I did not see the Presidential car or any of the persons in it.

In the hospital room to which Mrs. Johnson and I were taken, the shades were drawn—I think by Agent Youngblood. In addition to him, two or three other agents were there.

As I remember, we got our first specific report from Emory Roberts, one of the agents from the White House detail. He told us that President Kennedy had been very badly injured and that his condition was quite poor. He said that he thought we should make plans to get back to Washington immediately.

I asked about Governor Connally and was told that he, too, had been shot, but that his wound was not serious. I was told that Mrs. Kennedy and Mrs. Connally were uninjured and that no one else had been hurt.

Mrs. Johnson and I asked if we could see Mrs. Kennedy and Mrs. Connally. Agent Youngblood told me that I could not leave the room, and I followed his direction. Mrs. Johnson was allowed to leave for this purpose.

At some time during these events, Kenneth O'Donnell, Congressman Jack Brooks, Congressman Homer Thornberry, and Cliff Carter came into the room.

It was Ken O'Donnell who, at about 1:20 p.m., told us that the President had died. I think his precise words were, "He's gone." O'Donnell said that we should return to Washington and that we should take the President's plane for this purpose.

I found it hard to believe that this had happened. The whole thing seemed unreal—unbelievable. A few hours earlier, I had breakfast with John Kennedy; he was alive, strong, vigorous. I could not believe now that he was dead. I was shocked and sickened.

When Mr. O'Donnell told us to get on the plane and go back to Washington, I asked about Mrs. Kennedy. O'Donnell told me that Mrs. Kennedy would not leave the hospital without the President's body, and urged again that we go ahead and take *Air Force I* and return to Washington.

I did not want to go and leave Mrs. Kennedy in this situation. I said so, but I agreed that we would board the airplane and wait until Mrs. Kennedy and the President's body were brought aboard the plane.

It is, of course, difficult to convey an accurate impression of the period of time that we were in the hospital room. We were all stunned. I suppose we were in a state of shock and there was no time for the shock to wear off sufficiently so that the magnitude of our personal loss of this great man and good friend could express itself in words or in surface feelings.

I suppose, actually, that the only outlet for the grief that shock had submerged was our sharp, painful, and bitter concern and solicitude for Mrs. Kennedy.

Despite my awareness of the reasons for Mr. O'Donnell's insistence—in which I think he was joined by one or more of the Secret Service agents—that we board the airplane, leave Dallas, and go to Washington without delay, I was determined that we would not return until Mrs. Kennedy was ready, and that we would carry the President's body back with us if she wanted.

We left the room and were ushered by a cordon of agents to cars which were awaiting us. At Agent Youngblood's insistence, I entered one car and Mrs. Johnson another. Agent Youngblood and I were sitting in the back seat and Congressman Thornberry was in the front seat.

As we started away from the hospital, Congressman Albert Thomas came up to the car. He saw Congressman Thornberry —I don't think he saw me—and he asked the Congressman to wait for him. At my direction, the car stopped and picked him up and he sat in the front seat with Congressman Thornberry. I am sure this didn't take as much as a minute. Congressman Thornberry then climbed over and got into the back seat with us.

When we got to the airport, we proceeded to drive to the ramp leading into the plane, and we entered the plane.

We were ushered into the private quarters of the President's plane. It didn't seem right for John Kennedy not to be there. I told someone that we preferred for Mrs. Kennedy to use these quarters.

Shortly after we boarded the plane, I called Robert Kennedy, the President's brother and the Attorney General. I knew how grief-stricken he was, and I wanted to say something that would comfort him. Despite his shock, he discussed the practical problems at hand—problems of special urgency because we did not at that time have any information as to the motivation of the assassination or its possible implications. The Attorney General said that he would like to look into the matter of whether the oath of office as President should be administered to me immediately or after we returned to Washington, and that he would call back.

I thereafter talked with McGeorge Bundy and Walter Jenkins, both of whom urged that the return to Washington should not be delayed. I told them I was waiting for Mrs. Kennedy and for the President's body to be placed on the plane, and would not return prior to that time.

As I remember, our conversation was interrupted to allow the Attorney General to come back on the line. He said that the oath should be administered to me immediately, before taking off for Washington, and that it should be administered by a judicial officer of the United States. Shortly thereafter, the Deputy Attorney General, Mr. Katzenbach, dictated the form of oath to one of the secretaries aboard the plane.

I thought of Sarah Hughes, an old friend who is judge of the U.S. district court in Dallas. We telephoned Judge Hughes' office. She was not there, but she returned the call in a few minutes and said she would be at the airplane in 10 minutes. I asked that arrangements be made to permit her to have access to the airplane.

A few minutes later Mrs. Kennedy and the President's coffin arrived. Mrs. Johnson and I spoke to her. We tried to comfort her, but our words seemed inadequate. She went into the private quarters of the plane. I estimate that Mrs. Kennedy and the coffin arrived about a half hour after we entered the plane—just after 2 o'clock.

About a half hour later, I asked someone to find out if Mrs. Kennedy would stand with us during the administration of the oath. Mrs. Johnson went back to be with her. Mrs. Kennedy came and stood with us during the moments that the oath was being administered.

I shall never forget her bravery, nobility, and dignity.

I'm told that the oath was administered at 2:40 p.m. Mrs. Johnson and Mrs. Kennedy were at my side as Judge Hughes administered the oath of office.

The plane took off promptly after the swearing-in ceremonies. I then called President Kennedy's mother, Mrs. Rose Kennedy. She had previously been advised of the assassination. I told her of our grief and of our sorrow for her. I gave the telephone to Mrs. Johnson, who also tried to bring a word of comfort to the President's mother. I then called Nellie Connally, the Governor's wife, and told her of our concern for her and John, and tried to give her some comfort.

I then asked General Clifton, the military aide to the President, to call McGeorge Bundy in Washington to instruct him to ask the Cabinet members who were on their way to Japan to return immediately.

When we landed at the Andrews Air Force Base, I made a short statement for the press, radio, and television. In my heart, I asked for God's help that I should not prove unworthy of the responsibility which fate had thrust upon me.

LYNDON B. JOHNSON.

MRS. LYNDON B. JOHNSON

The statement of Mrs. Lyndon B. Johnson and covering letter:

THE WHITE HOUSE,
Washington, July 16, 1964.

The Honorable EARL WARREN,
The Chief Justice of the United States,
Washington, D.C.

MY DEAR MR. CHIEF JUSTICE: Mr. Lee Rankin, chief counsel to the President's Commission on the Assassination of President Kennedy, has advised me that the Commission would be interested to have a statement from me concerning my recollection of the events of November 22, 1963.

Beginning on November 30, and as I found time on the following 2 days, I dictated my recollection of that fateful and dreadful day on a small tape recorder which I had at The Elms, where we were then living. I did this primarily as a form of therapy—to help me over the shock and horror of the experience of President Kennedy's assassination. I did not intend that the tape should be used.

The quality of the tape recording is very poor, but upon considering your Commission's request, I decided to ask that the tape relating to November 22 be transcribed. I am sending the transcription to you with only a few, minor corrections. Perhaps it will serve your purposes. I hope so. In any event, it is a more faithful record of my recollection and impressions than I could produce at this late date.

Please accept, for yourself and the members of the Commission and its staff, my thanks and best wishes for the important task which you have undertaken and to which all of you have so generously dedicated yourselves.

Sincerely,

(S)   Lady Bird Johnson,
MRS. LYNDON B. JOHNSON.

[Enclosure.]

[Transcript from Mrs. Johnson's tapes relating to November 22, 1963]

10

It all began so beautifully. After a drizzle in the morning, the sun came out bright and beautiful. We were going into Dallas. In the lead car, President and Mrs. Kennedy, John and Nellie, and then a Secret Service car full of men, and then our car—Lyndon and me and Senator Yarborough. The streets were lined with people—lots and lots of people—the children all smiling; placards, confetti; people waving from windows. One last happy moment I had was looking up and seeing Mary Griffith leaning out of a window waving at me. Mary for many years had been in charge of altering the clothes which I purchased at a Dallas store.

Then almost at the edge of town, on our way to the Trade Mart where we were going to have the luncheon, we were rounding a curve, going down a hill, and suddenly there was a sharp loud report—a shot. It seemed to me to come from the right, above my shoulder, from a building. Then a moment and then two more shots in rapid succession. There had been such a gala air that I thought it must be firecrackers or some sort of celebration. Then, in the lead car, the Secret Service men were suddenly down. I heard over the radio system, "Let's get out of here," and our Secret Service man who was with us, Ruf Youngblood, I believe it was, vaulted over the front seat on top of Lyndon, threw him to the floor, and said, "Get down."

Senator Yarborough and I ducked our heads. The car accelerated terrifically fast—faster and faster. Then suddenly they put on the brakes so hard that I wondered if they were going to make it as we wheeled left and went around the corner. We pulled up to a building. I looked up and saw it said "Hospital." Only then did I believe that this might be what it was. Yarborough kept on saying in an excited voice, "Have they shot the President?" I said something like, "No; it can't be."

As we ground to a halt—we were still the third car—Secret Service men began to pull, lead, guide, and hustle us out. I cast one last look over my shoulder and saw, in the President's car, a bundle of pink, just like a drift of blossoms, lying on the back seat. I think it was Mrs. Kennedy lying over the President's body. They led us to the right, the left, and onward into a quiet room in the hospital—a véry small room. It was lined with white sheets, I believe.

People came and went—Kenny O'Donnell, Congressman Thornberry, Congressman Jack Brooks. Always there was Ruf right there, Emory Roberts, Jerry Kivett, Lem Johns, and Woody Taylor. There was talk about where we would go— back to Washington, to the plane, to our house. People spoke of how widespread this may be. Through it all, Lyndon was remarkably calm and quiet. Every face that came in, you searched for the answers you must know. I think the face I kept seeing it on was the face of Kenny O'Donnell, who loved him so much.

11

It was Lyndon as usual who thought of it first, although I wasn't going to leave without doing it. He said, "You had better try to see if you can see Jackie and Nellie." We didn't know what had happened to John. I asked the Secret Service men if I could be taken to them. They began to lead me up one corridor, back stairs, and down another. Suddenly I found myself face to face with Jackie in a small hall. I think it was right outside the operating room. You always think of her—or someone like her—as being insulated, protected; she was quite alone. I don't think I ever saw anyone so much alone in my life. I went up to her, put my arms around her, and said something to her. I'm sure it was something like, "God, help us all," because my feelings for her were too tumultuous to put into words.

And then I went in to see Nellie. There it was different because Nellie and I have gone through so many things together since 1938. I hugged her tight and we both cried and I said, "Nellie, it's going to be all right." And Nellie said, "Yes; John's going to be all right." Among her many other fine qualities, she is also tough.

Then I turned and went back to the small white room where Lyndon was. Mr. Kilduff and Kenny O'Donnell were coming and going. I think it was from Kenny's face and Kenny's voice that I first heard the words, "The President is dead." Mr. Kilduff entered and said to Lyndon, "Mr. President."

It was decided that we would go immediately to the airport. Quick plans were made about how to get to the car, who to ride in what. It was Lyndon who said we should go to the plane in unmarked cars. Getting out of the hospital into the cars was one of the swiftest walks I have ever made. We got in. Lyndon said to stop the sirens. We drove along as fast as we could. I looked up at a building and there already was a flag at half-mast. I think that is when the enormity of what had happened first struck me.

When we got to the airplane, we entered airplane No. 1 for the first time. There was a TV set on, and the commentator was saying, "Lyndon B. Johnson, now President of the United States." They were saying they had a suspect. They were not sure he was the assassin. The President had been shot with a 30–30 rifle. On the plane, all the shades were lowered. Lyndon said that we were going to wait for Mrs. Kennedy and the coffin. There was discussion about when Lyndon should be sworn in as President. There was a telephone call to Washington—I believe to the Attorney General. It was decided that he should be sworn in in Dallas as quickly as possible because of international implications, and because we did not know how widespread this incident was as to intended victims. Judge Sarah Hughes, a Federal judge in Dallas—and I am glad it was she—was called to come in a hurry.

Mrs. Kennedy had arrived by this time and the coffin, and

there—in the very narrow confines of the plane with Jackie on his left with her hair falling in her face, but very composed, and then Lyndon, and I was on his right, Judge Hughes with the Bible in front of her and a cluster of Secret Service people and Congressmen we had known for a long time—Lyndon took the oath of office.

It's odd at a time like that the little things that come to your mind and a moment of deep compassion you have for people who are really not at the center of the tragedy. I heard a Secret Service man say in the most desolate voice and I hurt for him, "We never lost a President in the Service," and then Police Chief Curry, of Dallas, came on the plane and said to Mrs. Kennedy, "Mrs. Kennedy, believe me, we did everything we possibly could."

We all sat around the plane. We had at first been ushered into the main private Presidential cabin on the plane—but Lyndon quickly said, "No, no" and immediately led us out of there; we felt that is where Mrs. Kennedy should be. The casket was in the hall. I went in to see Mrs. Kennedy and, though it was a very hard thing to do, she made it as easy as possible. She said things like, "Oh, Lady Bird, it's good that we've always liked you two so much." She said, "Oh, what if I had not been there? I'm so glad I was there." I looked at her. Mrs. Kennedy's dress was stained with blood. Her right glove was caked—that immaculate woman—it was caked with blood, her husband's blood. She always wore gloves like she was used to them. I never could. Somehow that was one of the most poignant sights—exquisitely dressed and caked in blood. I asked her if I couldn't get someone in to help her change, and she said, "Oh, no. Perhaps later I'll ask Mary Gallagher, but not right now."

She said a lot of other things, like, "What if I had not been there? Oh, I'm so glad I was there," and a lot of other things that made it so much easier for us. "Oh, Lady Bird, we've always liked you both so much." I tried to express something of how we felt. I said, "Oh, Mrs. Kennedy, you know we never even wanted to be Vice President and now, dear God, it's come to this." I would have done anything to help her, but there was nothing I could do to help her, so rather quickly I left and went back to the main part of the airplane where everyone was seated.

The ride to Washington was silent, strained—each with his own thoughts. One of mine was something I had said about Lyndon a long time ago—that he's a good man in a tight spot. I even remember one little thing he said in that hospital room, "Tell the children to get a Secret Service man with them."

Finally, we got to Washington, with a cluster of people watching. Many bright lights. The casket went off first; then Mrs. Kennedy. The family had come to join them, and then we followed. Lyndon made a very simple, very brief, and—I

13

think—strong, talk to the folks there. Only about four sentences, I think. We got in cars; we dropped him off at the White House, and I came home.

RALPH W. YARBOROUGH

The following affidavit was executed by Senator Yarborough of Texas on July 10, 1964.

PRESIDENT'S COMMISSION
ON THE ASSASSINATION OF   AFFIDAVIT
PRESIDENT JOHN F. KENNEDY

DISTRICT OF COLUMBIA, *ss:*

In response to the oral request of one of the attorneys for the Commission that I send you an affidavit for inclusion in the record of the assassination of President John F. Kennedy, I make the following statement:

On November 22, 1963, as the President and Mrs. Kennedy rode through the streets of Dallas, I was in the second car behind them. The first car behind the Presidential car was the Secret Service car; the second car behind them was Vice-President Lyndon Johnson's car. The driver and a secret service agent were on the front seat of the Vice-President's car. Vice-President Lyndon B. Johnson sat on the right side of the rear seat of the automobile, Mrs. Lyndon B. Johnson was in the center of the rear seat, while I sat on the left side of the rear seat.

After the Presidential motorcade had passed through the heart of downtown Dallas, experiencing an exceptionally warm and friendly greeting, as the motorcade went down the slope of Elm Street toward the railroad underpass, a rifle shot was heard by me; a loud blast, close by. I have handled firearms for fifty year, and thought immediately that it was a rifle shot. When the noise of the shot was heard, the motorcade slowed to what seemed to me a complete stop (though it could have been a near stop). After what I took to be about three seconds, another shot boomed out, and after what I took to be one-half the time between the first and second shots (calculated now, this would have put the third shot about one and one-half seconds after the second shot—by my estimate—to me there seemed to be a long time between the first and second shots, a much shorter time between the second and third shots—these were my impressions that day), a third shot was fired. After the third shot was fired, but only after the third shot was fired, the cavalcade speeded up, gained speed rapidly, and roared away to the Parkland Hospital.

I heard three shots and no more. All seemed to come from my right rear. I saw people fall to the ground on the embankment to our right, at about the time of or after the second shot, but before the cavalcade started up and raced away.

Due to the second car, with the secret service men standing on steps on the sides of it, I could not see what was happening in the Presidential car during the shooting itself. Some of the secret service men looked backward and to the right, in the general direction from which the rifle explosions seemed to come.

After the shooting, one of the secret service men sitting down in the car in front of us pulled out an automatic rifle or weapon and looked backward. However, all of the secret service men seemed to me to respond very slowly, with no more than a puzzled look. In fact, until the automatic weapon was uncovered, I had been lulled into a sense of false hope for the President's safety, by the lack of motion, excitement, or apparent visible knowledge by the secret service men, that anything so dreadful was happening. Knowing something of the training that combat infantrymen and Marines receive, I am amazed at the lack of instantaneous response by the Secret Service, when the rifle fire began. I make this statement in this paragraph reluctantly, not to add to the anguish of anyone, but it is my firm opinion, and I write it out in the hope that it might be of service in the better protection of our Presidents in the future.

After we went under the underpass, on the upward slope I could see over the heads of the occupants of the second car (Secret Service car) and could see an agent lying across the back or trunk of the Presidential car, with his feet to the right side of the car, his head at the left side. He beat the back of the car with one hand, his face contorted by grief, anguish, and despair, and I knew from that instant that some terrible loss had been suffered.

On arrival at the hospital, I told newsmen that three rifle shots had been fired. There was then no doubt in my mind that the shots were rifle shots, and I had neither then or now any doubts that any other shots were fired. In my opinion only three shots were fired.

The attached photograph from pages 24 and 25 of the *Saturday Evening Post* of December 14, 1963, shows the motorcade, as I remember it, an instant after the first shot. [Photograph is Yarborough Exhibit A.]

Given and sworn to this 10th day of July, 1964, at Washington, District of Columbia.

Signed this 10th day of July 1964.

> (S)   Ralph W. Yarborough,
> RALPH W. YARBOROUGH.

JOHN B. CONNALLY, JR.

The testimony of the Governor of Texas:
With Dr. Robert R. Shaw and Dr. Charles F. Gregory of Parkland Memorial Hospital present.

Mr. Specter. Well, just a very brief picture leading up to the trip, Governor, starting with whatever point you think would be most appropriate to give some outline of the origin of the trip.

A—Well, it had been thought that he should come to Texas for a period of many months, as a matter of fact. There was some thought given to it during 1962. The trip kept being delayed.

Finally in the fall of 1963 it was decided that he definitely should come, or should come in the fall of last year as opposed to waiting until this year, when his appearance might have more political overtones.

So I came up, I have forgotten the exact date, around the middle of October and talked to him about it, discussed the details, asked him what he would like to do.

He said he would like to do whatever he could do that was agreeable with me; it was agreeable with me that he more or less trust me to plan the trip for him, to tell him where he would like to go. About that time some thought was being given to having four fundraising dinners. His attitude on that was he wouldn't prefer that. He felt that the appearances would not be too good, that he would much prefer to have one if we were going to have any. I told him this was entirely consistent with my own thoughts. We ought not to have more than one fundraising dinner. If we did, it ought to be in Austin. If we could do it, I would like for him to see and get into as many areas of the State as possible while he was there.

He, on his own, had made a commitment to go to the dinner for Congressman Albert Thomas, which was being given the night of the 21st in Houston, so shortly, really before he got there, and when I say shortly I would say 2 weeks before he came, the plans were altered a little bit in that he landed originally in San Antonio in the afternoon about 1:30 of the afternoon of the 21st. From there we went to Houston, attended the Thomas dinner that night at about 8 o'clock.

After that we flew to Fort Worth, spent the night at the Texas Hotel, had a breakfast there the next morning, and left about 10 o'clock, 10:30, for the flight over to Dallas. . . .

Mr. Specter. What was the relative height of the jump seats, Governor, with respect to the seat of the President and Mrs. Kennedy immediately to your rear?

A—They were somewhat lower. The back seat of that particular Lincoln limousine, which is a specially designed and built automobile, as you know, for the President of the United States, has an adjustable back seat. It can be lowered or raised. I would say the back seat was approximately 6 inches higher than the jump seats on which Mrs. Connally and I sat.

Mr. Specter. Do you know for certain whether or not the movable back seat was elevated at the time?

A—No; I could not be sure of it, although I know there

16

were—there was a time or two when he did elevate it, and I think beyond question on most of the ride in San Antonio, Fort Worth, Houston, and Dallas, it was elevated. For a while—the reason I know is—I sat on the back seat with him during part of the ride, particularly in San Antonio, not in Dallas, but in San Antonio. The wind was blowing, and we were traveling fairly fast, and Mrs. Kennedy preferred to sit on the jump seat, and I was sitting on the back seat part of the time, and the seat was elevated, and I think it was on substantially all the trip.

Mr. Specter. Was the portion elevated, that where only the President sat?

A—No; the entire back seat.

Mr. Specter. Describe in a general way the size and reaction of the crowd on the motorcade route, if you would, please, Governor?

A—When we got into Dallas, there was quiet a large crowd at the airport to greet their President, I would say several thousand people.

Part way downtown, in the thinly populated areas of Dallas, where we traveled, the crowds were not thick and were somewhat restrained in their reaction. By restrained, I mean they were not wildly enthusiastic, but they were grown people. There was a mature crowd as we went through some of the residential areas. They applauded and they were obviously very friendly in their conduct.

But as we, of course, approached downtown, the downtown area of Dallas, going down the main street, the crowds were tremendous. They were stacked from the curb and even outside the curb, back against the back walls. It was a huge crowd. I would estimate there were 250,000 people that had lined the streets that day as we went down.

The further you went the more enthusiastic the response was, and the reception. It was a tremendous reception, to the point where just as we turned on Houston Street off of Main, and turned on Houston, down by the courthouse, Mrs. Connally remarked to the President, "Well, Mr. President, you can't say there aren't some people in Dallas who love you." And the President replied, "That is very obvious," or words to that effect.

So I would say the reception that he got in Dallas was equal to, if not more, enthusiastic than those he had received in Fort Worth, San Antonio, and Houston.

Mr. Specter. Are there any other conversations which stand out in your mind on the portion of the motorcade trip through Dallas itself?

A—No; actually we had more or less desultory conversation as we rode along. The crowds were thick all the way down on both sides, and all of us were, particularly the President and Mrs. Kennedy were, acknowledging the

17

crowds. They would turn frequently, smiling, waving to the people, and the opportunity for conversation was limited. . . .

Mr. Specter. Did the automobile stop at any point during this procession?

A—Yes; it did. There were at least two occasions on which the automobile stopped in Dallas and, perhaps, a third. There was one little girl, I believe it was, who was carrying a sign saying, "Mr. President, will you please stop and shake hands with me," or some—that was the import of the sign, and he just told the driver to stop, and he did stop and shook hands, and, of course, he was immediately mobbed by a bunch of youngsters, and the Secret Service men from the car following us had to immediately come up and wedge themselves in between the crowd and the car to keep them back away from the automobile, and it was a very short stop.

At another point along the route, a Sister, a Catholic nun, was there, obviously from a Catholic school, with a bunch of little children, and he stopped and spoke to her and to the children; and I think there was one other stop on the way downtown, but I don't recall the precise occasion. But I know there were two, but I think there was still another one. . . .

Mr. Specter. As to the comment which Mrs. Connally had made to President Kennedy which you just described, where on the motor trip was that comment made, if you recall?

A—This was just before we turned on Elm Street, after we turned off of Main.

Mr. Specter. Onto Houston?

A—Onto Houston, right by the courthouse before we turned left onto Elm Street, almost at the end of the motor-cade, and almost, I would say, perhaps a minute before the fatal shooting.

Mr. Specter. What was the condition of the crowd at that juncture of the motorcade, sir?

A—At that particular juncture, when she made this re-mark, the crowd was still very thick and very enthusiastic. It began to thin immediately after we turned onto Elm Street. We could look ahead and see that the crowd was beginning to thin along the banks, just east, I guess of the overpass.

Mr. Specter. Was there any difficulty in hearing such a conversational comment?

A—No, no; we could talk without any, and hear very clearly, without any difficulty, without any particular strain. We didn't do it again because in trying to carry on a conversation it would be apparent to those who were the spectators on the sidewalk, and we didn't want to leave the impression we were not interested in them, and so we just didn't carry on a conversation, but we could do so without any trouble.

Mr. Specter. As the automobile turned left onto Elm from Houston, what did occur there, Governor?

18

A—We had—we had gone, I guess, 150 feet, maybe 200 feet, I don't recall how far it was, heading down to get on the freeway, the Stemmons Freeway, to go out to the hall where we were going to have lunch and, as I say, the crowds had begun to thin, and we could—I was anticipating that we were going to be at the hall in approximately 5 minutes from the time we turned on Elm Street.

We had just made the turn, well, when I heard what I thought was a shot. I heard this noise which I immediately took to be a rifle shot. I instinctively turned to my right because the sound appeared to come from over my right shoulder, so I turned to look back over my right shoulder, and I saw nothing unusual except just people in the crowd, but I did not catch the President in the corner of my eye, and I was interested, because once I heard the shot in my own mind I identified it as a rifle shot, and I immediately—the only thought that crossed my mind was that this is an assassination attempt.

So I looked, failing to see him, I was turning to look back over my left shoulder into the back seat, but I never got that far in my turn. I got about in the position I am in now facing you, looking a little bit to the left of center, and then I felt like someone had hit me in the back.

Mr. Specter. What is the best estimate that you have as to the time span between the sound of the first shot and the feeling of someone hitting you in the back which you just described?

A—A very, very brief span of time. Again my trend of thought just happened to be, I suppose along this line, I immediately thought that this—that I had been shot. I knew it when I just looked down and I was covered with blood, and the thought immediately passed through my mind that there were either two or three people involved or more in this or someone was shooting with an automatic rifle. These were just thoughts that went through my mind because of the rapidity of these two, of the first shot plus the blow that I took, and I knew I had been hit, and I immediately assumed, because of the amount of blood, and, in fact, that it had obviously passed through my chest, that I had probably been fatally hit.

So I merely doubled up, and then turned to my right again and began to—I just sat there, and Mrs. Connally pulled me over to her lap. She was sitting, of course, on the jump seat, so I reclined with my head in her lap, conscious all the time, and with my eyes open; and then, of course, the third shot sounded, and I heard the shot very clearly. I heard it hit him. I heard the shot hit something, and I assumed again—it never entered my mind that it ever hit anybody but the President. I heard it hit. It was a very loud noise, just that audible, very clear.

Immediately I could see on my clothes, my clothing, I could

19

see on the interior of the car which, as I recall, was a pale blue, brain tissue, which I immediately recognized, and I recall very well, on my trousers there was one chunk of brain tissue as big as almost my thumb, thumbnail, and again I did not see the President at any time either after the first, second, or third shots, but I assumed always that it was he who was hit and no one else.

I immediately, when I was hit, I said, "Oh, no, no, no." And then I said, "My God, they are going to kill us all." Nellie, when she pulled me over into her lap—

Mr. Specter. Nellie is Mrs. Connally?

A—Mrs. Connally. When she pulled me over into her lap, she could tell I was still breathing and moving, and she said, "Don't worry. Be quiet. You are going to be all right." She just kept telling me I was going to be all right.

After the third shot, and I heard Roy Kellerman tell the driver, "Bill, get out of line." And then I saw him move, and I assumed he was moving a button or something on the panel of the automobile, and he said, "Get us to a hospital quick." I assumed he was saying this to the patrolman, the motorcycle police who were leading us.

At about that time, we began to pull out of the cavalcade, out of the line, and I lost consciousness and didn't regain consciousness until we got to the hospital. . . .

Governor, you have described hearing a first shot and a third shot. Did you hear a second shot?

A—No; I did not.

Mr. Specter. What is your best estimate as to the timespan between the first shot which you heard and the shot which you heretofore characterized as the third shot?

A—It was a very brief span of time; oh, I would have to say a matter of seconds. I don't know, 10, 12 seconds. It was extremely rapid, so much so that again I thought that whoever was firing must be firing with an automatic rifle because of the rapidity of the shots; a very short period of time.

Mr. Specter. What was your impression then as to the source of the shot?

A—From back over my right shoulder which, again, was where immediately when I heard the first shot I identified the sound as coming back over my right shoulder.

Mr. Specter. At an elevation?

A—At an elevation. I would have guessed at an elevation.

Mr. Specter. Excuse me.

A—Well, that is all.

Mr. Specter. Did you have an impression as to the source of the third shot?

A—The same. I would say the same. . . .

Mr. Specter. Did President Kennedy make any statement during the time of the shooting or immediately prior thereto?

A—He never uttered a sound at all that I heard.

Mr. Specter. Did Mrs. Kennedy state anything at that time?

A—Yes; I have to—I would say it was after the third shot when she said, "They have killed my husband."

Mr. Specter. Did she say anything more?

A—Yes; she said, I heard her say one time, "I have got his brains in my hand."

Mr. Specter. Did that constitute everything that she said at that time?

A—That is all I heard her say.

Mr. Specter. Did Mrs. Connally say anything further at this time?

A—All she said to me was, after I was hit when she pulled me over in her lap, she said, "Be quiet, you are going to be all right. Be still, you are going to be all right." She just kept repeating that. . . .

Mr. Specter. Did you observe any reaction by President Kennedy after the shooting?

A—No; I did not see him.

Mr. Specter. Did you observe any reaction by Mrs. Kennedy after the shooting?

A—I did not see her. This almost sounds incredible, I am sure, since we were in the car with them. But again I will repeat very briefly when what I believe to be the shot first occurred, I turned to my right, which was away from both of them, of course, and looked out and could see neither, and then as I was turning to look into the back seat where I would have seen both of them, I was hit, so I never completed the turn at all, and I never saw either one of them after the firing started, and, of course, as I have testified, then Mrs. Connally pulled me over into her lap and I was facing forward with my head slightly turned up to where I could see the driver and Roy Kellerman on his right, but I could not see into the back seat, so I didn't see either one of them.

Mr. Specter. When you turned to your right, Governor Connally, immediately after you heard the first shot, what did you see on that occasion?

A—Nothing of any significance except just people out on the grass slope. I didn't see anything that was out of the ordinary, just saw men, women, and children.

Mr. Specter. Do you have any estimate as to the distance which the President's automobile traveled during the shooting?

A—No; I hadn't thought about it, but I would suppose in 10 to 12 seconds, I suppose you travel a couple of hundred feet.

Mr. Specter. Did you observe any bullet or fragments of bullet strike the windshield?

A—No.

Mr. Specter. Did you observe any bullet or fragments of bullet strike the metal chrome?

A—No.

Mr. Specter. Did you experience any sensation of being

struck any place other than that which you have described on your chest?

A—No.

Mr. Specter. What other wounds, if any, did you sustain?

A—A fractured wrist and a wound in the thigh, just above the knee.

Mr. Specter. What thigh?

A—Left thigh; just above the knee.

Mr. Specter. Where on the wrist were you injured, sir?

A—I don't know how you describe it.

Mr. Specter. About how many inches up from the wrist joint?

A—I would say an inch above the wrist bone, but on the inner bone of the wrist where the bullet went in here and came out almost in the center of the wrist on the underside.

Mr. Specter. About an inch from the base of the palm?

A—About an inch from the base of the palm, a little less than an inch, three-quarters of an inch.

Mr. Specter. Were you conscious of receiving that wound on the wrist at the time you sustained it?

A—No, sir: I was not.

Mr. Specter. When did you first know you were wounded in the right wrist?

A—When I came to in the hospital on Saturday, the next morning, and I looked up and my arm was tied up in a hospital bed, and I said, "What is wrong with my arm?" And they told me then that I had a shattered wrist, and that is when I also found out I had a wound in the thigh.

Mr. Specter. Can you describe the nature of the wound in the thigh?

A—Well, just a raw, open wound, looked like a fairly deep penetration.

Mr. Specter. Indicating about 2 inches?

A—No; I would say about an inch, an inch and a quarter long is all; fairly wide, I would say a quarter of an inch wide, maybe more, a third of an inch wide, and about an inch and a quarter, an inch and a half long.

Mr. Specter. Were you conscious that you had been wounded on the left thigh at the time it occurred?

A—No.

Mr. Specter. Did you first notice that in the hospital on the following day also?

A—Yes.

Mr. Specter. In your view, which bullet caused the injury to your chest, Governor Connally?

A—The second one.

Mr. Specter. And what is your reason for that conclusion, sir?

A—Well, in my judgment, it just couldn't conceivably have been the first one because I heard the sound

22

of the shot. In the first place, I don't know anything about the velocity of this particular bullet, but any rifle has a velocity that exceeds the speed of sound, and when I heard the sound of that first shot, that bullet had already reached where I was, or it had reached that far, and after I heard that shot, I had the time to turn to my right, and start to turn to my left before I felt anything.

It is not conceivable to me that I could have been hit by the first bullet, and then I felt the blow from something which was obviously a bullet, which I assumed was a bullet, and I never heard the second shot, didn't hear it. I didn't hear but two shots. I think I heard the first shot and the third shot.

Mr. Specter. Do you have any idea as to why you did not hear the second shot?

A—Well, first, again I assume the bullet was traveling faster than the sound. I was hit by the bullet prior to the time the sound reached me, and I was in either a state of shock or the impact was such that the sound didn't even register on me, but I was never conscious of hearing the second shot at all.

Obviously, at least the major wound that I took in the shoulder through the chest couldn't have been anything but the second shot. Obviously, it couldn't have been the third, because when the third shot was fired I was in a reclining position, and heard it, saw it and the effects of it, rather—I didn't see it, I saw the effects of it—so it obviously could not have been the third, and couldn't have been the first, in my judgment.

Mr. Specter. What was the nature of the exit wound on the front side of your chest, Governor?

A—I would say, if the Committee would be interested, I would just as soon you look at it. Is there any objection to any of you looking at it?

The Chairman. No.

A—You can tell yourself.

I would say, to describe it for the record, however, that it, the bullet, went in my back just below the right shoulder blade, at just about the point that the right arm joins the shoulder, right in that groove, and exited about 2 inches toward the center of the body from the right nipple of my chest. I can identify these for you.

The bullet went in here—see if I properly describe that—about the juncture of the right arm and the shoulder.

Mr. Specter. Let the record show that the Governor has removed his shirt and we can view the wound on the back which he is pointing toward.

A—The other two are tubes that were inserted in my back by the doctors.

Mr. Specter. Dr. Shaw is present and he can, perhaps, describe with identifiable precision where the wounds are.

Dr. Shaw. There is the wound of the drain that has been specifically described. It was not as large as the scar indicated because in cleaning up the ragged edges of the wound, some of the skin was excised in order to make a cleaner incision. This scar—

Mr. Specter. Will you describe the location, Doctor, of that wound on the Governor's back?

Dr. Shaw. Yes. It is on the right shoulder, I will feet it, just lateral to the shoulder blade, the edge of which is about 2 centimeters from the wound, and just above and slightly medial to the crease formed by the axilla or the armpit, the arm against the chest wall.

Mr. Specter. What other scars are shown there on the Governor's back?

Dr. Shaw. The other scars are surgically induced. This is the incision that was made to drain the depth of the subscapular space.

Mr. Specter. And there you are indicating an incision at what location, please?

Dr. Shaw. Just at the angle of the shoulder blade. Here is the angle of the shoulder blade.

These incisions were never closed by suture. These incisions were left open and they healed by what we call secondary intention, because in this case there was what we call a Penrose drain, which is a soft-rubber drain going up into the depths of the shoulder to allow any material to drain. This was to prevent infection. The other small opening was the one in which the tube was placed through the eighth interspace.

Mr. Specter. Indicate its location, please, Doctor, on his back.

Dr. Shaw. This is lower on the right back in what we refer to as the posterior axillary line, roughly this line.

Mr. Specter. There you are drawing a vertical, virtually vertical line?

Dr. Shaw. Yes. It is on the right back, but getting close to the lateral portion of the chest. This also was a stab wound which was never sutured. There was a rubber drain through this that led to what we call a water seal bottle to allow for drainage of the inside of the chest.

Mr. Specter. Indicating again the second medically inflicted wound.

Dr. Shaw. Yes; that is right.

Mr. Specter. Will you now, Doctor, describe the location of the wound of exit on the Governor's chest, please?

Dr. Shaw. Yes. The wound of exit was beneath and medial to the nipple. Here was this V that I was indicating. It is almost opposite that. At the time of the wound there was a ragged oval hole here at least 5 centimeters in diameter, but the skin edges were excised, and here again this scar does not look quite as nice as it does during the more lateral portion of the surgically induced incision, because this skin was brought together under a little tension, and there is a little separation there.

Mr. Specter. Will you describe the entire scar there, Doctor, for the record, please?

Dr. Shaw. Yes. The entire surgical incision runs from the anterior portion of the chest just lateral to the, we call it, the condral arch. the V formed by the condral arch, and then extends laterally below the nipple, running up, curving up, into the posterior axillary portion or the posterior lateral wall of the chest.

Mr. Specter. What is the total length of the scar, Doctor?

Dr. Shaw. Twenty centimeters, about.

Mr. Dulles. Where was the center of the bullet wound itself in that scar about?

Dr. Shaw. Here.

Mr. Dulles. There?

Dr. Shaw. Yes. All of the rest of this incision was necessary to gain access to the depths of the wound for the debridement, for removing all of the destroyed tissue because of the passage of the bullet.

Mr. Dulles. Would you give us in your hand the area of declination from the entry to the—

Dr. Shaw. This way.

Mr. Dulles. Yes.

Mr. Specter. Can you estimate that angle for us, Doctor?

Dr. Shaw. We are talking about the angle now, of course, with the horizontal, and I would say—you don't have a caliper there, do you?

Dr. Gregory. Yes.

Dr. Shaw. I was going to guess somewhere between 25° and 30°.

Mr. Dulles. Sorry to ask these questions.

Governor Connally. That is fine. I think it is an excellent question.

Dr. Shaw. Well, this puts it right at 25°.

Mr. Specter. That is the angle then of elevation as you are measuring it?

Dr. Shaw. Measuring from back to front, it is the elevation of the posterior wound over the anteriór wound.

The Chairman. The course being downward back to front?

Dr. Shaw. Yes.

Governor Connally. Back to front.

The Chairman. Yes.

Dr. Shaw. At the time of the initial examination, as I described, this portion of the Governor's chest was mobile, it was moving in and out because of the softening of the chest, and that was the reason I didn't want the skin incision to be directly over that, because to get better healing it is better to have a firm pad of tissue rather than having the incision directly over the softened area.

Mr. Dulles. Doctor, would the angle be the same if the Governor were seated now the way he was in the chair?

Dr. Shaw. That is a good question. Of course, we don't know exactly whether he was back or tipped forward. But I don't think there is going to be much difference.

Mr. Dulles. Were you seated in about that way, Governor?

Governor Connally. Mr. Dulles, I would say I was in about this position when I was hit, with my face approximately looking toward you, 20° off of center.

Dr. Shaw. Yes; I got 27°. That didn't make much difference.

Mr. Specter. Is that reading taken then while the Governor is in a seated position, Doctor?

Dr. Shaw. Yes, seated; yes.

Representative Boggs. May I ask a question? How would his hand have been under those circumstances, Doctor, for the bullet to hit his wrist?

Dr. Gregory. I think it fits very well, really, remembering at the other end the trajectory is right here, and there would be no problem to pose his hands in that fashion, and if you will note, you can see it best from over here really, because you did see that the point of entry, and you can visualize his thigh, there is no problem to visualize the trajectory.

Mr. Dulles. Would you be naturally holding your hand in that position?

Dr. Gregory. It could be any place.

Governor Connally. It could be anywhere on that line, Mr. Dulles.

Mr. Chief Justice, you see this is the leg.

Dr. Shaw. Of course, the wound is much smaller than this.

Mr. Specter. Let the record show the Governor has displayed the left thigh showing the scar caused by the entry of the missile in the left thigh.

Dr. Gregory, will you describe the locale of that?

Dr. Gregory. Yes. This scar, excisional scar, is a better term, if I may just interject that——

Mr. Specter. Please do.

Dr. Gregory. The excisional scar to the Governor's thigh is located at a point approximately 10 or 12 centimeters above the adductor tubercule of the femur, placing it at the juncture of the middle and distal third of his thigh.

Mr. Specter. In lay language, Doctor, about how far is that up from the knee area?

Dr. Gregory. Five inches, 6 inches.

Mr. Specter. Governor Connally, can you recreate the position that you were sitting in in the automobile, as best you can recollect, at the time you think you were struck?

A—I think, having turned to look over my right shoulder, then revolving to look over my left shoulder, I threw my right wrist over on my left leg.

26

Mr. Specter. And in the position you are seated now, with your right wrist on your left leg, with your little finger being an inch or two from your knee?

A—From the knee.

Mr. Specter. And, Dr. Gregory, would that be in approximate alinement which has been characterized on Commission Exhibit——

Dr. Gregory. I think it fits reasonably well; yes, sir.

Mr. Specter. In a moment here I can get that exhibit.

Mr. Dulles. May I ask a question in the meantime?

A—Yes, sir.

Mr. Dulles. You turned to the right, as I recall your testimony, because you heard the sound coming from the right?

A—Yes, sir.

Mr. Dulles. How did you happen to turn then to the left, do you remember why that was?

A—Yes, sir; I know exactly. I turned to the right both to see, because it was an instinctive movement, because that is where the sound came from, but even more important, I immediately thought it was a rifleshot, I immediately thought of an assassination attempt, and I turned to see if I could see the President, to see if he was all right. Failing to see him over my shoulder, I turned to look over my left shoulder.

Mr. Dulles. I see.

A—Into the back seat, and I never completed that turn. I got no more than substantially looking forward, a little bit to the left of forward, when I got hit.

Representative Boggs. May I ask one of the doctors a question? What is the incidence of recovery from a wound of this type?

Dr. Gregory. I will defer the answer to Dr. Shaw. From the wrist, excellent so far as recovery is concerned. Functionally, recovery is going to be good, too, and Dr. Shaw can take on the other one.

Dr. Shaw. We never had any doubt about the Governor's recovery. We knew what we had to do and we felt he could recover. I think I indicated that to Mrs. Connally.

A—As soon as you got into the chest and found out what it was.

Representative Boggs. But there was a very serious wound, was there not, Doctor?

Dr. Shaw. Yes. It was both a shocking and painful wound, and the effects of the wound, the immediate effects of the wound, were very dangerous as far as Governor Connally was concerned, because he had what we call a sucking wound of the chest. This would not allow him to breathe. I think instinctively what happened, while he was riding in the car on the way to the hospital, he probably had his arm across, and he may have instinctively closed that sucking area to some extent. But they had to immediately put an occlusive dressing on it as soon as he got inside to keep him from sucking air in and out of the right chest.

Representative Boggs. Had hospitalization been delayed for about another half hour or so——

Dr. Shaw. That is speculation, but I don't think he could have maintained breathing, sufficient breathing, for a half hour with that type of wound. It is a little speculation. It would depend on how well he could protect himself. We have had instances where by putting their jackets around them like this, they could occlude this, and go for a considerable period of time. Airmen during the war instinctively protected themselves in this way.

Representative Boggs. You have no doubt about his physical ability to serve as Governor?

Dr. Shaw. None whatever. [Laughter.]

Senator Cooper. I am just trying to remember whether we asked you, Doctor, if you probed the wound in the thigh to see how deep it was.

Dr. Gregory. I did not, Senator. Dr. Tom Shires at our institution attended that wound, and I have his description to go on, what he found, what he had written, and his description is that it did not penetrate the thigh very deeply, just to the muscle, but not beyond that.

Representative Boggs. Just one other question of the Doctor. Having looked at the wound, there is no doubt in either of your minds that that bullet came from the rear, is there?

Dr. Gregory. There has never been any doubt in my mind about the origin of the missile; no.

Representative Boggs. And in yours?

Dr. Shaw. No.

Mr. Specter. Governor Connally, this is the exhibit which I was referring to, being 689. Was that your approximate position except—that is the alinement with your right hand being on your left leg as you have just described?

A—No; it looks like my right hand is up on my chest. But I don't know. I can't say with any degree of certainty where my right hand was, frankly.

Mr. Specter. Governor Connally——

A—It could have been up on my chest, it could have been suspended in the air, it could have been down on my leg, it could have been anywhere. I just don't remember.

I obviously, I suppose, like anyone else, wound up the next day realizing I was hit in three places, and I was not conscious of having been hit but by one bullet, so I tried to reconstruct how I could have been hit in three places by the same bullet, and I merely, I know it penetrated from the back through the chest first.

I assumed that I had turned as I described a moment ago,

28

placing my right hand on my left leg, that it hit my wrist, went out the center of the wrist, the underside, and then into my leg, but it might not have happened that way at all.

Mr. Specter. Were your knees higher on the jump seat than they would be on a normal chair such as you are sitting on?

A—I would say it was not unlike this, with the exception the knees might be slightly higher, perhaps a half an inch to an inch higher. . . .

Representative Boggs. This is a little bit off the subject, but it is pretty well established that the Governor was shot and he has recovered. Do you have any reason to believe there was any conspiracy afoot for somebody to assassinate you?

A—None whatever.

Representative Boggs. Had you ever received any threat from Lee Harvey Oswald of any kind?

A—No.

Representative Boggs. Did you know him?

A—No.

Representative Boggs. Had you ever seen him?

A—No.

Representative Boggs. Have you ever had any belief of, subsequent to the assassination of President Kennedy and your own injury, that there was a conspiracy here of any kind?

A—None whatever.

Representative Boggs. What is your theory about what happened?

A—Well, it is pure theory based on nothing more than what information is available to everyone, and probably less is available to me, certainly less than is available to you here on this Commission.

But I think you had an individual here with a completely warped, demented mind who, for whatever reason, wanted to do two things: First, to vent his anger, his hate, against many people and many things in a dramatic fashion that would carve for him, in however infamous a fashion, a niche in the history books of this country. And I think he deliberately set out to do just what he did, and that is the only thing that I can think of.

You ask me my theory, and that is my theory, and certainly not substantiated by any facts.

Representative Boggs. Going on again, Governor, and again using the word "theory," do you have any reason to believe that there was any connection between Oswald and Ruby?

A—I have no reason to believe that there was; no, Congressman. By the same token, if you ask me do I have any reason not to believe it, I would have to answer the same, I don't know.

Representative Boggs. Yes.

A—I just don't have any knowledge or any information about the background of either, and I am just not in a position to say.

29

Mr. Dulles. You recall your correspondence with Oswald in connection with Marine matters, when he thought you were still Secretary of the Navy?

A—After this was all over, I do, Mr. Dulles. As I recall, he wrote me a letter asking that his dishonorable discharge be corrected. But at the time he wrote the letter, if he had any reason about it at all, or shortly thereafter, he would have recognized that I had resigned as Secretary of the Navy a month before I got the letter, so it would really take a peculiar mind, it seems to me, to harbor any grudge as a result of that when I had resigned as Secretary prior to the receipt of the letter.

Mr. Dulles. I think I can say without violating any confidence, that there is nothing in the record to indicate that there was—in fact, Marina, the wife, testified, in fact, to the contrary. There was no animus against you on the part of Oswald, as you—

A—I have wondered, of course, in my own mind as to whether or not there could have conceivably been anything, and the only—I suppose like any person at that particular moment, I represented authority to him. Perhaps he was in a rebellious spirit enough to where I was as much a target as anyone else. But that is the only conceivable basis on which I can assume that he was deliberately trying to hit me.

Representative Boggs. You have no doubt about the fact that he was deliberately trying to hit you?

A—Yes, I do; I do have doubt, Congressman. I am not at all sure he was shooting at me. I think I could with some logic argue either way. The logic in favor of him, of the position that he was shooting at me, is simply borne out by the fact that the man fired three shots, and he hit each of the three times he fired. He obviously was a pretty good marksman, so you have to assume to some extent at least that he was hitting what he was shooting at.

On the other hand, I think I could argue with equal logic that obviously his prime target, and I think really his sole target, was President Kennedy. His first shot, at least to him, he could not have but known the effect that it might have on the President. His second shot showed that he had clearly missed the President and his result to him, as the result of the first shot, the President slumped and changed his position in the back seat just enough to expose my back. I haven't seen all of the various positions, but again I think from where he was shooting I was in the direct line of fire immediately in front of the President, so any movement on the part of the President would expose me.

The Chairman. Have you seen the moving pictures, Governor?

A—Yes, sir; I have, Mr. Chief Justice.

Mr. Specter. Was there any point of exit on your thigh wound?

30

A—No.

Mr. Specter. (to Dr. Gregory.) Would you give the precise condition of the right wrist, and cover the thigh, too?

Dr. Gregory. The present state of the wound on his wrist indicates that the linear scar made in the course of the excision is well healed; that its upper limb is about—

A—I thinks he wants you to describe the position of it.

Mr. Specter. Yes; the position.

Dr. Gregory. I was about to do that. The upper limb of it is about 5 centimeters above the wrist joint, and curves around toward the thumb distally to about a centimeter above the wrist joint.

Mr. Specter. What is the total length of that?

Dr. Gregory. The length of that excisional scar is about 4 centimeters, an inch and a half.

Mr. Specter. What is the wound appearing to be on the palmer side?

Dr. Gregory. The wound on the palmer side of the wrist is now converted to a well-healed linear scar approximately one-half inch in length, and located about three-quarters of an inch above the distal flexion crease.

Representative Boggs. What is the prognosis for complete return of function there?

Dr. Gregory. Very good, Congressman; very good. . . .

Mr. Specter. Governor Connally, in 1963 we were informed that Lee Harvey Oswald paid a visit to Austin, Tex., and is supposed to also have visited your office. Do you have any knowledge of such a visit?

A—No, sir.

Mr. Dulles. What date did you give?

Mr. Specter. 1963.

Representative Boggs. What date in 1963?

Mr. Specter. We do not have the exact date on that.

Representative Boggs. Excuse me just a minute. Would your office records indicate such a visit?

A—It might or might not, Congressman. We have—

Representative Boggs. That is what I would think.

A—We have there a reception room that is open from about 9:30 to 12 and from 2 to 4 every day, and depending on the time of the year there are literally hundreds of people who come in there. There would be as high as 80 at a time that come in groups, and a tour—this is a very large reception room which, frankly, we can't use for any other purpose because it is so useful for tourists, and they literally come in by the hundreds, and some days we will have a thousand people in that room on any given day. So for me to say he never was in there, I couldn't do that; and he might well have been there, and no record of it in the office.

We make no attempt to keep a record of all the people who come in. If they come in small groups or if they have appointments with me, or one of my assistants, yes, we do. We keep records of people who come in and want to leave a card or leave word that they dropped by. But I have no knowledge that he ever came by.

Mr. Specter. Do you have any recollection of your arrival at the hospital itself, at the Parkland Hospital?

A—Yes. I think when the car stopped the driver was obviously going at a very rapid rate of speed, and apparently, as he threw on the brakes of the car, it brought me back to consciousness.

Again, a strange thing—strange things run through your mind and, perhaps, not so strange under the circumstances, but I immediately—the only thought that occurred to me was that I was in the jump seat next to the door, that everyone concerned, was going to be concerned with the President; that I had to get out of the way so they could get to the President. So although I was reclining, and again Mrs. Connally holding me, I suddenly lurched out of her arms and tried to stand upright to get myself out of the car.

I got—I don't really know how far I got. They tell me I got almost upright, and then just collapsed again, and someone then picked me up and put me on a stretcher. I again was very conscious because this was the first time that I had any real sensation of pain, and at this point the pain in the chest was excruciating, and I kept repeating just over and over, "My God, it hurts, it hurts," and it was hurting, it was excruciating at that point. . . .

Mr. Specter. Governor Connally, other than that which you have already testified to, do you know of any events or occurrences either before the trip or with the President in Texas during his trip, or after his trip, which could shed any light on the assassination itself?

A—None whatever.

Mr. Specter. Do you know of any conversations involving anyone at all, either before the trip, during the trip, or after the trip, other than those which you have already related, which would shed any light on the facts surrounding the assassination?

A—None whatever.

Mr. Specter. Do you have anything to add which you think would be helpful to the Commission in any way?

A—No, sir; Mr. Specter, I don't.

I want to express my gratitude to the Commission for hearing me so patiently, but I only wish I could have added something more that would be helpful to the Commission on arriving at the many answers to so many of these difficult problems, but I don't.

I can only say that it has taken some little time to describe the events and what happened. It is rather amazing in retrospect when you think really what a short period of time it took for it to occur, in a matter of seconds, and if my memory is somewhat vague about precisely which way I was looking or where my hand or arm was, I can only say I hope it is understandable in the light of the fact that this was a very sudden thing. It was a very shocking thing.

I have often wondered myself why I never had the presence of mind enough—I obviously did say something; I said, "Oh, no, no, no," and then I said, "My God, they are going to kill us all."

I don't know why I didn't say, "Get down in the car," but I didn't. You just never know why you react the way you do and why you don't do some things you ought to do.

But I am again grateful to this Commission as a participant in this tragedy and as a citizen of this country, and I want to express, I think in behalf of millions of people, our gratitude for the time and energy and the dedication that this Commission has devoted to trying to supply the answers that people, I am sure, will be discussing for generations to come. I know it has been a difficult, long, laborious task for you, but I know that generations of the future Americans will be grateful for your efforts.

Representative Boggs. Governor, I would like to say that we have had fine cooperation from all of your Texas officials, from the attorney general of the State, and from his people and others who have worked with the Commission.

A—Well, we are delighted, and I am very happy that the attorney general is here with us today.

Senator Cooper. May I ask one question?

The Chairman. Yes, Senator Cooper.

Senator Cooper. Governor, at the time you all passed the Texas School Book Depository, did you know that such a building was located there? Were you familiar with the building at all?

A—Just vaguely, Senator.

Senator Cooper. But now when you heard the shot, you turned to your right because you thought, as you said, that the shot came from that direction. As you turned, was that in the direction of the Texas School Book Depository?

A—Yes, sir; it was.

Senator Cooper. Do you remember an overpass in front of you—

A—Yes, sir.

Senator Cooper. As you moved down?

A—Yes, sir.

Senator Cooper. Were you aware at all of any sounds of rifle-shots from the direction of the overpass, from the embankment?

A—No, sir; I don't believe there were such.

Senator Cooper. Well, you know, there have been stories.

A—Yes, sir; but I don't believe that.

Senator Cooper. I wanted to ask you if you were very con-

33

scious of the fact—you were conscious of a shot behind you, you were not aware of any shot from the embankment or overpass. The answer is what?

A—I am not aware of any shots from the overpass, Senator. Senator, I might repeat my testimony with emphasis to this extent, that I have all my life been familiar with the sound of a rifleshot, and that sound I heard I thought was a rifleshot, at the time I heard it I didn't think it was a firecracker, or blowout or anything else. I thought it was a rifleshot. I have hunted enough to think that my perception with respect to directions is very, very good, and this shot I heard came from back over my right shoulder, which was in the direction of the School Book Depository, no question about it. I heard no other. The first and third shots came from there. I heard no other sounds that would indicate to me there was any commotion or disturbance of shots or anything else on the overpass.

Senator Cooper. Would you describe again the nature of the shock that you had when you felt that you had been hit by a bullet?

A—Senator, the best way I can describe it is to say that I would say it is as if someone doubled his fist and came up behind you and just with about a 12-inch blow hit you right in the back right below the shoulder blade.

Senator Cooper. That is when you heard the first rifleshot?

A—This was after I heard the first rifleshot. There was no pain connected with it. There was no particular burning sensation. There was nothing more than that. I think you would feel almost the identical sensation I felt if someone came up behind you and just, with a short jab, hit you with a doubled-up fist just below the shoulder blade. . . .

Mr. Dulles. I have one or two. Governor, were you consulted at all about the security arrangements in connection with the Dallas visit?

A—No, sir; not really; no, sir; and let me add we normally are not.

Mr. Dulles. I realize that.

A—Mr. Dulles, the Secret Service, as you know, comes in, they work with both our department of public safety and the various city police, and the various localities in which we are going. So far as I know, there was complete cooperation on the part of everyone concerned, but I was not consulted. . . .

Mr. Dulles. Do you happen to recall in general when the decision was reached that the visit would include a trip to Dallas, or was that always a part?

A—I think it was always a part.

Mr. Dulles. Of the planning?

A—Yes; I think it was always a part. There was consideration given, if you had to leave out some place, let us leave out Dallas or let us leave out this one or that one, but there was no question, I don't think, in anyone's mind if we made more than one stop in the big cities that we were going to try to make them all, San Antonio, Houston, Dallas, and Fort Worth.

Mr. Dulles. You do not recall seeing anyone approach the car outside of those who were in the procession just prior to the shooting, anyone from the sidewalk or along the street there, in the park, which was on one side?

A—No, sir; I sure don't.

Mr. Dulles. You and one other happen to be the only witnesses who have indicated that they recognized it as being a rifleshot. The other witness, like you, was a huntsman. Most of the witnesses have indicated they thought it was a backfire; the first shot was a backfire or a firecracker.

Can you distinguish, what is there that distinguishes a rifleshot from a backfire or a firecracker? Can you tell, or is it just instinct?

A—I am not sure I could accurately describe it. I don't know that I have ever attempted to. I would say a firecracker or a blowout has more of a hollow, bursting kind of sound, as if you popped a balloon, or something of this sort. A rifleshot, on the other hand, to me has more of a ring, kind of an echo to it, more of a metallic sound to it. It is a more penetrating sound than a firecracker or a blowout. It carries—

Mr. Dulles. That gives me what I had in mind. I realize that. That is all I have, Mr. Chief Justice.

The Chairman. Thank you very much. We are very appreciative of the help you have given us.

Senator Cooper. May I ask just one question?

The Chairman. We hate to have you review all of this sordid thing again.

Senator Cooper. May I ask a rather general question? I would like to ask, in view of all the discussion which has been had, was there any official discussion of any kind before this trip of which you were aware that there might be some act of violence against the President?

A—No, sir.

Senator Cooper. Thank you.

A—No; let me say that there have been several news stories—

Senator Cooper. Yes, I know.

A—That purportedly quoted me about not wanting the President to ride in a motorcade or caravan in Dallas. That is very true. But the implication was that I had some fear of his life, which is not true.

The reason I didn't want him to do it at the time it came up was simply we were running out of time, and that, I thought, we were working him much too hard. This again was before the change, moving San Antonio to Thursday instead of having it all on one day, and I was opposed to a motorcade because they do drain energy, and it takes time to do it, and I didn't think we had the time.

35

But once we got San Antonio moved from Friday to Thursday afternoon, where that was his initial stop in Texas, then we had the time, and I withdrew my objections to a motorcade.

The Chairman. Thank you very much, Governor.

A—Thank you, sir.

MRS. JOHN B. CONNALLY

The testimony of the wife of the governor of Texas:

Mr. Specter. Mrs. Connally, tell us what happened at the time of the assassination.

A—We had just finished the motorcade through the downtown Dallas area, and it had been a wonderful motorcade. The people had been very responsive to the President and Mrs. Kennedy, and we were very pleased, I was very pleased.

As we got off Main Street—is that the main thoroughfare?

Mr. Specter. That is the street on which you were proceeding through the town, yes.

A—In fact the receptions had been so good every place that I had showed much restraint by not mentioning something about it before.

I could resist no longer. When we got past this area I did turn to the President and said, "Mr. President, you can't say Dallas doesn't love you."

Then I don't know how soon, it seems to me it was very soon, that I heard a noise, and not being an expert rifleman, I was not aware that it was a rifle. It was just a frightening noise, and it came from the right.

I turned over my right shoulder and looked back, and saw the President as he had both hands at his neck.

Mr. Specter. And you are indicating with your own hands, two hands crossing over gripping your own neck?

A—Yes; and it seemed to me there was—he made no utterance, no cry. I saw no blood, no anything. It was just sort of nothing, the expression on his face, and he just sort of slumped down.

Then very soon there was the second shot that hit John. As the first shot was hit, and I turned to look at the same time, I recall John saying, "Oh, no, no, no." Then there was a second shot, and it hit John, and as he recoiled to the right, just crumpled like a wounded animal to the right, he said, "My God, they are going to kill us all."

I never again——

Mr. Dulles. To the right was into your arms more or less?

A—No, he turned away from me. I was pretending that I was him. I never again looked in the back seat of the car after my husband was shot. My concern was for him, and I remember that he turned to the right and then just slumped down into the seat, so that I reached over to pull him toward

36

me. I was trying to get him down and me down. The jump seats were not very roomy, so that there were reports that he slid into the seat of the car, which he did not; that he fell over into my lap, which he did not.

I just pulled him over into my arms because it would have been impossible to get us really both down with me sitting and me holding him. So that I looked out, I mean as he was in my arms, I put my head down over his head so that his head and my head were right together, and all I could see, too, were the people flashing by. I didn't look back any more.

The third shot that I heard I felt, it felt like spent buckshot falling all over us, and then, of course, I too could see that it was the matter, brain tissue, or whatever, just human matter, all over the car and both of us.

I thought John had been killed, and then there was some imperceptible movement, just some little something that let me know that there was still some life, and that is when I started saying to him, "It's all right. Be still."

Now, I did hear the Secret Service man say, "Pull out of the motorcade. Take us to the nearest hospital," and then we took out very rapidly to the hospital.

Just before we got to Parkland, we made a right-hand turn, he must have been going very fast, because as he turned the weight of my husband's body almost toppled us both. . . .

We arrived at the hospital and sat there what seemed to me like an interminable time, and from what I know was just a few minutes, but the thoughts that went through my mind were how long must I sit here with this dying man in my arms while everybody is swarming over the President whom I felt very sure was dead, and just when I thought I could sit and wait no longer, John just sort of heaved himself up. He did not rise up in the car, he just sort of heaved himself up, and then collapsed down into the seat.

Mr. Specter. At that time you and Governor Connally were still on the jump seats of the car?

A—Yes, and they had not—the President was still—and Mrs. Kennedy were still in the back. . . .

Mr. Specter. Did President Kennedy say anything at all after the shooting?

A—He did not say anything. Mrs. Kennedy said, the first thing I recall her saying was, after the first shot, and I heard her say, "Jack, they have killed my husband," and then there was the second shot and then after the third shot she said, "They have killed my husband. I have his brains in my hand," and she repeated that several times, and that was all the conversation.

Mr. Specter. From point forward you say you had your eyes to the front so you did not have a chance——

A—Yes, because I had him, and I really didn't think about

looking back anyway, but I could just see the car rushing along, and people and things rushing past us. I remember thinking what a terrible sight this must be to those people, to see these two shot-up men, and it was a terrible horrifying thing, and I think that is about as I remember it.

Mr. Specter. What happened then after you got to the hospital?

A—We got to the hospital and, like I said, John heaved himself over. They still could not seem to get Mrs. Kennedy or the President out of the back of the car, but someone scooped him up in their arms and put him on a stretcher. There were two stretchers there, and then they took him off immediately to the emergency room, and they ran down the hall with the stretcher, and I just ran along with them.

They took him into the emergency room, and right behind us came the President on a stretcher, and they took him and put him in a room to the right. There was much commotion and confusion. There were lots of what I assumed were Secret Service men rushing in with machine guns, I guess, or tommy-guns. I am not real sure, they were big arms of some sort. There was no one—there were lots of people across the hall. There was no one with me and, of course, my thoughts then were, I guess like any other woman, I wondered if all the doctors were in the room on the left, and they were not taking too good care of my husband on the right. I shouldn't have worried about that, should I?

I knew no one in the hospital and I was alone. Twice I got up and opened the door into the emergency room, and I could hear John and I could see him moving, and I knew then that he was still alive.

I guess that time was short, too. It seemed endless. Somebody rushed out, I thought it was a nurse, and handed me one cuff link. I later read that it was a lady doctor.

They took him out of there very soon up to surgery, and I just left with him and waited in an office. . . .

As soon as Dr. Shaw found that he had some encouraging news, that the wounds were not as extensive as he had thought they could be or might be, he sent that word to me from the operating room, and that was good news.

I then asked if I couldn't go see Mrs. Kennedy, and they told me she had left the hospital. . . .

Mr. Dulles. I just have one question. Mrs. Connally, on one point your testimony differs from a good many others as to the timing of the shots. I think you said that there seemed to be more time between the second and third than between the first and the second; is that your recollection?

A—Yes. . . .

DAVID F. POWERS

The affidavit of a close friend and special assistant to President Kennedy:

I traveled to Texas with the Presidential party on November 21, 1963, on AF-1. After a stop in Houston, we spent the night in Fort Worth, Texas. On the evening of November 21st, we were discussing the size of the crowd in the Rice University Stadium at Houston, and the President asked me how I thought it compared with the crowd the last time he was there. I said that the crowd was about the same as the one which came to see him before but there were 100,000 extra people on hand who came to see Mrs. Kennedy. President Kennedy then made a comment to Mrs. Kennedy to the effect that she was a great asset on the trip and that seemed to make her happy, although at that particular moment she was very tired, having spent many hours that day traveling in the plane and on motorcades.

The next day we proceeded on to Dallas and arrived at Love Field at approximately 11:30 a.m. The President and Mrs. Kennedy were in high spirits and as they were leaving the plane I jokingly remarked to the two of them that they looked like Mr. and Mrs. America and that they should not both wave in the same direction as it would be too much for anyone to receive all that attention at once. . . . I was assigned to ride in the Secret Service automobile which proceeded immediately behind the President's car in the motorcade. That Secret Service follow-up automobile was an open car with two Special Agents in the front seat, two Special Agents in the rear seat and two Special Agents on each of the two running boards. I sat in the jump seat on the right side of the car and Kenneth O'Donnell sat in the jump seat on the left side of the car. . . .

When we passed through the heart of Dallas, the crowds were about ten deep. We then turned off of Main Street onto Houston and made the sharp swing to the left up Elm Street.

At that time we were traveling very slowly, no more than 12 miles an hour. In accordance with my custom, I was very much concerned about our timing and at just about that point I looked at my watch and noted that it was almost exactly 12:30 p.m., which was the time we were due at the Trade Mart. I commented to Ken O'Donnell that it was 12:30 and we would only be about five minutes late when we arrived at the Trade Mart. Shortly thereafter the first shot went off and it sounded to me as if it were a firecracker. I noticed then that the President moved quite far to his left after the shot from the extreme right hand side where he had been sitting. There was a second shot and Governor Connally disappeared from sight and then there was a third shot which took off the top of the President's head and had the sickening sound of a grapefruit splattering against the side of a wall. The total time be-

39

tween the first and third shots was about 5 or 6 seconds. . . .

CLINTON J. HILL

The testimony of the Secret Service agent responsible for the protection of Mrs. Kennedy:

Mr. Specter. Now, were you assigned to duties on the trip of President Kennedy to Texas in November 1963?

A—Yes, sir; I was.

Mr. Specter. Did you have any special duty assigned to you at that time?

A—Yes, sir.

Mr. Specter. In connection with the trip?

A—I was responsible for the protection of Mrs. Kennedy.

Mr. Specter. And, in a general way, what does that sort of an assignment involve?

A—I tried to remain as close to her at all times as possible, and in this particular trip that meant being with the President because all of their doings on this trip were together rather than separate. I would go over her schedule to make sure she knows what she is expected to do; discuss it with her; remain in her general area all the time; protect her from any danger. . . .

Mr. Specter. In which car in the motorcade were you positioned?

A—I was working the followup car, which is the car immediately behind the Presidential car. . . .

Mr. Specter. And how far was the President's car in front of the President's followup car during the course of the motorcade?

A—Approximately 5 feet.

Mr. Specter. Is there some well-established practice as to the spacing between the President's car and the President's followup car?

A—It would depend upon speed. We attempt to stay as close to the President's car as practical. At high rates of speed it is rather difficult to stay close because of the danger involved. Slow speeds, the followup car stays as close as possible so that the agents on the followup car can get to the Presidential car as quickly as possible. . . .

Mr. Specter. How were the agents armed at that time?

A—All the agents were armed with their hand weapons.

Mr. Specter. And is there any weapon in the automobile in addition to the hand weapons?

A—Yes. There is an AR-15, which is an automatic rifle, and a shotgun.

Mr. Specter. And where is the AR-15 kept?

A—Between the two agents in the rear seat.

Mr. Specter. How about the shotgun; where is that kept?

A—In a compartment immediately in front of the jump seats.

Mr. Specter. Is the President's followup car a specially constructed automobile?

A—Yes, sir; it is.

Mr. Specter. And what is the make and model and general description of that vehicle?

A—It is a 1955 Cadillac, nine-passenger touring sedan. It is a convertible type.

Mr. Specter. Was that automobile flown in specially from Washington for the occasion?

A—Yes; it was, sir.

Mr. Specter. Do you know how that automobile was transported to Dallas, Tex.?

A—Generally, it is flown in a C-130 by the Air Force. I am not sure how on this particular occasion. . . .

Mr. Specter. Did you have any occasion to leave the President followup car at any time?

A—When we finally did reach Main Street, the crowds had built up to a point where they were surging into the street. We had motorcycles running adjacent to both the Presidential automobile and the followup car, as well as in front of the Presidential automobile, and because of the crowds in the street, the President's driver, Special Agent Greer, was running the car more to the left-hand side of the street more than he was to the right to keep the President as far away from the crowd as possible, and because of this the motorcycles on the left-hand side could not get past the crowd and alongside the car, and they were forced to drop back. I jumped from the followup car, ran up and got on top of the rear portion of the Presidential automobile to be close to Mrs. Kennedy in the event that someone attempted to grab her from the crowd or throw something in the car.

Mr. Specter. When you say the rear portion of the automobile, can you, by referring to Commission Exhibit No. 345, heretofore identified as the President's automobile, specify by penciled "X" where you stood?

A—Yes, sir [indicating].

Mr. Specter. Will you describe for the record just what area it is back there on which you stood?

A—That is a step built into the rear bumper of the automobile, and on top of the rear trunk there is a handguard which you grab for and hang onto when you are standing up.

Mr. Specter. Are identical objects of those descriptions existing on each side of the President's car?

A—Yes, sir; they do. . . .

Mr. Specter. Now, had there been any instruction or comment about your performance of that type of a duty with respect to anything that President Kennedy himself had said in the period immediately preceding the trip to Texas?

A—Yes, sir; there was. The preceding Monday, the President was on a trip to Tampa, Fla., and he requested that the agents not ride on either of those two steps.

Mr. Specter. And to whom did the President make that request?

A—Assistant Special Agent in Charge Boring. . . .

Mr. Specter. And Special Agent Boring informed you of that instruction by President Kennedy?

A—Yes, sir; he did.

Mr. Specter. Did he make it a point to inform other special agents of that same instruction?

A—I believe that he did, sir.

Mr. Specter. And, as a result of what President Kennedy said to him, did he instruct you to observe that Presidential admonition?

A—Yes, sir.

Mr. Specter. How, if at all, did that instruction of President Kennedy affect your action and—your action in safeguarding him on this trip to Dallas?

A—We did not ride on the rear portions of the automobile. I did on those four occasions because the motorcycles had to drop back and there was no protection on the left-hand side of the car. . . .

Mr. Specter. Did you have any occasion to notice the Texas School Book Depository Building as you proceeded in a generally northerly direction on Houston Street?

A—Yes, sir. It was immediately in front of us and to our left.

Mr. Specter. Did you notice anything unusual about it?

A—Nothing more unusual than any other building along the way.

Mr. Specter. What is your general practice, if any, in observing such buildings along the route of a Presidential motorcade?

A—We scan the buildings and look specifically for open windows, for people hanging out, and there had been, on almost every building along the way, people hanging out, windows open.

Mr. Specter. And did you observe, as you recollect at this moment, any open windows in the Texas School Depository Building?

A—Yes, sir; there were. . . .

Well, as we came out of the curve, and began to straighten up, I was viewing the area which looked to be a park. There were people scattered throughout the entire park. And I heard a noise from my right rear, which to me seemed to be a firecracker. I immediately looked to my right, and, in so doing, my eyes had to cross the Presidential limousine and I saw President Kennedy grab at himself and lurch forward and to the left.

42

Mr. Specter. Why don't you just proceed, in narrative form, to tell us?

Representative Boggs. This was the first shot?

A—This is the first sound that I heard; yes, sir. I jumped from the car, realizing that something was wrong, ran to the Presidential limousine. Just about as I reached it, there was another sound, which was different than the first sound. I think I described it in my statement as though someone was shooting a revolver into a hard object—it seemed to have some type of an echo. I put my right foot, I believe it was, on the left rear step of the automobile, and I had a hold of the handgrip with my hand, when the car lurched forward. I lost my footing and I had to run about three or four more steps before I could get back up in the car.

Between the time I originally grabbed the handhold and until I was up on the car, Mrs. Kennedy—the second noise that I heard had removed a portion of the President's head, and he had slumped noticeably to his left. Mrs. Kennedy had jumped up from the seat and was, it appeared to me, reaching for something coming off the right rear bumper of the car, the right rear tail, when she noticed that I was trying to climb on the car. She turned toward me and I grabbed her and put her back in the back seat, crawled up on top of the back seat and lay there. . . .

Mr. Specter. Did you hear any more than two shots?

A—No, sir. . . .

Mr. Specter. When, in relationship to the second shot, did Mrs. Kennedy move out of the rear seat?

A—Just after it.

Mr. Specter. You say that it appeared that she was reaching as if something was coming over to the rear portion of the car, back in the area where you were coming to?

A—Yes, sir.

Mr. Specter. Was there anything back there that you observed, that she might have been reaching for?

A—I thought I saw something come off the back, too, but I cannot say that there was. I do know that the next day we found the portion of the President's head.

Mr. Specter. Where did you find that portion of the President's head?

A—It was found in the street. It was turned in, I believe, by a medical student or somebody in Dallas. . . .

Mr. Specter. Now, what action did you take specifically with respect to placing Mrs. Kennedy back in the rear seat?

A—I simply just pushed and she moved—somewhat voluntarily—right back into the same seat she was in. The President—when she had attempted to get out onto the trunk of the car, his body apparently did not move too much, because when she got back into the car he was at that time, when I got on top of the car, face up in her lap. . . .

43

After going under this underpass, I looked forward to the jump seats, where Mrs. Connally and Governor Connally were sitting. Mrs. Connally had been leaning over her husband. And I had no idea he had been shot. And when she leaned back at one time, I noticed that his coat was unbuttoned, and that the lower portion of his abdomen was completely covered with blood.

Mr. Specter. When was it that you first observed that?

A—Just after going under the underpass. . . .

Mr. Specter. Did Mrs. Kennedy say anything as you were proceeding from the time of the shooting to Parkland Hospital?

A—At the time of the shooting, when I got into the rear of the car, she said, "My God, they have shot his head off." Between there and the hospital she just said, "Jack, Jack, what have they done to you," and sobbed.

Mr. Specter. Was there any conversation by anybody else in the President's automobile from the time of the shooting to the arrival at Parkland Hospital?

A—I heard Special Agent Kellerman say on the radio, "To the nearest hospital, quick."

Mr. Specter. Any other comment?

A—He said, "We have been hit." . . .

Representative Boggs. Was Governor Connally conscious?

A—Yes, sir; he was.

Mr. Specter. Did Governor Connally say anything?

A—No, sir.

Mr. Specter. Did President Kennedy say anything?

A—No, sir. . . .

Mr. Specter. What did you observe as to President Kennedy's condition on arrival at the hospital?

A—The right rear portion of his head was missing. It was lying in the rear seat of the car. His brain was exposed. There was blood and bits of brain all over the entire rear portion of the car. Mrs. Kennedy was completely covered with blood. There was so much blood you could not tell if there had been any other wound or not, except for the one large gaping wound in the right rear portion of the head. . . .

Mr. Specter. Now, tell us what you did at the hospital from the time of arrival on, please.

A—I went into the emergency room with the President, but it was so small, and there were so many people in there that I decided I had better leave and let the doctors take care of the situation. So I walked outside; asked for the nearest telephone; walked to the nearest telephone. About that time Special Agent in Charge Kellerman came outside and said, "Get the White House."

I asked Special Agent Lawson for the local number in Dallas of the White House switchboard, which he gave to me. I called the switchboard in Dallas; asked for the line to be open to Washington, and remain open continuously. And then I asked for Special Agent in Charge Behn's office. Mr. Kellerman came out of the emergency room about that time, took the telephone and called Special Agent in Charge Behn that we had had a double tragedy; that both Governor Connally and President Kennedy had been shot. And that was about as much as he said. I then took the telephone and shortly thereafter Mr. Kellerman came out of the emergency room and said, "Clint, tell Jerry this is unofficial and not for release, but the man is dead." Which I did. During the two calls, I talked to the Attorney General, who attempted to reach me, and told him that his brother had been seriously wounded; that we would keep him advised as to his condition.

Mr. Specter. Where was Mrs. Kennedy all this time, if you know?

A—Immediately upon arrival, she went into the emergency room. And a few minutes afterward, she was convinced to wait outside, which she did, remained there the rest of the period of time that we were there.

Mr. Specter. And was there any pronouncement that the President had died?

A—Not that I know of. Apparently there was. I was requested by Mr. O'Donnell, one of the Presidential assistants, to obtain a casket, because they wanted to return to Washington immediately. I contacted the administrator of the hospital and asked him to take me where I could telephone the nearest mortuary, which I did, requested that their best available casket be brought to the emergency entrance in my name immediately.

Mr. Specter. And what action was taken as a result of that request by you?

A—The casket did arrive from the O'Neal Morturary, Inc., in their own hearse, which we then wheeled into the emergency room. I left the emergency room and asked that two of our agents, Special Agent Sulliman and Assistant Special Agent in Charge Stout clear all the corridors, and I checked the closest and most immediate route to the ambulance. We took the body from the hospital and departed the Parkland Hospital about 2:04 p.m. The ambulance was driven by Special Agent Berger. Special Agent in Charge Kellerman and Assistant Special Agent in Charge Stout were riding in the front seat; Mrs. Kennedy, Dr. Burkley, the President's body, and myself rode in the rear portion of the ambulance. . . .

Representative Boggs. May I ask a question? At the hospital in Texas, you had seen—had you seen the whole body, or just the back of the President's head?

A—I had seen the whole body, but he was still cold when I saw him.

Representative Boggs. At the morgue in Bethesda he was not cold?

A—Yes, sir; the autopsy had been completed, and the Law-

45

ler Morturary Co. was preparing the body for placement in a casket.

Representative Boggs. At this time did you see the whole body?

A—Yes, sir.

Representative Boggs. Did you see any other wound other than the head wound?

A—Yes, sir; I saw an opening in the back, about 6 inches below the neckline to the right-hand side of the spinal column.

Representative Boggs. Was there a frontal neck injury?

Mr. Hill. There was an area here that had been opened but—

Mr. Specter. You are indicating—

A—In the neck. It was my understanding at that time that this was done by a tracheotomy. . . .

ABRAHAM ZAPRUDER

The testimony of a Dallas dress manufacturer who took movies of the assassination:

Mr. Liebeler. Tell us what happened as you took these pictures.

A—Well, as the car came in line almost—I believe it was almost in line—I was standing up here and I was shooting through a telephoto lens, which is a zoom lens and as it reached about—I imagine it was around here—I heard the first shot and I saw the President lean over and grab himself like this (holding his left chest area).

Mr. Liebeler. Grab himself on the front of his chest?

A—Right—something like that. In other words, he was sitting like this and waving and then after the shot he just went like that.

Mr. Liebeler. He was sitting upright in the car and you heard the shot and you saw the President slump over?

A—Leaning—leaning toward the side of Jacqueline. For a moment I thought it was, you know, like you say, "Oh, he got me," when you hear a shot—you've heard these expressions and then I saw—I don't believe the President is going to make jokes like this, but before I had a chance to organize my mind, I heard a second shot and then I saw his head opened up and the blood and everything came out and I started—I can hardly talk about it [the witness crying].

Mr. Liebeler. That's all right, Mr. Zapruder, would you like a drink of water? Why don't you step out and have a drink of water?

A—I'm sorry—I'm ashamed of myself really, but I couldn't help it.

Mr. Liebeler. Nobody should ever be ashamed of feeling that way, Mr. Zapruder. I feel the same way myself. It was a terrible thing.

Let me go back now for just a moment and ask you how many shots you heard altogether.

A—I thought I heard two, it could be three, because to my estimation I thought he was hit on the second—I really don't know. The whole thing that has been transpiring—it was very upsetting and as you see—I got a little better all the time and this came up again and it to me looked like the second shot, but I don't know. I never even heard a third shot.

Mr. Liebeler. You didn't hear any shot after you saw him hit?

A—I heard the second—after the first shot—I saw him leaning over and after the second shot—it's possible after what I saw, you know, then I started yelling, "They killed him, they killed him," and I just felt that somebody had ganged up on him and I was still shooting the pictures until he got under the underpass—I don't even know how I did it. And then, I didn't even remember how I got down from that abutment there, but there I was, I guess, and I was walking toward—back toward my office and screaming, "They killed him, they killed him," and the people that I met on the way didn't even know what happened and they kept yelling, "What happened, what happened, what happened?" It seemed that they had heard a shot but they didn't know exactly what had happened as the car sped away, and I kept on just yelling, "They killed him, they killed him, they killed him," and finally got to my office and my secretary— I told her to call the police or the Secret Service—I don't know what she was doing, and that's about all. I was very much upset. Naturally, I couldn't imagine such a thing being done. I just went to my desk and stopped there until the police came and then we were required to get a place to develop the films. I knew I had something, I figured it might be of some help—I didn't know what. . . .

WILLIAM R. GREER

The testimony of the Secret Service agent driving the car in which President Kennedy was mortally wounded.

Mr. Specter. Now, would you tell us just what occurred as you were proceeding down Elm Street at that time?

A—Well, when we were going down Elm Street, I heard a noise that I thought was a backfire of one of the motorcycle policemen. And I didn't—it did not affect me like anything else. I just thought that it is what it was. We had had so many motorcycles around us. So I heard this noise. And I thought that is what it was. And then I heard it again. And I glanced over my shoulder. And I saw Governor Connally like he was starting to fall. Then I realized there was something wrong. I tramped on the accelerator, and at the same time Mr. Kellerman said to me, "Get out of here fast." And I cannot remember even the other shots or noises that was. I cannot quite remem-

47

ber any more. I did not see anything happen behind me any more, because I was occupied with getting away . . .

After he [Kellerman] had said to me, "Get out of here fast." He got the radio and called to the lead car, "Get us to a hospital fast, nearest hospital fast."

Mr. Specter. Do you recall whether he said anything else at that time?

A—After he had said to me, he said, "12:30," and that is all I remember him saying to me was 12:30, and he had communications with the cars but I don't remember what he had said to them.

Mr. Specter. Did he say just "12:30," or was it 12:30 used in a sentence?

A—He said "12:30." He looked at his watch, he said "12:30," and we were in the underpass at the time . . .

I came up alongside one or two motorcycle men and I called to them "get to a hospital fast." You know, I called to them "hospital."

Mr. Specter. Were you led to the hospital?

A—Yes, sir; I was led to the hospital by the police car who was preceding me.

Mr. Specter. Did you have any independent knowledge of the route from where you were?

A—No, sir.

Mr. Specter. From the point of assassination to the hospital?

A—No, sir; I didn't . . .

I didn't know how badly anyone really was injured. I had great thoughts the President was still living and that was the only thing I was thinking about was to get them in quick.

Mr. Specter. Did you observe anything specific which led you to the conclusion that the President was still living?

A—No, sir. When he was in the emergency room and I was there, I did see his chest expand and move, the movement of the chest a time or so . . .

I was inside the door, I know, I kept the door closed most of the time, let doctors and nurses in and out while he was—while they were working on him. I stayed inside the emergency room door.

Mr. Specter. Was there any special reason for you to leave part of the time?

A—No, sir; I didn't go any farther away than outside the door.

Mr. Specter. Were there any other Secret Service agents inside the emergency room at that time?

A—Not at that time; I was inside the door.

Mr. Specter. Where was Mrs. Kennedy at this time?

A—Mrs. Kennedy was outside the door. They got her a chair out there for a little while and then she insisted on coming in and she got in the corner for a little while there and stayed there a little while and I don't quite remember the time she went over to his body but she did go over there, and I don't remember how far along the doctors had been on him when that happened . . .

Mr. Specter. Have you ever had any reaction or thought at any time since the assassination that the shots came from the front of the car?

A—No, sir; I had never even the least thought that they could come. There was no thought in my mind other than that they were behind me . . .

Representative Ford. Did you hear the President say anything after the first shot?

A—No, sir; I never heard him say anything; never at any time did I ever hear him say anything.

Representative Boggs. Did Mrs. Kennedy say anything to you while you were driving to the hospital?

A—No, sir; she didn't . . .

ROY H. KELLERMAN

The testimony of the Secret Service Agent who was in charge of President Kennedy's trip to Texas:

Mr. Specter. What were your specific duties back on November 22 of 1963?

A—My specific duty, gentlemen, on the 22d of November of 1963, I was in charge of the detail for this trip of President Kennedy, for the trip to Texas in those 2 days. . . .

On November 22, the activities started at around 8:25 in the morning when the President, accompanied by the then Vice President Johnson, and a few congressional leaders walked out the front door, across this street which was a parking lot, and a few minutes' speech was made to the gathering there. It was a light drizzle at the time. From there we returned to the hotel and he attended a breakfast given by the chamber of commerce and, I believe it was, a citizens group of Fort Worth. On completion of the breakfast he returned to his suite. The weather was then changing. It had quit raining and it looked like it was going to break out and be a real beautiful day. In the neighborhood of 10 o'clock in the morning I received a call from Mr. Lawson, Special Agent Lawson, who had the advance from Dallas, Tex.

Mr. Specter. Mr. Lawson was with the Secret Service, was he?

A—Yes, sir; he is. He asked me to determine whether the bubbletop car that the President would ride in in Dallas that day should have the top down or remain up. . . .

Mr. Specter. With reference to the bubble top which you have heretofore described, of what is that composed?

A—It is composed of plastic, clear plastic substance. Its use would be for a weather matter whereby the President or his occupants can see out. It is not an enclosed car.

Mr. Specter. Is it bulletproof?

A—It is not bulletproof.

Mr. Specter. Is it bullet resistant in any way?

A—It's not bullet resistant.

Mr. Specter. Could you describe in a general way at this point what efforts, if any, have been made to obtain a bulletproof clear top for the President's automobile?

A—Presently?

Mr. Specter. Presently or heretofore.

A—I am going to have to go in the present day.

Mr. Specter. Fine.

A—This same vehicle, I understand, is being completed with a bullet-resistant top and sides. . . .

Representative Ford. Could the present top deflect in any way, destroy the accuracy of a shot?

A—This would be a guess, Mr. Congressman. I would think that it would be deterred for, let's say, the velocity of a missile coming in at great speed, I think it would deter it; I don't think it would eliminate—it still would enter the top.

Mr. Specter. Do you know how the President's automobile was transported from Washington, D.C., to Texas?

A—Yes, sir. The President's vehicle was transported to San Antonio by cargo aircraft. It was flown to San Antonio a day before the President arrived. It was then flown from San Antonio to Dallas, where it was used on November 22. This vehicle was not used in the other two stops at Houston and Fort Worth.

Senator Cooper. Do you know whether or not prior to November 22 the President's car had ever been equipped with a top which had the capacity to stop or deflect a bullet?

A—Never had been, Senator.

As I said earlier, the weather was clearing in Fort Worth; it was going to be a nice day. I asked Mr. Kenneth O'Donnell, who is President Kennedy's appointment secretary: "Mr. O'Donnell," I said, "the weather; it is slightly raining in Dallas, predictions of clearing up. Do you desire to have the bubbletop on the President's car or do you, or would you desire to have it removed for this parade over to the Trade Mart?"

His instructions to me were, "If the weather is clear and it is not raining, have that bubbletop off," and that is exactly what I relayed to Mr. Lawson. . . .

Mr. Specter. You described a radio. Will you tell us a little more fully what radio transmission there was in the motorcade, please?

A—Yes, sir. This lead car which Mr. Lawson was in has a portable radio. The President's car is next. This is equipped

50

with a permanent set radio on the same frequency as that gentleman up front. The next car is our Secret Service followup car which has a permanent installation. The Secret Service car, as I say, is equipped with a permanent installation which connects the President's car and the lead car. The next car in back of our Secret Service car was the then Vice President Johnson. The Secret Service agent in that car had a portable radio that he could read all three of us ahead. His car following was a small Secret Service followup car, and they, too, had a portable set, which could read all four. . . .

Mr. Specter. Describe the occupants of that car, indicating their positions, if you can, please.

A—Yes. The President—President Kennedy sat on the right rear seat. Next to him on the left seat was Mrs. Kennedy. On the right jump seat in front of President Kennedy was Governor Connally. On the left jump seat in front of Mrs. Kennedy was Mrs. Connally. I sat on the right passenger seat of the driver's seat, and Special Agent William Greer drove the vehicle.

Mr. Specter. How far were you behind the lead car? . . .

A—As we turned off Houston onto Elm and made the short little dip to the left going down grade, as I said, we were away from buildings, and were—there was a sign on the side of the road which I don't recall what it was or what it said, but we no more than passed that and you are out in the open, and there is a report like a firecracker, pop. And I turned my head to the right because whatever this noise was I was sure that it came from the right and perhaps into the rear, and as I turned my head to the right to view whatever it was or see whatever it was, I heard a voice from the back seat and I firmly believe it was the President's, "My God, I am hit," and I turned around and he has got his hands up here like this.

Mr. Specter. Indicating right hand up toward his neck?

A—That is right, sir. In fact, both hands were up in that direction.

Senator Cooper. Which side of his neck?

A—Beg pardon?

Senator Cooper. Which side of his neck?

A—Both hands were up, sir; this one is like this here and here we are with the hands—

Mr. Specter. Indicating the left hand is up above the head.

A—In the collar section.

Mr. Specter. As you are positioning yourself in the witness chair, your right hand is up with the finger at the ear level as if clutching from the right of the head; would that be an accurate description of the position you pictured there?

A—Yes. Good. There was enough for me to verify that the man was hit. So, in the same motion I come right back and grabbed the speaker and said to the driver, "Let's get out of here; we are hit," and grabbed the mike and I said, "Lawson, this is Kellerman,"—this is Lawson, who is in the front car. "We are hit; get us to the hospital immediately." Now, in the seconds that I talked just now, a flurry of shells come into the car. I then looked back and this time Mr. Hill, who was riding on the left front bumper of our followup car, was on the back trunk of that car; the President was sideways down into the back seat.

Mr. Specter. Indicating on his left side.

A—Right; just like I am here.

Mr. Specter. You mean, correct, left side?

A—Correct; yes, sir. Governor Connally by that time is lying flat backwards into her lap—Mrs. Connally—and she was lying flat over him.

Mr. Specter. Who was lying flat over him?

A—Mrs. Connally was lying flat over the Governor.

Mr. Specter. You say that you turned to your right immediately after you heard a shot?

A—Yes, sir.

Mr. Specter. What was the reason for your reacting to your right?

A—That was the direction that I heard this noise, pop.

Mr. Specter. Do you have a reaction as to the height from which the noise came?

A—No; honestly, I do not.

Representative Ford. Was there any reaction that you noticed on the part of Greer when the noise was noticed by you?

A—You are referring, Mr. Congressman, to the reaction to get this car out of there?

Representative Ford. Yes.

A—Mr. Congressman, I have driven that car many times, and I never cease to be amazed even to this day with the weight of the automobile plus the power that is under the hood; we just literally jumped out of the God-damn road.

Representative Ford. As soon as this noise was heard, or as soon as you transmitted this message to Lawson?

A—As soon as I transmitted to the driver first as I went to Lawson. I just leaned sideways to him and said, "Let's get out of here. We are hit."

Representative Ford. That comment was made to Greer; not to Lawson?

A—Yes, sir; that is right.

Representative Ford. And the subsequent message was to Lawson?

A—Correct. That is right.

Mr. Specter. With relationship to that first noise that you have described, when did you hear the voice?

A—His voice?

Mr. Specter. We will start with his voice.

A—OK. From the noise of which I was in the process of

turning to determine where it was or what it was, it carried on right then. Why I am so positive, gentlemen, that it was his voice—there is only one man in that back seat that was from Boston, and the accents carried very clearly.

Mr. Specter. Well, had you become familiar with the President's voice prior to that day?

A—Yes; very much so.

Mr. Specter. And what was the basis for your becoming familiar with his voice prior to that day?

A—I had been with him for 3 years.

Mr. Specter. And had you talked with him on a very frequent basis during the course of that association?

A—He was a very free man to talk to; yes. He knew most all the men, most everybody who worked in the White House as well as everywhere, and he would call you.

Mr. Specter. And from your experience would you say that you could recognize the voice?

A—Very much, sir; I would.

Mr. Specter. Now, I think you may have answered this, but I want to pinpoint just when you heard that statement which you have attributed to President Kennedy in relationship to the sound which you described as a firecracker.

A—This noise which I attribute as a firecracker, when this occurred and I am in the process of determining where it comes because I am sure it came off my right rear somewhere; the voice broke in right then.

Mr. Specter. At about the same time?

A—That is correct, sir. That is right.

Mr. Specter. Now, did President Kennedy say anything beside, "My God, I am hit."

A—That is the last words he said, sir.

Mr. Specter. Did Mrs. Kennedy say anything at that specific time?

A—Mr. Specter, there was an awful lot of confusion in that back seat. She did a lot of talking which I can't recall all the phrases.

Mr. Specter. Well, pinpoint—

A—But after the flurry of shots, I recall her saying, "What are they doing to you?" Now again, of course, my comparison of the voice of her speech—certainly, I have heard it many times, and in the car there was conversation she was carrying on through shock, I am sure.

Mr. Specter. Well, going back to the precise time that you heard the President say, "My God, I am hit," do you recollect whether she said anything at that time?

A—No.

Mr. Specter. Whether or not you can re-create what she said?

A—Not that I can recall right then, sir. This statement, or whatever she said, happened after all the shooting was over.

Mr. Specter. All right. Now, you have described hearing a noise which sounded like a firecracker and you have described turning to your right and described hearing the President's voice and, again, what was your next motion, if any, or movement, if any?

A—After I was sure that his statement was right that he was hit, turned from the back I come right down—

Mr. Specter. You just indicated that you had turned to the left. Had you turned to the left after hearing his voice?

A—Yes; certainly.

Mr. Specter. And what did you see? You have described what you saw in terms of position of his hands.

A—That was it.

Mr. Specter. What did you do next?

A—That is when I completely turned to my right and grabbed for the mike in the same motion, sideways telling the driver, "Let's get out of here; we are hit." . . .

As we arrived at the hospital I immediately got out of the car. Our followup car is in back of us, as you will recall. I yelled to the agents, "Get in"—"Go get us two stretchers on wheels."

In the meantime in a matter of seconds—I don't know how they got out so fast—I turned right around to the back door and opened it. By this time Mrs. Connally had raised up, and the Governor is lying in her lap, face up. His eyes are open and he is looking at me, and I am fairly sure he is alive. By this time I noticed the two stretchers coming out of the emergency room, and I said to the Governor, I said, "Governor, don't worry; everything is going to be all right." And he nodded his head, which I was fairly convinced that that man was alive.

By this time the stretcher is there. I get inside on one side of him, and Special Agent Hill on the other. Somebody is holding his feet, and we remove the Governor and put him on the stretcher and they take him in.

We then get in and help Mrs. Connally out. Our next move is to get Mrs. Kennedy off from the seat, which was a little difficult, but she was removed. Then Mr. Hill removed his coat and laid it over the President's face and shoulder. He and I among two other people—I don't know—we lifted up the President and put him on a stretcher and followed him right into the emergency room.

Gentlemen, this emergency room is a, it looks like a, checkerboard; it has a walkway down the center and a crossway and there are rooms on each side. President Kennedy was put into the one on the right, Governor Connally across on the left. And as we pushed the wheelchair in—we pushed the stretcher inside, the medical people just seemed to form right in, right there, and I walked around him and I wanted to look at this man's face, they had him face up.

54

Senator Cooper. The President?

A—The President; I am sorry. I did not see any wounds in that man's face.

Mr. Specter. Indicating with your hand at that moment the front part of his face?

A—Right, sir. . . .

Mr. Specter. What was the rearmost or uppermost portion of President Kennedy's head which you could observe at that time?

A—It was the hairline to the ear, sir.

Mr. Specter. Proceed.

A—Having all the medical people in there, my business is left in their hands. So I left. Mrs. Kennedy, incidentally, was still in there.

Mr. Specter. In where, sir?

A—In the emergency room with him. Which after a few minutes they convinced her to leave, and she sat outside the room while they were working over the President. I walked into this center area of this emergency room—and I am looking for a telephone—which there is a little doctor's office and I walked inside, and I am alone at that time, except one medic who was in there. There are two phones and I said, "Can I use either one of these phones to get outside?" and he said, "Yes; just pick one up."

By this time Mr. Lawson enters and also Mr. Hill. I asked Mr. Lawson for the telephone number of the Dallas White House switchboard. He immediately has it and I said to Mr. Hill, "Will you dial it, please?" By that time a medic comes into the room from President Kennedy's section and he asks if anybody knows the blood type of the President—President Kennedy. We all carry it. I produce mine, and that is what I believe they used; I am not sure. By this time the connection is made with the White House operator in Dallas, and I took the phone, identified myself, and I said, "Give me Washington. Please don't pull this line; let's leave it open."

I got the Washington operator and I said, identified myself, and I said, "Give me Mr. Behn."

Mr. Behn was in the office at the time, and I said—his name is Gerald Behn—and I said, "Gerry, we have had an incident here in Dallas. The President, the Governor have been shot. We are in the emergency room of the Parkland Memorial Hospital." I said, "Mark down the time." Of course, since that time until now we have disagreed on about 3 minutes. I said it is 12:38, which would be 1:38 Dallas time. I am sorry—Washington time.

Mr. Specter. Was that at the time you were talking to Mr. Behn?

A—To Mr. Behn; yes, sir.

Mr. Specter. And your version is that it is 12:38 Dallas time?

A—12:38. He said it was 12:41; he told me the next day.

Mr. Specter. May I interrupt you there for you to tell us how long after you arrived at the hospital did you make that telephone call to Mr. Behn, to the best of your recollection?

A—Three to five minutes. . . .

Mr. Specter. Mr. Kellerman, there is a report from the Federal Bureau of Investigation designated "Bureau File No. 105"—I believe there is an "S," although it is somewhat illegible on my copy—"S2555, report of Special Agent Robert P. Gemberling," dated December 10, 1963, which refers to an interview of you by Special Agent Francis X. O'Neill, Jr., and James W. Sibert, in which the following is set forth:

"He"—and this obviously refers to you—"advised that he heard a shot and immediately turned around looking past Governor Connally who was seated directly in back of him, to the President. He observed the President slumped forward and heard him say 'get me to a hospital.' Mr. Kellerman then heard Mrs. Kennedy say, 'Oh, no,' as the President leaned toward her." That is the end of the quotation. My question is: Did you hear him; did you hear President Kennedy say, "Get me to a hospital"?

A—No, sir.

Mr. Specter. Did you hear Mrs. Kennedy say, "Oh, no"?

A—No, sir.

Mr. Specter. Do you have any knowledge or explanation as to why you would have been so quoted in the report of the FBI?

A—When these two gentlemen talked to me, I don't know where they got those quotes, because the only two things that I told them, they were interested in what I heard from the people in the back seat, and one said "my God, I have been hit," which was President Kennedy, and Mrs. Kennedy said, "What are they doing to you?" . . .

Mr. Specter. How long, if at all, was she inside the emergency room with President Kennedy?

A—This I can't truly answer. However, I should say that, as for the casket being brought into the hospital, another gentleman came into this little doctor's room, his name I don't recall, but he represented himself to be from the Health Department or commission, some form. He said to me, he said, "There has been a homicide here, you won't be able to remove the body. We will have to take it down there to the mortuary and have an autopsy." I said, "No, we are not." And he said, "We have a law here whereby you have to comply with it."

With that Dr. Burkley walked in, and I said, "Doctor, this man is from some health unit in town. He tells me we can't remove this body." The Doctor became a little enraged; he said, "We are removing it." He said, "This is the President of the United States and there should be some consideration in an event like this." And I told this gentleman, I said, "You are

56

going to have to come up with something a little stronger than you to give me the law that this body can't be removed."

So, he frantically called everybody he could think of and he hasn't got an answer; nobody is home. Shortly he leaves this little room and it seems like a few minutes he is back and he has another gentleman with him, and he said, "This is"—the name escapes me—he said, "He is a judge here in Dallas," and he said, "He will tell you whether you can remove this body or not." I said, "It doesn't make any difference. We are going to move it," and I said, "Judge, do you know who I am?"

And he said, "Yes," and I said, "There must be something in your thinking here that we don't have to go through this agony; the family doesn't have to go through this. We will take care of the matter when we get back to Washington." The poor man looked at me and he said, "I know who you are," and he said, "I can't help you out." I said, "All right, sir." But then I happened to look to the right and I can see the casket coming on rollers, and I just left the room and let it out through the emergency entrance and we got to the ambulance and put it in, shut the door after Mrs. Kennedy and General McHugh and Clinton Hill in the rear part of this ambulance.

I am looking around for Mr. Greer and I don't spot him directly because I want to get out of here in a hurry, and I recognize Agent Berger and I said, "Berger, you get in the front seat and drive and, Mr. Stout, you get in the middle and I will get on this side," and as we are leaving—Mr. Lawson, I should say, was in a police car that led us away from Parkland Memorial Hospital. As we are leaving a gentleman taps on the driver's window and they roll it down and he says, "I will meet you at the mortuary." "Yes, sir." We went to the airport, gentlemen.

Mr. Specter. Who said, "Yes, sir"?

A—I did, sir. We went to the airport. In the meantime, Mr. Johnson had been taken to the airplane. They had secured the airport; nobody was there. They had removed seats off the rear part of the plane so we could put the body and the casket in it. As we got to the airport the ramp was there; we opened the door, and we moved the casket out and walked it right up to the plane. . . .

Mr. Specter. Now, then, you have specified the time of departure from Parkland Hospital and en route back to Love Field at what, sir?

A—We departed at 4 minutes after 2 from Parkland.

Mr. Specter. What time did you arrive at the President's plane?

A—2:14.

Mr. Specter. What were your next activities?

A—Our next time, we had waited until Judge Sarah Hughes had arrived for the swearing-in ceremonies.

Mr. Specter. What time did the swearing-in ceremonies occur?

A—2:37 p.m.

Mr. Specter. And what time did the plane depart from Dallas?

A—We left at 2:48.

Mr. Specter. Were you present during the swearing-in ceremonies?

A—Yes, sir.

Mr. Specter. In a general way, tell us who else was present there, recognizing that you don't know all the people there.

A—Yes. President Johnson, Mrs. Johnson, Mrs. Kennedy, Malcolm Kilduff. He was the press secretary for that trip. Congressman Thornberry, Congressman Thomas, Marie Fehmer, Mrs. Evelyn Lincoln, Jack Valenti, Bill Moyers, Special Agent Johns. There was another congressional man—I believe his name was Congressman Roberts—Brooks; I am sorry; Congressman Brooks. The picture was taken by Capt. Cecil Stoughton and myself.

Mr. Specter. What time did the President's plane arrive back at the Washington area?

A—May I look at my notes, sir?

Mr. Specter. Yes; you may. Identify for us, if you will, what notes you are referring to.

A—5:58 p.m. This is my report. . . .

By the time it took us to take the body from the plane into the ambulance, and a couple of carloads of staff people who followed us, we may have spent 15 minutes there. And in driving from Andrews to the U.S. Naval Hospital, I would judge, a good 45 minutes. So there is 7 o'clock. We went immediately over, without too much delay on the outside of the hospital, into the morgue. The Navy people had their staff in readiness right then. There wasn't anybody to call. They were all there. So at the latest, 7:30, they began to work on the autopsy. And, as I said, we left the hospital at 3:56 in the morning. Let's give the undertaker people 2 hours. So they were through at 2 o'clock in the morning. I would judge offhand that they worked on the autopsy angle 4½, 5 hours.

Mr. Specter. And were you present when the funeral director's personnel were preparing the body?

A—I was; yes, sir.

Mr. Specter. And about what time, then, did they complete their work?

A—They were all through at 3:30.

Mr. Specter. And what did you do immediately after they completed their work?

A—All right. Our communication between the Kennedy family and staff, who were on another floor in the hospital, was in this regard. We had telephone communication whereby we would tell them if the body is ready to be taken out of the morgue and into the ambulance. And they would hit the elevator and come right out the same way. So the 5 minutes it took to load the people in, we left the hospital morgue part at least at 3:50, and, as I say, we were off at 3:56, driving to the White House. . . .

KENNETH P. O'DONNELL

The testimony, in full, of a close friend and special assistant to President Kennedy:

Mr. Specter. Would you rise, please? Do you solemnly swear that the testimony you shall give in this deposition proceeding before the President's Commission on the Assassination of President Kennedy will be the truth, the whole truth, and nothing but the truth, so help you God?

A—I do.

Mr. Specter. Mr. O'Donnell, the purpose of our asking you to testify today is to obtain whatever knowledge you have about the origin of the trip to Texas by President Kennedy, the events during the trip, and the trip back to Washington, D.C., on November 22. With that general statement of purpose, I will ask you if you have any objection to giving a deposition at this time?

A—I do not.

Mr. Specter. Would you state your full name for the record, please?

A—Kenneth P. O'Donnell.

Mr. Specter. What were your duties on November 22, 1963?

A—I was special assistant to the President. I was in charge of his appointments and any itineraries that he might have.

Mr. Specter. How long had you served in that capacity?

A—I served as special assistant to the President since the inauguration, January 20, 1961, with the same duties.

Mr. Specter. Were you a party to the original conversations and decisions for President Kennedy to make a trip to Texas in November of 1963?

A—I was.

Mr. Specter. Would you outline the origin of that trip to Texas, please?

A—The origin of the trip I would think came from a conversation between the President, then Vice President Johnson, and myself. It concerned President Kennedy's desire, and President Johnson's desire that he come to Texas and spend some time there, looking forward to the campaign of 1964, in which Texas would play a very vital role in President Kennedy's view.

Mr. Specter. Approximately when did that first conversation occur, Mr. O'Donnell?

A—We had been discussing this for almost 6 or 7 months, but the time had never seemed quite right, either in the Vice President's mind or in Governor Connally's mind. Governor

Connally and the Vice President had discussed this. They arrived at a general agreement that it be done some time in the latter part of the month of November. I think this decision probably came in October, some time in October.

Mr. *Specter.* When had President Kennedy been in Dallas prior to the trip of November 1963?

A—The last time the President had been in Dallas was as a candidate for the Presidency.

I correct myself. He had been to—visit Speaker Rayburn in the hospital. I was not on that trip.

Mr. *Specter.* Then aside from the trip to see Speaker Rayburn, in the hospital, had the President been in Dallas at all since the campaign of 1960?

A—He had not.

Mr. *Specter.* Do you know approximately when it was that President Kennedy visited Speaker Rayburn in the hospital in Dallas?

A—I don't know exactly. It would be just before he passed away.

Mr. *Specter.* Does October 1961 sound about right to you?

A—It sounds about right.

Mr. *Specter.* And how many times had President Kennedy been to Texas between the campaign of 1960 and November 1963, if you know?

A—Well, he had been to the Speaker's funeral at Bonham. He had been to Houston, to see the new space center, and also he spoke at Rice Stadium. And he had been to El Paso, on a military inspection tour.

Mr. *Specter.* Are those, then, all the trips he made, to your knowledge?

A—That is all I can recollect at the moment.

Mr. *Specter.* In a general way, what was the purpose of the President's trip to Texas in November of 1963?

A—Well, he hadn't conducted any political activities in Texas. There were great controversies existing. There was a party problem in Texas that the President and the Vice President felt he could be helpful, as both sides of the controversy were supporting President Kennedy, and they felt he could be a bridge between these two groups, and this would be helpful in the election of 1964. I think that is the major reason for the trip.

Mr. *Specter.* Was President Kennedy motivated, to any extent at all, by his interest in making himself as President available to the people generally in every section of the country, including Texas?

A—Very definitely. The President's view of his responsibilities as President of the United States were that he meet the people, that he go out to their homes and see them, and allow them to see him, and discuss, if possible, the views of the world as he sees it, the problems of the country as he sees them. And he felt that leaving Washington for the President of the United States was most necessary—not only for the people, but for the President himself, that he expose himself to the actual basic problems that were disturbing the American people. It helped him in his job here, he was able to come back here with a fresh view of many things. I think he felt very strongly that the President ought to get out of Washington, and go meet the people on a regular basis.

Mr. Specter. Did he enjoy that exposure, strictly as a personal matter?

A—He enjoyed it very much. The President—liked people, and he liked to mingle with people.

Mr. Specter. When were the specific dates of November 21 and November 22 finally set as being the precise times for the trip to Texas?

A—Well, I am not clear in my recollection of that. I would think some time early in November. I know Thanksgiving was one of the problems we had to work with. We decided that would be the best time to go, in that general area, and we, in general, would keep a file—once we agreed we were going to Texas—we would keep a file on all the speaking engagements, all the invitations the President had received.

I would go to that file and select some that might look promising. One of them that I recollect was an invitation from Congressman Albert Thomas, or his committee, that was giving him an appreciation dinner—not the Congressman himself. And the President was very fond of Congressman Thomas, he was most helpful to him, and I knew he would want to go, if this was at all possible. I would think that probably had more to do with setting the actual definite dates of the 21st and 22d.

Mr. Specter. When, if you recall, was the Secret Service notified of the forthcoming trip to Texas?

A—I would think they would be notified around the first week in November. The general desire is that they have the specific information at least on the places that he might go 3 weeks prior to the trip.

Mr. Specter. And who among the members of the Presidential staff would be charged with the responsibility for coordinating the trip with the Secret Service?

A—That would be my responsibility. The manner in which we would set it up would be that I would notify the head here, who is Gerry Behn, and Gerry Behn would ask me when we were sending people down, so that his people and our people could go down at the same time. And I recollect that Jerry Bruno was one of them.

The first step would be to confer with the Governor, go over the general proposals that the Governor would make, and then bring it back to me. And I would go over it with the Governor and the Vice President and the President.

Mr. Specter. What planning was undertaken with respect

to the determination of the motorcade route through Dallas?

A—Well, I think once we arrived—we chose the four cities we were going into. And then the advance men and the Secret Service went out. Then we would work backwards from where we had to be at what time, and what things we had agreed we would do there. And the original—Dallas, as I recollect, was going to be an evening affair. The Governor thought the evening affair should be in Austin, and that we should hit Dallas around noontime.

Mr. Specter. When you say the evening affair, what are you referring to specifically there?

A—There was a political dinner which was to be conducted at Austin that evening, at the end of which the President was going with the Vice President to the ranch. This was a political fundraising dinner.

Mr. Specter. Now, had there been any conversation given at all to omitting a motorcade through Dallas?

A—None.

Mr. Specter. And what were the considerations behind the decision on having a motorcade through Dallas?

A—Well, we had a motorcade wherever we went. Particularly when we went to a large city, the purpose of going there was to give the President as much exposure to the people of Dallas and vice versa, the people of Dallas to the President, as possible.

The speaking engagement was a luncheon which was rather limited. And the President would not want to leave Dallas feeling that the only ones that were able to see him were a rather select group. So it would be automatic, and we would not even proceed with instructions, that the advance man and the Secret Service would, within the time allotted to them—would bring the President into Dallas, through an area which exposes him to the greatest number of people.

Mr. Specter. When was a decision made, if you recall, as to the precise route that the motorcade would follow through Dallas?

A—I don't recall. I would think it would be perhaps a week before the final decision was made. The President would not involve himself in anything like this. Once we agreed on where he would go, that was my responsibility to work it out. The normal course of events—they would say to me, "Do you want a motorcade in Dallas?" I would say, "Yes; this is how much time you have got." They would work out a motorcade. The Secret Service would time the route. Once they had worked out this point, they would come back to me and say, "We have accomplished the purpose you want." The Secret Service would say it takes so much time, the Governor would say "You have to be here at a certain time." Once all those are put together, the route is laid out and accepted.

Mr. Specter. Do you recall how long after the determination of the motorcade route that that information was transmitted to the press in Dallas?

A—I don't. I would think on the transmission to the press that that would not come from here anyway. That would come from down there. I would think the Governor's office would probably put that out. We would under normal circumstances inform through Mr. Salinger's office, I would inform him of the trip, and then I would give him a schedule that is given to me by the Secret Service, which would give the times, but no routes—times and locations, and would go along that he would arrive at 12 o'clock, address such and such a group at 1 o'clock. So we would not normally be privy—they could be saying to me, "We are going down 12th Street"—it would not mean anything to me. So I would think that our advance man and the Governor's advance man would make a decision on when they were going to announce the route.

I would think that was almost normal. You might say you wanted to do it 4 days ahead of time in New York, and the local fellow would really determine it—"Down here we do it this way."

Mr. Specter. Would the route be disclosed to the press as a matter of normal procedure in general as soon as it was ascertained?

A—Yes.

Mr. Specter. Were there any factors peculiar to Dallas which delayed the determination of the motorcade route?

A—The only factor that really did hold up a final decision was we had not been able to finally agree on where he would end up and where he would deliver the speech. There was a controversy between the Governor, and between some of the local democratic figures, and between our people, as to whether the place finally selected was the best place for the President to give the address. The Governor felt very strongly on it. And we finally acquiesced to his views. But I would think that came rather late in the game, and it would have altered the route quite dramatically.

Mr. Specter. Would you tell us if there was any consideration at all given to omitting Dallas as a stop on the trip in Texas?

A—I don't think so; no. I would think that the President would not have—once he had agreed to go to three or four other cities, that could not possibly go to Texas and avoid Dallas. It would cause more controversy—and it would not accomplish for us what really was the long-range purpose of the visit.

Mr. Specter. And the long-range purpose was what, sir?

A—Was to attempt to in some way bridge the gap between the two political groups in Texas who were at odds, and to assist the President and prepare for the 1964 campaign as best he could at this period of time.

Mr. Specter. What was the President's reaction towards Dallas generally, if you know, with respect to the current publicity about, say, Ambassador Stevenson's reception there?

A—Well, he was not in anyway concerned about it. I think that the President was a very charitable man. He felt that really the picture of Dallas as painted—and as a reflection of their press in many ways—was not the real picture of Dallas; that they were Americans like everybody else, that there were good and bad, and the fact that 50 shouting people didn't portray the city of Dallas. He had been there in the 1960 campaign when the Vice President had been spit upon, and the President received one of the finest receptions he ever got. He didn't carry the city. They opposed him. But they were not particularly different than anybody else. And that wouldn't concern him, and I think, very frankly, the more difficult it was the more he liked to go there. But I think he generally felt that the loud noises emanating from Dallas were a very small minority, and so reflected.

Mr. Specter. Had there been any discussion about limiting the trip to Texas to a 1 day venture?

A—I don't recollect any. I do know one of the original thoughts was that he go to this dinner in Austin, which was a political dinner. Whether there was any consideration in some other people's minds that he just go in for the dinner and leave, I know he, number 1, would not consider it.

Mr. Specter. Why not?

A—He would not consider it because he had a great aversion to going into any place to a fundraising political dinner in which he felt that the people that were there were not really representative of the people, but were politically committed people, where it was a business meeting. And he thought this reflected to some degree on the office of the Presidency, that on his only visit to Texas, or any other State in 3 years, that he came to raise money for a political party, that he owed to the people to expose himself to them. So he felt it was a duty of the Presidency to expose himself to the public. So he would not go to any place on a purely—but he certainly considered there were some political problems in Texas—that would also be in his judgment a bad political mistake. So I don't think there was ever any question that he would go some place else.

Mr. Specter. Did you accompany the President on all phases of the trip to Texas?

A—I was with him when he left. The only time that I was not with him was at Congressman Thomas' dinner. He went to the dinner. We ate at the hotel and went directly to the airport.

Mr. Specter. When did you depart, then, from Washington, on that trip to Texas?

A—Well, we left that morning by helicopter from the lawn. I think the records show it is 10:45. But the schedule was on time, certainly arriving there, and, as I recollect, we were on time pretty much the whole way as the schedule would reflect.

Mr. Specter. And from the helicopter at the White House lawn, where was your first stop by helicopter?

A—We stopped and boarded *Air Force 1* at Andrews Air Force Base.

Mr. Specter. Would the time of 11 a.m., as reflected in the records, be accurate as your point of departure, then, from Andrews Air Force Base?

A—Yes; I would think it would be.

Mr. Specter. And your first stop in Texas was what?

A—San Antonio.

Mr. Specter. Arrival time of 1:30 p.m.—would that be an accurate time of arrival, within a few minutes, say, of when you actually set down in San Antonio?

A—I would think that is right. As I say, we were on schedule, and the schedule would indicate we were due to arrive at 1:30.

Mr. Specter. What were the activities at San Antonio, Tex.?

A—We motorcaded through San Antonio and went to the Aerospace Medical Center, where the President made a speech, and from there to a second airport. We had moved *Air Force 1* from one airfield to another, on the other side of the city.

Mr. Specter. At the Aerospace Center, was there a dedication there of some new facilities?

A—Yes.

Mr. Specter. Was there any other public appearance, then, besides the one you mentioned, in San Antonio?

A—No.

Mr. Specter. To where did you go from San Antonio?

A—We flew to Houston.

Mr. Specter. And about what time did you arrive in Houston?

A—I would have to look at the record.

Mr. Specter. Was it late in the afternoon on November 21?

A—Late in the afternoon, I would think around 4 or 5 o'clock.

Mr. Specter. And what were the activities in Houston?

A—We drove from the airfield into the hotel. As I recollect, there were very large crowds.

Mr. Specter. Was that a motorcade procession, also?

A—Motorcade; and particularly as we got in downtown Houston, the crowds were very large, and very enthusiastic. Getting in the hotel was somewhat of a chore.

Mr. Specter. What public appearances did the President then make in Houston?

A—The President spoke at the appreciation dinner for Congressman Thomas. The records will show the location. I did not accompany him. And I went directly from the hotel to the airport, and met him as he got aboard the plane.

Mr. Specter. Approximately when did the Presidential party depart from Houston?

A—Well, I would have to guess again. I would think around 10:30 or 11 o'clock. The alternative was staying overnight in Houston, getting in early in the morning—or getting into Fort Worth late at night, and allowing the President a little more rest, and we selected going to Fort Worth that night.

Mr. Specter. What were the public appearances made by the President, then, in Fort Worth, Tex.?

A—He spoke at 8 o'clock that morning at a breakfast which was given by the business community, as I remember, came back up to his room, chatted for a few minutes, went back down. It had been raining. The sun had just come out. He went out and spoke to a group assembled in the parking lot and went back and departed for—came back upstairs, we chatted for a few minutes again, and then came back down and departed for Carswell.

Mr. Specter. And how did the President travel out of Fort Worth?

A—He left Fort Worth in an open car, traveled by car to Carswell.

Mr. Specter. And from Carswell, what was his mode of travel?

A—*Air Force 1* to Love Field, Dallas.

Mr. Specter. What were the weather conditions on the arrival at Love Field in Dallas?

A—The weather was clear, sunny, excellent weather.

Mr. Specter. What decision had been made as to whether to have an open car in Dallas?

A—The decision had been made to have an open—if the weather was good, he would ride in an open car.

Mr. Specter. And do you recall who made that decision?

A—Well, I would make that decision under normal circumstances. But it was almost an automatic decision, that whenever the weather was clear, he preferred to ride in an open car.

Mr. Specter. Do you recall at approximately what time the Presidential party arrived at Love Field, Tex.—Love Field, Dallas, Tex.?

A—I would think it would be around 11, 11:15. We were on time. We always allowed a few minutes at the airport, because he always shook hands with the crowd. So we left— my recollection is that we departed from Love Field approximately according to the schedule.

Mr. Specter. What were President Kennedy's activities at Love Field?

A—He had no scheduled activities. It was a matter of assembling the motorcade. He got off *Air Force 1,* and he went over to the crowd that was gathered around the rail, shook hands, went up and down.

Mr. Specter. What type of a crowd was it with respect to size?

A—It was a large crowd.

Mr. Specter. Would you tell us how the motorcade was constituted with respect to the general number of the cars and the way they were lined up, if you recall, please?

A—Well, I can't go more than—I got into the second car, and I didn't really look behind me. There was some controversy as to what Congressman sat in what car. We had a lot of Congressmen with us and a lot of dignitaries, and there was a lot of juggling around, which Mr. O'Brien was more involved with than I was, as to where Senator Yarborough and the Vice President and the Congressman sat. But it was a lengthy motorcade, more lengthy than normal. We always tried to keep them down as much as possible. But because of the number of Congressmen and the dignitaries involved.

Mr. Specter. How many cars were there ahead of yours?

A—Well, I think there was a scout car, which was the lead, the President's vehicle, and I was in the car right behind him, in the Secret Service followup car.

Mr. Specter. Who else besides you was in that car?

A—David Powers was with me. All the rest were agents.

Mr. Specter. Do you recall whether anything unusual occurred on the trip from Love Field down to the center of Dallas?

A—No; I thought it was normal—the crowds, going through the suburbs, were, I would say, from medium to heavy for that trip. I noted they were mostly white collar, mostly industrial places we passed by which I would say were highly technical. Therefore, the crowd reflected a middle to an upper class type. They were not unfriendly nor terribly enthusiastic. They waved. But were reserved, I thought.

Mr. Specter. Where were you seated in the car?

A—I was seated in the front jump seat—the jump seat.

Mr. Specter. On the left-hand side or the right-hand side?

A—Left-hand side.

Mr. Specter. And who sat on your immediate right?

A—Mr. Powers.

Mr. Specter. How many agents were there in front of you?

A—Well, there were the normal two or sometimes three in the front seat. I would not be clear as to how many there were. I would think there were about—just guessing—seven or eight agents in the car. Some on the running board, some seated, depending on the speed of the motorcade, or the activity.

Mr. Specter. Was there a front seat in the car, immediately ahead of you?

A—Yes.

Mr. Specter. And was that occupied by Secret Service agents?

A—It was.

Mr. Specter. And how about immediately to your rear? Was there a rear seat?

A—There was a rear seat. There were agents in that—again depending on the speed of the motorcade they were either on the running board, or as it slows up and the crowds got larger the agents would get on the running board. But as it moved along rather rapidly, as it did on the way in, they were seated most of the time.

Mr. Specter. Do you recall whether or not the President's automobile made any stops en route from the airport into the downtown area?

A—I don't recollect, clearly. I would be surprised if it did not. But I don't have any clear recollection.

Mr. Specter. Was it a usual practice for the President to make a stop on the motorcade?

A—If the crowds got too large, he would stop, or if he saw some child had gone to some great extreme with a sign, he would sometimes stop. Usually unless the crowds were particularly heavy, or indicated a need for a stop, he would not stop.

Mr. Specter. And what was the nature of the crowd in downtown Dallas?

A—The nature of the crowd was extremely heavy, one of the heaviest I have seen in any American city.

Mr. Specter. How did they compare with the crowds during the 1960 campaign in Dallas?

A—I would think probably heavier. but very close. They were both very large crowds, very enthusiastic. I think, as I have always noticed, to the President and candidate there is a different aura. But that would be the only difference I would notice in the crowd. There was a little bit more respect—still the same enthusiasm. At the last trip in Dallas he stopped the motorcade every 5 minutes—they mobbed the car. There was none of that. But they were in the middle of the street and off the sidewalks. So there was a very narrow lane to progress through. But they were still very orderly, but cheerful.

Mr. Specter. Did you have any specific reaction to the Dallas crowd in terms of what your expectation might have been about Dallas?

A—Well, I was pleased with it. As a politician, I was particularly pleased with it. I thought we had accomplished what we had come to Dallas to do, was, one, to establish the fact that the average person living in that city was no different than any other American, and that they respected and admired their President. And I felt one of the greatest things that does occur of a political nature is the Congressmen and the political leaders who had also been reading the same newspaper about how unpopular he was, it is good for them to see it really is not true, it is a reflection of a very small minority, and that the President of the United States was extremely popular in Dallas.

And that was the basic reason we went. And as we finished through the business section of town, that was my pleased impression.

Mr. Specter. Do you recall the scene when you left the Main

Street of downtown Dallas, with respect specifically to the presence of a large building which was immediately ahead of the motorcade?

A—I did not. I was looking at the crowd. And I frankly didn't look at the building, except when there were people in the windows. And as we made that turn, I had been standing—I remember I sat down. And as far as I was concerned, that was the end—we were then going to the luncheon—and I didn't notice any building at all.

Mr. Specter. Were you familiar with the identity of the specific plaza there, being known as Dealey Plaza?

A—I was not. I afterward have reflected on it many times.

Mr. Specter. Tell us what occurred then as you made that turn away from the crowded downtown Dallas area and headed toward the plaza area.

A—Well, I sat down. I remember saying to Dave Powers that it was a fantastic crowd. He agreed.

We turned. I remember the overpass. And then the shots occurred—which, at that time, I did not know were shots. My first impression was it was a firecracker. And then either somebody said, "He has been hit," or I noticed the slump—he had been waving out the right side of the car, and I noticed him slump over toward Mrs. Kennedy, and I realized then that they had been shots. But as fast as that realization occurred, I saw the third shot hit. It was such a perfect shot—I remember I blessed myself. I was rather convinced that was a fatal blow.

Mr. Specter. When you say you made a turn, which way did the motorcade turn?

A—Turned to the left.

Mr. Specter. And approximately how far behind the Presidential vehicle was the followup car at that time?

A—My guess would be 5 to 8 feet, the normal—when there are large crowds, pressing in on the side, they try to stay close. It was moving at a steady pace. The crowds were orderly. So he was at a normal—I would presume they were just about turning to step up the speed a little bit, because there would be no crowds from there.

Mr. Specter. What is your best estimate of the speed of the President's vehicle at that time?

A—Well, I would think we probably were going between 15 and 20, up until that moment, and I think he probably had just begun to accelerate probably up to about 25, somewhere in that vicinity.

Mr. Specter. Had the Secret Service followup car completed its left-hand turn prior to the time the shots rang out?

A—My recollection is they had, just about.

I don't recollect a separation of this nature. It was a slight sloping turn, as I remember, and I thought we were right together.

Mr. Specter. So that when you just indicated with your

hands, you were showing a pattern of the Secret Service car having made the turn and straightened up immediately behind the Presidential vehicle proceeding down the street?

A—That is my impression.

Mr. Specter. And was the overpass in sight at that time, did you say?

A—Yes; it was.

Mr. Specter. On which side of the car was President Kennedy seated?

A—He was on the right side.

Mr. Specter. The extreme right?

A—The extreme right.

Mr. Specter. And what was he doing with his hands prior to the time of the shooting, if you recall?

A—He was waving. We had just left the mass of crowds. But as we turned on the grass plot there were four or five people there, and I believe he waved to them.

Mr. Specter. Indicating a right-handed wave?

A—Yes.

Mr. Specter. Where was Governor Connally seated with respect to the President?

A—He was directly in front of the President.

Mr. Specter. Do you know whether or not the President's seat was raised or was it in its extreme low position at that time?

A—I would not know.

Mr. Specter. Do you know what the President's practice was as to whether or not the seat would be raised?

A—I don't know that, either.

Mr. Specter. Do you know what the controls were on the Presidential automobile for raising or lowering the President's seat?

A—No; I don't.

Mr. Specter. How many shots were there in all?

A—Three.

Mr. Specter. What is your best estimate as to the total time which elapsed from the first shot to the last shot?

A—I would say 5 to 6 seconds.

Mr. Specter. And was there any distinguishable tempo to the shots?

A—Yes; the first two came almost simultaneously, came one right after the other, there was a slight hesitation, then the third one.

Mr. Specter. And what was your reaction as to the source of the shots, if you had one?

A—My reaction in part is reconstruction—is that they came from the right rear. That would be my best judgment.

Mr. Specter. Was there any reaction by any of the other people around in any specific direction?

A—The agents all turned to the rear. I would think, watching the reaction of the President when the shot—the first shot hit—that it would be automatic it would have to have come from the rear. I think any experienced agent would make that assumption immediately.

Mr. Specter. And was the reaction of the agents which you have referred to as coming from the rear, to the right rear or to the left rear?

A—The reaction I note would be right rear. And, again, looking at the manner of the President's movement, I would think you would have to feel the thrust of the shot was from the right rear.

Mr. Specter. Now, what was there about the President's movement which leads you to that conclusion?

A—He was leaning out waving. He may have just been withdrawing his hand. And the shot hit him, and threw him to the left. He slumped on Mrs. Kennedy.

Mr. Specter. Were you able to determine a reaction on that slumping movement, as to whether it was the first, the second, or the third shot?

A—It was not the third shot. Whether it was the first or second, I would not know.

Mr. Specter. Do you think it could have been the second shot?

A—Yes; I do. If I had to pick one of the two, I think it might have been the second shot. It seemed to be—but, again, it is a foggy recollection—it seemed to have been that his movement coincided—with such a slight difference of time, that is just guesswork.

Mr. Specter. Did you observe any reaction of Governor Connally in the car?

A—I saw the Governor turn toward the President. The President, in that period of time, had been—they were one right behind the other. And the only reason I would even notice it was when the President had slumped to the left, the Governor then turned, and he was in my view. Otherwise, he would not have been. But the President slumped over, and, therefore, the Governor just turned and I could see him. I had no knowledge that he had been hit at that time.

Mr. Specter. When did you get the first knowledge that he had been hit?

A—When the third shot came. The President was hit. The motorcade accelerated. And one of the agents said, "The Governor has been hit, too."

Mr. Specter. Prior to the time that President Kennedy shifted to the left, then, could you see the Governor at all from your position?

A—Depending on how each one moved, normally, no. The President was directly behind the Governor. But if the President was over to the right waving, then you could see the Governor.

Mr. Specter. On the President's left when the Governor——

71

A—If the President was all the way to the right, the Governor, who was in front of him, would be visible to us. If they were both sitting, they were not. But they did confer back and forth. So the Governor was visible upon occasion. But when he turned around, it was really the first time I had been able to see him clearly.

Mr. Specter. At a time, though, when the President was on the extreme righthand side, waving, would the Governor then have been visible on the President's left or on his right?

A—He would be on his left.

Mr. Specter. Was the jump seat situated, if you know, to the precise front of the President to the right, to the left, or what?

A—I don't know.

Mr. Specter. What reaction did you observe, if any, as to Mrs. Kennedy during the shots?

A—Well, he slumped on her. She appeared to be immediately aware that something had happened. She turned toward him. And then the third shot hit. Obviously, she then knew what happened. She turned, looking at the backup car. Meanwhile Agent Hill had gotten off the car and started running up. She was clambering toward the back, and reached his hand, and he was on the car.

Mr. Specter. Did you observe any reactions in the President's car other than those which you have now testified about?

A—No.

Mr. Specter. At what point did the motocade accelerate?

A—It accelerated, I would think, right about at the time that Agent Hill grabbed onto the back of the car, which would be just a few seconds after the last shot.

Mr. Specter. And at what speed did the motorcade proceed en route to the hospital?

A—Very rapidly. I would guess between 60 and 70 miles an hour.

Mr. Specter. About how long did it take for the motocade to get to the hospital?

A—I would guess 5 to 10 minutes.

Mr. Specter. How far behind the President's car was the followup car in which you were riding at the time the President's car arrived at the hospital?

A—Right behind it, 5 or 6 feet.

Mr. Specter. What occurred at that time?

A—We got out of the car. David Powers got out of the car, went over to the President, and was not visible to me, and was crying, he laid on him. And then they came and took the President—that was the first time I really realized that Governor Connally had been badly hurt, as they also carried Governor Connally out.

Mr. Specter. What was Mrs. Kennedy doing at that time?

A—I believe somebody had helped her out and taken her into the hospital.

Mr. Specter. Was there a coat over President Kennedy at that time?

A—When they took him out, I was standing maybe 3 or 4 feet behind him. There was a wall of people between myself. I didn't see him, nor did I look.

Mr. Specter. Do you know who lifted the President out of the car?

A—I don't.

Mr. Specter. Do you know who lifted the Governor out of the car?

A—I don't.

Mr. Specter. By what means were they taken away from the vicinity of the car?

A—I think they had stretchers. As I say, I was far enough back at that moment that they were milling around, and so many people between my vision and what they were doing, I did not see. I could not be accurate on that.

Mr. Specter. What did you do next, Mr. O'Donnell?

A—I went into the hospital and went right to Mrs. Kennedy. She was seated right outside the room where they had placed the President. I would say she was in a total daze, and as yet not knowing whether there was any hope or not.

Mr. Specter. What were your activities in the period of time immediately following that moment?

A—Well, I stayed with her for a few minutes, and then no one seemed to be able to get any conclusive answer as to the President's condition. As I said, I had seen the shots so clearly, I had a pretty clear view. The first thing I had done—I asked them to get a priest, which they did immediately. I went into the room. There were four or five doctors there. Dr. Burkley I think was there. And I said, "I think we better get a definite answer one way or another—is there any hope at all?" I was unable to get a conclusive answer. But I think I got the answer I needed.

I don't know how Mrs. Kennedy was finally told. I may have told her about at that moment. Between the time and the time I knew definitely, I went to see the Vice President.

Mr. Specter. Who was with him at that time?

A—Mrs. Johnson was with him and an agent who at the time I did not know. I believe it is Youngblood.

Mr. Specter. Where was Vice President Johnson?

A—He was in a room across the hall. You had to go directly across what would probably be the reception room, which was open to the public, and into another room. And I recollect I turned to my right, and he was over more or less in the corner with a screen. He was standing on the right, Mrs. Johnson, I believe, was sitting, the agent was standing at the door.

Mr. Specter. And what conversations, if any, did you have with the then-Vice President Johnson?

A—I told him it looked very, very serious, and in my opinion that it was probably fatal. I hadn't been able to get a totally definite answer, but that I would let him know as soon as it was definite—but it looked pretty black.

I then left him. I don't recollect that he even commented. I left him and went back to Mrs. Kennedy, and within a very few minutes they confirmed the fact that the President was dead.

Mr. Specter. What did you do next?

A—As soon as I was assured that he was dead, and it was definite, I went back to the Vice President and informed him the President was dead, and that in my opinion he ought to get out of there as fast as he could. We had a general discussion. The President's first words to me were that we must look upon this in a sense that it might be a conspiracy of some nature, and that all security must be taken, and that we then discussed whether one of the possible movements might be to move the Presidential aircraft from Love Field to Carswell, where no route of departure could be laid out, and where there would be military security.

We discussed that. It was my opinion that his best movement was to move directly to Love Field. In fact, the routes would not be available anyway, because this was not a schedule —the departure from the hospital to the field would not be covered, if that were a possibility. And that it would be much better if he got to the field immediately, where he was under security and got aboard one of the aircraft.

Mr. Specter. Was there any discussion about his taking the presidential plane, AF–1, as opposed to AF–2?

A—There was not.

Mr. Specter. Did Vice President Johnson look to you in any way for a recommendation on his subsequent plans in terms of your being then in charge of the presidential party?

A—It was my impression that he did, that he, with the President gone—that he felt I was—had to assume a position of responsibility, both with regard to Mrs. Kennedy and as to himself. He asked me, as I recall—he asked me for my advice as to his departure and used the words, "I am in your hands now," at some point in the conversation.

But I did get the impression that he wanted official—that isn't the proper word—but that his movements should be approved by all concerned.

Mr. Specter. Have you now related all the conversation you had at that time with then-Vice President Johnson?

A—To the best of my recollection.

Mr. Specter. What did you do next, then?

A—Next after I left the Vice President, I went back to Mrs. Kennedy. On the way through the lobby I noted the newspapermen were clamoring for information. I met Kilduff. He said, "Should we announce it?" And I said I think that is a de-

74

cision that can only be made by the President "You better ask him." So that was the last I saw of Kilduff.

Mr. Specter. Who is Kilduff?

A—He is the assistant press secretary.

Mr. Specter. Malcolm Kilduff?

A—Malcolm Kilduff.

I then went back to Mrs. Kennedy, who was in a very understandably distraught condition. It was my opinion—I tried to in some way imply that she might leave and come with us, at least to get her out of that room. She was covered with blood.

Mr. Specter. Which room was she in then?

A—She was in the same room. She had not moved. She was sitting near the door.

Mr. Specter. That is the room where the President was treated by the Dallas doctors?

A—Yes; there is a little corridor. There were swinging doors. He was inside the swing door. She was not in the presence of the body.

Mr. Specter. What was her response to you?

A—Her response to me was she would not leave her husband's body. At that point, I realized that she would not. The doctor had continually attempted to get her to take some form of sedation. And she had consistently refused, and told me she would not take anything, that she was going to stay with her husband.

I realized that she was going to stay with her husband, no matter what anybody did, and there was no possible way of in any way getting her to leave. And so, therefore, the only alternative I could see was that we move the President. It is an assumption I probably would have arrived at anyway, but I arrived at it in this manner.

So I went out and got hold of Dr. Burkley and General McHugh, and one of the agents, and Andy Berger, as I recall, and told them to get a casket, to bring it back, and Dr. Burkley would have the doctors prepare the body for removal, and that we would proceed to the airport and go to Washington.

This was done very rapidly, as I recollect. It seems to me it wasn't more than half an hour that they arrived with the casket. I remember just before they arrived I got Dave Powers and said there was a little room in the back that we ought to just take Mrs. Kennedy under some subterfuge, and talk to her in the room while we brought the casket in, because I thought that might be the final blow. And we did, and—but she knew what was going on. She came out and said, "No, I want to watch it all." And she stood in the doorway, and thanked us for our attempt at being compassionate.

And then they took it in, and put the body in the casket.

We were then all prepared to go. The agents told me the

75

ambulance was ready, and they were prepared to move.

We—the casket was brought out about halfway, and a gentleman arrived who said that we would not be allowed to remove the body from the hospital until the necessary papers had been signed.

Mr. Specter. Do you know who he was?

A—I don't recollect who he was. I think he was—maybe from the coroner's office. My assumption is he would be.

But he took this position. We asked—I don't recollect who transmitted the message—that they speed this up as much as possible, and give us some idea how long it took to accomplish this. And they went out into this other little room where there were some telephones, and proceeded to call whoever it was necessary to call to get this permission.

We waited about 10 or 15 minutes, and Dr. Burkley and General McHugh were in the room, and Mr. O'Brien at some time. I went out again and asked them if they had an answer, and nobody seemed to be able to answer the question as to how long it might take, and whether it was a week or an hour.

So I was getting more concerned about Mrs. Kennedy's state all the time—although she appeared composed, as she had from the beginning.

Then a gentleman did arrive who has later been identified for me as a Judge Brown, who was on the telephone calling someone. It had been my assumption that upon his arrival that he had the power to permit us to depart. Dr. Burkley was talking to him in a very agitated manner. And the gentleman was very calm and cool and collected. If my recollection is clear, he said something to the effect that as of now this was just a homicide case, and there were certain things that had to be carried out, one of which I interpreted as an autopsy.

Mr. Specter. Who was it, Mr. O'Donnell, if you recall, who said this was just another homicide case?

A—My feeling is it was Brown, but I really would not be— in the excitement of the moment, the discussion of the autopsy, the signing of a certificate from the hospital, and the treatment of this as a homicide case, I would not want to be unfair and misinterpret who might have said it.

My recollection is it was indicated to us that the President is dead, the hospital has to perform certain functions, and the law must be met, no matter who it is, at this moment. In my own mind, when they said autopsy, I realized we were talking not about hours, but perhaps even days, which was an impossible situation for Mrs. Kennedy.

I talked to Dr. Burkley, and had him suggest to them that they could have a doctor come with us, he could accompany the body at all times, and that we would bring him immediately to the Naval Hospital, and that they could perform whatever necessary chores, and there would be no separation physically from the hospital and the performance of their autopsy.

They refused to consider this.

I in my own mind determined that we had no alternative but to just depart. So I went back in the room. I told Mr. O'Brien, and whoever else was assembled there, that we were going to leave. I notified the Secret Service and General Mc-Hugh, and told them to get ready to depart. We went in and took the body out. Mrs. Kennedy stood right behind it, I think totally unaware of the problems that were then existing, so perhaps confused as to the speed with which we were attempting to depart.

We pushed the casket out through the hall. This first gentleman that had come in, who, I presume, was from the coroner's office, shouted very loudly, "You can't do that, you can't leave here now." Nobody paid any attention to him. We pushed out through another set of swinging doors. I remember a Catholic priest was between this and the doorway, and was praying. It was most disconcerting because we were concerned at all times that some moment they would say stop, and I hated to think what might happen to Mrs. Kennedy if she had to go back and go through this all over again. So we brushed them all aside and came out the same way we had come in, through the same doors.

There was an ambulance there. Andy Berger was seated in the driver's seat. Several agents were there. The body was put into the ambulance, Mrs. Kennedy got in with it. We climbed into a car alongside of it, and we took off for the airport. I told the agents if they would signal ahead, that there were agents at the airfield, and that as soon as we came through the gate, they were to close the gate and let nobody else in.

Mr. Specter. That is the gate at the airfield?

A—Yes.

Mr. Specter. Do you recall approximately what time you left the hospital?

A—I haven't the vaguest idea.

Mr. Specter. Would you have any idea how long it was after you arrived at the hospital that you left the hospital?

A—I wouldn't—it was a couple of hours. But I wouldn't have any idea.

Mr. Specter. About how long did the trip take you from the hospital back to the airport?

A—I am guessing totally at time. I would think it seemed about 15 minutes. It wasn't a long period of time.

Mr. Specter. What occurred then?

A—The drive was uneventful. We went through the gate. We arrived at the Air Force—I didn't know whether it was 1 or 2, to be honest, until I saw the members of the crew. And they unloaded the casket. I remember they had a very, very difficult time getting it up, because of the narrowness of the ramp. It was very difficult for the Secret Service. It seemed at moments it might almost tumble; it was frightening.

77

We got on the plane. And the seats had been taken out on the left side, so they could lay the casket down. The casket was placed down. I told General McHugh to tell the pilot to take off.

Mr. Specter. Do you know whether or not President Johnson had been sworn in at that time?

A—At that time I didn't know President Johnson was on the plane. I did not know whether he had been. Subsequently I realized he had not been.

Mr. Specter. Was there any specific discussion, to your knowledge, or consideration, to your knowledge, of holding the Presidential plane until Mrs. Kennedy and President Kennedy's body arrived on that plane before departing for Washington?

A—There has been no discussion of that to my knowledge. Once the President—the Vice President left, I left him, I had not seen him again. I had been notified he had departed, I had been notified that he arrived, and that was the last I heard of it, until I got on the airplane.

Mr. Specter. What did you do next, after arriving on the airplane?

A—As I say, I told General McHugh to have the plane take off, still all of us under the assumption or apprehension that at some moment we either might not be granted clearance to take off, or that the hospital may have in some way gotten the police to intercept us—the difficulty of that to Mrs. Kennedy was incalculable. I was in a highly desperate strait to get that airplane in the air and back to Washington. As I say, I told General McHugh to tell the pilot to take off.

There was a delay of 2 or 3 minutes, and nothing happened. So I headed up for the cockpit myself, and I ran into McHugh in the meantime who said that President Johnson was aboard, and that he had ordered the pilot to delay, to hold up until he was sworn in. That was the first I knew he was aboard.

I would like to correct that. I must have known he was aboard, because I am sure he must have greeted Mrs. Kennedy as she came aboard. And he and Mrs. Johnson. But I don't have a clear recollection of that in my own mind.

Mr. Specter. Were you present when President Johnson was sworn in?

A—I was.

Mr. Specter. After you arrived back on AF-1, what did you do between that time and the time the plane was airborne?

A—Mrs. Johnson took Mrs. Kennedy into the President's room on *Air Force 1*. I remember she was reluctant to even go in there, but she persuaded her to. And——

Mr. Specter. Who was reluctant to go in?

A—Mrs. Kennedy. And I went up, and the President and I carried on a conversation, which, again my recollections might be hazy—that it had been brought to his attention that I had asked for the plane to take off, and that there was some difference of opinion between him and me. He said to me that he had called the Attorney General, and that the Attorney General had indicated that it was, if not mandatory, at least preferable that he be sworn in prior to the aircraft taking off. I didn't describe what I saw as the problems. I realized it was an inevitable delay. So I don't believe I commented on it. I just listened to him. We sat there.

I went up and talked to the pilot, to make sure they didn't let anybody on the plane, or put the ramps down for anybody, except the judge, under any circumstances. About 10 or 15 minutes later the judge arrived and the swearing in occurred.

Mr. Specter. How soon after the swearing in was the plane airborne, if you recall?

A—It was almost immediate—as soon as he was sworn in, the plane taxied out and took off.

Mr. Specter. On the return flight to Washington, where did you sit?

A—I sat with Mrs. Kennedy almost all the way. We came back—Mr. Powers, Mr. O'Brien, and I stayed in the back compartment. And then Mrs. Kennedy and I—I sat down with her, we sat that way all the way back. The President called me up on one or two occasions and asked me to stay up in the cabin, wanted to talk to me, but I felt I had to stay with Mrs. Kennedy. So I sat with her the whole trip.

Mr. Specter. What did you talk about?

A—We reminisced.

Mr. Specter. Did she have anything to eat on the trip back?

A—No; I think we both had a drink. I tried to get her to take a good strong drink. I had not much luck.

Mr. Specter. She drank part but not all?

A—As I recollect, she just wanted to talk. She talked all the way.

Mr. Specter. What did you do then after your arrival in Washington, D.C.? Or did you come back to Andrews Air Force Base?

A—We arrived at Andrews and meanwhile the Attorney General had been notified, the decision had been made that he would go to Bethesda.

Mr. Specter. Who made that decision, by the way?

A—Mrs. Kennedy.

Mr. Specter. That the autopsy should be performed?

A—I don't think she knew anything about an autopsy. The question is where the body went. We didn't tell her there was to be an autopsy. And the choice was Walter Reed or Bethesda. He being a Navy man, she picked Bethesda.

Mr. Specter. She chose Bethesda, as between Bethesda and Walter Reed?

A—She did.

Mr. Specter. Who made the decision there would be an autopsy, if you know?

A—I don't know who made the decision. I just think we all agreed—we arrived at Bethesda. The Attorney General was there. I think it was just our assumption that this was a necessary part.

Mr. Specter. How did you get from Andrews Air Force Base to Bethesda Naval Hospital?

A—By car.

Mr. Specter. About what time did you arrive at Andrews, if you recall?

A—I don't remember. It was dark. That is all I do recall.

Mr. Specter. About how long was the car trip from Andrews to Bethesda?

A—I would think 45 minutes.

Mr. Specter. And what did you do after your arrival at Bethesda?

A—When we arrived at Bethesda, we went immediately to some room, reception room, where the family was.

Mr. Specter. And how long did you stay there?

A—We stayed there, I would think, until 3 or 4 in the morning. We wanted to stay there until Mrs. Kennedy got back to the house.

We drove back to the White House with her.

Mr. Specter. At what time did you leave her at the White House?

A—I would think 4 or 5 in the morning.

Mr. Specter. After that, did you go home?

A—I did.

Mr. Specter. Who all was present with the family at Bethesda?

A—There was Mr. O'Brien, Mr. Powers—I don't recollect anybody else outside the family.

Mr. Specter. Who from the family was there?

A—As I remember, Jean Kennedy, the Attorney General and his wife, I think Pat and Eunice. There were some other people. Really there were two—there was one room inside, in which they were in, and there was one out in the reception.

Mr. Specter. What was on the balance of the itinerary in Texas after the planned luncheon at the Trade Mart at Dallas on November 22?

A—We were leaving Dallas and going to Austin, and Governor Connally had arranged one or two receptions, and then a large dinner in the evening, a fundraising dinner, and then the President was going to depart from there to the Vice President's ranch, and stay with them through Saturday, and then come back to Washington.

Mr. Specter. And was the estimated time of arrival at the LBJ Ranch about 10 p.m., on the evening of November 22?

A—That would be about right.

Mr. Specter. With the plan then being to depart for Washington on the 23d, Saturday?

A—Yes.

Mr. Specter. What was the President's attitude, in a general way, about Presidential protection—that is, President Kennedy's attitude about Presidential protection, Mr. O'Donnell?

A—Well, his general attitude was that the Secret Service—that there was no protection available to a President of a democracy such as the United States from a demented person who was willing to risk his own life; that if someone wanted to kill a President of the United States, who in a sense wears two hats—he is the leader of a political party as well as our Chief Executive—and by the nature of our system must mingle with crowds, must ride through our cities, and must expose himself to the American people—that the Secret Service would not be, other than the protection that they provide by the screening processes prior to the actual carrying out of a political trip—would not be able to guarantee 100 percent protection, considering one has to mingle with crowds of 50,000 or 100,000 people, and mingle with them at handshaking distance.

Mr. Specter. Had you ever discussed the dangers inherent in a motorcade, for example, with the President?

A—Not specifically in a motorcade. I don't think the President's view was—very frankly, we had discussed this general subject. We used to go on trips, and sit around in the evening and this would come up.

Mr. Specter. What was the President's view expressed during those conversations?

A—His view was that a demented person who was willing to sacrifice his own life could take the President's life. And that if it were to happen, I think his general view was it would happen in a crowded situation. I don't think it entered his mind that it might happen in the fashion as of a motorcade.

Mr. Specter. What was his reaction to that risk?

A—I think he felt that was a risk which one assuming the office of the Presidency of the United States inherited. It didn't disturb him at all.

Mr. Specter. When was the last conversation that you had with him on that general topic?

A—The last conversation I had with him on that general topic was the morning of the assassination.

Mr. Specter. Where did the conversation occur?

A—The conversation took place in his room, with Mrs. Kennedy and myself, perhaps a half hour before he left the Hotel Texas to depart for Carswell Air Force Base.

Mr. Specter. That was in Fort Worth?

A—That was in Fort Worth.

Mr. Specter. And tell us, as nearly as you can recollect, exactly what he said at that time, please.

A—Well, as near as I can recollect he was commenting to

his wife on the function of the Secret Service, and his interpretation of their role once the trip had commenced, in that their main function was to protect him from crowds, and to see that an unruly or sometimes an overexcited crowd did not generate into a riot, at which the President of the United States could be injured. But he said that if anybody really wanted to shoot the President of the United States, it was not a very difficult job—all one had to do was get a high building some day with a telescopic rifle, and there was nothing anybody could do to defend against such an attempt on the President's life.

Mr. Specter. What was Mrs. Kennedy's reaction to that philosophy?

A—I think—I think she had not quite thought of this at all. She certainly had not thought of it in this way. But I think the general tenor of the conversation was that she agreed that this was—in this democracy, this is inherent.

Mr. Specter. What had her reaction been to the trip to Texas up to that point?

A—She had enjoyed it. She had not been a girl who had loved campaigning. And I thought at the moment, at that very minute, that for the first time—the President and I were discussing a forthcoming trip to the west coast, and he had asked her if she would come, and she said she would be delighted to come, and she would like to go from now on.

The President was delighted. We were all delighted.

Mr. Specter. Had she been on any political trip before this trip to Texas?

A—No; she had not been on a political trip with us for quite awhile.

Mr. Specter. When was the trip immediately prior to the one to Texas that she was last on, if you recall?

A—I don't recall. I don't recall.

Mr. Specter. Was it during the 1960 campaign?

A—She was pregnant, as I recollect, during the 1960 campaign. She had been pregnant just prior to this. So that—and most of the other trips had been really the sort of thing that was difficult for Mrs. Kennedy to go on. But she had never evidenced to me quite as much interest in going on a—continuing to go on these trips, as she was after this.

Mr. Specter. Had she ever been to Texas prior to November 21, 1963?

A—Not to my recollection.

Mr. Specter. After the assassination, has she ever made any comment to you about that conversation which you had in the Hotel Texas in Fort Worth on the morning of November 22?

A—I have never dared bring that conversation up to Mrs. Kennedy.

Mr. Specter. Mr. O'Donnell, do you have any knowledge,

aside from the factors which you have set forth during your testimony today, concerning anyone involved in the shooting of the President?

A—No; I have no comment.

Mr. Specter. You say you have no knowledge?

A—I have no knowledge.

Mr. Specter. Do you have anything to add which you think would be helpful to the President's Commission in any way in its job of investigating all factors relating to the assassination of President Kennedy?

A—I do not.

Mr. Specter. One other detail, Mr. O'Donnell.

Did you have occasion to deal with any particular individuals from the city of Dallas itself during this trip, or in preparation for this trip?

A—No.

Mr. Specter. Mr. O'Donnell, under our practice, if you care to, we can make this transcript available to you to read and to sign.

Would you prefer that, or would you just as soon waive the signature, and have the transcript in its final form as it comes from the court reporter here?

A—I would like to read it.

Mr. Specter. Fine. We will make it available to you for reading and signature, sir. Thank you very much.

DR. CHARLES J. CARRICO

The testimony of the surgeon who was first to treat President Kennedy at Parkland Memorial Hospital, Dallas.

Mr. Specter. What experience have you had, if any, with gunshot wounds?

A—In the emergency room at Parkland, during my residence school and internship and residency, we have seen a fair number of gunshot wounds.

Mr. Specter. Could you approximate the number of gunshot wounds you have treated in the course of those duties?

A—In all probably 150, 200, something in that range.

Mr. Specter. What were your duties at Parkland Memorial Hospital on November 22, 1963?

A—At that time I was assigned to the elective surgery service, which is the general surgery service treating the usual surgical cases. I was in the emergency room evaluating some patient for admission.

Mr. Specter. What were you doing specifically in the neighborhood of 12:30 p.m. on that day?

A—At that time I had been called to the emergency room to evaluate a patient for admission to the hospital.

Mr. Specter. Were you notified that an emergency case involving President Kennedy was en route to the hospital?

A—Yes, sir.

Mr. Specter. What is your best estimate as to the time that you were notified that President Kennedy was en route to the hospital?

A—Shortly after 12:30 is the best I can do.

Mr. Specter. How long thereafter was it that he actually did arrive at Parkland, to the best of your recollection?

A—Within 2 minutes approximately.

Mr. Specter. And precisely where were you at Parkland when you first observed him?

A—When I first observed him I was in the emergency room, seeing—actually Governor Connally had been brought in first, as you know, Dr. Dulany and I had gone to care for Governor Connally and when the President was brought in I left Governor Connally and went to care for the President.

Mr. Specter. Will you describe briefly the physical layout of Parkland with respect to the point where emergency cases are brought up to the building and the general layout of the building into the emergency room.

A—The emergency entrance is at the back of the building. There is an ambulance ramp. Then immediately adjacent to the ambulance ramp are, of course, double doors, swinging doors and a corridor which is approximately 30 feet long and empties directly into the emergency room.

Then inside the emergency room are several areas, the surgical area consists of about eight booths for treating, examination and treatment of patients, and four large emergency operating rooms.

Two of these are specifically set aside for acutely ill, severely ill, patients and these are referred to as trauma rooms.

Mr. Specter. And were these trauma rooms used in connection with the treatment of President Kennedy and Governor Connally?

A—Yes, sir.

Mr. Specter. What precisely was the point where you met at his arrival?

A—The President was being wheeled into trauma room one when I saw him.

Mr. Specter. Who else, if anyone, was present at that time?

A—At that time, Dr. Don Curtis, Martin White.

The Chairman. Was he a doctor, too?

A—Yes, sir; Miss Bowron.

Mr. Specter. Who is Miss Bowron?

A—She is one of the nurses on duty at the emergency room.

Mr. Specter. Who was the first doctor to actually see the President?

A—I was.

Mr. Specter. Now, what did you observe as to the condition of President Kennedy when you first saw him?

A—He was on an ambulance cart, emergency cart, rather.

84

His color was blue white, ashen. He had slow agonal respiration, spasmodic respirations without any coordination. He was making no voluntary movements. His eyes were open, pupils were seen to be dilated and later were seen not to react to light. This was the initial impression.

Mr. Specter. What was the status of his pulse at the time of arrival?

A—He had no palpable pulse.

Mr. Specter. And was he making any movements at the time of arrival?

A—No voluntary movements, only the spasmodic respirations.

Mr. Specter. Was any heartbeat noted at his arrival?

A—After these initial observations we opened his shirt, coat, listened very briefly to his chest, heard a few sounds which we felt to be heartbeats and then proceeded with the remainder of the examination.

Mr. Specter. In your opinion was President Kennedy alive or dead on his arrival at Parkland.

A—From a medical standpoint I suppose he was still alive in that he did still have a heartbeat.

Mr. Specter. What action, if any, was taken with respect to the removal of President Kennedy's clothing?

A—As I said after I had opened his shirt and coat, I proceeded with the examination and the nurses removed his clothing as is the usual procedure.

Mr. Specter. Was President Kennedy wearing a back brace?

A—Yes; he was.

Mr. Specter. Would you describe as precisely as you can that back brace?

A—As I recall, this was a white cotton or some sort of fiber standard brace with stays and corset, in a corset-type arrangement and buckles.

Mr. Specter. How far up on his body did it come?

A—Just below his umbilicus, as I recall.

Mr. Specter. How far down on his body did it go?

A—I did not examine below his belt at that time.

Mr. Specter. Did you at any time examine below his belt?

A—I did not; no, sir.

Mr. Specter. Do you know if anyone else did?

A—Not in a formal manner.

Mr. Specter. What action did you take by way of treating President Kennedy on his arrival?

A—After what we have described we completed an initial emergency examination, which consisted of, as we have already said, his color, his pulse, we felt his back, determined there were no large wounds which would be an immediate threat to life there. Looked very briefly at the head wound and then because of his inadequate respirations inserted an endotracheal tube to attempt to support these respirations.

Mr. Specter. Specifically what did you do with respect to the back, Dr. Carrico?

A—This is a routine examination of critically ill patients where you haven't got time to examine him fully. I just placed my hands just above the belt, but in this case just above the brace, and ran my hands up his back.

Mr. Specter. To what point on his body?

A—All the way up to his neck very briefly.

Mr. Spector. What did you feel by that?

A—I felt nothing other than the blood and debris. There was no large wound there.

Mr. Specter. What source did you attribute the blood to at that time?

A—As it could have come from the head wound, and it certainly could have been a back wound, but there was no way to tell whether this blood would have come from a back wound and not from his head.

Mr. Specter. What action did you next take then?

A—At that time the endotracheal tube was inserted, using a curved laryngoscopic blade, inserting an endotracheal tube, it was seen there were some contusions, hematoma to the right of the larynx, with a minimal deviation of the larynx to the left, and ragged tissue below indicating tracheal injury.

The tube was inserted past this injury, and the cuff inflater was connected to a Bennett machine which is a respiratory assistor using positive pressure.

Mr. Specter. Will you describe briefly what you mean in lay terms by a cuffed endotracheal tube?

A—This is a plastic tube which is inserted into the trachea, into the windpipe, to allow an adequate airway, adequate breathing. The cuff is a small latex cuff which should prevent leakage of air around the tube, thus insuring an adequate airway.

Mr. Specter. Will you continue, then, to describe what efforts you made to revive the President.

A—After the endotracheal tube was inserted and connected, I listened briefly to his chest, respirations were better but still inadequate.

Dr. Perry arrived, and because of the inadequate respirations the presence of a tracheal injury, advised that the chest tube was to be inserted, this was done by some of the other physicians in the room.

At the same time we had been getting the airway inserted Dr. Curtis and Dr. White were doing a cutdown, venous section using polyethylene catheters through which fluid, medicine and blood could be administered.

Mr. Specter. Will you describe in lay language what you mean by a cutdown in relationship to what they did in this case?

A—This was a small incision over his ankle and a tube was

inserted into one of his veins through which blood could be given, fluid.

Mr. Specter. Is the general purpose of that to maintain a circulatory system?

A—Right.

Mr. Specter. In wounded parties?

A—Yes.

(At this point, Representative Ford entered the hearing room.)

Mr. Specter. Would you now proceed again to describe what else was done for the President in an effort to save his life?

A—Sure. Dr. Perry then took over supervision and treatment, and the chest tubes were inserted, another cutdown was done by Dr. Jones on the President's arm.

Fluid, as I said, was given, blood was given, hydrocortisone was given. Dr. Clark, the chief neurosurgeon, Dr. Bashour, cardiologist, was there or arrived, and a cardiac monitor was attached and although I never saw any electro-activity, Dr. Clark said there was some electrical activity of the heart which means he was still trying to——

Mr. Specter. What is Dr. Clark's position in the hospital?

A—He is chief of the neurosurgery department and professor of the neurosurgery.

Mr. Specter. Dr. Carrico, will you continue to tell us then what treatment you rendered the President?

A—When this electrocardiac activity ceased, close cardiac massage was begun. Using this, and fluids and airway we were able to maintain fairly good color, apparently fairly good peripheral circulation as monitored by carotid and radial pulses for a period of time. These efforts were abandoned when it was determined by Dr. Clark that there was no continued cardiac response. There was no cerebral response, that is the pupils remained dilated and fixed; there was evidence of anoxia.

Mr. Specter. Will you describe in lay language what anoxia means?

A—No oxygen.

Mr. Specter. Was cardiac massage applied in this situation?

A—Yes, sir; it was, excellent cardiac massage.

Mr. Specter. Were bloods administered to the President?

A—Yes, sir.

(At this point, Mr. Dulles entered the hearing room.)

Mr. Specter. Dr. Carrico, was any action taken with respect to the adrenalin insufficiency of President Kennedy?

A—Yes, sir; he was given 300 milligrams of hydrocortisone which is an adrenal hormone.

Mr. Specter. And what was the reason for the administration of that drug?

A—It was recalled that the President had been said to have adrenal insufficiency.

Mr. Specter. Now, at what time was the death of the President pronounced, Doctor?

A—At 1 o'clock.

Mr. Specter. Who pronounced the death of the President?

A—Dr. Clark, I believe.

Mr. Specter. Was that a precise time fixed or a general time fixed for the point of death?

A—This was a general time, sir.

Mr. Specter. What, in your opinion, was the cause of death?

A—The head wound, the head injury.

Mr. Specter. Will you describe as specifically as you can the head wound which you have already mentioned briefly?

A—Sure.

This was a 5- by 71-cm defect in the posterior skull, the occipital region. There was an absence of the calvarium or skull in this area, with shredded tissue, brain tissue present and initially considerable slow oozing. Then after we established some circulation there was more profuse bleeding from this wound.

Mr. Specter. Was any other wound observed on the head in addition to this large opening where the skull was absent?

A—No other wound on the head.

Mr. Specter. Did you have any opportunity specifically to look for a small wound which was below the large opening of the skull on the right side of the head?

A—No, sir; at least initially there was no time to examine the patient completely for all small wounds. As we said before, this was an acutely ill patient and all we had time to do was to determine what things were life-threatening right then and attempt to resuscitate him and after which a more complete examination would be carried out and we didn't have time to examine for other wounds.

Mr. Specter. Was such a more complete examination ever carried out by the doctors in Parkland?

A—No, sir; not in my presence.

Mr. Specter. Why not?

A—As we said initially this was an acute emergency situation and there was not time initially and when the cardiac massage was done this prevented any further examination during this time this was being done. After the President was pronounced dead his wife was there, he was the President, and we felt certainly that complete examination would be carried out and no one had the heart, I believe, to examine him then.

Mr. Specter. Will you describe, as specifically as you can then, the neck wounds which you heretofore mentioned briefly?

A—There was a small wound 5- to 8-mm. in size, located in the lower third of the neck, below the thyroid cartilage, the Adams apple.

Mr. Dulles. Will you show us about where it was?

A—Just about where your tie would be.

Mr. Dulles. Where did it enter?

A—It entered?

Mr. Dulles. Yes.

A—At the time we did not know——

Mr. Dulles. I see.

A—The entrance. All we knew this was a small wound here.

Mr. Dulles. I see. And you put your hand right above where your tie is?

A—Yes, sir; just where the tie——

Mr. Dulles. A little bit to the left.

A—To the right.

Mr. Dulles. Yes; to the right.

A—Yes. And this wound was fairly round, had no jagged edges, no evidence of powder burns, and so forth.

Representative Ford. No evidence of powder burns?

A—So far as I know.

Representative Ford. In the front?

A—Yes.

Mr. Specter. Have you now described that wound as specifically as you can based upon your observations at the time?

A—I believe so.

Mr. Specter. And your recollection at the time of those observations?

A—Yes; an even round wound.

Mr. Dulles. You felt this wound in the neck was not a fatal wound?

A—That is right.

Mr. Specter. That is, absent the head wound, would the President have survived the wound which was present on his neck?

A—I think very likely he would have.

Mr. Specter. Based on your observations on the neck wound alone did you have a sufficient basis to form an opinion as to whether it was an entrance or an exit wound?

A—No, sir; we did not. Not having completely evaluated all the wounds, traced out the course of the bullets, this wound would have been compatible with either entrance or exit wound depending upon the size, the velocity, the tissue structure and so forth.

Mr. Specter. Permit me to add some facts which I shall ask you to assume as being true for purposes of having you express an opinion.

First of all, assume that the President was struck by a 6.5 mm. copper-jacketed bullet from a rifle having a muzzle velocity of approximately 2,000 feet per second at a time when the President was approximately 160 to 250 feet from the weapon, with the President being struck from the rear at a downward angle of approximately 45 degrees, being struck on the upper right posterior thorax just above the upper border of the scapula 14 centimeters from the tip of the right acromion process and 14 centimeters below the tip of the right mastoid process.

Assume further that the missile passed through the body of the President striking no bones, traversing the neck and sliding between the large muscles in the posterior aspect of the President's body through a fascia channel without violating the pleural cavity, but bruising only the apex of the right pleural cavity and bruising the most apical portion of the right lung, then causing a hematoma to the right of the larynx which you have described, and creating a jagged wound in the trachea, then exiting precisely at the point where you observe the puncture wound to exist.

Now based on those facts was the appearance of the wound in your opinion consistent with being an exit wound?

A—It certainly was. It could have been under the circumstances.

Mr. Specter. And assuming that all the facts which I have given you to be true, do you have an opinion with a reasonable degree of medical certainty as to whether, in fact, the wound was an entrance wound or an exit wound?

A—With those facts and the fact as I understand it no other bullet was found this would be, this was, I believe, was an exit wound.

Mr. Specter. Were any bullets found in the President's body by the doctors at Parkland?

A—No, sir.

Mr. Specter. Was the President's clothing ever examined by you, Dr. Carrico?

A—No, sir; it was not.

Mr. Specter. What was the reason for no examination of the clothing?

A—Again in the emergency situation the nurses removed the clothing after we had initially unbuttoned enough to get a look at him, at his chest, and as the routine is set up, the nurses remove the clothing and we just don't take time to look at it.

Mr. Specter. Was the President's body then ever turned over at any point by you or any of the other doctors at Parkland?

A—No, sir.

Mr. Specter. Was President Kennedy lying on the emergency stretcher from the time he was brought into trauma room one until the treatment at Parkland Hosiptal was concluded?

A—Yes; he was.

Mr. Specter. At what time was that treatment concluded, to the best of your recollection?

A—At about 1 o'clock.

Mr. Specter. At approximately what time did you leave the trauma room where the President was brought?

A—I left right at one when we decided that he was dead.

Mr. Specter. And did the other doctors leave at the same time or did any remain in the trauma room?

A—I left before some of the other doctors, I do not remember specifically who was there. I believe Dr. Baxter was, Dr.

Jenkins was still there, I believe. And I think Dr. Perry was.

Mr. Specter. You have described a number of doctors in the course of your testimony up to this point. Would you state what other doctors were present during the time the President was treated, to the best of your recollection?

A—Well, I have already mentioned Dr. Don Curtis, the surgery resident; Martin White, an interne; Dr. Perry was there, Dr. Baxter, Dr. McClelland, a member of the surgery staff; Dr. Ronald Jones, chief surgery resident; Dr. Jenkins, chief of anesthesia; several other physicians whose names I can't remember at the present. Admiral Burkley, I believe was his name, the President's physician, was there as soon as he got to the hospital.

Mr. Specter. What is your view, Dr. Carrico, as to how many bullets struck the President?

A—At the time of the initial examination I really had no view. In view of what we have been told by you, and the Commission, two bullets would be my opinion. . . .

Mr. Specter. Were your views at that time consistent with the findings in the autopsy report, or did they vary in any way from the findings in that report?

A—As I recall, the autopsy report is exactly as I remember it.

Mr. Specter. Were your opinions at that time consistent with the findings of the autopsy report?

A—Yes. . . .

Mr. Specter. Dr. Carrico, have you changed your opinion in any way concerning your observations or conclusions about the situation with respect to President Kennedy at any time since November 22, 1963?

A—No.

Mr. Specter. Do you have any notes or writings of any sort in your possession concerning your participation in the treatment of President Kennedy?

A—None other than the letter to my children I mentioned to you.

Mr. Specter. Will you state briefly the general nature of that for the Commission here today, please.

A—This is just a letter written to my children to be read by them later, saying what happened, how I felt about it. And maybe why it happened, and maybe it would do them some good later.

Mr. Specter. Did you also make a written report which was made a part of the records of Parkland Hospital which you have identified for the record during the deposition proceeding?

A—Yes; I did.

Mr. Specter. Do those constitute the total of the writings which you made concerning your participation in the treatment of the President?

A—Right.

Mr. Dulles. You spoke of a letter to your children. I don't want to invade your privacy in this respect in any way, but is there anything in that letter that you think would bear on our considerations here by this Commission?

A—No; I don't believe so. This thing doesn't mention the treatment other than to say probably by the time they read the letter it will be archaic.

Mr. Dulles. You spoke about the causes of it all, I don't know whether——

A—Just a little homespun philosophy. I just said that there was a lot of extremism both in Dallas and in the Nation as a whole, and in an attitude of extremism a warped mind can flourish much better than in a more stable atmosphere.

Mr. Dulles. Thank you.

Mr. Specter. Dr. Carrico, was the nature of the treatment affected, in your opinion, in any way by the fact that you were working on the President of the United States?

A—I don't believe so, sir. We have seen a large number of acutely injured people, and acutely ill people, and the treatment has been carried out enough that this is almost reflex, if you will. Certainly everyone was emotionally affected. I think, if anything, the emotional aspect made us think faster, work faster and better.

Mr. Specter. Do you have anything to add which you think would be helpful to the Commission in its inquiry on the assassination of President Kennedy?

A—No, sir.

Mr. Specter. Those conclude my questions, Mr. Chief Justice.

The Chairman. Mr. Dulles, have you any questions to ask of the Doctor?

Mr. Dulles. Looking back on it, do you think it was probable that death followed almost immediately after this shot in the head?

A—Yes, sir; as I said——

Mr. Dulles. I was absent, I am sorry, at that time.

A—Yes, sir. Medically, I suppose you would have to say he was alive when he came to Parkland. From a practical standpoint, I think he was dead then.

The Chairman. Congressman Ford?

Representative Ford. When did you say that he arrived, when you first started working on the President?

A—It would only be a guess. Probably about 12:35. It was about 12:30 when I got in the emergency room, and I was there 2 or 3 minutes when we were called, and he was there within 2 or 3 minutes.

Representative Ford. So approximately from 12:35 until 1 the President was examined and treatment was given by you and others?

A—Yes.

Representative Ford. Have you read and analyzed the autopsy performed by the authorities at Bethesda?

A—I have not read it carefully. I have seen it. Mr. Specter showed me parts of it, and I had seen a copy of it earlier, briefly.

Representative Ford. Is there anything in it that you have read that would be in conflict with your observation?

A—Nothing at all in conflict. It certainly adds to the observations that we made.

COMMANDER JAMES J. HUMES

The testimony of the senior pathologist at the Naval Medical Center in Bethesda, Md., who performed the autopsy upon the body of President Kennedy:

Mr. Specter. Did you have occasion to participate in the autopsy of the late John F. Kennedy on November 22, 1963?

A—Yes, sir; I did.

Mr. Specter. What was your specific function in connection with that autopsy?

A—As the senior pathologist assigned to the Naval Medical Center, I was called to the Center by my superiors and informed that the President's body would be brought to our laboratories for an examination, and I was charged with the responsibility of conducting and supervising this examination; told to also call upon anyone whom I wished as an assistant in this matter, that I deemed necessary to be present.

Mr. Specter. Who did assist you, if anyone, in the course of the autopsy?

A—My first assistant was Commander J. Thornton Boswell, whose position is Chief of Pathology at the Naval Medical School, and my other assistant was Lt. Col. Pierre Finck, who was in the wound ballistics section of the Armed Forces Institute of Pathology. . . .

Mr. Specter. What time did the autopsy start approximately?

A—The President's body was received at 25 minutes before 8, and the autopsy began at approximately 8 p.m. on that evening. You must include the fact that certain X-rays and other examinations were made before the actual beginning of the routine type autopsy examination.

Mr. Specter. Precisely what X-rays or photographs were taken before the dissection started?

A—Some of these X-rays were taken before and some during the examination which also maintains for the photographs, which were made as the need became apparent to make such.

However, before the postmortem examination was begun, anterior, posterior and lateral X-rays of the head, and of the torso were made, and identification type photographs, I recall having been made of the full face of the late President. A photograph showing the massive head wound with the large defect that was associated with it. To my recollection all of these were made before the proceedings began.

Several others, approximately 15 to 20 in number, were made in total before we finished the proceedings. . . .

Mr. Specter. What time did this autopsy end?

A—At approximately 11 p.m. . . .

Mr. Specter. Will you now proceed to tell us what you observed with respect to the wound which is marked as appearing in the upper back or lower neck?

Mr. McCloy. Have you identified that?

Mr. Specter. The one on the side is 385 and the one of the rear view is 386. And that one is 387. For purposes of our record, if you will, put them in as 385 and 386 for our printed record. You might want to put them in chalk above them so you will see the one on the left is 385 and on the right is 386.

A—These exhibits again are schematic representations of what we observed at the time of examining the body of the late President.

Exhibit 385 shows in the low neck an oval wound which— excuse me, I wish to get the measurements correct. This wound was situated just above the upper border of the scapula, and measured 7 by 4 millimeters, with its long axis roughly parallel to the long axis of vertical column.

We saw—I would rather not discuss the situation of the anterior neck at this time or would you prefer it?

Mr. Specter. How would you prefer to do it, Dr. Humes?

A—I would prefer to discuss the wounds, two wounds, we saw posteriorly and the wound, other wound, of the skull before going to that. . . .

The wound in the low neck of which I had previously begun to speak is now posteriorly—is now depicted in 385, in 386 and in 388.

The second wound was found in the right posterior portion of the scalp. This wound was situated approximately 2.5 centimeters to the right, and slightly above the external occipital protuberance which is a bony prominence situated in the posterior portion of everyone's skull. This wound was then 2½ centimeters to the right and slightly above that point.

The third obvious wound at the time of the examination was a huge defect over the right side of the skull. This defect involved both the scalp and the underlying skull, and from the brain substance was protruding.

This wound measured approximately 13 centimeters in greatest diameter. It was difficult to measure accurately because radiating at various points from the large defect were multiple crisscrossing fractures of the skull which extended in several directions. . . .

These, then, were the three wounds which were quite obvious at the time of the examination. . . .

Mr. McCloy. Was the bullet moving in a direct line or had it begun to tumble?

A—To tumble?

That is a difficult question to answer. I have the opinion, however, that it was more likely moving in a direct line. You will note that the wound in the posterior portion of the occiput on Exhibit 388 is somewhat longer than the other missile wound which we have not yet discussed in the low neck. We believe that rather than due to a tumbling effect, this is explainable on the fact that this missile struck the skin and skull at a more tangential angle than did the other missile, and, therefore, produced a more elongated defect, sir. . . .

Mr. Dulles. Just one other question.

Am I correct in assuming from what you have said that this wound is entirely inconsistent with a wound that might have been administered if the shot were fired from in front or the side of the President: it had to be fired from behind the President?

A—Scientifically, sir, it is impossible for it to have been fired from other than behind. Or to have exited from other than behind.

Mr. McCloy. This is so obvious that I rather hesitate to ask it. There is no question in your mind that it was a lethal bullet?

A—The President, sir, could not possibly have survived the effect of that injury no matter what would have been done for him.

The Chairman. Mr. Specter.

Mr. Specter. What conclusions did you reach then as to the trajectory or point of origin of the bullet, Dr. Humes, based on 388?

A—We reached the conclusion that this missile was fired toward the President from a point above and behind him, sir. . . .

Mr. Specter. Did you have occasion to discuss that wound on the front side of the President with Dr. Malcolm Perry of Parkland Hospital in Dallas?

A—Yes, sir; I did. I had the impression from seeing the wound that it represented a surgical tracheotomy wound, a wound frequently made by surgeons when people are in respiratory distress to give them a free airway.

To ascertain that point, I called on the telephone Dr. Malcolm Perry and discussed with him the situation of the President's neck when he first examined the President, and asked him had he in fact done a tracheotomy which was somewhat redundant because I was somewhat certain he had.

He said, yes; he had done a tracheotomy and that as the point to perform his tracheotomy he used a wound which he had interpreted as a missile wound in the low neck, as the point through which to make the tracheotomy incision.

Mr. Specter. When did you have that conversation with him, Dr. Humes?

A—I had that conversation early on Saturday morning, sir.

Mr. Specter. On Saturday morning, November 23d?

A—That is correct, sir.

Mr. Specter. And have you had occasion since to examine the report of Parkland Hospital which I made available to you?

A—Yes, sir; I have. . . .

This report was written by doctor—or of the activities of Dr. James Carrico, Doctor Carrico in inserting the endotracheal tube noted a ragged wound of trachea immediately below the larynx.

The report, as I recall it, and I have not studied it in minute detail, would indicate to me that Doctor Perry realizing from Doctor Carrico's observation that there was wound of the trachea would quite logically use the wound which he had observed as a point to enter the trachea since the trachea was almost damaged, that would be a logical place in which to put his incision.

In speaking of that wound in the neck, Doctor Perry told me that before he enlarged it to make the tracheotomy wound it was a "few millimeters in diameter."

Of course by the time we saw it, as my associates and as you have heard, it was considerably larger and no longer at all obvious as a missile wound. . . .

This missile, to the best of our ability to ascertain, struck no bone protuberances, no bony prominences, no bones as it traversed the President's body. But it was a sharply delineated wound. It was quite regular in its outline. It measured, as I mentioned, 7 by 4 mm. Its margins were similar in all respects when viewed with the naked eye to the wound in the skull, which we feel incontrovertibly was a wound of entrance. . . .

We concluded that this missile depicted in 385 "C" which entered the President's body traversed the President's body and made its exit through the wound observed by the physicians at Parkland Hospital and later extended as a tracheotomy wound. . . .

Mr. McCloy. Quite apart from the President's clothing, now directing your attention to the flight of the bullet, quite apart from the evidence given by the President's clothing, you, I believe, indicated that the flight of the bullet was from the back, from above and behind. It took roughly the line which is shown on your Exhibit 385.

A—Yes, sir.

Mr. McCloy. I am not clear what induced you to come to that conclusion if you couldn't find the actual exit wound by reason of the tracheotomy.

A—The report which we have submitted, sir, represents our thinking within the 24–48 hours of the death of the President, all facts taken into account of the situation.

The wound in the anterior portion of the lower neck is physically lower than the point of entrance posteriorly, sir.

Mr. McCloy. That is what I wanted to bring out.

A—Yes, sir. . . .

Mr. Specter. Doctor Humes, as to points of entry on the body of the late President, how many were there in total?

A—Two, sir, as depicted in 385-C and 388-A.

Mr. Specter. And to point of exit, how many were there?

A—Two, sir, as depicted in 385-D and the vicinity of 388-B. I made the latter remark as was developed earlier, in that the size of the large defect in the skull was so great and the fragmentation was so complex that it was imposisble to accurately pinpoint the exit of the missile in the head wound. . . .

II. The Arrest

HOWARD LESLIE BRENNAN

The testimony of a 45-year-old steamfitter who was an eye-witness to the assassination from his position on a retaining wall about 90 feet from the Texas School Book Depository Building:

Mr. Belin. Mr. Brennan, could you please tell the Commission what happened from the time you sat on that retaining wall, what you saw?

A—I was more or less observing the crowd and the people in different building windows, including the fire escape across from the Texas Book Store on the east side of the Texas Book Store, and also the Texas Book Store Building windows. I observed quite a few people in different windows. In particular, I saw this one man on the sixth floor which left the window to my knowledge a couple of times. . . . As the parade came by, I watched it from a distance of Elm and Main Street, as it came on to Houston and turned the corner at Houston and Elm, going down the incline towards the railroad underpass. And after the President had passed my position, I really couldn't say how many feet or how far, a short distance I would say, I heard this crack that I positively thought was a backfire. . . . Then something, just right after this explosion, made me think that it was a firecracker being thrown from the Texas Book Store. And I glanced up. And this man that I saw previous was aiming for his last shot.

Mr. Belin. This man you saw previous? Which man are you talking about now?

A—The man in the sixth story window.

Mr. Belin. Would you describe just exactly what you saw when you saw him this last time?

A—Well, as it appeared to me he was standing up and resting against the left window sill, with gun shouldered to his right shoulder, holding the gun with his left hand and taking positive aim and fired his last shot. As I calculate a couple of seconds. He drew the gun back from the window as though he was drawing it back to his side and maybe paused for another second as though to assure hisself that he hit his mark, and then he disappeared.

And, at the same moment, I was diving off of that firewall and to the right for bullet protection of this stone wall that is a little higher on the Houston side.

Mr. Belin. Well, let me ask you. What kind of a gun did you see in that window?

A—I am not an expert on guns. It was, as I could observe, some type of a high-powered rifle.

Mr. Belin. Could you tell whether or not it had any kind of a scope on it?

A—I did not observe a scope.

Mr. Belin. Could you tell whether or not it had one? Do you know whether it did or not, or could you observe that it definitely did or definitely did not, or don't you know?

A—I do not know if it had a scope or not.

Mr. Belin. At the time you saw this man on the sixth floor, how much of the man could you see?

A—Well, I could see—at one time he came to the window and he sat sideways on the window sill. That was previous to President Kennedy getting there. And I could see practically his whole body, from his hips up. But at the time that he was firing the gun, a possibility from his belt up.

Mr. Belin. How much of the gun do you believe that you saw?

A—I calculate 70 to 85 percent of the gun.

Mr. Belin. Do you know what direction the gun was pointing.

A—Yes.

Mr. Belin. And what direction was the gun pointing when you saw it?

A—At somewhat 30 degrees downward and west by south.

Mr. Belin. Do you know down what street it was pointing?

A—Yes. Down Elm Street toward the railroad underpasses. . . .

Mr. Belin. Could you describe the man you saw in the window on the sixth floor?

A—To my best description, a man in his early thirties, fair complexion, slender but neat, neat slender, possibly 5-foot 10.

Mr. Belin. About what weight?

A—Oh, at—I calculated, I think, from 160 to 170 pounds.

Mr. Belin. A white man?

A—Yes.

Mr. Belin. Do you remember what kind of clothes he was wearing?

A—Light colored clothes, more of a khaki color.

Mr. Belin. Do you remember the color of his hair?

A—No. . . .

Mr. Belin. Now, taking you down to the Dallas Police Station, I believe you talked to Captain Fritz. And then what happened?

A—Well, I was just more or less introduced to him . . . and they told me they were going to conduct a lineup and wanted me to view it, which I did.

Mr. Belin. Do you remember how many people were in the lineup?

A—No; I don't. A possibility seven more or less one.

Mr. Belin. All right.

Did you see anyone in the lineup you recognized?

A—Yes.

Mr. Belin. And what did you say?

A—I told Mr. Sorrels and Captain Fritz at that time that Oswald—or the man in the lineup that I identified looking more like a closest resemblance to the man in the window than anyone in the lineup. . . .

Mr. Belin. As I understand your testimony, then, you said that you told him that this particular person looked the most like the man you saw on the sixth floor of the building there.

A—Yes, sir.

Mr. Belin. In the meantime, had you seen any pictures of Lee Harvey Oswald on television or in the newspapers?

A—Yes, on television. . . .

Mr. Belin. Now, is there anything else you told the officers at the time of the lineup?

A—Well, I told them I could not make a positive identification.

Mr. Belin. When you told them that, did you ever later tell any officer or investigating person anything different? . . .

A—I believe it was a Secret Service man from Houston.

Mr. Belin. What did he say to you and what did you say to him?

A—Well, he asked me—he said, "You said you couldn't make a positive identification."

He said, "Did you do that for security reasons personally, or couldn't you?"

And I told him I could with all honesty, but I did it more or less for security reasons—my family and myself.

Mr. Belin. What do you mean by security reasons for your family and yourself?

A—I believe at that time, and I still believe it was a Communist activity, and I felt like there hadn't been more than one eyewitness, and if it got to be a known fact that I was an eyewitness, my family or I, either one, might not be safe. . . .

Mr. Belin. Well, what happened in between to change your mind that you later decided to come forth and tell them you could identify him?

A—After Oswald was killed, I was relieved quite a bit that as far as pressure on myself of somebody not wanting me to identify anybody, there was no longer that immediate danger.

Mr. Belin. What is the fact as to whether or not your having seen Oswald on television would have affected your identification of him one way or the other?

A—That is something I do not know.

Mr. Belin. Mr. Brennan, could you tell us now whether you can or cannot positively identify the man you saw on the sixth floor window as the same man that you saw in the police station?

A—I could at that time—I could, with all sincerity, identify him as being the same man.

CHARLES DOUGLAS GIVENS

The testimony of the Texas School Book Depository employee who saw Oswald on the 6th floor of the building about 35 minutes before the assassination:

Mr. Belin. When did you see Lee Harvey Oswald next?

A—Next?

Mr. Belin. Yes.

A—Well, it was about a quarter till 12, we were on our way downstairs, and we passed him, and he was standing at the gate on the fifth floor.

I came downstairs, and I discovered I left my cigarettes in my jacket pocket upstairs, and I took the elevator back upstairs to get my jacket with my cigarettes in it. When I got back upstairs, he was on the sixth floor in that vicinity, coming from that way.

Mr. Belin. Coming from what way?

A—Toward the window up front where the shots were fired from. . . .

Mr. Belin. What did he say to you?

A—I say, "It's near lunch time."

He said, "No, sir. When you get downstairs, close the gate to the elevator."

That meant the elevator on the west side, you can pull both gates down and it will come up by itself.

MARRION L. BAKER

The testimony of the Dallas motorcycle policeman who was in the Kennedy motorcade and who is the first person known to have seen Oswald after the assassination:

Mr. Belin. When you heard the first shot or the first noise, what did you do and what did you see?

A—Well, to me, it sounded high and I immediately kind of looked up, and I had a feeling that it came from the building, either right in front of me or of the one across to the right of it.

Mr. Belin. What would the building right in front of you be?

A—It would be this Book Depository Building. . . .

Mr. Belin. How many shots did you hear?

A—Three.

Mr. Belin. All right. After the third shot, then, what did you do?

A—Well, I revved that motorcycle up and I went down to the corner. . . .

Mr. Belin. That is where you parked the motorcycle?

A—Yes. . . .

Mr. Belin. Then what did you do after surveying the situation?

A—I had it in mind that the shots came from the top of this building here.

Mr. Belin. By this building, you are referring to what?

A—The Book Depository Building.

Representative Boggs. You were parked right in front of the Building?

A—Yes, sir; ran right straight to it. . . . As I entered this lobby there were people going in as I entered. And I asked, I just spoke out and asked where the stairs or elevator was, and this man, Mr. Truly, spoke up and says, it seems to me like he says, "I am a building manager. Follow me, officer, and I will show you." . . .

Mr. Belin. What did you see Mr. Truly do?

A—He ran over there and pushed the button to get it down.

Mr. Belin. Did the elevator come down after he pushed the button?

A—No, sir; it didn't.

Mr. Belin. Then what did he do?

A—He hollered for it, said, "Bring that elevator down here."

Mr. Belin. How many times did he holler, to the best of your recollection?

A—It seemed like he did it twice.

Mr. Belin. All right.

Then what did he do?

A—I said let's take the stairs.

Mr. Belin. All right. Then what did you do?

A—He said, "Okay" and so he immediately turned around, which the stairs is just to the, would be to the, well, the west of this elevator.

Mr. Belin. All right.

A—And we went up them.

Mr. Belin. You went up the stairs then?

A—Yes, sir.

Mr. Belin. When you started up the stairs what was your intention at that time?

A—My intention was to go all the way to the top where I thought the shots had come from, to see if I could find something there, you know, to indicate that.

Mr. Belin. And did you go all the way up to the top of the stairs right away?

A—No, sir; we didn't.

Mr. Belin. What happened?

A—As I came out to the second floor there, Mr. Truly was ahead of me, and as I come out I was kind of scanning, you know, the rooms, and I caught a glimpse of this man. . . .

Mr. Belin. What did you do then?

A—I ran on over there—

Representative Boggs. You mean where he was?

A—Yes, sir. There is a door there with a glass . . . and then there is another door . . . and there is a hallway over there and a hallway entering into a lunchroom, and when I got to where I could see him he was walking away from me about 20 feet away from me in the lunchroom.

Mr. Belin. What did you do?

A—I hollered at him at that time and said, "Come here." He turned and walked right straight back to me. . . .

Representative Boggs. What did you say to him?

A—I didn't get anything out of him. Mr. Truly had come up to my side here, and I turned to Mr. Truly and I says, "Do you know this man, does he work here?" And he said yes, and I turned immediately and went on out up the stairs.

Representative Boggs. Let me ask one other question. You later, when you recognized this man as Lee Oswald, is that right, saw pictures of him?

A—Yes, sir. I had occasion to see him in the homicide office later that evening . . . and I went up there and made this affidavit.

Representative Boggs. After he had been arrested?

A—Yes, sir.

Mr. Dulles. Could you tell us anything more about his appearance, what he was doing, get an impression of the man at all? Did he seem to be hurrying, anything of that kind?

A—Evidently he was hurrying. . . .

Representative Boggs. When you saw him, was he out of breath, did he appear to have been running or what?

A—It didn't appear that to me. He appeared normal you know. . . .

Representative Boggs. That question about time I would like to establish.

How long would you say it was from the time that you first heard the shots until that episode occurred?

A—We went back and made two trial runs on that, and—

Mr. Belin. Was that on Friday, March 20?

A—Yes, sir. . . .

Mr. Dulles. Will you say from what time to what time, from the last shot? . . .

A—The first shot.

We simulated the shots and by the time we got there, we did everything that I did that day, and this would be the minimum, because I am sure that I, you know, it took me a little longer.

Mr. Dulles. I want to get clear in my mind and for the record, it started at the first shot and when did it terminate, when you saw Oswald?

A—When we saw Oswald.

Mr. Dulles. When you saw Oswald?

A—Yes, sir.

Mr. Dulles. And that time is how much?

A—The first run would be a minute and 30 seconds, and then we did it over, and we did it in a minute and 15 seconds.
. . .

Mr. Belin. Were we walking or running when we did this?

A—The first time we did it a little bit slower, and the second time we hurried it up a little bit.

Mr. Belin. Were we running or walking, when we moved, did we run or walk?

A—From the time I got off the motorcycle we walked the first time and then we kind of run the second time from the motorcycle on into the building.

Mr. Belin. All right. When we got inside the building did we run or trot or walk?

A—Well, we did it at kind of a trot, I would say, it wasn't a real fast run, an open run. It was more of a trot, kind of.

Mr. Belin. You mentioned the relationship between what we did on March 20 and what actually occurred on November 22. Would you estimate that what we did on March 20 was the maximum or minimum as for the time you took?

A—I would say it would be the minimum.

Mr. Belin. Did we make any or do any stopwatch tests about any route from the southeast corner of the sixth floor down to the [second floor] lunchroom?

A—Yes, sir; we made two test runs.

Mr. Belin. All right. Do you remember what the route was?

A—Yes, sir; we started on the sixth floor on the east side of the building.

Mr. Belin. All right.

A—We walked down the east wall.

Mr. Belin. We started at that particular corner?

A—Yes, sir; we started in the southeast corner.

Mr. Belin. All right. We walked down the east wall, you say?

A—That is right.

Mr. Belin. All right, then where did we go?

A—To the north wall and then we walked down the north wall to the west side of where the stairs was.

Mr. Belin. All right, we walked from the southeast corner to the northeast corner?

A—That is right.

Mr. Belin. Then along the northeast corner, around the elevators, do you remember who was with us when we did this?

A—Yes, sir. There was, it seems to me like his name was John—anyway, he was a Secret Service man.

Mr. Belin. John Howlett.

A—John Howlett. That is right, sir.

Mr. Belin. Did Mr. Howlett simulate anyone putting a gun in any particular place?

A—Yes, sir; he did.

Mr. Belin. And then what did we do when we got to the— where did he do that, do you remember?

A—that would be as we approached the stairway, there were some cases of books on the left-hand side there.

Mr. Belin. All right. And Secret Service Agent Howlett went over to these books and leaned over as if he were putting a rifle there?

A—That is right, sir.

Mr. Belin. Then what did he do?

A—Then we continued on down the stairs.

Mr. Belin. To the lunchroom?

A—That is right, sir.

Mr. Belin. Do you remember how long that took?

A—The first run with normal walking took us a minute and 18 seconds.

Mr. Belin. What about the second time?

A—And the second time we did it at a fast walk which took us a minute and 14 seconds.

MARY E. BLEDSOE

The testimony of a former landlady of Oswald's, who saw him on the bus he took after leaving the Texas School Book Depository Building:

Mr. Ball. All right, now, tell me what happened? . . .

A—Oswald got on. He looks like a maniac. His sleeve was out here [indicating]. His shirt was undone.

Mr. Ball. You are indicating a sleeve of a shirt?

A—Yes.

Mr. Ball. It was unraveled?

A—Was a hole in it, hole, and he was dirty, and I didn't look at him. I didn't want to know I even seen him, and I just looked off, and then about that time the motorman said the President had been shot. . . .

Mr. Ball. How close did he pass to you as he boarded the bus?

A—Just in front of me. Just like this [indicating].

Mr. Ball. Just a matter of a foot or two?

A—Uh-huh. . . .

Mr. Ball. How far had he been on the bus before he got off? Until the time he got on until the time he got off?

A—About three or four blocks. . . .

WILLIAM WAYNE WHALEY

The testimony of the cab driver who took Oswald to his rooming house after he got off the bus:

Mr. Ball. About 12:30 that day where were you?

A—Well, about 12:30 as you say, sir; I was at the Greyhound bus station. I have a copy of my trip sheet here. . . .

Mr. Ball. Were you standing at the Greyhound, at your cab stand at the Greyhound, long before you picked up another passenger?

A—No, sir, there was no one at the Greyhound stand and when I unloaded at the door I just pulled up about 30 feet to the stand and stopped and then I wanted a package of cigarettes, I was out so I started to get out and I saw this passenger coming so I waited for him. . . .

Mr. Ball. Did you notice how he was dressed?

A—Yes, sir. I didn't pay much attention to it right then. But it all came back when I really found out who I had. He was dressed in just ordinary work clothes. It wasn't khaki pants but they were khaki material, blue faded blue color, like a blue uniform made in khaki. Then he had on a brown shirt with a little silverlike stripe on it and he had on some kind of jacket, I didn't notice very close but I think it was a work jacket that almost matched the pants. . . .

Mr. Ball. Now, what happened after that, will you tell us in your own words what he did?

A—Well, on this which was the 14th trip when I picked up at the Greyhound I marked it 12:30 to 12:45.

Mr. Ball. You say that can be off 15 minutes?

A—That can be off either direction.

Mr. Ball. Anything up to 15 minutes, you say?

A—Yes, sir. . . .

Mr. Ball. Let's take the 12:30 trip, tell me about that, what the passenger said.

A—He said, "May I have the cab?"

I said, "You sure can. Get in." And instead of opening the back door he opened the front door, which is allowable there, and got in. . . . And he said, "500 North Beckley."

Well, I started up, I started to that address, and the police cars, the sirens was going, running crisscrossing everywhere, just a big uproar in that end of town and I said, "What the hell. I wonder what the hell is the uproar?"

And he never said anything. So I figured he was one of these people that don't like to talk so I never said any more to him.

But when I got pretty close to 500 block at Neches and North Beckley which is the 500 block, he said, "This will do fine," and I pulled over to the curb right there. He gave me a dollar bill, the trip was 95 cents. He gave me a dollar bill and didn't say anything, just got out and closed the door and walked around the front of the cab over to the other side of the street. Of course, traffic was moving through there and I put it in gear and moved on, that is the last I saw of him. . . .

Mr. Ball. I have some clothing here. Commission Exhibit No. 150, does that look like the shirt?

A—That is the shirt, sir. . . .

Mr. Ball. In other words, this is the shirt the man had on?

A—Yes, sir; that is the same one the FBI man had me identify.

Mr. Ball. This is the shirt the man had on who took your car at Lamar and Jackson?

A—As near as I can recollect as I told him. I said that is the shirt he had on because it had a kind of little stripe in it, light-colored stripe. I noticed that.

Mr. Ball. Here are two pair of pants, Commission Exhibit No. 157 and Commission Exhibit No. 156. Does it look anything like that?

A—I don't think I can identify the pants except they were the same color as that, sir. . . .

Mr. Ball. Here is Commission No. 162 which is a gray jacket with zipper.

A—I think that is the jacket he had on when he rode with me in the cab.

MRS. EARLENE ROBERTS

The testimony of the housekeeper at Oswald's rooming house in the 1000 block of North Beckley Street:

Mr. Ball. When is the first time you ever saw Lee Oswald?

A—The day he came in and rented the room—the 14th of October.

Mr. Ball. Had you ever heard of the man before?

A—No, and he didn't register as Oswald—he registered as O. H. Lee.

Mr. Ball. Did he sign his name?

A—O. H. Lee.

Mr. Ball. Did he sign his own name that way?

A—O. H. Lee—that's what he was registered as. . . .

Mr. Ball. Do you remember the day the President was shot?

A—Yes; I remember it—who would forget that? . . . He came home that Friday in an unusual hurry.

Mr. Ball. And about what time was this?

A—Well, it was after President Kennedy had been shot and I had a friend that said, "Roberts, President Kennedy has been shot," and I said, "Oh, no." She said, "Turn on your television," and I said "What are you trying to do, pull my leg?" And she said, "Well, go turn it on." I went and turned it on and I was trying to clear it up—I could hear them talking but I couldn't get the picture and he come in and I just looked up and I said, "Oh, you are in a hurry." He never said a thing, not nothing. He went on to his room and stayed about 3 or 4 minutes. . . .

Mr. Ball. When he came in the door, what did he do?

A—He just walked in—he didn't look around at me—he didn't say nothing and went on to his room.

Mr. Ball. Did he run?

A—He wasn't running, but he was walking pretty fast—he was all but running.

Mr. Ball. Then, what happened after that?

A—He went to his room and he was in his shirt sleeves but I couldn't tell you whether it was a long-sleeved shirt or what color it was or nothing, and he got a jacket and put it on—it was kind of a zipper jacket. . . .

A—Yes; it was a zipper jacket. How come me to remember it, he was zipping it up as he went out the door.

Mr. Ball. He was zipping it up as he went out the door?

A—Yes.

Mr. Ball. Then, when you saw him did you see any part of his belt?

A—No.

Mr. Ball. There is some suspicion that when he left there he might have had a pistol or a revolver in his belt; did you see anything like that?

A—No; I sure didn't.

Mr. Ball. Now, I show you Commission Exhibit No. 150—it is a shirt—have you seen that before?

A—Well, maybe I have. Now, that looks kind of like the dark shirt that he had on.

Mr. Ball. Now, when Oswald came in, he was in a shirt—does this shirt look anything like the shirt he had on?

A—It was a darker shirt he had on—I think it was a dark one, but whether it was long sleeve or short sleeve or what—I don't know.

Mr. Ball. Does the color of this shirt which I show you here, Commission Exhibit No. 150, look anything like the shirt he had on?

A—I'm sorry, I just don't know.

Mr. Ball. After he left the house and at sometime later in the afternoon, these police officers came out, did they?

A—Well, yes.

Mr. Ball. Now, after these police officers came out . . . did you see a gun holster in his room after they had searched it?

A—Yes—there was one of them little outfits—a little holster and they taken it out and where they got it—I don't know, but it was in the room. They had it in their hands, one of the men was holding it.

Mr. Ball. Had you ever seen that before?

A—No; I hadn't.

(In an affidavit filed with the Commission, Mrs. Roberts described what she knew of Lee Harvey Oswald's movements after he left the rooming house.) She said: "Oswald went out the front door. A moment later I looked out the window. I saw Lee Oswald standing on the curb at the bus stop just to the right, and on the same side of the street as our house. I just glanced out the window that once. I don't know how long Lee Oswald stood at the curb nor did I see which direction he went when he left there. . . .)

WILLIAM W. SCOGGINS

The testimony of a Dallas taxicab driver, who was one of several eyewitnesses to the shooting of Police Officer J. D. Tippit:

Mr. Dulles. What time was this, approximately, as far as you can recall?

A—Around 1:20 in the afternoon.

Mr. Belin. All right. Will you please state then what happened, what you saw, what you did, what you heard? . . .

A—Well, I first seen the police car cruising east. . . . He come from the west, going east on east Tenth.

Mr. Belin. Then what did you see? . . .

A—He stopped. When I saw he stopped, then I looked to see why he was stopping, you see, and I saw this man with a light-colored jacket on.

Mr. Belin. Did you see the police officer do anything?

A—I saw him get out of the police car. . . . Then he took about a step, I would say, or approximately one or two steps, and then I wasn't really—you know—I went back to my eating, and about that time I heard the shots.

Mr. Belin. How many shots did you hear?

A—Three or four, in the neighborhood. They was fast.

Mr. Belin. They were fast shots?

A—Yes; they were fast.

Mr. Belin. Then what did you do or say or hear?

A—Then I saw the man falling, grab his stomach and fall.

Mr. Belin. Which man did you see fall?

A—The policeman. I was excited when I heard them shots, and I started to get out. . . . I must have seen him fall as I was getting out of my cab, because I got out of the cab, and in the process of getting out of the cab I seen this guy coming around, so I got out of sight. . . . I got back behind the cab. . . .

Mr. Belin. When you saw the officer fall, when was the next place that you saw the man, or did you see him at the same time you saw the officer fall, the other man?

A—No. I saw him coming kind of toward me around that cutoff through there, and he never did look at me. He looked back over his left shoulder like that, as he went by. It seemed like I could see his face, his features and everything plain, you see.

Mr. Belin. Was he walking or running or trotting?

A—Kind of loping, trotting. . . .

Mr. Belin. Did you hear the man say anything?

A—I heard him mutter something like, "poor damn cop," or "poor dumb cop." He said that over twice, and the last, I don't know whether the middle word was "damn" or "dumb," but anyway, he muttered that twice.

Mr. Belin. Did you hear him say any other word or phrase?

A—No. . . .

Mr. Belin. [Now, let me ask you this question.] [First of all, do you remember] [or] Can you describe the man you saw on November 22 with the gun?

A—He was a medium-height fellow with, kind of a slender look, and approximately, I said 25, 26 years old, somewhere along there.

Mr. Belin. Do you remember the color of his hair?

A—Yes. It was light; let's see, was it light or not—medium brown, I would say.

Mr. Belin. Pardon?

A—Medium brown, I would say—now, wait a minute. Now, medium brown or dark.

Mr. Belin. Medium brown or dark hair?

A—Yes.

Mr. Belin. Was he a Negro or a white man?

A—White, light complected, not real brown.

Mr. Belin. Was he fat, average build or thin?

A—No, he was slender; not real slender, but you know—— . . .

Mr. Belin. They took you down about the time of the noon meal, is that correct; they took you to the police station?

A—Yes.

Mr. Belin. How many people were in the lineup, if you can remember?

A—Four.

Mr. Belin. Four? Did any one of the people look anything like—strike that. Did you identify anyone in the lineup?

A—I identified the one we are talking about, Oswald. I identified him.

Mr. Belin. You didn't know his name as Oswald at that time, did you, or did you not?

A—Yes, the next day I did. But, of course I didn't know what his name was the day that I picked him out.

Mr. Belin. You saw a man in the lineup?

A—Yes.

Mr. Belin. Did anyone tell you any particular man was Oswald in the lineup?

A—No. . . .

JOHNNY CALVIN BREWER

The testimony of the Dallas Shoe store manager who saw Oswald enter the Texas Theatre shortly after the shooting of Officer Tippit:

Mr. Belin. Would you describe what happened after you heard on the radio that an officer had been shot? . . .

A—I was in the store behind the counter, and I looked up and saw the man enter the lobby. . . . I heard the police cars coming and he stepped in. . . .

110

Mr. Belin. Will you describe the man you saw?

A—He was a little man, about 5'9", and weighed about 150 pounds is all.

Mr. Belin. How tall are you, by the way?

A—Six three. . . .

Mr. Belin. Then what did you see this man do?

A—He turned and walked out of the lobby and went up West Jefferson toward the theatre, and I walked out the front and watched him, and he went into the theatre.

Mr. Belin. What theatre is that?

A—Texas Theatre.

Mr. Belin. Why did you happen to watch this particular man?

A—He just looked funny to me. Well, in the first place, I had seen him some place before. I think he had been in my store before. And when you wait on somebody, you recognize them, and he just seemed funny. His hair was sort of messed up and looked like he had been running, and he looked scared, and he looked funny. . . .

Mr. Belin. Could you tell whether or not he bought a ticket?

A—No; he just turned and walked right straight in. . . .

Mr. Belin. All right. You saw this person Butch? (Warren H. Burroughs.)

A—Yes, sir.

Mr. Belin. You say he is the usher. . . .

A—Yes.

Mr. Belin. What did you and Butch do?

A—We walked down to the front of the theatre to the stage. First we checked the front exit, and it hadn't been opened. We went to the back and it hadn't been opened.

Mr. Belin. How could you tell that it hadn't been opened?

A—Well, you open it from the inside, and you raise a bar, and a rod sticks into a hole at the bottom and then you open it. When you close it, it doesn't fall back in. You have to raise the rod again to close it from the inside.

Mr. Belin. In other words, you have to close it from the inside?

A—You can close it from the outside, but it won't lock.

Mr. Belin. It was locked when you got there?

A—Yes.

Mr. Belin. So you knew that no one had left?

A—Yes.

Mr. Belin. Then what did you do?

A—We went back up front and went in the balcony and looked around but we couldn't see anything.

Mr. Belin. Now you first looked on the bottom floor and you did not see him?

A—Yes.

Mr. Belin. How many patrons were in the theatre at that time?

111

A—I couldn't really tell. There weren't many, but it was dark and we couldn't see how many people were in there. There were 15 or 20, I would say, at the most, upstairs and downstairs.

Mr. Belin. Together, 15 or 20?

A—Yes.

Mr. Belin. Then you went upstairs. Did you see him upstairs?

A—No; I couldn't see anything upstairs.

Mr. Belin. Did you hear any noises there?

A—When we first went down to the exit by the stage, we heard a seat pop up, but couldn't see anybody. And we never did see him.

But we went back and upstairs and checked, and we came down and went back to the box office and told Julia that we hadn't seen him.

Mr. Belin. Julia Postal is the cashier?

A—Yes; and she called the police, and we went—Butch went to the front exit, and I went down by the stage to the back exit and stood there until the police came.

Mr. Belin. Then what happened?

A—Well, just before they came, they turned the house lights on, and I looked out from the curtains and saw the man.

Mr. Belin. Where was he when you saw him?

A—He was in the center section about six or seven rows, from the back, toward the back. . . .

Mr. Belin. Then what happened?

A—I heard a noise outside, and I opened the door, and the alley, I guess it was filled with police cars and policemen were on the fire exits and stacked around the alley, and they grabbed me, a couple of them and held and searched me and asked me what I was doing there, and I told them that there was a guy in the theatre that I was suspicious of, and he asked me if he was still there.

And I said, yes, I just seen him. And he asked me if I would point him out.

And I and two or three other officers walked out on the stage and I pointed him out, and there were officers coming in from the front of the show, I guess, coming toward that way, and officers going from the back.

Mr. Belin. Then what did you see?

A—Well, I saw this policeman approach Oswald, and Oswald stood up and I heard some hollering, I don't know exactly what he said, and this man hit Patrolman McDonald.

Mr. Belin. You say this man hit Patrolman McDonald. Did you know it was Patrolman McDonald?

A—I didn't know his name, but I had seen him quite a few times around Oak Cliff. But I didn't know his name.

Mr. Belin. Then you later found out this was Patrolman McDonald?

A—Yes. . . .

M. N. McDONALD

The testimony of the Dallas police officer who arrested Oswald, after a scuffle, in the Texas Theatre:

Mr. Ball. Did you receive a report? . . .

A—Just as I got into the squad car, it was reported that a suspect was seen running into the Texas Theatre, 231 West Jefferson. . . .

Mr. Ball. What did you do?

A—Well, when I got to the front of the theater there was several police cars already at the scene, and I surmised that officers were already inside the theater.

So I decided to go to the rear, in the alley, and seal off the rear. . . . There were three other officers at the rear door. I joined them. We walked into the rear exit door over the alley.

Mr. Ball. What were their names?

A—Officer Hawkins, T. A. Hutson, and C. T. Walker. And as we got inside the door, we were met by a man that was in civilian clothes, a suit, and he told us that the man that acted suspiciously as he ran into the theater was sitting downstairs in the orchestra seats. . . . He was sitting at the rear of the theater alone.

Officer Walker and I went to the exit curtains that is to the left of the movie screen. I looked into the audience. I saw the person that the shoe store salesman had pointed out to us.

Mr. Ball. Were the lights on or off?

A—The lights were up, and the movie was playing at this time.

Mr. Ball. And could you see to the rear of the theater?

A—Yes, sir. . . .

As I got to the row where the suspect was sitting, I stopped abruptly, and turned in and told him to get on his feet. He rose immediately, bringing up both hands. He got this hand about shoulder high, his left hand shoulder high, and he got his right hand about breast high. He said, "Well, it is all over now."

As he said this, I put my left hand on his waist and then his hand went to the waist. And this hand struck me between the eyes on the bridge of the nose.

Mr. Ball. Did he cock his fist?

A—Yes, sir; knocking my cap off.

Mr. Ball. Which fist did he hit you with?

A—His left fist.

Mr. Ball. What happened then?

A—Well, whenever he knocked my hat off, any normal reaction was for me to go at him with this hand.

Mr. Ball. Right hand?

A—Yes. I went at him with this hand, and I believe I struck him on the face, but I don't know where. And with my hand, that was on his hand over the pistol.

113

Mr. Ball. Did you feel the pistol?

A—Yes, sir.

Mr. Ball. Which hand was—was his right hand or his left hand on the pistol?

A—His right hand was on the pistol.

Mr. Ball. And which of your hands?

A—My left hand, at this point.

Mr. Ball. And had he withdrawn the pistol—

A—He was drawing it as I put my hand.

Mr. Ball. From his waist?

A—Yes, sir.

Mr. Ball. What happened then?

A—Well, whenever I hit him, we both fell into the seats. While we were struggling around there, with this hand on the gun—

Mr. Ball. Your left hand?

A—Yes, sir. Somehow I managed to get this hand in the action also.

Mr. Ball. Your right hand?

A—Yes, sir. Now, as we fell into the seats, I called out, "I have got him," and Officer T. A. Hutson, he came to the row behind us and grabbed Oswald around the neck. And then Officer C. T. Walker came into the row that we were in and grabbed his left arm. And Officer Ray Hawkins came to the row in front of us and grabbed him from the front.

By the time all three of these officers had got there, I had gotten my right hand on the butt of the pistol and jerked it free.

Mr. Ball. Had you felt any movement of the hammer?

A—Yes, sir. When this hand—we went down into the seats.

Mr. Ball. When your left hand went into the seats, what happened?

A—It felt like something had grazed across my hand. I felt movement there. And that was the only movement I felt. And I heard a snap. I didn't know what it was at the time.

Mr. Ball. Was the pistol out of his waist at that time?

A—Yes, sir.

Mr. Ball. Do you know any way it was pointed?

A—Well, I believe the muzzle was toward me, because the sensation came across this way. To make a movement like that, it would have to be the cylinder or the hammer.

Mr. Ball. Across your left palm?

A—Yes, sir. And my hand was directly over the pistol in this manner. More or less the butt. But not on the butt.

Mr. Ball. What happened when you jerked the pistol free?

A—When I jerked it free, I was down in the seats with him, with my head, some reason or other, I don't know why, and when I brought the pistol out, it grazed me across the cheek here, and I put it all the way out to the aisle, holding it by the butt. I gave the pistol to Detective Bob Carroll at that point.

Mr. Ball. Grazed your left cheek?

A—Yes, sir.

Mr. Ball. Scratched—noticeable scratch?

A—Yes, sir; about a 4-inch scratch just above the eye to just above the lip.

Mr. Ball. Then what happened after that?

A—Well, the officers that had come to my aid started handcuffing him and taking him out of the theater.

Mr. Ball. What did he say—anything?

A—Well, he was cursing a little bit and hollering police brutality, for one thing.

Mr. Ball. What words did he use?

A—I couldn't recall the exact words. It was just mixed up words, people hollering and screaming when they get arrested.

Mr. Ball. What did he say about police brutality?

A—One thing, "Don't hit me any more." I remember that.

Mr. Ball. Did somebody hit him?

A—Yes, sir; I guess they did.

Mr. Ball. Who hit him, do you know?

A—No, sir; I don't, other than myself.

Mr. Ball. You know you hit him?

A—Yes, sir. . . .

J. W. FRITZ

The testimony of J. W. Fritz, captain of the Homicide and Robbery Bureau of the Dallas Police Department, who conducted much of the interrogation of Oswald:

Mr. Ball. What time did you arrive there?

A—We arrived at the hospital at 12:45, if you want that time, and at the scene of the offense at 12:58.

Mr. Ball. 12:58; the Texas School Book Depository Building.

A—Yes. . . .

Mr. Ball. What did you do when you got to this building?

A—Some officer told us they thought he was in that building, so we had our guns—

Mr. McCloy. Thought who was in the building?

A—The man who did the shooting was in the building. So, we, of course, took our shotguns and immediately entered the building and searched the building to see if we could find him. . . . We began searching the floors, looking for anyone with a gun or looked suspicious, and we searched through hurriedly through most all the floors. . . . It wasn't very long until someone called me and told me they wanted me to come to the front window, the corner window, they had found some empty cartridges.

Mr. Ball. That was on the sixth floor?

A—That is right; the sixth floor, corner window.

Mr. Ball. What did you do?

A—I told them not to move the cartridges, not to touch anything until we could get the crime lab to take pictures of them just as they were lying there and I left an officer assigned there to see that that was done, and the crime lab came almost immediately, and took pictures, and dusted the shelfs for prints. . . . A few minutes later some officer called me and said they had found the rifle over near the back stairway and I told them same thing, not to move it, not to touch it, not to move any of the boxes until we could get pictures. . . .

Mr. Ball. After the pictures had been taken of the rifle what happened then?

A—After the pictures had been made then I ejected a live shell, a live cartridge from the rifle.

Mr. Ball. And who did you give that to?

A—I believe that I kept that at that time myself. Later I gave it to the crime lab who, in turn, turned it over to the FBI. . . . About the time we finished Mr. Truly came and told me that one of his employees had left the building, and I asked his name and he gave me his name, Lee Harvey Oswald, and I asked his address. . . . I told them to drive me to city hall and see if the man had a criminal record and we picked up two other officers and my intentions were to go to the house [at Irving]. When I got to the city hall, I asked, because, I will tell you why I asked because while we were in the building we heard that our officer had been killed, someone came in and told me, I asked when I got to my office who shot the officer, and they told me his name was Oswald, and I said, "His full name?" And they told me and I said, "That is the suspect we are looking for in the President's killing."

So, I then called some of my officers to go right quickly, and asked them about how much evidence we had on the officer's killing and they told me they had several eye witnesses, and they had some real good witnesses, and I instructed them to get those witnesses over for identification just as soon as they could, and for us to prepare a real good case on the officer's killing so we would have a case to hold him without bond while we investigated the President's killing where we didn't have so many witnesses. . . .

Mr. Ball. Had he been brought into the station by that time?

A—He was at the station when we got there, you know.

Mr. Ball. Then you started to interrogate Oswald, did you?

A—Yes. sir.

Mr. Ball. And you called him into your room?

A—Yes, sir. . . .

Mr. Ball. Do you remember what you said to Oswald and what he said to you?

A—I can remember the thing that I said to him and what he said to me, but I will have trouble telling you which period

116

of questioning those questions were in because I kept no notes at the time, and these notes and things that I have made I would have to make several days later, and the questions may be in the wrong place.

Mr. Ball. What is your best memory of what you said to him when he first came in?

A—I first asked him as I do of most people something about where he was from, and where he was raised and his education, and I asked him where he went to school and he told me he went to school in New York for a while, he had gone to school in Fort Worth some, that he didn't finish high school, that he went to the Marines, and the Marines, and finished high school training in the Marines.

And I don't remember just what else. I asked him just the general questions for getting acquainted with him, and so I would see about how to talk to him, and Mr. Hosty [head of the FBI's Dallas office] spoke up and asked him something about Russia, and asked him if he had been to Russia, and he asked him if he had been to Mexico City, and this irritated Oswald a great deal and he beat on the desk and went into a kind of a tantrum.

Mr. Ball. What did he say when he was asked if he had been to Mexico City?

A—He said he had not been. He did say he had been to Russia, he was in Russia, I believe he said for some time. . . .

Mr. Ball. He hadn't been searched up to that time, had he?

A—Yes, sir; he had been searched.

Mr. Ball. Wasn't he searched later in the jail office?

A—He was searched, the officers who arrested him made the first search, I am sure. He had another search at the building and I believe that one of my officers . . . found some cartridges in his pocket in the room after he came to the city hall. I can't tell you the exact time when he searched him.

Mr. Ball. You don't have the record of the time when he was searched?

A—No.

Mr. Ball. You remember they found a transfer of Dallas Transit Company?

A—Yes, sir; found a transfer.

Mr. Ball. And some bullets?

A—Bullets; yes, sir. Cartridges. . . .

Mr. Ball. You had a showup that afternoon?

A—Yes, sir.

Mr. McCloy. May I ask what kind of bullets these were?

A—.38, cartridges for a .38 pistol.

Mr. McCloy. Pistol?

A—Yes, pistol cartridges.

Mr. Ball. You had a showup that afternoon?

A—That first showup was for a lady who was an eye witness. . . .

Mr. Ball. Do you remember her name?

A—Yes, Helen Markham. . . .

She looked at these people very carefully, and she picked him out and made the positive identification.

Mr. Ball. What did she say?

A—She said that is the man that I saw shoot the officer.

Mr. Ball. Who did she point out?

A—She pointed out Oswald; yes sir. . . .

Mr. Ball. Your records show the showup for Helen Markham was 4:45.

A—Yes, sir.

Mr. Ball. All right, now how long after that would you say you went back to your office and talked to him again?

A—I would say within, it would take us a few minutes, you know, to get him back from the showup, probably 15 minutes, something like that. . . .

Mr. Ball. Now, there was a time when you asked him where he worked and what he did?

A—Yes, sir. . . .

He told me he worked at the Texas School Book Depository. . . .

Mr. Ball. At that time didn't you know that one of your officers, Baker, had seen Oswald on the second floor?

A—They told me about that down at the bookstore. . . .

Mr. Ball. Did you question Oswald about that?

A—Yes, sir; I asked him about that and he knew that the officer stopped him all right. . . .

Mr. Ball. That same time you also asked him about the rifle.

A—I am not sure that is the time I asked him about the rifle. I did ask him about the rifle sometime soon after that occurred, and after the showup; I am not sure which time I asked him about the rifle.

Mr. Ball. Did you bring the rifle down to your office?

A—Not to him; not for him to see.

Mr. Ball. You never showed it to him?

A—No, sir. I asked him if he owned a rifle and he said he did not. I asked him if he had ever owned a rifle. He said a good many years ago he owned a small rifle but he hadn't owned one for a long time. I asked him if he owned a rifle in Russia and he said, "You know you can't own a rifle in Russia." He said, "I had a shotgun over there. You can't own a rifle in Russia." And he denied owning a rifle of any kind.

Mr. Ball. Didn't he say that he had seen a rifle at the building?

A—Yes, sir; he told me he had seen a rifle at the building 2 or 3 days before that Mr. Truly and some men were looking at.

Mr. Ball. You asked him why he left the building, didn't you?

A—Yes, sir.

Mr. Ball. He told you because he didn't think there would be any work?

A—Yes, sir.

Mr. Ball. Did you ask him what he did after he left the building?

A—Yes, sir.

Mr. Ball. What did he say?

A—He told me he went over and caught a bus and rode the bus to North Beckley near where he lived and went by home and changed clothes and got his pistol and went to the show. I asked him why he took his pistol and he said, "Well, you know about a pistol; I just carried it." Let's see if I asked him anything else right that minute. That is just about it.

Mr. Ball. Did you ask him if he killed Tippit?

A—Sir?

Mr. Ball. Did you ask him if he shot Tippit?

A—Oh, yes.

Mr. Ball. What did he say?

A—He denied it—that he did not. The only thing he said he had done wrong, "The only law I violated was in the show; I hit the officer in the show; he hit me in the eye and I guess I deserved it." He said, "That is the only law I violated." He said, "That is the only thing I have done wrong." . . .

Mr. Ball. Wasn't there some conversation also about what his political beliefs were?

A—I believe that is later. I asked him about his political beliefs and he said that he believed in fair play for Cuba. He said he was a member of the Fair Play for Cuba organization. They had headquarters in New York, had an office in New Orleans. . . .

Mr. Ball. Did you say anything to him about an attorney the first time you talked to him?

A—Yes, sir; the first time. He asked about an attorney, and I told him he certainly could have an attorney any time he wanted it. I told him he could have an attorney any time he liked, any attorney he wanted. I told him, I said, we will do it. He said he wanted an attorney in New York. And he gave me his name, Mr. Abt, and he said that is who he wanted, and I told him he could have anyone he liked. He said, well, he knew about a case that he had handled some years ago, where he represented the people who had violated the Smith Act, and he said, "I don't know him personally, but that is the attorney I want."

He said, "If I can't get him then I may get the American Civil Liberties Union to get me an attorney."

Mr. Ball. Was there anything said about calling him on the telephone?

A—A little bit later.

Mr. Ball. Not that time?

A—Not that minute. A little bit later, he asked something

119

else about an attorney and I said, "Did you call an attorney?" And he said, "You know I can't use the telephone." And I said, "Yes, you can; anybody can use a telephone." So, I told them to be sure to let him use a telephone and the next time I talked to him he thanked me for that, so I presume he called.

Mr. Ball. You don't know whether he called?

A—I don't know whether he did or not. . . .

Mr. Ball. Did—you have a rule in Texas, do you, that whatever a witness, a person in custody, says cannot be used against him unless he is warned?

A—We do have; yes, sir. We have to warn them before we can use the testimony. We have to warn them in the beginning before he is questioned.

Mr. Ball. Before he is questioned you must warn him?

A—Yes.

Mr. Ball. Before you questioned Oswald the first time, did you warn him?

A—Yes, sir.

Mr. Ball. What did you tell him? What were the words you used?

A—I told him that any evidence that he gave me would be used against him, and the offense for which the statement was made, that it would have to be voluntary, made of his own accord.

Mr. Ball. Did he reply to that?

A—He told me that he didn't want a lawyer and he told me once or twice that he didn't want to answer any questions at all. And once or twice he did quit answering any questions and he told me he did want to talk to his attorney, and I told him each time he didn't have to if he didn't want to. So, later he sometimes would start talking to me again.

Mr. Ball. Do you remember when you warned him again?

A—Yes, sir; I warned him two or three different times; yes, sir.

Mr. Ball. Do you remember when those times were?

A—No, sir; but during the afternoon.

Mr. Ball. They were—you were more or less continuously questioning through the afternoon, were you?

A—Yes, sir.

Mr. Ball. Now, at 7:10, he was arraigned in your office?

A—Yes, sir.

Mr. Ball. By arraign you mean he was informed of the charge against him?

A—That is right.

Mr. Ball. He wasn't asked to plea.

A—Before a judge, before a justice of the peace, a magistrate.

Mr. Ball. It is not your practice to ask for a plea at that stage, is it?

A—No, sir; we don't.

Mr. Ball. All you do is advise him of his rights and the charge against him?

A—That is right, I am not a lawyer, you might feel—I don't want to leave a bad impression, I am just telling you what we do.

Mr. Ball. What the practice is in Texas.

A—Yes, sir.

Mr. Ball. Did Oswald make any reply to Judge [David] Johnston? [who presided at the arraignment.]

A—He said a lot of sarcastic things to him.

Mr. Ball. What did he say?

A—Irritable, I can't remember all the things that he said. He was that way at each arraignment. He said little sarcastic things, some of the things were a little impudent things. . . .

Mr. Ball. Did you ever ask him if he had kept a rifle in the garage at Irving? [where Oswald's wife lived.]

A—Yes, sir; I did. I asked him and I asked him if he had brought one from New Orleans. He said he didn't.

Mr. Ball. He did not.

A—That is right.

I told him the people at the Paine residence said he did have a rifle out there, and he kept it out there and he kept it wrapped in a blanket and he said that wasn't true. . . .

Mr. Ball. Did you ever talk—you remember Wesley Frazier who came into the department and made a statement, do you, the boy who— . . .

Mr. Ball. A boy who lived in Irving who drove Oswald weekends back and forth from Irving.

A—Yes.

Mr. Ball. You remember you talked to him that night and he told about a package that Oswald carried into the Texas School Book Depository Building that morning.

A—Yes, sir; that is right.

Mr. Ball. Do you remember what that was?

A—He said he asked him what it was and he told him it was curtain rods.

Mr. Ball. Did you ever talk to Oswald about that?

A—Yes, sir; I did. . . .

Mr. Ball. What did you tell him?

A—I told him he had a package and put it in the back seat and it was a package about that long and it was curtain rods. He said he didn't have any kind of a package but his lunch. He said he had his lunch and that is all he had, and Mr. Frazier told me that he got out of the car with that package, he saw him go toward the building with this long package.

I asked him, I said, "Did you go toward the building carrying a long package?"

He said, "No. I didn't carry anything but my lunch."

Mr. Ball. Did Frazier ever tell you how long the package was?

121

A—He just measured, told me about that long.

Mr. Ball. Approximately how long?

A—I am guessing at this, the way he measured, probably 26 inches, 27 inches, something like that. Too short for the length of that rifle unless he took it down, I presume he took it down if it was in there, and I am sure it was.

Mr. Ball. Do you remember what time you—was it the way Frazier showed it to you—was it the size of a rifle that was broken down?

A—Yes, sir; it would be just about right.

Mr. Ball. Later that night you took him down to the show-uproom again, didn't you, when you had a press interview?

A—No, sir; I didn't have a press conference.

Mr. Ball. You didn't?

A—No.

Mr. Ball. Did you give any instructions to the press conference?

A—Yes, sir; the chief told me he wanted him brought down for a press conference, and I told my officers to take them down and I asked the chief to let me put it on the stage. I was a little bit afraid something might happen to him in front of that stage, someone in the crowd might hurt him but he said no, he wanted him out there in the front, and I told him I would like to put him on the stage so that the officers could jerk him inside the jail office if anything happened but he said no, he wanted him in front, so I told the officers to take him down.

I went down later to see how everything was going but I couldn't get in. The crowd had jammed clear back out into the hall. . . .

Mr. McCloy. May I ask you a question?

A—Yes, sir.

Mr. McCloy. Where was the—where did you first see the gun that was presumably used in the murder of Tippit?

A—Of Tippit?

Mr. McCloy. Tippit, yes; .38-caliber pistol.

A—The officers brought that in, you know, when they brought him in from the arrest at Oak Cliff.

Mr. McCloy. And they had that, you had seen it at about the time you first saw Oswald?

A—Well, a few minutes later.

Mr. McCloy. A few minutes later?

A—Yes, sir.

Mr. McCloy. It did show signs from your experience of having been recently fired?

A—I don't believe you can tell about that too well any more. You know the old style ammunition you could tell if a gun had been fired recently by the residue left in the barrel and smelling the barrel, but with the new ammunition they don't have that.

Mr. McCloy. And this was new ammunition that he was using?

A—Yes, sir; he was using new ammunition. . . .

Mr. McCloy. Did you see the gun in the position, the rifle I am talking about now.

A—Yes, sir.

Mr. McCloy. Did you see the rifle in the position in which it was found?

A—Yes, sir; I did.

Mr. McCloy. Where was it found?

A—It was found back near the stairway in a little—some boxes were stacked about this far apart, about that far apart. The rifle was down on the floor and partially under these boxes back near the stairway in the corner of the building.

Mr. McCloy. This was on the sixth floor?

A—Sixth floor; yes, sir.

Mr. McCloy. Nobody had touched it by the time you saw it?

A—No, sir; nobody touched it. They called me as soon as they saw it and I went back there and saw it.

Mr. McCloy. Then you say the rifle was then dusted?

A—Yes, sir.

Mr. McCloy. Does that mean the laboratory people had already come there then?

A—He came down from where he had been; he was on the same floor checking the empty cartridges, and he came back.

Mr. McCloy. Oh, yes.

A—To the back, when I called him, and he came back there and checked the rifle; yes, sir.

Mr. McCloy. When you went up to the sixth floor from which Oswald apparently had fired these shots, what did it look like there, what was the—how were things arranged there? Was there anything in the nature of a gun rest there or anything that could be used as a gun rest?

A—You mean up in the corner where he shot from, from the window?

Mr. McCloy. Yes.

A—Yes, sir; there were some boxes stacked there and I believe one box, one small box I believe was in the window, and another box was on the floor. There were some boxes stacked to his right that more or less blinded him from the rest of the floor. If anyone else had been on the floor I doubt if they could have seen where he was sitting.

Mr. McCloy. Did you see anything other— . . .

Mr. Dulles. When was the paper bag covering that apparently he brought the rifle in, was that discovered in the sixth floor about the same time?

A—No, sir; that was recovered a little later. I wasn't down there when that was found. . . .

Mr. Ball. Another thing, that day, at sometime during the

22d when you questioned Oswald, didn't you ask him about this card he had in his pocket with the name Alek Hidell?

A—I did; yes, sir.

Mr. Ball. What did you ask him about that?

A—I believe he had three of those cards if I remember correctly, and he told me that was the name that he picked up in New Orleans that he had used sometimes. One of the cards looked like it might have been altered a little bit and one of them I believe was the Fair Play for Cuba and one looked like a social security card or something. . . .

Mr. Ball. Now, the next morning or the next day you questioned him again, didn't you?

A—Let's see, that would be on the 23d.

Mr. Ball. You had another showup on the 23d in the afternoon, but apparently that morning before the showup you talked to him in your office?

A—Yes, sir. . . .

Mr. Ball. You learned certain things from your investigation of the day before, hadn't you?

A—Yes, sir.

Mr. Ball. One of them was you found he had a transfer, didn't you, in his pocket when he was arrested?

A—Yes, sir; I sure talked to him about the transfers.

Mr. Ball. All right. What did he say?

A—He admitted the transfer.

Mr. Ball. I don't want you to say he admitted the transfer. I want you to tell me what he said about the transfer.

A—He told me that was the transfer the busdriver had given him when he caught the bus to go home. But he had told me if you will remember in our previous conversation that he rode the bus or on North Beckley and had walked home but in the meantime, sometime had told me about him riding a cab.

So, when I asked him about a cab ride if he had ridden in a cab he said yes, he had, he told me wrong about the bus, he had rode a cab. He said the reason he changed, that he rode the bus for a short distance, and the crowd was so heavy and traffic was so bad that he got out and caught a cab. . . .

Mr. Ball. And you asked him [again,] didn't you, what he was doing at the time the President was shot?

A—Yes, sir; he told me he was having lunch when the President was shot.

Mr. Ball. With whom?

A—With someone called Junior, someone he worked with down there, but he didn't remember the other boy's name. . . .

Mr. Ball. But he said he had had lunch with Junior?

A—Yes, sir; and with someone else.

Mr. Ball. Did you find out that there was an employee named Junior, a man that was nicknamed Junior at the Texas School Book Depository?

A—Probably we have it here, some of the officers probably

did, we had all these people checked out. I didn't do it myself probably.

Mr. Ball. That same morning, you asked him also about his affiliations, didn't you ask him if he belonged to the Communist Party?

A—Yes, sir; I asked him if he belonged to the Communist Party.

Mr. Ball. What did he say?

A—He said he did not. He said he never had a card. He told me again that he did belong to the Fair Play for Cuba organization, that he was in favor of the Castro revolution and I don't remember what else he might have told me.

Mr. Ball. What about the pistol that he had on him when he was arrested, did you question him about that this morning?

A—That morning?

Mr. Ball. Your notes show that you did.

A—Yes, sir; I talked to him about the pistol and asked him where he got it.

Mr. Ball. What did he say?

A—He told me he had got it about 6 or 7 months before in Fort Worth but he wouldn't tell me where he got it. When I asked him a little further about that he told me he didn't want to talk any further about the pistol. . . .

Mr. Ball. Did you ever ask him what he thought of President Kennedy or his family?

A—Yes, sir; I asked him what he thought of the President.

Mr. Ball. What did he say?

A—What he thought about the family—he said he didn't have any particular comment to make about the President.

He said he had a nice family, that he admired his family, something to that effect. At one time, I don't have this in my report, but at one time I told him, I said, "You know you have killed the President, and this is a very serious charge."

He denied it and said he hadn't killed the President.

I said he had been killed. He said people will forget that within a few days and there would be another President.

Mr. Dulles. Did you say anything about Governor Connally?

A—No, sir; I don't think I questioned him about the Governor at that time. I might have asked him at one time. I remember telling him at one time he shot the Governor.

Mr. Dulles. Will you give us that?

A—He denied shooting any of them. . . .

Mr. Ball. In the meantime your officers had brought back from Irving some pictures that they found in the garage, hadn't they?

A—Yes, sir.

Mr. Ball. And you had had them blown up, hadn't you?

A—That is right.

Mr. Ball. What pictures—and you showed Oswald a picture at this time?

A—A picture of him holding a rifle and wearing the pistol. It showed a picture of him holding a rifle and wearing the pistol. I showed him first an enlarged picture. . . .

He said that wasn't his picture, he said, "I have been through that whole deal with all people in the cameras," he said, "One has taken my picture and that is my face and put a different body on it," He said, "I know all about photography, I worked with photography for a long time. That is a picture that someone else has made. I never saw that picture in my life." . . .

Mr. Ball. Did you ask him again about the rifle, did you ask him if that was the picture, that that rifle was his?

A—Yes, sir; I am sure I did.

Mr. Ball. Look at your notes.

A—All right, sir. Yes, sir; I did. I asked him again if that was his picture holding the rifle and he said it was not.

Mr. Ball. What did he say?

A—He denied it. He said he didn't have any knowledge of the picture at all. He said someone else had made it, he didn't know a thing about it or the rifle. . . .

Mr. Ball. Did you tell him that Frazier had told you that he had had a long parcel and placed it in the back seat? . . .

A—I remember telling him that someone told me that and I might have told him that two people saw him because not only Frazier but Frazier's sister saw that package, you know, and I did question him about that.

Mr. Ball. Did he say anything like this? "He might be mistaken or perhaps thinking about some other time when he picked me up."

A—That is probably right. . . .

Mr. Ball. Did you ask him why he had five live .38 caliber bullets in his shirt?

A—Yes; in his pocket?

Mr. Ball. Yes.

A—No; I didn't ask him that. . . .

Mr. Ball. In your report you have made a statement there of the conditions under which this interrogation proceeded, haven't you?

A—Yes; I did.

Mr. Ball. Will you tell us about that. You can describe it either as you state it here in your own words, but tell us what your difficulties were?

A—I can tell you in just a minute. My office is small as you know, it is a small office, it doesn't have too much room to begin with.

With all the outer office full of officers who all wanted to help and we were glad to have their assistance and help, and we appreciate it, but in the hallway we had some 200 news reporters and cameramen with big cameras and little cameras and cables running on the floors to where we could hardly get in and out of the office.

In fact, we had to get two police officers assigned to the front door to keep them out of the office so we could work.

My office is badly arranged for a thing of this kind. We never had anything like this before, of course, I don't have a back door and I don't have a door to the jail elevator without having to go through that hall for 20 feet, and each time we went through that hallway to and from the jail we had to pull him through all those people, and they, of course, would holler at him and say things to him, and some of them were bad things, and some were things that seemed to please him and some seemed to aggravate him, and I don't think that helped at all in questioning him. I think that all of that had a tendency to keep him upset.

Mr. Ball. What about the interview itself?

A—Now the interview itself inside, of course, we did have a lot of people in the office there to be interviewing a man. It is much better, and you can keep a man's attention and his thoughts on what you are talking to him about better I think if there are not more than two or three people.

But in a case of this nature as bad as this case was, we certainly couldn't tell the Secret Service and the FBI we didn't want them to work on it because they would have the same interest we would have, they would want to do anything they could do, so we, of course, invited them in too but it did make a pretty big crowd.

Mr. Ball. Did you have any tape recorder?

A—No, sir; I don't have a tape recorder. We need one, if we had one at this time we could have handled these conversations far better.

Mr. Ball. The Dallas Police Department doesn't have one?

A—No, sir; I have requested one several times but so far they haven't gotten me one. . . .

Mr. Ball. Was Oswald handcuffed at all times during the interrogation?

A—I believe he was; yes, sir, I believe we kept him handcuffed at all times. The first time we brought him in he was handcuffed with his hands behind him and he was uncomfortable and I had the officers change them and put his hands up front.

Mr. Ball. Was he fed any time during that day?

A—Yes, sir; he was. I don't remember buying him something to eat. I usually do, if they are hard up in jail at the time I buy something to eat but some of the other officers remember me buying him food but the only thing he would drink was I believe some milk and ate a little package of those crackers sandwiches and one of the other officers bought him a cup of coffee and that is all he would either eat or drink, that is all he wanted.

Mr. Ball. Now he talked to his wife and——

A—And his mother.

Mr. Ball. And his brother, Robert?

A—Yes, sir; I am pretty sure he did.

Mr. Ball. Where did he talk to them?

A—I believe that would be up in the jail. He didn't want them in my office. . . .

Mr. Ball. Is the jail wired so that you can listen to conversations?

A—No, sir; it isn't. Sometimes I wish I could hear some of the things they say but we don't. . . .

Mr. Dulles. What was Oswald's attitude toward the police and police authority?

A—You know I didn't have trouble with him. If we would just talk to him quietly like we are talking right now, we talked all right until I asked him a question that meant something, every time I asked him a question that meant something, that would produce evidence he immediately told me he wouldn't tell me about it and he seemed to anticipate what I was going to ask. In fact, he got so good at it one time, I asked him if he had had any training, if he hadn't been questioned before.

Mr. Dulles. Questioned before?

A—Questioned before, and he said that he had, he said yes, the FBI questioned him when he came back from Russia from a long time and they tried different methods. He said they tried the buddy boy method and thorough method, and let me see some other method he told me and he said, "I understand that."

Mr. Dulles. Did you ask him whether he had had any communist training or indoctrination or anything of that kind?

A—I asked him some questions about that and I asked him where he was in Russia. He told me he was in Russia, first I believe he told me, first I believe he said in Moscow, and then he said he went to Minsk, Russia, and I asked him what did you do, get some training, go to school? I suspected he had some training in sabotage from the way he talked and acted, and he said, "No, I worked in a radio factory." He acted like a person who was prepared for what he was doing. . . .

One time I asked him something about whether or not, either I asked him or someone else in there asked him, if he thought he would be better off, if he thought the country would be better off with the President killed and he said. "Well, I think that the Vice President has about the same views as the President has." He says he will probably do about the same thing that President Kennedy will do.

Mr. Dulles. Oswald said that to you?

A—Either to me or someone, it could be one of the other officers who asked that question while they were talking about him. . . .

Mr. Ball. Captain Fritz, from being with Oswald for a couple of days what were your impressions about him? Was he afraid, scared?

A—Was he afraid?

Mr. Ball. Yes.

A—No, sir; I don't believe he was afraid at all. I think he was a person who had his mind made up what to do and I think he was like a person just dedicated to a cause. And I think he was above average for intelligence.

I know a lot of people call him a nut all the time but he didn't talk like a nut. He knew exactly when to quit talking. He knew the kind of questions, I could talk to him as long as I wanted to if I just talked about a lot of things that didn't amount to anything. But any time I asked him a question that meant something he answered quick. . . .

JESSE E. CURRY

The testimony of the Chief of the Dallas Police Department concerning the treatment of Oswald while he was in police custody:

Mr. Dulles. How long were you at Love Field after the plane of the President left?

A—As I recall it was approximately an hour. . . .

Mr. Rankin. Then what did you do?

A—I returned to my office at city hall.

Mr. Rankin. Did you do anything about Lee Harvey Oswald at that time?

A—No. As I went into the city hall it was overrun with the news media.

Mr. Rankin. What did you do about that?

A—I didn't do anything. They were jammed into the north hall of the third floor, which are the offices of the criminal investigation division. The television trucks, there were several of them around the city hall. I went into my administrative offices, I saw cables coming through the administrative assistant office and through the deputy chief of traffic through his office, and running through the hall they had a live TV set up on the third floor, and it was a bedlam of confusion. . . .

Mr. Rankin. Did you inquire about whether permission had been given?

A—No; I didn't. We had in the past had always permitted free movement of the press around the city hall but we had never been faced with anything like this before where we had national and international news media descending upon us in this manner.

Mr. Rankin. Could you describe to the Commission the difference this time as compared with the ordinary case that you have handled?

A—Well, the ordinary case, perhaps we have two or three or maybe a half dozen reporters, we have a room for them on the third floor where they normally on assignment at city hall they stay in this room.

As prisoners are brought to and from the interrogation offices, it is necessary to bring them down the main corridor, and they usually are waiting there where they take pictures of them as they enter and as they leave and they sometimes try to ask them questions.

Mr. Dulles. What was Oswald's attitude toward the police? Have you any comment on that?

A—The only things I heard him say, he was very arrogant. He was very—he had a dislike for authority, it seemed, of anyone. . . .

Mr. Rankin. Did it ever come to your attention that he ever asked for or inquired about counsel?

A—Yes; I heard him say something. I asked if he had had an opportunity to use the phone and Captain Fritz told me they were giving him an opportunity to use the phone.

Mr. Rankin. What did he say about counsel?

A—As I recall he said he wanted to try to get in touch with John Abt.

Mr. Rankin. A-b-t?

A—A-b-t, I believe an attorney in New York, to handle his case and then if he couldn't get him he said he wanted to get someone from Civil Liberties Union.

Mr. Rankin. What did you do about that?

A—I told them to let him talk to them in an attempt to get his attorney and in an attempt to get some of his relatives so they could arrange for it.

Mr. Rankin. Will you describe how it was handled for him to be able to talk on the telephone?

A—We take them from their cells and we have two telephones that they are taken to, and they are put on these telephones and they are locked in, and a guard stands by while they make their calls. . . .

Mr. Rankin. Do you know whether an attorney from Dallas was offered to him and came to the jail?

A—There were some members of the Civil Liberties Union came to see us that night, and they said they were concerned with whether or not he was being permitted legal counsel.

Mr. Rankin. Did they talk to you?

A—No; they didn't talk to me. They talked to Professor Webster.

Mr. Rankin. How did this come to your attention?

A—He told me.

Mr. Rankin. I see. Now, tell us what he said.

A—He said that they had come down to see whether or not he was being permitted legal counsel, and Professor Webster is in the law school out at Southern Methodist University and he told them he thought he was being given an opportunity to get in touch with legal counsel, and they seemed satisfied then about it. We also got Mr. Nichols.

Mr. Rankin. Who is he?

A—He was president of the Dallas Bar Association or criminal bar. I don't know which, Louis Nichols, and——. . .

Dean Storey. Pardon me, it is Dallas Bar Association.

A—Dallas Bar Association.

The Chairman. Yes.

A—He went in to talk to him and to see whether or not he was getting an opportunity to receive counsel and he seemed pleased, I mean he had no complaints. He told him if he didn't get John Abt then he wanted someone from the Civil Liberties Union to come up and talk to him. Then Mr. Nichols then went out in front of the television cameras, I believe and made a statement to the effect that he had talked to him and he was satisfied that he was being given the opportunity for legal counsel.

The Chairman. On what day was this?

A—That was on the same day we arrested him.

The Chairman. That was Friday?

A—Yes.

Mr. Rankin. Do you know whether Mr. Oswald ever did obtain counsel?

A—I don't believe he did. But I do know he made some telephone contacts.

Mr. Rankin. Did the police department so far as you know interfere in any way with his obtaining counsel?

A—No, sir. . . .

GUY F. ROSE

The testimony of a detective in the Homicide and Robbery Bureau of the Dallas Police Department:

Mr. Ball. On the 22d of November 1963, were you on duty?

A—I went on duty shortly after the assassination. At the time of the assassination I was not on duty. . . .

Mr. Ball. Where did you go to work?

A—I reported to the homicide office. It's room 317 at the city hall.

Mr. Ball. Where did you go then?

A—There were some people in the office from the Book Depository and we talked to a few of them and then in just a few minutes they brought in Lee Oswald and I talked to him for a few minutes.

Mr. Ball. What did you say to him or did he say to you?

A—Well, the first thing I asked him was what his name was and he told me it was Hidell.

Mr. Ball. Did he tell you it was Hidell?

A—Yes; he did.

Mr. Ball. He didn't tell you it was Oswald?

A—No; he didn't, not right then—he did later. In a min-

131

ute—I found two cards—I found a card that said "A. Hidell."
And I found another card that said "Lee Oswald" on it, and
I asked him which of the two was his correct name. He
wouldn't tell me at the time, he just said, "You find out." And
then in just a few minutes Captain Fritz came in and he told
me to get two men and go to Irving and search his house. . . .

Mr. Ball. Did you have a search warrant?

A—No; we didn't.

Mr. Ball. How did you get in the house? . . .

A—Just as soon as we walked up on the porch, Ruth Paine
came to the door. She apparently recognized us—she said,
"I've been expecting you all," and we identified ourselves, and
she said, "Well, I've been expecting you to come out. Come
right on in."

Mr. Ball. Did she say why she had been expecting you?

A—She said, "Just as soon as I heard where the shooting
happened, I knew there would be someone out."

Mr. Ball. You took part in the search, didn't you?

A—Yes; I did.

Mr. Ball. What part did you take?

A—Well, I was the senior detective that was there, and so
I was sort of the spokesman for the group, I suppose, and
Stovall went into the bedroom of Marina Oswald—Marina
Oswald's bedroom, and I don't remember where Adamcik
went first, but I talked with Ruth Paine a few minutes and she
told me that Marina was there and that she was Lee Oswald's
wife and that she was a citizen of Russia, and so I called Captain Fritz on the phone and told him what I had found out
there and asked him if there was any special instructions, and
he said, "Well, ask her about her husband, ask her if her husband has a rifle."

I turned and asked Marina, but she didn't seem to understand. She said she couldn't understand, so Ruth Paine spoke
in Russian to her and Ruth Paine also interpreted for me,
and she said that Marina said—first she said Marina said "No,"
and then in a minute Marina said, "Yes, he does have."

So, then I talked to Captain Fritz for a moment and hung
up the phone and I asked Marina if she would show me where
his rifle was and Ruth Paine interpreted and Marina pointed
to the garage and she took me to the garage and she pointed
to a blanket that was rolled up and laying on the floor near
the wall of the garage and Ruth Paine said, "Says that that's
where his rifle is."

Well, at the time I couldn't tell whether there was one in
there or not. It appeared to be—it was in sort of an outline
of a rifle.

Mr. Ball. You mean the blanket had the outline of a rifle?

A—Yes; it did.

Mr. Ball. Was it tied at one end?

132

A—Yes sir; it was sort of rolled up, but it was flattened out from laying down and tied near the middle. I would say, with a cord and so I went on and picked the blanket up, but it was empty—it didn't have a rifle in it.

WILLIAM J. WALDMAN

The testimony of the vice president of Klein's Sporting Goods, Inc., the Chicago sporting goods company from which Oswald bought the assassination rifle:

Mr. Belin. I'm handing you what has been marked as an FBI Exhibit D–77 and ask you if you know what this is.

A—This is a microfilm record that—of mail order transactions for a given period of time. It was turned over by us to the FBI.

Mr. Belin. Do you know when it was turned over to the FBI?

A—It was turned over to them on November 23, 1963.

Mr. Belin. Now, you are reading from the carton containing that microfilm. Do you know whose initials are on there?

A—Yes; the initials on here are mine and they were put on the date on which this was turned over to the FBI concerned with the investigation.

Mr. Belin. You have on your premises a machine for looking at the microfilm prints?

A—Yes.

Mr. Belin. And you can make copies of the microfilm prints?

A—Yes.

Mr. Belin. I wonder if we can adjourn the deposition upstairs to take a look at these records in the microfilm and get copies of the appropriate records that you found on the evening of November 22.

A—Yes.

(Whereupon, the following proceedings were had at the microfilm machine.)

Mr. Belin. Mr. Waldman, you have just put the microfilm which we call D–77 into your viewer which is marked a Microfilm Reader-Printer, and you have identified this as No. 270502, according to your records. Is this just a record number of yours on this particular shipment?

A—That's a number which we assign for identification purposes.

Mr. Belin. And on the microfilm record, would you please state who it shows this particular rifle was shipped to?

A—Shipped to a Mr. A.—last name—H-i-d-e-l-l, Post Office Box 2915, Dallas, Tex.

Mr. Belin. And does it show any serial number or control number?

A—It shows shipment of a rifle bearing our control number VC–836 and serial number C–2766.

Mr. Belin. Is there a price shown for that?

A—Price is $19.95, plus $1.50 postage and handling, or a total of $21.45.

LT. COL. PIERRE A. FINCK

The testimony of a doctor and army expert on wound ballistics:

Mr. Specter. Based on your observations and conclusions, was President Kennedy shot from the front, rear, side or what?

A—President Kennedy was, in my opinion, shot from the rear. The bullet entered in the back of the head and went out on the right side of his skull, producing a large wound, the greatest dimension of which was approximately 13 centimeters.

Mr. Specter. And as to angle, was he shot from below, from level, from above, or what, in your opinion?

A—In my opinion, the angle can be determined only approximately due to the fact that the wound of entrance is fairly small and could give enough precision in the determination of the path, but the dimension of the wound of exit, letter B of Exhibit 388, is so large that we can only give an approximate angle. In my opinion, the angle was within 45 degrees from the horizontal plane.

Mr. Specter. Is that to say that there was a 45-degree angle of declination from the point of origin to the point of impact, from the point of origin of the bullet where the bullet came from a gun until the point where it struck President Kennedy?

The Chairman. In other words, you mean was he shot from above or below.

Mr. Specter. Yes.

A—I think I can only state, sir, that he was shot from above and behind.

MAJOR EUGENE D. ANDERSON

MASTER SERGEANT JAMES A. ZAHM

The testimony of two members of the Marine Corps who told about Oswald's marksmanship:

Mr. Specter. Based on what you see of Mr. Oswald's marksmanship capabilities from the Marine Corps records which you have before you, Major Anderson, how would you characterize him as a marksman?

Major Anderson. I would say that as compared to other Marines receiving the same type of training, that Oswald was a good shot, somewhat better than or equal to—better than the average let us say. As compared to a civilian who had not received this intensive training, he would be considered as a good to excellent shot.

Mr. Specter. Major Anderson, I now want to show you

certain photographs which have been heretofore identified and introduced into the Commission's record as a preliminary to asking your opinion on the difficulty of certain shots which I will identify.

First I show you Commission Exhibit No. 347 which is an overhead photograph of an area known as Dealey Plaza, which the record will show is the situs of the assassination of President Kennedy. I now show you Commission Exhibit No. 348 which is a photograph of the Texas School Book Depository Building with the letter "A" pointing to the half-opened window, that is the bottom portion of the window which is half opened, where other witnesses have testified that the assassin stood. Let me add as a factor for you to assume to be true, this the record will show is based upon eyewitnesses at the scene, that the weapon partly protruded from the window identified as letter "A" in Exhibit No. 348 pointing at an angle which is not completely in a straight line but very much in a straight line with the angle of the street being designated as Elm Street, which street runs on a downgrade of approximately 3°.

I now show you a document identified as Commission Exhibit No. 893, and a second document identified as Commission Exhibit No. 895, which depict frame No. 210 and frame No. 225 on photographs in the nature of moving pictures taken by Abraham Zapruder at the assassination site which the evidence indicates was the range of the first shot which struck President Kennedy in the lower portion of his neck, with that bullet striking at a distance from 176.9 feet to a distance of 190.8 feet. Stated differently, the evidence shows that somewhere between these two pictures President Kennedy was shot in the neck, and as the photograph of the rifle scope shows in the left-hand corner lower picture, that is the view through the telescopic lens which the marksman had based on onsite tests which were made in Dallas with a camera mounted looking through the scope on Commission Exhibit No. 139, which is the weapon identified as the assassination rifle. Now assuming those factors to be true for purposes of this next question, how would you characterize the difficulty of a shot at that range, which would strike the President in the lower portion of his neck at a spot indicated by a white mark on the back of the stand-in the photograph marked "Re-enactment"?

My question, then, is how would you characterize the difficulty or ease of that shot for a marksman with Mr. Oswald's capabilities?

A—In my opinion this is not a particularly difficult shot, and that Oswald had full capabilities to make this shot.

Mr. Specter. I now show you a document marked as Commission Exhibit No. 902, which characterizes what was believed to have been the shot which struck President Kennedy in the head at a distance from rifle in window to the President of 265.3 feet, with the photograph through rifle scope identified on the document being the view which the marksman had of the President at the time the President was struck in the head, and I ask you again for an opinion as to the ease or difficulty of that shot, taking into consideration the capabilities of Mr. Oswald as a marksman, evidenced by the Marine Corps documents on him.

A—I consider it to be not a particularly difficult shot at this short range, and that Oswald had full capabilities to make such a shot. . . .

Mr. Specter. Sergeant Zahm, I am now going to show you the same photographs which I showed to Major Anderson in setting the basis for asking you a hypothetical question on capabilities here. . . . Now assuming that the President was struck under those circumstances at a distance of from 176.9 feet to 190.8 feet, using a 6.5 mm Mannlicher-Carcáno rifle with a four-power scope, would a man with Oswald's marksmanship capabilities be able to complete such a shot and strike the target on the white mark there?

Sergeant Zahm. Very definitely.

Mr. Specter. How would you characterize that, as a difficult, not too difficult, easy, or how would you characterize that shot?

A—With the equipment he had and with his ability, I consider it a very easy shot.

Mr. Specter. Now taking a look at Commission Exhibit No. 902, which as the record will show, has been introduced into evidence to depict the shot which struck President Kennedy in the head at a distance from the rifle in the window to the part of the President's body being 265.3 feet. Assuming the same factors about using a Mannlicher-Carcáno rifle and pointing it down Elm Street as shown on Commission Exhibit No. 347, would a marksman of Mr. Oswald's capabilities using such a rifle with a 4-power scope be able to strike the President in the back of the head? Would Mr. Oswald possess the capability to complete such a shot which did, in this situation, strike the President in the back of the head?

A—Yes; I think that aiming at the mass of what portion of the President is visible at that distance and with his equipment, he would very easily have attained a hit, not necessarily aiming and hitting in the head. This would have been a little more difficult and probably be to the top of his ability, aiming and striking the President in the head. But assuming that he aimed at the mass to the center portion of the President's body, he would have hit him very definitely someplace, and the fact that he hit him in the head, but he could have hit, got a hit.

Mr. Specter. So you would have expected a man of Oswald's capabilities at a distance of 265.3 feet to strike the President someplace aiming at him under those circumstances?

A—Yes.

Mr. Specter. And within the range of where you would expect him to hit him, would that include the President's head?

A—Yes.

Mr. Specter. And how would you characterize that shot with respect to whether it was difficult or not difficult? . . .

A—I consider it still an easy shot, a little more difficult from the President's body position and increase in distance of approximately 40 feet, but I still consider it an easy shot for a man with the equipment he had and his ability.

Mr. Specter. Assuming that there were three shots fired in a range of 4.8 to 5.6 seconds, would that speed of firing at that range indicated in the prior questions be within Mr. Oswald's capabilities as a marksman?

—Yes.

Mr. Specter. What effect if any would the alinement of the street have on the moving vehicle in the way that it is shown on the picture, Exhibit No. 348?

A—This is a definite advantage to the shooter, the vehicle moving directly away from him and the downgrade of the street, and he being in an elevated position made an almost stationary target while he was aiming in, very little movement if any. . . .

SEBASTIAN F. LATONA

The testimony of an F.B.I. fingerprint expert who was questioned about prints found on a paper bag in which Oswald was believed to have carried the rifle to the school book depository that morning, on the rifle itself and on a book carton near the window from which the shots were fired:

Mr. Eisenberg. You stated I believe that you found a palmprint and a fingerprint on this paper bag?

A—That is correct.

Mr. Eisenberg. Did you find any other prints?

A—No; no other prints that we term of value in the sense that I felt that they could be identified or that a conclusion could be reached that they were not identical with the fingerprints or palmprints of some other person.

Mr. Eisenberg. Did you attempt to identify the palmprint and fingerprint?

A—The ones that I developed; yes.

Mr. Eisenberg. Were you able to identify these prints?

A—I—the ones I developed, I did identify.

Mr. Eisenberg. Whose prints did you find them to be?

A—They were identified as a fingerprint and a palmprint of Lee Harvey Oswald. . . .

Mr. Eisenberg. Now, Mr. Latona, I hand you Commission Exhibit 139 which, for the record, consists of the rifle found on the sixth floor of the TSBD building, and which was identified yesterday as the rifle—and the day before yesterday—as the rifle which fired the fatal bullets, and I ask you whether you are familiar with this weapon?

A—Yes; I am. . . .

Mr. Eisenberg. I now hand you a small white card marked with certain initials and with a date, "11-22-63." There is a cellophane wrapping, cellophane tape across this card with what appears to be a fingerprint underneath it, and the handwriting underneath that tape is "off underside of gun barrel near end of foregrip C 2766," which I might remark parenthetically is the serial number of Exhibit 139. I ask you whether you are familiar with this item which I hand you, this card?

A—Yes; I am familiar with this particular exhibit.

Mr. Eisenberg. Can you describe to us what that exhibit consists of, that item rather?

A—This exhibit or this item is a lift of a latent palmprint which was evidently developed with black powder. . . .

Mr. Eisenberg. Who did you get this exhibit, this lift from?

A—This lift was referred to us by the FBI Dallas office.

Mr. Eisenberg. And were you told anything about its origin?

A—We were advised that this print had been developed by the Dallas Police Department, and, as the lift itself indicates, from the underside of the gun barrel near the end of the foregrip.

Mr. Eisenberg. Now, may I say for the record that at a subsequent point we will have the testimony of the police officer of the Dallas police who developed this print, and made the lift; and I believe that the print was taken from underneath the portion of the barrel which is covered by the stock. Now, did you attempt to identify this print which shows on the lift Exhibit 637?

A—Yes; I did.

Mr. Eisenberg. Did you succeed in making identification?

A—On the basis of my comparison, I did effect an identification.

Mr. Eisenberg. And whose print was that, Mr. Latona?

A—The palmprint which appears on the lift was identified by me as the right palmprint of Lee Harvey Oswald. . . .

Mr. Eisenberg. I hand you now a small cardboard carton which has written on it "Box A" in red pencil and has various other marks which I won't go into, and I ask you whether you are familiar with this box, this carton?

A—Yes; I am.

Mr. Eisenberg. And did you examine this carton, Mr. Latona, to determine whether there were any identifiable latent fingerprints present? . . .

A—There were developed eight fingerprints and three palmprints.

Mr. Eisenberg. That is, a total of 13?

A—Nine fingerprints and four palmprints.

Mr. Eisenberg. Thirteen identifiable prints?

A—That is right. . . .

Mr. Eisenberg. So you found 13 identifiable prints, Mr. Latona. Were you able to identify any of these prints as belonging to a specific individual?

A—We were able to identify one fingerprint and one palmprint.

Mr. Eisenberg. And whose prints were they?

A—The fingerprint was identified as Harvey Lee Oswald.

Mr. Eisenberg. That is Lee Harvey Oswald?

A—That is right.

Mr. Eisenberg. And the palm?

A—The palmprint was identified also as Harvey Lee Oswald.

Mr. Eisenberg. Again Lee Harvey Oswald?

A—That is right.

ROBERT A. FRAZIER

The testimony of an FBI weapons expert on whether the cartridge cases and bullets and fragments later found had been fired from Oswald's rifle:

Mr. Eisenberg. Mr. Frazier, returning to the cartridge cases which were marked earlier into evidence as Commission Exhibits 543, 544, and 545, and which, as I stated earlier for the record, had been found next to the window of the sixth floor of the Texas School Book Depository, can you tell us when you received those cartridge cases?

A—Yes, sir; I received the first of the exhibits, 543 and 544, on November 23, 1963. They were delivered to me by Special Agent Vincent Drain of the Dallas FBI Office.

And the other one I received on November 27, 1963, which was delivered by Special Agents Vincent Drain and Warren De Brueys of the Dallas Office.

Mr. Eisenberg. After receiving these cartridge cases, did you clean them up or in any way prepare them for examination?

A—Yes. The bases were cleaned of a paint which was placed on them by the manufacturer. In spots this red lacquer on the base of the case was overlapping the head of the case where some of the microscopic marks were located, and some of that color was taken off.

Mr. Eisenberg. Why is that lacquer put on the cartridge cases?

A—It seals the primer area against moisture.

Mr. Eisenberg. Were there any other changes made in the preparation of the cartridge cases?

A—No, sir.

Mr. Eisenberg. You have examined the cartridge cases previously. Are they in the same condition now that they were

139

when you received them in the laboratory except for the cleaning of the lacquer?

A—Yes, sir; they are.

Mr. Eisenberg. After receiving the cartridge cases, did you examine them to determine whether they had been fired in Commission Exhibit 139 [the Oswald rifle]?

A—Yes, sir.

Mr. Eisenberg. When did you make the examinations?

A—On the dates I mentioned, that is, November 23, 1963, and November 27, 1963.

Mr. Eisenberg. And what were your conclusions, Mr. Frazier?

A—I found all three of the cartridge cases had been fired in this particular weapon. . . .

Mr. Eisenberg. Mr. Frazier, I now hand you Commission Exhibit 399, which, for the record, is a bullet, and also for the record, it is a bullet which was found in the Parkland Hospital following the assassination. Are you familiar with this exhibit?

A—Yes, sir. This is a bullet which was delivered to me in the FBI laboratory on November 22, 1963 by Special Agent Elmer Todd of the FBI Washington Field Office.

Mr. Eisenberg. Does that have your mark on it?

A—Yes, it does.

Mr. Eisenberg. The bullet is in the same condition as it was when you received it?

A—Yes, sir; except for the marking of my initials and the other examiners. There is a discoloration at the nose caused apparently by mounting this bullet in some material which stained it, which was not present when received, and one more thing on the nose is a small dent or scraped area. At this area the spectographic examiner removed a small quantity of metal for analysis.

Mr. Eisenberg. Did you prepare the bullet in any way for examination? That is, did you clean it or in any way alter it?

A—No, sir; it was not necessary. The bullet was clean and it was not necessary to change it in any way.

Mr. Eisenberg. There was no blood or similar material on the bullet when you received it?

A—Not any which would interfere with the examination, no, sir. Now there may have been slight traces which could have been removed just in ordinary handling, but it wasn't necessary to actually clean blood or tissue off of the bullet.

Mr. Eisenberg. Did you examine this exhibit to determine whether it had been fired in Exhibit 139?

A—Yes, sir.

Mr. Eisenberg. And what was your conclusion?

A—It was. Exhibit 399 was fired in the rifle 139.

Mr. Eisenberg. That is to the exclusion of all other rifles?

A—Yes, sir. . . .

HEINZ W. MICHAELIS

The testimony of an employee of the mail order company from which the revolver carried by Oswald at the time of his arrest was purchased:

Mr. Ball. Now, last fall did the Federal Bureau of Investigation visit your place of business and inquire as to the sale of a certain Smith & Wesson revolver?

A—Correct.

Mr. Ball. About what date?

A—I believe it was November the 30th, a Saturday.

Mr. Ball. And in searching your records for any such sale, to what particular record did you first look?

A—We started first, after having received the serial number, through our serial number book for this particular type of gun.

Mr. Ball. Now, what serial number did the FBI give you?

A—V, as in victory, 510210-65248.

Mr. Ball. Now, those two numbers signify what?

A—The first number, V510210, is commonly described as the butt number, while the second number, 65248, usually is described as the crane number. . . .

Mr. Ball. You have been testifying from a record which you have before you?

A—That is correct.

Mr. Ball. And that is a paper which has been marked for identification by the Federal Bureau of Investigation DL-28, Seaport Traders, Inc., No. A-5371.

Is that correct? You have been testifying from information contained on that?

A—Correct.

Mr. Ball. Will you tell me, describe that document and tell me its significance in your business?

A—This particular document is, after the order is processed, filed in our records under the name of the respective customer.

Mr. Ball. You mean after the revolver that was ordered by this mail order coupon, 135, has been packed and shipped, this invoice A-5371, is filed as a permanent record, is it, of the shipment?

A—Correct; filed under the name of the respective customer.

Mr. Ball. Now, this shows the words A. J. Hidell, P.O. Box 2915, Dallas, Tex. This appears on this invoice A-5371, does it not?

A—Yes.

Mr. Ball. It is described as an S. & W. .38 special, 2-inch Commando. What is the meaning of that?

A—Two inch is the barrel length. Commando is a description which we more or less gave because we have another 2-inch gun at a higher price and, in order that the order filler is able to identify between the two types, we have this type described as Commando.

Mr. Ball. Now, the No. 510210. What is the significance of that number?

A—It is the serial number of the gun in question.

CORTLANDT CUNNINGHAM

The testimony of one of the weapons experts who examined the cartridge cases found near the site of the murder of Officer J. D. Tippit and compared them with cartridges fired from the gun taken from Lee Harvey Oswald at the time of his arrest:

Mr. Eisenberg. Does this revolver have a serial number on it?

A—It does.

Mr. Eisenberg. Could you read that number to us, please?

A—V-510210.

Mr. Eisenberg. Is this serial number unique to this particular type of weapon?

A—Yes. Smith and Wesson does not duplicate numbers. You may have a similar number, but not with the prefix "V."

Mr. Eisenberg. So this is the only such weapon with this serial number that is in existence?

A—That is correct. As far as I know. I have never found one in my experience, and Smith and Wesson does not duplicate serial numbers in a particular series of weapons.

Mr. Eisenberg. Smith and Wesson claims not to duplicate?

A—That is correct. . . .

Mr. Eisenberg. For the record, I would like to state that these cartridge cases were found in the immediate proximity of the site at which Officer Tippit was killed. They were found on the ground near the street where Officer Tippit was killed on November 22.

Representative Ford. These are the ones that were found in the street near the automobile?

Mr. Eisenberg. Well, either in the street or in a lawn in front of a private residence, or semiapartment house. . . .

Mr. Chairman, I would like to have these four cartridge cases introduced into evidence as 594.

Representative Ford. They may be admitted.

Mr. Eisenberg. Now, Mr. Cunningham, could you describe the make of these cartridge cases?

A—Two of these cartridge cases are Remington-Peters .38 special cartridge cases. The other two cartridge cases are Western .38 Special cartridge cases.

Mr. Eisenberg. Now, you examined earlier six bullets which I told you had been—six cartridges which I told you had been taken from the chamber of the revolver which we have been looking at.

Those cartridges were divided into three Remington-Peters and three Western, were they not?

A—Yes, sir.

Mr. Eisenberg. So that—or 50-50. So that the division is the same, the division of the cartridge cases is the same, as between Remington-Peters and Western, as the division of the cartridges found—which I told you were found in the chamber?

A—Yes, sir.

Mr. Eisenberg. Did you examine the cartridge cases in Exhibit 594 in an attempt to determine whether they had been fired in Exhibit 143, the revolver, to the exclusion of all other revolvers?

A—I did.

Mr. Eisenberg. Can you tell us your conclusion?

A—As a result of my examination, it is my opinion that those four cartridge cases, Commission Exhibit 594, were fired in the revolver, Commission Exhibit 143, to the exclusion of all other weapons.

Mr. Eisenberg. When did you perform this examination, Mr. Cunningham?

A—On November 30, 1963.

Mr. Eisenberg. And how did you make the examination?

A—I first marked these cartridge cases upon receiving them. There were four. I would like to state, first of all that Special Agents Frazier and Killion also independently examined these four cartridge cases, and made the same comparisons that I am going to state. I am telling you what I found—although they independently arrived at the same conclusion.

The cartridge cases were first marked and examined for the presence of any individual characteristic marks on these cartridge cases whereby it would be possible to identify them as having been fired in a weapon. I then test-fired Commission Exhibit 143, using similar ammunition, and microscopically compared the four cartridge cases—one at a time—that is Commission Exhibit 594—with the tests obtained from the revolver, Commission Exhibit 143. . . .

DAVID L. JOHNSTON

The testimony of a Justice of the Peace of Dallas County:

Mr. Hubert. Were you the justice of peace that arraigned Oswald?

A—Yes; I arraigned Lee Harvey Oswald. . . . The first charge that was filed was for murder with malice of Officer J. D. Tippit of the Dallas Police Department in cause No. F-153, *The State of Texas* versus *Lee Harvey Oswald*. This complaint was filed at 7:05 p.m. on the 22nd day of November 1963.

Mr. Hubert. By whom?

A—By Capt. J. W. Fritz, captain of the homicide bureau, Dallas Police Department, was accepted by W. F. Alexander who is William F. Alexander, an assistant criminal district attorney of Dallas County, Tex., which was passed over to me at 7:05 p.m. The actual complaint was signed at 7:04 p.m. and I arraigned Lee Harvey Oswald at 7:10 p.m. on November 22, 1963, advising him of his constitutional rights and that he had to make no statement at all, and that any statement he made may be used in evidence against him for the offense concerning which this affidavit was taken, and remanded the defendant to the custody of the sheriff of Dallas County, Tex., with no bond as capital offense.

Mr. Hubert. Now, let's pass to the arraignment concerning President Kennedy. . . .

A—This was the arraignment of Lee Harvey Oswald for the murder with malice of John F. Kennedy, cause No. F-154, *The State of Texas* versus *Lee Harvey Oswald.* The complaint was filed at 11:25 p.m., was accepted by me at 11:26 p.m. It was filed at approximately 11:25 p.m. by Capt. J. W. Fritz, homicide bureau of the Dallas Police Department, and was accepted by Henry Wade, criminal district attorney, Dallas County, Tex., and was docketed as cause No. 154, F-154 at 11:26 p.m.

That arraignment was held at 1:35 a.m., November 23, 1963, in the identification bureau of the Dallas Police Department.

III. The Assassin

MRS. LEE HARVEY OSWALD

Testimony of the widow of the assassin:

Mr. Rankin. Mrs. Oswald, you be at your ease, and the interpreter will tell you what I ask and you take your time about your answers.

Will you state your name, please?

A—Marina, my name is Marina Nikolaevna Oswald. My maiden name was Prussakova.

Mr. Rankin. Where do you live, Mrs. Oswald?

A—At the present time I live in Dallas. . . .

Mr. Rankin. Mrs. Oswald, do you have a family?

A—I have two children, two girls, June will be 2 years old in February, and Rachel is 3 months old.

Mr. Rankin. Are you the widow of the late Lee Harvey Oswald?

A—Yes. . . .

Mr. Rankin. Do you recall the date that you arrived in the United States with your husband, Lee Harvey Oswald?

A—On the 13th of June, 1962—I am not quite certain as to the year—'61 or '62, I think '62.

Mr. Rankin. How did you come to this country?

A—From Moscow via Poland, Germany, and Holland we came to Amsterdam by train. And from Amsterdam to New York by ship, and New York to Dallas by air.

Mr. Rankin. Do you recall the name of the ship on which you came?

A—I think it was the SS *Rotterdam* but I am not sure.

Mr. Rankin. What time of the day did you arrive in New York?

A—It was—about noon or 1 p.m., thereabouts. It is hard to remember the exact time.

Mr. Rankin. How long did you stay in New York at that time?

A—We stayed that evening and the next 24 hours in a hotel in New York, and then we left the following day by air.

Mr. Rankin. Do you know whether or not you or your husband received any financial assistance for the trip to Texas at that time?

A—I don't know exactly where Lee got the money, but he said that his brother Robert had given him the money. But the money for the trip from the Soviet Union to New York was given to us by the American Embassy in Moscow.

Mr. Rankin. Do you recall what time of the day you left on the flight to Texas?

A—I think that by about 5 p.m. we were already in Texas.

Mr. Rankin. Did you go to Dallas or Fort Worth at that time?

A—In Dallas we were met by the brother, Robert, he lived in Fort Worth, and he took us from Dallas to Fort Worth and we stopped at the house.

Mr. Rankin. Who else stayed at Robert's house at that time besides your family?

A—His family and no one else.

Mr. Rankin. What did his family consist of at that time?

A—He and his wife and two children, a boy and a girl.

Mr. Rankin. How long did you stay at Robert's?

A—About 1 to 1½ months—perhaps longer, but no longer than 2 months.

Mr. Rankin. Were your relations and your husband's with Robert pleasant at that time?

A—Yes, they were very good. His brother's relationship to us was very good.

Mr. Rankin. Would you briefly describe what you did during that time when you were at Robert's?

A—The first time we got there we were, of course, resting for about a week, and I was busy, of course, with my little girl who was then very little. And in my free time, of course, I helped in the household.

Mr. Rankin. Did your husband do anything around the house or did he seek work right away?

A—For about a week he was merely talking and took a trip to the library. That is it.

Mr. Rankin. Then did he seek work in Fort Worth?

A—Yes.

Mr. Rankin. And when did he find his first job there?

A—While we were with Robert. It seems it was at the end of the second month that Lee found work. But at this time I don't remember the date ·exactly but his mother who lived in Forth Worth at that time rented a room and she proposed that we spend some time with her, that we live with her for some time.

Mr. Rankin. Did you discuss with your husband this proposal of your mother-in-law to have you live with her?

A—Well, she made the proposal to my husband, not to me. Of course, I found out about it.

Mr. Rankin. Did you and he have any discussion about it after you found out about it?

A—Yes, of course.

Mr. Rankin. You recall that discussion?

A—No. I only remember the fact.

Mr. Rankin. Did he find work after you left Robert's then?

A—Yes.

Mr. Rankin. You did move to be with your mother-in-law, lived with her for a time?

A—Yes, about 3 weeks. And then after 3 weeks Lee did not want to live with her any more and he rented an apartment.

Mr. Rankin. Do you know the reason why he did not want to live there any more?

A—It seemed peculiar to me and didn't want to believe it but he did not love his mother, she was not quite a normal woman. Now, I know this for sure.

Mr. Rankin. Did he tell you that at the time?

A—He talked about it but since he spoke in English to his mother, I didn't understand it. There were quite a few scenes when he would return from work he didn't want to talk to her. Perhaps she thought I was the reason for the fact that Lee did not want to talk to her. And, of course, for a mother this is painful and I told him that he should be more attentive to his mother but he did not change. I think that one of the reasons for this was that she talked a great deal about how much she had done to enable Lee to return from Russia, and Lee felt that he had done most of—the greatest effort in that respect and didn't want to discuss it.

Mr. Rankin. Where did he find work at that time?

A—Of course, if I had been told now I would have remembered it because I have learned some English but at that time I didn't know, but Lee told me that it wasn't far from Mercedes Street where we lived, and it was really common labor connected with some kind of metal work, something for buildings.

Mr. Rankin. Did he ever say whether he enjoyed that work?

A—He didn't like it.

Mr. Rankin. Do you recall how long he stayed at that job?

A—I don't know but it seemed to me that he worked there for about 3 or 4 months. Perhaps longer. Dates are one of my problems.

Mr. Rankin. Do you know whether he left that job voluntarily or was discharged?

A—He told me that he had been discharged but I don't know why.

Mr. Rankin. When you left the mother-in-law's house where did you go?

A—I have already said that we moved to Mercedes Street.

Mr. Rankin. Did you have an apartment there?

A—Yes, we rented an apartment in a duplex.

Mr. Rankin. Do you recall the address on Mercedes Street?

A—No, I don't remember the exact number.

Mr. Rankin. Will you describe the apartment, how many rooms it had?

A—Living room, kitchen, bath, and one bedroom.

Mr. Rankin. This was the first time since you had come to this country then that you had an opportunity to have a home of your own, is that right?

A—No, we had our own home in Russia.

Mr. Rankin. Did your husband work a full day at that time on this job?

A—Yes, sometimes he even worked on Saturdays.

Mr. Rankin. What did you do when he came home, did he help you with housework?

A—Yes. He frequently went to a library. He read a great deal.

Mr. Rankin. Do you recall any of the books that he read at that time?

A—No. I only know that they were books more of a historical nature rather than fiction or literature.

Mr. Rankin. In your story in Russian you relate the fact that he read a great deal of the time. Could you describe to the Commission just how that was? Did he go off by himself to read or how did he handle that?

A—He would bring a book from a library, sit in the living room and read. I was busy with housework, and that is the way it happened.

Mr. Rankin. Did you have differences between you about the time that he spent reading rather than devoting it to you or the other members of the family?

A—No. We did have quarrels about his relationship to his mother, the fact that he didn't want to change his relationship to his mother. I know that he read so much that when we lived in New Orleans he used to read sometimes all night long and in order not to disturb me he would be sitting in the bathroom for several hours reading.

Mr. Rankin. Did your quarrels start at that time when you were at Mercedes Street the first time?

A—Yes, we didn't have many quarrels.

Mr. Rankin. When you were at Mercedes Street did you have Robert visit you or did you visit him?

A—No, he came to us sometimes.

Mr. Rankin. Do you recall seeing any guns at Mercedes Street while you were there?

A—No.

Mr. Rankin. Did your mother-in-law come to see you at Mercedes Street?

A—Yes.

Mr. Rankin. Will you describe the relationship between your husband and your mother-in-law while he was at Mercedes Street?

A—She did not want us to move away to Mercedes Street, and Lee did not want to remain with her and did not even want her to visit us after that. Lee did not want her to know the address to which we were moving and Robert helped us in the move. I felt very sorry for her. Sometime after that she visited us while Lee was at work and I was quite surprised wondering about how she found out our address. An then we had a quarrel

148

because he said to me, "Why did you open the door for her, I don't want her to come here any more."

Mr. Rankin. During this period did your husband spend much time with the baby, June?

A—Yes. He loved children very much.

Mr. Rankin. Did you obtain a television set at that time?

A—Lee wanted to buy a television set on credit. He then returned it. Should I speak a little louder?

Mr. Rankin. Did Robert help any with the money or just in guaranteeing the payments?

A—I think that he only guaranteed the payments.

Mr. Rankin. Do you recall how much the television set cost?

A—No.

Mr. Rankin. So far as you know it was paid for out of your husband's income?

A—Yes.

Mr. Rankin. Were you still at Mercedes Street when he lost his job with the welding company?

A—Yes.

Mr. Rankin. Did he try to find another job in Fort Worth then?

A—Yes.

Mr. Rankin. Do you know how much he looked for jobs before he found one then?

A—He looked for work for some time but he could not find it and then some Russian friends of ours helped him find some work in Dallas.

Mr. Rankin. How long was he out of work?

A—It seems to me it was about 2 weeks; hard to remember, perhaps that long.

Mr. Rankin. Where did he find work in Dallas, do you remember the name?

A—I know it was some kind of a printing company which prepares photographs for newspapers.

Mr. Rankin. Was he working with the photographic department of that company?

A—Yes.

Mr. Rankin. Was he an apprentice in that work trying to learn it?

A—Yes, at first he was an apprenticé and later he worked.

Mr. Rankin. Do you know what his income was when he was working for the welding company?

A—I think it was about $200 a month, I don't know. I know it was a dollar and a quarter an hour.

Mr. Rankin. Did he work much overtime at that time?

A—Not too much but sometimes he did work Saturdays.

Mr. Rankin. Do you recall how much he received as pay at the printing company?

A—A dollar forty an hour.

Mr. Rankin. How many hours did he work a week, do you recall?

A—He usually worked until 5 p.m. But sometimes he worked later, and on Saturdays, too.

Mr. Rankin. The ordinary work week at that time was the 5-day week then, and the Saturdays would be an overtime period?

A—Yes.

Mr. Rankin. Who were the Russian friends who helped your husband find this job in Dallas?

A—George Bouhe.

Mr. Rankin. Did this friend and other Russian friends visit you at Mercedes Street?

A—Yes. When we lived at Fort Worth we became acquainted with Peter Gregory, he is a Russian, he lives in Fort Worth and through him we became acquainted with others.

Mr. Rankin. Will you tell us insofar as you recall, the friends that you knew in Fort Worth?

A—Our first acquaintance was Gregory. Through him I met Gali Clark, Mrs. Elena Hall. That is all in Fort Worth. And then we met George Bouhe in Dallas, and Anna Meller, and Anna Ray and Katya Ford.

Mr. Rankin. By your answer do you mean that some of those people you met in Dallas and some in Fort Worth?

A—George De Mohrenschildt—this was both in Fort Worth and Dallas, the names of my recital but they were well acquainted with each other, even though some lived in Dallas and some lived in Fort Worth.

Mr. Rankin. Will you please sort them out for us and tell us those you met in Dallas?

A—You mean by the question, who out of these Russians lives in Dallas?

Mr. Rankin. Or which ones you met in Dallas as distinguished from those you had already met in Fort Worth?

A—In Fort Worth I met the people from Dallas. There was George Bouhe, George De Mohrenschildt—no. Anna Meller and George Bouhe only, they were from Dallas, but I met them in Fort Worth.

Mr. Rankin. Did these friends visit you at your home in Fort Worth?

A—Yes, sometimes they came to visit us when they were in Dallas, they came to us. Sometimes they made a special trip to come and see us.

Mr. Rankin. Did you ever visit them in their homes?

A—Yes, when we lived in Fort Worth we went to Dallas several times to visit them.

Mr. Rankin. When you made these visits did you go to spend an evening or a considerable part of the time or were they short visits? Can you describe that?

A—We used to come early in the morning and leave at night. We would spend the entire day with them. We went there by bus.

150

Mr. Rankin. Did you have an automobile of your own at any time during this period?

A—No.

Mr. Rankin. Did any of these people have meals in your home when they visited you?

A—No. They usually brought—they usually came for short visits and they brought their own favorite vegetables such as cucumbers, George liked cucumbers.

Mr. Rankin. When you moved to Dallas, where did you live the first time?

A—I did not move to Dallas together with Lee. Lee went to Dallas when he found the job, and I remained in Fort Worth and lived with Elena Hall.

Mr. Rankin. For how long a period did you live with Mrs. Hall?

A—I think that it was about a month and a half.

Mr. Rankin. During that month and a half what did your husband do?

A—He had a job. He was working. He would call me up over the telephone but how he spent his time, I don't know.

Mr. Rankin. Do you know during that month and a half where he lived?

A—At first, I know that he rented a room in the YMCA but very shortly thereafter he rented an apartment. But where I don't know.

Mr. Rankin. During that month and a half did he come and see you and the baby?

A—Yes, two or three times he came to see us because he had no car. It was not very easy.

Mr. Rankin. Were these trips to see you on the weekends?

A—Yes.

Mr. Rankin. When he came did he also stay at the Hall's?

A—Yes.

Mr. Rankin. When you were staying at the Hall's did you pay them for your room and your meals?

A—No. No, she was very friendly toward us and she tried to help us.

Mr. Rankin. What did you and your husband do when he came to see you? Did he spend his time with you there in the home or did you go some place?

A—No, we didn't go anywhere.

Mr. Rankin. Did he do any reading there?

A—No. I remember that it was only a couple of times that he came for a weekend. Generally, he only came for a very short period of time, because he would come together with our friends, and they could not stay very long.

Mr. Rankin. When he came during that period did he discuss what he had been doing in Dallas, his work and other things?

A—He liked his work very much.

151

Mr. Rankin. After this month and a half did he find a place for you all to live together?

A—Yes, but it wasn't a problem there to find a place, no problem there to find a place.

Mr. Rankin. Did you then move to a home in Dallas?

A—Yes, on Elsbeth, Elsbeth Street in Dallas.

Mr. Rankin. Do you remember the number?

A—No.

Mr. Rankin. How did you move your things from Mrs. Hall's to the place on Elsbeth Street?

A—A friend who had a car helped us—I don't remember his name, Taylor, Gary Taylor.

The Chairman. Suppose we take a recess now for about 10 minutes to allow Mrs. Oswald to refresh herself.

(Short recess.)

The Chairman. The Commission may be in order.

Mr. Rankin. Did that require one or more trips to move your things from Fort Worth to Dallas when you went to Elsbeth Street?

A—One trip was enough.

Mr. Rankin. Did you observe any guns in your things when you moved?

A—No.

Mr. Rankin. What kind of place did you have at Elsbeth Street, was it rooms or an apartment?

A—An apartment.

Mr. Rankin. How many rooms in the apartment?

A—One living room, a bedroom, a kitchen, and the bathroom. It sounds very small for all of you but for us it was quite sufficient.

Mr. Rankin. Did you have a telephone there?

A—No.

Mr. Rankin. Do you recall what rent you paid?

A—It seems to me that it was $60, plus the utilities.

Mr. Rankin. That would be $60 a month?

A—Yes, and electricity and gas but the water was free. Sixty dollars a month including water.

Mr. Rankin. Did your husband help you with the housework at the address?

A—Yes, he always helped.

Mr. Rankin. What about his reading habits there, were they the same?

A—Yes, about the same.

Mr. Rankin. Can you tell us a little more fully about his reading? Did he spend several hours each evening in this reading?

A—Yes.

Mr. Rankin. Do you recall any of the books that he read at Elsbeth Street?

A—No. He had two books, two thick books on the history of the United States.

Mr. Rankin. Did your husband come home for a midday meal?

A—No.

Mr. Rankin. Did you go out in the evenings?

A—Yes.

Mr. Rankin. Where did you go?

A—Sometimes we went shopping to stores, and movies, though Lee really went to the movies himself. He wanted to take me but I did not understand English. Then on weekends we would go to a lake not far way or to a park or to a cafe for some ice cream.

Mr. Rankin. When you went to the lake or the park did you take food with you and have a picnic?

A—Yes.

Mr. Rankin. How did you get to the lake or the park, by bus or car, or what means of transportation?

A—It was only 10 minutes away, 10 minutes walking time from us.

Mr. Rankin. Were either you or your husband taking any schooling at that time?

A—Lee took English courses or typing courses. . . .

Mr. Rankin. About what time would he get home from work?

A—About 5 to 5:30.

Mr. Rankin. Then would you eat your evening meal?

A—Yes.

Mr. Rankin. How soon after that would he leave for the class?

A—When Lee took his courses he generally did not come home for dinner, usually he didn't.

Mr. Rankin. Did he practice his typewriting at home at all?

A—At home, no. But he had a book, a textbook on typing which he would review when he was at home.

Mr. Rankin. How soon after the class was over did he come home ordinarily?

A—Nine o'clock.

Mr. Rankin. Did he tell you anything about friends that he met at these classes?

A—No.

Mr. Rankin. While you were at Elsbéth Street do you recall seeing any guns in your apartment?

A—No.

Mr. Rankin. Do you remember exhibiting any guns to the De Mohrenschildt's while you were at Elsbeth Street?

A—That was on Neely Street, perhaps you are confused, this was on Neely Street.

Mr. Rankin. When did you move to Neely Street from the Elsbeth Street apartment?

A—In January after the new year. I don't remember exactly.

Mr. Rankin. Do you remember why you moved from Elsbeth to Neely Street?

A—I like it better on Neely Street. We had a porch there and that was more convenient for the child.

Mr. Rankin. What size apartment did you have on Neely Street?

A—The same type of apartment. . . .

Mr. Rankin. Did you have any differences with your husband while you were at Neely Street?

A—No. Well, there are always some reasons for some quarrel between a husband and wife, not everything is always smooth.

Mr. Rankin. I had in mind if there was any violence or any hitting of you. Did that occur at Neely Street?

A—No. That was on Elsbeth Street.

Mr. Rankin. Do you recall what brought that about?

A—Not quite. I am trying to remember. It seems to me that it was at that time that Lee began to talk about his wanting to return to Russia. I did not want that and that is why we had quarrels.

Mr. Rankin. Did you have discussions between you about this idea of returning to Russia?

A—Yes. Lee wanted me to go to Russia. I told him that that—Lee wanted me to go to Russia, and I told him that if he wanted me to go then that meant that he didn't love me, and that in that case what was the idea of coming to the United States in the first place. Lee would say that it would be better for me if I went to Russia. I did not know why. I did not know what he had in mind. He said he loved me but that it would be better for me if I went to Russia, and what he had in mind I don't know.

Mr. Rankin. Do you know when he first started to talk about your going to Russia?

A—On Elsbeth Street.

Mr. Rankin. Do you remember any occasion which you thought caused him to start to talk that way?

A—No, I don't.

Mr. Rankin. Do you know why he started to hit you about that?

A—Now, I think that I know, although at that time I didn't. I think that he was very nervous and just this somehow relieved his tension.

Mr. Rankin. Did you observe sometime when you thought he changed?

A—I would say that immediately after coming to the United States Lee changed. I did not know him as such a man in Russia.

Mr. Rankin. Will you describe how you observed these changes and what they were as you saw them?

A—He helped me as before, but he became a little more of a recluse. He did not like my Russian friends and he tried to forbid me to have anything to do with them.

154

He was very irritable, sometimes for a trifle, for a trifling reason.

Mr. Rankin. Did he tell you why he did not like your Russian friends?

A—I don't know why he didn't like them. I didn't understand. At least that which he said was completely unfounded. He simply said some stupid or foolish things.

Mr. Rankin. Will you tell us the stupid things that he said?

A—Well, he thought that they were fools for having left Russia; they were all traitors. I would tell him he was in the same position being an American in America but there were really no reasons but just irritation. He said that they all only like money, and everything is measured by money. It seems to me that perhaps he was envious of them in the sense they were more prosperous than he was. When I told him, when I would say that to him he did not like to hear that.

Perhaps I shouldn't say these foolish things and I feel kind of uncomfortable to talk about the foolish things that happened or what he said foolish things.

This is one of the reasons why I don't know really the reasons for these quarrels because sometimes the quarrels were just trifles. It is just that Lee was very unrestrained and very explosive at that time.

Mr. Rankin. Mrs. Oswald, we will ask you to be very frank with us. It isn't for the purpose of embarrassing you or your husband that we ask you these things but it might help us to understand and even if you will tell us the foolish and stupid things it may shed some light on the problem. You understand that?

A—I understand you are not asking these questions out of curiosity but for a reason.

Mr. Rankin. Did your husband indicate any particular Russian friends that he disliked more than others?

A—He liked De Mohrenschildt but he—because he was a strong person, but only De Mohrenschildt. He did not like Bouhe or Anna Meller.

Mr. Rankin. Did you ever tell him you liked these people?

A—Yes, I told him all the time that I liked these people and that is why he was angry at me and would tell me that I was just like they were. At one time I left him and went to my friends because he put me into—put me on the spot by saying, "Well, if you like your friends so much then go ahead and live with them," and he left me no choice.

Mr. Rankin. When was this, Mrs. Oswald?

A—On Elsbeth Street.

Mr. Rankin. How long were you gone from him then?

A—One week.

Mr. Rankin. Did he ask you to return?

A—Yes. I took June and I went to Anna Meller, took a cab and went there. I spent several days with her. Lee didn't know

155

where I was but he called up and about 2 or 3 days after I came to and we met at De Mohrenschildt's house and he asked me to return home. I, of course, did not want a divorce but I told him it would be better to get a divorce rather than to continue living and quarreling this way. After all this is only a burden on a man if two people live together and fight. I simply wanted to show him, too, that I am not a toy. That a woman is a little more complicated. That you cannot trifle with her.

Mr. Rankin. Did you say anything at that time about how he should treat you if you returned?

A—Yes. I told him if he did not change his character, then it would become impossible to continue living with him. Because if there should be such quarrels continuously that would be crippling for the children.

Mr. Rankin. What did he say to that?

A—Then he said that it would be—it was very hard for him. That he could not change. That I must accept him, such as he was. And he asked me to come back home with him right on that day but he left feeling bad because I did not go and remained with my friend.

Mr. Rankin. What did you say about accepting him as he was?

A—I told him I was not going to. Of course, such as he was for me he was good, but I wanted simply for the sake of the family that he would correct his character. It isn't that I didn't mean to say he was good for me, I meant to say that I could stand him, but for the sake of the children I wanted him to improve his behavior.

Mr. Rankin. Then did he get in touch with you again?

A—At that time there was very little room at Anna Meller's and it was very uncomfortable and I left and went to Katya Ford whose husband at that time happened to be out of town on business. I spent several days with Katya Ford but then when her husband returned I did not want to remain with her. And it was on a Sunday morning then when I moved over to Anna Ray. Lee called me and said he wanted to see me, that he had come by bus and he wanted to see me and he came that evening and he cried and said that he wanted me to return home because if I did not return he did not want to continue living. He said he didn't know how to love me in any other way and that he will try to change. . . .

Mr. Rankin. Do you recall the manner in which Lee brought up the idea of your going to Russia alone?

A—Quite simply he said it was very hard for him here. That he could not have a steady job. It would be better for me because I could work in Russia. That was all.

Mr. Rankin. Did you understand when he suggested it that he proposed that you go and he stay?

A—Yes. Now, I think I know why he had in mind to start his foolish activity which could harm me but, of course, at

156

that time he didn't tell me the reason. It is only now that I understand it. At that time when I would ask him he would get angry because he couldn't tell me.

Mr. Rankin. What would you say to him at that time?

A—I told him at that time that I am agreeable to going if he could not live with me. But he kept on repeating that he wanted to live with me but that it would be better for me, but when I wanted to know the reason he would not tell me.

Mr. Rankin. Is there something that you have learned since that caused you to believe that this suggestion was related to trying to provide for you or to be sure that you wouldn't be hurt by what he was going to do?

A—At that time I didn't know this. I only saw that he was in such a state that he was struggling and perhaps did not understand himself. I thought that I was the reason for that.

Mr. Rankin. Did he have a job then?

A—Yes.

Mr. Rankin. Did you feel that you were getting along on what he was earning?

A—Of course.

Mr. Rankin. Were you urging him to earn more so that he could provide more for the family?

A—No. We had enough.

Mr. Rankin. You were not complaining about the way you were living?

A—No. I think that my friends had thought, and it was also written in the newspapers that we lived poorly because for Americans $200 appears to be very little. But I have never lived in any very luxurious way and, therefore, for me this was quite sufficient. Some of the others would say, "well here, you don't have a car or don't have this or that." But for me it was sufficient. Sometimes Lee would tell me I was just like my friends, that I wanted to have that which they had. That I preferred them to him because they give me more, but that is not true.

Mr. Rankin. Did you understand when he suggested you return to Russia that he was proposing to break up your marriage?

A—I told him that I would go to Russia if he would give me a divorce, but he did not want to give me a divorce.

Mr. Rankin. Did he say why?

A—He said that if he were to give me a divorce that that would break everything between us, which he didn't want. That he wanted to keep me as his wife, but I told him that if he wants to remain in the United States I want to be free in Russia.

Mr. Rankin. During this period did he appear to be more excited and nervous?

A—Not particularly, but the later time he was more excited and more nervous but it was quite a contrast between the way he was in Russia.

157

Mr. Rankin. By the later time that you just referred to what do you mean? Can you give us some approximate date?

A—When we went to Neely Street. . . .

Mr. Rankin. Mrs. Oswald, as I recall you were telling us about these developments at Neely Street when you found that your husband was suggesting that you go back to Russia alone and you discussed that matter, and you thought it had something to do with the idea he had, which I understood you have discovered as you looked back or thought back later but didn't know at the time fully. Is that right?

A—That is correct.

Mr. Rankin. Could you tell us those things that you observed that caused you to think he had something in mind at that time, and I will ask you later, after you tell us, those that you discovered since or that you have obtained more light on since.

A—At that time I did not think anything about it. I had no reasons to think that he had something in mind. I did not understand him at that time.

Mr. Rankin. Do you recall the first time that you observed the rifle?

A—That was on Neely Street. I think that was in February.

Mr. Rankin. How did you learn about it? Did you see it some place in the apartment?

A—Yes, Lee had a small room where he spent a great deal of time, where he read—where he kept his things, and that is where the rifle was.

Mr. Rankin. Was it out in the room at that time, as distinguished from in a closet in the room?

A—Yes, it was open, out in the open. At first I think—I saw some package up on the top shelf, and I think that that was the rifle. But I didn't know. And apparently later he assembled it and had it in the room.

Mr. Rankin. When you saw the rifle assembled in the room, did it have the scope on it?

A—No, it did not have a scope on it.

Mr. Rankin. Did you have any discussion with your husband about the rifle when you first saw it?

A—Of course I asked him, "What do you need a rifle for? What do we need that for?"

He said that it would come in handy some time for hunting. And this was not too surprising because in Russia, too, we had a rifle.

Mr. Rankin. In Russia did you have a rifle or a shotgun?

A—I don't know the difference. One and the other shoots. You men. That is your business.

The Chairman. My wife wouldn't know the difference, so it is all right.

A—I have never served in the Army.

Mr. Rankin. Did you discuss what the rifle cost with your husband?

A—No.

Mr. Rankin. Was the rifle later placed in a closet in the apartment at Neely Street?

A—No, it was always either in a corner, standing up in a corner or on a shelf.

Mr. Rankin. Do you know what happened to the gun that you had in Russia? Was it brought over to this country?

A—No, he sold it there. I did not say so when I had the first interviews. You must understand this was my husband. I didn't want to say too much.

Mr. Rankin. Is this rifle at Neely Street the only rifle that you know of that your husband had after you were married to him?

A—Yes.

Mr. Rankin. Did you ever show that rifle to the De Mohrenschildts?

A—I know that De Mohrenschildts had said that the rifle had been shown to him, but I don't remember that.

Mr. Rankin. Do you recall your husband taking the rifle away from the apartment on Neely Street at any time?

A—You must know that the rifle—it isn't as if it was out in the open. He would hang a coat or something to mask its presence in the room. And sometimes when he walked out, when he went out in the evening I didn't know, because I didn't go into that room very often. I don't know whether he took it with him or not.

Mr. Rankin. Did you ever see him clean the rifle?

A—Yes. I said before I had never seen it before. But I think you understand. I want to help you, and that is why there is no reason for concealing anything. I will not be charged with anything.

Mr. Rankin. Did you see him clean the rifle a number of times?

A—Yes.

Mr. Rankin. Could you help us by giving some estimate of the times as you remember it?

A—About four times—about four or five times, I think.

Mr. Rankin. Did your husband ever tell you why he was cleaning the—that is, that he had been using it and needed to be cleaned after use?

A—No, I did not ask him, because I thought it was quite normal that when you have a rifle you must clean it from time to time.

Mr. Rankin. Did you ever observe your husband taking the rifle away from the apartment on Neely Street?

A—Now, I think that he probably did sometimes, but I never did see it. You must understand that sometimes I would be in the kitchen and he would be in his room downstairs, and he would say bye-bye, I will be back soon, and he may have taken it. He probably did. Perhaps he purely waited for an occasion when he could take it away without my seeing it.

Mr. Rankin. Did you ever observe that the rifle had been taken out of the apartment at Neely Street—that is, that it was gone?

A—Before the incident with General Walker, I know that Lee was preparing for something. He took photographs of that house and he told me not to enter his room. I didn't know about these photographs, but when I came into the room once in general he tried to make it so that I would spend less time in that room. I noticed that quite accidentally one time when I was cleaning the room he tried to take care of it himself.

I asked him what kind of photographs are these, but he didn't say anything to me.

Mr. Rankin. That is the photographs of the Walker house that you were asking about?

A—Yes. Later, after he had fired, he told me about it.

I didn't know that he intended to do it—that he was planning to do it.

Mr. Rankin. Did you learn at any time that he had been practicing with the rifle?

A—I think that he went once or twice. I didn't actually see him take the rifle, but I knew that he was practicing.

Mr. Rankin. Could you give us a little help on how you knew?

A—He told me. And he would mention that in passing—it isn't as if he said, "Well, today I am going"—it wasn't as if he said, "Well, today I am going to take the rifle and go and practice."

But he would say, "Well, today I will take the rifle along for practice."

Therefore, I don't know whether he took it from the house or whether perhaps he even kept the rifle somewhere outside. There was a little square, sort of a little courtyard where he might have kept it.

When you asked me about the rifle, I said that Lee didn't have a rifle, but he also had a gun, a revolver.

Mr. Rankin. Do you recall when he first had the pistol, that you remember?

A—He had that on Neely Street, but I think that he acquired the rifle before he acquired the pistol. The pistol I saw twice— once in his room, and the second time when I took these photographs.

Mr. Rankin. What period of time was there between when he got the rifle and you learned of it, and the time you first learned about the pistol?

A—I can't say.

Mr. Rankin. When you testified about his practicing with the rifle, are you describing a period when you were still at Neely Street?

A—Yes.

Mr. Rankin. Do you know where he practiced with the rifle?

160

A—I don't know where. I don't know the name of the place where this took place. But I think it was somewhere out of town. It seems to me a place called Lopfield.

Mr. Rankin. Would that be at the airport—Love Field?

A—Love Field.

Mr. Rankin. So you think he was practicing out in the open and not at a rifle range?

A—Yes.

Mr. Rankin. Do you recall seeing the rifle when the telescopic lens was on it?

A—I hadn't paid any attention initially.

I know a rifle was a rifle. I didn't know whether or not it had a telescope attached to it. But the first time I remember seeing it was in New Orleans, where I recognized the telescope. But probably the telescope was on before. I simply hadn't paid attention.

I hope you understand. When I saw it, I thought that all rifles have that.

Mr. Rankin. Did you make any objection to having the rifle around?

A—Of course.

Mr. Rankin. What did he say to that?

A—That for a man to have a rifle—since I am a woman, I don't understand him, and I shouldn't bother him. A fine life.

Mr. Rankin. Is that the same rifle that you are referring to that you took the picture of with your husband and when he had the pistol, too?

A—Yes. I asked him then why he had dressed himself up like that, with the rifle and the pistol, and I thought that he had gone crazy, and he said he wanted to send that to a newspaper. This was not my business—it was man's business.

If I had known these were such dangerous toys, of course— you understand that I thought that Lee had changed in that direction, and I didn't think it was a serious occupation with him, just playing around.

Mr. Rankin. Do you recall the day that you took the picture of him with the rifle and the pistol?

A—I think that that was towards the end of February, possibly the beginning of March. I can't say exactly. Because I didn't attach any significance to it at the time. That was the only time I took any pictures.

I don't know how to take pictures. He gave me a camera and asked me—if someone should ask me how to photograph, I don't know.

Mr. Rankin. Was it on a day off that you took the picture?

A—It was on a Sunday.

Mr. Rankin. How did it occur? Did he come to you and ask you to take the picture?

A—I was hanging up diapers, and he came up to me with

161

the rifle and I was even a little scared, and he gave me the camera and asked me to press a certain button.

Mr. Rankin. And he was dressed up with a pistol at the same time, was he?

A—Yes.

Mr. Rankin. You have examined that picture since, and noticed that the telescopic lens was on at the time the picture was taken, have you not?

A—Now I paid attention to it. A specialist would see it immediately, of course. But at that time I did not pay any attention at all. I saw just Lee. These details are of great significance for everybody, but for me at that time it didn't mean anything. At the time that I was questioned, I had even forgotten that I had taken two photographs. I thought there was only one. I thought that there were two identical pictures, but they turned out to be two different poses.

Mr. Rankin. Did you have anything to do with the prints of the photograph after the prints were made? That is, did you put them in a photographic album yourself?

A—Lee gave me one photograph and asked me to keep it for June somewhere. Of course June doesn't need photographs like that.

Mr. Rankin. Do you recall how long after that the Walker matter occurred?

A—Two, perhaps three weeks later. I don't know. You know better when this happened.

Mr. Rankin. How did you first learn that your husband had shot at General Walker?

A—That evening he went out, I thought that he had gone to his classes or perhaps that he just walked out or went out on his own business. It got to be about 10 or 10:30, he wasn't home yet, and I began to be worried. Perhaps even later.

Then I went into his room. Somehow, I was drawn into it— you know—I was pacing around. Then I saw a note there.

Mr. Rankin. Did you look for the gun at that time?

A—No, I didn't understand anything. On the note it said, "If I am arrested" and there are certain other questions, such as, for example, the key to the mailbox is in such and such a place, and that he left me some money to last me for some time, and I couldn't understand at all what can he be arrested for. When he came back I asked him what had happened. He was very pale. I don't remember the exact time, but it was very late.

And he told me not to ask him any questions. He only told me that he had shot at General Walker.

Of course I didn't sleep all night. I thought that any minute now the police will come. Of course I wanted to ask him a great deal. But in his state I decided I had best leave him alone—it would be purposeless to question him.

Mr. Rankin. Did he say any more than that about the shooting?

A—Of course in the morning I told him that I was worried, and that we can have a lot of trouble, and I asked him, "Where is the rifle? What did you do with it?"

He said, that he had left it somewhere, that he had buried it, it seems to me, somewhere far from that place, because he said dogs could find it by smell.

I don't know—I am not a criminologist.

Mr. Rankin. Did he tell you why he had shot at General Walker?

A—I told him that he had no right to kill people in peacetime, he had no right to take their life because not everybody has the same ideas as he has. People cannot be all alike.

He said that this was a very bad man, that he was a fascist, that he was the leader of a fascist organization, and when I said that even though all of that might be true, just the same he had no right to take his life, he said if someone had killed Hitler in time it would have saved many lives. I told him that this is no method to prove your ideas, by means of a rifle.

Mr. Rankin. Did you ask him how long he had been planning to do this?

A—Yes. He said he had been planning for two months. Yes —perhaps he had planned to do so even earlier, but according to his conduct I could tell he was planning—he had been planning this for two months or perhaps a little even earlier.

The Chairman. Would you like to take a little recess?

A—No, thank you. Better to get it over with.

Mr. Rankin. Did he show you a picture of the Walker house then?

A—Yes.

Mr. Rankin. That was after the shooting?

A—Yes. He had a book—he had a notebook in which he noted down quite a few details. It was all in English, I didn't read it. But I noticed the photograph. Sometimes he would lock himself in his room and write in the book. I thought that he was writing some other kind of memoirs, as he had written about his life in the Soviet Union.

Mr. Rankin. Did you ever read that book?

A—No.

Mr. Rankin. Do you know of anything else he had in it besides this Walker house picture?

A—No. Photographs and notes, and I think there was a map in there.

Mr. Rankin. There was a map of the area where the Walker house was?

A—It was a map of Dallas, but I don't know where Walker lived. Sometimes evenings he would be busy with this. Perhaps he was calculating something, but I don't know. He had a bus schedule and computed something.

After this had happened, people thought that he had a car, but he had been using a bus.

Mr. Rankin. Did he explain to you about his being able to use a bus just as well as other people could use a car—something of that kind?

A—No. Simply as a passenger. He told me that even before that time he had gone also to shoot, but he had returned. I don't know why. Because on the day that he did fire, there was a church across the street and there were many people there, and it was easier to merge in the crowd and not be noticed.

Mr. Rankin. Did you ask him about this note that he had left, what he meant by it?

A—Yes—he said he had in mind that if in case he were arrested, I would know what to do.

Mr. Rankin. The note doesn't say anything about Walker, does it?

A—No.

Mr. Rankin. Did you ask him if that is what he meant by the note?

A—Yes, because as soon as he came home I showed him the note and asked him "What is the meaning of this?"

Mr. Rankin. And that is when he gave you the explanation about the Walker shooting?

A—Yes.

I know that on a Sunday he took the rifle, but I don't think he fired on a Sunday. Perhaps this was on Friday. So Sunday he left and took the rifle.

Mr. Rankin. If the Walker shooting was on Wednesday, does that refresh your memory as to the day of the week at all?

A—Refresh my memory as to what?

Mr. Rankin. As to the day of the shooting?

A—It was in the middle of the week.

Mr. Rankin. Did he give any further explanation of what had happened that evening?

A—When he fired, he did not know whether he had hit Walker or not. He didn't take the bus from there. He ran several kilometers and then took the bus. And he turned on the radio and listened, but there were no reports.

The next day he bought a paper and there he read it was only chance that saved Walker's life. If he had not moved, he might have been killed.

Mr. Rankin. Did he comment on that at all?

A—He said only that he had taken very good aim, that it was just chance that caused him to miss. He was very sorry that he had not hit him.

I asked him to give me his word that he would not repeat anything like that. I said that this chance shows that he must live and that he should not be shot at again. I told him that I would save the note and that if something like that should be repeated again, I would go to the police and I would have the proof in the form of that note.

He said he would not repeat anything like that again.

By the way, several days after that, the De Mohrenschildts came to us, and as soon as he opened the door he said, "Lee, how is it possible that you missed?"

I looked at Lee. I thought that he had told De Mohrenschildt about it. And Lee looked at me, and he apparently thought that I had told De Mohrenschildt about it. It was kind of dark. But I noticed—it was in the evening, but I noticed that his face changed, that he almost became speechless.

You see, other people knew my husband better than I did Not always—but in this case.

Mr. Rankin. Was De Mohrenschildt a friend that he told—your husband told him personal things that you knew of?

A—He asked Lee not because Lee had told him about it, but I think because he is smart enough man to have been able to guess it. I don't know—he is simply a liberal, simply a man. I don't think that he is being accused justly of being a Communist.

Mr. Rankin. That is De Mohrenschildt that you refer to?

A—Yes.

Mr. Rankin. Did you tell the authorities anything about this Walker incident when you learned about it?

A—No.

Mr. Rankin. You have told the Secret Service or the FBI people reasons why you didn't. Will you tell us?

A—Why I did not tell about it?

First, because it was my husband. As far as I know, according to the local laws here, a wife cannot be a witness against her husband. But, of course, if I had known that Lee intended to repeat something like that, I would have told.

Mr. Rankin. Did he ask you to return the note to him?

A—He forgot about it. But apparently after that he thought that what he had written in his book might be proof against him, and he destroyed it.

Mr. Rankin. That is this book that you have just referred to in which he had the Walker house picture?

A—There was a notebook, yes, that is the one.

Mr. Rankin. What did you do with the note that he had left for you after you talked about it and said you were going to keep it?

A—I had it among my things in a cookbook. But I have two —I don't remember in which.

Mr. Rankin. Did your relations with your husband change after this Walker incident?

A—Yes.

Mr. Rankin. Will you describe to us the changes as you observed them?

A—Soon after that, Lee lost his job—I don't know for what reason. He was upset by it. And he looked for work for several days. And then I insisted that it would be better for him to go to New Orleans where he had relatives. I insisted

165

on that because I wanted to get him further removed from Dallas and from Walker, because even though he gave me his word, I wanted to have him further away, because a rifle for him was not a very good toy—a toy that was too enticing.

Mr. Rankin. Did you say that you wanted him to go to New Orleans because of the Walker incident?

A—No. I simply told him that I wanted to see his home town. He had been born there.

Mr. Rankin. When he promised you that he would not do anything like that again, did you then believe him?

A—I did not quite believe him inasmuch as the rifle remained in the house.

Mr. Rankin. Did you ask him to get rid of the rifle at that time?

A—Yes.

Mr. Rankin. After he shot at Walker, did you notice his taking the rifle out any more to practice?

A—No.

Mr. Rankin. Do you recall when you went to New Orleans?

A—I think it was in May. Lee went there himself, by himself. At that time, I became acquainted with Mrs. Paine, and I stayed with her while he was looking for work. In about one week Lee telephoned me that he had found a job and that I should come down.

Mr. Rankin. When did you first get acquainted with Mrs. Paine?

A—I think it was a couple of months earlier—probably in January.

Mr. Rankin. How did you happen to go to Mrs. Paine's house to stay? Did she invite you?

A—Yes; she invited me. I had become acquainted with her through some Russian friends of ours. We had visited with some people, and she was there. Inasmuch as she was studying Russian, she invited me to stay with her.

Mr. Rankin. Did you pay her anything for staying with her?

A—No, I only repaid her in the sense that I helped her in the household and that I gave her Russian language lessons. This, in her words, was the very best pay that I could give her. And she wanted that I remain with her longer.

But, of course, it was better for me to be with my husband.

Mr. Rankin. How did your husband let you know that he had found a job?

A—He telephoned me.

Mr. Rankin. Did you then leave at once for New Orleans?

A—Yes.

Mr. Rankin. And how did you get to New Orleans from Dallas?

A—Mrs. Paine took me there in her car. She took her children and my things and we went there.

166

Mr. Rankin. Did you have much in the way of household goods to move?

A—Everything—we could put everything into one car. But, in fact, most of the things Lee had taken with him. Because he went by bus.

Mr. Rankin. Did he take the gun with him to New Orleans?

A—I don't remember exactly, but it seems to me that it was not among my things.

Mr. Rankin. Where did you live at New Orleans?

A—Magazine Street. By the time I arrived there Lee already had rented an apartment. . . .

Mr. Rankin. Mrs. Oswald, did you discuss the Walker shooting with Mrs. Paine?

A—No. I didn't tell anyone. Apart from the FBI. That is after—that is later.

Mr. Rankin. When was it that you told the FBI about the Walker shooting?

A—About 2 weeks after Lee was killed.

Mr. Rankin. Before you went to New Orleans, had you seen anyone from the FBI?

A—The FBI visited us in Fort Worth when we lived on Mercedes Street.

Mr. Rankin. Was that in August 1962?

A—Probably.

Mr. Rankin. Do you know the names of the FBI agents that visited you then?

A—No. I don't remember that Lee had just returned from work and we were getting ready to have dinner when a car drove up and man introduced himself and asked Lee to step out and talk to him.

There was another man in the car. They talked for about 2 hours and I was very angry, because everything had gotten cold. This meant more work for me. I asked who these were, and he was very upset over the fact that the FBI was interested in him.

Mr. Rankin. Did that interview take place in the car?

A—Yes.

Mr. Rankin. Did your husband tell you what they said to him and what he said to them?

A—I don't know to what extent this was true, but Lee said that the FBI had told him that in the event some Russians might visit him and would try to recruit him to work for them, he should notify the FBI agents. I don't know to what extent this was true. But perhaps Lee just said that.

Mr. Rankin. Did your husband say anything about the FBI asking him to work for them?

A—No, he didn't tell me.

Mr. Rankin. Did he say anything more about what they said to him in this interview?

167

A—No, he didn't tell me verbatim, but he said that they saw Communists in everybody and they are very much afraid and inasmuch as I had returned from Russia.

Mr. Rankin. Did he tell you that they had asked him whether he had acted as an agent or was asked to be an agent for the Russians?

A—No.

Mr. Rankin. Do you recall any other——

A—Excuse me. They did ask him about whether the Russians had proposed that he be an agent for them.

Mr. Rankin. Did he tell you what he said to them in that regard?

A—He told me that he had answered no.

Mr. Rankin. After this interview by the FBI agents, do you recall any later interview with them and yourself or your husband before you went to New Orleans?

A—No, there were no other interviews.

The next time was in Irving, when I lived with Mrs. Paine. But that is after I returned from New Orleans.

Mr. Rankin. At New Orleans, who did your husband work for?

A—He worked for the Louisiana Coffee Co. But I don't know in what capacity. I don't think that this was very good job, or perhaps more correctly, he did not—I know that he didn't like this job.

Mr. Rankin. Do you know what he received in pay from that job?

A—$1.35 an hour, I think. I am not sure.

Mr. Rankin. How long did he work for this coffee company?

A—I think it was from May until August, to the end of August.

Mr. Rankin. Was he discharged?

A—Yes.

Mr. Rankin. And then was he unemployed for a time?

A—Yes.

Mr. Rankin. After you had discussed with your husband your going to Russia, was anything done about that?

A—Yes, I wrote a letter to the Soviet Embassy with a request to be permitted to return. And then it seems to me after I was already in New Orleans, I wrote another letter in which I told the Embassy that my husband wants to return with me.

Mr. Rankin. Do you recall the date of the first letter that you just referred to?

A—No. But that is easily determined.

Mr. Rankin. Were you asking for a visa to return to Russia?

A—Yes.

Mr. Rankin. Did you discuss with your husband his returning with you before you wrote the second letter that you have described?

A—I didn't ask him. He asked me to do so one day when

he was extremely upset. He appeared to be very unhappy and he said that nothing keeps him here, and that he would not lose anything if he returned to the Soviet Union, and that he wants to be with me. And that it would be better to have less but not to be concerned about tomorrow, not to be worried about tomorrow.

Mr. Rankin. Was this a change in his attitude?

A—Towards me or towards Russia?

Mr. Rankin. Towards going to Russia.

A—I don't think that he was too fond of Russia, but simply that he knew that he would have work assured him there, because he had—after all, he had to think about his family.

Mr. Rankin. Did you know that he did get a passport?

A—It seems to me he always had a passport.

Mr. Rankin. While he was in New Orleans, that he got a passport?

A—Well, it seems to me that after we came here, he immediately received a passport. I don't know. I always saw his green passport. He even had two—one that had expired, and a new one.

Mr. Rankin. Do you know when the new one was issued?

A—No. It seems to me in the Embassy when we arrived. I don't know.

But please understand me correctly, I am not hiding this. I simply don't know.

Mr. Rankin. Do you know about a letter from your husband to the Embassy asking that his request for a visa be considered separately from yours?

A—No, I don't.

Mr. Rankin. When you were at New Orleans, did your husband go to school, that you knew of?

A—No.

Mr. Rankin. Did he spend his earnings with you and your child?

A—Most of the time, yes. But I know that he became active with some kind of activity in a pro-Cuban committee. I hope that is what you are looking for.

Mr. Rankin. When did you first notice the rifle at New Orleans?

A—As soon as I arrived in New Orleans.

Mr. Rankin. Where was it kept there?

A—He again had a closet-like room with his things in it. He had his clothes hanging there, all his other belongings.

Mr. Rankin. Was the rifle in a cover there?

A—No.

Mr. Rankin. Did you notice him take it away from your home there in New Orleans at any time?

A—No. I know for sure that he didn't. But I know that we had a kind of a porch with a—screened-in porch, and I know that sometimes evenings after dark he would sit there with his

169

rifle. I don't know what he did with it. I came there by chance once and saw him just sitting there with his rifle. I thought he is merely sitting there and resting. Of course I didn't like these kind of little jokes.

Mr. Rankin. Can you give us an idea of how often this happened that you recall?

A—It began to happen quite frequently after he was arrested there in connection with some demonstration and handing out of leaflets.

Mr. Rankin. Was that the Fair Play for Cuba demonstration?

A—Yes.

Mr. Rankin. From what you observed about his having the rifle on the back porch, in the dark, could you tell whether or not he was trying to practice with the telescopic lens?

A—Yes. I asked him why. But this time he was preparing to go to Cuba.

Mr. Rankin. That was his explanation for practicing with the rifle?

A—Yes. He said that he would go to Cuba. I told him I was not going with him—that I would stay here.

Mr. Rankin. On these occasions when he was practicing with the rifle, would they be three or four times a week in the evening, after the Fair Play for Cuba incident?

A—Almost every evening. He very much wanted to go to Cuba and have the newspapers write that somebody had kidnaped an aircraft. And I asked him "For God sakes, don't do such a thing."

Mr. Rankin. Did he describe that idea to you?

A—Yes.

Mr. Rankin. And when he told you of it, did he indicate that he wanted to be the one that would kidnap the airplane himself?

A—Yes, he wanted to do that. And he asked me that I should help him with that. But I told him I would not touch that rifle.

This sounds very merry, but I am very much ashamed of it.

Mr. Rankin. Did you tell him that using the rifle in this way, talking about it, was not in accordance with his agreement with you?

A—Yes.

Mr. Rankin. What did he say about that?

A—He said that everything would go well. He was very self-reliant—if I didn't want to.

Mr. Rankin. Was there any talk of divorce during this period?

A—No. During this time, we got along pretty well not counting the incidents with Cuba. I say relatively well, because we did not really have—generally he helped me quite a bit and was good to me. But, of course, I did not agree with his views.

Mr. Rankin. At this time in New Orleans did he discuss with you his views?

A—Yes.

Mr. Rankin. What did he say about that?

A—Mostly—most of the conversations were on the subject of Cuba.

Mr. Rankin. Was there anything said about the United States —not liking the United States.

A—No. I can't say—he liked some things in Russia, he liked some other things here, didn't like some things there, and didn't like some things here.

And I am convinced that as much as he knew about Cuba, all he knew was from books and so on. He wanted to convince himself. But I am sure that if he had gone there, he would not have like it there. either. Only on the moon, perhaps.

Mr. Rankin. Did he tell you what he didn't like about the United States?

A—First of all, he didn't like the fact that there are fascist organizations here. That was one thing.

The second thing, that it was hard to get an education and hard to find work. And that medical expenses were very high.

Mr. Rankin. Did he say who he blamed for this?

A—He didn't blame anyone.

Mr. Rankin. Did he ever say anything about President Kennedy?

A—No. At least—I was always interested in President Kennedy and had asked him many times to translate articles in a newspaper or magazine for me, and he always had something good to say. He translated it, but never did comment on it. At least in Lee's behavior—from Lee's behavior I cannot conclude that he was against the President, and therefore the thing is incomprehensible to me. Perhaps he hid it from me. I don't know. He said that after 20 years he would be prime minister. I think that he had a sick imagination—at least at that time I already considered him to be not quite normal—not always, but at times. I always tried to point out to him that he was a man like any others who were around us. But he simply could not understand that.

I tried to tell him that it would be better to direct his energies to some more practical matters, and not something like that.

Mr. Rankin. Can you tell us what you observed about him that caused you to think he was different?

A—At least his imagination, his fantasy, which was quite unfounded, as to the fact that he was an outstanding man. And then the fact that he was very much interested, exceedingly so. in autobiographical works of outstanding statesmen of the United States and others.

Mr. Rankin. Was there anything else of that kind that caused you to think that he was different?

A—I think that he compared himself to these people whose

171

autobiographies he read. That seems strange to me, because it is necessary to have an education in order to achieve success of that kind. After he became busy with his pro-Cuban activity, he received a letter from somebody in New York, some Communist—probably from New York—I am not sure from where —from some Communist leader and he was very happy, he felt that this was a great man that he had received the letter from.

You see, when I would make fun of him, of his activity to some extent, in the sense that it didn't help anyone really, he said that I didn't understand him, and here, you see, was proof that someone else did, that there were people who understood his activity:

I would say that to Lee—that Lee could not really do much for Cuba, that Cuba would get along well without him, if they had to.

Mr. Rankin. You would tell that to him?

A—Yes.

Mr. Rankin. And what would he say in return?

A—He shrugged his shoulders and kept his own opinion. He was even interested in the airplane schedules, with the idea of kidnaping a plane. But I talked him out of it.

Mr. Rankin. The airplane schedules from New Orleans?

A—New Orleans—but—from New Orleans—leaving New Orleans in an opposite direction. And he was going to make it turn around and go to Cuba.

Mr. Rankin. He discussed this with you?

A—Yes.

Mr. Rankin. When did his Fair Play for Cuba activity occur —before or after he lost his job?

A—After he lost his job. I told him it would be much better if he were working, because when he didn't work he was busy with such foolishness.

Mr. Rankin. What did he say about that?

A—Nothing. And it is at that time that I wrote a letter to Mrs. Paine telling her that Lee was out of work, and they invited me to come and stay with her. And when I left her, I knew that Lee would go to Mexico City. But, of course, I didn't tell Mrs. Paine about it.

Mr. Rankin. Had he discussed with you the idea of going to Mexico City?

A—Yes.

Mr. Rankin. When did he first discuss that?

A—I think it was in August.

Mr. Rankin. Did he tell you why he wanted to go to Mexico City?

A—From Mexico City he wanted to go to Cuba—perhaps through the Russian Embassy in Mexico somehow he would be able to get to Cuba.

Mr. Rankin. Did he say anything about going to Russia by way of Cuba?

A—I know that he said that in the embassy. But he only said so. I know that he had no intention of going to Russia then.

Mr. Rankin. How do you know that?

A—He told me. I know Lee fairly well—well enough from that point of view.

Mr. Rankin. Did he tell you that he was going to Cuba and send you on to Russia?

A—No, he proposed that after he got to Cuba, that I would go there, too, somehow.

But he also said that after he was in Cuba, and if he might go to Russia, he would let me know in any case.

Mr. Rankin. Did he discuss Castro and the Cuban Government with you?

A—Yes.

Mr. Rankin. When did he start to do that?

A—At the time that he was busy with that pro-Cuban activity. He was sympathetic to Castro while in Russia, and I have also a good opinion of Castro to the extent that I know. I don't know anything bad about him.

Mr. Rankin. What did he say about Castro to you?

A—He said that he is a very smart statesman, very useful for his government, and very active.

Mr. Rankin. What did you say to him?

A—I said. "Maybe." It doesn't make any difference to me.

Mr. Rankin. Did you know he was writing to the Fair Play for Cuba organization in New York during this latter period in New Orleans?

A—Yes.

Mr. Rankin. Did he show you that correspondence?

A—No.

Mr. Rankin. How did you learn that?

A—He told me about it. Or, more correctly, I saw that he was writing to them. . . .

Mr. Rankin. Did your husband have any organization in his Fair Play for Cuba at New Orleans?

A—No, he had no organization. He was alone. He was quite alone.

Mr. Rankin. When did you learn about his arrest there?

A—The next day, when he was away from home overnight and returned, he told me he had been arrested.

Mr. Rankin. What did he say about it?

A—He was smiling, but in my opinion he was upset. I think that after that occurrence—he became less active, he cooled off a little.

Mr. Rankin. Less active in the Fair Play for Cuba?

A—Yes. He continued it, but more for a person's sake. I think that his heart was no longer in it.

Mr. Rankin. Did he tell you that the FBI had seen him at the jail in New Orleans?

A—No.

Mr. Rankin. Did he complain about his arrest and say it was unfair, anything of that kind.

A—No.

Mr. Rankin. Did you know he paid a fine?

A—Yes.

Mr. Rankin. Did you have anything to do with trying to get him out of jail?

A—No.

He was only there for 24 hours. He paid his fine and left. He said that the policeman who talked to him was very kind, and was a very good person.

Mr. Rankin. While you were in New Orleans, did you get to know the Murrets?

A—Yes. They are his relatives. I think that Lee engaged in this activity primarily for purposes of self-advertising. He wanted to be arrested. I think he wanted to get into the newspapers, so that he would be known.

Mr. Rankin. Do you think he wanted to be advertised and known as being in support of Cuba before he went to Cuba?

A—Yes.

Mr. Rankin. Do you think he thought that would help him when he got to Cuba?

A—Yes.

Mr. Rankin. Did he tell you anything about that, or is that just what you guess?

A—He would collect the newspaper clippings about his— when the newspapers wrote about him, and he took these clippings with him when he went to Mexico.

Mr. Rankin. Did the Murrets come to visit you from time to time in New Orleans?

A—Yes—sometimes they came to us, and sometimes we went to them.

Mr. Rankin. Was that a friendly relationship?

A—I would say that they were more of a family relationship type. They were very good to us. His uncle, that is the husband of his aunt, was a very good man. He tried to reason with Lee after that incident. Lee liked them very much as relatives but he didn't like the fact that they were all very religious.

When his uncle, or, again, the husband of his aunt would tell him that he must approach things with a more serious attitude, and to worry about himself and his family, Lee would say, "Well, these are just bourgeois, who are only concerned with their own individual welfare." . . .

Mr. Rankin. Did your husband ever tell you what he told the FBI agent when they came to the jail to see him?

A—No.

Mr. Rankin. After you wrote Mrs. Paine, did she come at once in response to your letter to take you back to Dallas?

A—Not quite at once. She came about a month later. She

apparently was on vacation at that time, and said that she would come after her vacation.

Mr. Rankin. Didn't she indicate that she was going to come around September 30, and then came a little before that?

A—No. In her letter to me she indicated that she would come either the 20th or the 21st of September, and she did come at that time.

Mr. Rankin. Did you move your household goods in her station wagon at that time?

A—Yes.

Mr. Rankin. Do you know whether or not the rifle was carried in the station wagon?

A—Yes, it was.

Mr. Rankin. Did you have anything to do with loading it in there?

A—No. Lee was loading everything on because I was pregnant at the time. But I know that Lee loaded the rifle on.

Mr. Rankin. Was the rifle carried in some kind of a case when you went back with Mrs. Paine?

A—After we arrived, I tried to put the bed, the child's crib together, the metallic parts, and I looked for a certain part, and I came upon something wrapped in a blanket. I thought that was part of the bed, but it turned out to be the rifle.

Mr. Rankin. Do you remember whether the pistol was carried back in Mrs. Paine's car too?

A—I don't know where the pistol was. . . .

Mr. Rankin. When you found the rifle wrapped in the blanket, upon your return to Mrs. Paine's, where was it located?

A—In the garage, where all the rest of the things were.

Mr. Rankin. In what part of the garage?

A—In that part which is closer to the street, because that garage is connected to the house. One door opens on the kitchen, and the other out in the street.

Mr. Rankin. Was the rifle lying down or was it standing up on the butt end?

A—No, it was lying down on the floor.

Mr. Rankin. When your husband talked about going to Mexico City, did he say where he was going to go there, who he would visit?

A—Yes. He said that he would go to the Soviet Embassy and to the Cuban Embassy and would do everything he could in order to get to Cuba.

Mr. Rankin. Did he tell you where he would stay in Mexico City?

A—In a hotel.

Mr. Rankin. Did he tell you the name?

A—No, he didn't know where he would stop.

Mr. Rankin. Was there any discussion about the expense of making the trip?

A—Yes. But we always lived very modestly, and Lee always had some savings. Therefore, he had the money for it.

Mr. Rankin. Did he say how much it would cost?

A—He had a little over $100 and he said that that would be sufficient.

Mr. Rankin. Did he talk about getting you a silver bracelet or any presents before he went?

A—It is perhaps more truth to say that he asked me what I would like, and I told him that I would like Mexican silver bracelets. But what he did buy me I didn't like at all. When he returned to Irving, from Mexico City, and I saw the bracelet, I was fairly sure that he had bought it in New Orleans and not in Mexico City, because I had seen bracelets like that for sale there. That is why I am not sure that the bracelet was purchased in Mexico.

Lee had an identical bracelet which he had bought in either Dallas or New Orleans. It was a man's bracelet.

Mr. Rankin. The silver bracelet he gave you when he got back had your name on it, did it not?

A—Yes.

Mr. Rankin. Was it too small?

A—Yes, I was offended because it was too small, and he promised to exchange it. But, of course, I didn't want to hurt him, and I said, thank you, the important thing is the thought, the attention.

Mr. Rankin. Did he discuss other things that he planned to do in Mexico City, such as see the bullfights or jai alai games or anything of that kind?

A—No, I was already questioned about this game by the FBI, but I never heard of it. But I had asked Lee to buy some Mexican records, but he did not do that.

Mr. Rankin. Do you know how he got to Mexico City?

A—By bus.

Mr. Rankin. And did he return by bus, also?

A—It seems, yes. Yes, he told me that a round-trip ticket was cheaper than two one-way tickets.

Mr. Rankin. Did you learn that he had a tourist card to go to Mexico?

A—No.

Mr. Rankin. If he had such a card, you didn't know it then?

A—No.

Mr. Rankin. After he had been to Mexico City, did he come back to Irving or to Dallas?

A—When Lee returned I was already in Irving and he telephoned me. But he told me that he had arrived the night before and had spent the night in Dallas, and called me in the morning.

Mr. Rankin. Did he say where he had been in Dallas?

A—It seems to me at the YMCA.

Mr. Rankin. Did he come right out to see you then?

A—Yes.

Mr. Rankin. Did he tell you anything about his trip to Mexico City?

A—Yes, he told me that he had visited the two embassies, that he had received nothing, that the people who are there are too much—too bureaucratic. He said that he has spent the time pretty well. And I had told him that if he doesn't accomplish anything to at least take a good rest. I was hoping that the climate, if nothing else, would be beneficial to him.

Mr. Rankin. Did you ask him what he did the rest of the time?

A—Yes, I think he said that he visited a bull fight, that he spent most of his time in museums, and that he did some sightseeing in the city.

Mr. Rankin. Did he tell you about anyone that he met there?

A—No.

He said that he did not like the Mexican girls.

Mr. Rankin. Did he tell you anything about what happened at the Cuban Embassy, or consulate?

A—No. Only that he had talked to certain people there.

Mr. Rankin. Did he tell you what people he talked to?

A—He said that he first visited the Soviet Embassy in the hope that having been there first this would make it easier for him at the Cuban Embassy. But there they refused to have anything to do with him.

Mr. Rankin. And what did he say about the visit to the Cuban Embassy or consulate?

A—It was quite without results.

Mr. Rankin. Did he complain about the consular or any of the officials of the Cuban Embassy and the way they handled the matter?

A—Yes, he called them bureaucrats. He said that the Cubans seemed to have a system similar to the Russians—too much red tape before you got through there.

Mr. Rankin. Is there anything else that he told you about the Mexico City trip that you haven't related?

A—No, that is all that I can remember about it.

Mr. Rankin. Do you recall how long he was gone on his trip to Mexico City?

A—All of this took approximately 2 weeks, from the time that I left New Orleans, until the time that he returned.

Mr. Rankin. And from the time he left the United States to go to Mexico City to his return, was that about 7 days?

A—Yes. He said he was there for about a week.

Mr. Rankin. When you were asked before about the trip to Mexico, you did not say that you knew anything about it. Do you want to explain to the Commission how that happened?

A—Most of these questions were put to me by the FBI. I do not like them too much. I didn't want to be too sincere with them. Though I was quite sincere and answered most of their questions. They questioned me a great deal, and I was very tired of them, and I thought that, well, whether I knew about it or didn't know about it didn't change matters at all, it didn't help anything, because the fact that Lee had been there was already known, and whether or not I knew about it didn't make any difference.

Mr. *Rankin.* Was that the only reason that you did not tell about what you knew of the Mexico City trip before?

A—Yes, because the first time that they asked me I said no, I didn't know anything about it. And in all succeeding discussions I couldn't very well have said I did. There is nothing special in that. It wasn't because this was connected with some sort of secret.

Mr. *Rankin.* Did your husband stay with you at the Paines after that first night when he returned from Mexico?

A—Yes, he stayed overnight there.

And in the morning we took him to Dallas.

Mr. *Rankin.* And by "we" who do you mean?

A—Ruth Paine, I and her children.

Mr. *Rankin.* Do you know what he did in Dallas, then?

A—He intended to rent an apartment in the area of Oak Cliff, and to look for work.

Mr. *Rankin.* Do you know whether he did that?

A—Yes, I know that he always tried to get some work. He was not lazy.

Mr. *Rankin.* Did he rent the apartment?

A—On the same day he rented a room, not an apartment, and he telephoned me and told me about it.

Mr. *Rankin.* Did you discuss the plans for this room before you took him to Dallas?

A—No. I asked him where he would live, and he said it would be best if he rented a room, it would not be as expensive as an apartment.

Mr. *Rankin.* Did he say anything about whether you would be living with him, or he would be living there alone?

A—No, I did not really want to be with Lee at that time, because I was expecting, and it would have been better to be with a woman who spoke English and Russian.

Mr. *Rankin.* Do you know where your husband looked for work in Dallas at that time?

A—No. He tried to get any kind of work. He answered ads, newspaper ads.

Mr. *Rankin.* Did he have trouble finding work again?

A—Yes.

Mr. *Rankin.* How long after his return was it before he found a job?

A—Two to three weeks.

Mr. *Rankin.* When he was unemployed in New Orleans, did he get unemployment compensation?

A—Yes.

Mr. Rankin. Do you know how much he was getting then?

A—$33 a week. It is possible to live on that money. One can fail to find work and live. Perhaps you don't believe me. It is not bad to rest and receive money.

Mr. Rankin. When he was unemployed in Dallas, do you know whether he received unemployment compensation?

A—We were due to receive unemployment compensation, but it was getting close to the end of his entitlement period, and we received one more check.

Mr. Rankin. Did you discuss with him possible places of employment after his return from Mexico?

A—No. That was his business. I couldn't help him in that. But to some extent I did help him find a job, because I was visiting Mrs. Paine's neighbors. There was a woman there who told me where he might find some work.

Mr. Rankin. And when was this?

A—I don't remember. If that is important, I can try and ascertain date. But I think you probably know.

Mr. Rankin. Was it shortly before he obtained work?

A—As soon as we got the information, the next day he went there and he did get the job.

Mr. Rankin. And who was it that you got the information from?

A—It was the neighbor whose brother was employed by the school book depository. He said it seemed to him there was a vacancy there.

Mr. Rankin. What was his name?

A—I don't know.

The Chairman. Well, I think we have arrived at our adjournment time. We will recess now until tomorrow morning at 10 o'clock. . . .

Mr. Rankin. Could you tell us about De Mohrenschildt? Was he a close friend of your husband?

A—Lee did not have any close friends, but at least he had—here in America—he had a great deal of respect for De Mohrenschildt.

Mr. Rankin. Could you describe that relationship. Did they see each other often?

A—No, not very frequently. From time to time.

Mr. Rankin. Did your husband tell you why he had so much respect for De Mohrenschildt?

A—Because he considered him to be smart, to be full of joy of living, a very energetic and very sympathetic person.

Mr. Rankin. We had a report that——

A—Excuse me. It was pleasant to meet with him. He would bring some pleasure and better atmosphere when he came to visit—with his dogs—he is very loud.

Mr. Rankin. Did you like him?

A—Yes. Him and his wife.

Mr. Rankin. Did you understand any of the conversations between your husband and De Mohrenschildt?

A—Yes, they were held in Russian.

Mr. Rankin. Did they discuss politics or the Marxist philosophy or anything of that kind?

A—Being men, of course, sometimes they talked about politics, but they did not discuss Marxist philosophy. They spoke about current political events.

Mr. Rankin. Did they have any discussions about President Kennedy or the Government in the United States at that time?

A—No, only George said that before he got married he knew Jackie Kennedy, that she was a very good, very sympathetic woman. Then he was writing a book, that is George, and with reference to that book he had written a letter to President Kennedy. This was with reference to the fact that John Kennedy had recommended physical exercise, walking and so on, and De Mohrenschildt and his wife had walked to the Mexican border. And he hoped that John Kennedy would recommend his book.

I don't know—perhaps this is foolishness.

Mr. Rankin. Did he say anything, or either of them say anything about President Kennedy at that time?

A—Nothing bad.

Mr. Rankin. When you referred to George, did you mean Mr. De Mohrenschildt?

A—Yes. I generally didn't believe him, that he had written a book. Sometimes he could say so, but just for amusement. . . .

Mr. Rankin. In the period of October 1962, you did spend some time with Mrs. Hall, did you not, in her home?

A—Yes.

Mr. Rankin. Will you tell us about how that happened?

A—When Lee found work in Dallas, Elena Hall proposed that I stay with her for some time, because she was alone, and I would be company.

Mr. Rankin. Did that have anything to do with any quarrels with your husband?

A—No.

Mr. Rankin. During that period of October of 1962, when your husband went to Dallas to get work, do you know where he lived?

A—I know that for—at first, for some time he stayed at the YMCA, but later he rented an apartment, but I don't know at what address. Because in the letters which he wrote me, the return address was a post office box.

Mr. Rankin. Do you know whether he stayed during that period part of the time with Gary Taylor?

A—No.

Mr. Rankin. Where did you live while your husband was

looking for work and staying at the YMCA and at this apartment that you referred to?

A—When he stayed at the YMCA he had already found work, and I was in Fort Worth.

Mr. Rankin. And where in Fort Worth were you staying then?

A—With Mrs. Hall.

Mr. Rankin. Did you notice a change, psychologically, in your husband during this period in the United States?

A—Yes.

Mr. Rankin. When did you first notice that change?

A—At—at Elsbeth Street, in Dallas. After the visit of the FBI, in Fort Worth. He was for some time nervous and irritable.

Mr. Rankin. Did he seem to have two different personalities then?

A—Yes.

Mr. Rankin. Would you describe to the Commission what he did to cause you to think that he was changing?

A—Generally he was—usually he was quite as he always was. He used to help me. And he was a good family man. Sometimes, apparently without reason, at least I did not know reasons, if any existed, he became quite a stranger. At such times it was impossible to ask him anything. He simply kept to himself. He was irritated by trifles.

Mr. Rankin. Do you recall any of the trifles that irritated him, so as to help us know the picture?

A—It is hard to remember any such trifling occurrences, sometimes such a small thing as, for example, dinner being five minutes late, and I do mean five minutes—it is not that I am exaggerating—he would be very angry. Or if there were no butter on the table, because he hadn't brought it from the icebox, he would with great indignation ask, "Why is there no butter?" And at the same time if I had put the butter on the table he wouldn't have touched it.

This is foolishness, of course. A normal person doesn't get irritated by things like that.

Mr. Rankin. Mrs. Oswald, I do not ask these questions to pry into your personal affairs, but it gives us some insight into what he did and why he might have done the things he did.

I hope you understand that.

A—I understand.

Mr. Rankin. Could you tell us a little about when he did beat you because we have reports that at times neighbors saw signs of his having beat you, so that we might know the occasions and why he did such things.

A—The neighbors simply saw that because I have a very sensitive skin, and even a very light blow would show marks. Sometimes it was my own fault. Sometimes it was really necessary to just leave him alone. But I wanted more attention. He was jealous. He had no reason to be. But he was jealous of even some of my old friends, old in the sense of age.

Mr. Rankin. When he became jealous, did he discuss that with you?

A—Yes, of course.

Mr. Rankin. What did he say?

A—I don't remember.

Basically, that I prefer others to him. That I want many things which he cannot give me. But that was not so. Once we had a quarrel because I had a young man who was a boyfriend —this was before we were married, a boy who was in love with me, and I liked him, too. And I had written him a letter from here. I had—I wrote him that I was very lonely here, that Lee had changed a great deal, and that I was sorry that I had not married him instead, that it would have been much easier for me. I had mailed that letter showing the post office box as a return address. But this was just the time when the postage rates went up by one cent, and the letter was returned. Lee brought that letter and asked me what it was and forced me to read it. But I refused. Then he sat down across from me and started to read it to me. I was very much ashamed of my foolishness. And, of course, he hit me, but he did not believe that this letter was sincere. He asked me if it was true or not, and I told him that it was true. But he thought that I did it only in order to tease him. And that was the end of it. It was a very ill-considered thing.

Mr. Rankin. Do you recall anything more that he said at that time about that matter?

A—Of course after he hit me, he said that I should be ashamed of myself for saying such things because he was very much in love with me. But this was after he hit me.

Generally, I think that was right, for such things, that is the right thing to do. There was some grounds for it.

Please excuse me. Perhaps I talk too much.

Mr. Rankin. When you had your child baptized, did you discuss that with your husband?

A—I knew that Lee was not religious, and, therefore, I did not tell him about it. I lived in Fort Worth at that time, while he lived in Dallas.

But when June was baptized, I told him about it, and he didn't say anything about it. He said it was my business. And he said, "Okay, if you wish." He had nothing against it. He only took offense at the fact that I hadn't told him about it ahead of time.

Mr. Rankin. Are you a member of any church?

A—I believe in God, of course, but I do not go to church— first because I do not have a car. And, secondly, because there is only one Russian Church. Simply that I believe in God in my own heart, and I don't think it is necessary to visit the church. . . .

Mr. Rankin. Did you think there was something in your husband's life in America, his friends and so forth that caused him to be different here?

A—No, he had no friends who had any influence over him. He himself had changed by comparison to the way he was in Russia. But what the reason for that was, I don't know.

Am I giving sufficient answers to your questions?

Mr. Rankin. You are doing fine.

Did your consideration of a divorce from your husband have anything to do with his ideas and political opinions?

A—No. The only reasons were personal ones with reference to our personal relationship, not political reasons.

Mr. Rankin. In your story you say that what was involved was some of his crazy ideas and political opinions. Can you tell us what you meant by that?

A—This was after the case, after the matter of the divorce. I knew that Lee had such political leanings.

Mr. Rankin. With regard to your Russian friends, did you find the time when they came less to see you and didn't show as much interest in you?

A—Yes.

Mr. Rankin. Can you give us about the time, just approximately when you noticed that difference.

A—Soon after arriving in Dallas. Mostly it was De Mohrenschildt who visited us. He was the only one who remained our friend. The others sort of removed themselves.

Mr. Rankin. Do you know why that was?

A—Because they saw that Lee's attitude towards them was not very proper, he was not very hospitable, and he was not glad to see them. They felt that he did not like them.

Mr. Rankin. Will you describe what you observed that caused you to think this, or how your husband acted in regard to these friends?

A—He told me that he did not like them, that he did not want them to come to visit.

Mr. Rankin. Did he show any signs of that attitude towards them?

A—Yes, he was not very talkative when they came for a visit. Sometimes he would even quarrel with them.

Mr. Rankin. When he quarreled with them, was it in regard to political ideas or what subjects?

A—Yes, they would not agree with him when he talked on political matters.

Mr. Rankin. Do you recall any conversation that you can describe to us?

A—Of course it is difficult to remember all the conversations. But I know that they had a difference of opinion with reference to political matters. My Russian friends did not approve of everything. I am trying to formulate it more exactly. They did not like the fact that he was an American who had gone to Russia. I think that is all. All that I can remember. . . .

Mr. Rankin. Did you ever have arguments with your husband about smoking and drinking wine, other things like that?

A—About drinking wine, no. But he didn't like the fact that I smoked, because he neither smoked nor drank. It would have been better if he had smoked and drank. . . .

Mr. Rankin. Did you notice any difference in his attitude towards your child after you saw this change in his personality?

A—No.

Mr. Rankin. Will you describe to the Commission how your husband treated the baby, and some of his acts, what he did?

A—He would walk with June, play with her, feed her, change diapers, take photographs—everything that fathers generally do.

Mr. Rankin. He showed considerable affection for her at all times, did he?

A—Yes. If I would punish June, he would punish me.

Mr. Rankin. When did you first meet Michael Paine?

A—After I became acquainted with Ruth and she visited me for the first time, she asked me to come for a visit to her. This was on a Friday. Her husband, Michael, came for us and drove us to their home in Irving.

Mr. Rankin. They were living together at that time, were they?

A—No.

Mr. Rankin. Did Michael Paine know Russian?

A—No.

Mr. Rankin. At the time of the Walker incident, do you recall whether your husband had his job or had lost it?

A—You had said that this had happened on a Wednesday, and it seems to me that it was on a Friday that he was told that he was discharged. He didn't tell me about it until Monday.

Mr. Rankin. But it was on the preceding Friday that he was discharged, was it not?

A—No, not the preceding Friday—the Friday after the incident. That is what he told me.

Mr. Rankin. If he had lost his job before the Walker incident, you didn't know it then?

A—No.

Mr. Rankin. On the day of the Walker shooting did he appear to go to work as usual?

A—Yes.

Mr. Rankin. And when did he return that day, do you recall?

A—Late at night, about 11.

Mr. Rankin. He did not come home for dinner then, before?

A—Yes, he had come home, and then left again.

Mr. Rankin. Did you notice any difference in his actions when he returned home and had dinner?

A—No.

Mr. Rankin. Did he appear to be excited, nervous?

A—No, he was quite calm. But it seemed to me that inside he was tense.

Mr. Rankin. How could you tell that?

A—I could tell by his face. I knew Lee. Sometimes when some thing would happen he wouldn't tell me about it, but I could see it in his eyes, that something had happened.

Mr. Rankin. And you saw it this day, did you?

A—Yes.

Mr. Rankin. When did he leave the home after dinner?

A—I think it was about 7. Perhaps 7:30.

Mr. Rankin. Did you observe whether he took any gun with him?

A—No. He went downstairs. We lived on the second floor. He said, "Bye-bye."

Mr. Rankin. Did you look to see if the gun had been taken when he did not return?

A—No, I didn't look to see. . . .

Mr. Rankin. Did you understand that he had used any assumed name about going to Mexico?

A—No.

Mr. Rankin. He never told you anything of that kind?

A—No. After Lee returned from Mexico, I lived in Dallas, and Lee gave me his phone number and then when he changed his apartment—Lee lived in Dallas, and he gave me his phone number. And then when he moved, he left me another phone number.

And once when he did not come to visit during the weekend, I telephoned him and asked for him by name—rather, Ruth telephoned him and it turned out there was no one there by that name. When he telephoned me again on Monday, I told him that we had telephoned him but he was unknown at that number.

Then he said that he had lived there under an assumed name. He asked me to remove the notation of the telephone number in Ruth's phone book, but I didn't want to do that. I asked him then, "Why did you give us a phone number, when we do call we cannot get you by name?"

He was very angry, and he repeated that I should remove the notation of the phone number from the phone book. And, of course, we had a quarrel. I told him that this was another of his foolishness, some more of his foolishness. I told Ruth Paine about this. It was incomprehensible to me why he was so secretive all the time.

Mr. Rankin. Did he give you any explanation of why he was using an assumed name at that time?

A—He said that he did not want his landlady to know his real name because she might read in the paper of the fact that he had been in Russia and that he had been questioned.

Mr. Rankin. What did you say about that?

185

A—Nothing. And also he did not want the FBI to know where he lived.

Mr. Rankin. Did he tell you why he did not want the FBI to know where he lived?

A—Because their visits were not very pleasant for him and he thought that he loses jobs because the FBI visits the place of his employment. . . .

Mr. Rankin. Did you notice any change in your husband after this trip to Mexico?

A—In my opinion, he was disappointed at not being able to get to Cuba, and he didn't have any great desire to do so any more because he had run into, as he himself said—into bureaucracy and red tape. And he changed for the better. He began to treat me better.

Mr. Rankin. Will you tell us how he treated you better?

A—He helped me more—although he always did help. But he was more attentive. Perhaps this was because he didn't live together with me but stayed in Dallas. Perhaps, also because we expected a child and he was in somewhat an elated mood.

Mr. Rankin. Did your husband have any money with him when he returned from Mexico?

Mrs. Oswald. Yes, he had some left. But I never counted how much money he had in his wallet. That is why I don't know.

Mr. Rankin. Was it a small or a large amount or do you know that?

A—What would be a large amount for me would not be a large amount for you.

Mr. Rankin. Well, can you give us any estimate of what you think he had?

A—He might have had $50 or $70, thereabouts. It is necessary sometimes to make a joke. Otherwise, it gets boring. . . .

Mr. Rankin. After your husband returned from Mexico, did you examine the rifle in the garage at any time?

A—I had never examined the rifle in the garage. It was wrapped in a blanket and was lying on the floor.

Mr. Rankin. Did you ever check to see whether the rifle was in the blanket?

A—I never checked to see that. There was only once that I was interested in finding out what was in that blanket, and I saw that it was a rifle.

Mr. Rankin. When was that?

A—About a week after I came from New Orleans.

Mr. Rankin. And then you found that the rifle was in the blanket, did you?

A—Yes, I saw the wooden part of it, the wooden stock.

Mr. Rankin. On the weekend before your husband got his job at the depository, did he spend that with you at the Paines?

A—Yes.

Mr. Rankin. Did he come home Friday or Saturday?

A—On a Friday.

Mr. Rankin. When he returned to Dallas on Monday, the 14th of October, did he tell you he was going to change his room?

A—No.

Mr. Rankin. Do you remember what your husband's pay was at the depository?

A—It seems to me that it was also $1.25.

Mr. Rankin. About how much a month did it run?

A—It seems to me it was $210 to $230.

Mr. Rankin. Do you recall the hours that he worked?

A—It seems that—it seems to me that it was from 8:30 a.m. to 5 p.m.

Mr. Rankin. And did he work the weekend or any overtime?

A—No. It does happen in that depository that they work overtime. But he did not have to work any.

Mr. Rankin. During the week when he was in Dallas and you were at Irving, did he call you from time to time?

A—Daily, twice.

Mr. Rankin. Did he leave his telephone number in Dallas with you?

A—Yes.

I don't have it, it was in Paine's notebook.

Mr. Rankin. Did he speak to you in Russian when he called you on the telephone?

A—Yes. Sometimes he would try to speak in English when someone was listening, and he didn't want them to know he spoke Russian—then he would try to speak in English. . . .

Mr. Rankin. On these weekends, did you ever observe your husband going to the garage, practicing with the rifle in any way?

A—No.

Mr. Rankin. Did you see him leave the house when he could have been going to the garage and practicing with his rifle?

A—No, he couldn't have practiced while we were at the Paine's, because Ruth was there. But whenever she was not at home, he tried to spend as much time as he could with me— he would watch television in the house. But he did go to the garage to look at our things that were there.

Mr. Rankin. And you don't know when he went there what he might have done with the rifle? Is that what you mean?

A—At least I didn't notice anything.

Mr. Rankin. Now, you have described your husband's—

A—Excuse me. I think that it takes considerable time to practice with a rifle. He never spend any great deal of time in the garage.

Mr. Rankin. You have described your husband's practicing on the back porch at New Orleans with the telescopic scope and the rifle, saying he did that very regularly there.

Did you ever see him working the bolt, the action that opens the rifle, where you can put a shell in and push it back—during those times?

A—I did not see it, because it was dark, and I would be in the room at that time.

But I did hear the noise from it from time to time—not often.

Mr. Rankin. Do you recall the weekend that you went to the hospital for your baby?

A—Very well.

Mr. Rankin. Did your husband go with you at that time?

A—No. Ruth drove me at that time. He remained with June because June was crying and we could not leave her with strangers. He wanted to go with me, but we couldn't arrange it any other way.

Mr. Rankin. After the baby was born, did he come and see you?

A—Yes.

Mr. Rankin. Did he say anything to you about the baby?

A—Every father talks a lot.

Mr. Rankin. Did he talk about the baby?

A—About me and the child—he was very happy. He even had tears in his eyes. . . .

Mr. Rankin. We have reports of FBI interviews the last part of October, that is October 29, and also November 1, and November 5. We would like to ask you about them, since some of them may have been with Mrs. Paine in your presence or with you.

Do you recall one on October 29th?

A—I don't remember the interview. Ruth interpreted—she talked to them.

Mr. Rankin. In order that the Commission will understand, whenever the FBI would try to ask you any questions, Mrs. Paine would interpret for you?

A—Yes.

Mr. Rankin. And would she at the same time answer things in English, too, herself?

A—Yes.

Mr. Rankin. So, in effect, the FBI was——

A—Excuse me—she loves to talk.

Mr. Rankin. The FBI was interviewing both of you at the same time, to some extent, is that right?

A—Yes. They asked her about Lee, as far as I know.

Mr. Rankin. Do you recall that you did have such an interview at Mrs. Paine's house when she acted as interpreter on November 1, 1963?

A—Yes.

Mr. Rankin. Were you present on November 5, 1963, when FBI agents Hosty and Wilson interviewed Mrs. Paine at her home?

A—I was in my room at that time busy with little Rachel, and I heard voices which I thought were voices of the FBI. I came out of the room and they were in a hurry to leave. They did not talk to me at that time, other than just a greeting.

Mr. Rankin. Do you know whether or not they had been talking to Mrs. Paine about you or your husband?

A—Yes. She told me about it, but I was not especially interested. She does not interpret quite exactly. She is hard to understand. But she told me that in general terms.

Mr. Rankin. You have told us about the fact that you got the telephone number of the FBI agent and gave it to your husband. Was that the November 1 interview when that happened?

A—Yes. . . .

Mr. Rankin. Now, did you report to your husband the fact of this visit, November 1, with the FBI agent?

A—I didn't report it to him at once, but as soon as he came for a weekend, I told him about it.

By the way, on that day he was due to arrive.

Mr. Rankin. That is on November 1?

A—Yes. Lee comes off work at 5:30—comes from work at 5:30. They left at 5 o'clock, and we told them if they wanted to they could wait and Lee would be here soon. But they didn't want to wait.

Mr. Rankin. And by "they" who do you mean? Do you recall the name of the other man beside Agent Hosty?

A—There was only one man during the first visit. I don't remember his name. This was probably the date because there is his name and the date.

Mr. Rankin. Now, what did you tell your husband about this visit by the FBI agent and the interview?

A—I told him that they had come, that they were interested in where he was working and where he lived, and he was, again, upset.

He said that he would telephone them—I don't know whether he called or not—or that he would visit them.

Mr. Rankin. Is that all you told him at that time about the interview?

A—No. I told him about the content of the interview, but now I don't remember.

Mr. Rankin. Do you remember anything else that happened in the interview that you could tell the Commission at this time?

A—I told you that I had told them that I didn't want them to visit us, because we wanted to live peacefully, and that this was disturbing to us.

Mr. Rankin. Was there anything else?

A—There was more, but I don't remember now.

Mr. Rankin. Now, during this period of time——

A—Excuse me. He said that he knew that Lee had been engaged in passing out leaflets for the Committee for Cuba, and he asked whether Lee was doing that here.

189

Mr. Rankin. Did you answer that question?

A—Yes.

Mr. Rankin. What did you say?

A—I said that Lee does not engage in such activities here. This was not like an interview. It was simply a conversation. We talked about even some trifles that had no relationship to politics.

Mr. Rankin. Do you know whether or not your husband had any interviews or conversations with the FBI during this period.

A—I know of two visits to the home of Ruth Paine, and I saw them each time. But I don't know of any interviews with Lee. Lee had told me that supposedly he had visited their office or their building. But I didn't believe him. I thought that he was a brave rabbit.

Mr. Rankin. Did your husband continue to call you daily from Dallas after he got his job?

A—Yes.

Mr. Rankin. Did he tell you what he was doing?

A—Usually he would call me during the lunch break, and the second time after he was finished work, and he told me that he was reading, that he was watching television, and sometimes I told him that he should not stay in his room too much, that he should go for a walk in the park.

Mr. Rankin. What did he say in answer to that?

A—Or I would tell him to go out and eat, and he said that he would listen to me. I don't know to what extent he fulfilled my requests. . . .

Mr. Rankin. Will you describe to us your relationship with your mother-in-law now?

A—After all of this happened I met with her at the police station. I was, of course, very sorry for her as Lee's mother. I was always sorry for her because Lee did not want to live with her.

I understood her motherly concern. But in view of the fact of everything that happened later, her appearances in the radio, in the press, I do not think that she is a very sound thinking woman, and I think that part of the guilt is hers. I do not accuse her, but I think that part of the guilt in connection with what happened with Lee lies with her because he did not perhaps receive the education he should have during his childhood, and he did not have any correct leadership on her part, guidance. If she were in contact with my children now, I do not want her to cripple them.

Mr. Rankin. Has she tried to see you since the assassination?

A—Yes, all the time.

Mr. Rankin. And have you seen her since that time?

A—Accidentally we met at the cemetery on a Sunday when I visited there, but I didn't want to meet with her, and I left. She didn't understand that I didn't want to meet with her and she accused the Secret Service personnel of preventing her from seeing me.

Mr. Rankin. Except for the time at the jail and at the cemetery, have you seen her since the assassination?

A—No.

Mr. Rankin. At the time you did see your mother-in-law, did you observe any difference in her attitude towards you?

A—Yes, of course.

Mr. Rankin. Will you describe that difference that you observed?

A—At first I said that I didn't see her any more. But after Lee was in jail I lived with her for some time at that inn.

Mr. Rankin. The Six Flags?

A—The Six Flags. And inasmuch as I lived with her and met with her every day I could see—I was able to see the change. At least if her relationship with me was good, it was not sincere. I think that she does not like me. I don't think that she simply is able to like me.

There were some violent scenes, she didn't want to listen to anyone, there were hysterics. Everyone was guilty of everything and no one understood her.

Perhaps my opinion is wrong, but at least I do not want to live with her and to listen to scandals every day.

Mr. Rankin. Did she say anything to indicate that she blamed you in connection with the assassination?

A—No, she did not accuse me of anything.

Mr. Rankin. In your presence, at any time, did she accuse Ruth Paine of being involved in causing the assassination or being directly involved?

A—No, she never accused Ruth Paine. She simply did not like her.

Mr. Rankin. Did she tell you why she didn't like Ruth Paine?

A—She told me but I didn't understand it because it was in English. She expresses more by rather stormy mimicry, thinking that that would get across and I would understand.

Mr. Rankin. You said that you didn't want to see Ruth Paine because you thought she wanted to see you for her own interests. Will you tell us what you meant by that?

A—I think that she wants to see me in her own selfish interests. She likes to be well known, popular, and I think that anything that I should write her, for example, would wind up in the press.

The reason that I think so is that the first time that we were in jail to see Lee, she was with me and with her children, and she was trying to get in front of the cameras, and to push her children and instructed her children to look this way and look that way. And the first photographs that appeared were of me with her children. . . .

Mr. Rankin. In one of your statements that you have given the FBI and the Secret Service you indicated that this particular weekend your husband stayed in Dallas—that is the 15th through the 17th of November. Does that refresh your memory?

A—Yes—the 15th to the 17th he remained in Dallas. That is, he didn't come that weekend.

But on the 13th he was not in Irving.

Mr. Rankin. That would be the weekend before the assassination, to refresh your memory again.

A—You see, this is why I was not surprised that he didn't come—that he came, rather, he had not come on Friday and Saturday, and on Sunday I called him over the telephone and this is when he had a quarrel over the fictitious name.

By the way, he didn't come because I told him not to come. He had wanted to come, he had telephoned.

Mr. Rankin. What did you tell him about not coming?

A—That he shouldn't come every week, that perhaps it is not convenient for Ruth that the whole family be there, live there.

Mr. Rankin. Did he say anything about that?

A—He said, "As you wish. If you don't want me to come, I won't."

Mr. Rankin. Were you quite angry with him about the use of the fictitious name?

A—Yes. And when he called me over the phone a second time I hung up and would not talk to him.

Mr. Rankin. Did you tell him why you were so angry?

A—Yes, of course.

Mr. Rankin. What did you say?

A—I said, "After all, when will all your foolishness come to an end? All of these comedies. First one thing then another. And now this fictitious name."

I didn't understand why. After all, it was nothing terrible if people were to find out that he had been in Russia.

Mr. Rankin. What did he say when you said that?

A—That I didn't understand anything.

Mr. Rankin. Do you remember an incident when he said you were a Czechoslovakian rather than a Russian?

A—Yes. We lived on Elsbeth Street, and he had told the landlady that I was from Czechoslovakia. But I didn't know about it, and when the landlady asked me, I told her I was from Russia. I told Lee about it that evening, and he scolded me for having said that.

Mr. Rankin. What did you say to him then?

A—That the landlady was very nice and she was very good to me and she was even pleased with the fact that I was from Russia.

Mr. Rankin. Did you object to your husband saying that you were from some country other than Russia?

A—Of course.

Mr. Rankin. What did you say to him about that?

A—I am not ashamed of the fact that I am from Russia. I can even be proud of the fact that I am Russian. And there is no need for me to hide it. Every person should be proud of his nationality and not be afraid or ashamed of it.

Mr. Rankin. What did he say in response to that?

A—Nothing.

Mr. Rankin. When he gave the fictitious name, did he use the name Hidell?

A—Where?

Mr. Rankin. When you called him that time.

A—Where?

Mr. Rankin. On the weekend, when you called him, you said there was a fictitious name given.

A—I don't know what name he had given. He said that he was under a fictitious name, but he didn't tell me which.

Mr. Rankin. Have you ever heard that he used the fictitious name Hidell?

A—Yes.

Mr. Rankin. When did you first learn that he used such a name?

A—In New Orleans.

Mr. Rankin. How did you learn that?

A—When he was interviewed by some anti-Cubans, he used this name and spoke of an organization. I knew there was no such organization. And I know that Hidell is merely an altered Fidel, and I laughed at such foolishness. My imagination didn't work that way.

Mr. Rankin. Did you say anything to him about it at that time?

A—I said that it wasn't a nice thing to do and some day it would be discovered anyhow.

Mr. Rankin. Now, the weekend of November 15th to 17th, which was the weekend before the assassination, do you know what your husband did or how he spent that weekend while he was in Dallas?

A—No, I don't.

Mr. Rankin. Do you know whether he took the rifle before he went into Dallas, that trip, for that weekend?

A—I don't know. I think that he took the rifle on Thursday when he came the next time, but I didn't see him take it. I assume that. I cannot know it.

Mr. Rankin. Except for the time in New Orleans that you described, and the time you called to Dallas to ask for your husband, do you know of any other time your husband was using an assumed name?

A—No, no more.

Mr. Rankin. Did you think he was using that assumed name in connection with this Fair Play for Cuba activity or something else?

A—The name Hidell, which you pronounced Hidell, was

in connection with his activity with the non-existing organization.

Mr. Rankin. Did you and your husband live under the name Hidell in New Orleans?

A—No.

Mr. Rankin. You were never identified as the Hidells, as far as you knew, while you were there?

A—No. No one knew that Lee was Hidell.

Mr. Rankin. How did you discover it, then?

A—I already said that when I listened to the radio, they spoke of that name, and I asked him who, and he said it was he.

Mr. Rankin. Was that after the arrest?

A—I don't remember when the interview took place, before the arrest or after.

Mr. Rankin. But it was in regard to some interview for radio transmission, and he had identified himself as Hidell, rather than Oswald, is that right?

A—No—he represented himself as Oswald, but he said that the organization which he supposedly represents is headed by Hidell.

Mr. Rankin. He was using the name Hidell, then, to have a fictitious president or head of the organization which really was he himself, is that right?

A—Yes.

Mr. Rankin. You have told us about his practicing with the rifle, the telescopic lens, on the back porch at New Orleans, and also his using the bolt action that you heard from time to time.

Will you describe that a little more fully to us, as best you remember?

A—I cannot describe that in greater detail. I can only say that Lee would sit there with the rifle and open and close the bolt and clean it. No, he didn't clean it at that time.

Yes—twice he did clean it.

Mr. Rankin. And did he seem to be practicing with the telescopic lens, too, and sighting the gun on different objects?

A—I don't know. The rifle was always with this. I don't know exactly how he practiced, because I was in the house, I was busy. I just knew that he sits there with his rifle. I was not interested in it.

Mr. Rankin. Was this during the light of the day or during the darkness?

A—During darkness.

Mr. Rankin. Was it so dark that neighbors could not see him on the porch there with the gun?

A—Yes.

Mr. Rankin. Now, during the week of the assassination, did your husband call you at all by telephone?

A—He telephoned me on Monday, after I had called him on Sunday, and he was not there.

194

Or, rather, he was there, but he wasn't called to the phone because he was known by another name.

On Monday he called several times, but after I hung up on him and didn't want to talk to him he did not call again. He then arrived on Thursday.

Mr. Rankin. Did he tell you he was coming Thursday?

A—No.

Mr. Rankin. Did you learn that he was using the assumed name of Lee as his last name?

A—I know it now, but I did not ever know it before.

Mr. Rankin. Thursday was the 21st. Do you recall that?

A—Yes.

Mr. Rankin. And the assassination was on the 22d.

A—This is very hard to forget.

Mr. Rankin. Did your husband give any reason for coming home on Thursday?

A—He said that he was lonely because he hadn't come the preceding weekend, and he wanted to make his peace with me.

Mr. Rankin. Did you say anything to him then?

A—He tried to talk to me but I would not answer him, and he was very upset.

Mr. Rankin. Were you upset with him?

A—I was angry, of course. He was not angry—he was upset. I was angry. He tried very hard to please me. He spent quite a bit of time putting away diapers and played with the children on the street.

Mr. Rankin. How did you indicate to him that you were angry with him?

A—By not talking to him.

Mr. Rankin. And how did he show that he was upset?

A—He was upset over the fact that I would not answer him. He tried to start a conversation with me several times, but I would not answer. And he said that he didn't want me to be angry at him because this upsets him.

On that day, he suggested that we rent an apartment in Dallas. He said that he was tired of living alone and perhaps the reason for my being so angry was the fact that we were not living together. That if I want to he would rent an apartment in Dallas tomorrow—that he didn't want me to remain with Ruth any longer, but wanted me to live with him in Dallas.

He repeated this not once but several times, but I refused. And he said that once again I was preferring my friends to him, and that I didn't need him.

Mr. Rankin. What did you say to that?

A—I said it would be better if I remained with Ruth until the holidays, he would come, and we would all meet together. That this was better because while he was living alone and I stayed with Ruth, we were spending less money. And I told him to buy me a washing machine, because with two children it became two difficult to wash by hand.

Mr. Rankin. What did he say to that?

A—He said he would buy me a washing machine.

Mr. Rankin. What did you say to that?

A—Thank you. That it would be better if he bought something for himself—that I would manage.

Mr. Rankin. Did this seem to make him more upset, when you suggested that he wait about getting an apartment for you to live in?

A—Yes. He then stopped talking and sat down and watched television and then went to bed. I went to bed later. It was about 9 o'clock when he went to sleep. I went to sleep about 11:30. But it seemed to me that he was not really asleep. But I didn't talk to him.

In the morning he got up, said goodbye, and left, and that I shouldn't get up—as always, I did not get up to prepare breakfast. This was quite usual.

And then after I fed Rachel, I took a look to see whether Lee was here, but he had already gone. This was already after the police had come. Ruth told me that in the evening she had worked in the garage and she knows that she had put out the light but that the light was on later—that the light was on in the morning. And she guessed that Lee was in the garage.

But I didn't see it.

Mr. Rankin. Did she tell you when she thought your husband had been in the garage, what time of the day?

A—She thought that it was during the evening, because the light remained on until morning.

Mr. Rankin. Why did you stay awake until 11:30? Were you still angry with him?

A—No, not for that reason, but because I had to wash dishes and be otherwise busy with the household—take a bath. . . .

Mr. Rankin. Mrs. Oswald, why did the use of this false name by your husband make you so angry? Would you explain that a little bit?

A—It would be unpleasant and incomprehensible to any wife if her husband used a fictitious name. And then, of course, I thought that if he would see that I don't like it and that I explained to him that this is not the smart thing to do, that he would stop doing it.

Mr. Rankin. Did you feel that you were becoming more impatient with all of these things that your husband was doing, the Fair Play for Cuba and the Walker incident, and then this fictitious name business?

A—Yes, of course. I was tired of it.

Every day I was waiting for some kind of a new surprise. I couldn't wait to find out what else would he think of.

Mr. Rankin. Did you discuss that with your husband at all?

A—Yes, of course.

Mr. Rankin. What did you say about that?

A—I said that no one needed anything like that, that for no reason at all he was thinking that he was not like other people, that he was more important.

Mr. Rankin. And what did he say?

A—He would seem to agree, but then would continue again in two or three days.

Mr. Rankin. Did you sense that he was not intending to carry out his agreement with you to not have another Walker incident or anything like that?

A—I generally didn't think that Lee would repeat anything like that. Generally, I knew that the rifle was very tempting for him. But I didn't believe that he would repeat it. It was hard to believe.

Mr. Rankin. I wasn't clear about when Mrs. Paine thought that your husband might have been in the garage and had the light on. Can you give us any help on the time of day that she had in mind?

A—In the morning she thought about it. But she didn't attach any significance to it at that time. It was only after the police had come that this became more significant for her.

Mr. Rankin. So she thought it was in the morning after he got up from his night's rest that he might have gone to the garage, turned on the light?

A—In my opinion, she thought that it was at night, or during the evening that he had been in the garage and turned on the light. At least that is what she said to me. I don't know.

Mr. Rankin. Did she indicate whether she thought it was before he went to bed at 9 o'clock?

A—I don't know. At first it seems it wasn't nine, it was perhaps ten o'clock when Lee went to bed. And first, Ruth went to her room and then Lee went. He was there after her.

Mr. Rankin. So he might have been in the garage sometime between 9 and 10? Was that what you thought?

A—Yes. But I think that he might have even been there in the morning and turned on the light.

Mr. Rankin. On this evening when you were angry with him, had he come home with the young Mr. Frazier that day?

A—Yes.

Mr. Rankin. When was the last time that you had noticed the rifle before that day?

A—I said that I saw—for the first and last time I saw the rifle about a week after I had come to Mrs. Paine.

But, as I said, the rifle was wrapped in a blanket, and I was sure when the police had come that the rifle was still in the blanket, because it was all rolled together. And, therefore,

197

when they took the blanket and the rifle was not in it, I was very much surprised.

Mr. Rankin. Did you ever see the rifle in a paper cover?

A—No.

Mr. Rankin. Could you describe for the Commission the place in the garage where the rifle was located?

A—When you enter the garage from the street it was in the front part, the left.

Mr. Rankin. By the left you mean left of the door?

A—It is an overhead door and the rifle was to the left, on the floor.

It was always in the same place.

Mr. Rankin. Was there anything else close to the rifle that you recall?

A—Next to it there were some—next to the rifle there were some suitcases and Ruth had some paper barrels in the garage where the kids used to play.

Mr. Rankin. The way the rifle was wrapped with a blanket, could you tell whether or not the rifle had been removed and the blanket just left there at any time?

A—It always had the appearance of having something inside of it. But I only looked at it really once, and I was always sure the rifle was in it. Therefore, it is very hard to determine when the rifle was taken. I only assumed that it was on Thursday, because Lee had arrived so unexpectedly for some reason.

Mr. Rankin. Did you believe that the reason for his coming out to see you Thursday was to make up?

A—I think there were two reasons. One was to make up with me, and the other to take the rifle. This is—this, of course, is not irreconcilable.

Mr. Rankin. But you think he came to take the rifle because of what you learned since. Is that it?

A—Yes, of course.

Mr. Rankin. Before this incident about the fictitious name, were you and your husband getting along quite well?

A—Yes.

Mr. Rankin. Did he seem to like his job at the depository?

A—Yes, because it was not dirty work.

Mr. Rankin. Had he talked about getting any other job?

A—Yes. When he went to answer some ads, he preferred to get some work connected with photography rather than this work. He liked this work relatively speaking—he liked it. But, of course, he wanted to get something better.

Mr. Rankin. Did you like the photographic work?

A—Yes. It was interesting for him. When he would see his work in the newspaper he would always point it out.

Mr. Rankin. He had a reference in his notebook to the word "Microdot." Do you know what he meant by that?

A—No.

Mr. Rankin. How did your husband get along with Mrs. Paine?

A—He was polite to her, as an acquaintance would be, but he didn't like her. He told me that he detested her—a tall and stupid woman. She is, of course, not too smart, but most people aren't.

Mr. Rankin. Did he ever say anything to indicate he thought Mrs. Paine was coming between him and you?

A—No.

Mr. Rankin. Did Mrs. Paine say anything about your husband?

A—She didn't say anything bad. I don't know what she thought. But she didn't say anything bad.

Perhaps she didn't like something about him, but she didn't tell me. She didn't want to hurt me by saying anything.

Mr. Rankin. I have understood from your testimony that you did not really care to go to Russia but your husband was the one that was urging that, and that is why you requested the visa, is that correct?

A—Yes.

Mr. Rankin. And later he talked about not only you and your child going, but also his going with you, is that right?

A—Yes.

Mr. Rankin. Do you know what caused him to make that change?

A—At one time—I don't remember whether he was working at that time or not—he was very sad and upset. He was sitting and writing something in his notebook. I asked him what he was writing and he said, "It would be better if I go with you."

Then he went into the kitchen and he sat there in the dark, and when I came in I saw that he was crying. I didn't know why. But, of course, when a man is crying it is not a very pleasant thing, and I didn't start to question him about why.

Mr. Rankin. Did he say to you that he didn't want you to leave him alone?

A—Yes.

Mr. Rankin. Did you at that time say anything to him about your all staying in this country and getting along together?

A—I told him, of course, that it would be better for us to stay here. But if it was very difficult for him and if he was always worried about tomorrow, then perhaps it would be better if we went.

Mr. Rankin. On the evening of the 21st, was anything said about curtain rods or his taking curtain rods to town the following day?

A—No, I didn't have any.

Mr. Rankin. He didn't say anything like that?

A—No.

Mr. Rankin. Did you discuss the weekend that was coming up?

A—He said that he probably would not come on Friday, and he didn't come—he was in jail.

Mr. Rankin. Did the quarrel that you had at that time seem to cause him to be more disturbed than usual?

A—No, not particularly. At least he didn't talk about that quarrel when he came. Usually he would remember about what happened. This time he didn't blame me for anything, didn't ask me any questions, just wanted to make up.

Mr. Rankin. I understood that when you didn't make up he was quite disturbed and you were still angry, is that right?

A—I wasn't really very angry. I, of course, wanted to make up with him. But I gave the appearance of being very angry. I was smiling inside, but I had a serious expression on my face.

Mr. Rankin. And as a result of that, did he seem to be more disturbed than usual?

A—As always, as usual. Perhaps a little more. At least when he went to bed he was very upset.

Mr. Rankin. Do you think that had anything to do with the assassination the next day?

A—Perhaps he was thinking about all of that. I don't think that he was asleep. Because, in the morning when the alarm clock went off he hadn't woken up as usual before the alarm went off, and I thought that he probably had fallen asleep very late. At least then I didn't think about it. Now I think so.

Mr. Rankin. When he said he would not be home that Friday evening, did you ask him why?

A—Yes.

Mr. Rankin. What did he say?

A—He said that since he was home on Thursday, that it wouldn't make any sense to come again on Friday, that he would come for the weekend.

Mr. Rankin. Did that cause you to think that he had any special plans to do anything?

A—No.

Mr. Rankin. Did you usually keep a wallet with money in it at the Paines?

A—Yes, in my room at Ruth Paine's there was a black wallet in a wardrobe. Whenever Lee would come he would put money in there, but I never counted it.

Mr. Rankin. On the evening of November 21st, do you know how much was in the wallet?

A—No. One detail that I remember was that he had asked me whether I had bought some shoes for myself, and I said no, that I hadn't had any time. He asked me whether June needed anything and told me to buy everything that I needed for myself and for June—and for the children.

This was rather unusual for him, that he would mention that first.

200

Mr. Rankin. Did he take the money from the wallet from time to time?

A—No, he generally kept the amount that he needed and put the rest in the wallet.

I know that the money that was found there, that you think this was not Lee's money. But I know for sure that this was money that he had earned. He had some money left after his trip to Mexico. Then we received an unemployment compensation check for $33. And then Lee paid only $7 or $8 for his room. And I know how he eats, very little.

Mr. Rankin. Do you know what his ordinary lunch was?

A—Peanut butter sandwich, cheese sandwich, some lettuce, and he would buy himself a hamburger, something else, a coke.

Mr. Rankin. And what about his evening meal? Do you know what he ate in the evening meal?

A—Usually meat, vegetables, fruit, dessert.

Mr. Rankin. Where would he have that?

A—He loved bananas. They were inexpensive.

The place where he rented a room, he could not cook there. He said that there was some sort of a cafe across the street and that he ate there.

Mr. Rankin. Did he ever tell you what he paid for his evening meal?

A—About a dollar, $1.30.

Mr. Rankin. What about his breakfast? Do you know what he had for breakfast ordinarily?

A—He never had breakfast. He just drank coffee and that is all.

Not because he was trying to economize. Simply he never liked to eat.

Mr. Rankin. Mr. Reporter, will you note the presence of Mr. Ruben Efron in the hearing room. He also knows Russian.

On November 21, the day before the assassination that you were describing, was there any discussion between you and your husband about President Kennedy's trip or proposed trip to Texas, Dallas and the Fort Worth area?

A—I asked Lee whether he knew where the President would speak, and told him that I would very much like to hear him and to see him. I asked him how this could be done.

But he said he didn't know how to do that, and didn't enlarge any further on that subject.

Mr. Rankin. Had there ever been——

A—This was also somewhat unusual—his lack of desire to talk about that subject any further.

Mr. Rankin. Can you explain that to us?

A—I think about it more now.

At that time, I didn't pay any attention.

Mr. Rankin. How did you think it was unusual? Could you explain that?

A—The fact that he didn't talk a lot about it. He merely

201

gave me—said something as an answer, and did not have any further comments.

Mr. Rankin. Do you mean by that usually he would discuss a matter of that kind and show considerable interest?

A—Yes, of course, he would have told who would be there and where this would take place.

Mr. Rankin. Did you say anything about his showing a lack of interest at that time?

A—I merely shrugged my shoulders.

Mr. Rankin. Now, prior to that time, had there been any discussion between you concerning the proposed trip of President Kennedy to Texas?

A—No.

Mr. Rankin. While you were in New Orleans, was there any discussion or reference to President Kennedy's proposed trip to Texas?

A—No.

Mr. Rankin. Did your husband make any comments about President Kennedy on that evening, of the 21st?

A—No.

Mr. Rankin. Had your husband at any time that you can recall said anything against President Kennedy?

A—I don't remember any—ever having said that. I don't know. He never told me that.

Mr. Rankin. Did he ever say anything good about President Kennedy?

A—Usually he would translate magazine articles. They were generally good. And he did not say that this contradicted his opinion. I just remembered that he talked about Kennedy's father, who made his fortune by a not very—in a not very good manner. Disposing of such funds, of course, it was easier for his sons to obtain an education and to obtain a government position, and it was easier to make a name for themselves.

Mr. Rankin. What did he say about President Kennedy's father making his fortune?

A—He said that he had speculated in wine. I don't know to what extent that is true.

Mr. Rankin. When he read these articles to you, did he comment favorably upon President Kennedy?

A—I have already said that he would translate articles which were good, but he would not comment on them.

Mr. Rankin. Can you recall——

A—Excuse me. At least when I found out that Lee had shot at the President, for me this was surprising. And I didn't believe it. I didn't believe for a long time that Lee had done that. That he had wanted to kill Kennedy—because perhaps Walker was there again, perhaps he wanted to kill him.

Mr. Rankin. Why did you not believe this?

A—Because I had never heard anything bad about Kennedy from Lee. And he never had anything against him.

Mr. Rankin. But you also say that he never said anything about him.

A—He read articles which were favorable.

Mr. Rankin. Did he say he approved of those articles?

A—No, he didn't say anything. Perhaps he did reach his own conclusions reading these articles, but he didn't tell me about them.

Mr. Rankin. So apparently he didn't indicate any approval or disapproval as far as he was concerned, of President Kennedy?

A—Yes, that is correct. The President is the President. In my opinion, he never wanted to overthrow him. At least he never showed me that. He never indicated that he didn't want that President.

Mr. Rankin. Did you observe that his acts on November 21st the evening before the assassination, were anything like they were the evening before the Walker incident?

A—Absolutely nothing in common.

Mr. Rankin. Did he say anything at all that would indicate he was contemplating the assassination?

A—No.

Mr. Rankin. Did he discuss the television programs he saw that evening with you?

A—He was looking at TV by himself. I was busy in the kitchen. At one time when we were—when I was together with him they showed some sort of war films, from World War II. And he watched them with interest.

Mr. Rankin. Do you recall films that he saw called "Suddenly," and "We were Strangers" that involved assassinations?

A—I don't remember the names of these films. If you would remind me of the contents, perhaps I would know.

Mr. Rankin. Well, "Suddenly," was about the assassination of a president, and the other was about the assassination of a Cuban dictator.

A—Yes, Lee saw those films.

Mr. Rankin. Did he tell you that he had seen them?

A—I was with him when he watched them.

Mr. Rankin. Do you recall about when this was with reference to the date of the assassination?

A—It seems that this was before Rachel's birth.

Mr. Rankin. Weeks or months? Can you recall that?

A—Several days. Some five days.

Mr. Rankin. Did you discuss the films after you had seen them with your husband?

A—One film about the assassination of the president in Cuba, which I had seen together with him, he said that this was a fictitious situation, but that the content of the film was similar to the actual situation which existed in Cuba, meaning the revolution in Cuba.

Mr. Rankin. Did either of you comment on either film being like the attempt on Walker's life?

A—No. I didn't watch the other film.

Mr. Rankin. Was anything said by your husband about how easy an assassination could be committed like that?

A—No. I only know that he watched the film with interest, but I didn't like it.

Mr. Rankin. Do you recall anything else he said about either of these films?

A—Nothing else. He didn't tell me anything else. He talked to Ruth a few words. Perhaps she knows more.

Mr. Rankin. By Ruth, you mean Mrs. Paine?

A—They spoke in English.

Yes.

Mr. Rankin. And did Mrs. Paine tell you what he said to her at that time?

A—No.

Mr. Rankin. Do you recall your husband saying at any time after he saw the film about the Cuban assassination that this was the old-fashioned way of assassination?

A—No.

Mr. Rankin. Do you recall anything being said by your husband at any time about Governor Connally?

A—Well, while we were still in Russia, and Connally at that time was Secretary of the Navy, Lee wrote him a letter in which he asked Connally to help him obtain a good character reference because at the end of his Army service he had a good characteristic—honorable discharge—but that it had been changed after it became known he had gone to Russia.

Mr. Rankin. Had it been changed to undesirable discharge, as you understand it?

A—Yes. Then we received a letter from Connally in which he said that he had turned the matter over to the responsible authorities. That was all in Russia.

But here it seems he had written again to that organization with a request to review. But he said from time to time that these are bureaucrats, and he was dissatisfied.

Mr. Rankin. Do you know when he wrote again?

A—No.

Mr. Rankin. Was that letter written from New Orleans?

A—I don't know. I only know about the fact, but when and how, I don't know.

Mr. Rankin. Did your husband say anything to you to indicate he had a dislike for Governor Connally?

A—Here he didn't say anything.

But while we were in Russia he spoke well of him. It seems to me that Connally was running for Governor and Lee said that when he would return to the United States he would vote for him.

Mr. Rankin. That is all that you remember that he said about Governor Connally?

A—Yes.

Mr. Rankin. With regard to the Walker incident, you said that your husband seemed disturbed for several weeks. Did you notice anything of that kind with regard to the day prior to the assassination?

A—No.

Mr. Rankin. On November 22, the day of the assassination, you said your husband got up and got his breakfast. Did you get up at all before he left?

A—No. I woke up before him, and I then went to the kitchen to see whether he had had breakfast or not—whether he had already left for work. But the coffee pot was cold and Lee was not there.

And when I met Ruth that morning, I asked her whether Lee had coffee or not, and she said probably, perhaps he had made himself some instant coffee.

But probably he hadn't had any breakfast that morning.

Mr. Rankin. Then did he say anything to you that morning at all, or did he get up and go without speaking to you?

A—He told me to take as much money as I needed and to buy everything, and said goodbye, and that is all.

After the police had already come, I noticed that Lee had left his wedding ring.

Mr. Rankin. You didn't observe that that morning when your husband had left, did you?

A—No.

Mr. Rankin. Do you know approximately what time your husband left that morning?

A—I have written it there, but I have now forgotten whether it was seven or eight. But a quarter to eight—I don't know. I have now forgotten.

Mr. Rankin. What time was he due for work?

A—He was due at work at 8 or 8:30. At 7:15 he was already gone.

Mr. Rankin. Do you know whether he rode with Wesley Frazier that morning?

A—I don't know. I didn't hear him leave.

Mr. Rankin. Did you ever see a paper bag or cover for the rifle at the Paine's residence or garage?

A—No.

Mr. Rankin. Did you ever see a bag at any time?

A—No.

Mr. Rankin. Where did your husband have his lunch? Did he take a sandwich to the depository, or did he go home to his rooming house for lunch? Do you know?

A—He usually took sandwiches to lunch. But I don't know whether he would go home or not.

Mr. Rankin. Had your husband ever left his wedding ring at home that way before?

A—At one time while he was still at Fort Worth, it was inconvenient for him to work with his wedding ring on and he would remove it, but at work—he would not leave it at home. His wedding ring was rather wide, and it bothered him.

I don't know now. He would take it off at work.

Mr. Rankin. Then this is the first time during your married life that he had ever left it at home where you live?

A—Yes.

Mr. Rankin. Do you know whether your husband carried any package with him when he left the house on November 22nd?

A—I think that he had a package with his lunch. But a small package.

Mr. Rankin. Do you know whether he had any package like a rifle in some container?

A—No.

Mr. Rankin. What did you do the rest of the morning, after you got up on November 22nd?

A—When I got up the television set was on, and I knew that Kennedy was coming. Ruth had gone to the doctor with her children and she left the television set on for me. And I watched television all morning, even without having dressed. She was running around in her pajamas and watching television with me.

Mr. Rankin. Before the assassination, did you ever see your husband examining the route of the parade as it was published in the paper?

A—No.

Mr. Rankin. Did you ever see him looking at a map of Dallas like he did in connection with the Walker shooting?

A—No.

Mr. Rankin. How did you learn of the shooting of President Kennedy?

A—I was watching television, and Ruth by that time was already with me, and she said someone had shot at the President.

Mr. Rankin. What did you say?

A—It was hard for me to say anything. We both turned pale. I went to my room and cried.

Mr. Rankin. Did you think immediately that your husband might have been involved?

A—No.

Mr. Rankin. Did Mrs. Paine say anything about the possibility of your husband being involved?

A—No, but she only said that "By the way, they fired from the building in which Lee is working."

My heart dropped. I then went to the garage to see whether the rifle was there, and I saw that the blanket was still there, and I said, "Thank God." I thought, "Can there really be such a stupid man in the world that could do something like that?" But I was already rather upset at that time—I don't know why. Perhaps my intuition.

I didn't know what I was doing.

Mr. Rankin. Did you look in the blanket to see if the rifle was there?

A—I didn't unroll the blanket. It was in its usual position, and it appeared to have something inside.

Mr. Rankin. Did you at any time open the blanket to see if the rifle was there?

A—No, only once.

Mr. Rankin. You have told us about that.

A—Yes.

Mr. Rankin. And what about Mrs. Paine? Did she look in the blanket to see if the rifle was there?

A—She didn't know about the rifle.

Perhaps she did know. But she never told me about it.

I don't know.

Mr. Rankin. When did you learn that the rifle was not in the blanket?

A—When the police arrived and asked whether my husband had a rifle, and I said "Yes."

Mr. Rankin. Then what happened?

A—They began to search the apartment. When they came to the garage and took the blanket, I thought, "Well, now, they will find it."

They opened the blanket but there was no rifle there.

Then, of course, I already knew that it was Lee. Because, before that, while I thought that the rifle was at home, I did not think that Lee had done that. I thought the police had simply come because he was always under suspicion.

Mr. Rankin. What do you mean by that—he was always under suspicion?

A—Well, the FBI would visit us.

Mr. Rankin. Did they indicate what they suspected him of?

A—They didn't tell me anything.

Mr. Rankin. What did you say to the police when they came?

A—I don't remember now. I was so upset that I don't remember what I said.

Mr. Rankin. Did you tell them about your husband leaving his wedding ring that morning?

A—No, because I didn't know it.

Mr. Rankin. Did you tell them that you had looked for the gun you thought was in the blanket?

A—No, it seems to me I didn't say that. They didn't ask me.

Mr. Rankin. Did you watch the police open the blanket to see if the rifle was there?

A—Yes.

Mr. Rankin. Did Mrs. Paine also watch them?

207

A—It seems to me, as far as I remember.

Mr. Rankin. When the police came, did Mrs. Paine act as an interpreter for you?

A—Yes. She told me about what they had said. But I was not being questioned so that she would interpret. She told me herself. She very much loved to talk and she welcomed the occasion.

Mr. Rankin. You mean by that she answered questions of the police and then told you what she had said?

A—Yes.

Mr. Rankin. And what did she tell you that she had said to the police?

A—She talked to them in the usual manner, in English, when they were addressing her.

But when they addressed me, she was interpreting.

Mr. Rankin. Do you recall the exact time of the day that you discovered the wedding ring there at the house?

A—About 2 o'clock, I think. I don't remember. Then everything got mixed up, all time.

Mr. Rankin. Did the police spend considerable time there?

A—Yes.

Mr. Rankin. Do you remember the names of any of the officers?

A—No, I don't.

Mr. Rankin. How did they treat you?

A—Rather gruff, not very polite. They kept on following me. I wanted to change clothes because I was dressed in a manner fitting to the house. And they would not even let me go into the dressing room to change.

Mr. Rankin. What did you say about that?

A—Well, what could I tell them?

I asked them, but they didn't want to. They were rather rough. They kept on saying, hurry up.

Mr. Rankin. Did they want you to go with them?

A—Yes.

Mr. Rankin. Did you leave the house with them right soon after they came?

A—About an hour, I think.

Mr. Rankin. And what were they doing during that hour?

A—They searched the entire house.

Mr. Rankin. Did they take anything with them?

A—Yes—everything, even some tapes—Ruth's tapes from a tape recorder, her things. I don't know what.

Mr. Rankin. Did they take many of your belongings?

A—I didn't watch at that time. After all, it is not my business. If they need it, let them take it.

Mr. Rankin. Did they give you an inventory of what they took?

A—No.

Mr. Rankin. You have never received an inventory?

A—No.

Mr. Rankin. Do you know what they took?

A—No. I know that I am missing my documents, that I am missing Lee's documents, Lee's wedding ring.

Mr. Rankin. What about clothing?

A—Robert had some of Lee's clothing. I don't know what was left of Lee's things, but I hope they will return it. No one needs it.

Mr. Rankin. What documents do you refer to that you are missing?

A—My foreign passport, my immigration card, my birth certificate, my wedding certificate—marriage certificate, June's and Rachel's birth certificates. Then various letters, my letters from friends. Perhaps something that has some bearing—photographs, whatever has some reference—whatever refers to the business at hand, let it remain.

Then my diploma. I don't remember everything now.

Mr. Rankin. What documents of your husband's do you recall that they took?

A—I didn't see what they took. At least at the present time I have none of Lee's documents.

Mr. Rankin. The documents of his that you refer to that you don't have are similar to your own that you described?

A—Yes. He also had a passport, several work books, labor cards. I don't know what men here—what sort of documents men here carry. . . .

Mr. Rankin. In some newspaper accounts your mother-in-law has intimated that your husband might have been an agent for some government, and that she might have—did have information in that regard.

Do you know anything about that?

A—The first time that I hear anything about this.

Mr. Rankin. Did you ever know——

A—That is all untrue, of course.

Mr. Rankin. Did you ever know that your husband was at any time an agent of the Soviet Union?

A—No.

Mr. Rankin. Did you ever know that your husband was an agent of the Cuban government at any time?

A—No.

Mr. Rankin. Did you ever know that your husband was an agent of any agency of the United States Government?

A—No.

Mr. Rankin. Did you ever know that your husband was an agent of any government?

A—No.

Mr. Rankin. Do you have any idea of the motive which induced your husband to kill the President?

A—From everything that I know about my husband, and of the events that transpired, I can conclude that he wanted in

209

any way, whether good or bad, to do something that would make him outstanding, that he would be known in history.

Mr. Rankin. And is it then your belief that he assassinated the President, for this purpose?

A—That is my opinion. I don't know how true that is.

Mr. Rankin. And what about his shooting at General Walker? Do you think he had the same motive or purpose in doing that?

A—I think that, yes.

Mr. Rankin. After the assassination, were you coerced or abused in any way by the police or anyone else in connection with the inquiry about the assassination?

A—No.

Mr. Rankin. Did you see or speak to your husband on November 22d, following his arrest?

A—On the 22d I did not see him.

On the 23d I met with him.

Mr. Rankin. And when you met with him on the 23d, was it at your request or his?

A—I don't know whether he requested it, but I know that I wanted to see him.

Mr. Rankin. Did you request the right to see your husband on the 22d, after his arrest?

A—Yes.

Mr. Rankin. And what answer were you given at that time?

A—I was not permitted to.

Mr. Rankin. Who gave you that answer?

A—I don't know. The police.

Mr. Rankin. You don't know what officer of the police?

A—No.

Mr. Rankin. Where did you spend the evening on the night of the assassination?

A—On the day of the assassination, on the 22d, after returning from questioning by the police, I spent the night with Mrs. Paine, together with Lee's mother.

Mr. Rankin. Did you receive any threats from anyone at this time?

A—No.

Mr. Rankin. Did any law enforcement agency offer you protection at that time?

A—No.

Mr. Rankin. When you saw your husband on November 23d, the day after the assassination, did you have a conversation with him?

A—Yes.

Mr. Rankin. And where did this occur?

A—In the police department.

Mr. Rankin. Were just the two of you together at that time?

A—No, the mother was there together with me.

Mr. Rankin. At that time what did you say to him and what did he say to you?

A—You probably know better than I do what I told him.

Mr. Rankin. Well, I need your best recollection, if you can give it to us, Mrs. Oswald.

A—Of course he tried to console me that I should not worry, that everything would turn out well. He asked about how the children were. He spoke of some friends who supposedly would help him. I don't know who he had in mind. That he had written to someone in New York before that. I was so upset that of course I didn't understand anything of that. It was simply talk.

Mr. Rankin. Did you say anything to him then?

A—I told him that the police had been there and that a search had been conducted, that they had asked me whether we had a rifle, and I had answered yes.

And he said that if there would be a trial, and that if I am questioned it would be my right to answer or to refuse to answer. . . .

Mr. Rankin. Your ill feeling towards the FBI was due to the fact that you thought they were trying to obtain evidence to show your husband was guilty in regard to the assassination?

A—Yes.

Mr. Rankin. But you have said since the assassination that you didn't want to believe it, but you had to believe that your husband had killed President Kennedy, is that right?

A—Yes. There were some facts, but not too many, and I didn't know too much about it at that time yet. After all, there are in life some accidental concurrences of circumstances. And it is very difficult to believe in that.

Mr. Rankin. But from what you have learned since that time, you arrived at this conclusion, did you, that your husband had killed the President?

A—Yes. Unfortunately, yes.

Mr. Rankin. And you related those facts that you learned to what you already knew about your life with him and what you knew he had done and appeared to be doing in order to come to that conclusion?

A—Yes.

Mr. Rankin. When you saw your husband on November 23d, at the police station, did you ask him if he had killed President Kennedy?

A—No.

Mr. Rankin. Did you ask him at that time if he had killed Officer Tippit?

A—No. I said, "I don't believe that you did that, and everything will turn out well."

After all, I couldn't accuse him—after all, he was my husband.

Mr. Rankin. And what did he say to that?

A—He said that I should not worry, that everything would

211

turn out well. But I could see by his eyes that he was guilty. Rather, he tried to appear to be brave. However, by his eyes I could tell that he was afraid.

This was just a feeling. It is hard to describe.

Mr. Rankin. Would you help us a little bit by telling us what you saw in his eyes that caused you to think that?

A—He said goodbye to me with his eyes. I knew that. He said that everything would turn out well, but he did not believe it himself.

Mr. Rankin. How could you tell that?

A—I saw it in his eyes.

Mr. Rankin. Did your husband ever at any time say to you that he was responsible or had anything to do with the killing of President Kennedy?

A—After Kennedy—I only saw him once, and he didn't tell me anything, and I didn't see him again.

Mr. Rankin. And did he at any time tell you that he had anything to do with the shooting of Officer Tippit?

A—No.

Mr. Rankin. Did you ever ask your husband why he ran away or tried to escape after the assassination?

A—I didn't ask him about that.

Mr. Rankin. On either November 22d, or Saturday, November 23d, did anyone contact you and advise you that your husband was going to be shot?

A—No. . . .

Mr. Rankin. After the assassination, did the police and FBI and the Secret Service ask you many questions?

A—In the police station there was a routine regular questioning, as always happens. And then after I was with the agents of the Secret Service and the FBI, they asked me many questions, of course—many questions. Sometimes the FBI agents asked me questions which had no bearing or relationship, and if I didn't want to answer they told me that if I wanted to live in this country, I would have to help in this matter, even though they were often irrelevant. That is the FBI.

Mr. Rankin. Do you know who said that to you?

A—Mr. Heitman and Bogoslav, who was an interpreter for the FBI.

Mr. Rankin. You understand that you do not have to tell this Commission in order to stay in this country, don't you, now?

A—Yes.

Mr. Rankin. You are not under any compulsion to tell the Commission here in order to be able to stay in the country.

A—I understand that.

Mr. Rankin. And you have come here because you want to tell us what you could about this matter, is that right?

A—This is my voluntary wish, and no one forced me to do this.

Mr. Rankin. Did these various people from the police and the Secret Service and the FBI treat you courteously when they asked you about the matters that they did, concerning the assassination and things leading up to it?

A—I have a very good opinion about the Secret Service, and the people in the police department treated me very well. But the FBI agents were somehow polite and gruff. Sometimes they would mask a gruff question in a polite form. . . .

Mr. Rankin. Is there anything else about your treatment by law enforcement officials during this period that you would like to tell the Commission about?

A—I think that the FBI agents knew that I was afraid that after everything that had happened I could not remain to live in this country, and they somewhat exploited that for their own purposes, in a very polite form, so that you could not say anything after that. They cannot be accused of anything. They approached it in a very clever, contrived way.

Mr. Rankin. Was there anyone else of the law enforcement officials that you felt treated you in that manner?

A—No. As for the rest, I was quite content. Everyone was very attentive towards me. . . .

Mr. Rankin. Mrs. Oswald, I asked you if you asked your husband about his efforts to escape, why he did that. I will ask you now whether in light of what you said about his seeking notoriety in connection with the assassination, in your opinion how you explain his efforts to escape, which would presumably not give him that notoriety.

A—When he did that, he probably did it with the intention of becoming notorious. But after that, it is probably a normal reaction of a man to try and escape.

Mr. Rankin. You will recall that in the interviews, after the assassination, you first said that you thought your husband didn't do it, do you?

A—I don't remember it, but quite possibly I did say that.

You must understand that now I only speak the truth.

Mr. Rankin. Recently you said that you thought your husband did kill President Kennedy.

A—I now have enough facts to say that.

Mr. Rankin. Can you give us or the Commission an idea generally about when you came to this latter conclusion, that he did kill President Kennedy?

A—Perhaps a week after it all happened, perhaps a little more. The more facts came out, the more convinced I was.

Mr. Rankin. You have stated in some of your interviews that your husband would get on his knees and cry and say that he was lost. Do you recall when this happened?

A—That was in New Orleans.

Mr. Rankin. Was it more than one occasion?

A—When he said that, that was only once.

Mr. Rankin. And do you know what caused him to say that?

213

A—I don't know.

Mr. Rankin. You don't know whether there was some occasion or some happening that caused it?

A—No.

Mr. Rankin. Did your mother-in-law ever indicate that she had some particular evidence, either oral or documentary, that would decide this case?

A—Yes, she always said that she has a pile of papers and many acquaintances.

Mr. Rankin. Did you ever ask her to tell you what it was that would be so decisive about the case?

A—I would have liked to ask her, but I didn't speak any English. And then I didn't believe her. What documents could she have when she had not seen Lee for one year, and she didn't even know we lived in New Orleans?

I think that is just simply idle talk, that she didn't have anything.

Perhaps she does have something.

But I think that it is only she who considers that she has something that might reveal, uncover this.

Mr. Rankin. Has there been any time that you wanted to see your mother-in-law that you have been prevented from doing so?

A—Never.

I don't want to see her, I didn't want to.

Mr. Rankin. Mrs. Oswald, I am going to ask you about differences between you and your mother-in-law, not for the purpose of embarrassing you in any way, but since we are going to ask her to testify it might be helpful to the Commission to know that background.

I hope you will bear with us.

Have you had some differences with your mother-in-law?

A—I am sorry that you will devote your time to questioning her, because you will only be tired and very sick after talking to her. I am very much ashamed to have this kind of relationship to my mother-in-law. I would like to be closer to her and to be on better terms with her. But when you get to know her, you will understand why. I don't think that she can help you.

But if it is a formality, then, of course.

Mr. Rankin. Mrs. Oswald, can you describe for the Commission your differences so the Commission will be able to evaluate those differences?

A—Well, she asserts, for example, that I don't know anything, that I am being forced to say that Lee is guilty in everything, that she knows more.

This is what our differences are.

Mr. Rankin. And have you responded to her when she said those things?

A—She said this by means of newspapers and television. I haven't seen her.

214

I would like to tell her that, but it is impossible to tell her that, because she would scratch my eyes out.

Mr. Rankin. Are there any other differences between you and your mother-in-law that you have not described?

A—No, there are no more.

Mr. Rankin. Do you know of any time that your husband had money in excess of what he obtained from the jobs he was working on?

A—No.

Mr. Rankin. He had his unemployment insurance when he was out of work. Is that right?

A—Yes.

Mr. Rankin. And then he had the earnings from his jobs, is that right?

A—Yes.

Mr. Rankin. Now, beyond those amounts, do you know of any sum of money that he had from any source?

A—No.

Mr. Rankin. Do you know whether he was ever acting as an undercover agent for the FBI.

A—No.

Mr. Rankin. Do you believe that he was at any time?

A—No.

Mr. Rankin. Do you know whether or not he was acting as an agent for the CIA at any time?

A—No.

Mr. Rankin. Do you believe that he was?

A—No.

Mr. Rankin. Did you know Jack Ruby, the man that killed your husband?

A—No.

Mr. Rankin. Before the murder of your husband by Jack Ruby, had you ever known of him?

A—No, never.

Mr. Rankin. Do you know whether your husband knew Jack Ruby before the killing?

A—He was not acquainted with him. Lee did not frequent nightclubs, as the papers said.

Mr. Rankin. How do you know that?

A—He was always with me. He doesn't like other women. He didn't drink. Why should he then go?

Mr. Rankin. Do you know any reason why Jack Ruby killed your husband?

A—About that, Jack Ruby should be questioned.

Mr. Rankin. I have to ask you, Mrs. Oswald.

A—He didn't tell me.

Mr. Rankin. And do you know any reason why he should?

A—I don't know, but it seems to me that he was a sick person at that time, perhaps. At least when I see his picture in the paper now, it is an abnormal face.

Mr. Rankin. Has your husband ever mentioned the name Jack Ruby to you?

A—No.

Mr. Rankin. He never at any time said anything about Jack Ruby that you can recall?

A—No, never. I heard that name for the first time after he killed Lee.

I would like to consult with Mr. Thorne and Mr. Gopadze.

The Chairman. You may.

(Brief recess)

The Chairman. All right.

Mr. Rankin. Mrs. Oswald, would you like to add something to your testimony?

A—Yes. This is in connection with why I left the room. I will tell you why I left the room.

I consulted with my attorney, whether I should bring this up. This is not a secret. The thing is that I have written a letter, even though I have not mailed it yet, to the attorney—to the prosecuting attorney who will prosecute Jack Ruby. I wrote in that letter that even—that if Jack Ruby killed my husband, and I felt that I have a right as the widow of the man he killed to say that, that if he killed him he should be punished for it. But that in accordance with the laws here, the capital punishment, the death penalty is imposed for such a crime, and that I do not want him to be subjected to that kind of a penalty. I do not want another human life to be taken. And I don't want it to be believed because of this letter that I had been acquainted with Ruby, and that I wanted to protect him.

It is simply that it is pity to—I feel sorry for another human life. Because this will not return—bring back to life Kennedy or the others who were killed. But they have their laws, and, of course, I do not have the right to change them. That is only my opinion, and perhaps they will pay some attention to it. That is all. . . .

Mr. Rankin. Now, Mrs. Oswald, we will turn to some period in Russia, and ask you about that for a little while.

Can you tell us the time and place of your birth?

A—I was born on July 17, 1941, in Severo Dvinsk, in the Arkhangelskaya Region.

Mr. Rankin. Who were your parents?

A—Names?

Mr. Rankin. Yes, please.

A—My mother was Clogia Vasilyevna Proosakova. She was a laboratory assistant.

Mr. Rankin. And your father?

A—And I had a stepfather. I had no father. I never knew him.

Mr. Rankin. Who did you live with as a child?

A—With my stepfather, with my mother, and sometimes with my grandmother—grandmother on my mother's side.

Mr. Rankin. Did you live with your grandparents before you went back to live with your mother and your stepfather?

A—Yes, I lived with my grandmother until I was approximately five years old.

Mr. Rankin. And then you moved to live with your mother and your stepfather, did you?

A—Yes.

Mr. Rankin. And was that in Leningrad?

A—After the war, we lived in Moldavia for some time. After the war it was easier to live there, better to live there. And then we returned to Leningrad where we lived with my stepfather's mother—also with my half brother and half sister.

Mr. Rankin. What was your stepfather's business?

A—He was an electrician in a power station in Leningrad.

Mr. Rankin. Did you have brothers and sisters?

A—Yes.

Mr. Rankin. How many?

A—One brother, one sister—from my mother's second marriage.

Mr. Rankin. How old were they?

A—How old are they, or were they?

Mr. Rankin. Are they—I mean in comparison with your age. Were they three or four years older than you?

A—My brother is 5 years younger than I am. My sister is probably 9 years younger than I am. About four years between brother and sister.

Mr. Rankin. Do you know whether your stepfather was a member of the Communist Party?

A—No.

Mr. Rankin. That is, you don't know, or you know he was not?

A—No, I know that he was not a member.

Mr. Rankin. Did you live for a period with your mother alone?

A—No. After my mother's death, I continued to live with my stepfather, and later went to live in Minsk, with my uncle— my mother's brother.

Mr. Rankin. What was your stepfather's name?

A—Alexandr Ivanovich Medvedev.

Mr. Rankin. When did you leave the home of your stepfather?

A—In 1961. No—1959.

Mr. Rankin. What was your grandfather's occupation?

A—On my mother's side?

Mr. Rankin. Yes.

A—He was a ship's captain.

Mr. Rankin. Was he a member of the Communist Party?

A—No. He died shortly after the war.

Mr. Rankin. Which war?

A—Second.

Mr. Rankin. Did you get along well with your grandparents?

A—Yes, I was their favorite.

Mr. Rankin. Did you get along with your stepfather?

A—No. I was not a good child. I was too fresh with him.

Mr. Rankin. Did your mother and your stepfather move to Zguritsa?

A—That is in Moldavia, where we lived. That is after the war. It was a very good life there. They still had some kulaks, a lot of food, and we lived very well.

After the war, people lived there pretty well, but they were dekulakized subsequently.

By the way, I don't understand all of that, because these people worked with their own hands all their lives. I was very sorry when I heard that everything had been taken away from them and they had been sent somewhere to Siberia where after living in the south it would be very cold.

Mr. Rankin. Did your mother have any occupation?

A—Yes, laboratory assistant—I said that.

Mr. Rankin. Was she a member of the Communist Party?

A—No.

Mr. Rankin. Do you recall when your mother died?

A—In 1957.

Mr. Rankin. Did you receive a pension after your mother's death?

A—Yes.

Mr. Rankin. How much was it?

A—All children received pensions.

We received for it 3520 rubles, the old rubles.

Mr. Rankin. Was that called a children's pension?

A—Yes. It was paid up to majority, up to the age of 18.

Mr. Rankin. And was it paid to you directly or to your stepfather?

A—It was paid to me directly.

Mr. Rankin. Did your brother and sister get a similar pension?

A—Yes.

Mr. Rankin. Did your stepfather adopt you?

A—No, I was not adopted.

Mr. Rankin. What was your relationship with your half brother? Did you get along with him?

A—I loved them very much, and they loved me.

Mr. Rankin. And your half sister, too?

A—Yes. They are very good children. Not like me.

Mr. Rankin. Will you tell us what schools you went to?

A—At first I went to school in Moldavia, and later in Leningrad, in a girl's school and then after finishing school I studied in a pharmaceutical institute—pharmaceutical school, rather than institute.

Mr. Rankin. Where was the pharmaceutical school?

A—In Leningrad.

Mr. Rankin. Did you go through high school before you went to the pharmaceutical school?

A—Yes. . . .

Mr. Rankin. Were you a good student?

A—I was capable but lazy. I never spent much time studying. You know, everything came to me very easily. Sometimes my ability saved me. My language, you know—I talk a lot, and get a good grade.

Mr. Rankin. Did you work part-time while you were going to school?

A—Yes. The money which I received on the pension was not enough, and therefore I had to work as well as study.

Mr. Rankin. And what did you do in working?

A—At first I worked in a school cafeteria, school lunchroom. This was good for me, because I also got enough to eat that way.

And then I felt the work was not for me, that it was too restricted, and then I worked in a pharmacy. Then when I graduated I worked in a pharmacy as a full-fledged pharmacist—as a pharmacist's assistant.

Mr. Rankin. Before you graduated, how much were you paid for your work?

A—I think I received 36 per month—this is new rubles—at that time it was still 360 old rubles. But I could eat there three times a day. And then this was a lunchroom that was part of a large restaurant where everyone liked me and I always was treated to all sorts of tidbits and candy. I remember they had some busboys there who always saved something for me.

Mr. Rankin. Did you save any money while you were working before you graduated?

A—I don't know how to save money. I like to make presents.

Mr. Rankin. Where did you work after you graduated?

A—I was assigned to work in Leningrad, but my stepfather didn't want me to remain with him because he thought perhaps he would marry again, and, therefore, I left.

But he hasn't married up until now.

Mr. Rankin. I hand you Exhibit 20, and ask you if you know what that is.

A—This is my diploma. My goodness, what did they do with my diploma?

I can't work with it. The government seal is missing. Who will give me a new diploma?

Mr. Rankin. Mrs. Oswald, I want to explain to you—the Commission hasn't done anything to your diploma. We are informed that——

A—They should have treated it a little more carefully, though.

Mr. Rankin. The process was trying to determine fingerprints. It wasn't our action.

A—There must be many fingerprints on there. All of my

teachers and everybody that ever looked at it. I am sorry—it is a pity for my diploma. . . .

Mr. Rankin. In this job that you obtained after you left the school, what were your duties?

A—When I worked in the pharmacy?

Mr. Rankin. Yes.

A—I worked in a hospital pharmacy. I prepared prescriptions. After the rounds every day, the doctors prescribed prescriptions, and the nurses of each department of the hospital enter that in a book, and turn it over to the pharmacy for preparation, where we again transcribed it from the nurses' book as a prescription and prepared it.

Mr. Rankin. Were you assigned to a particular job or did you go out and get the job? How was that arranged?

A—Generally upon graduation there is an assignment. I was sent to work to a drug warehouse in Leningrad. But this work was not very interesting, because everything was in packages. It is more of a warehousing job. And, therefore, if I had wanted to change I could have changed to any pharmacy. This assignment is only performed in order to guarantee that the graduate has a job. But the graduate can go to work somewhere else.

Mr. Rankin. How long did you stay in this first job?

A—I was there for three days, which is a probationary period, intended to have the employee familiarize himself with his duties. I didn't like that work, and I went to Minsk, and worked there. I worked there in my own specialty with pleasure. But the reference which I received after I was going to the United States was not very good, because they were very dissatisfied with the fact that I was going to the United States. They could not understand how could it be that a good worker could leave. . . .

Mr. Rankin. Did you belong to any organizations during this period in Minsk?

A—First I was a member of the Trade Union. Then I joined the Comsomol, but I was discharged after one year.

Mr. Rankin. Do you know why you were discharged?

A—I paid my membership dues regularly, and at first they didn't know who I was or what I was, but after they found out that I had married an American and was getting ready to go to the United States, I was discharged from the Comsomol. They said that I had anti-Soviet views, even though I had no anti-Soviet views of any kind.

Mr. Rankin. Do you think that they thought you had anti-Soviet views because you married an American?

A—They didn't say that.

Mr. Rankin. Did they give any reason, other than the fact that you had them?

A—They never gave that as a direct reason, because the Soviet Government was not against marrying an American.

But every small official wants to keep his place, and he is afraid of any troubles. I think it was sort of insurance.

Mr. Rankin. Was there any kind of a hearing about your being let out of the Comsomol?

A—Oh, yes.

Mr. Rankin. Did you attend?

A—I didn't go there, and they discharged me without me— I was very glad. There was even a reporter there from Comsomol paper, Comsomol Pravda, I think. He tried to shame me quite strongly—for what, I don't know. And he said that he would write about this in the paper, and I told him "Go ahead and write."

But he didn't write anything, because, after all, what could he write?

Mr. Rankin. Did you make any objection to being removed from the Comsomol?

A—No.

Mr. Rankin. Did you belong to any social clubs there?

A—No.

Mr. Rankin. Did you belong to any culture groups?

A—No.

Mr. Rankin. Did you go out with groups of students in the evening?

A—Of course.

Mr. Rankin. After you came to the United States, did you correspond with some of these friends?

A—Yes, but these were not the same friends. They were generally some girl friends before I was married and some friends we made later.

Mr. Rankin. Did you have a social life there at Minsk?

A—Of course.

Mr. Rankin. What did that social life consist of? Did you go to parties or to the opera or theater, or what?

A—Sometimes we met at the home of some friends. Of course we went to the opera, to the theater, to concerts, to the circus. To a restaurant.

Mr. Rankin. When did you first meet Lee Oswald?

A—The first time when I went to a dance, to a party. And there I met Lee.

Mr. Rankin. Do you recall the date?

A—On March 4th.

Mr. Rankin. What year?

A—1961.

Mr. Rankin. Where did you meet him?

A—In Minsk.

Mr. Rankin. Yes—but can you tell us the place?

A—In the Palace of Trade Unions.

Mr. Rankin. What kind of a place is that? Is that where there are public meetings?

A—Sometimes they do have meetings there. Sometimes it is also rented by some institutes who do not have their own halls for parties.

Mr. Rankin. They have dances?

A—Yes. Every Saturday and Sunday.

Mr. Rankin. Did someone introduce you to him?

A—Yes.

Mr. Rankin. Who introduced you?

A—I had gone there with my friends from the medical institute, and one of them introduced me to Lee.

Mr. Rankin. What was his name?

A—Yuri Mereginsky.

Mr. Rankin. Do you know by what name Lee Oswald was introduced to you?

A—Everyone there called him Alec, at his place of work, because Lee is an unusual, cumbersome name. For Russians it was easier—this was easier.

Mr. Rankin. Is Alec a name close to Lee, as far as the Russian language is concerned?

A—A little. Somewhat similar.

Mr. Rankin. Did you know that Lee Oswald was an American when you first met him?

A—I found that out at the end of that party, towards the end of that party, when I was first introduced to him, I didn't know that.

Mr. Rankin. Did that make any difference?

A—It was more interesting, of course. You don't meet Americans very often.

Mr. Rankin. After this first meeting, did you meet him a number of times?

A—Yes.

Mr. Rankin. Can you describe just briefly how you met him and saw him?

A—After the first meeting he asked me where he could meet me again. I said that perhaps some day I will come back here again, to the Palace. About a week later I came there again with my girl friend, and he was there.

Mr. Rankin. And did he have a period that he was in the hospital there?

A—I had arranged to meet with him again. I had already given him a telephone number. But he went to a hospital and he called me from there. We had arranged to meet on a Friday, and he called from the hospital and said he couldn't because he was in the hospital and I should come there, if I could.

Mr. Rankin. Did you learn what was wrong with him then?

A—He was near the ear, nose and throat section and it seems that he had something wrong with his ears and also the glands or polyps.

Mr. Rankin. Did you visit him regularly for some period of time?

A—Yes, quite frequently, because I felt sorry for him being there alone.

Mr. Rankin. And did you observe a scar on his left arm?

A—He had a scar, but I found that out only after we were married.

Mr. Rankin. What did you find out about that scar?

A—When I asked him about it, he became very angry and asked me never to ask about that again.

Mr. Rankin. Did he ever explain to you what caused the scar?

A—No.

Mr. Rankin. Did you ever learn what caused the scar?

A—I found out here, now, recently.

Mr. Rankin. Did you learn that he had tried to commit suicide at some time?

A—I found that out now.

Mr. Rankin. During the time Lee Oswald was courting you, did he talk about America at all?

A—Yes, of course.

Mr. Rankin. What do you recall that he said about it?

A—At that time, of course, he was homesick, and perhaps he was sorry for having come to Russia. He said many good things. He said that his home was warmer and that people lived better.

Mr. Rankin. Did he talk about returning?

A—Then? No.

Mr. Rankin. Did he describe the life in America as being very attractive?

A—Yes. At least in front of others he always defended it.

Mr. Rankin. Did he——

A—It is strange to reconcile this. When he was there he was saying good things about America.

Mr. Rankin. And when he was talking only to you, did he do that, too?

A—Yes.

Mr. Rankin. Before you were married, did you find out anything about his plans to return to America?

A—No.

Mr. Rankin. Did you learn anything before you were married about the fact that there might be some doubt whether he could return to the United States?

A—Once before we were married we had a talk and I asked him whether he could return to the United States if he wanted to, and he said no, he could not.

Mr. Rankin. Did he tell you why?

A—No. At that time, he didn't. He said that when he had arrived, he had thrown his passport on a table and said that he would not return any more to the United States. He thought that they would not forgive him such an act.

223

Mr. Rankin. Before you were married, did you ever say to him you would like to go to the United States?

A—No.

Mr. Rankin. Can you tell us what attracted you to him?

A—I don't know. First, the fact that he was—he didn't look like others. You could see he was an American. He was very neat, very polite, not the way he was here, not as you know him here. And it seemed that he would be a good family man. And he was good.

Mr. Rankin. Did you talk about many things when you were together, when he was courting you?

A—We talked about everything, about the moon and the weather.

Mr. Rankin. Where was he living at that time?

A—In Minsk. By the way, on the same street where I lived.

Mr. Rankin. Did he have an apartment?

A—Yes. By the way, this was the same apartment where I had dreamed to live. I didn't know about it yet. It had a very beautiful balcony, terrace. I would look at that building sometimes and say it would be good to visit in that building, visit someone there, but I never thought that I would wind up living there.

Mr. Rankin. Can you describe the number of rooms there were in his apartment?

A—We had a small room—one room, kitchen, foyer, and bathroom. A large terrace, balcony.

Mr. Rankin. Do you know what he paid for rent?

A—For two it was quite sufficient. Seven and a-half rubles per month.

Mr. Rankin. Wasn't that pretty cheap for such a nice apartment?

A—Yes, it was cheap.

Mr. Rankin. Was this apartment nicer than most in this city?

A—No, in that city they have good apartments because the houses are new. That is, on a Russian scale, of course. You cannot compare it to private houses people live in here.

Mr. Rankin. Did he have an automobile?

A—Oh, no. In Russia this is a problem. In Russia it is difficult to have an automobile.

Mr. Rankin. Did he have a television set?

A—No. Only a radio receiver, a record player.

Mr. Rankin. Did you have a telephone?

A—No—I don't like television.

Mr. Rankin. Why?

A—The programs are not always interesting, and you can get into a stupor just watching television. It is better to go to the movies.

Mr. Rankin. What was his occupation at this time?

A—He worked in a radio plant in Minsk.

Mr. Rankin. Do you know what his work was?

224

A—As an ordinary laborer—metal worker. From that point of view, he was nothing special. I had a greater choice in the sense that many of my friends were engineers and doctors. But that is not the main thing.

Mr. Rankin. Did others with a similar job have similar apartments?

A—The house in which we lived belonged to the factory in which Lee worked. But, of course, no one had a separate apartment for only two persons. I think that Lee had been given better living conditions, better than others, because he was an American. If Lee had been Russian, and we would have had two children, we could not have obtained a larger apartment. But since he was an American, we would have obtained the larger one. It seems to me that in Russia they treat foreigners better than they should. It would be better if they treated Russians better. Not all foreigners are better than the Russians.

Mr. Rankin. Did he say whether he liked this job?

A—No, he didn't like it.

Mr. Rankin. What did he say about it?

A—First of all, he was being ordered around by someone. He didn't like that.

Mr. Rankin. Anything else?

A—And the fact that it was comparatively dirty work.

Mr. Rankin. Did he say anything about the Russian system, whether he liked it or not?

A—Yes. He didn't like it. Not everything, but some things.

Mr. Rankin. Did he say anything about Communists and whether he liked that?

A—He didn't like Russian Communists. He said that they joined the party not because of the ideas, but in order to obtain better living conditions and to get the benefit of them.

Mr. Rankin. Did it appear to you that he had become disenchanted with the Soviet system?

A—Yes, he had expected much more when he first arrived.

Mr. Rankin. Did he ever tell you why he came to Russia?

A—Yes. He said he had read a great deal about Russia, he was interested in seeing the country, which was the first in the Socialist camp about which much had been said, and he wanted to see it with his own eyes. And, therefore, he wanted to be not merely a tourist, who is being shown only the things that are good, but he wanted to live among the masses and see.

But when he actually did, it turned out to be quite difficult. . . .

Mr. Rankin. Now, do you recall that you said to your husband at any time that he was just studying Marxism so he could get attention?

A—Yes.

Mr. Rankin. In order to cause him not to be so involved in some of these ideas, did you laugh at some of his ideas that he told you about, and make fun of him?

225

A—Of course.

Mr. Rankin. Did he react to that?

A—He became very angry.

Mr. Rankin. And did he ask you at one time, or sometimes, not to make fun of his ideas?

A—Yes.

Mr. Rankin. Now, returning to the period in Russia, while your husband was courting you, did you talk to him, he talk to you, about his childhood?

A—No, not very much. Only in connection with photographs, where he was a boy in New York, in the zoo. Then in the Army—there is a snapshot taken right after he joined the Army.

Mr. Rankin. Did he tell you about anything he resented about his childhood?

A—He said it was hard for him during his childhood, when he was a boy, because there was a great age difference between him and Robert, and Robert was in some sort of a private school. He also wanted to have a chance to study, but his mother was working, and he couldn't get into a private school, and he was very sorry about it.

Mr. Rankin. In talking about that, did he indicate a feeling that he had not had as good an opportunity as his brother Robert?

A—Yes.

Mr. Rankin. When he talked about his service in the Marines, did he tell you much about what he did?

A—He didn't talk much about it, because there wasn't very much there of interest to me. But he was satisfied.

Mr. Rankin. Did he indicate that he was unhappy about his service with the Marines?

A—No, he had good memories of his service in the Army. He said that the food was good and that sometimes evenings he had a chance to go out.

Mr. Rankin. Did he say anything about his mother during this period of time?

A—This was before we were married. I had once asked Lee whether he had a mother, and he said he had no mother. I started to question him as to what had happened, what happened to her, and he said that I should not question him about it.

After we were married, he told me that he had not told me the truth, that he did have a mother, but that he didn't love her very much.

Mr. Rankin. Did he tell you why he didn't love her?

A—No.

Mr. Rankin. Do you recall anything more he said about his brother Robert at that time?

A—He said that he had a good wife, that he had succeeded fairly well in life, that he was smart and capable.

226

Mr. Rankin. Did he say anything about having any affection for him?

A—Yes, he loved Robert. He said that when Robert married Vada that his mother had been against the marriage and that she had made a scene, and this was one of the reasons he didn't like his mother.

Mr. Rankin. Did he say anything about his half brother, by the name of Pic—I guess the last name was Pic—Robert Pic?

A—He said that he had a half brother by the name of Pic from his mother's first marriage, but he didn't enlarge upon the subject. It is only that I knew he had a half brother by that name.

He said that at one time they lived with this John Pic and his wife, but that his wife and the mother frequently had arguments, quarrels. He said it was hard for him to witness these scenes, it was unpleasant.

Mr. Rankin. Did you regard your husband's wage or salary at Minsk as high for the work he was doing?

A—No. He received as much as the others in similar jobs.

Mr. Rankin. Did your husband have friends in Minsk when you first met him?

A—Yes.

Mr. Rankin. How did he seem to get along with these friends?

A—He had a very good relationship with them.

Mr. Rankin. Did he discuss any of them with you?

A—Yes.

Mr. Rankin. Will you tell us when you married your husband?

A—April 30, 1961.

Mr. Rankin. Was there a marriage ceremony?

A—Not in a church, of course. But in the institution called Zags, where we were registered.

Mr. Rankin. Was anyone else present at the ceremony?

A—Yes, our friends were there.

Mr. Rankin. Who else was there?

A—No one besides my girlfriends and some acquaintances. My uncle and aunt were busy preparing the house, and they were not there for that reason.

Mr. Rankin. After you were married did you go to live in your husband's apartment there?

A—Yes.

Mr. Rankin. Did you buy any new furniture?

A—Yes.

Mr. Rankin. When was your baby born?

A—February 15, 1962.

Mr. Rankin. What is her name?

A—June Lee Oswald.

Mr. Rankin. Did you stop working before the birth of the baby?

A—Yes.

Mr. Rankin. Did you return to work after the baby was born?

A—No.

Mr. Rankin. How did you and your husband get along during the period that you were in Minsk, after you were married?

A—We lived well. . . .

Mr. Rankin. Did your husband engage in any Communist Party activities while he was in the Soviet Union?

A—Not at all—absolutely not.

Mr. Rankin. Do you know whether he was a member of any organization there?

A—I think that he was also a member of a trade union, as everybody who works belongs to a trade union. Then he had a card from a hunting club, but he never visited it. He joined the club, apparently.

Mr. Rankin. Did he go hunting while he was there?

A—We only went once, with him and with my friends.

Mr. Rankin. Was that when he went hunting for squirrels?

A—If he marked it down in his notebook that he went hunting for squirrels, he never did. Generally they wanted to kill a squirrel when we went there, or some sort of a bird, in order to boast about it, but they didn't.

Mr. Rankin. Were there any times while he was in the Soviet Union after your marriage that you didn't know where he went?

A—No.

Mr. Rankin. When did you first learn that he was planning to try to go back to the United States?

A—After we were married, perhaps a month later.

Mr. Rankin. Did you discuss the matter at that time?

A—We didn't discuss it—we talked about it—because we didn't make any specific plans.

Mr. Rankin. Do you recall what you said about it then?

A—I said, "Well, if we will go, we will go. If we remain, it doesn't make any difference to me. If we go to China, I will also go."

Mr. Rankin. Did you and your husband make a trip to Moscow in connection with your plans to go to the United States?

A—Yes. We went to the American Embassy.

Mr. Rankin. Did your husband make a trip to Moscow alone before that? About his passport?

A—He didn't go alone. He actually left a day early and the following morning I was to come there.

Mr. Rankin. I understand that he didn't get any permission to make this trip to Moscow away from Minsk. Do you know whether that is true?

A—I don't know about this. I know that he bought a ticket and he made the flight.

Mr. Rankin. According to the practice, then, would he be

permitted to go to Moscow from Minsk without the permission of the authorities?

A—I don't know whether he had the right to go to Moscow. Perhaps he did, because he had a letter requesting him to visit the Embassy. But he could not go to another city without permission of the authorities.

Mr. Rankin. When the decision was made to come to the United States, did you discuss that with your family?

A—First when we made the decision, we didn't know what would come of it later, what would happen further. And Lee asked me not to talk about it for the time being.

Mr. Rankin. Later, did you discuss it with your family?

A—Later when I went to visit the Embassy, my aunt found out about it, because they had telephoned from work, and she was offended because I had not told her about it. They were against our plan.

Mr. Rankin. Did you tell your friends about your plans after you were trying to arrange to go to the United States?

A—Yes.

Mr. Rankin. Was there some opposition by people in the Soviet Union to your going to the United States?

A—Somewhat. You can't really call that opposition. There were difficult times.

Mr. Rankin. Can you tell us what you mean by that?

A—First, the fact that I was excluded from the Comsomol. This was not a blow for me, but it was, of course, unpleasant. Then all kinds of meetings were arranged and members of the various organizations talked to me. My aunt and uncle would not talk to me for a long time.

Mr. Rankin. And that was all because you were planning to go to the United States?

A—Yes.

Mr. Rankin. Were you hospitalized and received medical treatment because of all of these things that happened at that time, about your leaving?

A—No.
What?

Mr. Rankin. Did you have any nervous disorder in 1961 that you were hospitalized for?

A—I was nervous, but I didn't go to the hospital. I am nervous now, too.

Mr. Rankin. Then you went to Kharkov on a vacation, didn't you?

A—Yes.
If you have a record of the fact that I was in the hospital, yes, I was. But I was in the hospital only as a precaution because I was pregnant. I have a negative Rh factor, blood Rh factor, and if Lee had a positive they thought—they thought that he had positive—even though he doesn't. It turned out that we both had the same Rh factor. . . .

229

Mr. Rankin. Were you aware of your husband's concern about being prosecuted with regard to his returning to the United States?

A—Yes, he told me about it. He told me about it, that perhaps he might even be arrested.

Mr. Rankin. Was he fearful of prosecution by the Soviet Union or by the United States?

A—The United States.

Mr. Rankin. Do you recall any time that the Soviet authorities visited your husband while you were trying to go to the United States?

A—No.

Mr. Rankin. What was the occasion for your traveling to Kharkov in 1961?

A—My mother's sister lives there, and she had invited me to come there for a rest because I was on vacation.

Mr. Rankin. Did anyone go with you?

A—No.

Mr. Rankin. How long did you stay?

A—Three weeks, I think.

Mr. Rankin. Did you write to your husband while you were gone?

A—Yes.

Mr. Rankin. Was your aunt's name Mikhilova?

A—Mikhilova, yes.

Mr. Rankin. Was there any reason why you took this vacation alone and not with your husband?

A—He was working at that time. He didn't have a vacation. He wanted to go with me, but he could not.

Mr. Rankin. Do you know what delayed your departure to the United States?

A—No.

Mr. Rankin. There was some correspondence with the Embassy about your husband returning alone. Did you ever discuss that?

A—Yes.

Mr. Rankin. What did he say about that, and what did you say?

A—He said that if he did go alone, he feared that they would not permit me to leave, and that he would, therefore, wait for me.

Mr. Rankin. What did you say?

A—I thanked him for the fact that he wanted to wait for me.

Mr. Rankin. Where did you stay in Moscow when you went there about your visa?

A—At first, we stopped at the Hotel Ostamkino. And then we moved to the Hotel Berlin, formerly Savoy.

Mr. Rankin. How long were you there on that trip?

A—I think about 10 days, perhaps a little longer. . . .

Mr. Rankin. Do you know any reason why your husband

was permitted to stay in the Soviet Union when he first came there?

A—I don't know.

Mr. Rankin. Do you know why——

A—Many were surprised at that—here and in Russia.

Mr. Rankin. Do you know why he went to Minsk, or was allowed to go to Minsk?

A—He was sent to Minsk.

Mr. Rankin. By that, you mean by direction of the government?

A—Yes.

Mr. Rankin. Did your husband do any writing while he was in the Soviet Union that you know of?

A—Yes, he wrote a diary about his stay in the Soviet Union. . . .

Mr. Rankin. Do you recall that you or your husband were contacted at any time in the Soviet Union by Soviet intelligence people?

A—No.

Mr. Rankin. During the time your husband was in the Soviet Union, did you observe any indication of mental disorder?

A—No.

Mr. Rankin. How did he appear to get along with people that he knew in the Soviet Union?

A—Very well. At least, he had friends there. He didn't have any here.

Mr. Rankin. How much time did you spend in Amsterdam on the way to the United States?

A—Two or three days, it seems to me.

Mr. Rankin. What did you do there?

A—Walked around the city, did some sightseeing.

Mr. Rankin. Did anybody visit you there?

A—No.

Mr. Rankin. Did you visit anyone?

A—No.

Mr. Rankin. What hotel did you stay in?

A—We didn't stop at a hotel. We stopped at a place where they rent apartments. The address was given to us in the American Embassy.

Mr. Rankin. Do you recall what you paid in the way of rent?

A—No, Lee paid it. I don't know.

Mr. Rankin. How did your husband spend his time when he was aboard the ship?

A—I was somewhat upset because he was a little ashamed to walk around with me, because I wasn't dressed as well as the other girls. Basically, I stayed in my cabin while Lee went to the movies and they have different games there. I don't know what he did there. . . .

Mr. Rankin. Mrs. Oswald, can you tell us what your husband was reading in the Soviet Union after you were married, that you recall?

A—He read the Daily Worker newspaper in the English language.

Mr. Rankin. Anything else?

A—It seems to me something like Marxism, Leninism, also in the English language. He did not have any choice of English books for reading purposes.

Mr. Rankin. Was he reading anything in Russian at that time?

A—Yes, newspapers, and nothing else.

Mr. Rankin. No library books?

A—No. It was very hard for him.

Mr. Rankin. Did he go to any schools while he was in the Soviet Union that you know of?

A—No. . . .

Mr. Rankin. Some of the Commissioners have a question or two, or a few questions. If you will permit them, they would like to address them to you.

Representative Boggs. Mrs. Oswald, this question has already been asked you, but I would like to ask it again.

I gather that you have reached the conclusion in your own mind that your husband killed President Kennedy.

A—Regretfully, yes.

Representative Boggs. During the weeks and months prior to the assassination—and I think this question has also been asked—did you ever at any time hear your late husband express any hostility towards President Kennedy?

A—No.

Representative Boggs. What motive would you ascribe to your husband in killing President Kennedy?

A—As I saw the documents that were being read to me, I came to the conclusion that he wanted in any—by any means, good or bad, to get into history. But now that I have heard a part of the translation of some of the documents, I think that there was some political foundation to it, a foundation of which I am not aware.

Representative Boggs. By that, do you mean that your husband acted in concert with someone else?

A—No, only alone.

Representative Boggs. You are convinced that his action was his action alone, that he was influenced by no one else?

A—Yes, I am convinced.

Representative Boggs. Did you consider your husband a Communist?

A—He told me when we were in New Orleans that he was a Communist, but I didn't believe him, because I said, "What kind of a Communist are you if you don't like the Communists in Russia?"

Representative Boggs. Did he like the Communists in the United States?

232

A—He considered them to be on a higher level and more conscious than the Communists in Russia.

Representative Boggs. Did you consider your husband a normal man in the usual sense of the term?

A—He was always a normal man, but where it concerned his ideas, and he did not introduce me to his ideas, I did not consider him normal.

Representative Boggs. Maybe I used the wrong terminology. Did you consider him mentally sound?

A—Yes; he was smart and capable. Only he did not use his capabilities in the proper direction. He was not deprived of reason—he was not a man deprived of reason.

Representative Boggs. Thank you, Mr. Chairman. Thank you.

The Chairman. Senator Cooper, did you have any questions to ask?

A—No one knows the truth, no one can read someone else's thoughts, as I could not read Lee's thoughts. But that is only my opinion.

Senator Cooper. Mrs. Oswald, some of the questions that I ask you you may have answered—because I have been out at times.

I believe you have stated that your husband at times expressed opposition to or dislike of the United States or of its political or economic system, is that correct?

A—As far as I know, he expressed more dissatisfaction with economic policy, because as to the political matters he did not enlighten me as to his political thoughts.

Senator Cooper. Did he ever suggest to you or to anyone in your presence that the economic system of the United States should be changed, and did he suggest any means for changing it?

A—He never proposed that, but from his conversations it followed that it would be necessary to change it. But he didn't propose any methods.

Senator Cooper. Did he ever say to you or anyone in your presence that the system might be changed if officials were changed or authorities of our country were changed?

A—No, he never said that to me.

Senator Cooper. Did he ever express to you any hostility toward any particular official of the United States?

A—I know that he didn't like Walker, but I don't know whether you could call him an official.

Senator Cooper. May I ask if you ever heard anyone express to him hostility towards President Kennedy?

A—No, never. . . .

The above testimony was given by Mrs. Oswald, the wife of Lee Harvey Oswald, during a four-day appearance before the Commission in February, 1963. She was subsequently recalled before the Commission in June for the following testimony:

Mr. Rankin. Mrs. Oswald, we would like to have you tell about the incident in regard to Mr. Nixon that you have told about since we had your last examination. Could you tell us what you know about that incident, first, when it happened insofar as you can recall?

A—I am very sorry I didn't mention this before. I prefer that you ask me the questions and that will help me to remember what there is.

Mr. Rankin. Can you tell us what Mr. Nixon it is, was it Richard Nixon, the former Vice President of the United States that you were referring to?

A—I only know one Nixon and I think it was Richard Nixon which it was all about.

Mr. Rankin. Can you fix the date when this occurrence did happen? Approximately?

A—It was a weekend before he went to New Orleans and after the Walker business I think. But I might be mistaken as to whether or not this was a weekend because I am basing this on the fact that my husband was home and he wasn't—wasn't always employed and he was at home weekdays as well sometimes, so I can't be entirely sure that it was a weekend.

Mr. Rankin. Can you place the place of the various homes you had that this happened?

A—Neely Street.

Mr. Rankin. At the Neely Street house. Do you know what time of day it occurred?

A—This was in the morning.

Mr. Rankin. Who was there?

A—Just my husband and me.

Mr. Rankin. Now, will you describe in detail just what happened. Mrs. Oswald, when you are answering the questions will you try to break up your answers, and let the interpreter try to translate; I think it will be helpful in not having the interpreter have to try to remember everything of a long answer. Do you understand me? . . .

A—It was early in the morning and my husband went out to get a newspaper, then he came in and sat reading the newspaper. I didn't pay any attention to him because I was occupied with the housework.

Then he got dressed and put on a good suit. I saw that he took a pistol. I asked him where he was going, and why he was getting dressed. He answered, "Nixon is coming. I want to go and have a look." I said, "I know how you look," or rather, "I know how you customarily look, how you customarily take a look," because I saw he was taking the pistol with him rather than I know how you look in the sense that you are dressed, how you look at things is what I mean.

Mr. Rankin. Had it come to your attention, Mrs. Oswald, that Mr. Nixon was going to be in Dallas prior to that time?

234

A—No; it did not.

Mr. Rankin. Had you seen anything in the newspapers or heard anything over the radio or television?

A—No; we didn't have TV. I didn't see this in the newspaper.

Mr. Dulles. Do you know what newspaper it was in which your husband read this report?

A—No; Dallas Morning News maybe. It was a morning paper.

Mr. Rankin. Do you know whether there was any information at all in the papers about Mr. Nixon planning to come to Dallas about that time?

A—I didn't ever read the newspaper and I did not know; therefore, didn't know whether there was any information in the newspapers prior to this time about Vice President Nixon's arrival in Dallas. . . .

Mr. Rankin. What did your husband say that day about Richard Nixon, when he got this gun and dressed up. Did he tell you anything about him?

A—No; I just didn't know what to do, you know.

Mr. Rankin. How did you know he was interested in doing something about Mr. Nixon at that time?

A—My husband just said that Nixon is coming to Dallas.

Mr. Rankin. Then what did you do?

A—First I didn't know what to do. I wanted to prevent him from going out.

Mr. Rankin. Did you say anything to him?

A—I called him into the bathroom and I closed the door and I wanted to prevent him and then I started to cry. And I told him that he shouldn't do this, that he had promised me.

Mr. Rankin. Are you referring to his promise to you that you described in your prior testimony after the Walker incident?

A—Yes; that was the promise.

Mr. Rankin. Do you recall the bathroom, how the door closes? Does it close into the bathroom on Neely Street or from the outside in?

A—I don't remember now. I don't remember. I only remember that it was something to do with the bathroom.

Mr. Rankin. Did you lock him into the bathroom?

A—I can't remember precisely.

Mr. Rankin. Do you recall how the locks were on the bathroom door there?

A—I can't recall. We had several apartments and I might be confusing one apartment with the other.

Mr. Rankin. Is it your testimony that you made it impossible for him to get out if he wanted to?

A—I don't remember.

Representative Ford. Did he try to get out of the bathroom?

A—I remember that I held him. We actually struggled for

several minutes and then he quieted down. I remember that I told him that if he goes out it would be better for him to kill me than to go out.

Mr. Dulles. He is quite a big man and you are a small woman.

A—No; he is not a big man. He is not strong.

Mr. Dulles. Well, he was 5 feet 9, and you are how tall?

A—When he is very upset, my husband is very upset he is not strong and when I want to and when I collect all my forces and want to do something very badly I am stronger than he is.

Mr. Dulles. You meant mentally or physically?

A—I am not strong but, you know, there is a certain balance of forces between us.

Mr. Dulles. Do you think it was persuasion, your persuasion of him or the physical form or both that prevented him from going?

A—I don't think it was physically, physical prevention because if he—I couldn't keep him from going out if he really wanted to. It might have been that he was just trying to test me. He was the kind of person who could try and wound somebody in that way. Possibly he didn't want to go out at all but was just doing this all as a sort of joke, not really as a joke but rather to simply wound me, to make me feel bad. . . .

Mr. Rankin. Had your husband said anything before or did he say anything at that time in regard to Mr. Nixon showing any hostility, friendship, or anything else?

A—Showing any hostility or friendship toward Mr. Nixon?

Mr. Rankin. Yes; toward Nixon.

A—I don't remember him saying anything—I don't remember but he didn't tell me. I don't remember him saying anything of that sort. I only remember the next day he told me that Nixon did not come. Excuse me. . . .

Mr. Rankin. What else happened about this incident beyond what you have told us?

A—He took off his suit and stayed home all day reading a book. He gave me the pistol and I hid it under the mattress.

Mr. Rankin. Did you say anything more than you have told us to him about this matter at that time?

A—I closed the front door to the building that day and when we were quarreling about—when we were struggling over the question of whether or not he should go out I said a great deal to him.

Mr. Rankin. What did you say to him then?

A—I don't remember.

Mr. Rankin. Just tell us in substance?

A—I really don't remember now. I only remember that I told him that I am sorry of all these pranks of his and especially after the one with General Walker, and he had promised me, I told him that he had promised me——

Mr. Rankin. Did he say anything in answer to that?

A—I don't remember.

Mr. Dulles. As I recall, in your previous testimony there was some indication that you had said that if he did the Walker type of thing again you would notify the authorities. Did that conversation come up at this time with your husband?

A—Yes; I said that. But he didn't go at that time and after all he was my husband.

Mr. Dulles. Does—do you mean you said it again at the time of the Nixon incident?

A—Yes; I told him that but you must understand that I don't speak English very well, and for that reason I used to keep a piece of paper with me, and I had it, you know, what piece of paper I am talking about. At that time I didn't know how to go in police station; I don't know where it was.

Mr. McKenzie. Was that the passport?

A—No. After the incident with Walker——

Mr. Rankin. Was that paper the Walker incident note that you have described in your testimony?

A—Yes.

Representative Ford. When you put the pistol under the mattress, what happened to the pistol from then on?

A—That evening he asked for it and said that nothing was going to happen, and that he said he wouldn't do anything and took the pistol back. And put it into his room.

Mr. Dulles. Did you keep the, what you call, the Walker note with you all the time or did you have in a particular place where you could go and get it and show it to him?

A—I had it all the time. I kept it in a certain place initially and then I put it in the pages of a book.

Senator Cooper. Mr. Rankin, would you ask the witness to state again what Lee Oswald's promise was to her that he had made at the time of the Walker incident?

Mr. Rankin. Will you relate the promise that your husband made to you right after the discovery of the Walker incident by you?

A—This wasn't a written promise.

Mr. Rankin. No.

A—But in words it was more or less that I told him that he was very lucky that he hadn't killed—it was very good that he hadn't killed General Walker. I said it was fate that—it was fate that General Walker not be killed and therefore he shouldn't try such a thing again.

Mr. Rankin. What did he say in answer to that?

A—He said perhaps I am right. I myself didn't believe what I was saying because I didn't believe that he was fated. I was just trying to find some way of dissuading my husband to do such a thing again. Do you understand what I mean?

Mr. Rankin. Yes. Did he say that he would or would not do that again, that is what I want to know.

A—At the time I did definitely convince him that I was

right, and at the time he said that he would not do such a thing again.

Mr. Rankin. Now, when you talked to him about the Nixon incident and persuaded him not to go out and do anything to Mr. Nixon, did you say anything about your pregnancy in trying to persuade him?

A—Yes.

Mr. Rankin. What did you say about that?

A—Yes; I told him that I was pregnant.

Mr. Rankin. Did you observe his action at the time of this Nixon incident, how he acted?

A—How he reacted to this?

Mr. Rankin. How he reacted to your interfering with him?

A—At first he was extremely angry, and he said, "You are always getting in my way." But then rather quickly he gave in, which was rather unusual for him. At the time I didn't give this any thought, but now I think it was just rather a kind of nasty joke he was playing with me. Sometimes Lee was—he had a sadistic—my husband had a sadistic streak in him and he got pleasure out of harming people, and out of harming me, not physically but emotionally and mentally. . . .

Mr. Dulles. Was there any reason why you didn't tell the Commission about this when you testified before?

A—I had no—there is no particular reason. I just forgot. Very likely this incident didn't make a very great impression on me at that time.

Mr. Dulles. Now, before the death of President Kennedy, of course, you knew that your husband had purchased a rifle?

A—Yes.

Mr. Dulles. You knew that he had purchased a pistol?

A—Yes.

Mr. Dulles. And a knife?

A—No; what kind of knife?

Mr. Dulles. Did he have a knife?

A—He had a little pocket knife; I think.

Mr. Dulles. You knew that he had told you that he had tried to kill General Walker?

A—Yes.

Mr. Dulles. And, of course, as you said you heard him make a threat against Nixon.

A—Yes.

Mr. Dulles. Did you have some fear that he would use these weapons against someone else?

A—Of course; I was afraid.

Mr. Dulles. What?

A—Of course; I was afraid.

Mr. Dulles. You thought that he might use his weapons against someone?

A—After the incident with Nixon I stopped believing him.

Mr. Dulles. You what?

A—I stopped believing him.

Mr. Dulles. Why?

A—Because he wasn't obeying me any longer, because he promised and then he broke his promise.

Mr. Dulles. Would you repeat that?

A—Because he wasn't obeying me any more. He promised and, he made a promise and then he broke it.

Mr. Dulles. That is my question. Having been told that—isn't it correct he told you that he shot at General Walker? He made a promise to you that he wouldn't do anything like that again, you heard him threaten Vice President Nixon, didn't it occur to you then that there was danger that he would use these weapons against someone else in the future?

A—After the incident with Walker, I believed him when he told me that he wouldn't use the weapons any longer.

Mr. Dulles. I remember you testified before and I asked you if you had heard him threaten any official or other person and your answer was no.

A—Because I forgot at that time about the incident with Nixon.

Mr. Dulles. I want to ask you again: In view of the fact that you knew—in view of the fact that he had threatened Walker by shooting at him, and he threatened Vice President Nixon can you not tell this Commission whether after that he threatened to hurt, harm any other person?

A—Nobody else. Perhaps I shoud be punished for not having said anything about all this, but I was just a wife and I was trying to keep the family together, at that time. I mean to say. I am talking, of course, of the time before President Kennedy's death. And if I forget to say anything now, I am not doing it on purpose.

Mr. Dulles. I am just asking questions. Will you say here that he never did make any statement against President Kennedy?

A—Never.

Mr. Dulles. Did he ever make any statement about him of any kind?

A—He used to read and translate articles from the newspaper about Kennedy to me and from magazines, favorable articles about Kennedy. He never commented on them and he never discussed them in any way but because of his translations and his reading to me he always had a favorable feeling about President Kennedy because he always read these favorably inclined articles to me. He never said that these articles never were true, that he was a bad President or anything like that.

Mr. Dulles. I didn't catch the last.

A—He never said these articles were not true or that President Kennedy was a bad President or anything like that. . . .

Mr. Rankin. Did the FBI tell you that the reason they were asking about whether there was a mistake as to whether it was Mr. Nixon or Vice President Johnson was because there was a report in Dallas papers about Vice President Johnson going to Dallas around the 23d of April?

A—Yes; they did tell me this. They said that at this time there was only one announcement in the newspapers of anyone coming and that was Vice President Johnson.

Mr. Rankin. But you still are certain it was Mr. Nixon and not Vice President Johnson?

A—Yes, no. I am getting a little confused with so many questions. I was absolutely convinced it was Nixon and now after all these questions I wonder if I am right in my mind.

Mr. Rankin. Did your husband——

A—I never heard about Johnson. I never heard about Johnson. I never knew anything about Johnson. I just don't think it was Johnson. I didn't know his name.

Mr. Rankin. Did your husband during the Nixon incident say Mr. Nixon's name several times or how many times.

A—Only once.

Mr. Rankin. Now, you said that your husband went to get the pistol in the room. Will you tell us what room that was that he went to get the pistol?

A—It was a small sort of storeroom. Just to the left off the balcony as you come in; it is just on the left from the balcony.

Mr. Rankin. Was it out, was the pistol out in the room or was it in a closet?

A—This room contained only a table and some shelves, and the pistol was not on the table. It was hidden somewhere on a shelf.

Representative Ford. Was the rifle in that room, too?

A—Yes.

Mr. Rankin. Where was the rifle in the room?

A—Sometimes it was in the corner, sometimes it was up on a shelf. Lee didn't like me to go into this room. That is why he kept it closed all the time and told me not to go into it. Sometimes he went in there and sat by himself for long periods of time.

Mr. Dulles. By closed, do you mean locked?

A—He used to close it from the inside. I don't remember what kind of lock it was. Possibly it was just a—some kind of a tongue——. . .

Mr. Rankin. Did you ever consider telling the police about the Walker and Nixon incidents?

A—I thought of this but then Lee was the only person who was supporting me in the United States, you see. I didn't have any friends, I didn't speak any English and I couldn't work and I didn't know what would happen if they locked him up and I didn't know what would happen to us. Of course, my reason told me that I should do it but because of circumstances I couldn't do it. . . .

Mr. Rankin. When you were telling about the Nixon inci-

dent you referred to your husband's sadistic streak. Do you recall that?

A—Yes.

Mr. Rankin. Can you tell us a little more about that, how it
showed?

A—Anytime I did something which didn't please him he
would make me sit down at a table and write letters to the
Russian Embassy stating that I wanted to go back to Russia.
He liked to tease me and torment me in this way. He knew
that this—he just liked to torment me and upset me and hurt
me, and he used to do this especially if I interfered in any of
his political affairs, in any of his political discussions. He
made me several times write such letters.

Mr. Dulles. I have just one question: What did you or your
husband do with these letters that you wrote? Did any of them
get mailed or did they all get destroyed?

A—He kept carbons of these letters but he sent the letters
off himself.

Mr. Dulles. To the Russian Embassy?

A—Yes; he didn't give me any money to buy stamps. I never
had any pocket money of my own.

Mr. Rankin. But the letters to the Embassy you are referring
to are actual letters and requested—requests—they weren't
practice letters or anything of that kind to punish you, were
they?

A—Yes; they were real letters. I mean if my husband didn't
want me to live with him any longer and wanted me to go back,
I would go back, not because I wanted to go back but I didn't
have any choice. . . .

*Recalled again before the Commission in September, Mrs.
Oswald gave the following testimony:*

Senator Russell. It seems to me that I recall once or twice
in this testimony when you had had some little domestic
trouble, as all married couples have, that he had cried, which
is most unusual for a man in this country—men don't cry
very often, and do you think that he cried despite the fact
that he wasn't very devoted to you and loved you a great deal?

A—The fact that he cried, and on one occasion he begged
me to come back to him—he stood on his knees and begged me
to come back to him—whether that meant that he loved me—
perhaps he did. On the other hand. the acts that he committed
showed to me that he didn't particularly care for me.

Senator Russell. You think then that his acts that he committed outside your domestic life within the family, within the
realm of the family, was an indication that he did not love you?

A—The fact that he made attempts on the lives of other
people showed to me that he did not treasure his family life
and his children, also the fact that he beat me and wanted to
send me to the Soviet Union.

Senator Russell. And you think that the fact that he promised you after the Walker incident that he would never do anything like that again but did, is an indication that he didn't love you?

A—Logically—yes. That shows to me that he did not love me. At times he cried, and did all sorts of helpful things around the house. At other times he was mean. Frankly, I am lost as to what to think about him.

And I did not have any choice, because he was the only person that I knew and I could count on—the only person in the United States.

Senator Russell. Did he beat you very often, Mrs. Oswald, strike you hard blows with his fists? Did he hit you with his fists?

A—When he beat me, sometimes he would beat me hard and sometimes not too hard. Sometimes he would leave a black eye and sometimes he wouldn't, depending on which part of me he would strike me. When we lived in New Orleans he never beat me up.

Senator Russell. Did he ever beat you in Russia before you came to this country?

A—No.

Senator Russell. Had you ever heard of any husband striking his wife in Russia?

A—It seems that beating of wives by the Russian husbands is a rather common thing in the Soviet Union and that is why I was afraid to marry a Russian.

Senator Russell. I see. Do they beat them with anything other than their hands?

There was a law in my State at one time that a man could whip his wife as long as he didn't use a switch that was larger than his thumb. That law has been repealed.

But, did they ever whip their wives with anything other than their hands in Russia?

A—I do not know. I was not interested in what manner they beat their wives.

Senator Russell. That's difficult for me to believe—that a very charming and attractive girl who was being courted by a number of men, I would have thought you would have been greatly interested in all the aspects of matrimony?

A—How would I know?

Senator Russell. How would you know it—well, by general conversation. Don't people talk about those things all over the world—in Russia and everywhere else?

A—That's different there.

Senator Russell. People are very much the same, aren't they, all over the world? If a man in the neighborhood gets drunk and beats and abuses his wife and children, isn't that discussed by all the people in the block—in that area?

A—Sometimes during a life of 20 years with a husband, everything will be all right, and then some occasion will arise or something will happen that the wife will learn about what kind of person he is.

I know of one family in the Soviet Union in Minsk, where a husband was married to a woman 17 years, and he just went to another woman.

For 1 year.

For 1 year—then he came back to the first one full of shame and repentance and he cried and she took him back in. He lived with her for 3 days and then left her again. He was excluded from the party.

Senator Russell. Excommunicated from the party?

A—Expelled from the party.

But he took all the possessions of their common property when he left.

Senator Russell. I'm taking too much time, and I will hurry along. Did he ever beat you badly enough, Mrs. Oswald, for you to require the services of a doctor, a physician?

A—No.

Senator Russell. Did he ever strike you during your pregnancy, when you were pregnant?

A—Yes; he did strike me.

Senator Russell. What reason did he give for striking you, usually?

A—Well, the reasons were if—they were very petty—I can't even remember what the reasons were after this quarrel was over. Sometimes he would tell me to shut up, and I don't take that from him.

I'm not a very quiet woman myself.

Senator Russell. "I'm not—" what?

A—I'm not a quiet woman myself and sometimes it gets on your nerves and you'll just tell him he's an idiot and he will become more angry with you.

Enraged. When I would call him an idiot, he would say, "Well, I'll show you what kind of an idiot I am," so he would beat me up.

Senator Russell. Did you ever strike him?

A—I would give him some in return. . . .

Senator Russell. Did you ever strike him with anything other than your hand?

A—Well, I think at one time I told him that if he would beat me again, I will hurl a radio, a transistor radio, and when he did strike me, I threw the radio at him.

Senator Russell. You missed him?

A—No—it broke. I missed him.

Senator Russell. Yes, she missed him.

A—I tried not to hit him. . . .

Representative Boggs. May I just ask one or two questions? Have you seen Mrs. Marguerite Oswald at any time since you first appeared before the Commission?

A—No.

Representative Boggs. Have you heard from her?

A—No.

Representative Boggs. You've had no communication from her either directly or indirectly?

A—No.

She tried to get in touch with me.

Through Attorney McKenzie.

Representative Boggs. And you refused to see her?

A—Yes.

I think that she may have been bad influence with the children—improper influence with the children.

I feel that—I hardly believe—that Lee Oswald really tried to kill President Kennedy.

I feel in my own mind that Lee did not have President Kennedy as a prime target when he assassinated him.

Representative Boggs. Well, who was it?

A—I think it was Connally. That's my personal opinion that he perhaps was shooting at Governor Connally, the Governor of Texas.

Senator Russell. You've testified before us before that Lee told you he was coming back to Texas—if he was back in Texas, he would vote for Connally for Governor. Why do you think he would shoot him?

A—I feel that the reason that he had Connally in his mind was on account of his discharge from the Marines and various letters they exchanged between the Marine Corps and the Governor's office, but actually, I didn't think that he had any idea concerning President Kennedy.

Representative Boggs. Well, now, my next question is—did he ever express any hostility to Governor Connally?

A—He never expressed that to me—his displeasure or hatred of Connally, but I feel that there could have been some connection, due to the fact that Lee was dishonorably discharged from the Corps, and there was an exchange of letters between the Governor's Office and Lee. That's my personal opinion.

Representative Boggs. Just a minute. Excuse me, Senator.

I asked you in February, Mrs. Oswald, I said, "What motive would you ascribe to your husband in killing President Kennedy?" And, you said, "As I saw the documents that were being read to me, I came to the conclusion that he wanted by any means, good or bad to get into history, and now that I've read a part of the translation of some of the documents, I think that there was some political foundation to it, a foundation of which I am not aware."

And then you go on and you express no doubt in your mind that he intended to kill President Kennedy.

A—Did I say that, this last time in Dallas? The last time in Dallas, apparently there was some misunderstanding on the part of my answers to the Commission, because I was told by Mr. McKenzie that it wasn't reported accurately.

The record should read that on the basis of the documents that I have read, I have no doubt—that I had available to me to read—I had no doubt that he did——

Mr. Gopadze. That he could kill him——

Mr. Gregory. Could or have wanted to—could have wanted to——

Mr. Gopadze. He could kill—she doesn't say "want"—he could have killed him.

Representative Boggs. Let's straighten this out because this is very important.

A—Okay.

Representative Boggs. I'll read it to you, "I gather that you have reached the conclusion in your own mind that your husband killed President Kennedy?" You replied, "Regretfully—yes."

Now, do you have any reason to change that?

A—That's correct. I have no doubt that he did kill the President.

Representative Boggs. Now, the other answer as I read it was: "On the basis of documents that you had seen presented at the Commission hearings"—isn't that right?

A—The word "documents" is wrong—the facts presented—that's what I mean.

Representative Boggs. Again we get back to the question of motive. You said again today that you are convinced that Lee Oswald killed President Kennedy.

You said something additionally today, though, and that is that you feel that it was his intention not to kill President Kennedy, but to kill Governor Connally.

Now, am I correct in saying that she had not said this previously?

Mr. Rankin. Ask her that.

Representative Boggs. Let's get an answer. I think this answer is quite important.

A—On the basis of all the available facts, I have no doubt in my mind that Lee Oswald killed President Kennedy.

At the same time, I feel in my own mind as far as I am concerned, I feel that Lee—that my husband perhaps intended to kill Governor Connally instead of President Kennedy.

Representative Boggs. Now, let me ask you one other question: Assuming that this is correct, would you feel that there would be any less guilt in killing Governor Connally than in killing the President?

A—I am not trying to vindicate or justify or excuse Lee as my husband. Even if he killed one of his neighbors, still it wouldn't make much difference—it wouldn't make any difference—a killing is a killing. I am sorry. . . .

Senator Russell. I am concerned about this testimony, Mrs. Oswald, about your believing now that Lee was shooting at

Connally and not at the President, because you did not tell us that before.

A—At that time I didn't think so, but the more I mull over it in my own mind trying to get it in my own mind what made him do what he did, the more I think that he was shooting at Connally rather than President Kennedy.

Senator Russell. Now, did you not testify before that Lee wrote a letter to Connally when he was Secretary of the Navy about the nature of his Marine discharge?

A—Yes.

Senator Russell. And that when he got a letter back, you asked him what it was?

A—Yes.

Senator Russell. And he said, "Well, it's just some Bureaucrat's statement"?

A—Yes.

Yes.

Senator Russell. Did you not further testify that Lee said in discussing the gubernatorial election in Texas that if he were here and voting, that he would vote for Connally?

A—Yes.

Senator Russell. Now do you think he would shoot and kill a man that he would vote for, for the Governor of his state?

A—The only reason is—I am trying to analyze, myself, there was a reason—more reason to dislike Connally as a man than he had for Kennedy.

Senator Russell. Well, she testified before that he had spoken, as far as Lee spoke favorably of anyone, that he had spoken favorably of both Kennedy and of Governor Connally.

A—He also told me that he was favorable toward Connally, while they were in Russia. There is a possibility that he changed his mind, but he never told her that.

Senator Russell. Well, I think that's about as speculative as the answers I've read here. He might have changed his mind, but he didn't tell her anything about it, as she testified—that discussing politics in Texas, that he said that if he were here when they had the election, that he would vote for John Connally for Governor, and that was after he got the letter about the Marine Corps.

A—That happened in Russia when he received some kind of pamphlet with a picture of Connally, a separate time, at which time he remarked that when he returned, if and when he returned to Texas he would vote for Connally.

Senator Russell. That's right—that's exactly right, but yet now you say that he was his prime target.

I want to know what Connally had done to Lee since he got back from Russia that would cause him to change his mind, to shoot him? .

A—I do not know, but there is a possibility that Lee became

246

hateful of Connally because the matter of this dishonorable discharge was dragging so long.

Senator Russell. Yes; but Connally had left the Navy, where he had anything to do with the discharge, before he got the pamphlet about his being a candidate for Governor?

A—I am not sure when that particular thing happened, whether Mr. Connally was the Secretary of the Navy or what he was doing.

Senator Russell. Well, it's a matter of common knowledge that he ran for Governor after he resigned as Secretary of the Navy.

A—I don't know.

Senator Russell. Did you not know that when Mr. Connally was running for Governor of Texas, he was no longer Secretary of the Navy and had nothing to do with the Marine Corps?

A—Yes, I knew—I knew that he was not the Secretary of the Navy any more because Lee told me that Connally stated in the letter to Lee that he was no longer Secretary of Navy and hence he couldn't do anything for him, and that Connally referred the petition to the proper authorities. . . .

Senator Russell. Do you have any facts on which you base your opinion now that Lee Oswald was shooting and was intending to kill Connally rather than President Kennedy?

A—I have no facts whatsoever. I simply express an opinion which perhaps is not logical at all, but I am sorry if I mixed everybody up.

Senator Russell. You haven't mixed anybody up, except I think that you have your evidence terribly confused.

A—No; I have no facts whatsoever. I'm sorry I told them that.

Senator Russell. Do you know whether or not Lee knew Connally personally or did he know that he was going to be in this motorcade at all?

A—No; I did not know whether Lee knew or ever contacted the Governor personally, and I don't know whether Lee knew that the Governor would be in the motorcade. . . .

NELSON DELGADO

Testimony of a serviceman who was a friend of Lee Harvey Oswald in the Marine Corps:

Mr. Liebeler. But you do remember that when you would walk into the room Oswald would be sitting there with this book [Das Kapital] and it would be open?

A—Yes; and then he had this other book. I am still trying to find out what it is. It's about a farm, and about how all the animals take over and make the farmer work for them. It's really a weird book, the way he was explaining it to me, and that struck me kind of funny. But he told me that the farmer represented the imperialistic world, and the animals were the workers, symbolizing that they are the socialist people, you know, and that eventually it will come about that the socialists will have the imperialists working for them, and things like that, like these animals, these pigs took over and they were running the whole farm and the farmer was working for them.

Mr. Liebeler. Is that what Oswald explained to you.

A—Yes.

Mr. Liebeler. Did you tell the FBI about this?

A—Yes.

Mr. Liebeler. Did they know the name of the book?

A—No.

Mr. Liebeler. The FBI did not know the name of the book?

A—No.

Mr. Liebeler. Do you want to know the name of the book?

A—Yes.

Mr. Liebeler. It is called the Animal Farm. It is by George Orwell.

A—He didn't tell me. I asked him for the thing, but he wouldn't tell me. I guess he didn't know. The Animal Farm. Did you read it?

Mr. Liebeler. Yes.

A—Is it really like that?

Mr. Liebeler. Yes; there is only one thing that Oswald did not mention apparently and that is that the pigs took over the farm, and then they got to be just like the capitalists were before, they got fighting among themselves, and there was one big pig who did just the same thing that the capitalist had done before. Didn't Oswald tell you about that?

A—No; just that the pigs and animals had revolted and made the farmer work for them. The Animal Farm. Is that a socialist book?

Mr. Liebler. No.

A—That is just the way you interpret it; right?

Mr. Liebeler. Yes; I think so. It is actually supposed to be quite an anti-Communist book.

A—Is it really? . . .

RUTH HYDE PAINE

The testimony of the woman with whom Mrs. Lee Harvey Oswald was living at the time of the assassination:

Mr. Jenner. Now, you have an entry in your diary, and I quote it on the 24th of April, 1963: "Lee and Marina."

A—Yes.

Mr. Jenner. Was that an entry made after the fact?

A—No; I judge that was——

Mr. Jenner. Now, please give me your best recollection.

A—That was the plan to meet, knowing Lee was no longer

working; it was there for not only a meeting with Marina, but I expected to see them both at the apartment.

Mr. Jenner. So that is confined to the meeting you expected to have with Lee and Marina that morning when you went there and, to your surprise, you found that Mr. Oswald was all packed to go to New Orleans.

A—All packed and looking for a cab; yes.

Mr. Jenner. How long did Marina remain in your home on that occasion?

A—She stayed then until May 9—well, excuse me, she stayed until the 10th of May.

Mr. Jenner. You have an entry, do you not, in your diary as to the May 9th or 10th.

A—Yes.

Mr. Jenner. Read it.

A—It says now going over to the 11th "New Orleans."

Mr. Jenner. And you have written across then "May 10 and May 11," is that right?

A—Yes.

Mr. Jenner. What does the "New Orleans" signify, please?

A—Lee called on the evening of the 9th to say he had work.

Mr. Jenner. You recall that?

A—I recall that definitely. Marina says, "Papa naslubet," "Father loves us," "Daddy loves us, he got work and he wanted us to come." She was very elated.

Mr. Jenner. This is Marina talking to you?

A—I could see as she talked on the phone.

Mr. Jenner. You overheard this conversation?

A—Afterward. She said over and over, "Papa naslubet," "Daddy loves us," "Daddy loves us."

Mr. Jenner. She was elated?

A—She was elated and, let's see, we tried to think when we could leave, and first said over the phone that we would leave on the morning of the 11th. But I thought it would be too long to do all this in one day, and we accelerated our preparations and left midday on the 10th which got us to Shreveport.

Mr. Jenner. Before we get into this, and I would like to cover this interim period before any adjournment today; there was a 16-day period now, approximately, maybe we will limit it to 15 days, that Marina stayed with you in your home.

A—That is right.

Mr. Jenner. Did you have conversations with her about her husband?

A—Yes.

Mr. Jenner. About their life in Russia?

A—Well, even going so far as to wonder——

Mr. Jenner. During this 15-day period?

A—Yes. We had such conversations.

Mr. Jenner. Would you please relate to us your discussions

249

with Marina with respect to her husband Lee Harvey Oswald?

A—Well, she wondered if he did, in fact, love her.

Mr. *Jenner*. What did she say?

A—She said she supposed most couples had at some time wondered about this. She wondered herself whether she loved him truly. She talked some of her few months of dating that she had in Minsk, and of living there.

Mr. *Jenner*. That is before her marriage to Lee Harvey?

A—Yes. At some point, and I want to tell you this, whether it is appropriate or whether it happened later in October, I can't be certain, but I think in May she told me she had written a letter to a previous boyfriend, and that this letter had come back because she had put insufficient postage on it, and Lee had found it at the door coming back through the mail, and had been very angry.

Mr. *Jenner*. Did she go beyond that?

A—She did not. To tell me what was in the letter, you mean?

Mr. *Jenner*. I am not thinking so much within the letter. Did she go beyond stating that he was merely only angry? Was there any discussion about his having struck her?

A—No; none. No, none. She never mentioned to me ever that Lee had struck her.

Mr. *Jenner*. And during all the visits you ever had with her, all the tete-a-tetes, her living with you on this occasion we now describe as 15½ days, and in the fall, was there any occasion when Marina Oswald related to you any abuse, physical abuse, by her husband, Lee Harvey Oswald, with respect to her?

A—There was never any such occasion.

Mr. *Jenner*. Never any such occasion. And in particular this incident?

A—She related this incident, but it did not include anything further than he had been very angry and hurt.

Mr. *Jenner*. Up to this time, that is, the time she came to you on the 24th, had you ever seen any bruises——

A—No; I never saw her——

Mr. *Jenner*. On her person?

A—No; I never saw her bruised.

Mr. *Jenner*. At no time that you have ever seen her or known her, have you ever seen her bruised?

A—At no time.

Mr. *Jenner*. So that there has been no occasion when you have seen it, or been led to believe, she had been subjected to any physical abuse by her husband?

A—That is right.

Mr. *Jenner*. Was there any discussion during these 15 days of any occasion when Marina had gone off to live with someone else?

A—No. I think she told me that in the fall.

Mr. *Jenner*. I see. As long as I have raised that, would you please give us the time and the occasions and tell us what occurred?

A—When she told me?

Mr. Jenner. What she said. When was this?

A—This probably was in October. She told me that the previous year she had——

Mr. Jenner. 1962?

A—Yes. She had in the fall, she had gone to a friend's home, left Lee. She described his face as she left, as shocked and dismayed and unbelieving.

Mr. Jenner. Unbelieving?

A—In a sense that she was truly walking out on him.

Mr. Jenner. Yes. Excuse me. Did she put it in those terms, that she was leaving?

A—She was leaving; yes.

Mr. Jenner. She left him?

A—Yes; and went to stay with a friend. Then moved to the home——

Mr. Jenner. Did she name the friend?

A—She did not name the friend; no. The friend's name came up in another connection, but I had no way of making the connection until after I learned about this to whom she referred.

Mr. Jenner. Do you now recall the name?

A—She went to Katya Ford's.

The Chairman. To the Fords?

A—To Katya, being the friend, Mrs. Ford.

The Chairman. Mrs. Ford.

A—And then moved. She did tell me this. She had moved on the weekend to a different home. Then Lee came there, pleaded for her to come back, promised that everything would be different. She went back and she reported—as she reported it to me, things were no different.

Mr. Jenner. Were not different?

A—Were not different.

Mr. Jenner. Did you undertake a discussion with her as to what the things were that were disturbing her?

A—That offended her that much? No; I did not.

Mr. Jenner. That led her to leave her husband?

A—No.

Mr. Jenner. There was no discussion of that?

A—No.

Mr. McCloy. Did you ever witness any altercations?

A—Indeed I saw them argue a good deal.

Mr. McCloy. Sharp arguments?

A—Yes.

Mr. Dulles. But no violence of any kind?

A—No physical violence.

Mr. McCloy. Any profanity?

251

A—I am not sure I know Russian profanity. He was very curt and told her to shut up quite a great deal.

Mr. Jenner. In your presence?

A—Yes.

Mr. Jenner. In the presence of others?

A—Particularly in New Orleans the first time when we went down, when I took her to New Orleans in May, he was very discourteous to her, and they argued most of that weekend. I was very uncomfortable in that situation, and he would tell her to shut up, tell her, "I said it, and that is all the discussion on the subject."

Representative Ford. What were the kinds of discussions that prompted this?

A—I can't recall that, and I have already had my brain picked trying to, with other people trying to, to recall what was the difficulty. I do recall feeling that the immediate things they were talking about were insufficient reason for that much feeling being passed back and forth, and I wondered if I wasn't adding to the strain in the situation, and did my best to get back to Texas directly. But the—well, I do recall one thing, yes—we arrived with a big load of blackberries that we bought from a vendor along the street.

Representative Ford. On the way down?

A—On the way down, on the road, and ate them, and then, he, one morning, started to make blackberry wine, and she bawled him out for it, what a waste of good blackberries, and she said, "What do you think you are doing? Ruining all this." And he proceeded, and argued about it, but thought he should, you know, defend himself. On this occasion she was making the attack in a sense and didn't think he should do it this way, and then, so, under fire and attack, he continued. But then the next day she observed that he had tossed it all out and lost heart after the argument, and decided it wasn't——

Mr. Dulles. He tossed out the wine?

A—He tossed it out; yes.

Mr. Jenner. You detected, then, irritability as between them. Is that a fair statement?

A—That is accurate.

Mr. Jenner. And anger rose to the surface pretty easily?

A—Very easily.

Mr. Jenner. What was your impression? Of course he hadn't seen her then for a couple of weeks.

A—That is right.

Mr. Jenner. Tell us about it—when she came in. Did they embrace?

A—Yes. We arrived at his uncle's in one section of New Orleans, and had a very friendly half hour or so——

Mr. Jenner. Was he there?

A—Yes; he was there. He introduced her and little June,

252

and played with June, on his shoulders, perhaps. At any rate, he was very glad to see the baby, and was congenial and outgoing. We talked with the relatives for a short time.

Then the uncle drove them to the apartment—I was following with my children in my car—drove to the apartment he had rented, which was in a different section of the city. And Lee showed her, of course, all the virtues of the apartment that he had rented. He was pleased that there was room enough, it was large enough that he could invite me to stay, and the children, to spend the night there. And he pointed out this little courtyard with grass, and fresh strawberries ready to pick, where June could play. And a screened porch entryway. And quite a large living room. And he was pleased with the furniture and how the landlady had said this was early New Orleans style. And Marina was definitely not as pleased as he had hoped. I think he felt—he wanted to please her. This showed in him.

Mr. Jenner. Tell us what she said. What led you to that conclusion?

A—She said it is dark, and it is not very clean. She thought the courtyard was nice, a grass spot where June could play, fenced in. But there was very little ventilation. We immediately were aware there were a lot of cockroaches.

Mr. Jenner. Was she aware of this, and did she comment on that?

A—I don't know as anything was said. He was pretty busy explaining. He was doing his best to get rid of them. But they didn't subside. I remember noticing that he was tender and vulnerable at that point, when she arrived.

Mr. Jenner. He was tender?

A—Hoping for—particularly vulnerable, hoping for approval from her, which she didn't give. It wasn't a terribly nice apartment. And she had been disappointed, because when we first arrived she thought that the home we were going to was the apartment.

Mr. Jenner. She thought the Murrets' home?

A—Yes. So when we came up to the Murrets' home, she said, "This is lovely, how pleased I am." So that she was in—disappointed by contrast with the apartment that she really had to live in.

Representative Ford. She expressed this?

A—She expressed her disappointment; yes; and didn't meet his hopes to be pleased with it.

Mr. Dulles. As compared with their previous place of residence, how was the New Orleans apartment? It was bigger, I gather.

A—It was larger. It was darker, less well ventilated. It was on the first floor, the other was upstairs. I would say they were comparable in cost and in attractiveness.

Mr. Jenner. What about vermin?

A—I didn't see any vermin at the first place. But then I didn't spend the night there.

Mr. Jenner. So the welcoming was cordial?

A—The welcoming was cordial.

Mr. Jenner. They seemed to have a fine relationship at that moment?

A—Yes.

Mr. Jenner. But as the weekend progressed, and she saw the new apartment, all the time you were there, you were aware of friction and irritability?

A—Yes.

Mr. Jenner. Going back to the 15 days again, was there any discussion during this period, again, on the subject of Mr.— of Lee Oswald wishing Marina to return to Russia?

A—I believe I made definite, but only verbal, an invitation for her to stay on with me, past the time of the baby's birth, if she wished to.

Mr. Jenner. I take it—I will get into that. But I take it your answer to my question first is yes.

A—Yes.

Mr. Jenner. Now, tell us what that discussion was.

A—Well——

Mr. Jenner. And how it arose.

A—Well, we still discussed the possibility of her coming back to have the baby here—although by no means a definite —definitely planned.

Mr. Jenner. Excuse me. I am a little confused. When you say coming back to have the baby here——

A—It was assumed she would go to New Orleans when he called, but we talked about the possibility of her coming back to Dallas. I said she was still welcome to if she wants to, if it seems appropriate, to come here to have the baby.

Mr. Dulles. That was to your house, you mean?

A—Yes; to stay at my house before, or especially right after the baby's birth, where I could look after June while she was in the hospital and later. June didn't take readily to strangers. She did like me and was comfortable with me, so I felt she might want to have someone she knew and got along with.

Mr. Jenner. But in this connection, was there a discussion between you and Marina Oswald subject to her husband wishing her to return to Russia?

A—I don't believe she again said that he was after her to return.

Mr. Jenner. Well, then, on the whole, your answer to my question would be no.

A—That is right. As far as I recall, it came up only once in our discussions prior to New Orleans. . . .

Mr. Jenner. Now, you received in May or on or about May,

or shortly after May 25, 1963, another note from Marina Oswald, did you not?

A—This was postmarked May 25.

Mr. Jenner. After you had taken her to New Orleans?

A—That is correct. This was the first letter I received from her from New Orleans.

Mr. Jenner. And you have kindly produced the original of that letter for the Commission, have you not?

A—Yes.

Mr. Jenner. Is that correct?

A—Yes; it is. . . .

Mr. Jenner. She has supplied me with an interpretation. In the first paragraph it reads and I quote, and you follow me, please. I will read the whole paragraph:

"Here it is already a week since I received your letter. I can't produce any excuses as there are no valid reasons. I am ashamed to confess that I am a person of moods and my mood currently is such that I don't feel much like anything. As soon as you left all love stopped and I am very hurt that Lee's attitude toward me is such that I feel each minute that I bind him. He insists that I leave America which I don't want to do at all. I like America very much and I think that even without Lee I would not be lost here. What do you think?"

Had you had any discussion with Marina when you were in New Orleans on the subject matters which I have just read to you from the first paragraph of her letter, Commission Exhibit No. 408?

A—There was no such discussion in New Orleans.

Mr. Jenner. What impact did this have on you, Mrs. Paine, when you received this letter and read that first paragraph?

A—It was a repetition, or similar to something she had told me late in March, which I have already put on the record yesterday, saying basically that he wanted her to go back, wanted to send her back to the Soviet Union.

Mr. Jenner. And to send her back alone, is that correct?

A—That was the impression I carried.

Mr. Jenner. Was there ever any occasion, during all your acquaintance with the Oswalds, when there was any suggestion or implication that if she returned to Russia, at his request, that he would accompany her?

A—There was no such suggestion.

Mr. Jenner. Was it always that she was to go to Russia alone?

A—As she described it, it carried from her the feeling that she was being sent away.

Mr. Jenner. What about the little child, June?

A—June with her.

Mr. Jenner. Was to accompany her to Russia. Now, the second paragraph, if I may:

"This is the basic question which doesn't leave me day or

night. And again Lee has said to me that he doesn't love me. So you see we came to mistaken conclusions. It is hard for you and me to live without a return of our love interest gone. How would it all end?"

Had there been discussions between you and Marina Oswald on the subject of whether or not her husband had love for her, and in that area?

A—What I particularly recall is what I mentioned yesterday, when he telephoned her and said he had found a job and wanted her to come—

Mr. Jenner. This was just before going to New Orleans?

A—Just before going to New Orleans.

Mr. Jenner. In the spring?

A—Right. She said "Papa loves us," as I have testified. She had wondered to me during the 2 weeks previous whether he did, whether she loved him. But was clearly elated by his call and gradually came to her own conclusions. Really, I had no ground upon which to make a conclusion.

Mr. Dulles. She was speaking in Russian then to you?

A—Yes.

Mr. Jenner. Now, were you impressed that this paragraph, however, was not consistent with her immediate response at the time that telephone call had been made to her?

A—It showed me there was not as much change as she had hoped.

Mr. Jenner. Did you have any discussion with her on this subject when you were in New Orleans, and when you took her or when you were taking her from Irving, Tex., to New Orleans?

A—No.

Mr. Jenner. None whatsoever. When you were in New Orleans, Mrs. Paine, did you tour any night clubs?

A—No.

Mr. Jenner. Did you or Marina ever evidence any interest in touring Bourbon Street, for example?

A—You are talking about the spring visit?

Mr. Jenner. Yes; I am.

A—We went to the French Quarter during the day.

Mr. Jenner. Please identify whom you include when you say "we."

A—Lee, Marina, I, and three children.

Mr. Jenner. Did all of you, including Lee, go to the French Quarter?

A—Yes; we did.

Mr. Jenner. Did you tour the Bourbon Street areas, Royal Street, and the other areas?

A—No; we did not.

Mr. Jenner. Will you tell us without any length—you did not. This was a tourist visit of the French Quarter, is that right?

A—Yes.

Mr. Jenner. In the day?

A—Yes.

Mr. Jenner. With the children?

A—Yes.

Mr. Jenner. Was anything said during the course of that tourist visit about visiting Bourbon Street at night rather than in the daytime?

A—I don't recall that there was anything said.

Mr. Jenner. Was there any discussion about Lee Oswald visiting or frequenting night clubs?

A—None.

Mr. Jenner. Either in Dallas, or in New Orleans or in Irving, Tex.?

A—None; at any time.

Mr. Jenner. Did any one of you tour Bourbon Street at night during that spring visit?

A—No.

Mr. Jenner. Any discussion of the subject?

A—Not to my recollection.

Mr. Jenner. Was there a subsequent occasion when you did visit Bourbon Street at night?

A—In September, when I visited again in New Orleans. Shall I tell that?

Mr. Jenner. Yes; please, because there is a measure of contrast to that I would like to bring out.

A—Marina and I and our three small children went down in the early evening and walked along the street.

Mr. Jenner. Would you tell us how that came about, whether Lee Oswald accompanied you?

A—He did not accompany us. He was asked if he wanted to go, and he said he did not. Marina was interested in my seeing Bourbon Street at night simply as a tourist attraction.

Mr. Jenner. And you two girls took your children?

A—Yes.

Mr. Jenner. Did she take June?

A—Yes.

Mr. Jenner. You two girls walked down Bourbon Street?

A—And one of us very pregnant.

Mr. Jenner. And observed everything from the outside. You didn't go inside any night clubs?

A—No. In fact, when I realized we weren't permitted, we went on.

Mr. Jenner. You had small children?

A—Yes.

Mr. Jenner. Was there any discussion with Mr. Oswald at that time or with Marina which led you to form a judgment as to whether he was a man who might or would, or had frequented night clubs?

A—I judged he was not such a person.

Mr. Jenner. In all your experiences with the Oswalds from

257

February, sometime in February 1963. even to the present date, had any mention been made of Lee Oswald frequenting night clubs?

A—None.

Mr. Jenner. Or of Marina at any time?

A—No mention of her.

Mr. Dulles. Did you get the impression when you made this trip that Marina had previously made the trip herself, that she seemed to know the surroundings?

A—This occurs in the next paragraph of the letter she wrote in May, so I knew she had been herself.

Mr. Dulles. She had been there before?

A—Yes. From the letter I judge with Lee accompanying her.

Mr. Jenner. Mrs. Paine, if you will pardon me. Mr. Reporter, will you read the question?

(Question read.)

Mr. Jenner. Would you answer just that question?

A—Yes.

Mr. McCloy. She did answer it.

Mr. Jenner. I didn't think she did.

Mr. Dulles. I think she said "yes."

Mr. Jenner. Now the letter of May 25th to you does make reference to visits to the French Quarter, is that correct?

A—Yes.

Mr. Jenner. Gentlemen of the Commission, that portion of the letter reads as follows:

"Now a bit about the impressions I have received this week. Last Saturday we went to Aunt Lillian's"—Aunt Lillian, Mrs. Paine, is Lee Oswald's aunt?

A—Yes.

Mr. Jenner. Mrs. Murret?

A—Mrs. Murret.

Mr. Jenner. "And leaving June with her we are at the lake. Lee wanted to catch crabs but caught nothing. I have a very high opinion of his relatives."

By the way, what was your opinion of his relatives?

A—I met them only once. I thought them to be very nice.

Mr. Jenner. "Straightforward and kind people. To me they are very attentive. I like them. We have been to the French Quarter in the evening. It is a shame you didn't manage to get there in the evening. For me it was especially interesting as it was the first time in my life I had seen such. There were many night clubs there. Through the open doors were visible barrel covered dancing girls (so as not to say entirely unclothed). Most of them had really very pretty, rare figures and if one doesn't think about too many things then one can like them very much. There were a great many tourists there. For the most part very rich. We have been to the near park again."

That is all of that paragraph dealing with the nightclubs.

258

Now, did you ever know a man or person by the name of Jack Rubinstein or Jack Ruby?

A—No.

Mr. Jenner. Prior to November 24, 1963?

A—No.

Mr. Jenner. Did you ever hear of any such individual?

A—No, I did not.

Mr. Jenner. Had you frequented a nightclub in Irving or in Dallas prior to November 24, 1963?

A—Not at any time. In either town.

Mr. Jenner. You and your husband Michael were not in the habit of visiting, frequenting nightclubs?

A—No.

Mr. Jenner. It is a fact, is it not, Mrs. Paine that neither you nor Mr. Paine attended nightclubs at all?

A—That is correct.

Mr. Jenner. Is this true prior to your moving to Irving?

A—Yes.

Mr. Jenner. Was there anything that occurred during all these months of your acquaintance with the Oswalds that did or might have led you to any opinion as to Lee's frequenting of nightclubs or his acquaintance with nightclubs or his being intimate with nightclub people?

A—During the entire time, is that your question?

Mr. Jenner. Yes. Let us end the day for you for this purpose at November 22, 1963?

A—He was, I would say, actively disinterested in going down to Bourbon Street in the last weekend in September.

Mr. Jenner. But even prior to that time?

A—It was the 21st.

Mr. Jenner. Had anything occurred by way of a remark at all that made an impression on you in the area of his being acquainted possibly with any nightclub people, any entertainers?

A—There had been no hint of any sort that he was acquainted with nightclub people?

Mr. McCloy. Whether in Dallas, New Orleans or Irving?

A—That is right. Of course, I had not talked to him a great deal up to the New Orleans trip. Then after that time there was also no hint or mention of any nightclub people. After that time in New Orleans he did refuse table wine at my home, so I got the impression of him as a person who didn't like to drink.

Mr. Jenner. During all your acquaintance with Lee Harvey Oswald, did you ever see him take a drink of spirits, intoxicating spirits?

A—It is possible he had beer at the initial party on the 22nd of February, that is as far as I can remember.

Mr. Jenner. What impression did you have of him as a man of temperance?

259

A—He teased Marina about liking wine as if it displeased him mildly. . . .

Mr. Jenner. Now, did you write Marina on or about the 11th of July?

A—I have a rough draft of that date.

Mr. Jenner. I hand you a document of two pages which has been identified as Commission Exhibit No. 410.

(The document referred to was marked Commission Exhibit No. 410 for identification.)

Would you please tell us what that document is?

A—This is the rough draft, to which I just referred, written to Marina.

Mr. Jenner. And you thereupon prepared the final draft and sent it?

A—That is correct.

Mr. Jenner. This represents, does it not, your best recollection of the contents of the letter, the letter in its final form as you transmitted it to Marina?

A—I think this is probably a very accurate representation of the letter in its final form. It was the first time I put on paper an invitation to her to come and stay with me for anything more than a few weeks around the birth of the baby.

Mr. Jenner. Have you supplied the Commission with a translation of your letter?

A—Yes; I have.

Mr. Jenner. And that appears at the bottom of page 7 of your notes which you have supplied to me?

A—That is correct.

Mr. Jenner. I direct your attention, if I may, and the attention of the Commission as interpreted by Mrs. Paine, the first sentence reads, "Dear Marina, if Lee doesn't wish to live with you any more and prefers that you go to the Soviet Union, think about the possibility of living with me."

You just said—is that the portion of your letter which you say this is the first invitation you made to Marina to come to live with you generally?

A—This was the first written invitation.

Mr. Jenner. I see.

A—I had made an informal invitation face to face when she was staying the first week in May, but felt as I made it that she didn't take this seriously.

Mr. Jenner. Now, you go on in your letter and you make reference, for example, to—let's take the second paragraph of your letter appearing at the top of page 8 of your notes, "You know I have long received from my parents, I live dependent a long time. I would be happy to be an aunt to you and I can. We have sufficient money. Michael will be glad. This I know. He just gave me $500 for the vacation or something necessary. With this money it is possible to pay the doctor and hospital in October when the baby is born, believe God. All will be well for you and the children. I confess that I think that the opportunity for me to know you came from God. Perhaps it is not so but I think and believe so."

Had you discussed this matter with your husband?

A—Yes; I had.

Mr. Jenner. And you were still living separate and apart at that time?

A—Yes. But I felt so long as I was not yet earning, he would be the one, in fact, who was supporting all of us.

Mr. Jenner. I think the Commission might be interested in that. You were not taking this action, either in the earlier stage in the early spring or in the summer of inviting Marina to live with you without discussing that with your husband even though you and your husband at that time were separated?

A—That is correct.

Mr. Jenner. Did you do anything, Mrs. Paine, in this connection with respect to keeping Lee Oswald informed of your invitations and your communications in this area with Marina?

A—I wrote into the letter that I hoped—well you might just read the last paragraph.

Mr. Jenner. Would you mind reading it?

A—I will read it, the last paragraph in the letter, and I might say that the entire letter I wrote with the possibility in mind that he should see this.

Mr. Jenner. Did you desire that he do see it?

A—I wanted him to—her to feel free to show it to him. I didn't want her to come to my house if this offended or injured him, if this was in some way—

(At this point, Senator Cooper entered the hearing room.)

Mr. Jenner. Divisive?

A—If he did in fact want to keep his family together, I certainly wanted him to, but if the bulk of his feelings lay on the side of wanting to be away, separated from Marina, then I thought it was legitimate for him to have that alternative, although it was not legitimate for him to simply send her back if she didn't want to go.

Mr. Jenner. Send her back where?

A—To the Soviet Union, if she didn't want to go. So in this light I will read the last paragraph of Commission Exhibit 410:

"I don't want to hurt Lee with this invitation to you. Only I think that it would be better that you and he do not live together if you do not receive happiness. I understand how Michael feels. He doesn't love me and wants a chance to look for another life and another wife. He must do this, it seems, and so it is better for us not to live together. I don't know how Lee feels. I would like to know. Surely things are hard for him now, too. I hope that he would be glad to see you with me where he can know that you and the children will receive everything that is necessary and he would not need to worry about it. Thus he could start life again."

Mr. Jenner. Mrs. Paine, having all this in mind and what you have testified to up to now, would you please tell the gentlemen of the Commission the factors and motivations you had in inviting Marina to come live with you; first to have her baby, next on a more extended scale, all of the factors that motivated you in your offer, in your own words?

A—The first invitation, just to come for a few weeks at the time of the birth is a simpler question, I will answer that first.

I felt that she would need someone simply to take care of her older child for the time that she was in the hospital, and that things would be easier for her if she didn't have to immediately take up the full household chores upon returning from the hospital. This was a very simple offer.

Mr. Jenner. That was all that motivated you at that time?

A—Now, in asking her to come and stay for a more extended period, I had many feelings. I was living alone with my children, at that time, had been since the previous fall, nearly a year, at the time this letter is written. I had no idea that my husband might move back to the house. I was tired of living alone and lonely, and here was a woman who was alone and in a sense also, if Lee, in fact didn't want to be with her, and further she was a person I liked. I had lived with her 2 weeks in late April and early May. I enjoyed her company.

Further, being able to talk Russian with her added a wider dimension to my rather small and boring life as a young mother. I didn't want to go out and get a job because I wanted to be home with my children, but on the other hand, I saw a way to, and that is part of what studying Russian altogether is for me, a way to make my daily life more interesting. I also felt when I first heard in March that Lee was wanting to send Marina back, that is how it was presented to me, that it just seemed a shame that our country couldn't be a more hospitable thing for her if she wanted so much to stay, that I thought she should have that opportunity.

I was pleased that she liked America, and thought that she should have a chance to stay here and raise her children here as she wished.

I might say also if I had not been living alone I would not have undertaken such an invitation. My house is small and it wouldn't have gone with married life. . . .

Mr. Jenner. You were about to state to the Commission Marina Oswald's reaction to your series of invitations. Is that correct?

A—Yes.

Mr. Jenner. Would you proceed then?

A—As reflected in this letter. This was the third letter I received from her after a space of over a month, and I had been very concerned about her. I was much relieved to get it. She said she had been to the doctor and her condition was normal. She responded to this series of four letters of which we have

262

three in rough draft, saying—shall I read in some of the things said?

Mr. Jenner. To the extent that you desire to do so. We will not read the whole letter, it is quite long; that which is pertinent to what you have in mind.

A—Well, that for a considerable period Lee has been good to her, she writes. He talks a lot about the coming baby.

Mr. Jenner. Perhaps you might pick out—there are only about four sentences.

A—"He has become more attentive and we hardly quarrel".

Mr. Jenner. This indicates a change somewhat in relationship and would you please read that portion of the letter?

A—Yes.

Mr. Dulles. Could we have the date of this letter once again?

A—The date of the letter. We have no date on the letter. It was written somewhere between July 18 and July 21, which is the date of my reply.

Mr. Jenner. That is how you identify it?

A—Yes.

Representative Ford. This is 1963?

A—Right. Again, "He has become much more attentive and we hardly quarrel. True I have to give in a great deal. It could not be otherwise. But if one wants peace then it is necessary to give in. We went to the doctor, my condition is normal."

And she thanks me for the invitation and thanks Michael also and says:

"I would try to take advantage of it if things really become worse, if Lee becomes coarse with me again and treats me badly." . . .

Representative Boggs. When did she return to your home?

A—She came with me from New Orleans, leaving there the 23d of September and arriving in Irving the 24th of September.

Representative Boggs. And she lived with you in Irving from the 24th of September until the 23d?

A—The morning of the 23d.

Representative Boggs. Of November?

A—She left the morning of the 23d, she left expecting to come back.

Representative Boggs. During that period of time did Lee Oswald live there?

A—No.

Representative Boggs. He visited there on weekends?

A—He visited there on weekends.

Representative Boggs. How well did you know Lee Oswald?

A—Insufficiently well.

Representative Boggs. What do you mean by that?

A—Well, I regret, of course, very deeply that I didn't perceive him as a violent man.

263

Representative Boggs. You saw no evidence of violence in him at any time?

A—No, I didn't. He argued with his wife but he never struck her. I never heard from her of any violence from him.

Representative Boggs. Did he ever express any hostility toward anyone while he was talking with you?

A—Not of a violent or——

Representative Boggs. Did he ever express any political opinions to you?

A—Yes, he called himself a Marxist. He said that on the occasion after Stevenson had been in town in relation to the United Nations Day.

Mr. Jenner. Adlai Stevenson?

A—Adlai Stevenson, and Lee had been to a meeting of the National Indignation Committee held another night that week, and he was at our home the following Friday night and commented that he didn't like General Walker.

This is the only thing I heard from him on the subject.

Representative Boggs. Did he ever express any violence toward General Walker?

A—No.

Representative Boggs. Did he ever discuss President Kennedy with you?

A—He never mentioned Kennedy at all.

Representative Boggs. Did you see the rifle that he had in the room in your home?

A—In the garage, no.

Representative Boggs. In the garage, you never saw one?

A—I never saw that rifle at all until the police showed it to me in the station on the 22d of November.

Representative Boggs. Were you at home when the FBI interviewed Marina and Lee?

A—The FBI never interviewed Marina and me; I was waiting to hear your question.

Representative Boggs. At your home?

A—The FBI never interviewed Marina and Lee at my home. The FBI was there one afternoon and talked to Marina through me; they never saw Lee Oswald in my home. I told them he would be there on a weekend.

Representative Boggs. Did you ever discuss politics with Marina?

A—As close as we would come, I would say, would be what I have mentioned about Madam Nhu; she was interested in what the family would do. She also said to me that she thought Khrushchev was a rather coarse, country person. She said that she admired Mrs. Kennedy a great deal, and liked, this is all before, liked President Kennedy very much.

Mr. Jenner. This was all before November 22?

A—Yes.

Representative Boggs. Were you aware of the fact that Lee

returned to your home the night before the assassination?

A—Yes.

Representative Boggs. Were you curious about that in view of the fact that he seldom came except on weekends?

A—It was the first time he had come without asking permission to come. He came after he and his wife had quarreled, and Marina and I said to one another, we took this to be as close as he could come to an apology, and an effort to make up.

Representative Boggs. That was the reason you thought he had come?

A—But I didn't inquire of him.

Representative Boggs. You did not know that the next morning when he left he had a rifle?

A—No.

Representative Boggs. Did you see him when he left that morning?

A—No, I didn't.

Representative Boggs. Have you been active in politics yourself?

A—No; I vote. And I am a member of the League of Women Voters, that is the extent of my activity. . . .

Representative Boggs. You never formed any opinion about Lee Oswald as a person?

A—I formed many, and I would like to make that a special area.

Representative Boggs. Would you just tell me just in a sentence or two, I know you could go into it in greater detail, but was your opinion favorable? Was it unfavorable, or what?

A—I disliked him actively in the spring when I thought he just wanted to get rid of his wife and wasn't caring about her, wasn't concerned whether she would go to the doctor. I then found him much nicer, I thought, when I saw him next in New Orleans in late September, and this would be a perfectly good time to admit the rest of the pertinent part of this letter to my mother written October 14, because it shows something that I think should be part of the public record, and I am one of the few people who can give it, that presents Lee Oswald as a human person, a person really rather ordinary, not an ogre that was out to leave his wife, and be harsh and hostile to all that he knew.

But in this brief period during the times that he came out on weekends, I saw him as a person who cared for his wife and his child, tried to make himself helpful in my home, tried to make himself welcome although he really preferred to stay to himself.

He wasn't much to take up a conversation. This says, "Dear Mom," this is from Commission Exhibit No. 425, "Lee Oswald is looking for work in Dallas. Did my last letter say so? Probably not. He arrived a week and a half ago and has been look-

265

ing for work since. It is a very depressing business for him, I am sure. He spent last weekend and the one before with us here and was a happy addition to our expanded family. He played with Chris"—my 3-year-old, then 2—"watched football on the TV, planed down the doors that wouldn't close, they had shifted and generally added a needed masculine flavor"——

Mr. Jenner. Wait a second.

A—"And generally added a needed masculine flavor. From a poor first impression I have come to like him. We saw the doctor at Parkland Hospital last Friday and all seems very healthy" and this refers to Marina. "It appears that charges will be geared to their ability to pay."

Representative Boggs. Were you——

A—May I go on?

Representative Boggs. Yes; surely. Finish.

A—This was an intervening section where he was the most human that I saw him, and, of course, it has been followed by my anger with him, and all the feeling that most of us have about his act. But it seems to me important, very important, to the record that we face the fact that this man was not only human but a rather ordinary one in many respects, and who appeared ordinary.

If we think that this was a man such as we might never meet, a great aberration from the normal, someone who would stand out in a crowd as unusual, then we don't know this man, we have no means of recognizing such a person again in advance of a crime such as he committed.

The important thing, I feel, and the only protection we have is to realize how human he was though he added to it this sudden and great violence beyond——

Representative Boggs. You have no doubt about the fact that he assassinated President Kennedy?

A—I have no present doubt.

Representative Boggs. Do you have any reason to believe he was associated with anyone else in this act or it was part of a conspiracy?

A—I have no reason to believe he was associated with anyone.

Representative Boggs. Did you ever see him talking with anyone else, in conversation with anybody else or get mail at your home?

A—I never saw him talking with anyone else. He received all his mail from home, third class for the most part perhaps one letter from Russia.

Representative Boggs. Did he have telephone calls at your home of a mysterious nature?

A—No.

Mr. Jenner. Excuse me, did he ever have a telephone call at your home mysterious or otherwise?

A—No; never.

Representative Boggs. You then would be surprised if he were part of any group?

A—I would be very surprised. For one thing, I judged, I had to wonder whether this man was a spy or someone dangerous to our Nation. He had been to the Soviet Union and he had come back and he didn't go as a tourist. He went by his own admission intending to become a Soviet citizen and then came back.

Representative Boggs. What about Marina—go ahead and finish.

A—Then the FBI came, as I thought they well might, interested in this man who had been to the Soviet Union and I felt that if he had associations this would be very easy for them to know. I didn't see any, but would tend to point to the possibility of his being a spy or subversive. But I didn't see any such and I felt happy that they were charged with the responsibility of knowing about it.

Representative Boggs. Did you see any indication of any connection of Marina with any group that might be considered unusual?

A—No; no one called her.

Representative Boggs. Did she have any letters?

A—She received a letter from a friend in the Soviet Union which she showed to me and mentioned to me.

Representative Boggs. Was this just a normal letter?

A—Girl friend.

Representative Boggs. What is your present relationship with Marina?

A—I have seen her once since the assassination. That was a week ago Monday. It was the first time since the morning of the 23d when she left my house, both of us expecting she would come back to it that evening. In the intervening period I wrote her a collection of letters trying to determine what her feelings were and whether it was suitable for me to write and see her.

I am presently confused, as I was then, as to how to best be a friend to her. I don't know what is appropriate in this situation.

By that I mean during the time I was writing the letters to her and not getting an answer when she was with Mr. Martin.

Representative Boggs. Was your conversation last Monday friendly?

A—Yes.

Mr. McCloy. Might I ask one question?

You said that Lee had mentioned General Walker and indicated that he didn't like General Walker. Can you elaborate on that a little bit, to what extent, how violent was he in his expression?

A—No; it wasn't violent at all. It was more of, oh, well,

more not giving him much credit even, but it was done briefly, this was in passing, so my recollection is hazy. But certainly there was no strong expression.

Mr. McCloy. No vehemence about it?

A—Absolutely not, I would have remembered that. And I recall that Marina said nothing. . . .

Representative Boggs. There is one item I might bring out along the line you were inquiring about.

You gave some consideration, did you not, Mrs. Paine, during this period, as to whether Mr. Oswald, Lee Harvey Oswald, could or might have been a Russian agent.

A—Yes.

Mr. Jenner. And we discussed this yesterday, as I recall?

A—Briefly.

Mr. Jenner. And what conclusions did you come to on that score and why?

A—I thought that he was not very intelligent. I saw as far as I could see he had no particular contacts. He was not a person I would have hired for a job of any sort, no more than I would have let him borrow my car.

Mr. Jenner. Did you give consideration in that connection? Did his level of intelligence affect your judgment as to whether the Russian Government would have hired him?

A—Yes.

Mr. Jenner. How did it affect you?

A—I doubted they would have hired him. I kept my mind open on it to wonder.

Mr. Jenner. And you had doubt why?

A—Simply because he had gone to the Soviet Union and announced that he wanted to stay, and then came back, and I wasn't convinced that he liked America.

Mr. Jenner. Did your judgment of him, and as to his level of intelligence, affect your decision ultimately that the Russian Government might not or would not have hired him because he was not a man of capacity to serve in such a way for the Russian Government?

A—Yes; that affected my judgment.

Mr. Dulles. Have you any idea as to his motivation in the act, in light of what you have said in the assassination?

A—It is conjecture, of course, but I feel he always felt himself to be a small person; and he was right. That he wanted to be greater, or noticed, and Marina had said of him he thinks he is so big and fine, and he should take a more realistic view of himself and not be so conceited. . . .

A—And I feel that he acted much more from the emotional pushings within him than from any rational set of ideas, and—

Mr. Dulles. Emotional pushings toward aggrandizement you have in mind is what you said?

A—Yes. . . .

Mr. Jenner. Now, that is one incident.

A—That is one incident. Another refers to a rough draft of a letter that Lee wrote and left this rough draft on my secretary desk.

Mr. Jenner. Would you describe the incident? In the meantime, I will obtain the rough draft here among my notes.

A—All right. This was on the morning of November 9, Saturday. He asked to use my typewriter, and I said he might.

Mr. Jenner. Excuse me. Would you please state to the Commission why you are reasonably firm that it was the morning of November 9? What arrests your attention to that particular date?

A—Because I remember the weekend that this note or rough draft remained on my secretary desk. He spent the weekend on it. And the weekend was close and its residence on that desk was stopped also on the evening of Sunday, the 10th, when I moved everything in the living room around; the whole arrangement of the furniture was changed, so that I am very clear in my mind as to what weekend this was.

Mr. Jenner. All right, go ahead.

A—He was using the typewriter. I came and put June in her highchair near him at the table where he was typing, and he moved something over what he was typing from, which aroused my curiosity.

Mr. Jenner. Why did that arouse your curiosity?

A—It appeared he didn't want me to see what he was writing or to whom he was writing. I didn't know why he had covered it. If I had peered around him, I could have looked at the typewriter and the page in it, but I didn't.

Mr. Jenner. It did make you curious?

A—It did make me curious. Then, later that day, I noticed a scrawling handwriting on a piece of paper on the corner at the top of my secretary desk in the living room. It remained there.

Sunday morning I was the first one up. I took a closer look at this, a folded sheet of paper folded at the middle. The first sentence arrested me because I knew it to be false. And for this reason I then proceeded—— . . .

Mr. Jenner. That is interesting You noticed that the document was in English.

A—Oh, yes.

Mr. Jenner. You saw it. And it was folded at what point, now that you have the transcript of it before you?

A—At the top of what I could see of the paper. In other words, it was just below the fold. It said, "The FBI is not now interested in my activities."

Mr. Jenner. Is that what arrested your attention?

A—Yes.

Mr. Jenner. What did you do?

A—I then proceeded to read the whole note, wondering, knowing this to be false, wondering why he was saying it. I was

269

irritated to have him writing a falsehood on my typewriter, I may say, too. I felt I had some cause to look at it.

Mr. Jenner. May I have your permission, Mr. Chairman. The document is short. It is relevant to the witness' testimony, and might I read it aloud in the record to draw your attention to it?

Mr. McCloy. Without objection.

Mr. Jenner. Mrs. Paine, would you help me by reading it, since you have it there.

A—Do you want me to leave out all the crossed out——

Mr. Jenner. No; I wish you would indicate that too.

A—"Dear Sirs:

"This is to inform you of events since my interview with comrade Kostine in the Embassy of the Soviet Union, Mexico City, Mexico."

(Discussion off the record.)

A—He typed it early in the morning of that day because after he typed it we went to the place where you get the test for drivers. It was that same day.

Mr. Jenner. It was election day and the driver's license place was closed, is that correct?

A—Yes.

Mr. Jenner. And that was November 9?

A—Yes.

Mr. Jenner. Now you have reached the point where you are reading the letter on the morning of November 10.

A—That is right; after I had noticed that it lay on my desk the previous evening.

"I was unable to remain in Mexico City (because I considered useless—)"—because—it is crossed out.

Mr. Jenner. Excuse me, Mr. Chairman. In this transcript wherever there are words stricken out, the transcriber has placed those words in parenthesis and transcribed the words, but then has written the words "crossed out" to indicate in the original the words crossed out.

Proceed, Mrs. Paine.

A—"Indefinitely because of my (visa—crossed out) Mexican visa restrictions which was for 15 days only.

"(I had a—crossed out) I could not take a chance on applying for an extension unless I used my real name so I returned to the U.S.

"I and Marina Nicholyeva are now living in Dallas, Texas. (You all ready ha—crossed out).

"The FBI is not now interested in my activities in the progressive organization FPCC of which I was secretary in (New Orleans, La.—crossed out) New Orleans, Louisiana since I (am—crossed out) no longer (connected with—crossed out) live in that state.

"(November the November—crossed out) the FBI has visited us here in Texas on November 1st. Agent of the FBI James P. Hasty warned me that if I attempt to engage in FPCC activities

270

in Texas the FBI will again take an 'interest' in me. The agent also 'suggested' that my wife could 'remain in the U.S. under FBI protection', that is, she could (refuse to return to the— crossed out) defect from the Soviet Union. Of course I had my wife strongly protested these tactics by the notorious FBI.

"(It was unfortun that the Soviet Embassy was unable to aid me in Mexico City but—crossed out) I had not planned to contact the Mexico City Embassy at all so of course they were unprepared for me. Had I been able to reach Havana as planned (I could have contacted—crossed out) the Soviet Embassy there (for the completion of would have been able to help me get the necessary documents I required assist me—crossed out) would have had time to assist me, but of course the stuip Cuban consule was at fault here. I am glad he has since been replaced by another."

Mr. Jenner. Now I would like to ask you a few questions about your reaction to that. You had read that in the quiet of your living room on Sunday morning, the 10th of November.

A—That is correct.

Mr. Jenner. And there were a number of things in that that you thought were untrue.

A—Several things I knew to be untrue.

Mr. Jenner. You knew to be untrue. Were there things in there that alarmed you?

A—Yes; I would say so.

Mr. Jenner. What were they?

A—To me this—well, I read it and decided to make a copy.

Mr. Jenner. Would having the document back before you help you?

A—No, no. I was just trying to think what to say first. And decided that I should have such a copy to give to an FBI agent coming again, or to call. I was undecided what to do. Meantime I made a copy.

Mr. Jenner. But you did have the instinct to report this to the FBI?

A—Yes.

Mr. Jenner. And you made a copy of the document?

A—And I made a copy of the document which should be among your papers, because they have that too. And after having made it, while the shower was running, I am not used to subterfuge in any way, but then I put it back where it had been and it lay the rest of Sunday on my desk top, and of course I observed this too.

Mr. Jenner. That is that Lee didn't put it away, just left it out in the room?

A—That he didn't put it away or didn't seem to care or notice or didn't recall that he had a rough draft lying around. I observed it was untrue that the FBI was no longer interested in him. I observed it was untrue that the FBI came—

Mr. Jenner. Why did you observe that that was untrue?

A—Well, the FBI came and they asked me, they said——

Mr. Jenner. Had the FBI been making inquiries of you prior to that time?

A—They had been twice.

Mr. Jenner. November 1 and—

A—November 1, and they told me the 5. I made no record of it whatever.

Mr. Jenner. But it was a few days later?

A—Yes; a few days later. And the first visit I understood to be a visit to convey to Marina that if any blackmail pressure was being put upon her, because of relatives back home, that she was invited, if she wished, to talk about this to the FBI. This is a far cry from being told she could defect from the Soviet Union, very strong words, and false both.

Mr. Jenner. Did you ever hear anything at all insofar as the FBI is concerned reported to you by Marina or Lee Harvey Oswald during all of your acquaintance with either of them of any suggestion by the FBI or anybody else that Marina defect in that context to the United States?

A—No, absolutely not.

Mr. Jenner. Or anything of similar import?

A—Nothing of similar import.

Mr. Jenner. I limited it to the FBI. Any agency of the Government of the United States?

A—Nothing of that sort.

Mr. Jenner. And did you see or observe anything during all of that period of your acquaintance, which stimulated you to think at all or have any notion that any agency of the Government of the United States was seeking to induce her to defect?

A—To the United States?

Mr. Jenner. To the United States.

A—No, and her terminology in view of it was so completely different from such stereotyped and loaded words that I was seeing as I read this. What I was most struck with was what kind of man is this.

Mr. Jenner. Is who?

A—Why is Lee Oswald writing this? What kind of man? Here is a false statement that she was invited to defect, false statement that the FBI is no longer interested, false statement that he was present, "they visited I and my wife."

Mr. Jenner. Was he present?

A—He was not present. False statement that "I and my wife protested vigorously." Having not been present he could not protest.

Mr. Jenner. He was not present when the FBI interviewed you on November 1. Was Marina present then?

A—She was present.

Mr. Jenner. And was Marina present when the FBI came later on November 5?

A—She came into the room just after basically the very short visit was concluded.

Mr. Jenner. The second interview was a rather short one?

A—The second interview was conducted standing up. He simply asked me did I know the address. My memory had been refreshed by him since.

Mr. Jenner. The first interview, however, was a rather lengthy one?

A—But it was not strictly speaking an interview.

Mr. Jenner. What was it?

A—It was, as Mr. Hosty has described to me later, and I think this was my impression too of it at the time, an informal opening for confidence. He presented himself. He talked. We conversed about the weather, about Texas, about the end of the last World War and changes in Germany at the time.

He mentioned that the FBI is very careful in their investigations not to bring anyone they suspect in public light until they have evidence to convict him in a proper court of law, that they did not convict by hearsay or public accusation.

He asked me, and here I am answering why I thought it was false to say the FBI is no longer interested in Lee Oswald; he asked first of all if I knew did Lee live there, and I said "No." Did I know where he lived? No, I didn't, but that was in Dallas.

Did I know where he worked? Yes, I did.

And I said I thought Lee was very worried about losing this job, and the agent said that well, it wasn't their custom to approach the employer directly. I said that Lee would be there on the weekend, so far as I knew, that he could be seen then, if he was interested in talking to Lee.

I want to return now to the fact that I had seen these gross falsehoods and strong words, concluding with "notorious FBI" in this letter, and gone to say I wondered whether any of it was true; including the reference to going to Mexico, including the reference to using a false name, and I still wonder if that was true or false that he used an assumed name, though I no longer wonder whether he had actually gone.

Mr. Jenner. There was a subsequent incident in which you did learn that he used an assumed name, was there not?

A—Yes, a week later.

Mr. Jenner. We will get to that in a moment. But was this——

A—But this was the first indication that I had that this man was a good deal queerer than I thought, and it didn't tell me, perhaps it should have but it didn't tell me just what sort of a queer he was. He addressed it "Dear Sirs." It looked to me like someone trying to make an impression, and choosing the words he thought were best to make that impression, even including assumed name as a possible attempt to make an impression on someone who was able to do espionage, but not to my mind necessarily a picture of someone who was doing espionage,

273

though I left that open as a possibility, and thought I'd give it to the FBI and let them conclude or add it to what they knew.

I regret, and I would like to put this on the record, particularly two things in my own actions prior to the time of the assassination.

One, that I didn't make the connection between this phone number that I had of where he lived and that of course this would produce for the FBI agent who was asking the address of where he lived.

Mr. Jenner. I will get to that, Mrs. Paine.

A—Well, that is regret 1.

Mr. Jenner. I don't want to cover too many subjects at the moment.

A—But then of course you see in light of the events that followed it is a pity that I didn't go directly instead of waiting for the next visit, because the next visit was the 23d of November.

Mr. Jenner. Now I am going to get to that. What did you do with your copy of the letter?

A—I put my copy of the letter away in an envelope in my desk. I then, Sunday evening, also took the original. I decided to do that Sunday evening.

Mr. Jenner. He had left?

A—No, he had not left.

Mr. Jenner. He had not left?

A—I asked the gentlemen present, it included Michael, to come in and help me move the furniture around. I walked in and saw the letter was still there and plunked it into my desk. We then moved all the furniture. I then took it out of the desk and placed it.

Mr. Jenner. When did you take it out of the desk?

A—I don't think he knew that I took it. Oh, that evening or the next morning, I don't recall.

Mr. Jenner. And this was the 10th of November?

A—Yes.

Mr. Jenner. Did you have any conversation with him about that?

A—No. I came close to it. I was disturbed about it. I didn't go to sleep right away. He was sitting up watching the late spy story, if you will, on the TV, and I got up and sat there on the sofa with him saying, "I can't speak," wanting to confront him with this and say, "What is this?" But on the other hand I was somewhat fearful, and I didn't know what to do.

Representative Ford. Fearful in what way?

A—Well, if he was an agent, I would rather just give it to the FBI, not to say "Look, I am watching you" by saying "What is this I find on my desk."

Mr. Jenner. Were you fearful of any physical harm?

A—No; I was not.

Representative Ford. That is what I was concerned about.

A—No; I was not, though I don't think I defined my fears. I sat down and said I couldn't sleep and he said, "I guess you are real upset about going to the lawyer tomorrow."

He knew I had an appointment with my lawyer to discuss the possibility of a divorce the next day, and that didn't happen to be what was keeping me up that night, but I was indeed upset about the idea, and it was thoughtful for him to think of it. But I let it rest there, and we watched the story which he was interested in watching. And then I excused myself and went to bed.

Mr. Jenner. What did you do ultimately with your draft of the letter and the original?

A—The first appearance of an FBI agent person on the 23d of November, I gave the original to them. The next day it probably was I said I also had a copy and gave them that. I wanted to be shut of it.

Mr. Jenner. So I take it, Mrs. Paine, you did not deliver either the original or the copy or call attention to the original or the copy with respect to the FBI.

A—Prior.

Mr. Jenner. Prior to the 23d did you say?

A—That is right.

Mr. Jenner. And what led you to hold onto this rather provocative document?

A—It is a rather provocative document. It provoked my doubts about this fellow's normalcy more than it provoked thoughts that this was the talk of an agent reporting in. But I wasn't sure.

I of course made no—I didn't know him to be a violent person, had no thought that he had this trait, possibility in him, absolutely no connection with the President's coming. If I had, hindsight is so much better, I would certainly have called the FBI's attention to it. Supposing that I had?

Mr. Jenner. If the FBI had returned, Mrs. Paine, as you indicated during the course of your meeting with the FBI November 1, would you have disclosed the document to the FBI?

A—Oh, I certainly think so. This was not something I was at all comfortable in having even.

Mr. Jenner. Were you expecting the FBI to return?

A—I did expect them to come back. As I say, I had said that Lee was here on weekends and so forth. It might have been a good time to give them this document. But as far as I knew, and I know now certainly, they had not seen him and they were still interested in seeing him. . . .

Mr. Jenner. Of course we all know the blanket to which we are referring, which I will ask you about in a moment. I might show it to you at the moment, or at least ask you if it is the blanket. I am exhibiting to the witness Commission Exhibit No. 140. Is this blanket familiar to you?

A—Yes, it is.

Mr. Jenner. And give us the best recollection you have when you first saw it.

A—My best recollection is that I saw it on the floor of my garage sometime in late October. . . .

Mr. Jenner. In what shape, that is form, was the blanket when you first saw it? And I take it you first saw it in your garage.

A—That is my recollection.

Mr. Jenner. And it was subsequent to the time that you and Marina had returned to Irving?

A—Yes.

Mr. Jenner. And you are certain that you did not see the blanket in your station wagon when you arrived in Irving?

A—I do not recall seeing the blanket in my station wagon. . . .

About like so.

Mr. Jenner. For the record if you please. Mr. Chairman, the length of the form is just exactly 45 inches, and it is across exactly 12 inches.

Representative Ford. That is across lying flat.

Mr. Jenner. Across lying flat, thank you.

Now, what else about the form of the blanket did you notice on the occasion when you first saw it on your garage floor? Anything else?

A—I recall from either that occasion or another that there were parallel strings around it.

Mr. Jenner. Tied?

A—Into a bundle, yes, 3 or 4.

Mr. Jenner. Let's proceed with the 21st. Did anything occur on the 21st with respect to Lee Harvey Oswald, that is a Thursday?

A—I arrived home from grocery shopping around 5:30, and he was on the front lawn. I was surprised to see him.

Mr. Jenner. You had no advance notice?

A—I had no advance notice and he had never before come without asking whether he could.

Mr. Jenner. Never before had he come to your home in that form without asking your permission to come?

A—Without asking permission; that is right.

Mr. Jenner. And he was out on the lawn as you drove up, on your lawn?

A—That is right. Playing with June and talking with Marina, who was also out on the lawn.

Mr. Jenner. And you were, of course, surprised to see him?

A—Yes.

Mr. Jenner. Did you park your car in the driveway as usual?

A—Yes.

Mr. Jenner. Did you walk over to speak with him?

A—Yes, got out, very likely picked some groceries out of the car and he very likely picked some up too, and this is I judge what may have happened.

Mr. Jenner. Tell the Commission what was said between you and Lee Oswald?

A—Between me and Lee Oswald?

Mr. Jenner. Yes, on that occasion.

A—That is not what I recall. I recall talking with Marina on the side.

Mr. Jenner. First. Didn't you greet him?

A—Yes; I greeted him.

Mr. Jenner. And then what did you do, walk in the house?

A—As we were walking in the house, and he must have preceded because Marina and I spoke in private to one another, she apologized.

Mr. Jenner. Was Marina out on the lawn also?

A—Yes, sir. She apologized for his having come without permission and I said that was all right, and we said either then or later—I recall exchanging our opinion that this was a way of making up the quarrel or as close as he could come to an apology for the fight on the telephone, that his coming related to that, rather than anything else.

Mr. Jenner. That was her reaction to his showing up un-invited and unexpectedly on that particular afternoon, was it?

A—Well, it was rather my own, too.

Mr. Jenner. And it was your own?

A—Yes.

Mr. Jenner. And because of this incident of the telephone call and your not being able to reach him, and the subsequent talk between Lee and Marina in which there had been some anger expressed, you girls reached the conclusion the afternoon of November 21 that he was home just to see if he could make up with Marina?

A—Yes.

Mr. Jenner. Do I fairly state it?

A—Yes.

Mr. Jenner. What did you do that evening? Did you have oc-casion to note what he did?

A—We had dinner as usual, and then I sort of bathed my children, putting them to bed and reading them a story, which put me in one part of the house. When that was done I realized he had already gone to bed, this being now about 9 o'clock. I went out to the garage to paint some children's blocks, and worked in the garage for half an hour or so. I noticed when I went out that the light was on.

Mr. Jenner. The light was on in the garage?

A—The light was on in the garage.

Mr. Jenner. Was this unusual?

A—Oh, it was unusual for it to be on; yes. I realized that I felt Lee, since Marina had also been busy with her children, had gone out to the garage, perhaps worked out there or gotten something. Most of their clothing was still out there, all of their winter things. They were getting things out from time to time, warmer things for the cold weather, so it was not at all remarkable that he went to the garage, but I thought it careless of him to have left the light on. I finished my work and then turned off the light and left the garage.

Mr. *Jenner*. Have you completed that now?

A—Yes.

Mr. *Jenner*. You stated he was in the garage, how did you know he was in the garage?

Mr. *McCloy*. She didn't state that.

A—I didn't state it absolutely. I guessed it was he rather than she. She was busy with the children and the light had been on and I know I didn't leave the light on.

Mr. *Jenner*. Then, I would ask you directly, did you see him in the garage at anytime from the time you first saw him on the lawn until he retired for the night?

A—No.

Mr. *Jenner*. Until you retired for the night?

A—No.

Mr. *Jenner*. Was he out on the lawn after dinner or supper?

A—I don't believe so.

Mr. *Jenner*. Did you hear any activity out in the garage on that evening?

A—No; I did not.

Mr. *Jenner*. Any persons moving about?

A—No.

Mr. *Jenner*. The only thing that arrested your attention was the fact that you discovered the light on in the garage?

A—That is right.

Mr. *Jenner*. Before you retired?

Representative Ford. You discovered that when you went out to work there?

A—When I went out to work there.

Mr. *McCloy*. When you went out there, did you notice the blanket?

A—I don't recall specifically seeing the blanket. I certainly recall on the afternoon of the 22d where it had been.

Mr. *Dulles*. Was there any evidence of any quarreling or any harsh words between Lee Harvey and Marina that evening that you know of?

A—No.

Mr. *Jenner*. Was there a coolness between them?

A—He went to bed very early, she stayed up and talked with me some, but there was no coolness that I noticed. He was quite friendly on the lawn as we——

Mr. *Jenner*. I mean coolness between himself and—between Lee and Marina.

A—I didn't notice any such coolness. Rather, they seemed

278

warm, like a couple making up a small spat, I should interject one thing here, too, that I recall as I entered the house and Lee had just come in, I said to him, "Our President is coming to town."

And he said, "Ah, yes," and walked on into the kitchen, which was a common reply from him on anything. I was just excited about this happening, and there was his response. Nothing more was said about it.

Mr. Dulles. I didn't catch his answer.

A—"Ah, yes," a very common answer.

Mr. Jenner. He gave no more than that laconic answer?

A—That is right.

Mr. Jenner. Had there been any discussion between you and Marina that the President was coming into town the next day?

A—Yes.

Mr. Jenner. Did she say anything on that subject in the presence of Lee that evening?

A—I don't recall anything of that sort. . . .

Mr. Jenner. Now, as you and Marina sat that evening, folding the ironing, what did you discuss?

A—I don't recall specifically.

Mr. Jenner. Was there any discussion that might serve to refresh your recollection, any discussion of the fact that Lee Oswald had come home or come to Irving in the first place on a Thursday afternoon, which is unusual, or that he had come home unannounced and without invitation, which also as you have testified was unusual? Wasn't there any discussion between you and Marina, speculation at least on your part as to why he was home?

A—Yes, there was discussion. I can't recall exactly what time in the evening it took place but I recall the content of the discussion.

Mr. Jenner. You tell us about it.

A—She suggested that he was making up the quarrel that they had had because of her attempt to reach him by telephone, and I agreed, concurred with that judgment of it.

Mr. Jenner. What was the attitude that evening?

A—He was very warm and friendly.

Mr. Jenner. Was there anything unusual about his attitude and conduct that evening?

A—Nothing except he went to bed a little earlier than he normally would have on a Sunday evening before work.

Mr. Jenner. Were you conscious of the fact that he was retiring a little earlier than he normally would?

A—Yes.

Mr. Jenner. And did you speculate in your mind as to why that might be?

A—No. I knew that he would go to bed as early as 10 o'clock say on the Sunday evening before going to work the next day. This was just, still early.

Mr. Jenner. What was Marina's attitude toward him that evening? Was she reserved because of this quarrel?

A—No. I think she felt the best thing was to pass it by and not discuss it. . . .

Mr. Jenner. You awakened when in the morning?

A—At 7:30.

Mr. Jenner. And when you awakened, immediately after you awakened what did you do?

A—When I awoke I felt the house was extremely quiet and the thought occurred to me that Lee might have overslept. I wondered if he had gotten up in time to get off around 7 o'clock because I knew he had to go to meet Wesley Frazier to catch his ride. I looked about and found a plastic coffee cup in the sink that had clearly been used and judged he had had a cup of coffee and left.

Mr. Jenner. Did you see any other evidence of his having had breakfast?

A—That was all he normally had for breakfast.

Mr. Jenner. A plastic coffee cup with some remains in it of coffee?

A—Instant coffee; yes.

Mr. Jenner. What was his habit with respect to his breakfast when he made his visits?

A—It was very normal for him to take coffee.

Mr. Jenner. Was Marina up and about when you arose at 7:30?

A—No; she was not.

Mr. Jenner. Do you have a recollection of the garage area? Was the door to the garage, the entrance to the garage from the kitchen, closed or open?

A—It was closed. Would it help if I tried to narrate what happened?

Mr. Jenner. Yes.

Mr. McCloy. Go ahead and narrate.

A—I fixed breakfast for myself and my children, turned on the television set to hear President Kennedy speak in Fort Worth, and had breakfast there. I left the house about 9 with my little girl and boy, because she had a dentist appointment, the little girl. I left the television set on, feeling that Marina might not think to turn it on, but I knew that she would be interested to see President Kennedy.

I then was gone until nearly noon, 11:30 or so, both to the dentist and on some errands following that, came back and there was coverage of the fact of the motorcade in Dallas, but there was no television cameras showing it, as you know, and Marina thanked me for having left the television set on. She said she woke up in kind of a bad mood, but she had seen the arrival of President Kennedy and Mrs. Kennedy at the airport in Dallas, and had been thrilled with this occasion and with the greeting he had received, and it had lifted her spirits.

Very shortly after this time, I had only just begun to prepare the lunch, the announcement was made that the President had been shot, and I translated this to Marina. She had not caught it from the television statement. And I was crying as I did the translation. And then we sat down and waited at the television set, no longer interested in the preparing of lunch, and waited to hear further word.

I got out some candles and lit them, and my little girl also lighted a candle, and Marina said to me, "Is that a way of praying?", and I said "Yes, it is, just my own way." And it was well over an hour before we heard definitely that the President was dead.

Mr. Jenner. How did that come to your attention?

A—It was announced on the television. I think it was even still in the intervening time. It was announced on the television that the shot which was supposed to have killed the President was fired from the Texas School Book Depository Building on Elm.

Mr. Jenner. Did you communicate that to her?

A—Marina at this time was in the yard hanging some clothes. I recall going out to her and telling her this.

Mr. Jenner. What did she say?

A—I don't believe she said anything. I then also——

Mr. Jenner. Excuse me. You say "I don't believe she said anything." Is it your recollection?

A—I don't recall anything at all that she said.

Mr. Jenner. Would you——

Mr. McCloy. You told her that you had heard over the television?

A—I heard that the shot had been made——

Mr. McCloy. Coming from the Texas School Book Depository?

A—Schoolbook depository, and I believe I also said I didn't know there was a building on Elm.

Senator Cooper. Why did you go out to tell her, this fact?

A—I felt this was terribly close, somebody working in that building had been there. I thought Lee might be able to say somewhat about what happened, had been close to the event. This was my thought, that we would know somebody who would be able to give or possibly give a first-hand——

Senator Cooper. Did you have any thought at all that Lee Oswald might have been the man who fired the shot?

A—Absolutely none; no.

Mr. Jenner. Why was that, Mrs. Paine?

A—I had never thought of him as a violent man. He had never said anything against President Kennedy, nor anything about President Kennedy. I had no idea that he had a gun. There was nothing that I had seen about him that indicated a man with that kind of grudge or hostility.

Mr. McCloy. But you told this to Marina because of the association of Lee Oswald with the schoolbook depository?

A—Yes, I then proceeded to hang some clothes.

Mr. Jenner. She did not comment?

A—She did not comment.

Mr. Jenner. Made no comment?

A—That is my recollection, that she made no comment. I then helped hang the clothes. My recollection skips then to being again in front of the television listening, and it was then that we heard that the President was dead. We were both sitting on the sofa.

Mr. Jenner. Marina had come in from the yard?

A—Yes.

Mr. Jenner. From the hanging of the clothes?

A—I don't recall whether we came in together or whether she preceded me into the house while I finished hanging up the clothes. But I do recall then next sitting on the sofa when the announcement was definitely made that the President was dead. And she said to me "What a terrible thing this was for Mrs. Kennedy and for the two children." I remember her words were, "Now the two children will have to grow up without the father." It was very shortly after this we were still sitting on the sofa.

Mr. McCloy. Just take a little time and compose yourself.

A—My neighbor, Mrs. Roberts, came in, really I think to see if we had heard, and——

Senator Cooper. Why don't you rest a few minutes?

A—I can proceed. I recall my feeling of anger with her for not being more upset, or she didn't appear to me to be, any more than reporting a remarkable news item. Then it was shortly after that that the bell rang and I went to the door and met some six officers from the sheriff's office and police station.

Mr. Jenner. Was this approximately 3:30 p.m.?

A—Oh, I think it was earlier, but I wouldn't be certain. I know that we had put our children to bed. They were all taking a nap, though I am not certain. Yes, my little girl was asleep also. I cried after I had heard that the President was dead, and my little girl was upset, too, always taking it from me more than from any understanding of the situation. And she cried herself to sleep on the sofa, and I moved her to her bed, and Christopher was already asleep in his crib. June was in bed asleep.

Mr. Jenner. Was Marina emotional at all? Did she cry?

A—No. She said to me, "I feel very badly also, but we seem to show that we are upset in different ways." She did not actually cry.

Mr. McCloy. May I go back a moment there, if I may. You said you were sitting on the sofa—that she and you were sitting on the sofa. While you were listening or looking at the tele-

282

vision, was there any announcement over the television of a suspicion being cast at Lee?

A—It had just been announced that they had caught someone in a theatre, but there was no name given.

Mr. McCloy. So up to this point there was no suggestion that Lee was involved?

A—No; not until the time the officers came to the door.

Mr. McCloy. Not until the officers came?

A—Do you want to ask me about that?

Mr. Jenner. Yes. Now, the officers came to the door——

Mr. McCloy. Pardon me. Were you asking a question?

Mr. Jenner. I was waiting for you.

Mr. McCloy. Senator Cooper reminded me that there were comments, apparently to the effect that somebody from that building had fired the shots. Did you hear that when you were sitting on the sofa with Marina? Did you hear that comment on the television?

A—No; that was earlier.

Mr. McCloy. That was even earlier?

A—Yes; before it was announced that he was dead.

Senator Cooper. But when you were all sitting there——

A—It was at that point that I went out to the yard to tell her.

Senator Cooper. To tell her?

A—Yes.

Senator Cooper. After that when you went back in and you all were sitting on the sofa and she was there, were there any other comments over the television that someone from this building had fired the shot or that any suspects from——

A—You mean, someone associated with the building?

Senator Cooper. Yes.

A—No; that was not said.

Senator Cooper. There was nothing else said about that?

A—No; just that the shot came from the building.

Mr. McCloy. Nothing else that you heard?

A—Nothing else about it.

Mr. Jenner. Mrs. Paine, you do have a definite recollection that you communicated to Marina out in the yard that the shot had come from the Texas School Book Depository?

A—Yes.

Mr. Jenner. And what did she do when you communicated that to her, apart from what she said? You told us what she said. What did she do? Did she come in the house?

A—I don't recall.

Mr. Jenner. Did she enter the garage?

A—I don't know. I never saw her enter the garage, but my recollection is that I was outside hanging clothes after I told her this, but what I can't recall is whether she remained with me hanging the clothes or whether she went in the house.

Mr. Jenner. She might have gone into the house?

A—She might have gone into the house.

Mr. Jenner. But, in any event, you do not recall her entering the garage following your advising her of the announcement that the shot had come, or was thought to have come from the Texas School Book Depository?

A—I do not recall.

Senator Cooper. When you went out to tell her, was she hanging clothes?

A—She was hanging clothes.

Senator Cooper. Then did you go help her, and then both of you were hanging clothes?

A—I then helped her. What I can't remember is whether she remained and finished the job with me. I remember I finished, remained until they were all hung.

Senator Cooper. Do you remember at anytime after that whether or not you were hanging clothes alone?

A—That is what I am not certain about. I could well have been.

Mr. Jenner. At anytime that afternoon, in any event, up to the time that the policeman rang your doorbell, did you observe or were you aware that Marina had entered the garage?

A—I wasn't aware that she had entered, if she did. . . .

Mr. Jenner. How many police officers were there?

A—There were six altogether, and they were busy in various parts of the house. The officer asked me in the garage did Lee Oswald have any weapons or guns. I said no, and translated the question to Marina, and she said yes; that she had seen a portion of it—had looked into—she indicated the blanket roll on the floor.

Mr. Jenner. Was the blanket roll on the floor at that time?

A—She indicated the blanket roll on the floor very close to where I was standing. As she told me about it I stepped onto the blanket roll.

Mr. Jenner. This might be helpful. You had shaped that up yesterday and I will just put it on the floor.

A—And she indicated to me that she had peered into this roll and saw a portion of what she took to be a gun she knew her husband to have, a rifle. And I then translated this to the officers that she knew that her husband had a gun that he had stored in here.

Mr. Jenner. Were you standing on the blanket when you advised——

A—When I translated. I then stepped off of it and the officer picked it up in the middle and it bent so.

Mr. Jenner. It hung limp just as it now hangs limp in your hand?

A—And at this moment I felt this man was in very deep trouble and may have done——

Mr. McCloy. Were the strings still on it?

A—The strings were still on it. It looked exactly as it had at

284

previous times I had seen it. It was at this point I say I made the connection with the assassination, thinking that possibly, knowing already that the shot had been made from the School Book Depository, and that this was a rifle that was missing, I wondered if he would not also be charged before the day was out with the assassination.

Mr. Jenner. Did you say anything?

A—No; I didn't say that.

Mr. Jenner. When the officer picked up the blanket package, did you hear any crinkling as though there was paper inside?

A—No crinkling.

Mr. Jenner. None whatsoever. When you stepped on the package, did you have a feeling through your feet that there was something inside the package in the way of paper.

A—Not anything in the way of paper.

Mr. Jenner. Or wrapping.

A—Or anything that crinkled; no. I did think it was hard but that was my cement floor.

Mr. Jenner. But definitely you had no sensation of any paper inside?

A—No such sensation.

Mr. Jenner. Of the nature or character of the wrapping paper you identified yesterday.

A—No; and when he picked it up I would think such paper would rattle, but there was no such sound. Marina said nothing at this time. She was very white, and of course I judged——

Mr. Jenner. Did she blanch?

A—She is not a person to immediately show her feelings necessarily. She was white. I wouldn't say that it was a sudden thing. I can't be certain that it was sudden at that point.

Representative Ford. How close was she standing to it.

A—From here to there, about 6 feet.

Mr. Jenner. Proceed.

A—The officers then said they would like me and Marina to go down to the police station, and I said well, I would seek to try to get a baby-sitter to come to stay with the children so that we might accompany them. About this time, we then left the garage as I recall, because then Michael Paine arrived at the front door. I was in the living room when he came. And I said "Did you know to come" and he said that he had heard Oswald's name mentioned on the radio, and had come over directly, for which I may say I was very glad.

Mr. Jenner. Where was Marina in the meantime?

A—Marina remained in the house with the children. Lynn by this time had awakened as I recall. Christopher was still sleeping and I think June was also. And I said I would walk over to my neighbors to ask if—there was something that intervened I just remembered. I first went and asked my immediate neighbor, Mrs. Roberts, if she could keep the children for a short time in the afternoon, but she was just on her way to go somewhere. She couldn't. So then I went to the home of the person I normally have for a baby-sitter. It was now after school or this babysitter would not have been there, which brings us to 3:30 perhaps. And I asked the mother if the young girl, teenage girl, could come and stay at the house. I was accompanied to the house by one of the officers. As we left the house I said "Oh, you don't have to go with me." Oh, he said, he'd be glad to. And then it occurred to me he had been assigned to go with me, and I said "come along." It was the first I have ever experienced being in the company of people who suspected me of anything, and of course that is their business.

We did arrange then for the girls to come back, one or two, I forget whether it was two of the daughters or one that came then to my house to stay with the children. As I came back, I noticed the officers carrying a number of things from the house, and I looked into the back of one of the cars. It was across the street from my house, and saw he had three cases of 78 records of mine, and I said, "You don't need those and I want to use them on Thanksgiving weekend. I have promised to lead a folk dance conference on the weekend. I will need those records which are all folk dance records and I doubt that you might get them back at that time."

And I said, "that is a 16 mm projector. You don't want that. It is mine."

And he took me by the arm and he said, "We'd better get down to the station. We have wasted too much time as it is." And I said, "I want a list of what you are taking, please." Or perhaps that was before. As much answer as I ever got was "We'd better get to the station." Then I evidently had made them nervous because when we got back from this car to the house, Marina wanted to change from slacks as I had already done to a dress. They would not permit her to do that. I said "She has a right to, she is a woman, to dress as she wishes before going down." And I directed her to the bathroom to change. The officer opened the bathroom door and said no, she had no time to change. I was still making arrangements with the babysitters, arranging for our leaving the children there, and one of the officers made a statement to the effect of "we'd better get this straight in a hurry Mrs. Paine or we'll just take the children down and leave them with juvenile while we talk to you."

And I said "Lynn, you may come too" in reply to this. I don't like being threatened. And then Christopher was still sleeping so I left him in the house and Lynn, my daughter, and Marina took her daughter and her baby with her to the police station, so we were quite a group going into town in the car. Michael was in one car, Marina and I and all the children were in another with three police officers as I recall. One of them spoke some Czech, tried to understand what was being said. The one in the front seat turned to me and said "Are you a Communist," and I said, "No, I am not, and I don't even feel the need of a Fifth

286

Amendment." And he was satisfied with that. We went on then to the police station, and waited until such time as they could interview us. They interviewed Michael at one point separately.

Mr. Jenner. Separately?

A—And they interviewed Marina while I was present. . . .

Mr. Jenner. Was it agreed that Marina would stay at your house that night?

A—Yes; certainly all her baby things were there. So, we went back there. We were taken back by police officers.

Mr. Jenner. Everybody assumed she would return back to your home?

A—Oh, yes.

Mr. Jenner. Was there any discussion that would indicate any reluctance on the part of anybody that she return to your home?

A—None.

Mr. Jenner. None whatsoever by anybody?

A—That is correct, none whatsoever by anybody.

The police officers brought us back to my home. It was by this time dark, and I think it was about 9 o'clock in the evening. I asked Michael to go out and buy hamburgers at a drive-in so we wouldn't have to cook, and we ate these as best we could, and began to prepare to retire. We talked. I have a few specific recollections of that period that I will put in here.

Just close to the time of retiring Marina told me that just the night before Lee had said to her he hoped they could get an apartment together again soon. As she said this, I felt she was hurt and confused, wondering how he could have said such a thing which indicated wanting to be together with her when he must have already been planning something that would inevitably cause separation. I asked her did she think that Lee had killed the President and she said, "I don't know." And I felt that this was not something to talk about really anyway. But my curiosity overcame my politeness. . . .

Representative Ford. Did you take your children shopping?

A—Always. Then about 3:30 or 4 I got a telephone call.

Mr. Jenner. The phone rang?

A—The phone rang; I answered it.

Mr. Jenner. Did you recognize the voice?

A—I recognized the voice but I don't recall what he said.

Mr. Jenner. What did the voice say?

A—The voice said: "This is Lee."

Mr. Jenner. Give your best recollection of everything you said and if you can, please, everything he said, and exactly what you said.

A—I said, "Well, Hi." And he said he wanted to ask me to call Mr. John Abt in New York for him after 6 p.m. He gave me a telephone number of an office in New York and a residence in New York.

Mr. Jenner. Two telephone numbers he gave you?

A—Yes.

287

Mr. Jenner. One office and one residence of Mr. John Abt. Did he say who Mr. John Abt was?

A—He said he was an attorney he wanted to have.

Mr. Jenner. Represent him?

A—To represent him. He thanked me for my concern.

Mr. Jenner. Did he tell you or ask you what you were to do or say to Mr. Abt if you reached him?

A—I carried the clear impression I was to ask him if he would serve as attorney for Lee Oswald.

Mr. Jenner. All right.

Have you given the substance of the conversation in as much detail, of the entire conversation, as you now can recall?

A—There is a little more that is——

Senator Cooper. Why don't you just go ahead and tell it as you remember it, everything that he said and you said?

A—I can't give the specific words to this part but I carry a clear impression, too, that he sounded to me almost as if nothing out of the ordinary had happened.

I would make this telephone call for him, would help him, as I had in other ways previously. He was, he expressed gratitude to me. I felt, but did not express, considerable irritation at his seeming to be so apart from the situation, so presuming of his own innocence, if you will, but I did say I would make the call for him.

Then he called back almost immediately. I gather that he had made the call to me on the permission to make a different call and then he got specific permission from the police to make a call to me and the call was identical.

Mr. Jenner. This is speculation?

A—This is speculation but the content of the second call was almost identical.

Mr. Jenner. The phone rang?

A—He asked me to contact John Abt.

Mr. Jenner. He identified himself and he asked you to make the call?

A—Yes.

Mr. Jenner. What did he say?

A—He wanted me to call this lawyer.

Mr. Jenner. Did you express any surprise for him to call back almost immediately giving you the same message that he had given previously?

A—I think somebody must have said, that the officers had said he could call, make this call.

Mr. Jenner. Did you say anything about the fact that he had already just called you about the same subject matter?

A—He may have added.

Mr. Jenner. Did you, please?

A—No. I was quite stunned that he called at all or that he thought he could ask anything of me, appalled, really.

288

Mr. McCloy. Did he say he was innocent, or did he just have this conversation with respect to the retention of a counsel?

A—That is all.

Mr. Jenner. At no time during either of those conversations did he deny that he was in any way involved in this situation?

A—He made no reference to why he was at the police station or why he needed a lawyer.

Mr. Jenner. He just assumed that you knew he was at the police station, did he?

A—That is right. . . .

A—In this interim then, I suppose I talked to some more news people but I want to get to the next important point which was that Lee called again.

Mr. Jenner. A third time?

A—I really call the first two one, but it was twice dialed.

Mr. Jenner. Fix the time, please.

A—It was around 9:30 in the evening.

Mr. Jenner. Who was home? Was your husband there on that occasion?

A—I don't recall.

Mr. Jenner. Was anyone else other than your children and yourself in your home at the time of the receipt of the call in the evening?

A—It could only have been Michael. I would remember someone else.

Mr. Jenner. But you have no definite recollection that even he was present?

A—No.

Mr. Jenner. All right. The phone rang, you answered it.

A—Yes.

Mr. Jenner. Did you recognize the voice?

A—I recognized the voice.

Mr. Jenner. Whose was it?

A—It was Lee Oswald's.

Mr. Jenner. What did he say and what did you say?

A—He said, "Marina, please," in Russian.

Mr. Jenner. Please, Mrs. Paine, did he speak to you in English in the conversations in the afternoon or in Russian?

A—He spoke in English the entire conversation.

Mr. Jenner. The two in the afternoon?

A—Yes.

Mr. Jenner. Now, however, he resorted to Russian, did he?

A—Yes. He planned to speak to Marina.

Mr. Jenner. I beg your pardon?

A—He planned to speak to Marina, and this opening phrase was one he normally used calling as he had many previous times to speak to her.

Mr. Jenner. He was under the assumption, you gathered, that Marina was in your home?

A—He certainly was.

Mr. Jenner. All right.

A—And I would be fairly certain that I answered him in English. I said she was not there, that I had a notion about where she might be, but I wasn't at all certain. That I would try to find out. He said, he wanted me to—he said he thought she should be at my house. He felt irritated at not having been able to reach her. And he wanted me to——

Mr. Jenner. Did he sound irritated?

A—Yes; he sounded just a slight edge to his voice. And he wanted me to deliver a message to her that he thought she should be at my house.

Mr. Jenner. And he so instructed you?

A—Yes.

Mr. Jenner. That is what he said?

A—Yes. That was so far as I remember, the entire conversation.

Mr. Jenner. What response did you give to his direction?

A—I said I would try to reach her. . . .

GEORGE S. De MOHRENSCHILDT

Testimony of George S. De Mohrenschildt, a Russian-born businessman who befriended Oswald in Dallas:

Mr. Jenner. Give me your impression of him at that time—your first impression.

A—The first impression and the last impression remain more or less the same. I could never get mad at this fellow.

Mr. Jenner. Why?

A—Sometimes he was obnoxious. I don't know. I had a liking for him. I always had a liking for him. There was something charming about him, there was some—I don't know. I just liked the guy—that is all.

Mr. Jenner. When you reached home, you reported on this——

A—You know, he was very humble—with me he was very humble. If somebody expressed an interest in him, he blossomed, absolutely blossomed. If you asked him some questions about him, he was just out of this world. That was more or less the reason that I think he liked me very much.

Mr. Jenner. Yes; he did. It is so reported, and Marina has so said.

Well, that first visit didn't give you any opportunity to observe the relations between Marina and Lee, I assume?

A—I already noticed then that the couple—that they were not getting along, right away.

Mr. Jenner. What made you have that impression?

A—Well, there was a strained relationship there. You could feel that. And, you know how it is—you can see that the couple —that they are not very happy. You could feel that. And he was not particularly nice with her. He didn't kiss her. It wasn't a loving husband who would come home and smile and kiss his wife, and so on and so forth. He was just indifferent with her. He was more interested in talking to me than to her. That type of attitude.

Mr. Jenner. But you did notice throughout all your acquaintance with him that he blossomed when you paid attention to him, let us say?

A—Exactly.

Mr. Jenner. You drew him into conversation or situations—especially when you asked something about him?

A—Yes; exactly. I think that is his main characteristic. He wanted people to be interested in him, not in Marina. And she remained quite often in the background. . . .

Mr. Jenner. What was your understanding of the difficulties they were having?

A—Why was he physically beating her?

The difficulties were this: She was—just incompatibility. They were annoying each other, and she was all the time annoying him. Having had many wives, I could see his point of view. She was annoying him all the time—"Why don't you make some money?", why don't they have a car, why don't they have more dresses, look at everybody else living so well, and they are just miserable flunkeys. She was annoying him all the time. Poor guy was going out of his mind.

Mr. Jenner. And you and your wife were aware of this, were you?

A—Yes.

Mr. Jenner. And had discussed it——

A—We told her she should not annoy him—poor guy, he is doing his best, "Don't annoy him so much." And I think I mentioned before one annoying thing. She openly said he didn't see her physically—right in front of him. She said, "He sleeps with me just once a month, and I never get any satisfaction out of it." A rather crude and completely straightforward thing to say in front of relative strangers, as we were.

Mr. Jenner. Yes.

A—I didn't blame Lee for giving her a good whack on the eye. Once it was all right. But he also exaggerated. I think the discussions were purely on that basis—purely on a material basis, and on a sexual basis, those two things—which are pretty important. . . .

I did not take him seriously—that is all.

Mr. Jenner. I know you didn't. Why didn't you?

A—Well——

Mr. Jenner. You are a highly sophisticated person.

A—Well, he was not sophisticated, you see. He was a semi-educated hillbilly. And you cannot take such a person seriously. All his opinions were crude, you see. But I thought at the time he was rather sincere.

291

Mr. Jenner. Opinion sincerely held, but crude?

A—Yes.

Mr. Jenner. He was relatively uneducated.

A—Oh, yes.

Mr. Jenner. Quite, as a matter of fact—he never finished high school.

A—Yes; I did not even know that.

Mr. Jenner. Did you have the feeling that his views on politics were shallow and surface?

A—Very much so.

Mr. Jenner. That he had not had the opportunity for a study under scholars who would criticize, so that he himself could form some views on the subject?

A—Exactly. His mind was of a man with exceedingly poor background, who read rather advanced books, and did not understand even the words in them. He read complicated economical treatises and just picked up difficult words out of what he has read, and loved to display them. He loved to use the difficult words, because it was to impress one.

Mr. Jenner. Did you think he understood it?

A—He did not understand the words—he just used them. So how can you take seriously a person like that? You just laugh at him. But there was always an element of pity I had, and my wife had, for him. We realized that he was sort of a forlorn individual, groping for something.

Mr. Jenner. Did you form any impression in the area, let us say, of reliability—that is, whether our Government would entrust him with something that required a high degree of intelligence, a high degree of imagination, a high degree of ability to retain his equilibrium under pressure, a management of a situation, to be flexible enough?

A—I never would believe that any government would be stupid enough to trust Lee with anything important.

Mr. Jenner. Give me the basis of your opinion.

A—Well, again, as I said, an unstable individual, mixed-up individual, uneducated individual, without background. What government would give him any confidential work? No government would. Even the government of Ghana would not give him any job of any type.

Mr. Jenner. You used the expression "unstable." Would you elaborate on that?

A—Well, unstability—his life is an example of his instability. He switched allegiance from one country to another, and then back again, disappointed in this, disappointed in that, tried various jobs. But he did it, you see, without the enjoyment of adventure—like some other people would do in the United States, a new job is a new adventure, new opportunities. For him it was a gruesome deal. He hated his jobs. He switched all the time. . . .

Mr. Jenner. Did you form an impression of him, Mr. De

292

Mohrenschildt, as to his reliability in a different sense now—that is, whether he was reasonably mentally stable or given to violent surges of anger or lack of control of himself?

A—Of course, he was that. The fact that we took his wife away from him, you know, was the result of his outbursts and his threats to his wife.

Mr. Jenner. What kind of threats?

A—Well, that he will beat the hell out of her. I think Marina told me that he threatened to kill her. . . .

Mr. Jenner. Did Marina smoke?

A—Yes. Oh, boy, this is an interesting question. She loved to smoke and would smoke as many cigarettes as she could lay her hands on. And you know, Oswald did not smoke and forbade her to smoke. This is the reason—one of the reasons they fought so bitterly—because he would take the cigarette away from her and slap her.

Mr. Jenner. In your presence?

A—In my presence, would take the cigarette away from her and push her, "You are not going to do that", in a dictatorial way. So I would say, "Now, stop it, let her smoke." And then he would relax. But that is the type of person he was. But not in our presence—when we were away, Marina said he would not let her smoke nor drink, I think. He refused to let her drink either. And she liked to have a drink. With all her defects, she is more or less a normal person, and rather happy-go-lucky, a very happy-go-lucky girl.

Mr. Jenner. What about his drinking?

A—I never saw him drink. Maybe he would take a very little, but I never saw him drink more than half a glass—as far as I remember. I didn't pay too much attention. Maybe that is why he was tense, because he did not drink enough. He was always tense. That guy was always under some kind of pressure.

Mr. Jenner. You have that impression?

A—Yes; always some kind of pressure.

Mr. Jenner. And this was an inward pressure, you thought?

A—Yes; some inward pressure. . . .

Mr. Jenner. Did that ever arise, discussions as to why—possibly affecting his desire to return to the United States?

A—I do not recall that. The most important answer I think I got from Oswald—and that was one of the reasons we liked him and thought that he was rather intelligent in his estimation of Soviet Russia—is the fact that we asked him, both my wife and I, "Why did you leave Soviet Russia", and he said very sincerely, "Because I did not find what I was looking for."

Mr. Jenner. And did you ask him what he was looking for?

A—A Utopia. I knew what he was looking for—Utopia. And that does not exist any place.

293

Mr. Jenner. This man could not find what he was looking for anywhere in this world.

A—He could not find it in the States, he could not find it any place.

Mr. Jenner. He could find it only in him.

A—Exactly. He could find it in himself, in a false image of grandeur that he built in himself. But at the time that we knew him that was not so obvious. Now you can see that, as a possible murderer of the President of the United States, he must have been unbelievably egotistical, an unbelievably egotistical person.

Mr. Jenner. Do you know what paranoia is?

A—Yes.

Mr. Jenner. Well——

A—I know it very well.

Mr. Jenner. Did you notice——

A—Because I am interested in medicine.

Mr. Jenner. Did you notice any tendencies—this may be rationalization, of course, now that you are thinking back.

A—I would call him a stage below definite paranoia, which means a highly neurotic individual. But even an M.D. would not give you a right definition, or a right demarcation between the two. . . .

Mr. Jenner. What impression, if you have any, do you have with respect to his sexual habits? Did you ever have any thoughts?

A—Yes.

Mr. Jenner. As to whether he was a homosexual?

A—No.

Mr. Jenner. He was not in your opinion?

A—I don't think so, I think he was an asexual person, asexual, and as I told you before, Marina was bitterly complaining about her lack of satisfaction. This is really the time that we decided just to drop them you see. One of the reasons you see we decided not to see them again, because we both found it revolting, such a discussion of marital habits in front of relative strangers as we were, see. . . .

Mr. Jenner. Was there any occasion when it came to your attention that there was any alarm on Marina's part with respect to Lee possibly inflicting some harm on Vice President Nixon, or former Vice President Nixon?

A—No.

Mr. Jenner. That doesn't ring a bell at all?

A—It doesn't ring a bell at all. But what I wanted to underline, that was always amazing to me, that as far as I am concerned he was an admirer of President Kennedy.

Mr. Jenner. I was going to ask you about that.

Tell me the discussions you had in that connection. Did you have some discussions with him?

A—Just occasional sentences, you know. I think once I

mentioned to him that I met Mrs. Kennedy when she was a child you know, she was a very strong-willed child, very intelligent and very attractive child you see, and a very attractive family, and I thought that Kennedy was doing a very good job with regard to the racial problem, you know. We never discussed anything else. And he also agreed with me, "Yes, yes, yes; I think it is an excellent President, young, full of energy, full of good ideas."

Mr. Jenner. Did he ever indicate any resentment of Mr. Kennedy's wealth?

A—That is definitely a point there, you know. He did not indicate, but he hated wealth, period, you see. Lee Oswald hated wealth, and I do not recall the exact words, but this is something that you could feel in him, you see. And since he was very poor, you know, I could see why he did, you see. I even would tell him sometimes, "That is ridiculous. Wealth doesn't make happiness and you can be poor and be happy, you can be wealthy and be very unhappy; it doesn't matter." I met a lot of wealthy people in my life and found that quite a few of them are very unhappy and I have met quite a few poor people and they are very happy. So it is nothing to be jealous of. . . .

JEANNE De MOHRENSCHILDT

The testimony of Mrs. De Mohrenschildt, who was a friend of the Oswalds in Dallas:

Mr. Jenner. Now, Mrs. De Mohrenschildt, you had discussions with both Marina and Lee about their difficulties?

A—Yes; we had them at the same time, in the same room.

Mr. Jenner. Now, what were the reasons that she advanced as to any—as to her dissatisfaction?

A—What was the reasons what?

Mr. Jenner. What were the reasons she said why she was dissatisfied with him?

A—Oh, there was quite a few reasons. And I tell you—it was strange for me to hear from a young girl like that to speak so, how you say it—so boldly, about sex, for instance. I was shocked by it, you know—because in my times, even I was twice as old as she.

Mr. Jenner. Will you please tell me what she said?

A—Well, she said her husband doesn't satisfy her. She just— and he is just too busy with his things, he doesn't pay enough attention to her.

Mr. Jenner. That was one reason?

A—That is one of the main reasons, yes.

And the second reason, he was cruel with her—for instance, she likes to smoke, and he would forbid her to smoke. Any little argument or something—like once something—she didn't fill his bathtub, he beat her for it. And, also, he didn't like for her to have a drink of wine. She liked wine very much. She wasn't a drunk or anything, but she likes to drink wine. And he would object to that, too. And that was their main disagreements.

And then with the baby, he was absolutely fanatical about the child. He loved that child. You should see him looking at the child, he just changed completely. He thought that she was not too good with the child. The child was already spoiled to no end. Every time the child makes a noise, she picked it up. If she is not there in a second to pick the child up, Lee is after her— why is the baby crying? And the baby is extremely difficult, because it doesn't know anybody but her or Lee. Nobody could pick her up. And she is constantly with her. She had the child with her all the time, from our observations. She just couldn't take it. It was very, very difficult. And still at the same time, she didn't do much to free herself from it.

Mr. Jenner. What were Marina's personal habits? Was she clean and neat? Did she keep her home clean and neat? Or did her laziness spill over in those areas?

A—Well, it was halfway, because it seems to be neat, and still not very—she was not a woman to arrange the home or make a home. I don't think so. And I don't know enough about it, because they had so few things, and they were so poor. So what can you make a home out of, nothing. You cannot really judge. You cannot. I am sure if she has things to do it with, I am sure she will.

At that particular time, she could not. She didn't have enough things to make a home. The apartments they were living in in Dallas were miserable, very, very poor. . . .

Mr. Jenner. From your contacts with him, you had the impression he had been disappointed in Russia?

A—I asked him, "Why did you come back, if you were such a brave big hero and you threw the passport?"

And as she told me, "In the American Ambassador's face in Moscow."

He said, "Here is your passport, now I am going to be a Soviet citizen."

And I said, "How come you are back?"

He said, "I didn't find what I was looking for."

Mr. Jenner. Oswald said that?

A—That was Oswald's answer. "I didn't find what I was looking for."

So, to me, the answer was the stupid kid decided to be obnoxious, and thinking he was a big hero went over there, and learned the hard way, burned himself, and decided to come back, and our Government was wonderful to help him at the time. And he was very conscientious about paying the debt, very conscientious. He paid it back, I think, the first thing, out of the first salary, in spite how hard it was for them to live. Those are the things.

And I don't know of anybody saying anything good about

him. And that made me a little mad. Nobody said anything good about him. He had a lot of good qualities. He had a lot of terrible qualities, but certainly to compare him with that horrible Ruby—Oswald had a lot of good qualities. And if people would be kinder to him, maybe, you know—maybe he wouldn't be driven to be so, and wouldn't do anything like that. I don't know whether he did or not, anyway. But he would not be involved in it.

But I have the impression that he was just pushed, pushed, pushed, and she was probably nagging, nagging, nagging.

Mr. Jenner. You found her to be a nagger?

A—Yes; oh, yes; she ribbed him even in front of us. . . .

Mr. Jenner. Now, I asked you as to the sources of difficulty, and you related them. Did she twit him about his inability to make enough money so that she could live better?

A—Yes. That was one complaint. Another complaint, sex-wise, he wasn't satisfactory for her. In fact, she was almost sick that she wasn't getting enough sex, which I never heard of before. I didn't know such things can happen to people, you know.

We saw, ourselves, he was a little difficult—for instance, with the baby. I also objected that he didn't let her smoke. After all, she is supposed to be a grown woman. He was definitely domineering—it has to be just like he said and that is it. He always had a feeling that he is the boss, and she has to—just nothing, just wipe the floor with her. This man. So we objected to that.

Mr. Jenner. Now, you were going to tell me the basis on which you formed your opinion as to her, you say, nagging. You used the term "ribbing." This was not jocular, was it—not joking? It was irritating?

A—It was irritating. That he was a big shot, reading, reading, reading.

Mr. Jenner. Would say that in your presence?

A—Yes.

Mr. Jenner. She would ridicule him, in other words?

A—Yes, in a way, yes. She said things that will hurt men's pride. That definitely was. . . .

ELENA A. HALL

The testimony of Mrs. Hall, with whom Mrs. Lee Harvey Oswald lived briefly in Fort Worth, Tex.:

Mr. Liebeler. The first time that Marina came to your house, can you remember exactly when that was?

A—In July. Sometime in July.

Mr. Liebeler. And you noticed even in July that she had been bruised, is that correct?

A—Yes.

Mr. Liebeler. But it wasn't until October or November——

A—October when she moved.

Mr. Liebeler. That you learned that she had gotten those bruises as a result of her husband beating her, is that right?

A—Yes.

Mr. Liebeler. At the time in October that Marina lived in your house, did she discuss with you her marital relations with Oswald?

A—Yes. Well, she is, I think she is very nice girl. And I told her, "Marina, you are in such a difficult financial situation, you'd better not have children for quite a while, and when you have a better financial situation, you can have them." And she said, "Well, I don't know."

And I told her, "If you want to, I have a lady doctor, Dr. Taylor. If you want me, I will take you there. She will give you some things." And she said, "No; I don't think so."

She said, "Our married life is so strange that I don't think I ever will have any children any more," because he was very cold to her.

Mr. Liebeler. Did Marina indicate at that time that she and Oswald did not have normal sexual relations.

A—Very seldom. The thing that she told me, "Very seldom."

Mr. Liebeler. Tell me everything that you can remember about that subject that Marina told you.

A—That was the only thing that was worrying me, her to not have children, because they are in such bad shape, and that is the only thing she told me.

And I said, "If you think you want any more." So it is none of my business, you know.

Mr. Liebeler. Is that all that Marina said about that subject?

A—We didn't talk any more, because it was my suggestion to her to not have children, and she told me that, and that was all.

Mr. Liebeler. Did she ever tell you that Oswald would—was not very much of a man in that sense?

A—Yes. That is what she told me.

Mr. Liebeler. They very seldom had sexual relations?

A—Yes, sir.

Mr. Liebeler. Did you ever discuss that question with her any other time?

A—No.

Mr. Liebeler. Did you form an impression as to how Lee and Marina were getting along with each other at the time that Marina lived in your house, other than what we have already talked about?

A—No. Couple of times I told her, "Why do you argue with him about little things," and she said, "Oh, because he is not a man." That is what she told me. For instance, I like hot peppers and he didn't like it. Well, is nothing wrong with a man who doesn't like peppers. John doesn't like it at all. And at the table they were eating, and I ate the peppers, and he wouldn't touch, and she said, "He is afraid of everything, hot peppers."

And he said, he don't like it, and they had argument about that. And after he left I said, "Marina, you shouldn't do that because, well, some people like them and some don't."

Well, things like that, she would start with him and they had an argument. Probably if I wouldn't be there, they would have a fight or something.

Mr. Liebeler. Did you ever have the feeling that Marina was a good wife to Oswald, or did you have the feeling that she was not particularly a good wife?

A—Well, she is a little bit lazy one, and she can sleep 48 hours a day. That is the only thing. And maybe they had trouble because of this and little things, like I said about the peppers and so on.

Mr. Liebeler. Did you ever see or hear of Marina making fun of Oswald in front of other people?

A—Who?

Mr. Liebeler. Marina making fun of Lee?

A—Oh, yes; she would do it.

Mr. Liebeler. Can you think of any specific examples?

A—She always was complaining about him. He was not a man. He is afraid. I don't know, not complete, I guess, or something like that. Not complete man.

Mr. Liebeler. This may not seem to be too important, but we are not just curious, it might have a bearing on the Commission's determination of what kind of man Oswald was and what kind of person he was.

Did Marina make fun of Oswald's sexual inability in front of other people, or was it a more general thing?

A—Generally. I never heard sexual nothing; no. Only when I asked her about this, she told me. And that was, we don't talk any more about this. I didn't hear it. Maybe somebody else did. I didn't.

Mr. Liebeler. You had the feeling, I gather from what you said, that if there were difficulties in the Oswald marriage, they were not entirely Lee Oswald's fault? It also would be some of the fault of Marina?

A—Yes.

Mr. Liebeler. What is your opinion?

A—I think that she is stubborn, real stubborn, and she would pick up something little and go on and have an argument for nothing. . . .

DR. RENATUS HARTOGS

Testimony of a New York psychiatrist who interviewed Oswald in 1953 and a report on his examination.

Mr. Liebeler. In your capacity as chief psychiatrist for the

Youth House did you have occasion at any time to interview Lee Harvey Oswald?

A—Yes.

Mr. Liebeler. Would you tell us when that was and all that you can remember about that interview in your own words.

A—That is tough. I remember that—actually I reconstructed this from what I remembered from the seminar. We gave a seminar on this boy in which we discussed him, because he came to us on a charge of truancy from school, and yet when I examined him, I found him to have definite traits of dangerousness. In other words, this child had a potential for explosive, aggressive, assaultive acting out which was rather unusual to find in a child who was sent to Youth House on such a mild charge as truancy from school.

This is the reason why I remember this particular child, and that is the reason why we discussed him in the seminar.

I found him to be a medium-sized, slender, curlyhaired youngster, pale-faced, who was not very talkative, he was not spontaneous. He had to be prompted. He was polite. He answered in a somewhat monotonous fashion. His sentences were well structured. He was in full contact with reality.

Mr. Liebeler. He was?

A—He was in full contact with reality. I found his reasoning to be intensely self-centered, his judgment also centering around his own needs, and the way he looked at life and his relationships with people. This was mostly in the foreground. So this is what I remember actually. . . . [Youth House report entered in record].

"This 13-year-old, well-built, well-nourished boy was remanded to Youth House for the first time on charge of truancy from school and of being beyond the control of his mother as far as school attendance is concerned. This is his first contact with the law.

"He is—tense, withdrawn and evasive boy who dislikes intensely talking about himself and his feelings. He likes *the* give the impression that he doesn't care about others and rather likes to keep himself so that he is not bothered and does not have to make the effort of communicating. It was difficult to penetrate the emotional wall behind which this boy hides—and he provided us with sufficient clues, permitting us to see intense anxiety, shyness, feelings of *awkwardness* and insecurity as the main reasons for his withdrawal tendencies and solitary habits. Lee told us: 'I don't want a friend and I don't like to talk to people.' He describes himself as stubborn and according to his own saying likes to say 'no.' Strongly resistive and negativistic features were thus noticed—but psychotic mental content was denied and no indication of psychotic mental changes were arrived at.

"Lee is a youngster with superior mental endowment functioning presently on the bright normal range of mental effi-

300

ciency. His abstract thinking capacity and his vocabulary are well developed. No retardation in school subjects could be found in spite of his truancy from school. Lee limits his interests to reading magazines and looking at the television all day long. He dislikes to play with others or to face the learning situation in school. On the other hand he claims that he is 'very poor' in all school subjects and would need remedial help. The discrepancy between the claims and his actual attainment level show the low degree of self-evaluation and self-esteem at which this boy has arrived presently, mainly due to feelings of general inadequacy and emotional discouragement.

"Lee is the product of a broken home—as his father died before he was born. Two older brothers are presently in the United States Army—while the mother supports herself and Lee as an insurance broker. This occupation makes it impossible for her to provide adequate supervision of Lee and to make him attend school regularly. Lee is intensely dissatisfied with his present way of living, but feels that the only way in which he can avoid feeling too unhappy is to deny to himself competition with other children or expressing his needs and wants. Lee claims that he can get very angry at his mother and occasionally has hit her, particularly when she returns home without having bought food for supper. On such occasions she leaves it to Lee to prepare some food with what he can find in the kitchen. He feels that his mother rejects him and really has never cared very much for him. He expressed the similar feeling with regard to his brothers who live pretty much on their own without showing any brotherly interest in him. Lee has vivid fantasy life, turning around the topics of omnipotence and power, through which he tries to compensate for his present shortcomings and frustrations. He did not enjoy being *together* with other children and when we asked him whether he prefers the company of boys to *the one* of girls—he answered—'I dislike everybody.' His occupational goal is to join the Army. His mother was interviewed by the Youth House social worker and is described by her as a 'defensive, rigid, self-involved and intellectually alert' woman who finds it exceedingly difficult to understand Lee's personality and his withdrawing behavior. She does not understand that Lee's withdrawal is a form of violent but silent protest against his neglect by her—and represents his reaction to a complete absence of any real family life. She seemed to be interested enough in the welfare of this boy to be willing to seek guidance and help as regards her own difficulties and her management of Lee. . . ."

MRS. MYRTLE EVANS

Testimony of a woman who was a friend of Oswald's mother in New Orleans:

Mr. Jenner. What about Lee?

A—Well, Lee was a smart boy. He was no dummy. He was a bit of a bookworm, I would say.

Mr. Jenner. Tell me more about that.

A—Well, he had hair like his mother for example, but he was a loner. That's what the children all said, but of course, I didn't pay too much attention to that, but he didn't bring boys in the house, I mean, and he would always seem to prefer being by himself.

Mr. Jenner. He wouldn't bring boys into the house?

A—No; he never did, that I know of. He would come home, and he would get his books and his music, and then when he wanted supper, or something to eat, he would scream like a bull. He would holler, "Maw, where's my supper?" Some of the time Margie would be downstairs talking to me or something, and when he would holler at her, she would jump up right away and go and get him something to eat. Her whole life was wrapped up in that boy, and she spoiled him to death. Lee was about 13 about that time, I think, along in there.

MRS. MARGUERITE OSWALD

The testimony of the mother of Lee Harvey Oswald:

Mr. Rankin. If you could start out and tell us within the period that Lee Oswald returned from the Soviet Union on, whatever you know about it, in your own way, and then we will go back to the other matters later.

Is that all right?

A—Yes, sir—anything is just fine. I am willing to help in any way possible.

I wanted to state it clearly in the beginning.

I received a speedletter from the State Department stating that Lee would leave Moscow, and how he would leave and arrive in New York—on June 13, 1962. I was on a case in Crowell, Tex. I am a practical nurse. And I was taking care of a very elderly woman, whose daughter lived in Fort Worth, Tex.

So I was not able to leave and meet Lee.

Robert, his brother, met him, and Lee went to Robert's home.

Approximately about a week later—I could not stand it any more—I called the daughter and had her come to take care of her mother, and took 3 days off, and went to Fort Worth to see Lee and Marina.

Marina is a beautiful girl. And I said to Lee, "Marina, she doesn't look Russian. She is beautiful."

He says, "Of course not. That is why I married her, because she looks like an American girl."

I asked her where he had met her, and he said he met her at a social function, a community function.

I said, "You know, Lee, I am getting ready—I was getting ready to write a book on your so-called defection.

"I had researched it and came to Washington in 1961, and, by the way, asked to see President Kennedy, because I had a lot of extenuating circumstances at the time because of the defection."

He said, "Mother, you are not going to write a book."

I said, "Lee, don't tell me what to do. I cannot write the book now, because, Honey, you are alive and back."

But, at the time, I had no way of knowing whether my son was living or dead, and I planned to write the book.

"But don't tell me what to do. It has nothing to do with you and Marina. It is my life, because of your defection."

He said, "Mother, I tell you you are not to write the book. They could kill her and her family."

That was in the presence of my son Robert Oswald and his wife.

Mr. Rankin. Can you tell us about what date that was?

A—Let's see. Lee arrived in New York on June 13, and—now, I have a letter stating, from Lee, that he is arriving in New York on June 13th. However, he plans to go to Washington for a day or two. So I have no way of knowing, Mr. Rankin, whether he came straight from New York to my son's home, or if he stayed in New York and came to Washington a few days.

But I have the letter stating that.

But I have no way of knowing.

Mr. Rankin. Was this conversation within about a week of the time that he came back?

A—Yes, approximately. That is correct.

So I stayed in Fort Worth 2 or 3 days. I did not live at Robert's home. I rented a motel. In fact, the lady of the mother I was taking care of paid my motel expenses while I was in Fort Worth. But I went there every day.

While I was there—Marina is a pharmacist. I have a medical book, and Lee was saying that he was losing his hair, and how he had become bald, because of the cold weather in Texas.

So I got the medical book, looking up baldness, and the treatment for baldness, and Marina came by and she read the prescriptions.

So I said, "Lee, she reads English," and he said, "Mother, that is Latin, of course, that is universal."

So because it was a medical conversation, Lee said he had an operation while in the Soviet Union on his throat.

I am sorry—but all of the confusion of myself being there and the daughter-in-law, the Russian girl—that was never gone into. That is all I know.

But that was also said in the presence of my son Robert—that he had an operation on his throat while in the Soviet Union.

Mr. Rankin. Did he say when that was?

A—No, sir; that was all that was said.

As I say, with all the confusion of Marina, we were so thrilled with Marina, with the children and all, there was quite a bit of confusion.

Now, I left, and I went back to Crowell on my job.

While I was in Robert's home, Lee immediately was out job-hunting. And I felt very bad about that, because they had come 10,000 miles by ship, by plane, and by train, which was an awfully hard trip with a young baby, and I thought he should at least have a week or two before he would look for work.

But I want you to know that immediately Lee was out looking for work.

And this is the time that Lee had gone to the public stenographer, made the statement that he was writing a book.

You probably have that information. It was highly publicized.

I, myself, gave him the $10 that he gave the public stenographer.

I bought Marina clothes, and brought clothes to her while at my daughter-in-law's house, bought diapers for the baby. And Marina had more clothes when she arrived in the States than I now have.

So what I am trying to state is as we go further into the story, it has been stated that my son neglected Marina, and that she didn't have any clothes. The Russian people have stated that all throughout Texas in the papers. And that is not true. I happen to know, because I, myself, bought Marina three dresses. And my daughter-in-law bought dresses, and my daughter-in-law's sister, which I would like to have as a witness, bought clothes for Marina. So there is this conflicting testimony.

Mr. Rankin. What daughter-in-law was that?

A—Robert's wife. And Robert's wife's sister, who is a schoolteacher, bought clothes for Marina.

Mr. Rankin. Is she married?

A—No. She is a schoolteacher. She is single.

So that story there is incorrect.

So then I went back to Crowell, Tex., and I was not satisfied in my mind because the way they lived. They only had a two-bedroom house. As you know, Robert has two children. And there was another couple with another child.

So Lee immediately began looking for work.

So I decided that I would quit this job and help the children all I could. So I did. I gave notice. And I came to Fort Worth, and I rented an apartment at the Rotary Apartments, which is on West 7th and Summit. And Lee and Marina then came to live with me.

Mr. Rankin. How long did they stay at Robert's?

A—They stayed at Robert's approximately 2 or 3 weeks, sir.

So then they came to live with me.

While there, I said to Lee—I am ahead of my story.

Lee and Marina had sent me wonderful gifts, and I have the gifts, from Russia. A box of tea, very fine tea, a Russian scarf,

304

pure linen napkins, embroidered with my initial, a box of candy for Christmas that has a Russian Santa Claus on it.

I said to Lee, "Lee, I want to know one thing. Why is it you decided to return back to the United States when you had a job in Russia, and as far as I know you seemed to be pretty well off, because of the gifts that you have sent me. And you are married to a Russian girl, and she would be better off in her homeland than here. I want to know."

He said, "Mother, not even Marina knows why I have returned to the United States."

And that is all the information I ever got out of my son.

"Not even Marina knows why I have returned to the United States."

Mr. Rankin. How did you get along when you were there together with Marina and your son?

A—Well, that was a very happy month, Mr. Rankin. Marina was very happy. She had the best home, I believe, that she had ever had. And Lee—I was taking Lee out to work every morning, looking for work, through the unemployment commission, and ads in the paper. And I was taking care of the baby and doing the cooking, and Marina was helping clean up. And she would wash the dishes. And Lee and Marina would go for long walks every afternoon, and I would take care of the baby. Marina would sing around the house, and watch the television and comment on different programs, programs that she had seen in Russia.

She knew—there was a picture with Gregory Peck, and she said, "Mama, I know Gregory Peck."

And she was singing Santa Lucia.

And here again in my stupidity, I said to Lee, "Lee, she knows English, she is singing Santa Lucia."

He said, "Mother, that is an international song."

Marina was very happy, and I was very happy to have the children.

And Lee desperately looked for work.

He was offered several good jobs from the State Employment Office of Texas. One in particular, I remember he said that he regretted not getting the job, but they told him because his wife was not an American citizen, that they would not be able to hire him.

He met obstacles all the way.

This one particular woman at the Texas employment agency took an interest in Lee and went out all the way to give Lee clues for jobs. And I, myself, took Lee job-hunting every day.

And it is through the employment office that he became employed 3 weeks later, after he was in my home, by the Leslie Manufacturing Co. in Fort Worth, which is a sheetmetal place.

Mr. Rankin. Now, while Marina was living with you there, and your son, and the little baby——

A—June.

Mr. Rankin. Did you talk to Marina, and did she speak English to you?

A—Yes, she spoke English, Mr. Rankin. Like she would say—and we used the dictionary when she didn't understand.

She would say—I would say, "Marina, you now nurse your baby."

"Yes, Mama. The time."

Or "No time."

With motions—"no time, Mama."

She spoke English.

Mr. Rankin. What I would like to find out for the Commission, if we can, in regard to speaking English, did you think she was able to talk English fluently, or did you think she was in the process of learning it?

A—She was in the process of learning. But she understood more than she could talk.

And I have a letter from Lee stating that Marina also speaks and understands French, that she had learned at grammar school.

Mr. Rankin. Did you know French?

A—No, sir.

Mr. Rankin. So you could not tell?

A—I could not tell.

And I didn't think a thing of it.

And, of course, Marina and Lee spoke Russian all the time, even in front of me.

And you asked about this time—it was a very happy time. They would sit at the table. They were playing a game, and I said to Lee, "What is it you are doing?"

Because they were always talking in Russian.

"Mother, we are playing a game which is similar to American tic-tac-toe."

And they also taught each other. They had books. They are both children—very intelligent and studious. Lee was teaching Marina English, and Marina was teaching him some things that he wanted to know about Russia, in my home.

Mr. Rankin. Now, you were saying that he got this job at the Leslie Manufacturing Co.

A—Yes, sir.

And then his first pay—he kept his first pay. And then the second pay, he rented the home on Mercedes Street, which is the south side, and approximately 10 blocks from where I lived at the Rotary Apartment, and approximately 10 blocks from where he was to work.

Lee had no car, and Lee walked to and back from work, which helped to save money.

Now, you must understand that this couple had no money, and had nothing. I gave them some dishes, and some silverware, and just a few little things that I could help out with.

But Lee did have the first week's pay.

306

THE EXHIBITS

A selection of key exhibits
presented in Hearings before the Warren Commission
on the Assassination of President Kennedy.

COMMISSION EXHIBIT 697.
The President and Mrs. Kennedy in the motorcade in Dallas.

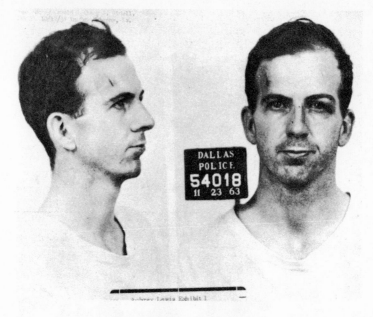

LEWIS (AUBREY L.) EXHIBIT No. 1.
Police identification photograph of Lee Harvey Oswald.

2

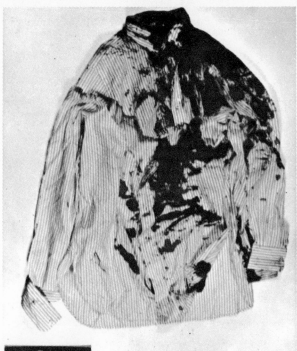

COMMISSION EXHIBITS 394 & 395.
Shirt and tie worn
by President Kennedy
at time of assassination.

3

Statement of Charles J. Price, Administrator, Parkland Memorial
Hospital, concerning the treatment of President Kennedy
and Governor Connally.

TOP SECRET

1:52 p.m.
November 27, 1963

As best I can recall, I was sitting at my desk looking out
the window with the thought in mind that it had turned out to be perfect weather for the President's visit and that it might be possible
to allow some of the employees to go out to the Boulevard to watch the
Presidential motorcade go by.

About that time, Robert G. Holcomb came into my office with
the Budget work sheets he had been revising and stated that the budget
revisions had been completed and that the budget was in balance. I
thanked him, told him to just leave them on my desk and that I would
review it later. Bob turned and left the office.

I looked at my watch, saw that it was 12:35 and thought, well
it's too late to make arrangements for the personnel to go out to the
Boulevard now; then it flashed through my mind that the luncheon rather
than the return motorcade was scheduled to start at 12:30 and that my
secretary would know definitely the time the luncheon was scheduled and would be
over.

As I was getting up to go check the time with her, I heard
sirens in the distance and about that time, Bob Holcomb hollered, "Jack,
something's going on." By that time I was almost to Fayetta's desk, the
phone rang - she answered, held it out to me and said, "Mr. Price, it's
for you."

As I took the phone, I turned to look out the window and while
the voice on the other end said, "This is Phyllis, the President's been
shot and they're bringing him to our Emergency Room," I saw two motorcycles sweep around the corner at Harry Hines into our grounds - it
appeared that they came up the left lane rather than the far side.

TOP SECRET

Bob Holcome was standing in the **TOP SECRET** door entrance of the Administrator's Office. I pointed to him and said, "Emergency Room," turned and asked where Steve was - was told that he wasn't in the office and said "get him" then I took off for the Emergency Room.

In the Emergency Room hall I told Bob to get Chief and all the help we could to control entrances and then I rushed down to the triage desk, asked the nurse if they had been notified, was told that they had, saw Mrs. Doris Nelson in the corridor and asked her if everything was ready. She said "Yes" and she and I went to the Surgery area to check. Most of the patients had been moved and the area cleared so I went back to the triage area.

Just about the time we reached the triage area a patient on a stretcher was being wheeled in feet first, a group of men were bending over the patient, mainly around the waist to head region - a coat had been thrown over the patient's chest and head. I did not know who this patient was. The stretcher paused momentarily at the triage desk, I grabbed the end of the stretcher; the patient was lying with feet toward me with coat thrown over upper body, secret service, FBI and other attendants were huddled over him. I grabbed the end of the stretcher and said this way as I pulled it down the corridor to the surgical area, around the corner and into the hallway entrance between Trauma 1 and Trauma 2 where Mrs. Nelson was standing. I relinquished my hold on the stretcher to Mrs. Nelson, turned and started back out the way we came in. As I reached the corner of the examining booths, the door opened and another stretcher was wheeled in. With a shock I first saw Mrs. Kennedy walking on the left side of the stretcher as the patient was being wheeled in head first and this patient also had a coat thrown over the upper portion of the body. I watched as the stretcher passed me and was wheeled into Trauma 1. At first I wondered what had happened to Mrs. Kennedy

TOP SECRET

5

as the right lower part of ~~her dress and her~~ right leg looked as
though it had been thickly painted and was shocked when I realized
that it was not paint, but blood. There were 8 to 10 secret service
or FBI men closely following and around the stretcher.

I did not recognize any of the people with the first
patient nor know who the patient was until later. In the first
few seconds before the motorcade had arrived at the Emergency entrance, the rumor that everyone had been shot had swept the area.
After she wheeled the stretcher in to Trauma 1, Mrs. Nelson's eye
caught mine and I knew that the President was either dead or dying
from her shocked expression.

I turned and told the personnel standing around the nurses
station and the crowd congregating from the X-ray entrance to go
back to their stations, that we would tell them what was going on
when we knew more ourselves.

I then left this area and went back to the triage area where
I was told that all the patients were in. About this time, a colored
lady in hysterics came in with a child apparently 3 to 5 years old
in her arms. The child had blood on its face and blood was streaked
down the right side of the face. It appeared to have blood from the
corner of the mouth. An orderly and an aide were standing nearby
and one of them took the child and we helped the mother to sit down
at the chair at the triage desk.

Again, I was told that all the patients were in and that
Governor Connally had been taken to the Operating Room.

Mr. Davis was down in the area and I asked him to help
control the crowds and to assist our guards and Chief Wright along
these lines. There were numerous questions from clerks and other
personnel regarding the phones, which the reporters had come in and
grabbed, some had left messages to be called and I instructed the

personnel to hang the photo up and not to hold any of the lines. I turned to go into the Minor Medicine area and bumped into Pete (?). I told him to help see that every entrance was under control. I then went into Minor Medicine, saw Mrs. Johnson sitting with her back to the wall, facing my way. There were several men in the last booth on the left, one of the men turned and said, "He is okay," so I left the area and went back down the corridor, telling personnel to go back to their stations and close all doors.

I went out to the Admitting area, a guard was posted on the door, so I told all the personnel milling about around the elevators and the Admitting Office to go back to their stations, that we would let them know what was happening as soon as we could. I went back to the Emergency surgical area and as I walked in, a nurse said, please, Mr. Price, do something about the press. They are swamping us and the switchboard is frantic. About that time, I saw Steve, who told me that the White House Press representatives were here, and that they had issued orders that only they would make any statements or releases. He asked about setting up a press room in one of the classrooms and I told him that he knew best how to handle the press and to go ahead and use his own judgment and use whatever facilities he needed to cover the situation, as well as to make announcements concerning the location of the press room, telephones, etc.

I then instructed all personnel that Steve was handling the press and that any inquiries should be referred to him and they should be directed to room 101.

I then went back to stand before the hallway entrance to Trauma #1 to help keep the personnel back and to restrict entrance into the area.

Dr. Kemp Clark **TOP SECRET** he could be of assistance.
I directed him to Trauma #1, shortly thereafter Dr. Don Seldin came to
me and asked if he could help. Told him he could best help by getting
interns, residents and other personnel not on duty in the area back
to their stations. He said he would check and get Major Medicine
cleared out to help relieve congestion.

About that time Dr. Clark came out of Trauma #1 and told me
that the president was dead and that he would sign the death certificate.

While we were talking, one of the secret service men came to
me with a request that we get a priest as soon as possible. I had
started to try to contact Ken Pepper when I saw Steve and told him to
try to get a priest as soon as possible. I turned to Dr. Clark and
asked his assistance in getting personnel, both medical and hospital
who were not directly involved with patients, back to their stations.

By this time guards had been posted at all doors so they
were instructed to keep doors closed and not let anyone in until they
had been identified by Administrative or nursing service personnel
in the area. About this time Steve came up and whispered to me
that the President was dead.

I left the area and went back to the triage area and an FBI
man was out there. He whispered to me, "Don't let anyone know when
the President died - security." About that time the priest came in
the door and I started with him back down the corridor, ran into Steve,
and asked him to please escort the priest into the Trauma room. I
made a complete check of the corridor, asking the personnel to please
close their doors and stay in their rooms and then went back into the
Emergency area.

During this time Mrs. Kennedy was sitting on a brown metal
chair with left side almost in line with the trauma room door. She
was composed but apparently in shock. She still had on her bloodstained

TOP SECRET

gloves, her face was smudge~~d and a~~ppa~~rently~~ ~~no~~body had done anything
for her. This disturbed me deeply, and the first opportunity I had
to catch Mrs. Nelson, I asked her to please do something for Mrs.
Kennedy. Mrs. Nelson told me that she was as worried as I about
her, but that the secret service would not let anyone touch her or
do anything for her. While talking with Mrs. Nelson, one of the
secret service men who had been bruised or had a minor injury came
to me and asked if there were another way that the President and
Mrs. Kennedy could be taken out of the building. I told him there
was a tunnel exit and that if he would come with me, I would walk it
off for him. We walked down to inspect the tunnel, then returned to
the surgery area of the Emergency Room.

During the time that we had been gone, Senator Yarbrough,
several ladies from the Presidential party, Mayor Cabell, and other
dignataries had come into the Emergency Room. Prior to this, I had
been told that Senator Yarbrough had been taken to the Blood Bank in
shock and had been checked to be sure that he was all right. My
·impression was that the lady with him in the Emergency room was Mrs.
Lincoln, the President's private secretary, but I had never seen her
and didn't know for sure; but I got them chairs, reassured a patient
in the first booth on the left, pulled the curtain and seated them
in front of the curtain. I then went and got them some coffee, saw
Mayor Cabell standing at a corner of the opposite booth, introduced
myself and asked if I could get him some coffee - he refused. While
I was talking with him, Steve passed by and I told him for God's sake
to get Mrs. Kennedy at least a cup of water. The coffee was hot and
                                     it
I was afraid that if xkx were handed to her, it would burn her. He got
a cup of water from the nursing station, handed it to a secret service
man, who gave it to her. She murmured a soundless "Thank you" and drank it.

About this time, from behind me, came to me and asked
how we could move the president's body. He asked if we had a casket,
a basket or anything that we could get to move the body immediately.
I told him that we had nothing like that, but that we had several
military installation nearby where we could get a casket, or we
could get one from a local funeral director. He asked me to wait
where I was, stating he would be back in just a minute.

I noticed that Steve had started out of the area with a
secret service man and asked where he was going. He ~~stated that he~~
said to get a casket, and I told him to wait a minute as someone had
just asked me about one and had asked that no further action be taken
at that time. Another man in the group who had been talking with
Mrs. Kennedy and the other secret service agents near her came to me
and asked that we get a casket of any kind from any place the quickest
possible way.

I then turned to Steve and relayed the request to him, and
asked that he see what could be done about it. I had just gone to
the corridor to check the personnel when Mr. Maher came in through
the entrance near the Admitting Office and stated that he would like
to speak to Mrs. Kennedy. I told him that I could get him into the
Emergency Room, but that I doubted that he would be allowed to speak
with Mrs. Kennedy. ~~I told him that I could get him into the Emergency~~
~~Room, but that I doubted that he would be allowed to speak with~~
~~Mrs. Kennedy~~. While I was talking with him, another secret service
man grabbed me by the arm and asked if I knew an alternate route
the Johnson's could use for an exit. I told him I had walked out an
alternate route with another agent a few minutes ago and that if he
would come with me, I would show him. We went to the Emergency Room
elevator, one of the maintenance men was ~~in it~~, manually operating it, and I told him to take
us to the basement. About that time, one of the residents breathlessly

ran in with two units of blood and said he had to get to the second
floor immediately, it was an extreme emergency, so I instructed the
elevator operator to go to second, and then to take us on down to the
basement. The secret service agent and I "ran" the alternate route,
then when we got back to the Emergency Room area, he asked me to show
him where the Johnsons were. We went through the center of the
Emergency Room to Minor Medicine, but the Johnson's were gone. Two
colored aides were standing on the window sill looking out the window,
and the agent and I parted the slats and looked out at the crowds.

About that time another agent came in the door and said,
"My God, they've gone." Both men left hurriedly. I went back to
the surgical area after checking all entrances again and had just
opened the door leading from the surgical area into the main corridor
when I heard a scuffle outside. Chief Wright was there and Mrs.
Nelson was coming in the door rather shaken. A man in a light gray
speckled suit was sprawled on the floor. I asked Nelson if everything were under control and what happened. She said that an FBI
man had tried to enter the area without showing his credentials and
that a secret service agent had knocked him winding. Several secret
service agents had at this time rushed to the scene. I saw the
man get up and heard him say as I was closing the door, "You're not
in control now - what's your name."

I checked the surgical area again, then left and went back
up the corridor, talked briefly to the guards and was almost in the
surgical area when I heard murmurs and turned and saw the casket
being rolled in. As they passed the triage desk, someone shouted,
"Stop those reporters." Several (three, I think) of the men supposedly
helping with the casket were reporters. I ran up, noticed that Steve
was on the right side, so I ran to the left side and with Mrs. Nelson

at the end of the casket **TOP SECRET** to the door where
I turned back to prevent anyone else from going in. Mr. O'Neal
had a brief conference with a secret service man regarding embalming
and then they moved off. Shortly thereafter, Dr. Earl Rose was
seen in the area. He was very pale and agitated and stated that
according to the law, the body could not be moved without an order
from a justice of the peace or a decision made about a medicolegal.
There was a frantic questioning of the people in the Emergency Room
as to where a justice of the peace could be located.

Someone said Justice of the Peace Wards (or Hall) was
across the hall in front of the Lab. I ran over and asked if he were
there and directed him to the nurses station where Drs. Rose, Clark and
a bevy of secret service men were in conference. These few minutes
seemed interminable and the tensions increasingly mounted. Finally
when I saw that they were getting ready to move the casket, I left
and went up the corridor, asking everyone to move back and to clear
the way. I asked a guard to stand in the waiting room door and a
policeman to please clear the other entrances. I stood at the south
end of the center of the corridor with my back to the wall as the
casket was wheeled up the corridor. As the procession came, it was
lead by secret service men, Mrs. Kennedy was walking on the ~~right~~ _left_ side
of the casket
with her right hand encased in a bloodstained glove resting on the
casket near the head. The O'Neal funeral home personnel were pushing
from behind while Mr. O'Neal was at the head. As the casket passed I
could not resist the impulse to place my hand on it briefly as it
passed as an expression of our sorrow and grief and _in_ a final salute.

At the time the casket passed the cashier's office, I looked
at my watch - the time was 2:20 p.m. I watched the hearse leave, then
went back into the Blood Bank where Dr. Guy insisted that I have a cup
of coffee and teased me about my appearance, stating that I looked like

TOP SECRET

I needed some blood myself. I told them that I was all right and went back into the Emergency Room area. I saw Mrs. Nelson and told her that I wanted to see her in her office. I then went and got a cup of coffee for her and one for myself, and went into her office, smoked a cigarette, but couldn't drink the coffee, while we talked. I asked her to get summary statements from all of her personnel while the events were still fresh in their minds, then I came back to my office.

Shortly after coming to my office, Dr. Carter Pannill came in and asked if he could assist in any way. I asked him to please stay in the office as there might be some medical questions or questions pertaining to faculty members that he could help me with. Shortly thereafter Dr. Clark came in followed by Dr. Seldin. Dr. Clark gave us a run down on what had happened in Trauma 1 and gave us the details as he saw them. Dr. Clark stated that he would contact all of the medical personnel involved and get statements from them before he left that day in order that we could get the facts while they were fresh and get the personal versions correlated. While we were discussing these things, Pete came in and I asked him to go down and ask Mrs. Nelson for a resume which I had discussed with her previously. Later Pete brought back the attached statement.

Then later Dr. Tom Shires and other personnel who had been working with Governor Connally came in. Dr. Shires told us briefly his experience of having just finished his lecture in Houston, and being whisked back by jet to operate on the Governor. Dr. Seldin left with the request that we call him if he could be of any assistance to us.

We assisted wit **TOP SECRET** iting dignataries, a
number of questions pertaining to arrangements for the Governor's
welfare, his staff, his family and many friends. One question in
particular was a question about some of our colored personnel being
scheduled for duty for the Governor.

I left the office quite late that night.

COMMISSION EXHIBIT 385.
Schematic drawing showing side view of entry and exit wounds
to neck area of President Kennedy.

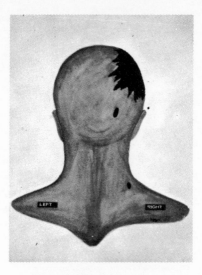

Commission Exhibit 386.
Schematic drawing showing view from posterior aspect of entry
wound to neck area and also the skull wound.

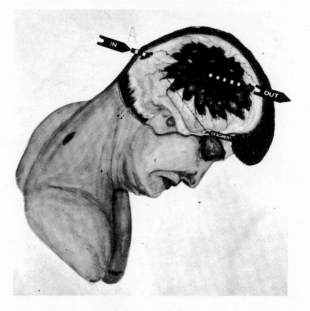

Commission Exhibit 388.
Schematic drawing showing skull wound as viewed from above.

POLICE DEPARTMENT
CITY OF DALLAS
CPS-J6-566

ARREST REPORT
ON
INVESTIGATIVE PRISONER

RT. THUMB PRINT

FIRST NAME	MIDDLE NAME		LAST NAME		DATE	TIME
LEE	HARVEY		OSWALD		11-22-63	1 40 PM

RACE

WHITE ☐ COLORED ☐	SEX MALE ☒ FEMALE ☐	AGE 24	DATE OF BIRTH OCT 15-39	HOME ADDRESS 1026 N. BECKLEY

ADDRESS WHERE ARREST MADE 231 W JEFFERSON	TYPE PREMISES (IF BUSINESS, GIVE TRADE NAME ALSO) THEATRE

CHARGE INV. MURDER	BUSINESS WHERE ARREST MADE HAS: BEER LICENSE ☐ LIQUOR LICENSE ☐ STATE LIC. NO.

HOW ARREST MADE ON VIEW ☒ CALL ☐ WARRANT ☐	LOCATION OF OFFENSE (IF OTHER THAN PLACE OF ARREST)

COMPLAINANT (NAME—RACE—SEX—AGE)	HOME ADDRESS—PHONE NO.	BUSINESS ADDRESS—PHONE NO.

WITNESS	HOME ADDRESS—PHONE NO.	BUSINESS ADDRESS—PHONE NO.

WITNESS	HOME ADDRESS—PHONE NO.	BUSINESS ADDRESS—PHONE NO.

PROPERTY PLACED IN POUND (MAKE, MODEL, LICENSE NO. OF AUTO) PROPERTY PLACED IN PROPERTY ROOM

NAMES OF OTHERS ARRESTED AT SAME TIME IN CONNECTION WITH THE SAME OR SIMILAR OFFENSE

NAME OF AND/OR INFORMATION CONCERNING OTHER SUSPECTS NOT APPREHENDED

OTHER DETAILS OF THE ARREST

This man shot and killed President John F. Kennedy and Police Officer J. D. Tippit. He also shot and wounded Governor John Connally.

CHECK ALL ITEMS WHICH APPLY:
DRUNK ☐ DRINKING ☐ CURSED ☐ RESISTED ☐ FOUGHT ☐   INJURED BEFORE ARREST ☐   INJURED DURING OR AFTER ARREST ☐   OFFICER(S) INJURED ☐   SPECIAL REPORT ☐

ARRESTING OFFICER M. N. MCDONALD	I. D. NO. 1175	ARRESTING OFFICER K.E. LYONS	I. D. NO. 1276
OTHER OFFICER LT. E.L. CUNNINGHAM	I. D. NO.	OTHER OFFICER P.L. BENTLEY	I. D. NO. 526

INVESTIGATION ASSIGNED TO	CHARGE FILED	FILED BY	DATE	DATE - TIME TO CO. JAIL

RELEASED BY	DATE - TIME	H.C. BOND BY	DATE - TIME	COURT	DATE	TIME

DISTRIBUTION: (REMOVE CARBON—CHECK ORIGINAL FOR RECORDS BU—CHECK COPY FOR EACH BUREAU CONCERNED)
RECORDS BUREAU ☐ SPEC. SER. BUREAU ☐ HOMICIDE ROBBERY ☐ AUTO THEFT ☐ BURGLARY THEFT ☐ FORGERY ☐ JUVENILE ☐ TRAFFIC ☐ ☐

USE REVERSE SIDE IF MORE SPACE NEEDED

105

COMMISSION EXHIBIT 2003.
Arrest report of Oswald.

COMMISSION EXHIBIT 744.
Dallas police officer M. N. McDonald who arrested Oswald.

IN THE NAME AND BY THE AUTHORITY OF THE STATE OF TEXAS.

PERSONALLY APPEARED before me the undersigned authority this affiant, who after being by me duly sworn, deposes and says your Affiant has good reason to believe and does believe that one

Lee Harvey Oswald

hereinafter styled Defendant, heretofore on or about the *22nd* day of *November* A. D. 19*63* in the County of Dallas and State of Texas, did unlawfully *then and there voluntarily and with Malice aforethought kill John F. Kennedy by shooting him with a gun*

Against the peace and dignity of the State.   David Johnston Exhibit No. 4

Sworn to and subscribed before me this the

22 day of *November* A. D. 19*63*

Henry Wade
Assistant Criminal District Attorney of
Dallas County, Texas.

Affiant.

JOHNSTON EXHIBIT 4.
Sworn affidavit charging Oswald with murder
of President Kennedy.

YOUTH HOUSE

SOCIAL WORKER'S REPORT

BRONX 5/7/53

Case No. 26996   Date of Admission   4/16/53

Name   OSWALD, LEE   Age   18   October   1939
                                                Day   Mo.   Year
Address   825 East 179th Street, Bronx, N Y. Father Lee (Dec)

Social Worker   Evelyn Strickman   Mother   Margarite

PSYCHIATRIC STUDY

Lee Oswald is a seriously detached, withdrawn youngster of thirteen, remanded to Youth House for the first time on a charge of truancy. There is no previous court record.

Laconic and taciturn, Lee answered questions, but volunteered almost nothing about himself spontaneously. Despite the fact that he is very hard to reach, Lee seems to have some ability to relate which in view of the solitary existence he has been leading, is somewhat surprising. There is a rather pleasant, appealing quality about this emotionally starved, affectionless youngster which grows as one speaks to him, and it seems fairly clear that he has detached himself from the world around him because no one in it ever met any of his needs for love.

Lee said he was at Youth House for truancy and that his truancy was caused by his preference for other things, which he considered more important. Questioning as to what these things were elicited the answer "Oh, just things" but it was finally learned that Lee spent all of his time looking at television and reading various magazines. He said his truancy never became serious until he moved up here from Fort Worth, Texas, about five or six months ago. He never liked school, however, and never formed close relationships with other people.

By persistent questioning, the information received from Lee was as follows: his father died before he was born and he doesn't know a thing about him. He has no curiosity about his father, says he never missed having one, and never thought to ask about him. His mother was left with three children, John, 21, in the Coast Guard and stationed in New York for the last two years; Robert, 18, a pilot in the Air Force Marines and Lee. Lee said his mother supported them by working as an insurance broker and she was on the go all day long. He doesn't remember anyone else taking care of him and he thinks she either left him in the care of his older brothers or else that he shifted for himself. She would leave early in the morning and come home around seven or eight at night after a hard day's work. Occasionally he went

18

with her, but found her frequent stops to sell insurance boring, while he waited for her in the car.

Lee ate lunch in school and often made his own meals at night. When his mother did make meals, he was often dissatisfied with them, and complained to her that she just threw things together. Her answer was that she was too tired after a hard day's work to feel like fussing.

Lee saw little of his brothers, partially because of the difference in their ages and partially because the older boys were either working or going out with their own friends, so that they didn't want Lee tagging after them. Lee spent very little time with the boys in his neighborhood, and preferring to be alone, when he came in from school would watch television or read magazines. It was during this period that he was already experiencing difficulty in school. He said it wasn't because he couldn't do the work, but he never felt like it or thought it was very important. He learned to read adequately but felt he had trouble in English grammar and arithmetic. He denied any feelings of inferiority in relation to the other boys in his class.

After Lee's brothers entered the service and John was stationed in New York, his mother decided to come here to be near John. They drove up five or six months ago, and moved into John's apartment in Manhattan. Questioning revealed that while Lee felt John was glad to see them, his sister-in-law, Marjorie, was unhappy about their sharing the apartment until they could find a place of their own and she made them feel unwelcome. Lee had to sleep in the living room during this period although there was five rooms in the apartment and he admitted that this made him feel as he always did feel with grownups—that there was no room for him. His face lost its usual impassive expression for a moment when he talked about John's baby, however and he said he had a good deal of fun playing with it.

Lee's mother finally found an apartment of her own on the Grand Concourse in the Bronx and she also found a job as an assistant manager in a woman's clothing shop. This meant that she was away from home all day. Lee made his own meals and spent all his time alone because he didn't make friends with the boys in the neighborhood. He withdrew into a completely solitary and detached existence where he did as he wanted and he didn't have to live by any rules or come into contact with people. He stayed in bed until eleven or twelve, got up and made himself something to eat and then sat and looked at magazines. When they first came to New York, his mother enrolled him in a private Lutheran Academy because he thought he would like this. After two months he didn't find school interesting or important so he started to truant. He was then transferred to a public school in the Bronx at which point he stopped going to school altogether.

When questioned about his mother's reaction to this he said she told him to go to school "but she never did anything about it." When he was asked if he wished that she would do something he nodded and finally emerged with the fact that he just felt his mother "never gave a damn" for him. He always felt like a burden that she had to tolerate, and while she took care of the material needs, he never felt that she was involved with him in any way or cared very much what happened to him. When Lee and his mother are home togther, he is not uncomfortable with her, but they never have anything to say to each other. She never punishes him because she is the kind of person who just lets things ride. It was hard for him to say whether she acted the same way towards his brothers, because he never noticed. Although his brothers were not as detached as his mother was, he experienced rejection from them, too, and they always pushed him away when he tried to accompany them. They never met any of his needs. He said he had to be "my own father" because there was never any one there for him. His mother bought his clothes without consulting him (which he didn't mind too much) and gave him an occasional quarter, but she was completely detached from him and they had little communication with each other. He felt that she was very much like him, in a way, because she didn't talk much. She has a few friends who visit occasionally, but she is equally silent with them. Lee feels that his mother has always left him to shift pretty much for himself and showed no concern about him whatsoever.

Lee was able to respond to expressions of understanding for his lonely situation, but he denied that he really felt lonely. Questioning elicited the information that he feels almost as if there is a veil between him and other people through which they cannot reach him, but he prefers this veil to remain intact. He admitted, however, the tearing aside of the veil in talking to a social worker was not as painful as he would have anticipated. He was not comfortable in talking but he was not as disturbed in talking about his feelings as he thought he might be. When this was used as an opportunity to inquire into his fantasy life, he responded with a reminder that "this is my own business." He agreed to answer questions if he wanted to, rejecting those which upset him and acknowledged fantasies about being powerful, and sometimes hurting or killing people, but he refused to elaborate on this. None of these fantasies involved his mother, incidentally. He also acknowledged dreaming but refused to talk about the dreams other than to admit that they sometimes contained violence, but he insisted that they were pleasant. Lee's developmental history was negative except for a mastoid operation and a tonsillectomy when he was about seven. He remembers that the operations frightened him, but nothing else about them.

Talk about future planning produced the fact that Lee wanted to return home, and his assurance that he would run away if he were placed in a boarding school. Being away from home means a loss of his freedom and privacy to him, and he finds it disturbing living with other boys, having to take showers with them and never being alone. He was away to camp several times during his life and he enjoyed it, but it was very different than his present experiences. He was willing to acknowledge that home offered him very little but he said he wanted it this way. If he could have his own way, he would like to be on his own and join the Service. While he feels that living that close to other people and following a routine would be distasteful he would "steel" himself to do it. Since he rejected placement, the possibility of a return home with casework help was broached. Lee finally decided that although he didn't really want help, and would prefer to remain as solitary as he has always been if it came to a choice between placement and going to a caseworker, he would chose the latter. He said, too, that if it were a choice between placement and going back to school, he would make an effort to return to school and go regularly.

Observation of Lee's relationship with other boys during his stay at Youth House showed that he detached himself completely, and repulsed any efforts at friendship by others. Although he reacted favorably to supervision and did whatever was asked of him without comment when on his floor he sat by himself and read. At 8:15 every evening he asked to be excused so that he could go to bed. The other boys appeared to respect his seclusion and didn't force themselves on him. He did not encourage conversation with anyone, and when asked questions was very terse in his replies. He was very neat and clean and always finished his work before going out to the floor.

In the recreation area he was usually quiet and withdrawn sitting by himself. If he did become involved in any minor altercation he was very hostile and belligerent and somewhat defiant of supervision. He seemed to be respected by group members who left him alone.

This pattern of behavior was also noted in school, where he was quiet, cooperative and respectful of authority but avoided contact with members of his group. He seemed timid and fearful of physical contact.

There was some very minimal movement in his relationship with his social worker, although it was so small as to be almost not noticeable. Ordinarily when approached he remained polite but uncommunicative but when he was shown some special attention and concern when he had an earache, he responded somewhat. He never sought his caseworker out, and asked for nothing, nor did he volunteer anything further about himself.

Mrs. Oswald, Lee's mother was seen for an interview at Youth House. She is a smartly dressed, gray haired woman, very self-possessed and alert and superficially affable. Essentially, however, she was revealed as a defensive, rigid, self-involved person [illegible] in accepting and relating to people.

One of the first things Mrs. Oswald demanded to know was why Lee was at Youth House but she gave no opportunity to explain the purpose of his stay here and instead wanted to know if he had received a complete physical examination. She had not been satisfied with a recent examination particularly with the genitalia. When she was told that our examination had revealed nothing unusual, she looked at once relieved and disappointed.

Mrs. Oswald gave what she termed her "analysis" of the situation as the move from Fort Worth to New York as being the reason for Lee's truancy. She herself had been very discomfited by the change, and said she was sorry she came, since she is finding it difficult to adjust to New York. At home where she was also a manager in women's shops, she had found her "help" with whom she made it a point never to mix, very respectful but here she complained of their arrogance. Furthermore, she found living conditions difficult. After her confidence was gained somewhat Mrs. Oswald said that she had come from Fort Worth to be near John, because Lee was left so much alone after Robert joined the Service. Her eyes filled with tears as she said there had been an exchange of letters and telephone calls with John anxious for her to come, only to find out on arrival that her daughter-in-law was extremely cold. The daughter-in-law is only 17 and went out of her way to let Mrs. Oswald know she could not stay with them permanently. Mrs. Oswald said she had had no such intention, although she did expect her daughter-in-law to put her up until she could find an apartment and a job. She was so uncomfortable there, however, that she took Lee and moved into a very inadequate basement apartment, where Lee seemed to become very depressed. As soon as she could she found an apartment in the Bronx and he seemed to perk up considerably.

According to Mrs. Oswald, she never had any difficulty with Lee in Fort Worth and she disclaimed any knowledge of his truanting there. She said he had always been a very quiet boy, as was John and she felt they were like her, while Robert was like their father. Even when Lee was little, he never mixed freely with other children and she wanted it this way because she had always been a working woman who didn't want to have to worry about his wandering off or associating with other children. She instructed him to stay in the yard and he always did so. If other boys came to play with him that was all right, although when other boys did approach him to play, he usually preferred to be by himself. She thought this was in his nature and that one couldn't change a person's nature. She didn't see anything strange about his seclusiveness and said she was not a gregarious person herself and she had never felt the need to make friends.

Questioning revealed that Mrs. Oswald had lost her husband when she was seven months pregnant with Lee. He died suddenly one morning of a heart attack and in a burst of confidence she confided that since then, she has not spoken to his family. He died at 6 A.M. and she wanted him buried the same day because her thought was for herself and the child she was carrying and she didn't think she could do her husband any good by an elaborate funeral or a wake. His family was horrified and said they never saw anything as cold as this. They have avoided her since and she had to rely on neighbor's help when Lee was born. She justified herself at great length as not cold but "sensible."

When it was offered that it must have been difficult for her to be both parents as well as the breadwinner, proudly she said she had never found it so. She felt she was a very independent, self-reliant person, who never needed help from anyone, and who pulled herself up by her own bootstraps. Her mother died when she was only two, and her father raised six children with the help of housekeepers in a very poor section of New Orleans of mixed racial groups. She always had "high-falutin" ideas and managed to make something of herself.

After her husband died, Mrs. Oswald stayed at home for two years, taking care of the children and living on the insurance her husband left. When this ran out, she placed the two older boys in a Lutheran Home and moved in with her sister who took care of Lee while she worked. At one point, Mrs. Oswald moved out and took a furnished room because she felt she had to have a free mind to work, and couldn't be bothered with a child. When her sister began to complain, however, since she had a houseful of children of her own, Mrs. Oswald placed Lee in the Lutheran Home for three or four months too and then brought all the children home again.

After she reconstituted the family she left the boys pretty much to their own devices since she was working all kinds of hours and did not get home until late at night. All the boys were extremely quiet, rather withdrawn children who made little demand on her and played by themselves. Of this she was very proud. Lee had a completely uneventful development except for the mastoid operation when he was five, but he was a very stoical child, who never complained of pain. Mrs. Oswald bathed all the children herself until they were 11 or 12, when, she said in an embarrassed manner, they got a little too old for "me to look at". Her feeling was that New York City laws were in a large measure responsible for Lee's continued truancy and that if they had left things to her to handle, she could have managed him. John also had been a truant and she let him go out to work until he decided that he wanted to go back to school. At first she had not been aware that Lee was truanting, since he dressed and left every morning, but when she found out, she talked to him and made several visits to the school, but got nowhere. She warned him that he could be put away, but Lee didn't believe her. She thought the biggest mistake was the way the Bureau of Attendance approached the boy, and said they were making a "criminal out of him." She wanted to be able to raise her own child the way she saw fit. She agreed that if truancy were carried to a certain extent it could be a problem. She would not agree that Lee's seclusiveness was a problem, although she finally admitted that there was something not quite right about the fact that he was entirely alone. She wouldn't be worried if he saw boys in school during the day and then wanted to be alone, but if he was alone all day and half the night it didn't look so good. She listened attentively to the possible alternatives the court might order to solve the problem, but she was angry at the idea of probation saying that this wasn't a "real chance." She also felt that involvement with a social worker was "talking to a stranger" and she didn't think this was a "real chance" either. She thought that he ought to have a chance to see if he could go to school without any probation officer or social worker to interfere and then, if he played hookey for even one day, he ought to be put away in a home. Her plan seemed to be more of an expression of her need to assert her own volition against authority than any understanding of Lee. She didn't seem to see him as a person at all, but as an extension of herself.

Lee Oswald is a seriously withdrawn, detached and emotionally isolated boy of 13, who is at Youth House for the first time on a charge of truancy. Lee came here from Fort Worth, Texas with his mother, about six months ago and he has been unable to make an adjustment in New York. The root of his difficulties which produced warning signals before he ever came here, seems to lie in his relationship with his mother. Lee feels that while she always cared for his material needs she was never really involved with him and didn't care very much what happened to him. There was no one in his family who could meet his needs for love and interest since his father died of a heart attack two months before he was born and two older brothers now 21 and 18 were involved

24

with their own friends and activities and repulsed his advances. Lee became a seclusive child who was thrown upon himself and his own resources and he never made friends with other children. His mother who worked and who, when he was an infant, demonstrated her need to shift responsibility for him by leaving him with her sister and then placing him for awhile in a Home, appears to be a rigid, self-involved woman with strong ideas and she has little understanding of this boy's behavior nor of the protective shell he has drawn around himself in his effort to avoid contact with people which may result in hurt for him. It is possible that her own negative attitude about casework help and probation officers may communicate itself to Lee, interfering with his chances for help. On the other hand there would be little accomplished by placing him in the impersonal setting afforded by an institution without seeing, first, if he can be reached in therapy. Despite his withdrawal, he gives the impression that he is not so difficult to reach as he appears and patient, prolonged effort in a sustained relationship with one therapist might bring results. There are indications that he has suffered serious personality damage but if he can receive help quickly this might be repaired to some extent.

COMMISSION EXHIBIT 2595.
Marina Oswald in Minsk, Russia.

COMMISSION EXHIBIT 2629.
Lee and Marina Oswald
on train leaving Russia.

COMMISSION EXHIBIT 2622.
Marina, June, and Lee Oswald in Minsk.

Nov. 3 1957

I, Lee Harvey Oswald, do hereby request that my present United States citizenship be revoked.

I appeared in person, at the consulate office of the United States Embassy, Moscow, on Oct 31st, for the purpose of signing the formal papers to this effect. This legal right I was refused at that time.

I wish to protest against this action, and against the conduct of the official of the United States consular service who acted on behalf of the United States government.

My application, requesting that I be considered for citizenship in the Soviet Union is now pending before the Supreme Soviet of the U.S.S.R.. In the event of acceptance, I will request my government to lodge a formal protest regarding this incident.

HOV. 06. 1959

MOSCOW

Lee Harvey Oswald

COMMISSION EXHIBIT 912.
Declaration of Oswald to U.S. Embassy requesting his citizenship be revoked.

27

May, 1961

"Dear Sirs:

"In regards to your letter of March 24. I understand the reasons for the necessity of a personal interview at the Embassy, however, I wish to make it clear that I am asking not only for the right to return to the United States, but also for full guarantees that I shall not, under any circumstances, be persecuted for any act pertaining to this case. I made that clear from my first letter, although nothing has been said, even vaguely, concerning this in my correspondence with the Embassy. Unless you honestly think that this condition can be met, I see no reason for a continuance of our correspondence, instead I shall endeavor to use my relatives in the United States, to see about getting something done in Washington.

"As for coming to Moscow, this would have to be on my own initiative and I do not care to take the risk of getting into a awkward situation unless I think it worthwhile. Also, since my last letter I have gotten married.

"My wife is Russian, born in Leningrad, she has no parents living and is quite willing to leave the Soviet Union with me and live in the United States.

"I would not leave here without my wife so arrangements would have to be made for her to leave at the same time as I do.

"The marriage stamp was placed on my present passport, after some trouble with the authorities, so my status as far as the USSR is concerned, is the same as before, that is 'without citizenship.'

"So with this extra complication I suggest you do some checking up before advising me further.

"I believe I have spoken frankly in this letter. I hope you do the same in your next letter.

"Sincerely yours,

/s/ Lee Harvey Oswald"

COMMISSION EXHIBIT 973.
Letter from Oswald to U.S. Embassy, Moscow,
asking to be allowed to return to United States.

①

Кажется что всё это вчера, а прошло уже 3 года — срок не слишком большой, но прошел дней, как один день. И много воды утекло с тех пор, и много пере-мен. Было то самое произошло

COMMISSION EXHIBIT 994.
Excerpts from Marina Oswald's narrative of her life.

TRANSLATION OF COMMISSION EXHIBIT NO. 993

It seems as though it all happened yesterday, and three years already gone by—not a very long period of time, but it has passed as fast as a single day. Much water has flowed by, and there have been many changes.

You might be interested to know how I met Lee Oswald, and how we lived. It was an ordinary life, not unusual in any way. It is the way the enormous majority of people live in the world. But it seems to me as though it was in some way marked by fate. Even now I can confidently say that this was fate. And may those who do not believe in fate excuse me.

. . . This is how it happened: Lee and I met in Minsk. This is a rather large, provincial city of the USSR, the capital of the Belorussian Republic, with a population of 500,000. And among this comparatively large number of people, two found each other. Myself a Russian—my future husband an American. We represented different worlds, different continents, but we were united by fate.

It was, I think, a Thursday, the 4th of March, although I do not remember precisely, in 1961. I had already been in Minsk more than a year. It is still cold there in March, with snow, frost, wind—the winter does not want to pass, although the approach of spring can be felt. And even people's hearts begin to beat in a different way—at least that's the way it appears to young people. I was 19 years old. I had many admirers, but then, all girls, when they get married, can say the same. One of them was Sasha P. He studied in the Medical Institute, and I know that he was head over heels in love with me, although he knew I had plenty of defects. I was not attracted to him, although this was not because he was a bad-looking fellow. Quite to the contrary, many young girls were dying to have him as a close friend. He was very smart, studied both hard and successfully, was handsome, and from a good family. Today he is a good doctor (in Russia people become specialists very early—at the age of 23 or 24). . . .

One day Sasha invited me to a social evening at the Medical Institute, and I knew that Anatoli would be there too. You see what a frivolous girl I was. Sasha forced me to promise that I would be there and gave me an invitation. . . .

Sasha was with his friends from the institute. One of his friends introduced me to Lee, calling him Alik (all his friends, and the

29

people with whom he worked, called him Alik, in that way rebaptising him with a Russian name, since the name Lee sounds too unusual in Russian). But he did not say that Lee was an American, and when Lee invited me to dance, and we started to talk, I decided that he was from one of the Baltic countries, since he talked with an accent. But later that same evening I found out that Lee was an American. The mother of the acquaintance who introduced us had been in the United States with Russian tourists, and was telling of her impressions. For that reason her son, who had known Alik previously, invited him to this dance. But I had come late, and didn't hear all this.

I liked Lee immediately. He was very polite and attentive, and I felt that he liked me too, since he tried not to miss any dances with me. He got nervous if anyone else managed to invite me first. Later, when we were married, Lee told me that he noticed me as soon as I came into the dance hall. Don't think that I have an especially high opinion of myself or am anything unusual, but I can say that my youth, and the fact that I had just come in from the cold—had their effect. By then the girls were already tired, whereas I had just taken off my overcoat—so that I had a fresh look and was not pale like the others. I remember having on my favorite dress made of red Chinese brocade (Lee liked this dress afterwards), and my hair was done a la Brigitte Bardot. That evening I even liked myself. You see how I am boasting; but I am writing what I felt. It's all true. Lee told me afterwards that he sees me come into the hall and thought how he might get to meet me. It showed on his face that he was glad to meet me when one of his friends led him over to the group of young people in which I was standing. . . .

That evening Sasha and Alik took me home. We were alone in the street for a few moments, when Lee asked when and where he could see me. I told him that perhaps I would come again to the dances at the place where we met but did not make any precise promise. But when, a week later, I went again with a friend to a dance—Lee was there. That evening he came home with me, and I introduced him to my Aunt. My Aunt liked his modesty and politeness, also the fact that he was very neat. She told me with a laugh that only an American was lacking in my collection. No one yet (nor I myself) thought that this was my future husband. We agreed to meet, I think, the next Saturday, but the day before, Lee was taken to the hospital and telephoned me asking me to visit him. But he rang three evenings in a row before he was able to tell me this, since when he rang I was away with my friends. I liked Lee, but I did not consider him seriously, and therefore I continued to go out with my friends—since you have to do something with your free evenings. When I came to the hospital to visit Lee, he was very glad, and hadn't expected it. I don't know why he thought so badly of me. I remember bringing some canned apricots—and didn't realize that this was his favorite dessert. Intuition told me what his taste would be. In general, I felt sorry for this young man who had come from a different continent and was completely alone although he had friends. And I think that he felt himself alone in a foreign country. Even if one likes a lot in a foreign country, still there is more which is unusual. For instance, Lee was surprised to find out that in all the stores of the USSR the prices of groceries are the same. For example, if you buy sugar, it costs the same in every store.

I remember one of our meetings in the hospital. It was Easter. and I brought him a colored egg. He was delighted that we had the same custom as in the United States. My uncle and aunt are non-believers, but this custom is very ancient and still survives in people. Some people don't believe in God, but color eggs just to change the pattern of their days, but many still believe. And although Lee also did not believe in God he was very pleased that I had done this and thought it had helped to bring us closer. In any case, it seems to me that he became more sympathetic toward me. Believe me that I didn't do this on purpose—I didn't know your customs, I just wanted to show what ours were. In general Lee had a very sickly look, and this made people sorry for him. I and my aunt were very sorry for him, for the fact that he was alone, and she was very cordial and even tender with him. While Lee was still in the hospital he told me that he wanted us to become engaged and said that I should not see anyone else. I promised, but did not take it seriously, since I did not yet love Lee, but was just sorry for him.

Then, after a successful operation (I think they cut out some glands or polyps in his nose—I am not sure) Lee was discharged from the hospital. We met very often, sometimes at our house, sometimes at his. We walked in the street. I very much enjoyed walking in the streets of Minsk in the spring—it is cold, but spring is coming on. Later Lee admitted that these walks in the snowy streets were a great lesson to him, since he could not stand cold weather, being from the South in the United States. Actually, after living in the warm climate of Texas or Louisiana, it is difficult to live in such a comparatively cold place.

When Lee and I met, my friends used to come along too and we would dance and drink coffee and tea. The boys and girls would try to show off their knowledge of English and ask Lee how various English words were pronounced. Everyone had a gay time. Lee had a lot of classical records, and he loved to listen to them when we were alone. He did not like noisy company and rather preferred to be alone with me. I remember one of these evenings when we drank tea with pastry and kisses. Then (please excuse my vulgarity, due to youth) the tea was very tasty. I never again drank such tea or ate such pastry—ha ha! Lee told me that he wanted us to get married and to stay here forever. He had a small darling one-room apartment with a balcony, a bathroom, gas, kitchen, and a separate entrance—quite enough for two, especially if they were young. I told him that I would become his wife (since I had already fallen in love with him) but that we should wait several months since it was a little embarrassing in front of our friends to get married so quickly. But Lee agreed to wait only until the first of May. It was already warm. We planted some flowers on the balcony in honor of my agreeing to marry him. On April 20 we applied to the ZAGS (after getting my uncle's and aunt's permission), and we were told that we had to wait ten days (a whole ten days) before they would know whether we could get married, since Lee did not have Soviet citizenship. After ten days, which was very long for us. we got married. It was one of the happiest days in my life. Alik too, I think, was very happy that we were allowed to get married. He only calmed down on the day of our marriage; before that he went every day to the ZAGS to find out if we were to get permission. Only after our wedding did he finally believe that what we wanted had really happened. We did not believe that it was possible. I remember that Lee brought me some early narcissi, and we went to the ZAGS with our friends. We came back on foot; the sun was shining; it was a warm Sunday, and everything was beautiful. By the way, after the birth of June I found a dried narcissus from my bouquet in Alik's Russian-English dictionary. But when we were living in New Orleans he gave this dictionary to the public library and remembered this only in Dallas. He became very upset at losing this flower. But let's go back to the story. The happy month of May was our honeymoon month. On May 1 we strolled in the streets of Minsk in the warm spring rain and got soaked through, but did not notice it. Of course we were both working but we had the evenings after 5 o'clock and Sundays entirely to ourselves. We ate in restaurants, in the first place because I did not have time to cook dinner (in Russia there are none of those frozen and prepared foods that you have in the United States) and in the second place because I did not know how to cook properly. We went out to Youth Lake to go boating, went to the movies, and walked in the park. My friends often came to see us and we would have a good time listening to music, dancing or playing cards. In Russia Lee was sociable and liked youthful company. He and I loved classical music. We had many Tchaikovsky records, as he was Lee's favorite composer, and also Grieg, Liszt, Rimsky-Korsakov, Schumann. Lee's favorite opera was the Queen of Spades. In Russia a film was made of this opera, a beautiful film. Lee went to it four or five times and at home I even came to be jealous of this opera. After work he would immediately start playing this record, not once but several times. We often went to the opera theater, the conservatory or the circus. Lee liked to visit my uncle and aunt. My aunt was especially sorry for Lee since he was alone in our country, and treated us like her own children. She tried to make things as agreeable as possible for Lee, told me that I should not bother him with little things. We bought some furniture and many of my friends envied the way we lived. Lee was very anxious to have a child and was very grieved when the honeymoon was over and there was no sign of a baby. Sometime in the middle of June we were out on a lake near Minsk with one of his friends who spoke English very well lying in the sun and swimming. That was a wonderful day, and that evening Lee told me that he was sure that after the required time, starting from that day, we would have a baby. I did not believe it, but a week later we were eating in a cafe and I fainted. I think this was the first sign of the baby. It was a great joy for us and for my aunt. She has no children and she was very anxious to take care of my (sic) grandchildren. I felt fairly well, but the doctors told me that I might lose the baby since I had RH negative blood. Lee was very upset by this, but when he had his own blood checked, it turned out that he was also RH negative. Only a very small percentage have RH negative blood, and this very unusual coincidence—in which both husband and wife were RH negative—pleased us very much.

Before our marriage I asked Lee if he might sometime return to the United States. He answered that he thought not. After our wedding Lee told me that several months earlier he mailed a request to the American Embassy to return home, but had not received an answer, and for that reason thought that it was impossible. He asked if I would go back with him to the United States if he got permission. I answered that if he was my husband, I would go with him wherever he went. It was all the same to me if it was China, Africa, or the United States. Lee told the Embassy that he had gotten married, and that we both wanted to go back to the United States. They suggested that we visit the American Embassy in Moscow, which we did in July. I submitted an application to the American Embassy for an entry visa into the United States, and a request to the USSR Ministry of Foreign Affairs for an exit visa. After this there was another wait, and we did not know how long it might be. But by New Year's I received an answer from the American Embassy that I had been granted permission to come to the United States. We then had to wait for my permission to leave the USSR. Lee, being a foreigner, could obtain an exit visa anytime he wanted, as soon as he was ready to go. This is the right of foreigners. The American Embassy suggested that Lee leave by himself, before me, but he refused. My relatives and friends were unhappy that we could go so far away, perhaps never to return.

We met the New Year with great hopes for the change in our lives. My girl friends felt sorry that we were leaving and at the same time were envious that I would see so many new things. After all, it is interesting to see new countries, to see how others live on the earth. To tell the truth, in the place where I worked, not everyone took the same attitude. Some even tried to persuade me to divorce Lee and remain in the Soviet Union. I don't know why they were frightened at the idea of my departure for America —probably it was the effect of habit. But it is certain that youth is afraid of nothing. And then my intuition told me that the same kind of ordinary people live in America as everywhere else. And they would not have anything against me as long as I did not do anything wrong. What is more, I very much wanted to see with my own eyes my husband's home—America, about which people talk and write so much.

On February 14 we were visiting a friend of mine and had a wonderful evening. We were both very gay, and I joked that Lee would send me to the hospital the next day, although we were not expecting the baby until February 30 (sic). As it happened, I woke up at six o'clock in the morning and told Lee that perhaps we should go to the hospital. Lee was terribly pleased and frightened. It was very funny to watch his suffering, as though he was the one who had to go to the hospital. He was hurrying me on, but I was not in any great pain and did not want to go. After lengthy persuasion on the part of Lee we went to the hospital at 9:00 a.m. As though it was deliberate, no taxi was to be found. With difficulty we squeezed into a bus. Lee's face showed how nervous he was. I had never seen him look like that before. It was February, cold and slippery, with snow on the ground. And Lee thought that something was sure to happen between the bus and the hospital. I worked in the drug store by the clinical hospital and for that reason decided to have the baby in that hospital. After all, I knew the doctors and the nurses and felt somewhat at home there. If something happened they would help me quicker. Anyway, at 9:10 we got to the hospital safely, and Lee went off to work. And at 9:55 our daughter was born. Alik had not yet made it to work when they telephoned his place of work and congratulated him on his daughter. So his friends knew before him that he was a father. In Russia women stay ten days in the hospital after having a baby, if all is normal; for three or four days they are not even allowed to get up from the bed. And no one except the mother sees the baby, in order to prevent infection from outsiders. The father and the relatives do not have the right to visit the maternity ward. I think this is a good idea. But nonetheless I was visited by my friends who were studying in the Medical Institute and who did their clinical practice in this hospital. Several times I even managed to meet Lee, since my drug store was located on the first floor of this building and I was on the third. This is illegal, so there is a sin on my soul, but I wanted to see Lee very much. He was very glad to have a daughter as though he had not been dreaming of a son. He even said that a girl is better for the mother, but that the next one would have to be a son. After 10 long days I was discharged from the hospital and was met by a whole crowd of relatives and friends. It was cold and both Lee and I were afraid that if the girl took even a breath of cold air she would get sick. Stupid young father and mother. Lee even forbade anyone to come into the room where the baby was kept until they got warm after coming from the street. The first day of my arrival home, February 23, was a very joyful day in our lives. Lee was so agitated that he couldn't even talk. He was more worried than I was. We both ran around the apartment, rushed hither and yon, were very busy, but achieved no results. The little one was so small and helpless that we didn't know what to do with her and were afraid to pick her up. And at night time neither of us slept but kept listening to make sure that our daughter was still alive. Lee was afraid that something could happen to the baby at night and that we would not notice it. The girl was very quiet and she did not give us too much trouble. I can say that Lee at that time was a very good husband and a very good father. He always helped me around the house, picked up things, cleaned the floor, washed the dishes. And when the baby was born he even washed and ironed the diapers because we did not have a washing machine. Of course, I did not try to profit by this and not do anything myself. But I was very pleased that my husband was sharing these chores with me.

We named our daughter June—in honor of the month of June, the month in which the life of one more human being in our family began. Lee loved June very much. It seemed to me that he didn't love me any more, but just the daughter. This, of course, was not true. These are two different kinds of love.

In the evening of February 23 my aunt had a birthday party at her house. But I was afraid to go with a small baby to a place where there were a lot of people. So I sent Lee to congratulate my aunt and waited a long time for him to return. Lee came home at 11:00 o'clock and, to my surprise, he was drunk. This is the first time I saw Lee drunk, and it was terribly funny. He had to drink vodka in honor of his newborn daughter, and since there were a lot of toasts, my American, who was not used to Russian vodka, could not hold it and became drunk. It was really terribly funny to see him; he said a lot of silly things to me and to his daughter, and was extremely happy. I have to say that in this condition he was not rowdy but very obedient and went straight to bed. Lee never drank and didn't like to drink, but was willing to celebrate an event such as the birth of a daughter. The first two weeks were a worrisome time, but then we both quieted down and decided that nothing would happen to our daughter, since everything was all right, and thus we became normal parents. All my girl friends came to visit our daughter, brought new toys, and sewed little dresses for her in the evenings. Everybody loved her, and my aunt was especially pleased to have a granddaughter. As a joke she even used to ask us to give June to her.

In the middle of May I received my Soviet exit visa. We went first to Moscow to put our documents in their final form, i.e., to obtain a foreign passport for myself, to exchange some money (to get dollars for rubles), and to buy a ticket. In Moscow we stayed several days in the Hotel Ostankino, and then transferred to the Berlin, since it was closer to the center of town.

The last days in the USSR were spent in a frantic rush. There was a lot to be done and this took up a lot of time. Basically Lee took care of the packing, since I was occupied with June.

We had saved a little money, and in addition we had money from the sale of our furniture and some other things. This we exchanged for dollars, but of course it was not enough to buy a ticket and to get a start in the United States. So Lee borrowed some money from the American Embassy. From Moscow we took the train to Warsaw, Berlin, and Amsterdam. Holland, that small and cozy country, pleased me most of all. We went through Holland on a Sunday. The bells were ringing in the churches, and people were going to church. It was sunny, and everything was very quiet. It seemed that the people here had never known trouble, and everything was like a fairy tale; even the houses in Holland look like ones in a fairy tale, with lots of glass and light. Holland is a very, very clean country, surely the cleanest country in the world. We lived in an apartment in Amsterdam for three days, and our landlady was so neat that we were even afraid to lie down on the sheets for fear of getting them dirty. Do not think that they thought we were dirty. In America, it seems, they cannot wash so clean, although there are even more facilities for it. It depends upon the people. In Amsterdam we bought a ticket on a boat for New York. It was already June, but in Holland it was still cold. We wore our overcoats. On June 13, we arrived in New York. Rain was falling, and it was rather cold. The fact that it was raining seemed to me a good sign. In Russia they say that if rain falls, for instance, during a wedding, the people will be happy or rich. Silly person that I was, I thought that perhaps here we would be happy, money did not matter, the most important thing was peace in the family, and then we would overcome any difficulties.

Upon our arrival in America Lee became very preoccupied since all the responsibility was on him. And we had a number of problems: a quite large debt, no work (in America this is still a problem), and we still didn't know how and where we would live. From the hotel in New York Lee telephoned his brother Robert who proposed that we live for the time being with him in Fort Worth. We bought a ticket on an airplane and the closer we got to Texas the more we undressed. In New York you could wear an overcoat, it was still rather cold. But by Atlanta it was already very hot. I remember that we took a short rest in Atlanta for several minutes while the airplane was being readied for its further flight. We went out to take a breath of fresh air. And people were eying us askance. I cannot boast about the way we were dressed. And even June was dressed in Russian style. In Russia children are dressed in diapers, that is to say their arms and legs are wrapped in diapers—the result being that they look something like an Egyptian mummy. I am looking at myself now with different eyes and think what a comical sight we must have been then.

In Dallas we were met by Robert and his family. I was very ashamed of how sloppy we looked. We were both very tired from the trip and didn't have anything very good to wear anyway, not to speak of the way my hair must have looked. I am afraid that Robert also was ashamed of having such a relative as myself. But they are very good people and did not say anything to me; quite to the contrary, they helped me get used to the new country. . . .

And so we lived with Robert. At first we rested a little from our trip, and Lee started looking for a job. Alas, this was not very easy. I remember especially that Lee did not have any particular skill. Finally we had a stroke of luck and Lee found a job, although not a very enviable one. He worked as a machinist in some little factory which turns out metal products for homes. But for the beginning, even this was good and better than living off other people. Although Robert's family treated us very well, one can only go so far. And besides we still owed a debt for our travel expenses. After Robert. Lee's mother proposed that we live for a while with her. We lived with her for two or three weeks and then took an apartment on Mercedes Street. Lee went to work and during my free time I took June and used to enjoy looking around the stores. Montgomery Ward, a very large store, was across the street. Everything was fine; Lee did not like his work very much, but he understood that it would enable us to live and pay off our debts. One day Lee came home from work and had not yet changed his clothes when some man knocked at the door. He turned out to be an FBI agent and asked Lee to come into a car, which he had parked across the street, and talk. There was one other man in the car. They talked for two hours, and I started getting angry at these uninvited guests, since it is no fun to heat up dinner several times. Lee came home very upset but tried not to show it. But from his face and from his behavior I could see that this visit distressed him very much. He did not say what he had talked about with these men, and I did not try to question him since it was so unpleasant for him. This all happened at Robert's house in Fort Worth.

Lee saw that it was actually quite boring for me, and that I was very lonely after the first holiday impression had passed and nothing remained but worries and housework. One day he told me that he had met a Russian who had been living there for a long time, and that he had invited him home. Subsequently, through this person, we found out that there are a lot of Russians in Dallas, and we met many of them. In this way I acquired new friends, and Russian ones besides. This was very agreeable for me. My Russian friends were extremely kind to me, and helped a great deal; but Lee did not like them very much, probably because they did not take his side in political discussions. I am ashamed to say that I am not particularly competent, and not very interested, in politics, and therefore I cannot say precisely what these discussions were about. But people view things in different ways, and the same happens here. Therefore it seemed to me normal that my friends did not understand and did not support Lee. But I was not happy that because of this he started being disagreeable to my friends and even to me, because I tried to maintain contact with them. I was hurt that Lee so avoided people and wanted me to do the same. We started to quarrel. In general, our family life began to deteriorate after we arrived in America. Lee was always hot-tempered, and now this trait of character more and more prevented us from living together in harmony. Lee became very irritable, and sometimes some completely trivial thing would drive him into into a rage. I myself do not have a particularly quiet disposition, but I had to change my character a great deal in order to maintain a more or less peaceful family life. In the end of September Lee lost his job. But it was a good thing that we had already paid off our debt to the American government. All the same, things were rather difficult. In spite of everything our Russian friends helped us. One of our friends helped Lee find a job in Dallas. He started working in the Printing Company in Dallas, and for the time being I lived with my Russian acquaintances in Fort Worth. Lee rented a room in Dallas and came to see me from time to time. But he wrote letters and telephoned. No matter how much we quarreled, I knew he loved me and the family, and I trusted him. We quarreled only because he had a difficult character and because that was the only way he could love. But he did not think that these quarrels could break up the family, and so I forgave him everything.

Lee was very pleased with his new job, and soon (in the end of October) I came to live with him in Dallas. We rented an apartment on Elsbeth Street in Dallas. In our spare time we walked in the park and around the city, visiting our Russian friends. In the evening Lee went two or three times a week to an evening school in Dallas—studying typing. I thought that this would be useful. But he did not finish the course, since he got tired of it. One day we had a serious quarrel because Lee told the landlady a lie about my being from Russia. He told her that I was from Czechoslovakia. And when the landlady asked me, I told her that I was from Russia, not knowing what Lee had told her. In this way a misunderstanding arose. I did not understand why Lee was hiding the fact that he was married to a Russian. But I refused to tell a lie. He got angry at me, said that I did not understand anything, and that I was not supporting him. I answered that it was hard to understand such stupidity, and that he was simply stupid. Then he told me that if I didn't like it I could go where I wanted. I was terribly hurt. I had no one there close to me except him and if this man rejected me, why should I stand in his way. I took June and left Lee to go to my Russian acquaintances. Three days later Lee telephoned them and wanted to see me and talk to me. We met, and Lee asked me to come home, saying that everything would be all right. But I refused, since I wanted to show him that I had a character too as well as self respect, and that he couldn't trample on this self respect too much. Before this all happened Lee had even hit me at times, for absolute trifles. Of course my heart wanted to return to him, but I didn't try to show him this. I wanted him to see that family life is not a plaything, and that he had to be more serious about it. Then it seemed to me that Lee didn't love me any more, and although it was very hard to turn him down, I told him that I didn't want to live any longer with a person who hurt me without any reason, and that I wanted a divorce. I saw that Lee went home extremely upset, and I felt that this might teach him a lesson. Of course I did not want a divorce, since I loved Lee, but I would have done it if he had not so insisted and begged me to come home. One Sunday when I was still living with my friends, Lee came to visit. We talked alone in the room, and I saw him cry for the first time. What woman's heart can resist this, especially if she is in love? Lee begged me to come back, asked my forgiveness, and promised that he would try to improve, if only I would come back. Do not think that I am boasting—as if to say look how he loves her and he is even crying. But knowing Lee's character, I can say that this is perhaps the first time in his life that he had to go and ask someone a favor, and, what is more, show his tears. Then I felt that this man is very unhappy, and that he cannot love in any other way. All of this, including the quarrels, mean love in his language. I saw that if I did not go back to him, things would be very hard for him. Lee was not particularly open with me about his feelings, and always wore a mask. Then I felt for the first time that this person was not born to live among people, that among them he was alone. I was sorry for him and frightened. I was afraid that if I did not go back to him something might happen. I didn't have anything concrete in mind, but my intuition told me that I couldn't do this. Not because I am anything special, but I knew that he needed me. I went back to Lee. He tried to be better in his relations with me. But broke down at times all the same. What can you do when a person has been this way all his life? You can't reform him at once. But I decided that if I had enough patience, everything would be better, and that this would help him. I understood that our unappealing material situation had its effect. Lee was terribly unhappy that he could not give those things which other husbands can give their wives. This could be felt especially after we had visited my friends who lived much better than we. Lee suspected (although there was no reason for it) that I blamed him for his inability to get along in life. And because he thought about this more than I did, he used to get angry at me and would criticize me for my friends. Again we quarreled, but I forget hurts quickly and was ready to forgive —especially my unsuccessful husband.

When we were not quarreling I was very happy with my Lee. He helped me with the house work, and took care of June. He devoted a great deal of time to June. He also read a great deal. He used to bring home dozens of books from the library and just swallowed them down, even reading at night. Sometimes it seemed to me that he was living in another world which he had constructed for himself, and that he came down to earth only to go to work, to earn money for his family, to eat, and to sleep. Perhaps this is not true, but, in my opinion, he had two lives, spending most of his time in his own separate life. Previously, in Russia I had not noticed this, since he was not so withdrawn. Only once when he was writing a book about his life in Russia he went off by himself and would become irritated if people bothered him. Of course this "book" was in English, and I didn't read it. Therefore I cannot tell about everything written in it. He was not particularly talkative about his memoirs.

For Thanksgiving we went to Robert's house in Fort Worth. I liked this good American holiday; it is very agreeable to celebrate it. In the station Lee asked me if I wanted to hear the music from the movie Exodus. I did not know this movie, but I liked the music very much. Lee paid a lot for this record, played it several times, and said that it was one of his favorite melodies. Now that Lee is no longer alive, I like this melody even more, since it is associated with happy memories. Lee was in a very gay mood, we joked a lot, fooled around, photographed one another in the station and laughed at how silly we were getting. At Robert's house everything was also very gay and in a holiday mood. Even more because Lee met his half brother whom he had not seen for several years. There was lots to talk about and to remember. Later we came home and resumed our ordinary everyday life. It is a good thing anyway that people have holidays—to get a good change.

The next holiday was Christmas, which we celebrated at the house of my friends. There were very many people, and it was noisy and gay. It is very agreeable to see people with happy faces. I was very pleased to see how nicely the city was decorated for Christmas, and how people were hurrying to buy their Christmas presents. The way Christmas is celebrated here is very beautiful. This was my first Christmas in America, but could I have thought then that I would celebrate the next one without Lee.

New Year's was very dull for us as we stayed home. Lee went to bed early, and I sat up and thought about Russia and my friends there. It was very depressing especially when I thought of my home, my relatives, who were making merry, and I was not with them, but sitting alone and unhappy. After New Year's we moved to a new apartment on the next street. There we had a balcony. This reminded us a little of Russia, and it was convenient for June, since she was beginning to crawl. On the balcony Lee set out boxes for flowers. But the flowers which he planted did not grow, since the weather here was rather warm for Russian flowers, the seeds of which we had brought with us. These were the seeds of flowers which we had liked when Lee and I took walks in the Minsk Botanical Gardens. The winter here was very warm and I was not used to the absence of snow. But Lee was happy, since he could not stand the cold, especially the Russian winter. When we lived here I was already somewhat out of contact with my Russian friends, since they did not particularly like Lee, nor he them. And although I wanted to see my friends more often, I knew that Lee would not be too satisfied with that, and I wanted to maintain peace in our family. Nonetheless, every now and then, one of my friends would visit me in order that I would not die of boredom. One day we were invited to a friend's house, where I met Ruth Paine, who was studying Russian here in America and wanted to improve her conversational knowledge. We began to see each other. Ruth would come to see me with her children. This was very good both for me and for June. She was growing up alone and becoming terribly wild, so the company of other children was good for her. Sometimes we went out on picnics at a nearby lake. Lee loved to fish, and we would look and rejoice if he caught a little fish. Several times I even made soup out of the fish which we caught by our own efforts. Several times we went to visit Ruth who lived in Irving.

At this time I was pregnant. Lee was very anxious to have a son and was sure that the next child would be a boy. I did not feel very well. Ruth's company was very good for me, since we two women could talk about our own problems. But of course I could not tell her everything which was tormenting me, for example, that my Lee wanted to kill General Walker.

It happened like this: I knew that Lee had a rifle but did not pay any particular attention to it. Many men have rifles. How could I have known what this rifle was meant for? I had enough worries of my own already. One day Lee stayed out very late. I should note that he was extremely punctual and always came home on time. I thought that he had been delayed by his lessons in school, but it was already after eleven. I started to get uneasy, and when I went into the room where he usually read and occupied himself with his own affairs, I found there a note for me, which told me what I should do in case he was arrested. I was puzzled as to why he should be arrested, and when Lee returned, I showed him this note and asked him what it meant. His face was unrecognizable and asked me not to ask him any questions, only saying that he had recently taken a shot at General Walker. Then he turned on the radio, but didn't hear any news about it. You can imagine how I felt. I thought a policeman would any many and told Lee this. But he answered that I should not worry ahead of time. He did not know how this had all ended, and only in the morning he heard on the radio that an attempt had been made against Walker and that he had not been killed. I demanded of Lee an explanation of why he had done this. He answered that this person belonged to a Fascist organization, and that it would be better for everyone if he were dead. I answered that he did not have the right to kill a person, regardless of who he was. To this Lee answered that if Hitler had been killed early enough, people would not have suffered so much, and there would not have been a war. Of course I agree with his opinion of Hitler, but I was very happy that he had not hit Walker. I asked Lee where his rifle was, where he had left it, since someone might find it. He answered that he had buried it. Several days later he brought it home. I was glad that all this ended so favorably for us and for Walker. I asked Lee not to do such a thing again, and he promised me not to. I told him that I would keep this note and that if he tried anything similar I would go to the police. Several days later Lee told me that he no longer had a job. God, one more misfortune on my head! Lee said that it would be better for me if I returned to Russia. Lee became even more withdrawn and was not particularly kind in his relations with me. I decided that it would be better to go back to Russia and no longer be a weight to a person who, in addition, does such terrible things. I wrote a letter to the Soviet Embassy in Washington requesting a visa. In the meantime I decided that if Lee did not have a job, it would be better to go to a different city. I was also afraid that in Dallas Lee would be very tempted to repeat his attempt on Walker. I suggested that we leave for New Orleans—Lee's home town. There he had relatives. I thought that he would be ashamed to do the same things there as he had done in Dallas. I wanted to get as far as possible from the occasion of sin. Ruth Paine offered to have me live with her in Irving until Lee found a job. I lived with her a week, and during this time Lee went to New Orleans. Two weeks later Lee telephoned that he had found a job and that I should come. Ruth agreed to take us to New Orleans, and besides she wanted to see the city. When we arrived in New Orleans Lee rented an apartment near his work. He worked in the Louisiana Coffee Company.

My first impression of New Orleans was very good. I liked the wonderful beach. The French quarter was very interesting. But this is all more for tourists. When you live a rather busy life, and don't have much time to visit restaurants and the various places of amusement, I think that you would no longer like New Orleans. What is more, the mosquitoes are terribly vicious. I could hardly stand the humid and hot weather, and it was even more difficult in view of my condition. But our family life in New Orleans was more peaceful. Lee took great satisfaction in showing me the city where he was born. We often went to the beach, the zoo, and the park. Lee liked to go and hunt crabs. It is true, that he was not very pleased with his job. . . . We did not have very much money, and the birth of a new child involved new expenses. It was rather difficult. I saw that it was very hard for Lee and thought it would be better to go back to Russia. Of course it would be difficult to leave Lee, but one day, to my great pleasure, Lee said that he wanted to go back with me. After all, it would be better for him to have a steady job there and not to have to worry about the next day. As before, Lee spent a great deal of time reading. Then he discovered a new activity. He started to spread pro-Cuban leaflets in the city. I was not exactly happy with this occupation of his, but it seemed to me better than his "games" with the rifle, as in Dallas. To tell the truth, I sympathized with Cuba. I have a good opinion of this new Cuba, since when I was living in Russia I saw a lot of excellent movies about the new life in Cuba. After seeing these films and reading the literature, I came to think that the people were satisfied with their new life, and that the revolution had given to many work, land, and a better life than they had had before. When I came to the United States, and people told me that they did not love Fidel Castro, I did not believe them. In Russia we did not think this way, since we had only heard good things about him. Of course, I do not know from personal experience what conditions are like there, since I have never been to Cuba. I have formed an opinion only on the basis of films, books, and newspapers. If I see in a movie that people are happy, I cannot say that that is bad.

But I did not support Lee since I felt that he was too small a person to take so much on himself. He became conceited about doing such an important job and helping Cuba. But I saw that no one here agreed with him. So why do it? And even more in view of the fact that Cuba will get along by itself, without Lee Oswald's help. I thought it was better for him to take care of his family. Lee and I quarreled about this, especially one day when he was arrested and spent the night in jail. I think that this somewhat cooled off his passion. But he spoke on the radio and had discussion with anti-Cubans. It was a pity that I could not understand very much English and do not know what he said. After having been arrested, however, Lee distributed pro-Cuban literature with somewhat less ardor and activity than before.

In the end of August Lee lost his job here too. We were receiving unemployment compensation. Lee looked for a job but couldn't find one. Our situation was not especially prosperous, and Lee began to think more and more about returning to Russia.

I wrote Ruth Paine a letter about our situation. She very kindly offered me to come with June to her to live as long as I wanted. At this time she and her children were spending the summer vacation with her parents and her friends, and she wrote that she would come and pick me up in the end of September. On September 20 Ruth came to see us, and several days later June and I went to Irving. Ruth wanted me to help her with her conversational Russian and to be her friend, since she was rather bored and lonely at home alone. At that time she was not living with her husband.

Lee remained in New Orleans and said that he would try to find a job there or in some other place, and, if he could not find one there, would come to Dallas. I did not want the baby to be born in New Orleans, since I did not like that city (perhaps undeservedly). I liked Dallas better. After two weeks Lee telephoned and said that he had come to Irving and that if we could meet him at the bus station that would be fine, since he did not have an automobile and it was rather far to Ruth Paine's house by bus. Ruth's car was being repaired at that time, and Lee hitch-hiked his way there. This was, it seemed, October 3 or 4. Lee spent the night with us and the next morning Ruth and I took him to Dallas (the repairs having been finished that evening). We had some things to do in Dallas and dropped Lee off in Oak Cliff. He went off to rent a room to live in while in Dallas looking for work. He lived in Dallas and I lived in Irving with Ruth Paine. It was very nice for me to have her as my friend, since she helped me very much in the time before the child was born. She was even more useful in this respect, since she went with me to the doctor, and if we did not have transportation she could take me to the hospital. I was very happy to live with Ruth Paine not because she was useful, but because I liked her company. We two women could talk heart to heart. We got to know each other better and enjoyed spending many evenings together chattering about this and that.

Lee called twice a day, was worried about my health and about June. He came to us by bus every weekend and we would meet him. Lee hadn't yet found a job. One day we were with a neighbor of Mrs. Paine, and there was another woman there. We were conversing (or rather everyone was talking except me, since I did not speak English but only understood it). Ruth said that my husband could not find a job. This woman said that her brother worked in the School Book Depository and there was apparently an opening there. That day Ruth telephoned the Depository, but they did not give a definite answer, only asking that he come the next day. When Lee called that evening we told him the news, and the next day at 10 o'clock in the morning Lee went there to ask about the job. During the lunch break he told us delightedly that he had been accepted. This was October 14 or 16. The brother of the neighbor who had helped find the job brought Lee over on Friday and took him back on Monday morning. This was a very nice young man, and it was very kind of him to do it.

In the beginning of October I remember that an FBI agent came to see our neighbor and asked her who was living with Ruth Paine. She answered that a Russian woman was living there with her child, but that she didn't know her name or anything special about her. We were not home then and for that reason he did not come to see us. The next day he paid us a visit and talked with Mrs. Paine, questioning her about Lee. She said that Lee was living in Dallas and gave his telephone number. He left his own name and telephone number. A week later he came again with some other young man and they left in precisely five minutes. I don't know what he talked about with Ruth Paine, but she said that he asked if I had any difficulties with the USSR, meaning if they were bothering me here in Dallas, if Soviet agents came to see me. I think this was worse than nonsense. He did not talk with me, and as soon as I appeared in the room he hastened to leave. I have trouble now remembering the precise dates involved; perhaps I am mixing things up. I remember his first visit after visiting our neighbors came about two weeks after the birth of our daughter Rachel (Rachel was born October 20). It was a Friday. We were expecting Lee to come at 5:30 and told him that if he wanted to talk to Lee, he could wait a little longer. But he left without seeing Lee. We told Lee about this, and he became very upset that they were again concerning themselves with him.

On the eve of October the 18th, we celebrated Lee's birthday at Ruth Paine's House. Her husband was there. Lee was in a very good mood, since he had a job and was expecting a son. He stayed with us through the weekend, and on Sunday the 20th in the evening our daughter was born. Lee stayed at Ruth Paine's on Monday, since June was quieter when her father was there. Monday Lee visited me in the hospital. He was very happy at the birth of another daughter and even wept a little. He said that two daughters were better for each other—two sisters. He stayed with me about two hours. In his happiness he said a lot of silly things and was very tender with me, and I was very happy to see that Lee had improved a little, i.e., that he was thinking more about his family. In general, we got along very well together after he came to Irving. Lee said that by working and living alone in Dallas he could save a little money to buy a washing machine (not a new one, of course) for me, since, with two children there would be more washing. I wanted us to buy an automobile, since it is very awkward not to have a car and to be dependent on others. Lee did not insist on this since it was rather beyond our means. I asked him to learn how to drive. And when Lee came to see us, she taught him. But he did not display any particular desire to learn. Even so, the lessons were successful, and he turned out to be a capable student.

Actually, while I was living with Ruth, Lee and I had one quarrel over his renting a room in Dallas without giving his real name. It happened like this: On Friday, Lee, as usual, wanted to come to see us, but I told him that he did not have to come so often now. On Sunday I got lonesome and telephoned Lee, or rather Ruth telephoned, but there we were informed that no one lived there by that name. When on Monday Lee telephoned me from work I told him about this. He answered that he did not want any unnecessary questions as to why he talked Russian on the telephone. He said that he did not want people to get curious about his having been in Russia and that I should erase his telephone number from Ruth's address book. I answered that I did not have the right to do this. What's the sense of giving a telephone number if you conceal your real name, and if even I did not know it. He insisted, and I said that he was stupid and hung up. Therefore I was not surprised when Lee came to Irving on Thursday (instead of Friday evening). He said that he was lonesome. Ruth was not home. She had gone to the store to buy groceries. He came at 5:30 in the evening. He played with June on the street for a long time, helped me, was very tender, and tried to make up, but I was offended at him for this incident of the telephone. Lee said that he was sick of living alone, that it was better for him to take an apartment and to take me there. But I did not agree, saying that I would live a little longer with Ruth Paine, since she was helping me with the child and treated me very well. Lee said that I did not love him if I preferred to live so long with Ruth Paine. But I thought it was better to stay with Ruth Paine until Christmas, better to celebrate the holiday there with friends. Of course, if I had known what was going to happen, I would have agreed without further thought. Perhaps (if Lee was planning anything) he staked everything on a card. That is, if I agreed to his proposal to go with him to Dallas, he would not do what he had planned, and, if I did not, then he would. That evening Lee was not particularly agitated and did not in any particular way reveal his thoughts. Only when I told him that Kennedy was coming the next day to Dallas and asked how I could see him—on television, of course—he answered that he did not know. I was busy around the house and Lee went to bed at 10 o'clock. He was asleep when I came into our room at 12:30.

In the morning I did not usually get up to make breakfast for Lee—he always did that himself. At 7:00 a.m. the alarm clock rang, but Lee did not get up. After 10 minutes I woke him up and began to feed Rachel. He said that I should not get up, got dressed, said good-bye, and went out. I was busy with our daughter and did not hear when he left the house. But at 7:25, when I went into the kitchen, Lee had already gone. I looked to see if he had drunk his coffee, but the coffee pot was cold. I was surprised that he had not eaten breakfast. The previous evening Lee had said that he would not come on Friday, as it was inconvenient to come so often. That morning Ruth went with her children to the doctor, and I was watching the television set and was in a very joyful and friendly mood seeing how happy the people were to greet the President. Then Ruth came home and we continued to look at the television set. We were both feeling wonderful. But all of a sudden it was announced that someone had shot at the President. We were both terribly upset and waited impatiently for news of Kennedy's condition. Ruth said that the President had died. I was so shocked by this that I wept freely. I do not know why but I cried for the President as though I had lost a close friend, although I am from a completely different country and know very little about him. But all that I knew about him was good. I was very sorry for Jacqueline and her children. And I asked myself why fate was so cruel. Why good people leave this world so early while some bad ones have the luck to live for a long time. Then Ruth said that the shot had come from the building where Lee worked. My heart missed a beat and I thought did my "crazy" husband do this. But the news reports were all different. In the beginning no one knew who had done this. Everything was mixed up. *I went into the garage where Lee kept all our things to see if his rifle was in place. But the rifle which was wrapped in a blanket was there. I began to breathe easier but nonetheless I could not quite come to myself.* Then all of a sudden some policemen came and began to search. They asked if Lee had a rifle. I answered that he had. But when they went into the garage and picked up the blanket, the rifle was not there. *When I looked I saw this blanket, which lay in its usual position as though there was something inside it.* I had seen this rifle three weeks earlier when I became curious as to what was lying there wrapped up in a blanket; I thought that it was some metal pieces of June's bed. I had picked up the edge of the blanket and seen the rifle stock. But when it turned out that the rifle was not there I did not know what to think. After the search we went to the police station together with Ruth and her children, since the police said that Lee had been arrested. Although 99 percent of the evidence was against my husband I nonetheless thought that he had not done it; I did not want to believe this fearful truth. I thought it was some sort of misunderstanding, since, after all, Lee had always been under suspicion. After being questioned by the police I met Lee's mother and his brothers there. That day they did not permit us to see Lee himself. I returned with Lee's mother to Ruth's house in Irving. The next day I went with Lee's mother to the police to see Lee. We met. I talked with Lee, he asked about the children, soothed me, and told me not to worry. Everything would be all right, and all would be cleared up. If I had known that I was seeing him for the last time! Although he was a criminal, he was still my husband. And I ask forgiveness if I talk here a great deal about my own feelings. Saturday evening, together with Lee's mother and my children. I went to a hotel room which had been rented to us by some people from Life Magazine. They said it would be more convenient and easier if we did not go back to Ruth's house, since there were many people there who wanted to know more news and more details. On Sunday we went to see Lee again. Some Secret Service agents were with us. They said that that morning, when Lee was being taken to another prison, someone had shot him, and then I learned that my husband had died. It was a great sorrow for me to be left with two little babies, not knowing English, and without any money. But I thought that if my husband actually did this deed, God judged correctly. After all, it is easier to die unexpectedly than on the electric chair under present laws. After my husband's death things were extremely difficult. But I am very grateful to those Americans who thought about me and my children. The moral support was so important for me that I found the strength and the faith to remain in this country in the expectation of a better life. I am very, very grateful to the Secret Service agents who treated me so well and took such good care of me. Although some of the letters which I received accused these wonderful people of preventing me from seeing others. I am free to do anything I want. It's only that after everything which has happened I do not feel well enough to see anyone; I have no particular desire. I am a little offended at the FBI agents who have been tormenting me every day with their trivial questionings, some of which have absolutely nothing to do with Lee's case; for example, what sort of furniture we had in Russia, how many people lived in our house and their ages, not to mention questions about my friends and relatives. I think that they should not count on my practically becoming their agent if I desire to stay and live in the United States. In conclusion, I would like to thank all Americans for being, on the whole, such real and genuine people. I would like to thank them for having helped me without blaming me. I hope that I will find here a good future.

COMMISSION EXHIBIT 171.
Scene during Oswald's funeral.

ARREST REPORT
ON
INVESTIGATIVE PRISONER

FIRST NAME	MIDDLE NAME	LAST NAME	DATE	TIME	RT. THUMB PRINT
JACK		Ruby	11-24-62	M	I. D. NUMBER / ARREST NUMBER

RACE	SEX	AGE	DATE OF BIRTH	HOME ADDRESS
WHITE ☒ COLORED ☐	MALE ☒ FEMALE ☐	52	3-19-11	223 So. Ewing

ADDRESS WHERE ARREST MADE: 10½ So. Harwood Basement City Hall

TYPE PREMISES (IF BUSINESS, GIVE TRADE NAME ALSO): City Hall

CHARGE: Inv. Murder

HOW ARREST MADE: ON VIEW ☒ CALL ☐ WARRANT ☐

BUSINESS WHERE ARREST MADE HAS: BEER LICENSE ☐ LIQUOR LICENSE ☐ STATE LIC. NO.

LOCATION OF OFFENSE (IF OTHER THAN PLACE OF ARREST)

COMPLAINANT (NAME—RACE—SEX—AGE) HOME ADDRESS—PHONE NO. BUSINESS ADDRESS—PHONE NO.

WITNESS HOME ADDRESS—PHONE NO. BUSINESS ADDRESS—PHONE NO.

WITNESS HOME ADDRESS—PHONE NO. BUSINESS ADDRESS—PHONE NO.

PROPERTY PLACED IN POUND (MAKE, MODEL, LICENSE NO. OF AUTO) PROPERTY PLACED IN PROPERTY ROOM

NAMES OF OTHERS ARRESTED AT SAME TIME IN CONNECTION WITH THE SAME OR SIMILAR OFFENSE

NAME OF AND/OR INFORMATION CONCERNING OTHER SUSPECTS NOT APPREHENDED

OTHER DETAILS OF THE ARREST

This Subject Shot and Killed Lee Harvey Oswald.

CHECK ALL ITEMS WHICH APPLY:
DRUNK ☐ DRINKING ☐ CURSED ☐ RESISTED ☐ FOUGHT ☐ INJURED BEFORE ARREST ☐ INJURED DURING OR AFTER ARREST ☐ OFFICER(S) INJURED ☐ SPECIAL REPORT ☐

	I. D. NO.			I. D. NO.
ARRESTING OFFICER: L. C. Graves	702	ARRESTING OFFICER: W. J. Harrison		579
OTHER OFFICER: W. J. Cutchew	1111	OTHER OFFICER: R. L. Lowery		1081

INVESTIGATION ASSIGNED TO CHARGE FILED: Murder—Capt Fritz FILED BY DATE: 11-24-63 DATE-TIME TO CO. JAIL

RELEASED BY DATE y TIME H.C. BOND BY DATE-TIME COURT DATE TIME

DISTRIBUTION: (REMOVE CARBON—CHECK ORIGINAL FOR RECORDS BU.—CHECK COPY FOR EACH BUREAU CONCERNED)
RECORDS BUREAU ☐ SPEC. SER. BUREAU ☐ HOMICIDE ROBBERY ☐ AUTO THEFT ☐ BURGLARY THEFT ☐ FORGERY ☐ JUVENILE ☐ TRAFFIC ☐
USE REVERSE SIDE IF MORE SPACE NEEDED

COMMISSION EXHIBIT 2003.
Arrest report of Ruby.

48

ARMSTRONG EXHIBIT 5300-A.
Ruby and two entertainers in front of his nightclub.

SHERIFF'S DEPARTMENT
COUNTY OF DALLAS, TEXAS

Before me, the undersigned authority, on this the __22nd__ day of ____November____ A. D. 19 ____ 63

personally appeared ___Arnold Louis Rowland___ , Address ____3026 Hamerly St.,____

DOB 4-29-45 POB: Corpus Christi, Texas Dallas, Texas

Age_____ , Phone No.___FE 7 1861___

Deposes and says:-

    I am a student at Adamson High School in Dallas, Texas. I am employed on weekends at the Pizza Inn located on West Davis Avenue in Dallas. At approximately 12:10 P.M. today, my wife Barbara and I arrived in downtown Dallas and took position to see the President's motorcade. We took position at the west entrance of the Sheriff's Office on Houston Street. We stood there for a time talking about various things and were talking about the security measures that were being made for the president's visit in view of the recent trouble when Mr. Adlai Stevenson had been a recent visitor to Dallas. It must have been 5 or 10 minutes later when we were just looking at the surrounding buildings when I looked up at the Texas Book building and noticed that the second floor from the top had two adjoining windows which were wide open, and upon looking I saw what I thought was a man standing back about 15 feet from the windows and was holding in his arms what appeared to be a hi powered rifle because it looked as though it had a scope on it. He appeared to be holding this at a parade rest sort of position. I mentioned this to my wife and merely made the remark that it must be the secret service men. This man appeared to be a white man and appeared to have a light colored shirt on, open at the neck. He appeared to be of slender build and appeared to have dark hair. In about 15 minutes President Kennedy passed the spot where we were standing and the motorcade had just turned west on Elm heading down the hill when I heard a noise which I thought to be a back fire. In fact some of the people around laughed and then in about 8 seconds I heard another report and in about 3 seconds a third report. My wife, who had ahold, of my hand, started running and dragging me across the street and I never did look up again at this window.

This statement is true and correct to the best of my knowledge and belief.

Arnold L. Rowland

Subscribed and sworn to before me on this the ___22nd___ day of ____November____ A. D. 19 ___63___

Rosemary Allen

Notary Public, Dallas County, Texas

DECKER EXHIBIT 5323.
Eyewitness statement to Dallas County Sheriff's office.

SHERIFF'S DEPARTMENT
COUNTY OF DALLAS, TEXAS

Before me, the undersigned authority, on this the __22nd__ day of __November__ A. D. 19 63

personally appeared __Howard Leslie Brennan__, Address __6014 Woodard__
Dallas, Texas

Age __44__, Phone No. __EV 1-2713__

Deposes and says:-   I am presently employed by the Wallace and Beard Construction Company as a Steam fitter and have been so employed for about the past 7 weeks. I am working in the Katy Railroad yards at the West end of Pacific Street near the railroad tracks. We had knocked off for lunch and I had dinner at the cafeteria at Record and Main Street and had come back to see the President of the United States. I was sitting on a ledge or wall near the intersection of Houston Street and Elm Street near the red light pole. I was facing in a northerly direction looking not only at Elm street but I could see the large red brick building across the street from where I was sitting. I take this building across the street to be about 7 stories anyway in the east end of the building and the second row of windows from the top I saw a man in this window. I had seen him before the President's car arrived. He was just sitting up there looking down apparently waiting for the same thing I was to see the President. I did not notice anything unusual about this man. He was a white man in his early 30's, slender, nice looking, slender and would weigh about 165 to 175 pounds. He had on light colored clothing but definitely not a suit. I proceeded to watch the President's car as it turned left at the corner where I was and about 50 yards from the intersection of Elm and Houston and to a point I would say the President's back was in line with the last window I have previously described I heard what I thought was a back fire. It run in my mind that it might be someone throwing firecrackers out the window of the red brick building and I looked up at the building. I then saw this man I have described in the window and he was taking aim with a high powered rifle. I could see all of the barrel of the gun. I do not know if it had a scope on it or not. I was looking at the man in this window at the time of the last explosion. Then this man let the gun down to his side and stepped down out of sight. He did not seem to be in any hurry. I could see this man from about his belt up. There was nothing unusual about him at all in appearance. I believe that I could identify this man if I ever saw him again.

H. L. Brennan

Subscribed and sworn to before me on this the __22nd__ day of __November__ A. D. 19 63

Notary Public, Dallas County, Texas

DECKER EXHIBIT 5323.
Eyewitness statement to Dallas County Sheriff's office.

SHERIFF'S DEPARTMENT
COUNTY OF DALLAS, TEXAS

Before me, the undersigned authority, on this the __22nd__ day of __November__ A. D. 19 _63_

personally appeared __Amos Lee Euins_____, Address __411 Avenue F__

Age __15__, Phone No. __WH 3-9701__   Dallas, Texas

Deposes and says:-
      I am presently going to school at Franklin D. Roosevelt High School and am in the 9th grade. I got out of school this morning to see the President of the United States when he came to Dallas. I was standing on the corner of Elm and Houston street. From where I was standing I could look across the street and see a large red brick building. I saw the President turn the corner in front of me and I waved at him and he waved back. I watched the car on down the street and about the time the car got near the black and white sign I heard a shot. I started looking around and then I looked up in the red brick building. I saw a man in a window with a gun and I saw him shoot twice. He then stepped back behind some boxes. I could tell the gun was a rifle and it sounded like an automatic rifle the way he was shooting. I just saw a little bit of the barrel, and some of the trigger housing. This was a white man, he did not have on a hat. I just saw this man for a few seconds. As far as I know, I had never seen this man before.

Amos Lee Euins

Subscribed and sworn to before me on this the ____22nd____ day of ____November____ A. D. 19 _63_

Jones

Notary Public, Dallas County, Texas

DECKER EXHIBIT 5323.
Eyewitness statement to Dallas County Sheriff's office.

COMMISSION EXHIBIT 673.
Oswald's shirt worn day of assassination.

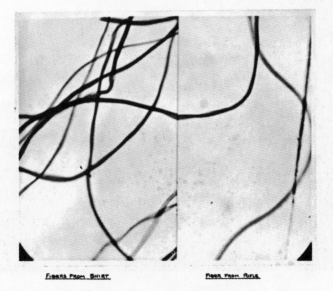

FIBERS FROM SHIRT

FIBER FROM RIFLE

COMMISSION EXHIBIT 676.
Physical evidence showing match between Oswald's shirt and
shirt fibres found on assassination rifle.

COMMISSION EXHIBITS 569 AND 570.
Ballistics evidence showing identical markings of assassination
bullet and a test bullet fired from Oswald's rifle.

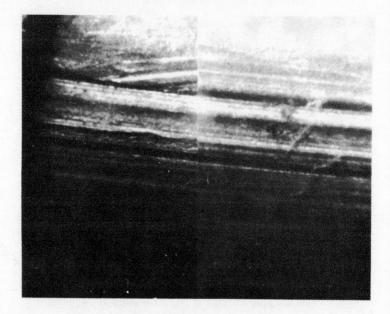

C 14   C 3

UNITED STATES DEPARTMENT OF JUSTICE

FEDERAL BUREAU OF INVESTIGATION

WASHINGTON, D.C. 20535

July 27, 1964

Honorable J. Lee Rankin
General Counsel
The President's Commission
200 Maryland Avenue, Northeast
Washington, D. C.

Dear Mr. Rankin:

I have received your letter of July 23, 1964. As you know, the Dallas Police Department lifted a latent impression off the underside of the gun barrel near the end of the foregrip of the rifle recovered on the sixth floor of the Texas School Book Depository Building. The Identification Division of the FBI determined this was a palm print which was identical with the right palm of Lee Harvey Oswald.

With respect to your specific question, no representative of this Bureau has made statements of any type to the press concerning the existence or nonexistence of this print.

Sincerely yours,

J. Edgar Hoover

COMMISSION EXHIBIT 2584.
Letter from J. Edgar Hoover confirming FBI fingerprint
identification of Oswald.

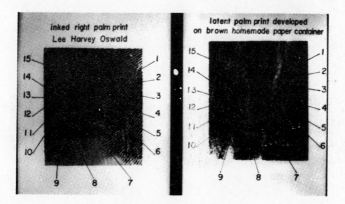

COMMISSION EXHIBIT 636.
Fingerprint evidence.

55

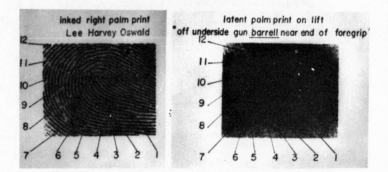

COMMISSION EXHIBIT 637.
Fingerprint evidence.

COMMISSION EXHIBIT 640.
Fingerprint evidence.

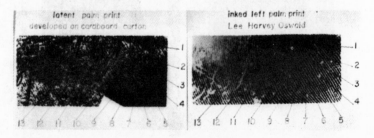

COMMISSION EXHIBIT 646.
Fingerprint evidence.

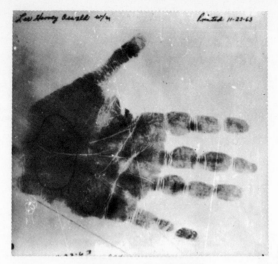

COMMISSION EXHIBIT 651.
Fingerprint evidence.

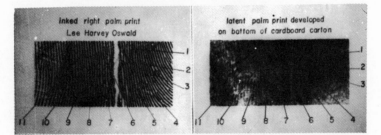

COMMISSION EXHIBIT 652.
Fingerprint evidence.

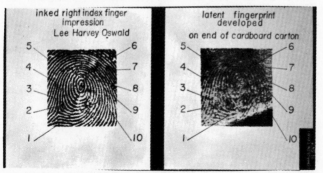

COMMISSION EXHIBIT 647.
Fingerprint evidence.

57

COMMISSION EXHIBIT 2585.
FBI report on claims made by Thomas G. Buchanan
in book WHO KILLED KENNEDY.

UNITED STATES DEPARTMENT OF JUSTICE
FEDERAL BUREAU OF INVESTIGATION

In Reply, Please Refer to
File No.

WASHINGTON 25, D.C.

June 3, 1964

"WHO KILLED KENNEDY?"
By Thomas G. Buchanan

CLAIMS AND RESULTS OF INVESTIGATION

1.   CLAIM: The railway overpass toward which the
President's motorcade was heading when the assassination shots
were fired was left unguarded on November 22, 1963, "contrary
to the most elementary security provisions." Page 81.

INVESTIGATION: Our inquiry shows that the railway
overpass was guarded by a patrolman of the Dallas Police Department
on November 22, 1963, at the time the President's motorcade
approached that point. In addition, there were several individuals
who were on the overpass at the time the President was killed.
None of the above individuals has furnished any evidence that an
assassin fired at the President from the overpass.

2.   CLAIM: The doctors who attended President Kennedy
at Parkland Memorial Hospital, Dallas, reportedly told reporters
that the first shot struck the President in the throat from the
front and that the second shot struck the right side of his head,
apparently coming from behind the President's car. According to
Buchanan, several weeks after the assassination doctors at
Parkland Memorial Hospital, following a visit by Secret Service
Agents showing them a document described as the autopsy report at
Bethesda Naval Hospital, retracted their original statement
concerning the nature of the throat wound. These doctors also
stated that a new wound discovered at the autopsy had not been
noticed in Dallas inasmuch as President Kennedy was lying on his
back during efforts made to sustain his life and a back wound
consequently would have been hidden from them. Pages 82-86.

INVESTIGATION: Doctors at Parkland Memorial Hospital
did not retract previous statements made by them but did state
that their efforts had been directed at keeping the President alive
and not at performing an autopsy. The autopsy report prepared at

the Bethesda Naval Hospital concludes that the throat wound was
an exit-type wound and that all the bullets striking President Kennedy
were fired from a point behind him.

3. CLAIM: Oswald was one of the worst shots in the
Marines or for that matter in any other military service. Page 81.

INVESTIGATION: Buchanan himself has stated that Oswald
was in the "sharpshooter" class in his shooting in the Marine Corps.
In addition, Buchanan has admitted that the "sharpshooter" class
is an intermediate class between "expert" on the top and "marksman"
on the bottom.

4. CLAIM: The FBI denied reports that Oswald had been
seen repeatedly driving a car into a Dallas rifle range for target
practice. Page 91.

INVESTIGATION: The FBI has made no such public denial.
However, our investigation has shown that Oswald was lacking in
ability to drive a car.

5. CLAIM: The FBI in an off-the-record briefing denied
that palmprints were found on the rifle associated with the
assassination of President Kennedy. Page 93.

INVESTIGATION: The FBI made no such denial. As a
matter of fact, the FBI Identification Division identified a latent
impression taken by the Dallas Police Department from the barrel of
the rifle as the right palmprint of Oswald. It is noted that
Mark Lane, in the "National Guardian" of December 19, 1963, alleged
that the FBI in off-the-record briefings had announced that "no
palm prints were found on the rifle."

6. CLAIM: The paraffin test made of Oswald's hands
and right cheek following his arrest by the Dallas Police Department
showed a residue of gunpowder on his hands but none on his cheek.
Therefore, according to Buchanan, the test proves that Oswald could
not have fired a rifle inasmuch as the rifle would have deposited
residue of gunpowder on his right cheek. Pages 93-96.

INVESTIGATION: The paraffin test has been found by the
FBI Laboratory to be extremely unreliable and inconclusive as to
whether or not a person has fired a weapon.

7. CLAIM: A photographer filmed the sixth-floor
window of the Texas School Book Depository building at 12:30
the day of the assassination. This photograph shows two silhouettes
in the stockroom and a clock on top of the building indicating the
time as 12:30. Pages 96-97.

INVESTIGATION: Such a photograph is not known to the FBI.
However, the FBI has a copy of a photographic print made from a
movie film reportedly taken at the assassination scene. In the
print an object appears in the window from which the assassination
shots were fired. This photograph has been examined by the FBI
Laboratory and the U.S. Navy Photographic Interpretation Center,
Suitland, Maryland, and the conclusion was reached that the image
seen in the window does not depict the form of a person or persons
and is probably a stack of boxes later determined to have been in
the room. No clock on top of the building appears in this photograph.

8. CLAIM: No employee who had access to the lunch-
room at the Texas School Book Depository would have eaten his lunch
on the sixth floor - "especially not Oswald, since it risked
additional incrimination." However, an "outsider," hiding for a
period of time prior to the assassination in the room on the sixth
floor, would have required food. Pages 96-98.

INVESTIGATION: An employee of the Texas School Book
Depository has advised that he ate lunch near the third double
window on the southeast corner of the building on the sixth floor,
sometime between 11:30 a.m. and 12 noon on November 22, 1963. The
employee has stated that he left the remnants of his lunch,
includ ng bones of fried chicken, near the window after he had
finished eating. He has also stated that he left the sixth floor

a few minutes after noon to join two fellow employees who were eating their lunch on the fifth floor of the building. He has stated that he did not see Oswald or anyone else at the windows on the south side of the building during the time he was on the sixth floor for lunch.

9. CLAIM: Oswald would have had to have been "the fastest runner since the great Olympic title holder, Jesse Owens," to have fired the assassination shots, hidden the rifle on the sixth floor, descended to the second floor lunchroom, and obtained a soft drink from a dispensing machine before the building superintendent, Roy S. Truly, and a Dallas policeman confronted Oswald at the second floor lunchroom. Pages 98-100.

INVESTIGATION: A survey was conducted by FBI Agents to determine the time taken by various routes and speeds to follow Oswald's actions immediately after the assassination shots. It is noted that the survey was conducted at a fast walk except in areas where an individual would have walked at a normal pace so as not to arouse suspicion. The survey showed that, walking from the window on the sixth floor via stairways, it would have taken Oswald about one minute and forty-five seconds to reach the front door of the Texas School Book Depository. The longest period of time to make the same journey, allowing 30 seconds in the lunchroom and involving the use of a passenger elevator for part of the descent to the second floor, was found to be three minutes and forty-nine seconds. It is noted that Truly has advised that he and the police officer arrived at the lunchroom on the second floor of the building in about two or three minutes after the assassination took place.

10. CLAIM: The assassin who fired at President Kennedy from the railway overpass fled the scene and left the murder weapon on that bridge behind him. Page 107.

INVESTIGATION: Our investigation has failed to develop any indication that a second rifle used in the assassination was found near the railway overpass and that a second assassin was involved in the killing of President Kennedy.

11. CLAIM: The name of the rifle used in the assassination appeared on the rifle. Page 108.

INVESTIGATION: Examination of the rifle used in the assassination does not reveal the name of the manufacturer of the weapon. However, it is noted that there is an inscription thereon that the rifle was made in Italy.

12. CLAIM: The Post Office Box in Dallas to which Oswald had the rifle mailed was kept under both his name and that of "A. Hidell." Page 111.

INVESTIGATION: Our investigation has revealed that Oswald did not indicate on his application that others, including an "A. Hidell," would receive mail through the box in question, which was Post Office Box 2915 in Dallas. This box was obtained by Oswald on October 9, 1962, and relinquished by him on May 14, 1963.

13. CLAIM: A detailed and "remarkably correct description" of Oswald was sent out over the police radio in Dallas at 12:36 p.m., November 22, 1963. Pages 114-116.

INVESTIGATION: The radio logs of the Dallas Police Department and the Dallas County Sheriff's Office show that no description of Oswald or any suspect in the assassination was broadcast at 12:36 p.m., November 22, 1963. Beginning at 12:43 p.m. and 12:49 p.m., respectively, and continuing until Oswald was taken into custody, the Dallas Police Department and the Dallas County Sheriff's Office broadcast descriptions of an unnamed suspect described as a slender white male, 30 years old, five feet ten inches tall, 155 or 165 pounds, who was possibly carrying a rifle. This suspect was reportedly seen running from the Texas School Book Depository after the assassination. A description of Oswald taken from background information and the autopsy report on him indicates he was 24 years old, five feet nine inches tall, weighed an estimated

150 pounds and had brown hair and blue-gray eyes. Although the
descriptions broadcast approximated Oswald's height and weight,
those descriptions were not accurate as to his age and lacked
specific details regarding the colors of his hair and eyes. No
broadcasts were made before Oswald's arrest that named Oswald as
a suspect or gave a description of him. It is also noted that
inquiry has shown that Oswald did not become a suspect until he was
reported missing from the book building at approximately 12:50 p.m.

14. CLAIM: Police knew Oswald's boardinghouse address,
1026 North Beckley Street. The sources of his address were the
records of the Texas School Book Depository, the "Red Squad" of
the Dallas Police Department, and the FBI, which had been given
that address by Mrs. Ruth Paine, with whom Oswald's wife was living
at the time. Page 119.

INVESTIGATION: The records of the Texas School Book
Depository did not show his address as 1026 North Beckley Street,
but did contain Mrs. Paine's residence in Irving, Texas, as his
address. The Dallas Police Department has denied that it had any
record of Oswald prior to the time of the assassination. Also,
Mrs. Paine had not advised the FBI of Oswald's boardinghouse address
prior to the assassination.

15. CLAIM: Dallas Police Officer J. D. Tippit was not
in favor with his superiors in the Dallas Police Department and
had gone ten years without a promotion. Page 120.

INVESTIGATION: A copy of the Dallas Police Department file
on Police Officer J. D. Tippit furnished by that Department has
been reviewed by this Bureau. While the file shows that

disciplinary action was taken against Tippit on several occasions,
it contains no information that he was "out of favor." The file,
however, shows that Tippit had received several commendations for
his performance of duty both from civilian sources and from the
Dallas Police Department. Superiors and associates have advised
that he was an average officer who was well liked and was not
overly ambitious. Several associates have stated that Tippit had
taken promotional examinations but they had no information as to
the results. A review of the file fails to disclose any reference
to promotional examinations offered or taken by Tippit. While he
was not promoted to a grade higher than patrolman, Tippit did
receive so-called "service" raises in salary on a periodic basis.

16. CLAIM: Police Officer Tippit, Jack Ruby and Oswald
all lived within a few blocks of each other. Page 121.

INVESTIGATION: A survey by the Dallas Office of this
Bureau has indicated that by the most direct routes available,
Tippit's residence was seven miles from Ruby's residence and from
Oswald's boardinghouse and that the distance between Ruby's
residence and Oswald's boardinghouse was one and three-tenths miles.

17. CLAIM: Jack Ruby and Dallas Police Officer Tippit
were described by Ruby's sister, Mrs. Eva Grant, to reporters as
"like two brothers." Page 121.

INVESTIGATION: Mrs. Grant has stated that at no time
before or after the assassination has she made such a statement to
any reporter or group of reporters. She has also advised that she
would not make such a statement under any circumstances, since it
would be completely untrue and without foundation.

18. CLAIM: There are standing orders for police in
Dallas as in other cities that radio cars of the type Tippit was
driving must have two policemen in them. Page 121.

INVESTIGATION: It is true that Tippit was alone in his
police car; however, it has been determined from officials of the
Dallas Police Department that their policy requires about 80 percent
of the patrolmen working the day shift, 7 a.m. to 3 p.m., as Tippit
was on the day of the assassination, to work alone and that Tippit
was one of the patrolmen assigned to work alone on that day.

19. CLAIM: Tippit was violating another order not to drive out of the sector of the city to which he had been assigned. Tippit was meant to be in downtown Dallas at the time he intercepted Oswald, shortly after Oswald had left his boardinghouse at 1026 North Beckley Street. Page 122.

INVESTIGATION: A review of Tippit's file in the Dallas Police Department and the radio log of that Department does not show that Tippit should have been in downtown Dallas at the time he confronted Oswald. The radio log shows that at 12:54 p.m. he advised the police radio dispatcher he was in the Oak Cliff area and that he was told to remain available for any emergency coming in. The Dallas Police file on Tippit shows that Tippit was moved from his regular area to cover an area closer to the assassination scene.

20. CLAIM: There are witnesses - "anonymous, it seems" - who saw Oswald run into a vacant lot, eject the spent shells from his revolver after shooting, and reload that revolver. Page 126.

INVESTIGATION: Our inquiry has developed witnesses and these witnesses, not anonymous as claimed by Buchanan, have advised that they saw Oswald apparently trying to unload his revolver near the location where Tippit was shot.

21. CLAIM: Oswald was arrested in the Texas Theater at 1:36 p.m. on November 22, 1963. Page 126.

INVESTIGATION: The radio log of the Dallas Police Department shows that Oswald was reported in the Texas Theater at 1:45 p.m., by a squad car. The same radio log shows that shortly after 1:51 p.m., the radio dispatcher received a report of the arrest of Oswald. The radio log of the Dallas County Sheriff's Office shows that at 1:53 p.m., the report was given that Oswald had been taken into custody.

22. CLAIM: The Dallas Police officers who arrested Oswald "beat him up" after they had disarmed him. Page 126.

INVESTIGATION: A Special Agent of this Bureau on the scene at the time of the arrest of Oswald has advised that Oswald was not mistreated and that no force was used to subdue him other than that necessary to overcome his armed resistance.

23. CLAIM: Oswald was first questioned "exclusively about the Tippit murder." Police, as long as they were able to maintain the prisoner in isolation, permitted him to think that he was just a suspect in that murder. Page 127.

INVESTIGATION: Special Agents of this Bureau were present during the early hours of questioning of Oswald at Dallas Police Headquarters, at which time Oswald vigorously denied having shot President Kennedy and Tippit.

24. CLAIM: Oswald insisted on his right to see a lawyer, making this demand before reporters, yet for two days of "persistent questioning" this right was "relentlessly denied him." Page 127.

INVESTIGATION: Oswald was advised following his arrest of his right to counsel by both a Dallas police officer and by FBI Agents present during the early interrogation of Oswald. Oswald, when arraigned at about 7 p.m., November 22, 1963, was advised by Justice of the Peace David Johnston of his right to an attorney's services. Late that night representatives of the Dallas Civil Liberties Union went to the Dallas Police Department and later departed satisfied that Oswald had been advised of this right. There is no indication Oswald made any attempt to contact an attorney on November 22, 1963. Again on November 23, 1963, Oswald was advised by a Dallas police official of his right to have an attorney. At that time Oswald indicated he wished to call attorney John J. Abt of New York City. He was taken from his cell on three separate occasions on that date to place collect calls via public telephones in the Dallas Police Headquarters, but on each occasion he was unable to make contact with Abt in New York City. Abt is an attorney who has represented the Communist Party, USA, in its litigation on several occasions with the Government of the U. S.

25. CLAIM: The Texas School Book Depository is owned and operated by the city government of Dallas and, therefore, Oswald was a municipal employee. Pages 131, 143, 151 and 155.

INVESTIGATION: The Texas School Book Depository is not a government agency of any municipality, county, state or Federal jurisdiction. It is a private concern which receives and distributes books to its various customers, including educational institutions. Therefore, Oswald, in his employment at the Texas School Book Depository, was not a municipal employee.

26. CLAIM: Among the papers found on Oswald by the Dallas Police Department was the name of Joseph Hosty of the Dallas Office of the FBI. In addition, information on papers found on Oswald recorded Hosty's home telephone number, office telephone number and car license number. This information appeared in the "Houston Post" and the source was reported to be Assistant District Attorney William Alexander. Page 149.

INVESTIGATION: The Hosty referred to by Buchanan is undoubtedly Special Agent James P. Hosty, Jr., of our Dallas Office. Oswald's address directory, which was found by the Dallas Police Department in Oswald's boardinghouse room, did not contain Special Agent Hosty's home telephone number. The directory did contain, however, his correct name, the telephone number and street address of the Dallas FBI Office, and the entry "MU 8605" or "MV 8605." Special Agent Hosty gave his name and the Dallas Office telephone number and street address to Mrs. Ruth Paine in contacting her on November 1, 1963, regarding Oswald's residence. Mrs. Paine has stated that she gave that data to Oswald. Marina Oswald has stated that she recorded Special Agent Hosty's license number on an occasion when he was at the Paine residence and gave it to Oswald. The 1962 license number of the automobile assigned to Special Agent Hosty on November 1, 1963, was MU 8605.

27. CLAIM: The "Philadelphia Inquirer" of December 8, 1963, contained an article stating that Hosty had seen Oswald shortly after he had left New Orleans in September, 1963. Page 149.

INVESTIGATION: Special Agent Hosty has furnished an affidavit stating that at no time prior to the assassination of President Kennedy had he ever seen or talked to Oswald. In addition, Hosty stated that he had never made any attempt to develop him as an informant or source of information.

28. CLAIM: Oswald was a double agent. Page 149.

INVESTIGATION: The Director of the FBI, John Edgar Hoover, has furnished the Commission with an affidavit categorically denying that Oswald was ever an informant of the FBI, was ever assigned a symbol number in that capacity, and was ever paid any amount of money by the FBI in any regard. It is noted that the Central Intelligence Agency has denied that Oswald was ever associated with it in any capacity.

29. CLAIM: The Walter-McCarran Act specifically calls for anyone who has attempted to renounce his U.S. citizenship to file an affidavit stating why he believes he should receive a U.S. passport. Page 151.

INVESTIGATION: The Internal Security Act of 1950 (Walter-McCarran Act) contains no reference to an affidavit required by a U.S. citizen who has attempted to expatriate himself.

30. CLAIM: It appears that the FBI knew Oswald possessed the alleged assassination rifle prior to the assassination of President Kennedy because it would seem unlikely that within one day the FBI could trace the rifle as coming from a mail order house in Chicago. Page 153.

INVESTIGATION: The FBI had no knowledge that Oswald possessed the assassination rifle prior to the assassination of President Kennedy. The tracing of the rifle purchased by Oswald under an assumed name from the mail order house in Chicago was completed by the FBI on November 23, 1963, regardless of Buchanan's claim.

31. CLAIM: Oswald's rifle was not taken away from him even though on April 10, 1963, there was good reason to suspect he had already used it to attempt to kill General Edwin A. Walker. Page 153.

INVESTIGATION: The FBI did not investigate the attempted assassination of General Walker on April 10, 1963, and had no reason to regard Oswald as a suspect in that attempted murder until December 3, 1963, when Marina Oswald furnished information that Oswald had, on the night in question, attempted to kill General Walker. The Dallas Police Department has also indicated that it had no record of Oswald prior to the assassination and had never developed or considered Oswald as a suspect in the attempted shooting of General Walker.

32. CLAIM: It can be inferred from the fact that General Walker's name and telephone number were in Oswald's notebook that Oswald and General Walker were known to each other. Page 154.

INVESTIGATION: Our investigation has developed no indication that Oswald and General Walker were known to each other. General Walker has been publicly quoted as saying he did not know anything about Oswald until Oswald was arrested for the assassination of the President.

And then the second week's pay. And he rented this home which was $59.50 a month. It was a nice little one-bedroom furnished duplex, in a nice neighborhood, convenient to his work.

But then that leaves the boy broke.

I brought food into the house. I never like to talk about the other members of the family, because to me that is speculation. But I know that Robert brought food, also, in the house. And they were not in want. Marina nursed June.

Now, it has been stated in the paper that the Russian friends have gone into the home and they are talking about this home, and found that they were in desperate straits, that there was no food in the house, and no milk for the baby.

I say Marina nursed the baby.

They may have walked into this home, where maybe they didn't have at that particular time any milk in the box. Maybe Lee was going to bring groceries home. But I know they were not in destitute circumstances in that respect.

They had no money and didn't have anything. I brought groceries, and I brought a roll of scotch toweling. I had bought two packs and I gave them one.

And the next day when I went by, the scotch toweling was in the kitchen, on a coat hanger, with a nail.

And I think that is real nice, a young couple that doesn't have any money, that they can use their imagination, and put up the scatch toweling to use on a coat hanger. They are just starting married life in a new country. And they have no money. But here is the point. The Russian friends, who were established, and had cars and fine homes, could not see this Russian girl doing without. They are the ones that interfered. They are the ones that interfered, and were not happy the way this Russian girl—and within a short time, then, this Russian girl had a playpen, had a sewing machine, had a baby bed, and a Taylor Tot. And this all came out in the paper—that they supplied this to the girl, because she was in need of these things.

I say it is not necessary for a young couple to have a playpen for a baby. We have millions and millions of American couples in the United States that cannot afford playpens for the children. I, myself, have been in that position.

So I think those things were immaterial.

The point I am trying to bring out is that these Russian friends have interfered in their lives, and thought that the Russian girl should have more than necessary.

And my son could not supply these things at that particular time. He was just starting to work.

This, to me, is very strong in my mind, that there are a lot of Russian friends that were made immediately, that have interfered and have publicly stated—a circle of friends, approximately eight or nine, that would not give their names in the paper, they were interviewed by Mr. Tinsley of the Star Telegram—that has downed Lee for every way possible.

So these are the Russian friends who are established with cars, and didn't think that the Russian girl was getting a good break in America.

Mr. Rankin. Were there any differences between you and Lee Oswald or Marina while they were in your home? Did you have any quarrels?

A—No, sir. no, sir, none at all.

Now, there was one thing. And I will point out the character of my son, and what I am saying about the playpen and so on.

Now, this was all done within a few weeks time. They moved there—they left my home in July, and they moved there in August, and then they moved to Dallas in October. So it was in this period of time that all these things were accumulated from Russian friends.

And no man likes other people giving—interfering in his way of living, and giving all these things to his wife that he himself cannot supply. This is a human trait, I would say.

Now, I want to bring this story up.

I could not afford to buy a bed for my grandchild, because I have worked prior to this for nothing. The job that I had quit I was making $25 a week, gentlemen—a 24-hour live-in job. The jobs prior to this I worked for $10 a week, 7 days a week, a live-in job.

Because of Lee's so-called defection, and my accident, the way I was treated, left destitute, without any medical or compensation, I decided to devote my life to humanity, and I became a practical nurse. And I have worked for $5 a week, living in the place.

So I had no money, I had $200 saved, when I came to Fort Worth, and that is what I rented the house with, and bought the food with.

So then that leaves me broke.

So I gave up a job in order to help this girl.

So to get back now to the home, Mr. Rankin—we had no quarrels. This month was beautiful. Marina was very happy.

I had the car and the television, and we went around.

As I say, they were free to go and come like they want. They would take long walks.

If you are not familiar with Fort Worth, Tex., from the Rotary Apartment to Leonard Brothers is approximately 3 miles, and they used to walk there, and they came home—Marina came home with a Cancan petticoat and some hose that Lee bought here with a few dollars that Robert and I had given him—he spent on his wife.

So that was a very happy time.

Now, when they lived in the home on Mercedes Street that he rented, I was employed as an OB, a nurse, in Fort Worth, Tex., at an OB's salary. And that salary, gentlemen, will astonish you. I worked, lived in, for $9 a day, 24 hours duty.

On an OB case—I am very busy with the baby all day long because people are coming in and out, giving presents and so on. I have a 10 o'clock feeding for the baby. And it is approximately 11 o'clock before I am through and in bed. The baby is up again at 2 o'clock. It is approximately 3:30 before I am through again with the baby. The baby is up again at 5:30. And it is approximately—then my day starts. I am stressing the point that I worked for $9 a day during all that, a $9 a day job. So that is 7 days a week, $63.

Now, this is the first time I have had a nurse's salary, I want you to understand.

So with my first pay, I bought Marina clothes, I bought the baby clothes, and I brought food into this home. I went all out for Marina. I just love her, and was just thrilled to death with her. And I bought a highchair. I could not afford a bed, because I didn't have enough money to buy the bed. So that is why I bought the clothes and things of that sort. But I bought the baby a highchair.

Mr. Rankin. How did Marina treat you then?

A—Fine. But then Marina was not satisfied with the things that I bought her.

As you see, the way I am properly dressed—I don't say I mean to be the height of fashion, but I have—before becoming a nurse I was in the business world, and I have been a manager in the merchandise field. So I do know clothes.

And I bought her some shorts. And she wanted short shorts, like the Americans. She pictured America in her mind evidently.

And I bought her a little longer shorts.

And "I no like, Mama."

I said, "Marina, you are a married woman and it is proper for you to have a little longer shorts than the younger girls."

"No, Mama."

And I will stress this—that Marina was never too happy— "No, Mama, no nice, no, Mama, no this."

That was perfectly all right. I thought she didn't understand our ways. I didn't feel badly about it.

I am going to get back to the highchair, to give you a picture of my son.

I bought the highchair and brought it over there, and Lee was not at home. And Marina didn't know what a highchair was. And she told me in Russian. I said, "How do they feed babies in Russia?" By this time, June was 4 or 5 months old, just getting ready to sit up.

"We put baby on lap, Mama, and baby eat on lap."

And so a highchair to me, I think, was new to Marina.

So approximately 2 or 3 days later I go over there and Lee says to me, "Now, Mother, I want you to understand right here and now—I want you to stop giving all these gifts to me and my wife. I want to give Marina whatever is necessary, the best I can

309

do. I want you to keep your money and take care of yourself, because today or tomorrow you take sick, and you spend all your money on us, I will have to take care of you." Which makes very good sense.

But he strongly put me in my place about buying things for his wife that he himself could not buy.

Mr. Rankin. What did you say to that?

A—I agreed with him. And I said—the shock of it—I realize what a mother-in-law I was in interfering. And, of course, that is part that we mothers-in-law do unconsciously. We try to help out our children, and in a way we are interfering in their life. They would rather have their own way of doing things.

And I realize that I had interfered, and the boy wanted to take care of his wife. So no more was said about it.

I go into many homes, being a nurse, and I see this problem also, where the mothers and mothers-in-law bring things, and the men strongly object to it—they would rather do without, and have their wife do without, and they themselves be the master of the home.

So then I realized I was being a foolish mother-in-law, and that he was perfectly right.

I should save my money and take care of myself. He had a wife and baby to take care of. If I didn't have any money, he might have to take care of me. So I agreed with that.

Mr. Rankin. Did Marina say anything about that?

A—Well, no, Marina didn't know—unless she understood the English part. I have no way of knowing, you see.

Mr. Rankin. All right. Tell us what happened after that, then.

A—Now, let me think just a minute.

This, gentlemen, is very emotional to me, because it is a humanitarian side that I am trying to bring out. Material things are involved to me that are of no consequence. And I am trying to point out the fact that these Russian people seemed to think that the Russian girl should have material things.

And all through my story, I can prove things that have happened of this nature.

Yes—I will continue.

I was on the OB case for very wealthy people. I then became a nurse and by word of mouth I had worked in the finest homes in Fort Worth at this salary. I have worked for Ammon Carter, Jr., who is the owner of the Star Telegram. I have worked in his home. I have worked for Dr. Ross seven weeks in his home. I have worked for Mayor Vandergriff. I took care of his last baby in his home. And I can go on and on.

So I have been employed in over 200 homes at this salary. So I know the difference of working in very poor homes, people on welfare, that I worked in, and then working in the rich homes. So I have experience, gentlemen, is what I am trying to say.

So I mentioned to Mrs. Rosenthal that Lee and Marina didn't have a baby bed, and Lee didn't have work clothes. He had had

310

his suits from the United States yet with him when he went to Russia. But he needed work clothes since he got this job.

She said, "Mrs. Oswald, what build is he?"

And I told her. And he was about the same build as her husband.

So she got out a lot of work clothes that her husband didn't want. However, she asked me $10 for 12 pairs of used pants. And I would not buy—give her $12. Here is a very wealthy woman, and she knows the story. And she knows that I have no money. And yet she expects me to pay for his used clothing. And so I have this principle about me. And I did not buy the used clothing, the clothing for Lee.

Now, Lee is having a birthday, which is October 18th. And this is approximately the 6th or 7th of October.

Now, this Sunday, October 12th, I went—this is very important, gentlemen—I went to this home and I was there—I asked to get off an hour or two to see the children, from this OB case at the Rosenthals. I went to see my son and daughter-in-law, and they were nicely dressed. And while there, about 10 minutes, a young couple came into the home, approximately the same age as Marina and Lee, and they had a little boy who I would say was about 6 or 8 months older than June. The woman put the little boy in the playpen with June, and June went to touch him, and Marina got up and said, "Oh, no, hurt baby." She spoke in English. So I said, "Do you speak Russian?" to this couple. And they said, "No, we don't. We are Americans. But my father"—and I will have to say this—"or grandfather"—I do not know which—"is a Russian, from Siberia, and that is how we know Marina and Lee."

So the conversation was general. And in the general conversation—now, this couple was from Dallas, visiting my family in Fort Worth. The conversation was general.

And she said, "Lee, my father has this place of business in Dallas, and will offer you a job in Dallas."

I said, "Lee, I didn't know that you wanted to give up your job and work in Dallas, because the Rosenthals that I am working for, her father owns the meatpacking house in Dallas, and she has told me that he employs hundreds of people, and if ever any time that you are in need, to go see her father, that she would be sure that he would give you a job."

So, gentlemen, this was on a Sunday.

I made coffee, and the house was in order. There was nothing packed.

Lee got paid on a Friday, from the Leslie Sheetmetal Works.

Monday Lee and Marina packed their belongings and went to Dallas.

The point I am bringing, is that Lee had no idea of quitting his job in Fort Worth, because he was not packed. This was on a Sunday. And this couple offered a job in Dallas. And their father, her grandfather, was a Russian, and Lee went to Dallas

311

on a Monday, and worked for the Arts Graphic. I do not know
—but you probably have that information. His very first job
there.

Mr. Rankin. Do you know whether he was discharged by the
Leslie people?

A—No, sir. he was not discharged by the Leslie people. He
just didn't show up. He was paid on a Friday, and that Monday
he did not show up for work, because he came to Dallas.

The point I am bringing out is this job was also offered to Lee
from a Russian father. He had no idea of moving. There was
nothing packed.

Now, I understand that my son Robert helped him to move.
And the way I know this—I went there on a Tuesday, and the
children had gone, because they had left on a Monday. So then
I went to Robert's home, and Robert was at work. So I was all
upset. They didn't tell me they were leaving.

I said to Veda, "Marina and Lee are no longer there, the
house is vacant."

Mr. Rankin. You spoke someone's name.

A—Veda, V-e-d-a, Robert's wife is Veda. I said they had to
move yesterday.

She said "Robert helped them to move, and they gave us the
food in the refrigerator."

I said it came up all of a sudden, and I told the story about
the couple being there.

Mr. Rankin. Do you know the name of that couple?

A—No, sir. And I have not been able to find out.

I have asked Mrs. Paine recently, and she said she does not
remember. And the night I was in Mrs. Paine's home, I asked
Marina and Mrs. Paine, and they did say a name. Marina would
know the name of the couple. But I do not have that information.

Mr. Rankin. And was he the owner of this business?

A—The father was the owner of the business. And this was
an American couple. And they did not speak Russian, either
one. The father was a Russian, or the grandfather—that owned
this place of business.

Mr. Rankin. I think you said the grandfather before.

A—I said either the father or the grandfather. I cannot be
sure.

It was the girl's father or grandfather, and not the boy.

So I told my daughter-in-law about this, and she knew about
it.

So now here is something that I would like to have my daughter-in-law as a witness.

It has been stated in the paper that my son was giving Marina
black eyes and possibly had beat her. And this is by the Russian
people.

Now, living in this home in Fort Worth, I had gone by several times I had a day off, and Marina was not at home.

312

I said to her, "Marina, Mama come to see you yesterday. You no home." She didn't answer.

I said, "Marina, Mama come see you. You no home, Marina."

"No. I go to lady's house to take English lessons."

Mr. Rankin. Do you know who she was speaking of?

A—I do not know for a fact. But my son Robert will know. And that is why it is important to call him. That is what I am trying to say, Chief Justice Warren. These others will know this part of my story, give you the facts.

I am assuming it is Mr. Peter Gregory's wife that started these lessons. But Marina was taking English lessons.

Now, they lived at a corner house, and there is Carol Street, and opposite Carol Street is a parking lot for Montgomery Ward. They live approximately two blocks from Montgomery Ward. So I had gone by, as I am stating, several times. You have to understand—this is just 6 or 7 weeks that they are in this home.

Mr. Rankin. You say "they." I am sorry to interrupt.

A—Marina and Lee, in this home.

Then Marina was not home. I could not understand where so fast that they could have so many friends, that this Russian girl didn't speak English and know her way about, could be gone all day long. That worried me.

So I sat in the car on Montgomery Ward's parking lot, where I could see the house, because I wanted to see who Marina was going to come home with.

The door was open. I went in the house and no one was there.

By this time, I was wondering how she could be gone all the time, being a stranger in town.

I sat in the car all day long. She didn't show up.

Finally, I went home, had my supper, left my apartment, and on the way going back to the house Lee was leaving Montgomery Ward.

Now, they did not have a phone. I am just assuming—this is not a fact—that Lee went to a telephone trying to locate his wife, because I was coming from Montgomery Ward. He got in the car with me, and we had about a block to go. I entered the home with Lee, and I said, "Lee where is Marina?" Of course, I knew that she wasn't home, because I had stayed in the car all day.

He said, "Oh, I guess she is out with some friends."

"Would you like me to fix your supper?"

"No, she will probably be home in time to fix my supper?"

So I left. I am not going to interfere in their married life. But I did offer to fix him supper. And I went back to make sure Marina still wasn't home.

I walked in the home with my son.

So approximately 2 days later—not approximately, but 2 days later I went to the home and my son was reading, he read

313

continuously—in the living room, and Marina was in the bedroom, I could not see Marina. And I said to Lee, "Tell Marina, I am here."

Marina made no appearance.

So I went into the bedroom, and she was nursing June with her head down. And I started to talk. And she still had her head down. And I came around to the front and I saw Marina with a black eye.

Now, gentlemen, I don't think any man should hit his wife, as is stated in the paper, or beat his wife. But I will say this. There may be times that a woman needs to have a black eye. I am not condoning the act. But I strongly am saying that this girl was not home. And this man was working. And I saw, myself, that this man came home and didn't have any food. This couple doesn't have a maid or anyone to give this working man food. And I think it was her duty to be home and have his supper ready.

That is a little thing, maybe. But to me it shows the character of what I am trying to bring out.

And so there may have been reasons that the children fought. And I also know that many, many couples fight, of our finest people, because I made it clear before that I have worked in these very fine homes, and have seen very fine people fight. I have seen a gentleman strike his wife in front of me. We know this happens. It is not a nice thing to do. But it happens in our finest homes. I am not condoning the act. But I am telling you that there probably was reasons, we will say. The woman has a black eye, and he is a louse—he gave her a black eye, but we must consider why did he give her a black eye. We always must consider the second aspect of the case.

Mr. Rankin. Did she take the baby with her when you looked——

A—Yes, sir, she took—always the baby was with her.

Mr. Rankin. Did you ask Marina how she got the black eye or anything about it?

A—Yes, in the bedroom. I was shocked.

"Mama—Lee." Just like that.

So I went in the living room and I said, "Lee, what do you mean by striking Marina?"

He said, "Mother, that is our affair."

And so that ended. I wasn't going to interfere any further.

Now, this has been publicly stated by the Russian friends, that he beat his wife. I don't know if he did beat his wife. I happened to see the black eye. I know that he hit her and gave her a black eye. Marina said so, and my son has said so. But how many times does this happen, I don't know.

But I am trying to point out that I don't approve of it. But I am trying to point out that everything is not according to Hoyle, as we say in our American way of life.

Mr. Rankin. Is there any other time that you recall that you saw that she had bruises or a black eye?

A—No, sir; that is the only time.

And then the children moved to Dallas.

Now, this will end that part of the story.

I have accepted and I have the public papers, in 1959, when Lee went to Russia—I made a statement that as an individual I thought he had a right to make up his own mind in the decision to do what he wanted. I am of that nature, because, gentlemen, today or tomorrow I may decide to go to Russia, I will go. We are taught that in America, that we have the right to do what we want as an individual. So I publicly stated in 1959 that Lee had a right, if he wanted to live in that country. And I think it was courage that he did so, instead of staying in America and talking about America, and living here and downing his country. It took courage to go and live where he wanted to live.

I was criticized highly for making that statement. And it is published in 1959—as far back as that.

So I will get back now to when the children left.

They did not tell me they had left.

So I accepted the fact that my son Lee did not want me to know that he was in Dallas.

Why I accepted the fact is because of Lee's so-called defection.

I have had it very hard. Mr. Rankin, and gentlemen—I have lost jobs, I was in a position, if I was in a home and television was on, and something political was on television, and the people commented, I felt it was necessary to keep quiet, because of it. Because of the defection I thought if I would express my views they might think I was a Communist like my son was supposed to be. And in many a home I have been in—after three or four days they would tell me my services were not needed.

I cannot say, sure it was because of Lee's defection. However, I feel sure that it is, because I am a respected person, and a very good nurse, as has been stated in the paper. And my jobs were gotten from word of mouth.

But you must understand that I deal with a lot of people. So naturally it is natural that some of them would feel resentful against me because of my son defecting to Russia and presumably being a Communist.

Mr. Rankin. Did you ever find out where Marina was that day that you tried to locate her?

A—No, sir, no sir, that ended that.

So I respected my son's wish, since he didn't want to tell me where he was in Dallas, that I would accept that fact.

Now, gentlemen, this may seem hard that I accept these things. But it is not. I am self-supporting. I have a life of my own. And if Lee decides that that is the way he wants it, I am not going to grieve and worry about it. I have to get my sleep in order to work. I have the ability of accepting things, the

315

ability granted me by the grace of God, because of my difficulty in life. I have been a widow. I have had many, many obstacles, and I have tried to face them. And my faith gets stronger. I do accept things.

As now, I accept the death of my son. I don't brood over that. I have that ability of doing that.

So I just accepted the fact—when Lee gets ready to let me know where he is, fine—up until that time, it is his privilege to do what he wants.

Now, that is the last contact I have had with Marina and Lee until the news broke in Dallas that Lee was picked up because of the assassination of President Kennedy.

Mr. Rankin. Tell us about this period you were talking about, when he went to Dallas. Was that before or after the time he went to New Orleans?

A—That was before the time, sir—he lived—from my apartment, the Rotary Apartments, when Lee got the job he lived on Mercedes Street from the end of July, I would say, or the beginning of September, until October, when he left to go to Dallas.

Mr. Rankin. What year was that?

A—That was in 1963.

Mr. Rankin. You mean '62?

A—I am sorry—1962. And that was the last I had seen of Marina and Lee.

Mr. Rankin. Did you ever find where they were in Dallas?

A—No, sir. I explained before that I made no attempt. I thought when they get ready to let me know, that is fine. Up until then, I had to do my own work and take care of myself. And I do respect other people's privileges. If that is the way they want it, fine.

When they get ready to let me know, I will welcome them. If not, I will go about my own business.

Mr. Rankin. Had you learned they had gone to New Orleans?

A—I had not learned of that until after the assassination. I knew nothing, I had no contact with them.

So, then, the next thing we should start then would be the Dallas—the assassination.

Mr. Rankin. Whatever you know.

A—Well, I was on a case in a rest home, and I had a 3 to 11 shift. I was dressed, ready to go to work. I was watching—I am a little ahead of my story.

I watched the television in the morning before I was dressed. And Richard Nixon was in Dallas, and he made a television appearance approximately 2 hours before President Kennedy was to arrive in Dallas. And, as a layman, I remember saying, "Well, the audacity of him, to make this statement against President Kennedy just an hour or two before his arrival in Dallas."

And then I had my lunch, and I dressed, with my nurse's

uniform on, to go to work, for the 3 to 11 shift. And I have to leave home at 2:30. So I had a little time to watch the Presidential procession.

And while sitting on the sofa, the news came that the President was shot. And there was a witness on television, a man and a little girl on television. However, I could not continue to watch it. I had to report to work.

So I went in the car, and approximately seven blocks away I turned the radio on in the car. I heard that Lee Harvey Oswald was picked up as a suspect.

I immediately turned the car around and came back home, got on the telephone, called Acme Brick in Fort Worth, and asked where Robert was, because he had been traveling, and I must get in touch with Robert immediately, because his brother was picked up as a suspect in the assassination. So they had Robert call me.

Robert didn't know that Lee was picked up.

Mr. Rankin. Was this the day of the assassination?

A—Yes, sir, the day of the assassination, they picked Lee up.

Mr. Rankin. And 3 to 11—that is in the afternoon?

A—This was 2:30, because I was on my way to work, and I had to be at work at 3 o'clock.

Mr. Rankin. Three in the afternoon is when you had to be at work?

A—Yes, sir, and it was 2:30 I heard the news and went back home.

I had Acme Brick call Robert to give him the news, and Robert called me, and he had not heard his brother was picked up.

Now, Robert is in Denton. So I called the Star Telegram, and asked that—if they could possibly have someone escort me to Dallas, because I realized I could not drive to Dallas. And they did. They sent two men to escort me to Dallas.

The name of one is Bob Shieffer, the other name I will have for you gentlemen.

Mr. Rankin. Who are those? Are those reporters?

A—Star Telegram reporters, sent by the Star Telegram editor to escort me to Dallas.

Now, upon arriving in Dallas, I did not ask—I did not want to talk to the police. I asked specifically to talk to FBI agents. My wish was granted, I was sent into a room. I have to backtrack my story.

The policemen do not know I am here—"I want to talk to FBI agents."

Mr. Rankin. What time of the day is this?

A—This is approximately 3:30. So I am escorted into an office, and two Brown FBI agents, they are brothers, I understand, and there was another man that I do not know the name.

Mr. Rankin. By that you mean their names were Brown?

A—Their names were Brown. And I have the correct names, also. But we were in this room, and I told them who I was. And

317

I said, "I want to talk with you gentlemen because I feel like my son is an agent of the government, and for the security of my country, I don't want this to get out."

But, first I said to them, "I want to talk to FBI agents from Washington."

"Mrs. Oswald, we are from Washington, we work with Washington."

I said, "I understand you work with Washington. But I want officials from Washington," and I believed they would be in town because of protecting the President.

I said, "I do not want local FBI men. What I have to say I want to say to Washington men."

Of course they wanted the news. They said, "Well, we work through Washington."

I said, "I know you do. But I would like Washington men." So I had no choice.

Mr. Rankin. Did you tell them why you thought he was an agent?

A—Yes, sir. I am coming to this.

So I said, "I have information that"—I told him who I was.

I said, "For the security of my country, I want this kept perfectly quiet until you investigate. I happen to know that the State Department furnished the money for my son to return back to the United States, and I don't know if that would be made public what that would involve, and so please will you investigate this and keep this quiet."

Of course that was news to them.

They left me sitting in the office. . . .

The Chairman. The Commission will be in order. Mrs. Oswald, you may continue with your statement.

A—Yes, sir. Now, we are in Mrs. Paine's home yet.

The Chairman. Yes. This is on the day of the assassination?

A—Yes, sir—the 22nd, Friday, the 22nd.

I am worried because Lee hasn't had an attorney. And I am talking about that, and Mrs. Paine said, "Oh, don't worry about that. I am a member of the Civil Liberties Union, and Lee will have an attorney, I can assure you."

I said to myself but when? Of course, I didn't want to push her, argue with her. But the point was if she was a member of the Union, why didn't she see Lee had an attorney then. So I wasn't too happy about that.

Now, gentlemen, this is some very important facts.

My daughter-in-law spoke to Mrs. Paine in Russian, "Mamma," she says. So she takes me into the bedroom and closes the door. She said, "Mamma, I show you." She opened the closet, and in the closet was a lot of books and papers. And she came out with a picture—a picture of Lee, with a gun.

It said, "To my daughter June"—written in English.

I said, "Oh, Marina, police." I didn't think anything of the picture.

Now, you must understand that I don't know what is going on on television—I came from the jailhouse and everything, so I don't know all the circumstances, what evidence they had against my son by this time. I had no way of knowing. But I say to my daughter, "To my daughter, June," anybody can own a rifle, to go hunting. You yourself probably have a rifle. So I am not connecting this with the assassination—"To my daughter, June," Because I would immediately say, and I remember—I think my son is an agent all the time—no one is going to be foolish enough if they mean to assassinate the President, or even murder someone to take a picture of themselves with that rifle, and leave that there for evidence.

So, I didn't think a thing about it. And it says "To my daughter, June." I said, "The police," meaning that if the police got that, they would use that against my son, which would be a natural way to think.

She says, "You take, Mamma."

I said, "No."

"Yes, Mamma, you take."

I said, "No, Marina. Put back in the book." So she put the picture back in the book. Which book it was, I do not know.

So the next day, when we are at the courthouse—this is on Saturday—she—we were sitting down, waiting to see Lee. She puts her shoe down, she says, "Mamma, picture." She had the picture folded up in her shoe.

Now, I did not see that it was the picture, but I know that it was, because she told me it was, and I could see it was folded up. It wasn't open for me to see. I said, "Marina." Just like that. So Robert came along and he says, "Robert"—I said, "No, no Marina." I didn't want her to tell Robert about the picture. Right there, you know. That was about the picture.

Mr. Rankin. Did you ever tell her to destroy the picture?

A—No. Now, I have to go into this. I want to tell you about destroying the picture.

Now, that was in Mrs. Paine's home. . . .

Mr. Rankin. Now, you were going to tell us about some further discussion of the picture you did see?

A—Yes—all right.

Now, so the next morning the two representatives of the Life Magazine, Mr. Allen Grant and Mr. Tommy Thompson come by at 9 o'clock with a woman, Russian interpreter, a doctor somebody. I have not been able to find this woman. I have called the universities, thinking that she was a language teacher, and I—maybe you have her name. But she is very, very important to our story.

And I do want to locate her, if possible.

During the night, I had decided I was going to take up their offer, because I would be besieged by reporters and everything. So why not go with the Life representatives, and let them pay my room and board and my daughter-in-law's. They came by at

9 o'clock, without calling, with this Russian interpreter. So Marina was getting dressed and getting the children dressed. He was taking pictures all the time.

Mr. Rankin. They came by where?

A—Mrs. Paine's home. And there was no hurry, though, to leave the home, because Mrs. Paine was most anxious for the Life representatives to talk to her and get these pictures and everything—whether Marina has any part in this I don't know, because they spoke Russian, and she didn't tell me about it. But I know Mrs. Paine did.

We left with the two Life representatives. They brought us to the Hotel Adolphus in Dallas. I immediately upon entering the hotel picked up the phone and called Captain Will Fritz, to see if Marina and I could see Lee at the jailhouse.

Mr. Rankin. Who is he?

A—He is one of the big men in Dallas on this case.

Mr. Rankin. The Chief of Detectives, or something like that?

A—Yes. And I called him from the hotel, and the man that answered the phone said he would relay my message to him, that I wanted to see if Marina and I could see Lee. I waited on the phone. He came back and said, "Yes, Mrs. Oswald, Captain Fritz said you may see Lee at 12 o'clock today."

We arrived at the Adolphus Hotel between 9:30 and 10:00.

Mr. Rankin. This was what day?

A—This was Saturday, November 23, the morning of Saturday, November 23.

While we were there, an FBI agent, Mr. Hart Odum entered the room with another agent, and wanted Marina to accompany him to be questioned.

Mr. Rankin. Were these FBI agents?

A—Yes, sir; Mr. Hart Odum is an FBI agent. And I said, "No, we are going to see Lee." We were all eating breakfast when he came in. I said, "No, we have been promised to see Lee. She is not going with you."

So he said, "Well, will you tell Mrs. Oswald, please"—to the interpreter, "I would like to question her and I would like her to come with me to be questioned."

I said, "It is no good. You don't need to tell the interpreter that, because my daughter-in-law is not going with you. We have been promised to see Lee. And besides Marina has testified, made her statement at the courthouse yesterday, and any further statements that Marina will make will be through counsel."

Mr. Odum said to the interpreter, "Mrs. Oswald"—to the interpreter—"will you tell Mrs. Oswald to decide what she would like to do and not listen to her mother-in-law."

I said, "It is no good to tell my daughter-in-law, because my daughter-in-law is not leaving here with you, Mr. Odum, without counsel."

And I had been telling Marina, "No, no."

She said, "I do, Mamma," she kept saying.

Just then my son, Robert, entered the room, and Mr. Odum said, "Robert, we would like to take Marina and question her."

He said, "No, I am sorry, we are going to try to get lawyers for both she and Lee."

So he left.

We went to the courthouse and we sat and sat, and while at the courthouse my son, Robert, was being interviewed by—I don't know whether it was Secret Service or FBI agents—in a glass enclosure. We were sitting—an office, a glass enclosed office. We were sitting on the bench right there.

Mr. Rankin. Where was this?

A—In the Dallas courthouse, on Saturday.

So we waited quite a while. One of the men came and said, "I am sorry that we are going to be delayed in letting you see Lee, but we have picked up another suspect."

I said to Marina, "Oh, Marina, good, another man they think maybe shoot Kennedy."

Mr. Rankin. Did you ask anything about who this suspect was?

A—No, sir; I did not. He just give the information why we would be delayed. We sat out there quite a while. The police were very nice. They helped us about the baby. We went into another room for privacy, for Marina to nurse Rachel. It was 2 or 3 hours before we got to see Lee. We went upstairs and were allowed to see Lee. This was in the jail—the same place I had been from the very beginning, and we were taken upstairs. And by the way, they only issued a pass for Marina and myself, and not for Robert. And Robert was very put out, because he thought he was also going to see his brother. Whether Robert saw his brother or not, I do not know, Mr. Rankin.

Mr. Rankin. About what time of day was this?

A—Just a minute now. We arrived there at 12 o'clock. This would be about 4 or 4:30 in the afternoon, before we got to see Lee.

Mr. Rankin. Was anyone else present when he saw you?

A—No. Marina and I were escorted back of the door where they had an enclosure and telephones. So Marina got on the telephone and talked to Lee in Russian. That is my handicap. I don't know what was said. And Lee seemed very severely composed and assured. He was well beaten up. He had black eyes, and his face was all bruised and everything. But he was very calm. He smiled with his wife, and talked with her, and then I got on the phone and I said, "Honey, you are so bruised up, your face. What are they doing?"

He said, "Mother, don't worry. I got that in a scuffle."

Now, my son would not tell me they had abused him. That was a boy's way to his mother—if he was abused, and it was shown in the paper his black eyes—he wouldn't tell how he got that. He said that was done in the scuffle. So I talked and said, "Is there anything I can do to help you?"

He said, "No, Mother, everything is fine. I know my rights, and I will have an attorney. I have already requested to get in touch with Attorney Abt, I think is the name. Don't worry about a thing."

Mr. Rankin. Did you say anything to him about another suspect?

A—No, sir, I did not. That was my entire conversation to him.

Gentlemen, you must realize this. I had heard over the television my son say, "I did not do it. I did not do it."

And a million of the other people had heard him. I say this. As a mother—I heard my son say this. But also as a citizen, if I had heard another man say, I didn't do it, I will have to believe that man, because he hasn't been—hasn't had the opportunity to present his side of the case. So here is my son. When I saw him people had said, "Did you ask him if he did it?"

No, sir. I think by now you know my temperament, gentlemen. I would not insult my son and ask him if he shot at President Kennedy. Why? Because I myself heard him say, "I didn't do it, I didn't do it."

So, that was enough for me, I would not ask that question.

Mr. Rankin. Who told you that there was—they had found another suspect?

A—One of the officers. That, sir, I don't know. He just walked in real fast while we were sitting down and said they had picked up another suspect, and it was in the paper that they had picked up another suspect at that particular time, which would have been approximately 1 o'clock that day.

Mr. Rankin. But you don't remember the officer's name?

A—No, sir, that is all he said and he left. He was just relaying why we would be delayed. But it was also published. I do not have the paper or the information. But I do know from the reporters, when I told my story, that part to them—they said that substantiates the newspaper story that they did pick up a suspect at that time.

Mr. Rankin. About how long did you and Marina spend there with your son?

A—I would say I spent about 3 or 4 minutes on the telephone, and then Marina came back to the telephone and talked with Lee. So we left. So Marina started crying. Marina says, "Mamma, I tell Lee I love Lee and Lee says he love me very much. And Lee tell me to make sure I buy shoes for June."

Now, here is a man that is accused of the murder of a President. This is the next day, or let's say about 24 hours that he has been questioned. His composure is good. And he is thinking about his young daughter needing shoes.

Now, June was wearing shoes belonging to Mrs. Paine's little girl, Marina told me—they were little red tennis shoes, and the top was worn. They were clean, and the canvas was showing by the toe part, like children wear out their toes.

I ask you this, gentlemen. If Marina had a hundred and some odd dollars in the house, why is it necessary that my son has to tell her at the jailhouse, remind her to buy shoes for his baby, for their child? Just a few dollars out of that hundred and some odd dollars would have bought shoes for this particular child.

Another way to look at this, as I stated previously—that the boy is concerned about shoes for his baby, and he is in this awful predicament. So he must feel innocent, or sure that everything is going to be all right, as he told me.

Mr. Rankin. Now, in this telephone conversation, when you talked to your son, can you explain a little bit to the Commission how that is? Was your son on the other side of a wall or something?

A—Yes, sir. My son was on the other side of the wall, and then back of the wall was a door with a peephole, where an officer was.

Now, we are going to come from the door, with the peephole and the officer, to my son. Then a glass partition and then glass partitions like telephone booths. But not really inclosed —just a little separation.

Mr. Rankin. So you could not reach in there and take your son's hand?

A—No, sir. We talked by telephone.

Mr. Rankin. And he had a telephone on his side, and——

A—And he had a telephone.

Mr. Rankin. And you talked back and forth?

A—Back and forth, that is right. That is the way we talked. And the boy was badly beat up. I have proof in the papers— his face, black eyes, all scratched up, his neck was scratched. He was badly beat up. But he assured me they were not mistreating him, that he got some of the bruises in the scuffle. As I say, the boy, if he was being mistreated, would not tell his mother that.

Mr. Rankin. And whatever Marina said to him was in Russian, and you didn't understand it?

A—No, sir, I did not understand. But I would say this, it seemed to be just an ordinary pleasant conversation. He was smiling. And she told me he said he loved her very much, she said she loved him, and told about buying the shoes for the baby. That is all she said. She did not tell me any other part of the conversation. And they talked quite a while. She talked with him twice. She talked with him the first time. I got on the phone. Then she talked to him again.

Mr. Rankin. Did it sound like there was any dispute or argument?

A—No. It was a pleasant conversation. But she did not volunteer to tell me what was said, and I did not ask her what was said. . . .

We had two beautiful suites—two, not one—completed rooms and baths, adjoining, at the Executive Inn. And that was the last time I had seen either representative. I was stranded with a Russian girl and two babies. I didn't realize in the beginning. But then it was time for food, and I had to order food. I told Marina to stay aside and that I would let the man in. She stayed in her room. I let this man in with the food, and then I became uneasy, that he might know who we were is what I was uneasy about, because I didn't realize the danger actually Marina and I were in.

I sensed we were alone. And there I was with a Russian girl. And I didn't want anybody to know who we were, because I knew my son had been picked up.

So this is where the picture comes in.

While there, Marina—there is an ashtray on the dressing table. And Marina comes with bits of paper, and puts them in the ashtray and strikes a match to it. And this is the picture of the gun that Marina tore up into bits of paper, and struck a match to it.

Now, that didn't burn completely, because it was heavy—not cardboard—what is the name for it—a photographic picture. So the match didn't take it completely.

Mr. Rankin. Had you said anything to her about burning it before that?

A—No, sir. The last time I had seen the picture was in Marina's shoe when she was trying to tell me that the picture was in her shoe. I state here now that Marina meant for me to to have that picture. from the very beginning, in Mrs. Paine's home. She said—I testified before—"Mamma, you keep picture."

And then she showed it to me in the courthouse. And when I refused it, then she decided to get rid of the picture.

She tore up the picture and struck a match to it. Then I took it and flushed it down the toilet.

Mr. Rankin. And what time was this?

A—This—now, just a minute, gentlemen, because this I know is very important to me and to you, too.

We had been in the jail. This was an evening. Well, this, then, would be approximately 5:30 or 6 in the evening.

Mr. Rankin. What day?

A—On Saturday, November 23. Now, I flushed the torn bits and the half-burned thing down the commode. And nothing was said. There was nothing said.

Mr. Rankin. That was at the Executive Inn?

A—At the Executive Inn.

Now, Mr. Hart Odum, the same FBI agent, that insisted upon my daughter-in-law going with him from the Adolphus Hotel, knocked on the door at the Executive Inn. I had had my robe and slippers on, and I pushed the curtain aside when he knocked. He said, "This is Mr. Odum."

So, I opened the door. This is very important. I would like to not talk about it. I would like to show you what I did. This is so important.

I opened the door just a little, because I had the robe off and I didn't want anybody to come in. The door is just ajar. I am going to take my shoes off, gentlemen, because I have this worked out. This is my height. He said, "Mrs. Oswald, we would like to see Marina."

I said, "Mr. Odum, I stated yesterday you are not going to see Marina. We are awful tired."

"Well, we just want to ask her one question."

"Mr. Odum, I am not calling my daughter. As a matter of fact, she is taking a bath."

She wasn't.

He said, "Mrs. Oswald, I would like to ask you a question."

I said, "Yes, sir." The door is ajar. This is my height. I wear bifocals, which enlarges things. And in his hand—his hand is bigger than mine—in the cup of his hand, like this, is a picture. And the two corners are torn off the picture. This is a very glossy black and white picture of a man's face and shoulder.

Now, Mr. Odum wasn't too tall. I need somebody else. Mr. Odum's hand with the picture—what I am trying to say—he is facing this way—showing me. So my eyes are looking straight at the picture. And I have nothing else to see but this hand and the picture, because the door is ajar. And there is nothing on the picture but a face and shoulders. There is no background or anything. So I can identify this picture amongst millions of pictures, I am so sure of it. It was a glossy black and white picture. So I said, "No, sir, believe me. I have never seen this picture in my life."

With that, he went off.

There was another man with him.

About an hour later the telephone rang, and it was Mrs. Paine. She said, "Mrs. Oswald, Lee called and he was very upset because Marina was not with me, and he asked me to get a lawyer for him, a Mr. Abt. I would like to talk to Marina."

So I put Marina on the telephone, and Marina said about two or three words.

So when she got off the telephone, I said—Now, Marina talks in Russian, gentlemen. I said, "Marina, Mrs. Paine told me that Lee called and you were not home at Mrs. Paine, and Lee tells Mrs. Paine to get a lawyer."

Marina didn't answer.

And I then sensed—well, now, why isn't she answering me? This is very peculiar.

And there was no more said about that conversation.

Mr. Rankin. Did you ask her about this lawyer?

A—Ask Marina?

Mr. Rankin. Yes.

A—No, sir. There was no more said about this conversation.

Mr. Rankin. You didn't say anything about Mr. Abt to her then?

A—No, sir. But here is the point to this whole thing.

The FBI agent would have to know where we were, and Mrs. Paine would have to know where we were, because of these two Life representatives, who, I am assuming, probably went back to Mrs. Paine's home in order to get more information. And she—they would have told her where we were, because no one knew where we were. This girl and I had no protection or anything. We were sent out there with this Mr. Allen Grant, the representative. And no one knew who we were. And Mr. Hart Odum would have to know where we were through Mrs. Paine, which is a normal procedure, let's say. He might have gone to Mrs. Paine's home looking for Marina there, and Mrs. Paine might have told him we were at the Executive Inn. I will grant that.

But the point I am going to make is that the picture was tried to be shown to Marina before the telephone conversation.

Now, if there are any questions why I say that, I would be happy to answer.

Mr. Rankin. Yes—why do you say that?

A—Because they wanted Marina——

Mr. Dulles. Could we get what picture this is? Is that the picture held in the hand?

A—Yes, sir—the picture that is held in the hand, that the FBI agent, Mr. Hart Odum showed me.

Mr. Rankin. I understand you didn't recognize who the picture was at all.

A—No. I told Mr. Hart Odum I had never seen the man before. "Believe me, sir," and he left.

So the picture was shown—was tried—had tried to be shown to my daughter-in-law, but they were not successful.

So then they received—Marina receives a telephone call.

Now, I am under the impression, since I know it was Mr. Jack Ruby's picture I saw—at the time I didn't.

Mr. Rankin. How do you know that?

A—Because I have seen his picture in the paper. Now I know it is Mr. Jack Ruby.

I am under the impression that Marina was threatened——

Mr. Rankin. What was the date now?

A—This is Saturday, November 23d. This is approximately 6:30 in the evening, that the FBI agent came. And the telephone call was later.

Now, I have no way of knowing whether Lee had permission to use the telephone. Remember, Lee is in jail.

Mr. Rankin. About what time do you think the telephone call was?

A—I would say it was about 7:30, 8 o'clock in the night.

Mr. Rankin. That was still on Saturday night?

A—Yes, sir, still on Saturday night at the Executive Inn. And that was after the picture was shown to me—she received this telephone call, and became very silent.

And the next day my son was shot.

Now, it is now that I have done investigation of this case that I believe that the picture was meant for Marina to see, meant for Marina to see.

Mr. Rankin. Why do you think that?

A—Because now it has been proven that Jack Ruby killed my son. And I think there is a connection there. Because Marina did not tell me about her conversation. And you men hold the answer whether Lee used the telephone from the jailhouse. I don't know that.

Mr. Rankin. You base that on just your own conclusion that you arrive at now, do you?

A—Yes—because of the FBI agent, Mr. Hart Odum, insistence on taking my daughter-in-law—and he being the same agent that came and showed the picture. And Mr. Ruby being the man that shot Lee—yes, these are definite conclusions.

Mr. Rankin. That is what you base it on?

A—Yes, sir, that is what I base it on.

Mr. Dulles. Do I understand correctly that Marina did not see the picture at any time?

A—That is correct, sir. But they tried awfully hard for Marina to see the picture.

Mr. Rankin. And when they could not show it to her——

A—They showed it to me—yes, sir.

Mr. Rankin. Have you ever seen that picture since?

A—On a Wednesday—Lee was shot on a Sunday—neither Marina nor I knew how he was shot. They kept it from us. You have to visualize this.

We were at the Six Flags with approximately 18 to 20 FBI agents, Secret Service men running in and out, a woman with a Russian girl and two sick babies, and the girl and I do not know what is going on.

Mr. Rankin. When you had gotten over to the Six Flags, you must have skipped something there—you were in the Executive Inn before.

A—Yes. I was going to make a point about letting you know why I didn't know.

Mr. Rankin. All right.

A—All right—let's go back to the Executive Inn.

So that night I was very upset and very worried. I realized that we were there alone. And we were not going to go in town, into Dallas. I wasn't going to take this Russian girl and the two babies. And the babies were all chapped. We had no diapers. We were not prepared for this. And it was hectic, gentlemen.

327

So all night long I am wondering how can I get in touch with Robert, what can I do.

And I was a little suspicious of Mrs. Paine. I was suspicious of Mrs. Paine from the time I entered her home. . . .

Mr. Rankin. Did you later learn at what time of that Sunday he was shot?

A—No, sir; I did not.

Mr. Rankin. You never did?

A—Not until about 3 days later. That is what I was telling you about Six Flags. I am trying to explain to you why I don't know these things is because we did not sit down and watch television and read papers. Marina and I—I had two sick babies there. There was a doctor coming in twice a day. I was a very busy woman. And the men were not telling us anything. They were not interested in us.

Mr. Rankin. Now after you told them that you wanted to stay in a hotel, you could be protected there, what happened?

A—Then, of course, nothing was said that they were going to give me my way. But we needed clothes—Marina and the baby needed clothes. So then they decided that they should go to Irving, through my suggestion and so on, and pick up clothes for Marina and the baby, because we were short on diapers. So they are going to Irving.

We got to Irving. There is police cars all around. So that is why I feel sure my son was shot.

Mr. Rankin. How far away is that from this Executive Inn?

A—I would think—now, this is just hearsay. But I would think it is about 12 to 15 or 18 miles.

When we reached there, they brought us to the chief of police's home. And there were cars all around.

As soon as the car stopped, the Secret Service agent said, "Lee has been shot."

And I said, "How badly?"

He said, "In the shoulder."

They brought Marina into the house.

Mr. Rankin. Did you ask him how he knew that?

A—It came over—I thought he had the radio in the car, Secret Serviceman, and he had talked to someone. This was all set up, sir, and I can prove to you. They didn't want us to know. They are now telling us this, Marina and I.

He talked, and then he turned around and said, "Lee has been shot."

I said, "How badly?"

He said, "In the shoulder."

I cried, and said, "Marina, Lee has been shot."

So Marina went into the chief of police's at Irving home, to call Mrs. Paine, to get the diapers and things ready. They decided and told us, with me in the car and Marina, that it would not be a good thing for us to go to Mrs. Paine's home and get these things, that Marina should go in the chief of police's home and call and tell Mrs. Paine what she wanted.

And one or two of the agents would go and get the things for Marina.

So I am sitting in the car with the agent. Marina is in the home now—remember.

So something comes over the mike, and the Secret Service agent says, "Do not repeat. Do not repeat."

I said, "My son is gone isn't he?"

And he didn't answer.

I said, "Answer me. I want to know. If my son is gone, I want to meditate."

He said, "Yes, Mrs. Oswald, your son has just expired."

Mr. Rankin. Now, which agent told you this?

A—This is the agent that was also now sent to me to protect me in Fort Worth, Tex.—Mr. Mike Howard, who was the agent that rode in the car with President Johnson, who was the agent that was at Six Flags, that was in charge, who was the agent that was assigned to protect Baine Johnson at the dormitory. He is also the same agent that was sent to protect me in Fort Worth, Tex.

Mr. Rankin. Now, who was the other agent that was with you that day? Was there another Secret Service agent with you?

A—He went into the home—he escorted Marina into the chief of police's home, and I do not know his name. And he is not the other agent that I want to know the name of.

Wait just a minute.

I don't know this man's name. But he is not the other agent that is involved.

Mr. Rankin. Now, about what time on that Sunday did you learn of your son's death?

A—Well, now, here is your time element. I said Robert and Mr. Gregory and the Secret Service were there approximately from 11:30. And I knew nothing about the shooting. And then we had to go to Irving and everything. Then they told us Lee was shot. So now we are bringing up to the time—it all fits in—which was 1 o'clock or 1:30.

As a matter of fact, then when I got the news, I went into the home, and I said, "Marina, our boy is gone."

We both cried. And they were all watching the sequence on television. The television was turned to the back, where Marina and I could not see it. They sat us on the sofa, and his wife gave us coffee. And the back of the television was to us. And the men and all, a lot of men were looking at the television. It probably just happened, because the man said, "Do not repeat." And I insisted.

They gave us coffee. . . .

Mr. Rankin. Was there any discussion between you and Marina about this?

A—About the shooting?

Mr. Rankin. Yes.

A—No. We didn't know. I was with Marina at the Executive Inn from the 22d until the shooting, the 24th—as I told you.

Then we left. And from the 24th to the 28th, at the Inn of the Six Flags, the agents and my son kept this from us. We did not know. We knew Lee was shot and dead. But we didn't know how. We didn't get to read a paper or watch television. We just had snatches of the television.

Mr. Rankin. Well, when you both learned that he was shot on that Sunday afternoon, did you and Marina say anything to each other?

A—Oh, yes. That is another story.

Immediately I said, "I want to see Lee." And Marina said, "I want see Lee, too."

And the chief of police and Mr. Gregory said, "Well, it would be better to wait until he was at the funeral home and fixed up."

I said, "No, I want to see Lee now."

Marina said, "Me, too, me want to see Lee."

They led us to believe that now they have taught her to do like this. But Marina has always spoken like that. I have acted as an interpreter for her, as I stated before, for an FBI agent. And she understood me. And he was satisfied that he didn't need an interpreter.

So she said, "I want to see Lee, too."

They didn't want us to see Lee, from the ugliness of it evidently. But I insisted, and so did Marina. So they could not do anything about it with the two women. So they decided to pacify us.

We got in the car. On the way in the car they were trying to get us to change our minds. And he said, Mr. Mike Howard— he was driving the car—"Mrs. Oswald for security reasons it would be much better if you would wait until later on to see Lee because this is a big thing."

I said, "For security reasons I want you to know that I am an American citizen, and even though I am poor I have as much right as any other human being, and Mrs. Kennedy was escorted to the hospital to see her husband. And I insist upon being escorted, and enough security to take me to the hospital to see my son."

Gentlemen, I require the same privilege.

So Mr. Mike Howard said, "All right, we will take you to the hospital.

"I want you to know when we get there we will not be able to protect you. Our security measures end right there. The police will then have you under protection. We cannot protect you."

I said, "That is fine. If I am to die, I will die that way. But I am going to see my son."

Mr. Gregory says—and in the most awful tone of voice, I will always remember this—remember, gentlemen, my son has been accused, I have just lost a son.

He said, "Mrs. Oswald, you are being so selfish. You are endangering this girl's life, and the life of these two children."

I want to elaborate on this. He is not thinking about me. He is thinking about the Russian girl. I am going to bring this over and over—that these Russian people are always considering this Russian girl. He snapped at me.

I said, "Mr. Gregory, I am not talking for my daughter-in-law. She can do what she wants. I am saying I want to see my son."

And so they brought us to the hospital. And Marina said, "I too want to see Lee."

After Mr. Gregory said that—"I, too, want to see Lee."

So then they did leave us at the entrance of the hospital, the Secret Service men, and then the police took over. We were escorted by the police in the hospital.

Mr. Rankin. About what time was that?

A—Well, I would not think it would be more than between 2 and 3 o'clock.

Mr. Rankin. Sunday afternoon?

A—Sunday, November 24th.

Mr. Rankin. And then what happened?

A—Then Mr. Perry, the doctor, came down. We were escorted into a room. And he came in. He said, "Now, you know the Texas law is that we have to have an autopsy on a body."

I said, "Yes, I understand."

And Marina understood.

Marina is a registered pharmacist.

So Marina understands these things. And Marina understood.

And he said, "Now, I will do whatever you ladies wish. I understand that you wish to see the body. However, I will say this. It will not be pleasant. All the blood has drained from him, and it would be much better if you would see him after he was fixed up."

I said, "I am a nurse. I have seen death before. I want to see my son now."

Marina—as I am trying to say, she understands English—she said, "I want to see Lee, too." So she knew what the doctor was saying.

We were escorted upstairs into a room. They said it was a morgue, but it wasn't. Lee's body was on a hospital bed, I would say, or a table—a table like you take into an operating room. And there were a lot of policemen standing around, guarding the body. And, of course, his face was showing. And Marina went first. She opened his eyelids. Now, to me—I am a nurse, and I don't think I could have done that. This is a very, very strong girl, that she can open a dead man's eyelids. And she says, "He cry. He eye wet." To the doctor. And the doctor said, "Yes."

Well, I know that the fluid leaves, and you do have moisture. So I didn't even touch Lee. I just wanted to see that it was my son.

So on the way, leaving the body in the room—I am in the room——

Mr. Rankin. You were satisfied it was your son?

A—Yes, sir. That is why I wanted to see the body. I wanted to make sure it was my son.

So while leaving the room, I said to the police—"I think some day you will hang your heads in shame."

I said, "I happen to know, and know some facts, that maybe this is the unsung hero of this episode. And I, as his mother, intend to provide this if I can."

And, with that, I left the room.

Then we were escorted into a room downstairs, and introduced to the chaplain. I have asked several reporters to give me the chaplain's name, because I wanted to have all this information for you. But you have to realize I just knew Thursday. And I have three times as many papers as I have here. So it has been a chore for me to do all this. But that is easy to find out—the name of the chaplain at Parkland Hospital. So I asked to speak to the chaplain in private. So I spoke to the chaplain in private, and I told him that I thought my son was an agent, and that I wanted him to talk to Robert. Robert does not listen to me, never has, and I have had very, very little conversation with Robert, ever since Robert has joined the Marines, because of the way our life has intervened.

Mr. Rankin. Did you tell the chaplain why you thought your son was an agent?

A—No, sir, but this is what I told the chaplain. No—I am always thinking of my country, the security of my country before I would say anything like that.

And I told you why I told the FBI men, because of the money involved, and I didn't know how the public would take this, because they helped a Marxist.

So I didn't tell him. But I did say I wanted him to talk to Robert, because we financially were in very poor straits. And then I wanted my son buried in the Arlington Cemetery.

Now, gentlemen, I didn't know that President Kennedy was going to be buried in Arlington Cemetery. All I know is that my son is an agent, and that he deserves to be buried in Arlington Cemetery. So I talked to the chaplain about this. I went into quite detail about this. I asked him if he would talk to Robert, because when I talked to Robert about it, as soon as

332

I started to say something he would say, "Oh, Mother, forget it."

So I asked the chaplain to talk to Robert about Lee being buried in the Arlington Cemetery.

Mr. Rankin. Did he report to you about it?

A—No, sir. But he did call Robert in. We were getting ready. The police were getting ready to escort us out of his office, and he said, "If you don't mind, I would like to talk to Robert Oswald just a minute."

So he brought Robert into the room he had taken me, and stayed in there a little while with Robert. So I feel sure that the chaplain relayed my message to him, because we were getting ready to leave, and he asked the police if he could talk to Robert.

Mr. Rankin. The chaplain never told you anything more about it?

A—No, sir. I have not seen the chaplain since.

Mr. Rankin. Did Robert say anything about it?

A—No, sir, Robert says nothing. I have tried to contact Robert for important matters, and Robert will not talk.

Lee was left handed. Lee wrote left handed and ate right handed. And I wanted to know if Lee shot left handed. Because on Lee's leaves, as I stated, they live out in the country, and Robert goes squirrel hunting, and all kinds of hunting. And on leaves from the Marines, Lee has gone out to this farmhouse, to Robert's family house, and he and his brother have gone squirrel hunting. And so Robert would know if Lee shot left handed, and he would not give me the information, gentlemen.

Mr. Rankin. Is Robert left handed?

A—Yes, Robert is left handed. I am left handed.

Mr. Rankin. Is John Pic left handed?

A—No, John is not.

Mr. Rankin. But you are?

A—Yes, sir.

Now, I write left handed, but I do everything else with my right hand.

But Lee was more left handed than I am.

I write left handed, but I do everything else with my right hand. But Lee was left handed.

Mr. Rankin. Was Lee Oswald's father left handed?

A—That I do not remember, Mr. Rankin. No—I am the left handed one. I would say no.

Now, there is another story. And we have stories galore, believe me—with documents and everything. . . .

Representative Ford. Where did you go after the Parkland Hospital? What happened then?

A—Oh, yes. This is interesting.

After the Parkland Hospital, then this Mike Howard said,

"Well, what we will do, we have a place, and this is where we will take them."

And they took us to the Inn of the Six Flags, which is on the outskirts of Arlington, Tex. They took us there.

And I am assuming that it is a Secret Service hideout or something, because they had made no arrangements or anything. We just were welcomed right in the Inn. They knew where to go. . . .

Mr. Rankin. Well, then, did you go to the funeral?

A—Well, let me get—we will get to the story of the ministers.

Mr. Rankin. All right.

A—Now, I was not consulted. Had Robert asked me—they are Lutheran, we are raised Lutherans. I have no church affiliation. I have learned since my trouble that my heart is my church. I am not talking against the church. But I go to church all day long, I meditate. And my work requires that I don't go to church. I am working on Sunday most of the time, taking care of the sick, and the people that go to church, that I work for, the families, have never once said, "Well, I will stay home and take care of my mother and let you go to church, Mrs. Oswald, today."

You see, I am expected to work on Sunday.

So that is why—I have my own church. And sometimes I think it is better than a wooden structure. Because these same people that expect me to work on Sunday, while they go to church, and go to church on Wednesday night—I don't consider them as good a Christian as I am—I am sorry.

Well—I would not have let Robert be so upset trying to get a Lutheran minister. If he could not get a Lutheran minister, I would have called upon another minister, because there would have been many, many ministers of many denominations that would have been happy to come and help the sorrowing family.

Well, a Reverend French from Dallas came out to Six Flags and we sat on the sofa.

Reverend French was in the center, I and Robert on the side. And Robert was crying bitterly and talking to Reverend French and trying to get him to let Lee's body go to church. And he was quoting why he could not.

So then I intervened and said, "Well, if Lee is a lost sheep, and that is why you don't want him to go to church, he is the one that should go into church. The good people do not need to go to church. Let's say he is called a murderer. It is the murderers and all we should be concerned about."

And that agent—I am going ahead of my story a little bit—that man right here——

Mr. Rankin. You are pointing to——

A—This agent right here. You may pass the picture around.

Mr. Rankin. The figure on the left hand of the picture you have just produced?

A—Yes, sir. I do not know his name. The man had the de-

334

cency to stay at the far end of the room, near the entrance door, while the minister and myself and Robert were sitting on the sofa. And when I said to the minister about the lost sheep, this agent, who I will have a much longer story to talk about, left the group and came and sat on the other sofa—there were two sofas and a cocktail table—and he said, "Mrs. Oswald, be quiet. You are making matters worse."

Now, the nerve of him—to leave the group and to come there and scold me.

This Mr. French, Reverend French, agreed that we would have chapel services, that he could not take the body into the church. And we compromised for chapel services.

However, when we arrived at the graveyard, we went to the chapel. There is the body being brought into the chapel. There is another picture. Here is another picture of the chapel.

Mr. Rankin. Before we go on——

A—And the chapel was empty. My son's body had been brought into the chapel, but Reverend French did not show up. And because there was a time for the funeral, the Star Telegram reporters and the police, as you see in the picture, escorted my son's body from the chapel and put it at the grave site. And when we went to the cemetery, we went directly to the chapel, because we were promised to have chapel services. And the chapel was empty. My son's body was not in it. Robert cried bitterly.

Mr. Rankin. Mrs. Oswald, can I interrupt a minute?

We will have the reporter identify this photograph that you just referred to, where the FBI agent is in the lefthand corner. . . .

And the FBI agent you refer to is in the upper lefthand corner of that exhibit.

A—That's right. And this is the other FBI agent, Mr. Mike Howard, who is going to be involved quite a bit. He is the one that was taking care of Baine Johnson. He is the one that they have now sent to protect me in Fort Worth. He was the lead man at Six Flags.

Mr. Rankin. And he stands right behind you there in that picture?

A—Yes, that is Mr. Mike Howard.

Mr. Rankin. Isn't he a Secret Service man?

A—Secret Service man—they are both Secret Service.

Representative Ford. That was the point I wanted to make, because she had said he was an FBI agent.

A—Yes—please interrupt. It is awful hard for me to remember and say things. So I appreciate you doing that. It is a long story. And I have many stories, gentlemen. I have many stories that I am sure you do not have. . . .

A—Now, I don't remember if I stated while at Six Flags that this particular agent identified as being to the left of the picture, while the television was on continuously—I have stated

335

before I never did sit down and watch it, because we were quite busy. And this was published in the Star Telegram by Mr. Blair Justice, and also on the radio.

He was very, very rude to me. Anything that I said, he snapped. And I took it for quite a while. At this particular time that they showed the gun on television, I said, "How can they say Lee shot the President? Even though they would prove it is his gun doesn't mean he used it—nobody saw him use it."

He snapped back and he said, "Mrs. Oswald, we know that he shot the President."

I then walked over to Mr. Mike Howard and I said, "What's wrong with that agent? That agent is about to crack. All he has done is taunt me ever since I have been here."

He said, "Mrs. Oswald, he was personal body guard to Mrs. Kennedy for 30 months and maybe he has a little opinion against you."

I said, "Let him keep his personal opinions to himself. He is on a job."

Now, there was another instance with this same agent. He followed Marina around continuously. I'm going to make this plain. He followed Marina around continuously. The pictures will always show him by Marina.

We were in the bedroom, and he was in the bedroom. And we were getting ready for the funeral.

Marina was very unhappy with the dress—they bought her two dresses. "Mama, too long." "Mama, no fit." And it looked lovely on her. You can see I know how to dress properly. I am in the business world as merchandise manager. And the dress looked lovely on Marina. But she was not happy with it.

I said, "Oh, honey, put your coat on, we are going to Lee's funeral. It will be all right."

And we had 1 hour in order to get ready for the funeral.

I said, "We will never make it. Marina is so slow."

She said, "I no slow. I have things to do."

I am trying to impress upon you that Marina understands English, and has always talked broken English.

Now, this agent was in the room and Robert was on the telephone. That is why he was allowed in the bedroom.

While Marina was complaining about her dress, my little grandbaby, 2 years old—and she is a very precious little baby, they are good children—was standing by her mother. And Marina was very nervous by this time. She was not happy with the dress. And Marina was combing her hair. She took the comb and she hit June on the head. I said, "Marina, don't do that." And this agent—I wish I knew his name—snapped at me and said, "Mrs. Oswald, you let her alone." I said, "Don't tell me what to say to my daughter-in-law when she was hitting my grandbaby on the head with a comb" in front of Robert Oswald.

Now, why did this man do these things?

Mr. Rankin. Are you saying that the agent did anything improper, as far as Marina was concerned?

A—Now, what do you mean when you say improper?

Mr. Rankin. Was there any improper relationship between them, as far as you know?

A—No. I am saying—and I am going to say it as strongly as I can—that I—and I have stated this from the beginning—that I think our trouble in this is in our own Government. And I suspect these two agents of conspiracy with my daughter-in-law in this plot.

The Chairman. With who?

A—With Marina and Mrs. Paine—the two women. Lee was set up, and it is quite possible these two Secret Service men are involved.

Mr. Rankin. Which ones are you referring to?

A—Mr. Mike Howard and the man that I did not—did not know the name, the man in the picture to the left. I have reason to think so because I was at Six Flags and these are just some instances that happened—I have much more stories to tell you of my conclusions. I am not a detective, and I don't say it is the answer to it. But I must tell you what I think, because I am the only one that has this information.

Now, here is another instance—

Mr. Rankin. What kind of a conspiracy are you describing that these men are engaged in?

A—The assassination of President Kennedy.

Mr. Rankin. You think that two Secret Service agents and Marina and Mrs. Paine were involved in that, in the conspiracy?

A—Yes, I do. Besides another high official. I will tell you the high official I have in mind when we go through that part of the story, if you please.

Mr. Rankin. Well, now, could you tell us what you base that on—because that is a very serious charge.

A—It is a very serious charge, and I realize that. I base that on what I told you, the attitude of this man, and Mike Howard's attitude also.

Now, I have to continue.

Mr. Rankin. Have you described that?

A—Yes. I have to continue.

While at Six Flags, Marina was given the red carpet treatment. Marina was Marina. And it was not that Marina is pretty and a young girl. Marina was under—what is the word—I won't say influence—these two men were to see that Marina was Marina. I don't know how to say it. Are you getting the point? Let me see if I can say it better.

Mr. Rankin. You mean they were taking care of her, or were they doing more than that?

A—More than taking care of Marina.

Mr. Rankin. Well, now, describe what more.

A—All right, I will describe it for you.

337

I am not quite satisfied with the way I said that. Let me get my thoughts together.

I noticed that—and of course as I have testified, the way the man treated me—and I was told he was a body guard for Mrs. Kennedy. We were at Six Flags on November 24th, at Lee's death, and on November 26th Marina and I—before November 26th—Marina and I were very, very friendly, very loving, everything was "Mama"—"Mama has a big heart." And we planned to live together.

I had an insurance policy that had expired on Lee. I was not able to keep up the premium. And I had $863. But however I had not looked at the policy for some years, and I was not quite sure that it was in force. But otherwise I had no money and no job. I had given up my job to come to the rescue. So I was very anxious to get home and get my papers and let them see the copies of everything I had, and to find out if I had my insurance policy, if it was in force, and also get some clothes.

From the 24th until the 26th I lived in my uniform, gentlemen. I did not have any clothes at the Six Flags. Yet Robert Oswald was taken to his home a couple of times to get clothes. And when I wanted to go home and get clothes, they put me off. One time I broke down crying. I said, "I don't understand it. You won't do anything for me, yet you drove Robert all the way to Denton to get clothes."

So the night of the 26th they took me home, and I got my papers. I found that my insurance policy was in force. So I said to Marina, "Marina, we all right. Mama has insurance policy, $800. You stay home with baby and mama work, or mama stay home with baby and you work, and at least we have a start."

"Okay, Mama. I not want big house, Mama. I want small place."

And this is the girl that has never had anything, and she only wanted small things. Fine.

On the date of the 22nd, approximately 10 o'clock—this was in the morning—I want to say something to Marina, and Marina shrugged me off and walked away.

Mr. Dulles. What date was this?

A—The 27th. That morning I had acted as interpreter for an FBI agent, and Mr. Mike Howard said, "Would you like us to get a Russian interpreter?" And he said, "No, Mrs. Oswald is doing fine." And he took the testimony from me as an interpreter. So, you see my daughter-in-law did understand English and answered me in her Russian broken English, because the FBI man was satisfied.

So when Marina shrugged me off, I thought right away that she thought—because I had to use the name Lee so many times —that I was hurting her husband, and maybe that is why she felt this way. So I thought maybe I am just imagining things.

338

So I waited quite a while, I would say half an hour. I went to Marina again. And she walked away and shrugged me off.

So I walked into the living room, where my son, Robert Oswald, and the Secret Service were and I said to Robert, "Robert, something is wrong with Marina. She won't have anything to do with me."

He said, "I know why. Marina has been offered a home by a very wealthy woman"—all of this was done without my knowledge—"by a very wealthy woman who will give her children education, and she didn't know how to tell you."

I said, "Well, Robert, why didn't you tell me?"

Of course when I said it, I was emotionally upset. I said, "Robert, why didn't you tell me?"

He said, "Because just the way you are acting now."

I said, "What do you mean the way I am acting now? I am acting in a normal fashion. You are telling me that you are taking my daughter-in-law and my grandchildren away from me, and I have lost my son, and my grandchildren and daughter are going to live with strangers. This is a normal reaction."

"Well, that is why we didn't tell you. We knew you would take it that way."

And that is the last time I have talked to my daughter-in-law, Marina. And that is the rift between Marina and I. There is no rift, sir? We were going to live together. But this home was offered Marina—and I will present this in evidence. . . .

Mr. Rankin. Mrs. Oswald, could you tell us first now, while you are fresh, about this conspiracy that you said that you knew about?

A—Yes—If you would like me to do it now. I was going to lead up to all the fundamentals, to my way of thinking. I have no proof, because naturally if I did I don't think we would be here.

But I feel like there is a lot of speculation about everything.

My way of thinking is because the involvement of myself at Six Flags and the way I was treated, as I have already put into the testimony, and as I stated yesterday, also, that I was supposed to be under protective custody, and I was not.

I wonder why I didn't have protective custody, why I am not important enough, with papers out of the vault, and appearing before the hearing, that Mr. Sorrels, head of the Secret Service, didn't give me protective custody, even though you, yourself, Mr. Rankin, required it.

These are the things I have to face that to me are very unusual.

Mr. Rankin. Well, it is such a serious charge to say that these two Secret Service men and your son and—I didn't understand for sure whether you included anyone else in your charge—were involved in a conspiracy to assassinate the President.

A—No, no——

Mr. Rankin. And your daughter-in-law.

A—That is not my statement. I said I thought that we have a plot in our own government, and that there is a high official involved. And I am thinking that probably these Secret Service men are part of it.

Now, I didn't say in a conspiracy—make it as strong as you did. I have made it strong. But I am under the impression that possibly there is a leak in our own government. . . .

Mr. Rankin. A leak is so much different from a conspiracy to assassinate the President, though.

A—Yes, but this leak—this could be the party involved in the assassination of the President—the high officials I am speaking of, I cannot pin it down to one sentence, gentlemen.

Mr. Rankin. Well, you named the Secret Service men, two of them.

A—That is right.

Mr. Rankin. Now, do you have anything that shows you that either of those men were involved in the conspiracy to assassinate President Kennedy?

A—I will answer that emphatically no. What I have stated is the way they treated me, sir. I elaborated the way these two men treated me—correct? I did that testimony yesterday.

So I have to consider these two men. I will put it that way.

Mr. Rankin. Let's consider Marina Oswald. Do you have anything that will show that she was involved in any conspiracy to assassinate President Kennedy?

A—I feel like Marina is involved and also Mrs. Paine, yes.

Mr. Rankin. Now, what do you have in that regard?

A—All right—because Marina—now this I have said to Mr. Jack Lengett, who is a New York Times newspaperman a long time ago. And I was ashamed to say it to anyone else. And I didn't tell it to him for a long time.

The story yesterday at the Six Flags, when I said to you Marina shrugged me off, and the second time she shrugged me off. The second time she said—and I would not say it now unless I had told Mr. Jack Lengett—she said, "You no have job."

In other words, since Marina was being offered a home, then you go to—"You don't have job."

Before she was satisfied to take $863 and live with me. I was giving her my money and giving her my love. And then, "You no have job."

I am trying to show you the disposition of my daughter-in-law. I love her. But I am trying to show you that there is two sides. I told you how she hit the little girl with the comb. "Mama, I no need you, Mama. You don't have job."

Mr. Rankin. Why does that show she was involved in any conspiracy?

A—Because I am going to try to show there is discrepancies all along. She was not supposed to speak English.

I testified that I, myself, questioned her for an FBI agent. I

340

acted as interpreter. So Marina did know English and understand English. So that is a question.

Mr. Rankin. I thought you said she spoke broken English.

A—Broken English. But she is not supposed to speak English at all, until now that she has learned English. That has been publicized over and over.

Mr. Rankin. And you think she could understand English fluently?

A—Yes, sir. I also told you when she lived with me that month in my home, how we conversed and talked. And yet the impression is that Marina came here and didn't speak English at all.

Mr. Rankin. How does that show she conspired to assassinate the President?

A—Because Marina now is not happy. Marina was very happy, I explained to you, the month she was with me in the beginning that they had rented this house. And then Marina made friends, very, very many friends. And Marina became discontented with Lee. Lee could not give her the things she wanted, what he told her about America. And Marina now has become discontented with me. I don't mean now—I mean at the Six Flags.

Mama always had a big heart. I quit a job to help these children, and that is perfectly all right. That is my nature.

But then, when she has somebody else, you are pushed aside.

I am trying to show this. And, as I go along—I cannot help but face this, gentlemen, it is a fact. I cannot help but face these things.

So I am under the impression—and this is speculation, like anything else—circumstantial evidence, let's say.

I am just a layman. That is what you have against my son. Nobody saw him with a rifle shoot the President. So you have mostly circumstantial evidence.

I have to think of all these things, who might be involved in this.

The Secret Service men, surely you will admit, did not guard our President properly.

Now, that was also stated in the newspaper by, I think it is, Secret Service Judge Baughman—am I saying that right? He is the one that—how Lee got out of the building, and why the President—there are many, many people that wonder. So I, too, am wondering.

So I say that President Kennedy was improperly guarded. And I am not the only one that says that, sir. So I have to consider that. I have to consider the way I, myself, was treated at Six Flags for the three days.

When I came here today—I have these notes, something very important about that particular incident at Six Flags, to back up my story with a witness. You don't have to take my word for it.

Mr. Rankin. What else is there now in regard to Marina that

341

caused you to think she conspired to kill President Kennedy?

A—Yes—because everything is laid out in Mrs. Paine's home and Marina's home. The gun was in the garage.

Mr. Rankin. Well, that doesn't make Marina do it, does it?

A—No, but Marina told the police that the gun was there the night before. She saw the gun in the garage the night before. She didn't see Lee take it that morning. But she made a statement that she saw the gun the night before.

The pictures of Lee with the rifle came from that home. If Lee is going to assassinate the President or anybody else, is he going to have photographs laying all around with the gun? No, sir.

And there is too much evidence pointing to the assassination and my son being the guilty one in this particular house.

All through the testimony, sir, everything has come from this particular house. And so I am a thinking person, I have to think.

Mr. Rankin. Why does that show that Marina had anything to do with the conspiracy?

A—Well, we are speculating, let's say. Marina is not happy. Lee can't give her any money and things. And she has made friends with these Russian folks that have cars and homes. And they are not happy because this Russian girl doesn't have anything. They are not happy about that.

And I am trying to show the disposition of the girl.

I love my daughter-in-law even now. Believe me, it is a sore spot to have to say this. But I have to face these facts of what I know.

Mr. Rankin. You realize it is a very serious charge.

A—Yes, sir. And it is also a serious charge that my son is the assassin of President Kennedy.

You see, we have two sides here. It is a very serious charge, because no one saw him shoot the President. And yet this is an international affair. And the conclusion has come to the conclusion that Lee Harvey Oswald has shot President Kennedy, and he alone. Lee Harvey Oswald, or Mr. J. Lee Rankin, or anyone in this room could not have been in that many places in 29 minutes time. It is utterly impossible.

And this has been gone over by hundreds of people. There are investigations. I have 1,500 letters, sir—not just letters of sympathy—people that are investigating this. And I don't read all thoroughly, and I am a layman. But he step by step has been taken, from what the resports said—that he was on the sixth floor, and then they saw him in the cafeteria drinking a Coca Cola, and the President came. Then he had to leave the building. He had so many blocks to walk before he caught a bus. He had to board the bus, he had to pay his fare, he had to get out of the bus, then he walked a few blocks, then he caught a taxicab, paid the taxi man, then he walked a few blocks, went to his home and got a coat. Then he walked a few more blocks and

342

shot the policeman. Then he walked a few more blocks and he was in the theater.

In 29 minutes time it cannot be done.

So I am convinced my son, and my son alone, if he is involved—I am a human being, and I say my son could have shot the President, and he could have been involved. I am not the type mother to think that he is perfect and he could not do it. But I say he did not do it alone—if he did it. Because it is utterly impossible.

And I do not believe my son did it.

I think my son was framed because, gentlemen—would his rifle be in the sixth floor window of the depository—unless you want to say my son was completely out of his mind. And yet there has been no statement to that effect. Wade has publicly said on the television when it happened that he is sane, he is well reasoned, he knows what he did. And Lee never did break, with his black eyes. He kept saying he was innocent. And yet in 12 hours time he was proven guilty. That doesn't make sense to me, an ordinary layman. So I have to consider who is involved.

Now, I am telling you that this girl was not happy with her situation. She had turned against me twice.

You, yourself, yesterday said that she testified that I told her to tear up the picture. God give me the grace—I did no such thing. My testimony is true.

So now she has lied there, I have found out.

And every evidence of any importance has come from this house. I have to face that.

Mr. Rankin. What else do you have that shows that she had any part in the conspiracy to assassinate the President?

A—Yes. I am under the impression that probably she—I think Lee is an agent. I have always thought that, and I have as much circumstantial evidence that Lee is an agent, that the Dallas police has that he is a murderer, sir.

Mr. Rankin. What do you base that on?

A—Well, I am going to tell my story. I have it all there. That is what I base it on.

Mr. Rankin. Can you tell us in summary?

A—No, sir, I don't think I want to tell it to you that way, because I cannot, almost.

Mr. Rankin. That is a very serious charge, that he was an agent, too.

A—Well, fine. So all right.

If I feel that way, sir, don't I have the right, the American way, to speak up and to tell you what I feel? Isn't that my privilege?

Mr. Rankin. Yes. But can't you tell us what you base it on?

A—Yes, sir, I will, as I go along, sir.

Mr. Rankin. Is that the only way you can tell it?

A—I don't see how I can say to you I know he is an agent,

and I have papers. I want to tell the whole story. I still have more papers. I have documents that I know you do not have, sir.

Mr. Rankin. Have you told us all that you know that would bear on your claim that Marina Oswald was——

A—Had a part in it.

Mr. Rankin. Had a part in it or conspired to assassinate the President?

A—Yes, sir—I cannot prove it. And I cannot prove Lee is an agent. I cannot prove these things.

But I have facts that may lead up to them. I cannot prove it, because if I did we would not be having this Commission, sir. I could say who shot President Kennedy.

Mr. Rankin. So in both cases of the agent—Lee being an agent, your son, and Marina Oswald and the Secret Service agents or anybody else conspiring with him for the assassination of President Kennedy, that is just suspicions. You cannot prove it—is that right?

A—I would not use the word suspicion, because I am not the type person to be suspicious and imagine things.

You may think so, because I am a woman. And this is my son. But my children were never tied to my apron strings.

And I can prove to you, in his defection in 1959, I made the statement that Lee, as an individual, had the right to think and do what he wanted to. They even said he was a Communist. If that is what he studied, and that is what he wanted to do, I accepted that, because that was his privilege as an individual. And that is public in 1959, my statement, which shows that I am not the sobbing mother kind because he has gone to Russia, and cry about it. I acknowledge that.

I have acknowledged that if the children, like Lee, went to Dallas, as I testified that yesterday, and didn't tell me he was going to Dallas—I don't grieve and lose my sleep over that. I have accepted that fact, because when Lee and Marina got ready to come to me that would be fine. In the meantime, I still have to live.

Mr. Rankin. Are you telling the Commission that your son was part of a conspiracy to assassinate the President?

A—I am saying that I realize that my son could possibly be part—yes—I realize he is a human being and he could possibly be in this, yes, sir.

Mr. Rankin. Are you saying he was?

A—No, I do not know. I am saying possibly he is involved.

Mr. Rankin. And you are saying possibly Marina was involved?

A—Well, exactly what I am trying to say. If I had proof, sir, I would give the proof in an affidavit and this case would be closed, like Mr. Wade said.

But I have as much right to my way of thinking as Mr. Wade has.

344

Mr. Rankin. You are saying that possibly the Secret Service agents were involved, too? You don't have any proof of that?

A—That is exactly what I have been trying to say. I have told you how I was treated, which has given me cause for this particular way of thinking—because I believe that my son is innocent. And I think that is the purpose of this Commission, is to hear all witnesses and arrive at a conclusion. Am I not right, gentlemen?

So this is my way of thinking. So grant me my way of thinking. If I am wrong, fine. But you may learn something.

Mr. Rankin. What about the high official now. Can you tell us who that was?

A—No, sir. I wish I did know. I have my own idea about that. I would rather not—because it is a high official—I would rather not give a name.

But I have my own very strong suspicions as to the official who he might be.

Mr. Rankin. We would appreciate your telling us within this group what you think.

A—Fine—and I expect to, Mr. Rankin. I am a person that is very outspoken, as you know by now, and I will certainly do that.

But will you grant me the privilege first of finding out the name of the man in the State Department that wrote the letter to Senator Tower, because it is an incorrect—it is incorrect—the whole testimony is incorrect.

Mr. Rankin. We will get that correspondence for you.

A—All right. I was going to go into something else, but while we are here, I will continue this.

And this, to me, will be in this line. And I think very important to you gentlemen. And you do not have a copy of what I am going to show you. I am the only person that has this copy.

I am sorry to take time, but these were not copied, sir. We sealed them up, and we were going to have them copied this afternoon. But I can get to this particular one. This is the defection. I have much more testimony than this. I have testimony, sir.

Mr. Rankin. Do you think that you can tell us the name of the high official you spoke about?

A—Yes, I think so. And I am going to tell you. But please do not ask me at this particular moment. I do not think this is the proper time for me to—it is just—I have no proof. Understand? As I said, it is my right to think and my analysis of the papers I have. I have papers where I can come to a conclusion, just like you gentlemen are going to have papers and witnesses and come to a conclusion.

Now, this particular instance——

Mr. Dulles. I wonder if we could not possibly explore that agent matter. I am very much interested in that. I cannot be here tomorrow. We laid all the groundwork for that.

The Chairman. Mr. Dulles would like to know her reasons for believing that he was an agent.

A—Yes, sir, I have two very long stories.

Mr. Dulles. I have to be absent, unfortunately, tomorrow, so I would like very much to have it.

Mr. Rankin. If you could go into that question, Mrs. Oswald, because Mr. Dulles is not going to be here tomorrow.

A—We have everything just so, and yet when we come here we don't have it. The International Rescue Committee is what I am looking for.

I have also the original application from the Albert Schweitzer coming that you gentlemen do not have.

The Chairman. Let's stay on one thing, please.

A—All right. I am a little excited now, because I meant to go story by story.

Gentlemen, I have at least four more stories to tell—two I don't think there are some parts you possibly can know about.

Mr. Rankin. Well, if you could tell why you think your son was an agent, it will help to get that taken care of this afternoon while Mr. Dulles can be with us. That is why I asked you that.

A—Yes, sir. We have a special file. You see, gentlemen, all morning long as I was in the backroom and we were copying things. We had everything just so. So now I don't know what condition they are in. Mr. Doyle and I worked on the papers again last night and we had them just so. And then when they were copied, evidently they were mixed up again.

Mr. Rankin. We tried to have you present so that would not happen, Mrs. Oswald. I guess you didn't accomplish that.

A—Well, they did take it into the other room, and we saw that they took it.

Well, I can be telling the story about it.

It is the International Rescue Committee, and a telegram.

I received a letter from Lee—this is going to be real short, Chief Justice Warren. It is going to continue this one story. And then I will go into the defection—is that right—because this will continue that.

A letter from Lee asking me to go to the Red Cross in Vernon—I was on a case there—and asking me to show the letter to the lady at the Red Cross. And this is from Moscow. This is the letter from Moscow. And telling her that all exit visas and everything had been documented and he is ready to come home, but he needs help financially to come home.

Evidently you have that information. That I know, sir.

Mr. Rankin. Yes.

A—So when I entered the Vernon Red Cross—now, this came with Lee's letter, Chief Justice Warren—the letter you have there direct from Moscow. That is why I have it, sir—because it was in Lee's letter asking me to go to the Red Cross in Vernon. So I have the original from Moscow.

I told the young lady, showed her the letter and showed her the paper. And I said, "Would you find out, please, the address of the International Rescue Committee? My son is in Russia and asked me to contact you."

She said, "What is your son doing in Russia?"

I said, "I don't know."

"You are his mother and you don't know what he is doing in Russia?"

I said, "Young lady, I said I do not know what he is doing in Russia."

"Well, I think anybody goes to Russia doesn't need any help to get back, they should stay over there."

So I said, "I am not interested in your personal opinion. I need help. Would you please contact, give me the address of the International Rescue Committee so I can continue to try to get money for my son to come home?"

She did not know of any address for the International Rescue Committee.

I asked her if she had a private line to Wichita Falls, which was approximately 40 miles away, which would be the next big city. She called Wichita Falls, and they did not know the address of the international committee.

So I called Robert and told Robert what I had and asked him to try to find out the address of the International Rescue Committee. However, he gave me no satisfaction.

Now, I sent a telegram—and you know this part of it—to the State Department, asking—I told them I was in a small town, Vernon, Tex., and I had received a letter from Lee asking me to get the address and help from the International Rescue Committee. But being a small town I had no success—could they help me out?

So they sent a telegram back with the address of the International Rescue Committee. That you have.

And this is Lee's letter—that goes with the other part.

Now, this young lady was very, very regalish. She didn't want to help anybody going to Russia. So when I received the telegram from the State Department, it was on a Saturday. I called her that morning. I was delayed 4 or 5 days. And to me it was very important, since my son and daughter-in-law had all documents finished with to get the money to come home, because I wanted that baby to be born here.

So I called her at her home and told her that I had the address from the State Department of the International Rescue Committee, and would she be so kind enough as to come to the office and write the letter for me.

She said, "Well, Mrs. Oswald, I don't have a key."

This is on a Saturday morning and she is in the courthouse. I said, "Do you mean to tell me you are in charge of the Red Cross and you don't have a key?"

"No, I don't."

"Well, young lady, you have delayed me 4 days, and I don't like your attitude. I am going to ask you especially to make a point to come to the office and get this in the mail for me. It is very important."

So, reluctantly, after much persuasion, she came.

So she wrote the letter to the International Rescue Committee, and handed it to me, and I mailed that letter—I mailed the letter.

This is dated January 22, 1962.

So she called me—her name—Mrs. Harwell. She is the only woman in the Red Cross office in Vernon, Tex.

She called me and told me she had received word from the International Rescue Committee. She read me this letter. So I said to Mrs. Harwell, "Do you mind if I take the letter, because I am very forgetful?"

So she took a scissors, gentlemen, and she cut this part out, which was her title and her address—it was addressed to her. This lady wanted no part of anybody in Russia—understand? So she cut this out.

But on the back page was the name. But that is why this space is here—she cut it out.

Now, the letter reads: "Since we had a call from the State Department on Mr. Oswald's case, your communication of January 14th did not come as a surprise."

So this young lady has followed up with a letter of her own to the International Rescue Committee.

"Since we have had a call from the State Department, your letter does not come as a surprise."

I mailed the first letter, and it was just—so she followed up her feelings about a boy in Russia.

Now, why does the State Department dicker with me—that is not the word—and then see fit to put in a personal call to the International Rescue Committee?

I would like to know who from the State Department called the International Rescue Committee.

There is my information there that I requested. Why is a call necessary?

Mr. Rankin. You think that shows there was a conspiracy?

A—I am wondering and questioning why a call is necessary, a call, when they had contacted—and I am showing you what I have here. I don't see any necessity of the State Department to call the International Rescue Committee.

And, gentlemen, you have a copy of this—Lee will not be helped.

I would like to know who called the International Rescue Committee from the State Department—yes, sir, I would.

Mr. Rankin. Yes, but you don't think that shows there is a conspiracy?

A—Well, no—now, Mr. Rankin, don't pin me down everything I say to the word conspiracy. I am trying to analyze a whole condensed program of things that are not correct. I am telling you about this. It could be just a simple thing, that he called. But I would like to know who called when it wasn't necessary to make a call, and Lee was not going to get the money. Read the letter.

Mr. Rankin. The reason I ask you about the conspiracy is because that is such a serious charge. And, as you say, if you could prove that, that would decide everything around here.

A—That is right. And I am going to see if I cannot show you these things.

Mr. Rankin. If you are speculating, which you have a right to do, that is something different.

A—Well, I have explained that I am speculating, that I have all these documents, that some of them don't make sense. That is what I am trying to tell you. I mentioned that before.

Mr. Rankin. You are not trying to say to the Commission that you have the proof that there was a conspiracy?

A—I have emphatically stated that I do not have the proof, because if I had the proof I would have an affidavit and give you gentlemen the proof. I made that clear two or three times. I wish I did have the proof, sir.

I think I said yesterday—it doesn't surprise me that there may be someone in our State Department or some official who would have part in this. He is a human being just like we are. He may have a title, but that doesn't make him a man back of the title.

Mr. Dulles. What is this conspiracy now, Mr. Rankin? Is this the conspiracy to do away with the President, or is this a different conspiracy?

Mr. Rankin. The conspiracy I was asking about was the conspiracy, she said, about the assassination of President Kennedy.

And she said that it involved the two Secret Service agents and her daughter-in-law and her son. That is the one I was asking about.

The Chairman. And Mrs. Paine.

A—And Mrs. Paine. I feel like the facts have come from this particular source.

Mr. Rankin. Now, as I understand she says now that she is speculating as to that being a possibility.

A—Well, now, Mr. Rankin, I have not changed my testimony, if you are implying that. I may not have put it in a position you understood. Because as I say, I certainly did not mean to imply that I had proof, because if I had proof I would not be sitting here taking all my energy and trying to show you this little by little. I would have had an affidavit and show you the proof. So if you want to call it speculation, call it speculation. I don't care what you call it. But I am not satisfied in my mind that things are according to Hoyle. And I believe that my son is innocent. And I also realize that my son could be involved. But I have no way of knowing these things unless I analyze the papers that I have, sir.

Mr. Rankin. The Commission would like to know what you base your assumption that your son was an agent on. Could you help us?

A—Would you like me to go into this story—I will start with my son's life from the very beginning.

Mr. Rankin. Can't we get down to——

A—No, sir, we cannot. I am sorry. This is my life. I cannot survive in this world unless I know I have my American way of life and can start from the very beginning. I have to work into this. I cannot answer these questions like in a court, yes or no. And I will not answer yes or no. I want to tell you the story. And that is the only way you can get a true picture. I am the accused mother of this man, and I have family and grandchildren, and Marina, my daughter-in-law. And I am going to do everything I can to try and prove he is innocent.

Mr. Rankin. Well, now, Mrs. Oswald, you are not claiming before this Commission that there was anything back at the beginning, at the early childhood of your son, in which you thought he was an agent?

A—Yes, sir—at age 16.

Mr. Rankin. Well, why don't you start with age 16, then.

A—Well, aren't you gentlemen—I have a letter from you, Mr. Rankin. Aren't you gentlemen interested in my son's life from the very beginning? I think you should, because it has been exploited in all the magazines and papers. And this is not my son is what I am trying to say. He is not a perfect boy, and I am not a perfect woman. But I can show a different side of Lee Harvey Oswald, which I hope to do to this Commission.

Mr. Rankin. Well, I plan to ask you about his early life and these other parts. But I thought it would be helpful if you would be willing to do it to tell the Commission, while Mr. Dulles is here, what you base this claim upon that your son was an agent of the Government.

A—Yes, and I would be happy to do it.

Mr. Rankin. If you have to go to when he was 16 years old as the first point, that will be fine.

But if you could cover that—then we will go on to other things.

A—All right. I have your word that you will let me have my life story from early childhood and Lee's life story from early childhood.

Now, I will start from age 16. Is that satisfactory?

Mr. Rankin. Would you do that? . . .

A—So Lee was determined at age 16—his birthday was going to be October 18th, right—and this was October 7th—was

350

going to join the Marines. So what Lee wanted me to do was falsify his birth certificate, which I would not do. And he kept after me, like a boy.

Now, this is a normal boy, wanting to join the Marines.

"I don't see why you don't just put that I am 17 years old."

I said, "Lee, We cannot do that."

He said, "Everybody else"—

I said, "No, I am not going to do it."

For 2 or 3 days Lee and I bickered back and forth about me falsifying his age. . . .

Lee, at age 16, read Robert's Marine manual back and forth. He knew it by heart. Robert had just gotten out of the Marines, and his manual was home. And Lee started to read communistic material along with that.

Mr. Rankin. What communistic material did he read?

A—It was a small book that he had gotten out of the library. And I knew he was reading it, Mr. Rankin.

Mr. Rankin. Was it in Marxism, or what was it about?

A—No— if you are saying the title is Marxism—no, sir, the title was not.

Mr. Rankin. Was it about communism?

A—It was more about communism. I knew he was reading it. But if we have this material in the public libraries, then certainly it is all right for us to read. And I think we should know about these things, and all of our scholars and educators and high school boys read subversive material, which we call subversive material. So I, as a mother, would not take the book away from him. That is fine. Lee is a reader. I have said from early childhood he liked histories and maps.

So that is fine.

What I am saying now—we are getting to this agent part.

He is with this recruiting officer and he is studying the Marine manual—he knew it back and forth. In fact, he would take the book and have me question some of the things. And he was reading communism.

Lee lived for the time that he would become 17 years old to join the Marines—that whole year.

Mr. Rankin. What did he do during that time?

A—Pardon?

Mr. Rankin. What did he do during that year?

A—What did he do during that year? He was working for— as a messenger for Tujaque and Son.

Mr. Rankin. He had quite a few jobs, did he not?

A—Yes. I can explain that to you.

His first job was Tujaque and Son, who was steamship people, and he was a messenger. And then he had a lot of friends.

Now, they say Lee didn't have friends. There were boys of his age—while he was working he had an opportunity to make friends, coming to my home. And one of the young men knew of a better paying job, where they had coffee breaks and everything, so Lee took that job, which was with a dental laboratory —if you have that information, sir.

And I think that is the only two jobs—no, Lee worked after school for Dolly Shoe Co. I was working there, in charge of the hosiery department, and Lee worked on Friday afternoon and Saturday as a shoe salesman.

That was his first job—while he went to school he worked there.

And then when he left school, as I told you, at age 16—the first job was Tujaque and Company, steamship, and then the dental laboratory. And that is the only jobs he had in New Orleans.

Mr. Rankin. Were there not times he didn't have any job during that year?

A—No, sir—because when we left New Orleans, Lee left this dental laboratory job—that is correct.

So I moved back to Fort Worth, Tex., because Robert did not want to live in New Orleans. Robert was raised in Texas, and has his girl friends and all his friends in Texas. So when Robert got out of the Marines, he wanted to live in Texas. So I know that Lee wants to join the Marines at age 17, so in the month of July 1956—and, gentlemen, I have always been broke, and I mean broke. About a week before rent time, we had it pretty hard in order to have that rent. Yet I take my furniture and ship it to New Orleans so Lee could be with his brother and we could be with the family—thinking maybe with Robert he would not join the Marines at age 17 and finish his schooling.

When Lee became age 17, October 18th, he joined the Marines.

The reason why he didn't go into the Marines until October 24th was the recruiting officer at the Marines could not understand his birth certificate, because his father had died 2 months before. So I had to send for an affidavit, even though I had the death notice from the paper and everything, and they could have—they could not understand that about that two months. I had to send to New Orleans for an affidavit of his father's death.

And so then Lee joined the Marines on October 24th.

From the 18th to the 24th every day Lee was leaving. We even laughed about it. Because he would leave in the morning and come home in the evening. And it was because he was born 2 months before his father—so he did join the Marines at age 18.

Now—that, Mr. Dulles, is the part you wanted to know. But, before, that has something to do with it. Lee——

Mr. Rankin. Mr. Dulles wanted to know what you based this idea that he was an agent on?

A—That is one part. That is the beginning of it, Mr. Dulles. I have much more. That is the beginning of it, sir. . . .

Mr. Rankin. Now, up to this point, you haven't told us anything that caused you to think he was an agent, have you?

A—Well, maybe, sir, I am not doing a very good job of what I am saying.

Mr. Rankin. What do you think you have said that caused you to think——

A—I have said that a Marine recruiting officer came to my home, and that Lee then continued reading Robert's manual by heart, and started reading communist literature. He is preparing himself to go into the Marine service—at age 17—this year before he actually joined the service. I am saying he is already preparing himself.

Mr. Rankin. To become an agent?

A—Yes, I think with the influence of this recruiting officer.

Mr. Rankin. You think the recruiting officer inspired him——

A—Yes, sir, influenced this boy.

Mr. Rankin. ——to read the communist literature?

A—Yes, sir—and Robert's Marine book.

Mr. Rankin. Is there anything else you base that on, except what you have told us?

A—About him being an agent?

Mr. Rankin. Yes.

A—Yes, sir, when I get through the whole story.

Mr. Rankin. I mean as far as the recruiting officer.

A—No. Otherwise than Lee's attitude. Lee read this manual. He knew it by heart. I even said, "Boy, you are going to be a general, if you ever get in the Marines."

Mr. Rankin. And you base the idea——

A—He had the idea.

Mr. Rankin. He was being prepared to become an agent, and inspired by this recruiting officer?

A—Yes, sir.

Mr. Rankin. By what you have told us about his reading the communist literature and this one pamphlet, and also the manual of the Marine Corps?

A—Yes, sir. And then living to when he is age 17 to join the Marines, which I knew, and which he did at age 17 on his birthday.

Mr. Rankin. Now, what else do you base your idea that he was—ever became an agent or was going to become an agent on?

A—Many, many things. We always watched—it is "I Led Three Lives"—the program—Philbrick. We always watched that. And when Lee returned from the service and the Marines, the three days—that program was on, and he turned it off. He said, "Mother, don't watch that, that is a lot of propaganda."

It has been stated publicly that the FBI did not know—didn't have Lee on the subversive list—I am probably not saying this

353

right, gentlemen—but the rightwing in Dallas. I don't know anything politically. The FBI and Secret Service had a list of names in Dallas of people that had to be watched, and Lee Harvey Oswald was not on that list. That would lead to believe there was some reason he was not on the list.

Mr. Rankin. Who did you get that from?

A—From the newspapers and all over. And there has been a lot of comment about this all through.

Now, I don't say it is correct. But what I have explained to you before—my way of thinking has to go with this, because I know the boy and the whole life, and you do not, sir.

Mr. Rankin. Well, I want to try to find out all you know about it.

A—Fine. And I want you to.

Also, Lee's letters—and I have them in the hotel—I didn't bring them, because I thought we were through, and you have the copies—most every letter from Lee tells me something.

When Lee is coming back from Russia he says, "I plan to stop over in Washington a while."

Lee says in the letter, "Marina's uncle is a major in the Soviet Union."

"I am an American citizen and I will never take Soviet citizenship."

If you will read every letter—if you think he is an agent—every letter is telling his mother—"If something happens to me, Mother, these are facts."

I might be elaborating. But I think my son is an agent. And these things piece by piece are going together, as far as I am concerned.

Representative Ford. When did you first think he was an agent?

A—When Lee defected. And I have always said a so-called defection, for this reason. . . .

Mr. Rankin. Did you think he was a Russian agent at this time?

A—No, sir; I did not think he was a Russian agent.

Representative Ford. I thought you answered in response to a question I asked, when you thought he was an agent, you said when he defected.

A—I might have said defected to Russia. No, sir; I never thought Lee was a Russian agent.

Representative Ford. I meant an agent of the United States. It is my recollection that you said when he defected to the Soviet Union, you then thought he was an American agent.

A—Yes, that is right. That is correct.

Mr. Rankin. What else caused you to think he was an American agent?

A—All right. I might be letting things out the way I am going. And I am very unhappy about this. Had I started with his childhood I could have worked up to age 15 very peacefully,

354

and you would have gotten everything. I hope I am not forgetting anything important. But now we have letters from the State Department.

Well, my trip to Washington has to come before the letters to the State Department, sir. So I am in conference with the three men. I showed them the letter from the—the application from the Albert Schweitzer College, and Lee's mail had been coming to my home. I didn't know whether he was living or dead. I did not want to mail these papers. So I made a personal trip to Washington.

I arrived at Washington 8 o'clock in the morning. I took a train, and borrowed money on an insurance policy I have, which I have proof. I had a bank account of $36, which I drew out and bought a pair of shoes. I have all that in proof, sir, the date that I left for the train. I was 3 nights and 2 days on the train, or 2 days and 3 nights. Anyhow, I took a coach and sat up.

I arrived at the station 8 o'clock in the morning and I called the White House. A Negro man was on the switchboard, and he said the offices were not open yet, they did not open until 9 o'clock. He asked if I would leave my number. I asked to speak to the President. And he said the offices were not open yet. I said, "Well, I have just arrived here from Fort Worth, Tex., and I will call back at 9 o'clock."

So I called back at 9 o'clock. Everybody was just gracious to me over the phone. Said that President Kennedy was in a conference, and they would be happy to take any message. I asked to speak to Secretary Rusk, and they connected me with that office. And his young lady said he was in a conference, but anything she could do for me. I said, "Yes, I have come to town about a son of mine who is lost in Russia. I do want to speak— I would like personally to speak to Secretary Rusk." So she got off the line a few minutes. Whether she gave him the message or what I do not know. She came back and said, "Mrs. Oswald, Mr. Rusk"—so evidently she handed him a note—and Mr. Boster was on the line—"that you talk to Mr. Boster, who is special officer in charge of Soviet Union affairs"—if I am correct. And Mr. Boster was on the line. I told him who I was. He said, "Yes, I am familiar with the case, Mrs. Oswald." He said, "Will an 11 o'clock appointment be all right with you?" This is 9 o'clock in the morning. So I said—this is quite an interesting story—I said, "Mr. Boster that would be fine. But I would rather not talk with you." I didn't know who Mr. Boster was. I said, "I would rather talk with Secretary of State Rusk. However, if I am unsuccessful in talking with him, then I will keep my appointment with you."

So I asked Mr. Boster—I said, "Mr. Boster, would you please recommend a hotel that would be reasonable?" He said, "I don't know how reasonable, Mrs. Oswald, but I recommend the Washington Hotel. It will be near the State Department and convenient to you."

So I went to the Washington Hotel. And as we know, gentlemen, there were nothing but men. They asked me if I had reservation. I said, "No, I didn't, but Mr. Boster of the State Department recommended that I come here." So they fixed me up with a room. I took a bath and dressed. I went to the appointment—because this is 9:30, I am on the phone, and I had to take a cab to the hotel. I arrived at Mr. Boster's office at 10:30.

But before arriving at Mr. Boster's office, I stopped at a telephone in the corridor, and I called Dean Rusk's office again, because I didn't want to see Mr. Boster, and I asked to speak to Dean Rusk. And the young lady said, "Mrs. Oswald, talk to Mr. Boster. At least it is a start."

So then I entered around the corridor into Mr. Boster's office. I have all the pictures of the State Department and everything to prove this story is true. I told the young lady, "I am Mrs. Oswald. I have an 11 o'clock appointment." Mr. Boster came out and said, "Mrs. Oswald, I am awfully glad you came early, because we are going to have a terrible snow storm, and we have orders to leave early in order to get home."

So he called Mr. Stanfield—the arrangements had been made —now, the other man—I don't have that name here for you, Mr. Rankin.

Mr. Rankin. Is it Mr. Hickey?

A—Yes, Mr. Hickey. You are correct.

So then we were in conference. So I showed the papers, like I am showing here. And I said, "Now, I know you are not going to answer me, gentlemen, but I am under the impression that my son is an agent." "Do you mean a Russian agent?" I said, "No, working for our Government, a U.S. agent. And I want to say this: That if he is, I don't appreciate it too much, because I am destitute, and just getting over a sickness," on that order.

I had the audacity to say that. I had gone through all of this without medical, without money, without compensation. I am a desperate woman. So I said that.

Mr. Rankin. What did they say to you?

A—They did not answer that. I even said to them, "No, you won't tell me." So I didn't expect them to answer that.

The Chairman. Did you mean you were seeking money from them?

A—No, sir. I didn't think that my son should have gone— in a foreign country, and me being alone. What I was saying was that I think my son should be home with me, is really what I implied.

The Chairman. Did you tell them that?

A—In the words that I said before—I didn't come out and say I want my son home. But I implied that if he was an agent, that I thought that he needed to be home.

Mr. Rankin. Did you say anything about believing that your son might know full well what he was doing in trying to defect

356

to the Soviet Union, he might like it better there than he did here?

A—I do not remember saying this. I know what I did say, and they agreed with me. I said—because I remember this distinctly. I said, "Now, he has been exploited all through the paper as a defector. If he is a defector"—because as we stated before, I don't know he is an agent, sir—and if he is a defector, that is his privilege, as an individual.

And they said, "Mrs. Oswald, we want you to know that we feel the same way about it." That was their answer.

Mr. Rankin. Did you say anything about possibly he liked the Soviet way of life better than ours?

A—I may have. I do not remember, sir. Honestly. I may have said that. I recall that they agreed with me, and they said, "We want him also to do what he wants to do."

So now this is January 2, 1961, is my trip to Washington. Approximately 8 weeks later, on March 22, 1961—which is 8 weeks—I received a letter from the State Department informing me of my son's address.

Mr. Rankin. Do you recall that they assured you there was no evidence he was an agent?

A—No, sir, there was no comment to that effect.

Mr. Rankin. And they told you to dismiss any such ideas from your mind?

A—No, sir.

Mr. Rankin. You are sure they didn't tell you that?

A—I am positive. I said to them, "Of course, I don't expect you to answer me." No, sir, there was nothing mentioned about the agent at all. And in fact, I would think, just as a layman, that the State Department would not even consider discussing that with me. But I mean it was not discussed. I am positive of that.

Mr. Rankin. If they recorded in a memorandum as of that date that they did say that to you, that would be incorrect?

A—That is incorrect, emphatically incorrect. That is incorrect. Because I said, "I don't expect you to tell me. But if he is an agent," I didn't think it was the thing to do.

Well, on January 21 was my trip to Washington, 1961. Approximately 8 weeks later, on March 22, 1961, I received a letter from the State Department informing me of my son's address, which you probably have, if you don't, sir, I have the copies. And also stating that my son wishes to return back to the United States—just 8 weeks after my trip to Washington.

Now, you want to know why I think my son is an agent. And I have been telling you all along.

Here is a very important thing why my son was an agent. On March 22 I receive a letter of his address and stating that my son wishes to return back to the United States. You have that, sir?

Mr. Rankin. Yes.

357

A—On April 30, 1961, he marries a Russian girl—approximately 5 weeks later.

Now, why does a man who wants to come back to the United States, 5 weeks later—here is the proof—April 30, 1961, is the wedding date—marry a Russian girl? Because I say—and I may be wrong—the U.S. Embassy has ordered him to marry this Russian girl. And a few weeks later, May 16, 1961, he is coming home with the Russian girl. And as we know, he does get out of the Soviet Union with the Russian girl, with money loaned to him by the U.S. Embassy. I may be wrong, gentlemen, but two and two in my books makes four. . . .

Mr. Rankin. Did you ever hear your son say anything against Governor Connally?

A—No, sir.

But here is what I have written down. The day at Robert's house, when I came in from the country, I, myself, gave Lee the copy—we had many copies—you showed me the copy—I gave him the copy and told him—I had written him and told him about the dishonorable discharge, but I did not send any papers, because I didn't want the Russians to know.

But when I came, I had a scrapbook, and I gave him a copy, Mr. Rankin, of the reason for dishonorable discharge. He says "Don't worry about it, mother. I can fix that. It is no problem."

So then the boy tried to fix it. And this is not a threat. My son is of this disposition, and he felt like he was a good marine. That I know. I would do the same. And I will read it now to Governor Connally: "I shall employ all means to right the gross mistake done to my family and my now dead son."

I expect to write to anybody officially to rectify this mistake.

I have shown this publicly at press conferences, and so I will employ all means to rectify this mistake—the mother of Lee Harvey Oswald. I intended to do that. That is my life's work.

I have the name of the man I talked to.

Chief Justice Warren—I will start from Lee as a baby, before I get to this.

Lee was born October 18, 1939, in New Orleans, La. His mother, Marguerite Claverie Oswald, his father's name was Robert Edward Lee, he was named after General Lee. The family's name is Harvey—his grandmother's name was Harvey. And so he was named Lee Harvey Oswald.

Lee was born 2 months after the death of his father, who died from a heart attack, coronary thrombosis.

Lee was a very happy baby.

I stayed home with the children as long as I could, because I believe that a mother should be home with her children.

I don't want to get into my story, though.

Lee had a normal life as far as I, his mother, is concerned. He had a bicycle, he had everything that other children had.

Lee has wisdom without education. From a very small child —I have said this before, sir, and I have publicly stated this in 1959—Lee seemed to know the answers to things without schooling. That type child, in a way, is bored with schooling, because he is a little advanced.

Lee used to climb on top of the roof with binoculars, looking at the stars. He was reading astrology. Lee knew about any and every animal there was. He studied animals. All of their feeding habits, sleeping habits. He could converse—and that is why he was at the Bronx Zoo when he was picked up for truancy—he loved animals.

Lee played Monopoly. Lee played chess. Lee had a stamp collection, and even wrote to other young men and exchanged stamps, sir.

And Lee read history books, books too deep for a child his age. At age 9 he was always instructed not to contact me at work unless it was an emergency, because my work came first —he called me at work and said, "Mother, Queen Elizabeth's baby has been born."

He broke the rule to let me know that Queen Elizabeth's baby had been born. Nine years old. That was important to him. He liked things of that sort.

He loved comics, read comic books. He loved television programs. But most of all he loved the news on radio and television. If he was in the midst of a story, a film—he would turn it off for news. That was important.

And I have stated in 1959, which is in print, that Lee loved maps. Lee would study maps, sir. And he could tell you the distance from here and there. And when he was home on leave, I was amazed. Something was said about an airplane trip. Immediately he knew how many miles in the air that that plane took.

Lee read very, very important things. And any and everything he could do.

Yet he played Monopoly, played baseball.

He belonged to the "Y." He used to go swimming. He would come by work with his head wet, and I would say, "Hurry home, honey, you are going to catch cold."

And I considered that, sir, a very normal life.

I am probably forgetting some things.

So then Robert joined the Marines in 1956—am I correct— that Robert joined the Marines?

No, Robert joined the Marines in 1952. We are now in Fort Worth, Tex., until 1952.

So then I decided, since I was working, I did not want Lee to be alone. Up until this time, sir, he had a brother. So I sold my home at 7400 Ewing Street, and went to New York City, not as a venture, but because my older son, John Edward Pic, lived in New York, and had lived in New York for years. He was in the Coast Guard, as a military man. He has now been in the service 14 years, and at that time it would have been approximately 8 or 9 years—I may be off because that is approximately. So he was stationed in New York. So I had no problem of selling my home and going there, thinking that John Edward would leave New York.

But the main thing was to be where I had family. And I moved to New York for that reason.

Mr. Rankin. About what date was that?

A—This was exactly August 1952, because I wanted to get there in time for Lee's schooling. And if I am not mistaken, Robert joined the Marines in July of 1952. And that was my reason for going.

I immediately enrolled Lee in a Lutheran school, because Lee was not confirmed—he was baptized in the Lutheran faith, but because of moving around—I had married Mr. Ekdahl in this period and so on, Lee was not confirmed.

I enrolled him in the Lutheran school which took him approximately an hour or longer by subway to get there. It was quite a distance. That is when we first arrived in New York.

I believe that Lee was in that school a very short time, 2 or 3 weeks, because at this time I was living in my daughter-in-law's home and son. And we were not welcome, sir. We were welcome for a few days. But then we were to get a place of our own—because her mother lived with her, and her mother had left to go visit a sister. So Lee and I could come to visit. But we were not going to live with John and his wife.

So we just stayed there a short time.

Mr. Rankin. Was there any time that you recall there was a threat of Lee Oswald against Mrs. Pic with a knife or anything like that?

Do you remember that?

A—Yes, I do. I am glad you said that.

My daughter-in-law was very upset. The very first time we went there—I stated before, and I am glad I said that—that we were not welcome. And immediately it was asked what did we plan to do, as soon as we put our foot in the house. And I had made it plain to John Edward that I was going to have a place of my own, that we were just coming there to get located.

My daughter-in-law resented the fact that her mother—this went on before I got there—that her mother had to leave the house and go visit a sister so I could come, John Edward's mother. I had never met my daughter-in-law. She didn't like me, and she didn't like Lee.

So she—what is the word to say—not picked on the child, but she showed her displeasure.

And she is a very—not, I would say so much an emotional person—but this girl is a New Yorker who was brought up in this particular neighborhood, which I believe is a poor section of New York.

The mother had lived in this home all her life. And this girl cursed like a trooper. She is—you cannot express it, Mr. Rankin—but not of a character of a high caliber.

At this particular time she had never been out of this neighborhood, or out of New York. And Lee loved the little baby. And he played with the baby and wanted to hold the baby and everything, which she objected.

We were not wanted, sir, from the very beginning. So there was, I think now—it was not a kitchen knife—it was a little pocket knife, a child's knife, that Lee had. So she hit Lee. So Lee had the knife—now, I remember this distinctly, because I remember how awful I thought Marjory was about this. Lee had the knife in his hand. He was whittling, because John Edward whittled ships and taught Lee to whittle ships. He puts them in the glass, you know. And he was whittling when this incident occurred. And that is what it occurred about, because there was scraps of wood on the floor.

So when she attacked the child, he had the knife in hand. So she made the statement to my son that we had to leave, that Lee tried to use a knife on her.

Now, I say that is not true, gentlemen. You can be provoked into something. And because of the fact that he was whittling, and had the knife in hand, they struggled.

He did not use the knife—he had an opportunity to use the knife.

But it wasn't a kitchen knife or a big knife. It was a little knife.

So I will explain it that way, sir.

So immediately then I started to look for a place.

I did find a place, I think, off the Concourse. I do not remember the street.

Mr. Rankin. Was that in the Bronx?

A—Off the Concourse, in the Bronx. And it was a basement apartment.

I had shipped some of my furniture. It was in a storehouse at this time. So I got it out and put it in this basement.

Lee had his own single bed. It was a one—one great big, big room. But we had the kitchen—regular New York type style—the kitchen and the bedroom and everything together, but large enough—a big one-room apartment. And there was a single bed that Lee slept on, and I slept on the studio couch.

Then Lee went to school.

Mr. Rankin. Was that Public School 117?

A—I have that information here.

Went to school in the neighborhood, Public School 117, which is a junior high school in the Bronx. It states here he attended 15 of 47 days. This is the place we were living that Lee was picked up by the truant officer in the Bronx Zoo.

I was informed of this at work, and I had to appear before a board, which I did.

Lee went back to school.

Then he was picked up again in the Bronx Zoo. And I had to appear before a board committee again.

361

Then the third time that Lee was picked up, we were—I never did get a subpena, but we were told that he had to appear at Children's Court. But I never—how I got the notice to appear at Children's Court—I am at a loss, sir.

But I did not contact at this time a lawyer or anything. I did not know. I did not think it was anything serious, because the Texas laws are not like the New York laws. In New York, if you are out of school one day you go to Children's Court. In Texas the children stay out of school for months at a time.

Lee had never done this. So I appeared with my son in court. There was a judge asked me if I want to be represented by court counsel. And I believe I said, yes, I believe I was represented by the court counsel at this particular time. And within a few minutes time—because there were hundreds of people sitting, waiting with their truant children, and it was just like this—you didn't take the time we are taking here, a half hour, to discuss the case. It was done immediately.

My child was taken from me in the courtroom.

Mr. Rankin. Had he been out of school quite a bit?

A—No, sir. At this time, he had not been out of school quite a bit.

So then I was given a slip of paper—no, I am sorry. I was told where to go, where Lee was, which was another office.

They took Lee from me in the courtroom, two men, officers, presumably. Then I went into another office and here was Lee. Lee was wearing his brother's Marine ring, just an ornament ring. They gave me Lee's ring and the things he had in his pocket, and told me that Lee was going to be at this home, which I think the name was the Warwick Home for Boys. And gave me a slip of paper and told me when I could visit Lee.

And that was all I knew at this particular time.

The child was immediately taken, and I was told to visit the child.

Now, I believe it was—this home was in Brooklyn. I may have the name wrong. It was an old, old home in Brooklyn.

So I went to visit my son.

And I hope some day to rectify this, because I think conditions of this kind in our United States of America are deplorable. And I want that to go down in the record.

Mr. Rankin. Did they tell you why he was taken to this home, your son?

A—For truancy, yes, sir.

So I had to stand single file approximately a block and a half, sir, with Puerto Ricans and Negroes and everything, and people of my class, single file, until we got to the main part of this building, which had a wire, a very heavy wire, partition wire, a man sitting back of the desk, but a man in the front of the gate that let me in. I had packages of gum and some candy for my son. And I sat down there. And the gum wrappers were taken off the gum, and the candy wrappers were taken off.

And my pocketbook was emptied. Yes, sir, and I asked why. It was because the children in this home were such criminals, dope fiends, and had been in criminal offenses, that anybody entering this home had to be searched in case the parents were bringing cigarettes or narcotics or anything.

So that is why I was searched.

So I was escorted into a large room, where there were parents talking with their children.

And Lee came out. He started to cry. He said, "Mother, I want to get out of here. There are children in here who have killed people, and smoke. I want to get out."

So then I realized—I had not realized until I went there what kind of place we had my child in.

We don't have these kinds of places in Texas or New Orleans, sir.

Then I realized what a serious thing this was. And this is when I decided I needed an attorney.

But Lee, I think was approximately in that home—I am not sure—5 or 6 weeks, which accounts for his truancy that the papers say that Lee was a truant, that he was out of school so long.

It is because he was in this home, sir. That accounts for a lot of the truancy.

Mr. Rankin. Did you talk to him about his truancy, say anything to him about it, or ask him about it, how he happened to stay out of school?

A—Yes, sir, I asked Lee.

Well, this comes in another part.

Mr. Rankin. All right.

A—So I left my son that day, and I think I visited him a couple of times after that. I am not quite sure.

But in the meantime, I engaged an attorney. I do not know the name of the attorney, and I wish I did.

When I told the attorney about Lee—and I have stated this at a press conference—he raised the roof, so as to say. He was indignant. I cannot quote his exact words. But what he said was that New York State picked up these boys and put them on a farm, and they pay these boys to work on this farm for the State of New York.

Now, I may not be saying this exactly. You may have the picture of the home.

But these boys work on the farm and are paid for it, I understand. That is all I can remember, sir, about this unpleasant thing, because I did not think it would ever come in my life, and after the time it happened I tried to put it out of my mind.

But now I am refreshed a little on that.

So Lee was in this home 5 or 6 weeks, I believe. You probably have the record.

So then we were asked to appear to court. I went into court with this attorney. And there, again, real fast we were in the courtroom and Lee was brought in, and Lee sat down by me. And I remember this distinctly, because Lee had ear trouble quite often. And I saw his ear running and I said, "Lee, you are having an earache." And the judge heard me saying something to Lee.

He said, "What did you tell your boy, Mrs. Oswald?"

I said, "Judge, I asked him if he had an earache."

I didn't know they were going to give me the child then.

So the judge talked to Lee and asked Lee if he was going to be good, and go back to school. Lee answered, "Yes, sir." And he said to me, "Mrs. Oswald, I understand that you and your daughter-in-law do not get along." I said, "That is correct." And he suggested that Lee would be much better off back in the open wide spaces that he was used to instead of in New York, where we had no family then, because the daughter-in-law and son were not friendly with us. And this judge suggested that. And the judge gave me my son, right then and there, gentlemen.

I left the courtroom with my boy. He was given to me in my custody.

Now, that is all I know of the case. The particular case.

From there, we went into an office where there was a probation officer, Mr. John Carro. Mr. Carro talked with Lee and asked Lee if he was going to go back to school.

"Yes, sir."

He reprimanded him a little bit—maybe not that, but gave him a little talk. And he said, "Lee, you are to report to me once a week for probation."

I am going to stress this.

I have been in this Commission 3 days. And you know I am very definite. So I was very definite with Mr. Carro. I did not mince my words. I said, "Mr. Carro, my son is not reporting to you once a week. This is not a criminal offense. He was picked up for truancy, he has assured the judge, promised the judge that he would be back to school. He has promised you he would be back to school. Let's give this boy a chance, and let's see if he will go to school."

"And then, Mr. Carro, if he doesn't go to school, then you can have him report to you."

Mr. Carro didn't take that graciously, which is true. When you don't agree with anyone over you, then you are in the minority, and you just as well make up your mind right then and there, that is it.

So from that time on Mr. Carro pestered me and Lee. Mr. Carro would call me at work, sir, and say that he had gone by the school, and that they were having trouble with Lee. And

364

I went to the school and talked to the principal and she said,
"Mrs. Oswald, what happened while the probation officer was
here—Lee moved the chair back, and it made a little noise."

And that is what Mr. Carro reported.

In plain words, gentlemen, Mr. Carro was indignant at my
attitude, because he was an official. . . .

Mr. Rankin. How did he [Lee] get along with you? Did you
get along well together?

A—Yes. Lee was a very quiet and studious boy. None of
my children gave me any trouble, thank God. We have no
police record, sir, or anything like that. And the children were
always more or less home. And particularly Lee. Lee would go
to the movies, and things like that. He was a normal boy. But
when he was home, he was most happy. And I am of this
disposition.

He could keep himself occupied—reading and when he
watched a football game on television, he would have the score
pad, and things of that sort. And so he was quite happy in his
own way.

Now, here is something very important.

While in New Orleans, in order to go to Arlington Heights
school, which is one of the ritziest schools in New Orleans, all
the wealthy people go there, and we happened to live in the
vicinity—Lee wanted a two-wheel bicycle, sir, and I bought
him one. So when school opened, Lee went to school on a
two-wheel bicycle. Can you picture this. A 16½-year-old boy
going to school on a bicycle, when all the other children had
their own cars? Just picture this. My children never did want
anything, and particularly Lee. . . .

Mr. Rankin. Did you ever hear your son say anything for or
against President Kennedy?

A—While Marina and Lee were in my home that month, and
I had a television—

Mr. Rankin. About what time was that?

A—This was July, 1962—when they stayed the month with
me. Yes, they were delighted with President Kennedy, both.

Mr. Rankin. What did they say about him?

A—Nothing political—just "Like President Kennedy." He
was telling Marina about President Kennedy. "I like President
Kennedy"—"I like, too."

My son has never said anything to me politically about anyone. My son loved the Marines, and loved his work and has
never, never said anything against—the only time I questioned
my son was ask him why he decided to come home, and he
said, "Not even Marina knows that." . . .

Mr. Rankin. Mrs. Oswald, you said that you would like to
turn now to telling us about your life. We would appreciate that
if you would do that.

A—Yes.

The Chairman. Mrs. Oswald, if you would prefer not to tell the story of your life, that is perfectly all right.

A—I want to tell the story but there is something else that upsets me.

The Chairman. It is perfectly all right if you don't wish to. You may take your time now and go right ahead.

A—I am sorry, you will have to excuse me about the story of my life, and Mr. Doyle knows why, but there is one part of the story of my life that will have a great connection with this, I believe.

I married Mr. Edwin Ekdahl who was an electrical engineer and a $10,000 a year man with an expense account. Mr. Ekdahl had a woman before he married me. Of course, I didn't know about it, sir. I made him wait a year before I married him, but the way I found this out, I received a telephone call, a telegram rather, he traveled—lots of times Lee and I traveled with him— stating he wouldn't return home when he was supposed to and for me not to meet him.

So, I called his office, I was familiar with, knew his secretary, and I was going to tell her that Mr. Ekdahl would be delayed 3 or 4 days. But immediately she said, "Mrs. Ekdahl, Mr. Ekdahl is not in, he has gone out to lunch."

So, I said, the general conversation went "When will he be back" and so on, and so that evening I took the car and I went to the Texas Electric Co., works for the Texaco, the main office in New York, but he was working in Fort Worth at the time, went to the building and saw him leave the building and I followed him and to an apartment house, saw him go into this apartment house.

Then I went back home, and my oldest son, John Edward Pic, who is in the service, had a friend at the house who was about 2 years older. I told them about what happened. So it was night by this time. The kids went with me.

I called Mr. John McClain, who is an attorney, and we live next door to Mr. McClain, and told him that I had seen Mr. Ekdahl go into a home when he was supposed to be out of town and what should I do.

He said, "Mrs. Oswald, just ring the phone. Do you know the woman?"

And I said, "Yes."

"Just ring the phone and let him know that you know he is there, that you saw him."

After I thought about it I thought that is not a good idea because he could leave and say he was just there on business and I wanted to catch him there.

So the kids and I planned that we would say she had a telegram, so we went up the stairs, I believe it was the second or the third floor, and the young man knocked on the door and said, "Telegram for Mrs. Clary"—was her name.

She said, "Please push it under the door" and I told him no; he said, "No, you have to sign for it."

So with that she opened the door to sign for it and with that I, my son, and with the other young man walked into the room and Mrs. Clary had on a negligee, and my husband had his sleeves rolled up and his tie off sitting on a sofa, and he said, "Marguerite, Marguerite, you have everything wrong, you have everything wrong."

He says, "Listen to me."

I said, "I don't want to hear one thing. I have seen everything I want to see, this is it."

My two boys, in military school, the two older boys, I am paying for the two older boys because I have sold a piece of property. I wanted to take care as long as I had money of my own children and when I married Mr. Ekdahl if he would support me and Lee I would be able to take care of John Edward, and Robert in military school, we couldn't have them with us because Mr. Ekdahl traveled.

This man never let me share with his insurance policies, beneficiary, in other words, I was another woman to him. I received $100 a month and that was it. That was all the money I had from Mr. Ekdahl, and when we traveled, for instance, we were in Santa Fe, N. Mex., and he was with all the businessmen, we would have to wait until Mr. Ekdahl got through, the baby and I, in order to eat, whether it was 2 or 3 o'clock in the evening because here I was, registered under Mrs. Ekdahl and I had a checking account, but under the name of Oswald, which was the money I was using for the children so it was kind of inconvenient for me to write a check under the name of Oswald.

I am trying to point out the kind of man he was.

I had a nice living in this sense. We lived in the finest hotels and we had the finest food because all of this was charged to his expense account but he gave me nothing but this $100. That was a standard thing and he expected me to account for every cent of the hundred dollars that I spent, which I refused to do.

So, we argued naturally, because this is not a marriage. Any man who marries a woman naturally shares, she shares in his bank account and in his insurance and so on and so forth.

I wanted to divorce Mr. Ekdahl naturally but my two boys as I have stated before were in the military school, and I wanted to wait until the end of the season, the school season.

So, Lee and I went to Covington, La., and I picked the boys up at military school because this was summer time—rather I wasn't back to him.

I left him and went back to him. But this particular time I picked the boys up at military school and we spent the summer in Covington, La., and by the way, I forgot to say that Lee had a beautiful voice and sang beautifully at age 6 in Covington, La., he sang a solo in the church, Silent Night, and that can be verified. This is a very small town and the only Lutheran Church there.

So, Mr. Ekdahl came to Covington, La., and I went back again to Mr. Ekdahl. But this time I went back to him I hadn't found out about the woman. I got excited. Then I found out about the woman, he rented a place on 8th Avenue a home.

And after I was there about a day I was in the yard hanging out some things and it was in the apartment house downstairs and a woman came along and I said, "How are you? I am Mrs. Ekdahl."

She looked astonished, and after I had made friends with her she informed me Mr. Ekdahl had a woman in this particular house while I was in Covington and she thought she was his wife but now I am the wife come.

Then I found out about the woman and we went to her apartment and caught her there. This is the end of the season by this time.

In the meantime Mr. Ekdahl filed suit for divorce from me. I thought I was sitting pretty. He didn't have anything on me. I had him for adultery with witnesses and everything and I didn't have an idea that he could sue me for a divorce, but Mr. Ekdahl did sue me for a divorce, and Mr. Ekdahl got the divorce. It was a jury case, and Mr. John McClain, was my attorney, the man I told you that I called to find out what to do.

Now, Mr. Fred Korth represented Mr. Ekdahl and when I walked into the courtroom, gentlemen, there were witnesses there that I had never seen before.

A Mr. George Levine, who is a very big businessman and who Mr. Ekdahl was representing in Fort Worth for the electrical part of his plant. I knew him this way.

One time we went to the circus with his wife, my husband, myself and Lee, before going to the circus we had dinner. Now, understand we are having dinner in a public place. From the dinner we go to the circus, we are in a public place and I want you to know that it is the only time I had seen Mr. George Levine,when Mr. George Levine rushed from work in his khaki pants and got on the witness stand swore how I nagged Mr. Ekdahl and how I threw bottles at him and so on and so forth.

There were other witnesses that I had never seen, sir, who swore how I nagged Mr. Ekdahl, and Mr. Ekdahl got his divorce from me.

Now, 2 days after the assassination, after Lee's death, while I am at Six Flags it comes over the radio that Mr. Korth knew the family, this happened in 1948, sir, then Mr. Korth knew the family, and that he had represented Mr. Ekdahl in divorce proceedings and, of course, talked to the reporters where they got the information that I hit him with a bottle and so on and so forth.

Now, that is my story there. I am not even guilty of that di-

368

vorce, as you see. This can be proved by my son John Edward Pic because he was a witness, sir.

I do not think I am going—I am not going to speculate but give my thoughts to anyone who would immediately make a statement that he had represented the mother of the accused assassin as an attorney years ago, and that I nagged Mr. Ekdahl and so on and so forth.

That was publicly announced about 2 days after my son was shot, sir.

Now, the name then, of course, he probably knew the name Oswald, but the name then was Ekdahl that I would say would stick in his mind more.

I will try to get to the very beginning of my life, Chief Justice.

The Chairman. Any time. Just take your time.

A—My mother died when I was quite young and my father raised us with housekeepers. My aunt lived in the neighborhood and I had a lot of cousins and a lot of aunts. My father was French, his name was Claverie, and my mother was German, the name is Stucke. All of my father's folks spoke French and my father spoke French to his sisters. I was a child of one parent, and yet I have had a normal life, a very hard normal life that I had been able to combat all by myself, sir, without much help from anyone.

I am saying that in reference to Lee being alone; there have been so many psychiatrists saying he was by himself and he had a father image and that is why he did the shooting. There are many, many children with one parent who are perfectly normal children and I happen to be one myself.

I had a very happy childhood. I sang. I sang from the kindergarten at grammar school, and all through grammar school I was the lead singer. I was one of the most popular young ladies in the school. I also play piano by ear. I don't know a note. I used to play the marching school song for the school children.

At my grammar school graduation I had the honor of wearing a pink dress instead of a white dress and sang the song "Little Pink Roses." So I had a very happy childhood and a very full childhood. I played the piano. We had house parties in those days and a lot of gatherings and it was everything Marguerite—and I also played a ukulele, so I have a very full happy childhood.

At the age of 17, I am ahead of my story—I have had 1 year high school education. I know that on my applications I had that I had completed high school but that is almost necessary to get a job.

But I had 1 year of high school education is all that I had, sir.

I then went to work at age 17, not quite 17, for one of the biggest corporation lawyers in New Orleans, La. The name then was DuFour, Rosen, Wolff, and Kammer. Mr. DuFour died while I was there and Mr. Kammer, I believe, is still living but they were corporation attorneys for that firm plus 4 or 5 other attorneys that handled divorce cases and similar cases and I was receptionist in the outer office.

So, everybody who came into the office had to state their business to me, because the attorneys were very busy, and if it was a particular case I had to know who to refer the party to this particular man.

So, naturally, I got a very large education, let's say, by doing this, and the mayor and everybody in the town, these are the largest attorneys, corporation attorneys in New Orleans, sir, and they were attorneys representing the New Orleans Public Service and big things of that sort, and the mayor and all used to call me the boss. When the mayor came in he had an appointment but I still had to ring the phone to see if the men were ready to see him. So they called me the boss.

I was also a maid in one of the carnival balls. I am a very poor young lady but a very, let's say, popular young lady.

My early childhood. We lived on the Phillips Street in New Orleans which was a very poor neighborhood. My father was one of the very first streetcar conductors and stayed on the very same line all these years until he retired and they gave him a citation because he was on the same line all those years from retirement, and we lived in a mixed neighborhood of Negroes and white, and my childhood I played with Negroes, sir, right next door to me was a lovely family that I grew up with this Negro family.

I married Mr. Edward John Pic, Jr., while working at the law firm. I was married to Mr. Pic two and a half years when I became with child, and he did not want any children. His family and my family tried to talk to him, and, well, his family almost beat him up to say, but nobody could do anything with him.

So, at 3 months I left Mr. Pic. Mr. Pic did not divorce me, and you have the records there of me divorcing Mr. Pic, contrary to all other stories, sir.

This child, John Edward Pic then I bore alone, without a husband. I was 3 months pregnant. I had 6 more months to go, and I had this child without a husband.

So, I have had two children without a husband present, Lee and the first child.

Mr. Oswald was an insurance agent, and he used to collect insurance at my sister's house, and the day that I left Mr. Pic he helped move my furniture, the things that I was going to take.

I didn't see Mr. Ekdahl for some time and—

The Chairman. Ekdahl or Oswald.

A—Mr. Oswald, sir, I am sorry.

John Edward and I were coming from the park one day, and Mr. Ekdahl picked—Mr. Oswald picked me up, and he was separated from his wife, however, not divorced but had been separated for a number of years, and I started dating Mr. Ekdahl and we decided to marry and he divorced his wife.

Mr. Rankin. You said Ekdahl again.

A—Oswald, I am sorry, and then he got the divorce proceeding. He was separated for a long time but never had been divorced from his wife but when we knew he was going to marry, and I also then got the divorce from Mr. Pic. I was not divorced from Mr. Pic, either. We were legally separated but I was not divorced from him.

So, Mr. Oswald and I married and of that marriage Robert was born 9 months later, and as you know consequently Lee, 2 months after his father had died.

Now, Mr. Oswald was a very good man. There was the only happy part of my life. When he died hardly anybody knew that John Edward Pic was not his son. He wanted to adopt John Edward, but because his father was supporting him which I think was only $18 a month, I explained to Lee that I thought we should save this money for the boys' education and let his own father support him and naturally we would educate and do all we could do but that was no more than right. So that is why he did not adopt John Edward.

Now, that is the story of my three marriages. I have been married approximately 9 years in the three times that I have been married, sir, and I would say, I am probably guilty of a lot of things but the initial guilt has never been mine in any of these marriages, the first marriage I had explained, the second marriage was death, and the third marriage was Mr. Ekdahl.

I think then you know the rest of the story, how I lived with my children and tried to support my children. . . .

JOHN EDWARD PIC

The testimony of Oswald's half-brother:

Mr. Jenner. Had you known, that Lee had entered the service?

A—Yes, sir; I knew this.

Mr. Jenner. Had enlisted in the Marines?

A—Yes, sir.

Mr. Jenner. And how had you learned that, through your mother?

A—Yes, sir; through my mother. . . . My mother told me some way or another, I don't remember, sir. This is how I learned about it, either by phone call or by letter or some way. Of course, I knew he would do it as soon as he reached the age.

Mr. Jenner. All right. Why did you know he would do it and tell us the circumstances upon which you, the facts upon which you base that observation?

A—He did it for the same reasons that I did it and Robert did it, I assume, to get from out and under.

Mr. Jenner. Out and under what?

A—The yoke of oppression from my mother.

Mr. Jenner. Had that been a matter of discussion between you and for example, between you and your brother Robert?

A—No, sir; it was just something we understood about and never discussed.

Mr. Jenner. And that would include Lee as well as your brother Robert; that is, you were all aware of it?

A—I know this includes my brother Robert. Of course, when I was 18 years old I didn't discuss things like this with Lee, who was much younger. . . .

Mr. Jenner. Was this 7-year spread as the years went on between you and Lee, did that affect your relationship with him as distinguished from your relationship with your brother Robert who was only 2 years younger?

A—Well, anything I was involved in Robert always was. Lee was left out because of the age difference. . . .

Mr. Jenner. What led up to and what were the circumstances involving or surrounding the visit of your mother and Lee to New York in the summer of 1952?

A—Well, Robert had joined the service in April 1952. It was the summer months, so Lee was not in school, and the trip to New York was feasible, being Lee would have no schooltime lost, it was my impression and also my wife's—meanwhile, I was married, you know, if you are interested in this.

Mr. Jenner. Yes; I am.

A—August 18, 1951, I married my wife Margaret Dorothy Fuhrman. . . .

Mr. Jenner. Did you hear anything to the effect that the reason why your mother and Lee had come to New York had anything to do with Lee's being given some sort of mental tests?

A—No, sir.

Mr. Jenner. Was there a period of time just before the enrollment of Lee in the New York Public School, that he attended for about a month a Lutheran denominational school?

A—I don't know, sir. . . .

Mr. Jenner. I see. All right.

A—At about the same time that Lee was enrolled in school that we had the big trouble. It seems that there was an argument about the TV set one day, and—between my wife and my mother. It seems that according to my wife's statement that my mother antagonized Lee, being very hostile toward my wife and he pulled out a pocketknife and said that if she made any attempt to do anything about it that he would use it on her, at the same time Lee struck his mother. This perturbed my wife to no end. So, I came home that night, and the facts were related to me.

Mr. Jenner. When the facts were related to you was your mother present, Lee present, your wife present? If not, who was present?

A—I think my wife told me this in private, sir. I went and asked my mother about it. . . .

Mr. Jenner. What did you say to your mother and what did she say to you?

A—I asked her about the incident and she attempted to brush it off as not being as serious as my wife put it. That Lee did not pull a pocketknife on her. That they just had a little argument about what TV channel they were going to watch. Being as prejudiced as I am I rather believed my wife rather than my mother. . . .

Mr. Jenner. Was your mother loving and affectionate toward you boys?

A—I would say for myself, sir, I wasn't to her.

Mr. Jenner. What is that?

A—I was not toward her.

Mr. Jenner. Why?

A—I had no motherly love feeling toward her. . . . It is my own opinion that she is out right now to make as much money as she can on her relationship with Lee Harvey Oswald. That is the only thing—I don't really believe she really believes he is innocent. I think she is out to make money than if she has to say he is guilty. I think she is a phony in the whole deal. . . .

MARK R. LANE

Testimony of a New York lawyer, who was retained by Mrs. Marguerite Oswald:

Mr. Rankin. Mr. Lane, the Commission has asked you a number of times to disclose to it the name of the informant that you said told you about having seen certain persons in the Carousel Club. Are you ready to disclose the name of that informant now?

A—I am ready, but as I told you when I gave you that information at the outset, I gave my word of honor to that person that I would not disclose his name unless he gave me permission to. I have gone to Dallas on two separate occasions to try to secure that permission. I have not been able to secure that permission. Nothing would make me happier than giving you the name of that person; but I have given my word of honor and, therefore, I am unable to give you that name. . . .

Mr. Rankin. The Commission has a number of times asked you by correspondence to disclose the name of that informant, and it now asks you in this proceeding, while you are under oath, to make that disclosure.

A—I will not do so, Mr. Rankin.

Mr. Rankin. Do you realize that the information you gave in closed session could have an unfavorable effect upon your country's interests in connection with this assassination and your failure to disclose the name of your informant would do further injury?

A—Mr. Rankin, I am astonished to hear that statement from you. There are 180 million Americans in this country. I am perhaps the only one who is a private citizen who has taken off the last 6 months to devote all of his efforts to securing whatever information can be found, and to making that known to this Commission, and publicly to the people of this country at great personal cost in terms of the harassment that I have suffered, in terms of the terrible financial losses that I have suffered. And to sit here today, after 6 months of this work, which I have given all to this Commission, voluntarily, and again have come here again today voluntarily to give you this information, and to hear you say that I am not cooperating with the Commission, and I am going to do harm to the country by not making information available to you astonishes me.

You have hundreds of agents of the FBI running all over the Dallas area—agents of the Secret Service, Dallas policemen. Are you telling me that in one trip to Dallas where I spent something like 2 days, I uncovered information which the whole police force of this Nation has not yet in 6 months been able to secure? I cannot believe that is a valid assessment of this situation. I cannot, Mr. Rankin.

The Chairman. Mr. Lane, may I say to you that until you give us the corroboration that you say you have, namely, that someone told you that that was a fact, we have every reason to doubt the truthfulness of what you have heretofore told us. And your refusal to answer at this time lends further strength to that belief. If you can tell us, and if you will tell us, who gave you that information, so that we may test their veracity, then you have performed a service to this Commission. But until you do, you have done nothing but handicap us.

A—I have handicapped you by working for 6 months and making all of the information which I have had available to you? I understand very fully your position, Mr. Chief Justice.

Mr. Rankin. Mr. Lane, what did you come down to tell us or inform the Commission about? You say you came here of your own volition in order to help us, and to give us information. Now, what information in light of the fact that I wrote you and asked you for two specific things—whatever information you had in any recorded form concerning your interview with Helen Markham, and secondly, the name of the informant, neither of which you are willing to disclose or have said anything to help the Commission on.

A—I came here at your request that I interrupt my trip in Europe to come back and testify before you. And I have done that.

The Chairman. By denying—by refusing to answer either question.

A—I think that—well, I have given you the reasons why I cannot answer the question. With reference to Mrs. Markham, I should tell you this, that I am hopeful that in the very near future I will be able to make that document available to you by securing permission from my client. But she has informed me at the present time that she is herself involved in securing some information relative to this whole matter, which you are familiar with, Mr. Rankin, and that she wishes there to be no discussion at all at this point about this matter.

Frankly, quite frankly, matters which have been given to this Commission in utmost confidence have appeared in the daily newspapers, and one cannot feel with great security that giving information to this Commission, even at secret hearings, means that the information will not be broadcast, and this is the problem which confronts us at the present time. . . .

The Chairman. Mr. Lane, you have manifested a great interest in Lee Harvey Oswald and his relationship to this entire affair. According to you, Mrs. Markham made a statement that would bear upon the probability of his guilt or innocence in connection with the assassination. Mrs. Markham has definitely contradicted what you have said, and do you not believe that it is in your own interest and in the interests of this country for you to give whatever corroboration you have to this Commission so that we may determine whether you or she is telling the truth?

A—I have given you all the information that I am permitted to give to you and to members of the Commission. I understand from Mr. Rankin that Mrs. Markham denies that she ever talked with me. Is that correct?

The Chairman. You needn't ask Mr. Rankin any questions. You won't answer the questions of this Commission, and he is not under examination by you at the present time.

A—I have answered questions. I spoke for about 85 pages, without a single question being put to me, because I was anxious to give to this Commission all the information in my possession.

The Chairman. Yes, but you did not give us all the information. You did not tell us that you had a recording of what Mrs. Markham said to you. Now, we ask you for verification of that conversation, because she has contradicted you. You say that you have a recording, but you refuse to give it to this Commission.

A—I am not in a position to give you that recording. I have made that quite plain. Because of a matter which has arisen in the last 3 or 4 days, which I was made aware of yesterday for the first time, I am not in a position to do that. Hopefully, I will be in a day or two.

The Chairman. We heard that when you were here in March—hopefully you would be able to tell us who this informant of yours was in Dallas concerning the so-called meeting between Jack Ruby and others in his nightclub. And we have been pursuing you ever since with letters and entreaties to give us that information so that we might verify what you have said, if it is a fact, or disproving it if it is not a fact. Here we pay your expenses from Europe, bring you over here, and without telling us at all that you won't answer that question, you come before the Commission and refuse to testify. Do you consider that cooperation?

A—Mr. Chief Justice, I believe I am the only citizen in this country who has devoted 6 months to securing information at his own expense. You talk about what it cost to go to Europe. I have gone to Europe twice, and I have paid for those trips myself. I have traveled all over this country. I have gone to Dallas five times. I have paid for those trips myself, and I am not in a position financially to do that, but I have done that to give you this information.

The Chairman. Were you getting evidence over in Europe?

A—No; I was discussing this case, because of the suppression in this country of the facts. I felt it important that somehow the American people be informed about what is taking place, and I found that practically the only way to inform the American people is to speak in Europe.

The Chairman. Have you charged admission for any of your speaking?

A—Have I charged admission?

The Chairman. Yes.

A—No; I have not charged admission.

The Chairman. Do you collect any money in this country at the speeches that you made?

A—Did I, personally, collect any money?

The Chairman. Did you have money collected?

A—I collected no money.

The Chairman. Did you have any money collected?

A—I did not.

The Chairman. Was there money collected at that meeting —at those meetings that you had?

A—I spoke at probably 40 different college campuses throughout the United States.

The Chairman. Was money collected at those places?

A—To my knowledge, at none of those meetings was money collected. At one or two or perhaps three other meetings, funds have been collected for the purpose of paying the salary of the secretary of this citizens committee of inquiry, and to pay the rent.

The Chairman. Who got the money?

A—The citizens committee of inquiry.

The Chairman. Who is the head of that?

A—I am the chairman of that.

The Chairman. Who else belongs to it?

A—Among others, Jessica Mitford, who is the author who

376

wrote "The American Way of Death," a best-selling book; Sterling Hayden, who is an actor; a number of attorneys, some in California, some in New York; and a number of others. I did not know that I was going to be questioned about the makeup of the citizens committee. Otherwise, I would have brought the entire membership list.

The Chairman. I didn't intend to ask you, but we are trying to get information about these different things that you considered vital in the assassination of the President. And it is a matter of great concern to the Commission that you are unwilling to tell us about those things that you considered bear upon the guilt or innocence of Lee Harvey Oswald. And it handicaps us greatly in what we are trying to do, because of the things that you do say when you are away from the Commission, and then when you refuse to testify before us as to those very things that you discuss in public.

A—I have not said anything in public, Mr. Chief Justice, that I have not said first before this Commission, or at one time before this Commission.

The Chairman. But, before your audiences, do you not claim to be telling the truth and to be verifying the things that you tell them, and then when you come here you refuse to give us the verification?

A—When I speak before an audience, I do hold myself out to be telling the truth, just as when I have testified before this Commission I have also told the truth. . . .

MAJOR GENERAL EDWIN A. WALKER

The testimony of a retired army officer who was shot at by Oswald:

Mr. Liebeler. It is my understanding that on the evening of April 10, 1963, some person fired a shot at you while you were in your home on Turtle Creek Boulevard; is that correct?

A—That is correct.

Mr. Liebeler. Would you tell us the circumstances surrounding that event, as you can now recall them?

A—I was sitting behind my desk. It was right at 9 o'clock, and most of the lights were on in the house and the shades were up. I was sitting down behind a desk facing out from a corner, with my head over a pencil and paper working on my income tax when I heard a blast and a crack right over my head.

Mr. Liebeler. What did you do then?

A—I thought—we had been fooling with the screens on the house and I thought that possibly somebody had thrown a firecracker, that it exploded right over my head through the window right behind me. Since there is a church back there, often there are children playing back there. Then I looked around and saw that the screen was not out, but was in the window, and this couldn't possibly happen, so I got up and walked

377

around the desk and looked back where I was sitting and I saw a hole in the wall which would have been to my left while I was sitting to my right as I looked back, and the desk was catercornered in the corner up against this wall. I noticed there was a hole in the wall, so I went upstairs and got a pistol and came back down and went out the back door, taking a look to see what might have happened.

Mr. *Liebeler*. Did you find anything outside that you could relate to this attack on you?

A—No, sir; I couldn't. As I crossed a window coming downstairs in front, I saw a car at the bottom of the church alley just making a turn onto Turtle Creek. The car was unidentifiable. I could see the two back lights, and you have to look through trees there, and I could see it moving out. This car would have been about at the right time for anybody that was making a getaway. . . .

Mr. *Liebeler*. Now do you have any knowledge or any information that would indicate that Oswald was involved in a conspiracy of any type on the assassination of the President?

A—I think he designated his own conspiracy when he said he was a member of the Fair Play for Cuba Committee. That to me is a definite recognition of conspiracy.

Mr. *Liebeler*. Suggesting that the Fair Play for Cuba Committee was involved?

A—I would say as a member of the Fair Play for Cuba Committee, it could not be segregated from being involved in it when one of its members does it, who thinks like they do.

Mr. *Liebeler*. Well, that is of course, your view. My question of you is this. Do you have any evidence or any knowledge that would indicate either the involvement of the Fair Play for Cuba Committee or any other individual or organization in a conspiracy or plot to assassinate the President?

The fact that Oswald may have been a member of this organization, which he was, of course, is a fact that can be viewed from many different ways. But my question to you is somewhat different from that, and that is, do you know of or have any evidence to indicate that this organization or any other organization or any other person was involved with Oswald in the assassination of the President?

A—My answer to you is that I have exactly the evidence that you have, which is evidence that it was involved in the conspiracy, because he said he was a member of the Fair Play for Cuba Committee, and I consider the objectives of the Fair Play for Cuba Committee a Communist activity and a conspiracy.

Mr. *Liebeler*. Do you know if anyone discussed the assassination with Oswald prior to the time that he assassinated the President, if he did the assassination; do you have any indication of that?

A—I have no personal knowledge that they did.

Mr. *Liebeler*. Do you have any indication that they did?

A—I certainly do.

Mr. Liebeler. Would you tell us what that is?

A—The indications seem to be not only mine, but all over the country that Rubenstein [Jack Ruby] and Oswald had some association.

Mr. Liebeler. Can you indicate to us what it was?

A—Well, I am wondering about one thing, how Rubenstein can take his car in to be fixed and Oswald can sign the ticket and pick up the car.

Mr. Liebeler. Now can you tell us when and where that happened?

A—I haven't been able to verify that it happened for sure, but I have been told that it happened.

Mr. Liebeler. Who told you that?

A—My information came from a repairman, from another fellow to a friend of mine, to me.

Mr. Liebeler. Could you give us the name of the person?

A—I don't think it is necessary. I think you have all the information, because the information also includes the fact that the records were picked up in the repair shop.

Mr. Liebeler. Whether we have the information or not, I am asking you if you know the name of that repairman who said that Oswald said he picked up his car?

A—No; I don't.

Mr. Liebeler. Do you know the name of the garage?

A—No; I don't. As I remember, it was a hotel garage.

Mr. Liebeler. Can you give us the name of the people that brought the information to you, so it can be traced back to this source? Who the garageman is, apparently as you say, that it came from a garageman somewhere.

A—No; I think your sources are better than mine on this.

Mr. Liebeler. That is not my question. My question is, do you know their names?

A—Yes; I do, but I am not telling.

Mr. Liebeler. So you are not going to tell us the names of these people?

A—Hold up. Off the record.

(Discussion off the record.)

A—We are all working in the best interests of this thing. I don't see where my sources of information have to be revealed. You know whether the information is any good or not, and I don't see any reason to get any more people involved than are already involved in it. The information is either correct or incorrect, and can be substantiated by your Commission, or it is not.

This that I am telling you is the information I have got. Now, if you all find out that it is absolutely necessary to your information, but revelation of the names of the people isn't necessary to your information with regard to the assassination. I think we have covered the assassination, and—as helpful as I can be—

don't think I wouldn't be delighted to see exactly all the truth that can probably come out of it, come out of it.

Mr. *Liebeler.* All we are asking you to do is give us whatever information you have that can help us in this investigation.

A—That I think we have covered, haven't we?

Mr. *Liebeler.* I don't know whether we have or not.

A—If you find out you need the further information that will really help the assassination story—we will leave it like this—I will do the best I can to cooperate on it, but I don't think it is necessary to reveal all the sources of my information, and the story which you all should have the basic facts. The basic facts are the records on the story and you either know whether or not they are true or not. I haven't done all this investigation.

Mr. *Liebeler.* Well, I am not able to make a determination as to whether or not the information that you have would be helpful to the Commission's work because I don't know what information you have.

A—Let's leave that, because if it is in the best interest of finding anything, that there is a hole in their findings, why we will reveal it.

Mr. *Liebeler.* I am going to let the question stand. I do ask you to tell me who advised you or who apprised you of information that Oswald picked up Jack Ruby's car, because I am not able to make a determination as to whether or not that information would be worthless to the Commission. It might be helpful and it might be that these people should be questioned by people on the Commission staff or by the FBI. So for that reason, I am compelled to let the question stand, and I do renew my request for you to give me the answer.

A—I will answer that at some later date if you find it necessary, I will reconsider it. . . .

Mr. *Liebeler.* Do you have any other information that would indicate any connection between Ruby and Oswald? By that question I do not mean to characterize the previous testimony.

A—If Oswald was the one that was at my house, I wonder where he was from the time he left until he got home, since the Las Vegas Club is not too far from my house.

Mr. *Liebeler.* Do you have any indication that Oswald went to that club?

A—No; I don't.

Mr. *Liebeler.* Do you have any other information that would suggest a connection between these two men?

A—I think the two boxes in the post office are very interesting.

Mr. *Liebeler.* Well, are you suggesting that because two men both happened to have post office boxes in the same post office, that that suggests there is some connection between them and indicates conspiracy to assassinate the President?

A—The boxes were rented the same week.

Mr. *Liebeler.* Were what?

380

A—I believe the boxes were arranged the same week in the post office.

Mr. Liebeler. Rented?

A—Rented.

Mr. Liebeler. You think that suggests a conspiracy between Oswald and Ruby to assassinate the President?

A—I think that is more information.

Mr. Liebeler. But I want to know.

A—That suggests a possible relationship. I think the fact that Rubenstein shot Oswald suggests plenty. I am convinced he couldn't have shot him except for one basic reason, and maybe many others, but to keep him quiet. That is what shooting people does. I think the whole city of Dallas is very interested. I would be interested in the information on a Professor Wolf, William T. Wolf.

Mr. Liebeler. Who is he?

A—William T.

Mr. Liebeler. What information is that?

A—The first man we found in the paper that seemed to have come to death after the attempted shot at me.

Mr. Liebeler. I am not familiar with the circumstances surrounding that. Would you tell me about Dr. Wolf?

A—William T. Wolf is a professor that was supposedly burned up in an apartment, which seems impossible to have burned a man up, a normal man with his normal faculties, because the apartment, he couldn't have been trapped in it on the first floor.

Mr. Liebeler. Did you know Dr. Wolf?

A—Never heard of him until I read about him in the paper, and I believe I read about him 8 days after they shot at me.

Mr. Liebeler. You think there is some connection between Dr. Wolf's death and the shot at you?

A—No; but I think there is some connection with respect to what is going on in Dallas.

Mr. Liebeler. Well, now, does this relate to the possibility of a conspiracy between Oswald and Ruby to assassinate President Kennedy?

A—I think many unusual deaths in the city of Dallas might show some indication of what is going on in Dallas, to include what happened on the 22d of November. And I would refer to one other, a professor by the name of Deen. His name is George C. Deen.

Mr. Liebeler. What has that got to do with the assassination of President Kennedy? What are the facts about it?

A—I would think it has to do with the investigation.

Mr. Liebeler. Well, in what way?

A—It seems rather mysterious that a young doctor of psychiatry at Timberlawn would, so far as I can tell, only show up in the obituary page.

Mr. Liebeler. What happened to this fellow?

A—Reported died of natural causes, I believe, or certainly nothing more than the obituary, so far as I can find.

Mr. Liebeler. Are you familiar with the organization known as The Minutemen?

A—In general terms.

Mr. Liebeler. Are you a member of that organization?

A—I am not.

Mr. Liebeler. Do you know of any connection between The Minutemen and the assassination of President Kennedy?

A—I do not.

Mr. Liebeler. Do you know of any conspiracy or connection on the part of any so-called rightwing organization and the assassination of President Kennedy?

A—I do not.

Mr. Liebeler. Do you know of any connection between any of the people who associate themselves with and who, shall we say, follow you as a political leader, and the assassination of President Kennedy?

A—No. People that follow me are for constitutional government. This is absolutely in violation of constitutional government. Very destructive to what we stand for.

Mr. Liebeler. So you say that there is no involvement of any kind or nature whatever between any of the organizations or people that associate with you or are involved with you in the assassination of President Kennedy?

A—I certainly know of none, and I certainly wouldn't be suspicious of any. I would be suspicious from the center to the left.

Mr. Liebeler. In any event, you don't have any knowledge of or information that would suggest to you any such conspiracy or involvement of any rightwing organization or person; is that correct?

A—That is correct. . . .

Mr. Liebeler. Do you have any other information that you think the Commission ought to have that we haven't already talked about?

A—Yes. I think the Commission should look into George De Mohrenschildt, if it hasn't.

Mr. Liebeler. What do you know about Mr. De Mohrenschildt?

A—I know that my information indicates that he lived next door to the professor that was supposed to have burned up.

Mr. Liebeler. Do you have any information that would connect De Mohrenschildt to the assassination of President Kennedy in any way?

A—I have the information the paper had that connected him with the Oswalds.

Mr. Liebeler. Yes?

A—Of course, it is common knowledge that De Mohrenschildt was associated with Oswald now.

382

Mr. Liebeler. Other than that, do you have any information to indicate that De Mohrenschildt was involved in any way with the assassination of President Kennedy?

A—Not directly.

General Watts. Do you have any indirect evidence?

A—I am tired of them blaming the rightwing, and I have had enough of this, and it is about time that the Commission cleared the city of Dallas.

Mr. Liebeler. Well, now, do you have any indirect indication or evidence that would associate De Mohrenschildt with the assassination of President Kennedy in any way?

A—I think it is very important that De Mohrenschildt knew Oswald. I think it is very interesting. My information is that De Mohrenschildt went to Haiti. I have nothing further to add. . . .

BERNARD WILLIAM WEISSMAN

The testimony of the signer of an advertisement placed in the Dallas Morning News on November 22, 1963:

Mr. Eisenberg. Mr. Weissman, I hand you this advertisement which I have labeled Weissman Exhibit No. 1, and ask you whether you are familiar with this advertisement?

A—Yes; I am.

Mr. Eisenberg. Are you the Bernard Weissman whose name appears at the bottom of this advertisement, as chairman?

A—Yes.

Mr. Eisenberg. Mr. Weissman, could you tell us how this advertisement came to be composed?

A—It is rather simple. A group of individuals in Dallas, friends of mine, got together and decided to express our feeling about the domestic and foreign policy of the Kennedy administration, and we felt that picketing, anything of the nature of picketing, and so forth, wouldn't go, since the Stevenson incident. We decided that the best way to get our point across would be to run an ad.

Mr. Eisenberg. When was this decision made?

A—The decision was made approximately a week or so before Kennedy's arrival in Dallas.

Mr. Eisenberg. That would be approximately November 15, 1963?

A—Approximately; a few days more, a few days less, in there.

Mr. Eisenberg. Who were the individuals who participated in this decision?

A—Larry Schmidt, Bill Burley, myself, and one or two other individuals who I would rather not mention. . . .

Mr. Weissman was recalled for further testimony:

Mr. Jenner. When did you first meet him? [Larrie Schmidt]

383

A—In Munich, Germany, about July or August of 1962. . . .

Mr. Jenner. . . . you met Larrie Schmidt in the Army?

A—Yes; I did.

Mr. Jenner. What other buddies did you have in the Army with whom you again renewed your acquaintance when you were discharged from the Army and went to Dallas?

A—Only one beside Larrie. That was Bill Burley. William Burley.

Mr. Jenner. What contact did you have with Mr. Larrie Schmidt and Mr. Burley after you left the Army, which eventually brought you to Dallas? . . .

A—Well, I got out of service on the 5th, and I spent the month of August looking for a job. During this time, I had been in contact with Larrie. I had telephoned him once during August. Things were pretty bad. I didn't have any money. As fas as I could ascertain he was broke himself. There wasn't any percentage in going to Dallas and not accomplishing anything. As a matter of fact, I had lost a good deal of confidence in Larrie in the year that he left Munich and was in Dallas, and the letters I got from him—he seemed to have deviated from our original plan. I wasn't too hot about going. He didn't seem to be accomplishing anything, except where it benefited him.

Mr. Jenner. You say he deviated from the original plan. What was the original plan?

A—Well, the original plan was to stay away from various organizations and societies that were, let's call them, radical, and had a reputation as being such.

Mr. Jenner. When you say radical, what do you mean?

A—I mean radical right. . . .

In any case Larrie wrote me easily a dozen letters imploring me to come down, telling me in one that he doesn't need me down there, but he would love to have my help because he can't accomplish anything without me, and in the next one saying, "Forget it, I don't need you," and so forth. As the letters came, they went with the wind, depending on what he was doing personally. And along about the end of October, I had been in contact with Bill [Burley]—he was in Baltimore, Md., selling hearing aids. He wasn't getting anywhere. He was making a living. . . .

Mr. Jenner. Excuse me. Why were you thinking of Dallas at this time?

A—Well, I kept getting these letters from Larrie. I tried to forget about it, and he constantly reminded me. Once or twice a week I would get a letter. And it was a question—I was almost obligated to go, because I had promised I would be there. And still having somewhat of a close relationship with Larrie, through my promises, I sort of felt morally obligated to go down there.

And, at the same time, it was new, different, exciting, it had a lot of promise for the future if it worked out.

So Adlai Stevenson was down there in the latter part of October. . . .

And I didn't pay too much attention to this—until the evening of Stevenson's speech at the Dallas Auditorium. And I

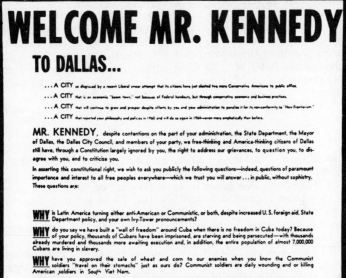

WELCOME MR. KENNEDY

TO DALLAS...

...A CITY so disgraced by a recent Liberal smear attempt that its citizens have just elected two more Conservative Americans to public office.

...A CITY that is an economic "boom town," not because of Federal handouts, but through conservative economic and business practices.

...A CITY that will continue to grow and prosper despite efforts by you and your administration to penalize it for its non-conformity to "New Frontierism."

...A CITY that rejected your philosophy and policies in 1960 and will do so again in 1964—even more emphatically than before.

MR. KENNEDY, despite contentions on the part of your administration, the State Department, the Mayor of Dallas, the Dallas City Council, and members of your party, we free-thinking and America-thinking citizens of Dallas still have, through a Constitution largely ignored by you, the right to address our grievances, to question you, to disagree with you, and to criticize you.

In asserting this constitutional right, we wish to ask you publicly the following questions—indeed, questions of paramount importance and interest to all free peoples everywhere—which we trust you will answer...in public, without sophistry. These questions are:

WHY is Latin America turning either anti-American or Communistic, or both, despite increased U.S. foreign aid, State Department policy, and your own Ivy-Tower pronouncements?

WHY do you say we have built a "wall of freedom" around Cuba when there is no freedom in Cuba today? Because of your policy, thousands of Cubans have been imprisoned, are starving and being persecuted—with thousands already murdered and thousands more awaiting execution and, in addition, the entire population of almost 7,000,000 Cubans are living in slavery.

WHY have you approved the sale of wheat and corn to our enemies when you know the Communist soldiers "travel on their stomachs" just as ours do? Communist soldiers are daily wounding and/or killing American soldiers in South Viet Nam.

WHY did you host, salute and entertain Tito — Moscow's Trojan Horse — just a short time after our sworn enemy, Khrushchev, embraced the Yugoslav dictator as a great hero and leader of Communism?

WHY have you urged greater aid, comfort, recognition, and understanding for Yugoslavia, Poland, Hungary, and other Communist countries, while turning your back on the pleas of Hungarian, East German, Cuban and other anti-Communist freedom fighters?

WHY did Cambodia kick the U.S. out of its country after we poured nearly 400 Million Dollars of aid into its ultra-leftist government?

WHY has Gus Hall, head of the U.S. Communist Party praised almost every one of your policies and announced that the party will endorse and support your re-election in 1964?

WHY have you banned the showing at U.S. military bases of the film "Operation Abolition"—the movie by the House Committee on Un-American Activities exposing Communism in America?

WHY have you ordered or permitted your brother Bobby, the Attorney General, to go soft on Communists, fellow-travelers, and ultra-leftists in America, while permitting him to persecute loyal Americans who criticize you, your administration, and your leadership?

WHY are you in favor of the U.S. continuing to give economic aid to Argentina, in spite of that fact that Argentina has just seized almost 400 Million Dollars of American private property?

WHY has the Foreign Policy of the United States degenerated to the point that the C.I.A. is arranging coups and having staunch Anti-Communist Allies of the U.S. bloodily exterminated.

WHY have you scrapped the Monroe Doctrine in favor of the "Spirit of Moscow"?

MR. KENNEDY, as citizens of these United States of America, we DEMAND answers to these questions, and we want them NOW.

THE AMERICAN FACT-FINDING COMMITTEE

"An unaffiliated and non-partisan group of citizens who wish truth"

BERNARD WEISSMAN,
Chairman

Commission Exhibit No. 1-31

P.O. Box 1792 — Dallas 21, Texas

got a long distance telephone call from Larrie, and he explained what had happened—that Stevenson had been struck by several individuals down there.

Mr. Jenner. Please call on your best recollection and tell us what he said to you. . . .

A—He said that big things are happening, and he went—this is before it hit the papers. He told me what had happened with Adlai Stevenson. . . .

And he said, "If we are going to take advantage of the situation, or if you are," meaning me, "you better hurry down here and take advantage of the publicity, and at least become known among these various rightwingers, because this is the chance we have been looking for to infiltrate some of these organizations and become known," in other words, go along with the philosophy we had developed in Munich. . . .

Mr. Jenner. What is CUSA, what was CUSA? What was its genesis?

A—Well, CUSA, the letters stand for the Conservatism USA, for lack of a better name. Larrie had originally founded this himself—as far as I know he had originally founded this himself in Munich some time in 1961.

Mr. Jenner. You mean it was a concept of his?

A—I don't know if it was his. But I was led to believe the concept was his; and when I became associated with him, almost a year after he had started to develop this organization —— . . .

Senator Cooper. May I ask a question there? I may have to leave in a few minutes. Was there any time when your organization drew up a list of organizations, of other organizations, that it wanted to infiltrate?

A—Yes.

Mr. Jenner. Do you have that list with you?

A—I don't know. I have lost an awful lot of it. I might.

Mr. Jenner. Would you look, please?

A—No; I don't have it.

Senator Cooper. May I ask, then—can he name from memory the organizations?

Mr. Jenner. Using your recollection, sir, and it appears to be very good, if I may compliment you——

A—Thank you.

Mr. Jenner. Would you do your best to respond to Senator Cooper's question by naming those various groups?

A—Yes. One was the NIC.

Mr. Jenner. When you use initials, will you spell out what the initials mean?

A—National Indignation Convention, headed by Frank McGee, in Dallas, Tex.

Young Americans for Freedom, which encompassed the southwest. The initials are YAF.

Mr. Jenner. Located in Dallas?

386

A—Regional headquarters in Dallas. John Birch Society.

Mr. Jenner. Where was the John Birch—was there a chapter or headquarters in Dallas?

A—There are several chapters in Dallas; yes. And as far as I can recollect, that is as far as we went.

Representative Boggs. What did you hope to accomplish by this infiltration, as you call it?

A—Well, I will be very blunt.

Representative Boggs. That is what I would like for you to be.

A—We were, you might say—at least I personally—this is my reason—I was sick and tired of seeing America as a weak sister all the time. And this is especially in the field of foreign affairs, where it seemed that our administration, whether it is the Eisenhower or the Kennedy administration, both of them, had no set, stable foreign policy. We were constantly losing ground all over the world. We were going to conference tables with everything to lose and nothing to gain, and coming away by losing.

And we hoped by developing a powerful political organization we could exert some influence on the government and eventually even put, you might say, our man in the White House, let's say, in order to obtain a stable policy—because we felt that the Communists were gaining ground all over the place, we were doing nothing but losing.

Representative Boggs. Did you have a candidate for the Presidency?

A—Excuse me?

Representative Boggs. Did you have a candidate—you said your man.

A—I wouldn't say we had a candidate. We had looked to Barry Goldwater as personifying Mr. Conservative. And we had stated in writing, though, that we would support him for the Presidency, but we were not obligated to support him or any other individual.

Representative Boggs. Are you still in this business?

A—No.

Representative Boggs. What are you doing now?

A—I am a salesman, I sell carpets.

Representative Boggs. You have given up this goal?

A—Well, if I had money I didn't know what to do with, I would get back into it—only I would do it myself, because I found that in order to accomplish these aims—I mentioned before I considered myself an idealist. I found in order to accomplish these goals I had to against my will prostitute my ideals in order to further the general cause of the organization.

Representative Boggs. What ideals did you find you had to prostitute?

A—I personally didn't want to associate with the John Birch Society.

Representative Boggs. You did not want to?

A—No; I did not.

Representative Boggs. Why didn't you?

A—Well; they are rather extreme, I thought. I didn't like some of the things they were doing. For example, I didn't want to spend my days and nights sneaking into bathrooms around the country, pasting up "Impeach Earl Warren" stickers. . . .

Representative Boggs. It has been established, I presume, who paid for this newspaper advertisement.

A—Well, this is something else. I am still not sure of who paid for it.

Mr. Jenner. The newspaper advertisement is Commission Exhibit No. 1031.

Representative Boggs. Did you bring the money in to pay for it?

A—Yes; I did.

Representative Boggs. Do you know where you got it?

A—I know where I got it. But I don't know where he got it from. I got it from Joe Grinnan.

Mr. Jenner. Joseph P. Grinnan, Room 811, Wilson Building, Dallas, Tex., independent oil operator in Dallas.

Representative Boggs. How did you happen to get it from him?

A—Well, Joe was the volunteer coordinator for the John Birch Society.

Representative Boggs. And how did he hand it to you—in a check or cash?

A—In cash.

Representative Boggs. How much was it?

A—It was a total of $1,462, I believe. We had 10 $100 bills one day, and the balance the following day. Now, as far as I know, Joe didn't put any of this money up personally, because I know it took him 2 days to collect it.

Representative Boggs. Do you think you know where he got it from?

A—I don't know. I really don't know.

Representative Boggs. He didn't tell you where he got it from?

A—No; he didn't.

Representative Boggs. But you are convinced in your own mind that it wasn't his money?

A—Yes; because he seemed to be—he didn't seem to be too solvent.

Representative Boggs. Did you solicit him for this money?

A—No; I didn't.

Representative Boggs. Who did?

A—I believe—well, I believe Larrie did. I think the idea for the ad originated with Larrie and Joe.

Representative Boggs. And Larrie solicited the money?

388

A—No; I don't think so. I think it was Joe who originally broached the subject.

Representative Boggs. How did you happen to end up with the money?

A—This was an expression of confidence, you might say, that Joe Grinnan had in me. . . .

Representative Boggs. Did you ever ask Joe where this money came from?

A—No; Joe was pretty secretive. I frankly didn't want to know. I was interested, but not that interested. And it didn't— it would have been a breach of etiquette to start questioning him, it seemed. . . .

Mr. Dulles. Did you suggest that this advertisement had been drafted before he collected the money?

A—Yes.

Mr. Dulles. And you used this advertisement as the basis for the collection of the money, or was it used for this purpose, as far as you know?

A—As far as I know; yes. . . .

Mr. Jenner. Tell us the genesis of the advertisement, the black border, the context, the text, the part which Mr. Grinnan played, you played, and Mr. Schmidt played in drafting it, how it came about, what you did, in your own words. How the idea arose in the first place—and then just go forward.

A—Well, after the Stevenson incident, it was felt that a demonstration would be entirely out of order, because we didn't want anything to happen in the way of physical violence to President Kennedy when he came to Dallas. But we thought that the conservatives in Dallas—I was told—were a pretty downtrodden lot after that, because they were being oppressed by the local liberals, because of the Stevenson incident. We felt we had to do something to build up the morale of the conservative element, in Dallas. So we hit upon the idea of the ad.

Mr. Jenner. Would you please tell us who you mean?

A—Me and Larrie, Larrie and Joe, and then all of us together. . . .

And I originally—well, I took the copy of the ad to the Dallas Morning News. . . .

Mr. Jenner. How many editions did this ad run for the $1,462?

A—One edition. It came out on the evening edition, on the 21st. and the morning of the 22d.

Mr. Jenner. Just one paper?

A—One edition, one paper.

Mr. Jenner. That is only the Dallas Morning News?

A—That is right.

Mr. Jenner. It was not in the other Dallas papers?

A—No.

Mr. Jenner. The Times Herald?

A—No. We felt—we didn't even go to the Times Herald.

We felt they would not even print it, because they are a very liberal paper, and we felt it would be a waste of time. We were convinced that the Morning News was conservative enough to print it. And they did.

Mr. Jenner. So the Dallas Morning News people were quite aware of the composition of the ad, and worked with you in putting it in final shape?

A—Yes; as a matter of fact, I had asked to show it to a Mr. Gray, who was the head of the advertising department, and they said no, that wouldn't be necessary, they just have to submit it to a judge something or other, a retired judge who was their legal advisor, and who would look at the ad to see if there was anything libelous in it, so to speak, or anything that the Morning News could be sued for. And I assume they did this, because they didn't let me know right away whether or not they could print it.

When I came back that afternoon, or the following morning—I don't recall which—and they said everything was okay, that it would go. . . .

Senator Cooper. May I ask this question: Would you state now to this Commission the idea of printing this ad was conceived by you and Larry Jones—what is the other's name?

A—Larrie Schmidt.

Senator Cooper. Alone, and there was no stimulation from any outside group or organization. Do you state that under oath?

A—There was stimulation.

Senator Cooper. From whom?

A—I assume from the Birch Society. In other words, I think the idea for the ad, for the something to do on the occasion of President Kennedy's visit—I think the idea for the something to do came from the Birch Society—whether Mr. Joe Grinnan or someone else, I don't know.

Senator Cooper. Was it communicated as an idea to you?

A—Larrie communicated the idea to me, said what do you think. I said, why not?

Senator Cooper. Which one of this group did the idea come to?

A—I don't know.

Senator Cooper. It didn't come to you?

A—No; it didn't come to me personally originally, no.

Mr. Dulles. What is the basis of your evidence of saying this was the Birch Society? How did you know that? Where did you get that?

A—Well, it came to a point where everything we were doing we had to go talk to Joe—big brother. And that is just the way it worked out.

Mr. Jenner. This is Joe Grinnan?

A—Yes. They were getting a grip on us, and Bill and I felt that we had to bust this grip somehow.

Mr. Dulles. Was he prominent in the Birch Society?

A—Yes: he was known.

Mr. Dulles. Joe Grinnan?

A—Yes; he was known as a coordinator. . . .

Mr. Jenner. In any of these negotiations that were carried on by you or your associates, was the name Jack Ruby ever mentioned as having any possible interest whatsoever in any of those groups?

A—Never.

Mr. Jenner. Did you hear of the name Jack Ruby or Jack Rubenstein up to—at anytime prior to November 24, 1963?

A—No; never.

Mr. Jenner. And do you have any information or any knowledge or any notion or feeling that Larrie Schmidt or any of your associates knew of or had any association with Jack Ruby or otherwise known as Jack Rubenstein?

A—I think I can state pretty emphatically no.

Mr. Jenner. Were there any communications of any kind or character, written notes, telephone calls, or otherwise, that you know about or knew about then to or from Jack Ruby?

A—Never.

Mr. Jenner. This is the first time we have mentioned the name Oswald. Had you ever heard the name Lee Harvey Oswald prior to your going to Dallas?

A—No.

Mr. Jenner. Did you hear of the name Lee Harvey Oswald at any time prior to November 22, 1963?

A—No.

Mr. Jenner. Was the name ever mentioned in your presence?

A—No.

Mr. Jenner. I take it from what you have said that you did not know a man by the name of Lee Harvey Oswald.

A—No. . . .

Mr. Jenner. And you were never in the Carousel Club at all; and you never were with Officer Tippit.

A—Right.

Mr. Jenner. Any place.

A—Any place.

Mr. Jenner. Mr. Weissman, it has been asserted that a meeting took place on November 14, 1963, in the Carousel Club between Officer Tippit and yourself—and I take it from your testimony that you vigorously deny that that ever took place.

A—Very definitely. . . .

IV. The Assassin's Killer

JACK L. RUBY

The testimony of the Dallas night club operator who killed Oswald opened with a plea that he be allowed to take a lie detector test. He said he first got word of the President's death while at the office of the Dallas Morning News placing an advertisement. He then continued:

Mr. Ruby. From the time that we were told that the President was shot, 35 minutes later they said he had passed away. In the meantime, I became very emotional. I called my sister at home. She was carried away terribly bad. And John Newnam happened to be there, and I know it is a funny reaction you have, you want other people to feel that you feel emotionally disturbed the same way as other people, so I let John listen to the phone that my sister was crying hysterically.

And I said to John, I said, "John I will have to leave Dallas." I don't know why I said that, but it is a funny reaction that you feel; the city is terribly let down by the tragedy that happened. And I said, "John, I am not opening up tonight."

And I don't know what else transpired there. I know people were just heartbroken. . . .

I left the building and I went down and I got my car, and I couldn't stop crying, because naturally when I pulled up to a stoplight and other people would be adjacent to me, I wouldn't want them to see me crying, because it looked kind of artificial.

And I went to the club and I came up, and I may have made a couple of calls from there. I could have called my colored boy, Andy, down at the club. I could have—I don't know who else I would have called, but I could have, because it is so long now since my mind is very much warped now.

You think that literally?

I went up to the club, and I told Andy, I said, "Call everyone and tell them we are not opening."

We have a little girl in Fort Worth I wanted to make sure he called her.

And a fellow by the name of Bell called and wanted to know if we were open.

And Kathy Kay called, and I said, "Definitely not."

And I called Ralph Paul, that owns the Bull Pen. He said, "Jack, being as everyone else is open"—because he knows I was pressed for money—and I said, "No, Ralph, I can't open."

He said, "Okay, if that is why, that is the way it's got to be."

So in the meantime, I had gone with Alice Nichols for some time, and I called her on the phone but she wasn't there, but I left the number on the pay phone for her to return the call, because I didn't want to keep the business phone tied up. And I hadn't spoken to her in maybe 9 months or a year. I don't know what I said to her, not many words, but just what happened.

I still remained around the club there. I am sure I was crying pretty bad. I think I made a long-distance call to California. This fellow had just visited me, and I had known him in the days back in Chicago when we were very young, in the real tough part of Chicago. His name is Al Gruber. . . .

When this thing happened, I called him. He said, "Yes, we are just watching on television." And I couldn't carry on more conversation. I said, "Al, I have to hang up."

Then I must have called my sister, Eileen, in Chicago.

Then a fellow came over to deliver some merchandise I had ordered over the phone, or Andy ordered. And we said, "What is the use of purchasing any merchandise of any kind, we are not interested in business." And I don't recall what I said, but I told him whatever money he received, to keep the change. I am not a philanthropist, but nothing bothered me at the time. I wasn't interested in anything.

Then I kept calling my sister, Eva, because she wanted me to come be with her.

Eva and I have a very complex personality. Very rarely can I be with her, but on this particular occasion, since she was carrying on so, I felt that I wanted to be with someone that meant something to me. I wanted to be with her.

And I kept calling her back, "I will be there." And so on. But I never did get there until a couple of hours later.

I finally left the club. . . . And I had been dieting, but I felt I wanted some food. I can't explain it. It would be like getting intoxicated at that particular time. It is amusing, but it is true.

I went over to the Ritz Delicatessen a block and a half away. Must have bought out the store, for about $10 worth of delicacies and so on. Went out to my sister's and stayed at her apartment.

Oh, I called from the apartment—my sister knew more of my calls than I did. I remember I think I called—I can't think of who I called.

Anyway, I am sure I made some calls of what had happened there. Somebody will have to piece me together from the time I got to my sister's apartment where I had partaken of the food.

Oh yes, I called Andy. This Andy Armstrong called me and said, "Don Safran wants you to call him."

This is rare for this gentleman, because he is a columnist for the Dallas Times Herald, because he never could get out any copy for my club. And he said, "Don Safran wants me to call him."

I called him, and he said, "Jack, are you going to be closed tonight?"

I said, "Yes."

He said, "Well, the Cabana and the Adolphus, the Century Room, are going to be closed."

I said, "Don, I am not asking you about any clubs that are going to be closed. I know I am going to be closed."

And he said, "Jack, that is what I want to know."

And I said, "You don't have to prompt me about who else is going to be closed."

I put the receiver down and talked to my sister, and I said, "Eva, what shall we do?"

And she said, "Jack, let's close for the 3 days." She said, "We don't have anything anyway, but we owe it to"—(chokes up).

So I called Don Safran back immediately and I said, "Don, we decided to close for Friday, Saturday, and Sunday."

And he said, "Okay."

Then I called the Morning News and I wanted to definitely make sure to change a copy of my ad to "Closed Friday, Saturday, and Sunday," something to that effect. . . .

I lie down and take a nap. I wake about 7 or 7:30. In the meantime, I think I called—the reason this comes back to me, I know I was going to go to the synagogue. . . . I went out to the synagogue and I went through the line and I spoke to Rabbi Silverman, and I thanked him for going to visit my sister at the hospital. She was in a week prior and had just gotten out. I don't remember the date.

Then he had a confirmation—this is the night prior to the confirmation. They serve little delicacies. So in spite of the fact of the mood I was in, I strolled into the place, and I think I had a little glass of punch. Nothing intoxicating, just a little punch they serve there. I didn't speak to anyone. One girl, Leona, said "Hello, Jack," and I wasn't in a conversational mood whatsoever.

I left the club—I left the synagogue and I drove by the Bali-Hai Restaurant. I noticed they were open. I took recognition of that.

I drove by another club called the Gay Nineties, and they were closed.

And I made it my business to drive down Preston Road. In my mind suddenly it mulled over me that the police department was working overtime. And this is the craziest thing that ever happened in a person's life. I have always been very close to the police department, I don't know why.

I felt I have always abided by the law—a few little infractions, but not serious—and I felt we have one of the greatest police forces in the world here, and I have always been close to them, and I visited in the office.

And over the radio I heard they were working overtime.

I stopped at the delicatessen called Phil's on Oak Lawn Avenue, and suddenly I decided—I told the clerk there I wanted him to make me some real good sandwiches, about 10 or 12, and he had already started on the sandwiches and I got on the phone.

I called an officer by the name of Sims and I said, "Sims, I hear you guys are working," and so on. I said, "I want to bring some sandwiches."

And he said, "Jack, we wound up our work already. We wound up what we were doing. We are finished what we were doing. I will tell the boys about your thoughtfulness, and I will thank them for you."

In the meantime, there is a fellow in town that has been very good to me named Gordon McLendon. Do you know him, Mr. Warren?

Chief Justice Warren. I think I do not.

A—He had been giving me a lot of free plugs. And all the while listening to the radio, I heard about a certain diskjockey, Joe Long, that is down at the station, giving firsthand information—I want to describe him—of Oswald.

Very rarely do I use the name Oswald. I don't know why. I don't know how to explain it—of the person that committed the act. [Pause to compose self.]

So before going down to the police station, I try to call KLIF but can't get their number.

I wanted to bring the sandwiches to KLIF so they would have the sandwiches, since they already started to make them up.

And I remember Russ Knight, a diskjockey—these names aren't familiar to you, but I have to mention them in order to refresh my memory.

His name was Moore, or something, and I tried to get information on the telephone, but they couldn't give me the phone number of his home.

I probably thought I could get the phone number, but after 6 p.m., you cannot get into the premises unless you have a "hot" number that is right to the diskjockey room.

So I couldn't get a hold of that. . . . .

I go down to the—I drive by—I leave the delicatessen—the clerk helped me with the sandwiches out to my car, and I thanked him. I told him, "These were going to KLIF, and I want you to make them real good."

He helped me with the sandwiches in the car. I got in the car and drove down toward town. I imagine it is about 4 or 5 miles to the downtown section from this delicatessen.

But prior to going into the station, I drove up McKinney Avenue to look over a couple of clubs to see if they were activating. I knew the club across from the Phil's Delicatessen and I knew the B. & B. Restaurant was open. That is a restaurant and I know the necessity for food, but I can't understand some of the clubs remaining open. It struck me funny at such a tragic time as that happening.

I drove down to Commerce and Harwood and parked my car with my dog—incidentally, I always have my dog with me —on the lot there, left the sandwiches in the car, went into the building of the police station, took the elevator up to the second floor, and there was a police officer there.

This is the first time I ever entered the building, gentlemen. The first time of that Friday. This time it must have been about—I mean the time, the time of my entering the building, I guess, was approximately 11:15 p.m.

The officer was there, and I said, "Where is Joe Long?"

I said, "Can I go and look for him?"

Evidently I took a little domineering part about me, and I was able to be admitted. I asked different reporters and various personalities there, "Are you Joe Long?," and I couldn't locate him.

I even had a police officer try to page him and he couldn't locate him.

I recognized a couple of police officers, Cal Jones and a few others, and I said "hello" to them.

And I am still looking for Joe Long, but I am carried away with the excitement of history.

And one fellow then—I am in the hallway there—there is a narrow hallway, and I don't recall if Captain Fritz or Chief Curry brings the prisoner out, and I am standing about 2 or 3 feet away from him, and there is some reporters that didn't know the various police officers, and I don't know whether they asked me or I volunteered to tell them, because I knew they were looking to find out who that was, and I said, "That was Chief Curry" or "That is Captain Fritz," or whoever it was.

I don't recall Henry Wade coming out in the hallway. He probably did. I don't recall what happened. . . .

Then suddenly someone asked, either the Chief or Captain Fritz, "Isn't there a larger room we can go into?"

They said, "Well, let's go down to the assembly room downstairs."

I don't know what transpired in between from the time that I had the officer page Joe Long up to the time I was standing about 3 feet away from Oswald. All the things—I don't recall if I am telling you everything that happened from that time, from the time I entered the building to the time I went down to the assembly room.

I went down to the assembly room down in the basement. I felt perfectly free walking in there. No one asked me or anything. I got up on a little table there where I knew I wasn't blocking anyone's view, because there was an abutment sticking out, and I had my back to the abutment, and I was standing there.

Then they brought the prisoner out and various questions were being shouted.

I noticed there was a chief county judge—Davidson, I can't think of his name, one of these precinct court judges, and they brought the prisoner out.

I don't recall if Chief Fritz, Captain Fritz was there, or Chief Curry. I know Henry Wade was there. And they started shouting questions and he said, "Is he the one?" And the question about the gun.

And they questioned Henry Wade, "what organization did he belong to," or something. And if I recall, I think Henry Wade answered, "Free Cuba."

And I corrected Henry Wade, because listening to the radio or KLIF, it stood out in my mind that it was "Fair Play Cuba." There was a difference.

So he said, "Oh yes, Fair Play Cuba," and he corrected that.

I don't know how long we remained there. There was a lot of questions thrown back and forth, and this District Attorney Henry Wade was answering them to the best he could.

From the way he stated, he let the reporters know that this was the guilty one that committed the crime.

He specifically stated that in that room, that he was the one.

It didn't have any effect in my mind, because whether the person had come out, whether he come out openly and publicly stated didn't have any bearing in my mind, because I wasn't interested in anything. All I knew, they had the prisoner. But the reporters like to know where they stand, "is he the one?"

We left out in the hallway, and I saw Henry Wade standing there, and I went over to him and said, "Henry, I want you to know I was the one that corrected you." I think it is a childish thing, but I met Henry Wade sometime back, and I knew he would recognize me.

By the way, it was "Fair Play Cuba," or something to that effect.

In the meantime, as I leave Henry Wade, two gentlemen pass by and I said, "Are you Joe Long?" He said, "No, why do you want Joe Long?"

And I said, "I got to get into KLIF. I have got some sandwiches."

And he said, "What about us?"

And I said, "Some other time."

And it so happened I found out Jerry Cunkle and Sam Pease, I found out they were the names, so I did get the number, because these fellows work for a rival radio station, and he gave me the number of KLIF.

And in the testimony of John Rutledge, if I recall now—this is the only time I had ever seen this person. When I went out the railing where the phone was at, people felt free to walk in.

In other words, I felt that I was deputized as a reporter momentarily, you might say.

So I called one of the boys at KLIF and I said to them, "I have sandwiches for you. I want to get over there." I said, "By the way, I see Henry Wade talking on the phone to someone. Do you want me to get him over here?"

And he said, "Yes, do that."

That is when everyone was beckoning Henry Wade, and I called him over and he talked on the phone to this boy.

And after he finished; I didn't even tell him what station it was. I said, "Here is somebody that wants to talk to you." And I felt he wouldn't turn it down.

And this fellow was very much elated that I brought him over there.

And I said, "Now, will you let me in?"

He said, "I will only leave the door open for 5 minutes." That was after the conversation was finished with Henry Wade.

I got ready to leave the building and I got up to the next floor and there was another diskjockey at KLIF, Russ Knight. He said, "Jack, where is everything happening?" And he had a tape recorder.

And I said, "Come on downstairs," and led him downstairs. And there was Henry Wade sitting there. And I said, "Henry, this is Russ Knight." And I left him there with Henry Wade, and I went to my car and drove over to KLIF, which is a block away from there.

And it was a little chilly that night, as I recall, but by bringing Russ Knight over to Henry Wade, I delayed too long to get to KLIF, and I had to wait 15 minutes until Russ Knight came from finishing his interview with Henry Wade.

I had the sandwiches with me and some soda pop and various things, and Russ Knight opened the door and we went upstairs. . . . I remained at KLIF from that moment on, from the time I got into the building, with Russ Knight. We talked about various things. I brought out the thought of this ad that Bernard Weissman had placed in the newspaper, and I also told Russ the one I admired by Gordon McLendon.

He came out with an editorial about the incident with Adlai Stevenson and all those things. He is one person that will immediately go to bat if anything is wrong. He will clarify it.

And I told Russ Knight there were some other things that were occurring at the time. So I remained there until about 2 a.m., and we all partook of the sandwiches and had a feast there. . . .

At 2 a.m., I left the building. I drove—I was going to go toward the Times Herald Building, because as a result—I very rarely go there for my weekend ad, because once I get the ad into the Morning News, which is the earlier issue, all I have to do is call the newspaper and they transpire the same ad that I had into the newspaper—into the Morning News.

And I promised one of the boys working in the Times Herald Building there—I was in the act, in the business of a twist-board deal I was promoting as a sales item by advertisement and mail order, and I had been evading him, or didn't have time to go out there because it was very late when I left the club, and I didn't want to stop, but because this was an early morning, I thought this would be the right time to go over there, plus the fact of changing my ad I had in the Morning News to the closing of 3 days, that I would go over there and maybe add a little more effectiveness to it in the way I wanted the ad placed.

As I was driving toward the Times Herald with the intention of doing these things, I heard someone honk a horn very loudly, and I stopped. There was a police officer sitting in a car. He was sitting with this young lady that works in my club, Kathy Kay, and they were very much carried away.

And I was carried away; and he had a few beers, and it is so bad about those places open, and I was a great guy to close; and I remained with them. . . .

And they talked and they carried on, and they thought I was the greatest guy in the world, and he stated they should cut this guy inch by inch into ribbons, and so on.

And she said, "Well, if he was in England, they would drag him through the streets and would have hung him." I forget what she said.

I left them after a long delay. They kept me from leaving. They were constantly talking and were in a pretty dramatic mood. They were crying and carrying on.

I went to the building of the Times Herald. I went to the Times Herald—may I read that, Joe? May I please?

(Joe Tonahill [Ruby Counsel] hands paper to Jack Ruby.)

Mr. Tonahill. Sam ever get your glasses?

A—Not yet. [Reading.] "This is the girl that"—what?— "that started Jack off." What is this other word?

Mr. Tonahill. Culminated?

A—That is untrue. That is what I wanted to read. (Throwing pad on table.)

Gentlemen, unless you get me to Washington, you can't get a fair shake out of me.

If you understand my way of talking, you have got to bring me to Washington to get the tests.

Do I sound dramatic? Off the beam?

Chief Justice Warren. No; you are speaking very, very rationally, and I am really surprised that you can remember as much as you have remembered up to the present time.

You have given it to us in detail.

A—Unless you can get me to Washington, and I am not a crackpot, I have all my senses—I don't want to evade any crime I am guilty of. But Mr. Moore, have I spoken this way when we have talked?

Mr. Moore. Yes.

A—Unless you get me to Washington immediately. I am afraid after what Mr. Tonahill has written there, which is unfair to me regarding my testimony here—you all want to hear what he wrote?

Chief Justice Warren. Yes; you might read it. If you need glasses again, try mine this time (handing glasses to Mr. Ruby).

A—(putting on glasses). "This is the girl"——

Mr. Tonahill. "Thing," isn't it?

A—"This is the thing that started Jack in the shooting."

Mr. Tonahill. Kathy Kay was talking about Oswald.

A—You are lying, Joe Tonahill. You are lying.

Mr. Tonahill. No; I am not.

A—You are lying, because you know what motivated me. You want to make it that it was a premeditation.

Mr. Tonahill. No.

A—Yes; you do.

Mr. Tonahill. I don't think there was any premeditation, but you go ahead and tell it your way. That is what we want you to do. That is what the Chief Justice wants.

A—Not when you specify this.

You are Senator Rankin?

Mr. Rankin. No; I am the general counsel for our Commission, Mr. Ruby.

Mr. Tonahill. You go on and keep telling it down to Caroline and the truth.

Chief Justice Warren. Mr. Ruby, may I suggest this, that if we are to have any tests, either a lie detector or, as you suggest, maybe a truth serum—I don't know anything about truth serum, but if we are to have it, we have to have something to check against, and we would like to have the rest of your story as you started to tell us, because you are now getting down to the crucial part of it, and it wouldn't be fair to you to have this much of it and then not have the rest.

A—Because the reason why, Joe knows from the time that I told Attorney Belli, and the story I wanted to tell on the stand, and Mr. Tonahill knows this isn't the time. The thought never entered my mind. He knows it.

Mr. Tonahill. I didn't say the thought entered your mind. I didn't say that.

A—You are inferring that.

Mr. Tonahill. Unconsciously, maybe, is what I meant to say.

A—Why go back to Friday, Joe?

Mr. Tonahill. You are going to come right down——

A—Why go back to Friday? That set me off.

Then it is a greater premeditation than you know is true.

Mr. Tonahill. I don't say it is premeditation. I never have. I don't think it is.

A—Because it never entered my mind when they talked

400

about, the officer, cutting him into bits. You would like to have built it up for my defense, but that is not it. I am here to tell the truth.

Mr. Tonahill. The psychiatrist said that to me.

A—You want to put that into my thoughts, but it never happened. I took it with a grain of salt what he said at that particular time.

Well, it is too bad, Chief Warren, that you didn't get me to your headquarters 6 months ago.

Chief Justice Warren. Well, Mr. Ruby, I will tell you why we didn't. Because you were then about to be tried and I didn't want to do anything that would prejudice you in your trial. And for that reason, I wouldn't even consider asking you to testify until your trial was over. That is the only reason that we didn't talk to you sooner.

And I wish we had gotten here a little sooner after your trial was over, but I know you had other things on your mind, and we had other work, and it got to this late date.

But I assure you, there is no desire on our part to let this matter go to any late date for any ulterior purpose. I assure you of that.

And as I told you at the beginning, if you want a test of some kind made, I will undertake to see that it is done. . . .

A—I am in the Times Herald Building. I go upstairs, naturally.

Chief Justice Warren. This is about what time?

A—This, I imagine, is—I left the KLIF at 2 a.m., and I spent an hour with the officer and his girl friend, so it must have been about 3:15 approximately. No; it wasn't. When you are not concerned with time, it could have been 4 o'clock.

Chief Justice Warren. It doesn't make any difference.

A—Forty-five minutes difference.

I am up there in the composing room talking to a guy by the name of Pat Gadash. He was so elated that I brought him this twist board, and I had it sealed in a polyethylene bag, but he wanted to see how it is demonstrated, how it was worked.

It is a board that is on a pivot, a ball bearing, and it has a tendency to give you certain exercises in twisting your body. So not that I wanted to get in with the hilarity of frolicking, but he asked me to show him, and the other men gathered around.

When you get into the movement of a ball bearing disk, your body is free to move. I know you look like you are having a gay time, because naturally if your body is so free of moving, it is going to look that way.

I am stating this in that even with my emotional feeling for our beloved President, even to demonstrate the twist board, I did it because someone asked me to.

You follow me, gentlemen, as I describe it?

401

Chief Justice Warren. Yes; I do.

A—Then we placed the ad in, and if I recall, I requested from Pat to put a black border around to show that the ad was in mourning, or something, because we were, everything was in mourning.

Bill, will you do that for me that you asked a minute ago? You said you wanted to leave the room.

Mr. Decker. I will have everyone leave the room, including myself, if you want to talk about it. You name it, and out we will go.

A—All right.

Mr. Decker. You want all of us outside?

A—Yes.

Mr. Decker. I will leave Tonahill and Moore. I am not going to have Joe leave.

A—If you are not going to have Joe leave——

Mr. Decker. Moore, his body is responsible to you. His body is responsible to you.

A—Bill, I am not accomplishing anything if they are here, and Joe Tonahill is here. You asked me anybody I wanted out.

Mr. Decker. Jack, this is your attorney. That is your lawyer.

A—He is not my lawyer.

(Sheriff Decker and law enforcement officers left room.)

Gentleman, if you want to hear any further testimony, you will have to get me to Washington soon, because it has something to do with you, Chief Warren.

Do I sound sober enough to tell you this?

Chief Justice Warren. Yes; go right ahead.

A—I want to tell the truth, and I can't tell it here. I can't tell it here. Does that make sense to you?

Chief Justice Warren. Well, let's not talk about sense. But I really can't see why you can't tell this Commission.

A—What is your name?

Mr. Ball. Joe Ball.

Chief Justice Warren. Mr. Joe Ball. He is an attorney from Los Angeles who has been working for me.

A—Do you know Belli too?

Mr. Ball. I know of him.

A—Ball was working with him. He knows Belli. You know Melvin Belli?

Mr. Ball. I am not acquainted with him.

Chief Justice Warren. No association of any kind.

Mr. Ball. We practice in different cities.

Chief Justice Warren. Five hundred miles away. Mr. Ball practices in Long Beach, and Mr. Belli practices in San Francisco. There is positively no connection between anybody in this room, as far as I know, with Mr. Belli. I can assure you of that.

A—Where do you stand, Moore?

Mr. Moore. Well, I am assigned to the Commission, Jack.

402

A—The President assigned you?

Mr. Moore. No; my chief did. And I am not involved in the investigation. I am more of a security officer.

A—Boys, I am in a tough spot, I tell you that.

Mr. Moore. You recall when I talked to you, there were certain things I asked you not to tell me at the time, for certain reasons, that you were probably going to trial at that time, and I respected your position on that and asked you not to tell me certain things.

A—But this isn't the place for me to tell what I want to tell.

Mr. Moore. The Commission is looking into the entire matter, and you are part of it, should be.

A—Chief Warren, your life is in danger in this city, do you know that?

Chief Justice Warren. No; I don't know that. If that is the thing that you don't want to talk about, you can tell me, if you wish, when this is all over, just between you and me.

A—No; I would like to talk to you in private.

Chief Justice Warren. You may do that when you finish your story. You may tell me that phase of it.

A—I bet you haven't had a witness like me in your whole investigation, is that correct?

Chief Justice Warren. There are many witnesses whose memory has not been as good as yours. I tell you that, honestly.

A—My reluctance to talk—you haven't had any witness in telling the story, in finding so many problems?

Chief Justice Warren. You have a greater problem than any witness we have had.

A—I have a lot of reasons for having those problems.

Chief Justice Warren. I know that, and we want to respect your rights, whatever they may be. And I only want to hear what you are willing to tell us, because I realize that you still have a great problem before you, and I am not trying to press you.

I came here because I thought you wanted to tell us the story, and I think the story should be told for the public, and it will eventually be made public. If you want to do that, you are entitled to do that, and if you want to have it verified as the thing can be verified by a polygraph test, you may have that, too.

I will undertake to do that for you, but at all events we must first have the story that we are going to check it against.

A—When are you going back to Washington?

Chief Justice Warren. I am going back very shortly after we finish this hearing—I am going to have some lunch.

A—Can I make a statement?

Chief Justice Warren. Yes.

A—If you request me to go back to Washington with you right now, that couldn't be done, could it?

Chief Justice Warren. No; it could not be done. It could not be done. There are a good many things involved in that, Mr. Ruby.

A—What are they?

Chief Justice Warren. Well, the public attention that it would attract, and the people who would be around. We have no place there for you to be safe when we take you out, and we are not law enforcement officers, and it isn't our responsibility to go into anything of that kind.

And certainly it couldn't be done on a moment's notice this way.

A—Well, from what I read in the paper, they made certain precautions for you coming here, but you got here.

Chief Justice Warren. There are no precautions taken at all.

A—There were some remarks in the paper about some crackpots.

Chief Justice Warren. I don't believe everything I read in the paper.

Mr. Moore. In that respect, the Chief Justice is in public life. People in public life are well aware they don't please everyone, and they get these threats.

Incidentally, if it is the part about George Senator talking about the Earl Warren Society, the Chief Justice is aware of that phase, and I am sure he would like to hear anything that you have to say if it affects the security.

Chief Justice Warren. Before you finish the rest of your statement, may I ask you this question, and this is one of the questions we came here to ask you.

Did you know Lee Harvey Oswald prior to this shooting?

A—That is why I want to take the lie detector test. Just saying no isn't sufficient.

Chief Justice Warren. I will afford you that opportunity.

A—All right.

Chief Justice Warren. I will afford you that opportunity. You can't do both of them at one time.

A—Gentlemen, my life is in danger here. Not with my guilty plea of execution.

Do I sound sober enough to you as I say this?

Chief Justice Warren. You do. You sound entirely sober.

A—From the moment I started my testimony, have I sounded as though, with the exception of becoming emotional, have I sounded as though I made sense, what I was speaking about?

Chief Justice Warren. You have indeed. I understood everything you have said. If I haven't, it is my fault.

A—Then I follow this up. I may not live tomorrow to give any further testimony. The reason why I add this to this, since you assure me that I have been speaking sense by then, I might be speaking sense by following what I have said, and the only thing I want to get out to the public, and I can't say it here, is with authenticity, with sincerity of the truth of everything and why my act was committed, but it can't be said here.

It can be said, it's got to be said amongst people of the highest authority that would give me the benefit of doubt. And following that, immediately give me the lie detector test after I do make the statement.

Chairman Warren, if you felt that your life was in danger at the moment, how would you feel? Wouldn't you be reluctant to go on speaking, even though you request me to do so?

Chief Justice Warren. I think I might have some reluctance if I was in your position, yes; I think I would. I think I would figure it out very carefully as to whether it would endanger me or not.

If you think that anything that I am doing or anything that I am asking you is endangering you in any way, shape, or form, I want you to feel absolutely free to say that the interview is over.

A—What happens then? I didn't accomplish anything.

Chief Justice Warren. No; nothing has been accomplished.

A—Well, then you won't follow up with anything further?

Chief Justice Warren. There wouldn't be anything to follow up if you hadn't completed your statement.

A—You said you have the power to do what you want to do, is that correct?

Chief Justice Warren. Exactly.

A—Without any limitations?

Chief Justice Warren. Within the purview of the Executive order which established the Commission. We have the right to take testimony of anyone we want in this whole situation, and we have the right, if we so choose to do it, to verify that statement in any way that we wish to do it.

A—But you don't have a right to take a prisoner back with you when you want to?

Chief Justice Warren. No; we have the power to subpena witnesses to Washington if we want to do it, but we have taken the testimony of 200 or 300 people, I would imagine, here in Dallas without going to Washington.

A—Yes; but those people aren't Jack Ruby.

Chief Justice Warren. No; they weren't

A—They weren't.

Chief Justice Warren. Now I want you to feel that we are not here to take any advantage of you, because I know that you are in a delicate position, and unless you had indicated not only through your lawyers but also through your sister, who wrote a letter addressed either to me or to Mr. Rankin saying that you wanted to testify before the Commission, unless she had told us that, I wouldn't have bothered you.

Because I know you do have this case that is not yet finished, and I wouldn't jeopardize your position by trying to insist that you testify.

So I want you to feel that you are free to refrain from testifying any time you wish.

But I will also be frank with you and say that I don't think it would be to your advantage to tell us as much as you have and then to stop and not tell us the rest. I can't see what advantage that would give you.

A—The thing is this, that with your power that you have, Chief Justice Warren, and all these gentlemen, too much time has gone by for me to give you any benefit of what I may say now.

Chief Justice Warren. No; that isn't a fact, because until we make our findings for the Commission, and until we make our report on the case, it is not too late.

And there are other witnesses we have who are yet to be examined. So from our standpoint, it is timely. We are not handicapped at all by the lateness of your examination.

A—Well, it is too tragic to talk about.

Mr. Rankin. Isn't it true that we waited until very late in our proceedings to talk to Mrs. Kennedy?

Chief Justice Warren. Yes; I might say to you that we didn't take Mrs. Kennedy's statement until day before yesterday. Mr. Rankin and I took her testimony then.

So we are not treating you different from any other witness.

A—I tell you, gentlemen, my whole family is in jeopardy. My sisters, as to their lives.

Chief Justice Warren. Yes?

A—Naturally, I am a foregone conclusion. My sisters Eva, Eileen, and Mary, I lost my sisters.

My brothers Sam, Earl, Hyman, and myself naturally—my in-laws, Harold Kaminsky, Marge Ruby, the wife of Earl, and Phyllis, the wife of Sam Ruby, they are in jeopardy of loss of their lives. Yet they have, just because they are blood related to myself—does that sound serious enough to you, Chief Justice Warren?

Chief Justice Warren. Nothing could be more serious, if that is the fact. But your sister, I don't know whether it was your sister Eva or your other sister——

A—Eileen wrote you a letter.

Chief Justice Warren. Wrote the letter to me and told us that you would like to testify, and that is one of the reasons that we came down here.

A—But unfortunately, when did you get the letter, Chief Justice Warren?

Chief Justice Warren. It was a long time ago, I admit. I think it was, let's see, roughly between 2 and 3 months ago.

A—Yes.

Chief Justice Warren. I think it was; yes.

A—At that time when you first got the letter and I was begging Joe Tonahill and the other lawyers to know the truth about me, certain things that are happening now wouldn't be happening at this particular time.

Chief Justice Warren. Yes?

A—Because then they would have known the truth about Jack Ruby and his emotional breakdown.

Chief Justice Warren. Yes?

A—Of why that Sunday morning—that thought never entered my mind prior to that Sunday morning when I took it upon myself to try to be a martyr or some screwball, you might say.

But I felt very emotional and very carried away for Mrs. Kennedy, that with all the strife she had gone through—I had been following it pretty well—that someone owed it to our beloved President that she shouldn't be expected to come back to face trial of this heinous crime.

And I have never had the chance to tell that, to back it up, to prove it.

Consequently, right at this moment I am being victimized as a part of a plot in the world's worst tragedy and crime at this moment.

Months back had I been given a chance—I take that back. Sometime back a police officer of the Dallas Police Department wanted to know how I got into the building. And I don't know whether I requested a lie detector test or not, but my attorney wasn't available.

When you are a defendant in the case, you say "speak to your attorney," you know. But that was a different time. It was after the trial, whenever it happened.

At this moment, Lee Harvey Oswald isn't guilty of committing the crime of assassinating President Kennedy. Jack Ruby is.

How can I fight that, Chief Justice Warren?

Chief Justice Warren. Well now, I want to say, Mr. Ruby, that as far as this Commission is concerned, there is no implication of that in what we are doing.

A—All right, there is a certain organization here——

Chief Justice Warren. That I can assure you.

A—There is an organization here, Chief Justice Warren, if it takes my life at this moment to say it, and Bill Decker said be a man and say it, there is a John Birch Society right now in activity, and Edwin Walker is one of the top men of this organization—take it for what it is worth, Chief Justice Warren.

Unfortunately for me, for me giving the people the opportunity to get in power, because of the act I committed, has put a lot of people in jeopardy with their lives.

Don't register with you, does it?

Chief Justice Warren. No; I don't understand that.

A—Would you rather I just delete what I said and just pretend that nothing is going on?

Chief Justice Warren. I would not indeed. I am only interested in what you want to tell this Commission. That is all I am interested in.

A—Well, I said my life, I won't be living long now. I know that. My family's lives will be gone. When I left my apartment that morning——

Chief Justice Warren. What morning?

A—Sunday morning.

Chief Justice Warren. Sunday morning.

A—Let's go back. Saturday I watched Rabbi Seligman. Any of you watch it that Saturday morning?

Chief Justice Warren. No; I didn't happen to hear it.

A—He went ahead and eulogized that here is a man that fought in every battle, went to every country, and had to come back to his own country to be shot in the back [starts crying]. I must be a great actor, I tell you that.

Chief Justice Warren. No.

A—That created a tremendous emotional feeling for me, the way he said that. Prior to all the other times, I was carried away.

Then that Saturday night, I didn't do anything but visit a little club over here and had a Coca-Cola, because I was sort of depressed. A fellow that owns the Pago Club, Bob Norton, and he knew something was wrong with me in the certain mood I was in.

And I went home and that weekend, the Sunday morning, and saw a letter to Caroline, two columns about a 16-inch area. Someone had written a letter to Caroline. The most heartbreaking letter. I don't remember the contents. Do you remember that?

Mr. Moore. I think I saw it.

A—Yes; and alongside that letter on the same sheet of paper was a small comment in the newspaper that, I don't know how it was stated, that Mrs. Kennedy may have to come back for the trial of Lee Harvey Oswald.

That caused me to go like I did; that caused me to go like I did.

I don't know, Chief Justice, but I got so carried away. And I remember prior to that thought, there has never been another thought in my mind; I was never malicious toward this person. No one else requested me to do anything.

I never spoke to anyone about attempting to do anything. No subversive organization gave me any idea. No underworld person made any effort to contact me. It all happened that Sunday morning.

The last thing I read was that Mrs. Kennedy may have to come back to Dallas for trial for Lee Harvey Oswald, and I don't know what bug got ahold of me. I don't know what it is, but I am going to tell the truth word for word.

I am taking a pill called Preludin. It is a harmless pill, and it is very easy to get in the drugstore. It isn't a highly prescribed pill. I use it for dieting.

I don't partake of that much food. I think that was a stimulus to give me an emotional feeling that suddenly I felt, which was so stupid, that I wanted to show my love for our faith, being of the Jewish faith, and I never used the term and I don't want to go into that—suddenly the feeling, the emotional feeling came within me that someone owed this debt to our beloved President to save her the ordeal of coming back. I don't know why that came through my mind.

And I drove past Main Street, past the County Building, and there was a crowd already gathered there. And I guess I thought I knew he was going to be moved at 10 o'clock, I don't know. I listened to the radio; and I passed a crowd and it looked—I am repeating myself—and I took it for granted he had already been moved.

And I parked my car in the lot across from the Western Union. Prior to that, I got a call from a little girl—she wanted some money—that worked for me, and I said, "Can't you wait till payday?" And she said, "Jack, you are going to be closed."

So my purpose was to go to the Western Union—my double purpose—but the thought of doing, committing the act wasn't until I left my apartment.

Sending the wire was when I had the phone call—or the money order.

I drove down Main Street—there was a little incident I left out, that I started to go down a driveway, but I wanted to go by the wreaths, and I saw them and started to cry again.

Then I drove, parked the car across from the Western Union, went into the Western Union, sent the money order, whatever it was, walked the distance from the Western Union to the ramp—I didn't sneak in. I didn't linger in there.

I didn't crouch or hide behind anyone, unless the television camera can make it seem that way.

There was an officer talking—I don't know what rank he had—talking to a Sam Pease in a car parked up on the curb.

I walked down those few steps, and there was the person that—I wouldn't say I saw red—it was a feeling I had for our beloved President and Mrs. Kennedy, that he was insignificant to what my purpose was.

And when I walked down the ramp—I would say there was an 8-foot clearance—not that I wanted to be a hero, or I didn't realize that even if the officer would have observed me, the klieg lights, but I can't take that.

I did not mingle with the crowd. There was no one near me when I walked down that ramp, because if you will time the time I sent the money order, I think it was 10:17 Sunday morning.

I think the actual act was committed—I take that back—was it 11 o'clock? You should know this.

Mr. Moore. 11:21.

A—No; when Oswald was shot.

Mr. Moore. I understood it to be 11:22.

A—The clock stopped and said 11:21. I was watching on that thing; yes. Then it must have been 11:17, closer to 18. That is the timing when I left the Western Union to the time of the bottom of the ramp.

You wouldn't have time enough to have any conspiracy, to be self-saving, to mingle with the crowd, as it was told about me.

I realize it is a terrible thing I have done, and it was a stupid thing, but I just was carried away emotionally. Do you follow that?

Chief Justice Warren. Yes; I do indeed, every word.

A—I had the gun in my right hip pocket, and impulsively, if that is the correct word here, I saw him, and that is all I can say. And I didn't care what happened to me.

I think I used the words, "You killed my President, you rat." The next thing, I was down on the floor.

I said, "I am Jack Ruby. You all know me."

I never used anything malicious, nothing like s.o.b. I never said that I wanted to get three more off, as they stated.

The only words, and I was highly emotional; to Ray Hall— he interrogated more than any other person down there—all I believe I said to him was, "I didn't want Mrs. Kennedy to come back to trial."

And I forget what else. And I used a little expression like being of the Jewish faith, I wanted to show that we love our President, even though we are not of the same faith.

And I have a friend of mine—do you mind if it is a slipshod story?

Chief Justice Warren. No; you tell us in your own way.

A—A fellow whom I sort of idolized is of the Catholic faith, and a gambler. Naturally in my business you meet people of various backgrounds.

And the thought came, we were very close, and I always thought a lot of him, and I knew that Kennedy, being Catholic, I knew how heartbroken he was, and even his picture—of this Mr. McWillie—flashed across me, because I have a great fondness for him.

All that blended into the thing that, like a screwball, the way it turned out, that I thought that I would sacrifice myself for the few moments of saving Mrs. Kennedy the discomfiture of coming back to trial.

Now all these things of my background, I should have been the last person in the world to want to be a martyr. It happens, doesn't it, Chief Warren?

I mean, for instance, I have been in the night club business, a burlesque house. It was a means of a livelihood. I knew persons of notorious backgrounds years ago in Chicago. I was

410

with the union back in Chicago, and I left the union when I found out the notorious organization had moved in there. It was in 1940.

Then recently, I had to make so many numerous calls that I am sure you know of. Am I right? Because of trying to survive in my business.

My unfair competition had been running certain shows that we were restricted to run by regulation of the union, but they violated all the rules of the union, and I didn't violate it, and consequently I was becoming insolvent because of it.

All those calls were made with only, in relation to seeing if they can help out, with the American Guild of Variety Artists. Does that confirm a lot of things you have heard?

Every person I have called, and sometimes you may not even know a person intimately, you sort of tell them, well, you are stranded down here and you want some help—if they konw of any official of the American Guild of Variety Artists to help me. Because my competitors were putting me out of business.

I even flew to New York to see Joe Glazer, and he called Bobby Faye. He was the national president. That didn't help. He called Barney Ross and Joey Adams. All these phone calls were related not in anyway involved with the underworld, because I have been away from Chicago 17 years down in Dallas.

As a matter of fact, I even called a Mr.—hold it before I say it—headed the American Federation of Labor—I can't think —in the State of Texas—Miller.

Chief Justice Warren. I don't know.

A—Is there a Deutsch I. Maylor? I called a Mr. Maylor here in Texas to see if he could help me out.

I want to set you gentlemen straight on all the telephone calls I had. This was a long time prior to what has happened. And the only association I had with those calls, the only questions that I inquired about, was if they could help me with the American Guild of Variety Artists, to see that they abolished it, because it was unfair to professional talent, abolish them from putting on their shows in Dallas. That is the only reason I made those calls. Where do we go from there?

Chief Justice Warren. Well, I will go back to the original question that I asked you. Did you ever know Oswald?

A—No; let me add—you are refreshing my mind about a few things.

Can I ask one thing? Did you all talk to Mr. McWillie? I am sure you have.

Voice. Yes.

A—He always wanted me to come down to Havana, Cuba; invited me down there, and I didn't want to leave my business because I had to watch over it.

He was a key man over the Tropicana down there. That was

411

during our good times. Was in harmony with our enemy of our present time.

Chief Justice Warren. Yes?

A—I refused. I couldn't make it. Finally he sent me tickets to come down, airplane tickets.

I made the trip down there via New Orleans, and so I stayed at the Volk's Apartments, and I was with him constantly.

And I was bored with the gambling, because I don't gamble, and there is nothing exciting unless you can speak their language, which is Spanish, I believe.

And that was the only environment. That was in August of 1959.

Any thought of ever being close to Havana, Cuba, I called him frequently because he was down there, and he was the last person to leave, if I recall, when they had to leave, when he left the casino.

As a matter of fact, on the plane, if I recall, I had an article he sent me, and I wanted to get it published because I idolized McWillie. He is a pretty nice boy, and I happened to be idolizing him.

When the plane left Havana and landed in the United States, some schoolteacher remarked that the United States is not treating Castro right. When they landed in the United States, this Mr. Louis McWillie slugged this guy for making that comment.

So I want you to know, as far as him having any subversive thoughts, and I wanted Tony to put it in the paper here. That is how much I thought of Mr. McWillie. And that is my only association.

The only other association with him was, there was a gentleman here that sells guns. He has a hardware store on Singleton Avenue.

Have I told this to you gentlemen? It is Ray's Hardware. His name is Ray Brantley.

This was—I don't recall when he called me, but he was a little worried of the new regime coming in, and evidently he wanted some protection.

He called me or sent me a letter that I should call Ray Brantley. He wanted some four little Cobra guns—big shipment.

So me, I should say myself rather, feeling no harm, I didn't realize, because he wasn't sending them to me, and I thought there was no crime, the man wanted protection, he is earning a livelihood.

I called Ray Brantley and I said, "Ray. McWillie called me." I don't remember if he sent me a letter or he called. He said he wants four little Cobras. or something like that.

He said "I know Mac. I have been doing business with him for a long time." Meaning with reference to when he was living in Texas. He did a lot of hunting and things like that.

Chief Justice Warren. Yes?

A—That was the only relationship I had of any mention, outside of phone calls, to Mr. McWillie, or any person from Havana, Cuba.

Chief Justice Warren. When was that?

A—Now the guns—am I correct? Did you ever go to check on it? On Ray Brantley?

Mr. Moore. No.

A—He denies I ever called. Evidently he feels, maybe he feels it would be illegal to send guns out of the country. I don't know if you gentlemen know the law. I don't know the law.

Chief Justice Warren. I don't know.

A—I kept—did I tell you this, Joe, about this?

Mr. Tonahill. Yes; you did.

A—That I wanted someone to go to Ray Brantley?

Mr. Tonahill. Yes.

A—When Phil Burleson came back with a letter signed, an affidavit that Ray Brantley said he never did receive a call from me, and the only gun he sent to McWillie was to the Vegas, but it came back that they didn't pick it up because it was a c.o.d. order.

This definitely would do me more harm, because if I tell my story that I called Ray Brantley, and he denies that he ever got a call from me, definitely that makes it look like I am hiding something.

Haven't I felt that right along, Joe?

Mr. Tonahill. You sure have, Jack.

A—Now, the reason I am telling you these things, I never knew Lee Harvey Oswald. The first time I ever have seen him was the time in the assembly room when they brought him out, when he had some sort of a shiner on his eye.

Chief Justice Warren. When was that little incident about the Cobras? About what year? That is all I am interested in.

A—Could have been prior to the early part of 1959.

Chief Justice Warren. Yes; all right.

A—That is the only call I made. And as a matter of fact, I didn't even follow up to inquire of this Mr. Brantley, whether he received it or what the recourse was. . . .

Mr. Rankin. How long did you spend in Cuba on this trip?

A—Eight days. A lot of your tourists were there. As a matter of fact, a lot of group tourists were going down, students of schools.

I mean, he had a way of purchasing tickets from Havana that I think he purchased them at a lesser price. He bought them from the travel agent in the Capri Hotel.

He bought them—did you meet McWillie?

Mr. Moore. I didn't.

Mr. Rankin. He was checked by the Commission in connection with this work.

Chief Justice Warren. There was some story in one of the

papers that you had been interested in shipping jeeps down to Cuba. Was there anything to that at all?

A—No; but this was the earlier part, when the first time Castro had ever invaded Cuba. There was even a Government article that they would need jeeps. I don't recall what it was, but I never had the facilities or the capabilities of knowing where to get jeeps.

But probably in conversation with other persons—you see, it is a new land, and they have to have a lot of things. As a matter of fact, the U. S. Government was wanting persons to help them at that particular time when they threw out the dictator, Batista.

And one particular time there was a gentleman that smuggled guns to Castro. I think I told you that, Mr. Moore; I don't remember.

Mr. Moore. I don't recall that.

A—I think his name was Longley out of Bay—something—Texas, on the Bayshore. And somehow he was, I read the article about him, that he was given a jail term for smuggling guns to Castro. This is the early part of their revolution.

Chief Justice Warren. Before the Batista government fell?

A—Yes; I think he had a boat, and he lived somewhere in Bay something, Bayshore, in the center part of Texas. Do you know him, Mr. Storey? Do you know this man?

Mr. Storey. No; I don't know him.

A—How can I prove my authenticity of what I have stated here today?

Chief Justice Warren. Well, you have testified under oath, and I don't even know that there is anything to disprove what you have said.

A—No; because I will say this. You don't know if there is anything to disprove, but at this moment, there is a certain organization in this area that has been indoctrinated, that I am the one that was in the plot to assassinate our President.

Mr. Rankin. Would you tell us what that is?

A—The John Birch Society.

Mr. Rankin. Can you tell us what basis you have for that, Mr. Ruby?

A—Just a feeling of it. Mr. Warren, you don't recall when I—Friday night after leaving the Times Herald, I went to my apartment and very impatiently awakened George Senator. As a matter of fact, used the words, as I state, "You will have to get up, George. I want you to go with me."

And he had been in bed for a couple of hours, which was about, I imagine, about 4:30 or a quarter to 5 in the morning.

And I called the club and I asked this kid Larry if he knew how to pack a Polaroid, and he said "Yes."

And I said, "Get up." And we went down and picked up Larry. And in the meantime, I don't recall if I stopped at the post office to find out his box number of this Bernard Weissman. I think the box number was 1792, or something to that; and then there was, it came to my mind when I left the Times Herald—I am skipping back—why I had awakened George.

I recall seeing a sign on a certain billboard "Impeach Earl Warren." You have heard something about that?

Chief Justice Warren. I read something in the paper, yes; that is all.

A—And it came from New Bedford, or Massachusetts; I don't recall what the town was.

And there was a similar number to that, but I thought at the time it would be the same number of 1792, but it was 1757.

That is the reason I went down there to take the Polaroid picture of it, because of that remaining in the city at the time.

What happened to the picture, I don't know. I asked Jim Bowie or Alexander to tell you.

Mr. Rankin. Did you know Weissman before that?

A—Never knew him. When I said Jim Bowie, no one says a word.

Mr. Bowie. We never have seen them.

A—They were in my person.

Mr. Bowie. But no evidence came?

A—No; it did not, never. As a matter of fact, I went to the post office to check on box 1792. I even inquired with the man in charge of where you purchase the boxes, and I said to him, "Who bought this box?"

And he said, "I can't give you the information. All I know is, it is a legitimate business box purchase."

And I checked the various contents of mail there.

Mr. Rankin. Did you know Officer Tippit?

A—I knew there was three Tippits on the force. The only one I knew used to work for the special services, and I am certain this wasn't the Tippit, this wasn't the man.

Mr. Rankin. The man that was murdered. There was a story that you were seen sitting in your Carousel Club with Mr. Weissman, Officer Tippit, and another who has been called a rich oil man, at one time shortly before the assassination. Can you tell us anything about that?

A—Who was the rich oil man?

Mr. Rankin. Can you remember? We haven't been told. We are just trying to find out anything that you know about him.

A—I am the one that made such a big issue of Bernard Weissman's ad. Maybe you do things to cover up, if you are capable of doing it.

As a matter of fact, Saturday afternoon we went over to the Turf Bar lounge, and it was a whole hullabaloo, and I showed the pictures "Impeach Earl Warren" to Bellocchio, and he saw the pictures and got very emotional.

And Bellocchio said, "Why did the newspaper take this ad of Weissman?"

And Bellocchio said, "I have got to leave Dallas."

And suddenly after making that statement, I realized it is his incapability, and suddenly you do things impulsively, and suddenly you realize if you love the city, you stay here and you make the best of it. And there were witnesses.

I said, "The city was good enough for you all before this. Now you feel that way about it." And that was Bellocchio.

As far as Tippit, it is not Tippitts, it is not Tippitts it is Tippit.

Mr. Rankin. This Weissman and the rich oil man, did you ever have a conversation with them?

A—There was only a few. Bill Rudman from the YMCA, and I haven't seen him in years.

And there is a Bill Howard, but he is not a rich oil man. He owns the Stork Club now. He used to dabble in oil.

Chief Justice Warren. This story was given by a lawyer by the name of Mark Lane, who is representing Mrs. Marguerite Oswald, the mother of Lee Harvey Oswald, and it was in the paper, so we subpenaed him, and he testified that someone had given him information to the effect that a week or two before President Kennedy was assassinated, that in your Carousel Club you and Weissman and Tippit, Officer Tippit, the one who was killed, and a rich oil man had an interview or conversation for an hour or two.

And we asked him who it was that told him, and he said that it was confidential and he couldn't tell at the moment, but that he would find out for us if whether he could be released or not from his confidential relationship.

He has never done it, and we have written him several letters asking him to disclose the name of that person and he has never complied.

A—Isn't that foolish? If a man is patriotic enough in the first place, who am I to be concerned if he wasn't an informer.

I am incarcerated, nothing to be worried about anyone hurting me.

Chief Justice Warren. Mr. Ruby, I am not questioning your story at all. I wanted you to know the background of this thing, and to know that it was with us only hearsay. But I did feel that our record should show that we would ask you the question and that you would answer it, and you have answered it.

A—How many days prior to the assassination was that?

Chief Justice Warren. My recollection is that it was a week or two. Is that correct?

A—Did anyone have any knowledge that their beloved President was going to visit here prior to that time, or what is the definite time that they knew he was coming to Dallas?

Chief Justice Warren. Well, I don't know just what those dates are.

A—I see.

Chief Justice Warren. I just don't know. Well, we wanted to ask you that question, because this man had so testified, and we have been trying ever since to get him to give the source of his information, but he will not do it, so we will leave that matter as it is.

A—No; I am as innocent regarding any conspiracy as any of you gentlemen in the room, and I don't want anything to be run over lightly. I want you to dig into it with any biting, any question that might embarrass me, or anything that might bring up my background, which isn't so terribly spotted—I have never been a criminal—I have never been in jail—I know when you live in the city of Chicago and you are in the livelihood of selling tickets to sporting events, your lucrative patrons are some of these people, but you don't mean anything to those people. You may know them as you get acquainted with them at the sporting events or the ball park.

Chief Justice Warren. The prizefights?

A—The prizefights. If that was your means of livelihood, yet you don't have no other affiliation with them, so when I say I know them, or what I have read from stories of personalities that are notorious, that is the extent of my involvement in any criminal activity.

I have never been a bookmaker. I have never stolen for a living. I am not a gangster I have never used a goon squad for union activities.

All I was was a representative to sound out applications for the American Federation of Labor, and if the employees would sign it, we would accept them as members.

I never knew what a goon looked like in Chicago, with the exception when I went to the service.

I never belonged to any subversive organization. I don't know any subversive people that are against my beloved country.

Mr. Rankin. You have never been connected with the Communist Party?

A—Never have. All I have ever done in my life—I had a very rough start in life, but anything I have done, I at least try to do it in good taste, whatever I have been active in.

Mr. Rankin. There was a story that you had a gun with you during the showup that you described in the large room there.

A—I will be honest with you. I lied about it. It isn't so. I didn't have a gun. But in order to make my defense more accurate, to save your life, that is the reason that statement was made.

Mr. Rankin. It would be quite helpful to the Commission if you could—in the first place, I want to get the trip to Cuba. Was that in 1959?

A—Yes; because I had to buy a $2 ticket, a pass to get through Florida.

Mr. Rankin. Did you have any other trip to Cuba?

A—Never; that is the only one that I made. . . .

Mr. Rankin. I think, Mr. Ruby, it would be quite helpful to the Commission if you could tell, as you recall it, just what you said to Mr. Sorrels and the others after the shooting of Lee Harvey Oswald. Can you recall that?

A—The only one I recall Mr. Sorrels in, there were some incorrect statements made at this time.

Mr. Rankin. Can you tell us what you said?

Congressman Ford. First, tell us when this took place.

Mr. Rankin. How soon after the shooting occurred?

A—Well, Ray Hall was the first one that interrogated me. Wanted to know my whole background.

Mr. Rankin. Can you tell us how soon it was? Within a few minutes after the shooting?

A—No; I waited in a little room there somewhere upstairs in —I don't know what floor it was. I don't recall.

Mr. Rankin. Where did this occur, on the third floor?

A—One of those floors. I don't know whether it was the third or second. If you are up on an elevator——

Mr. Rankin. Can you give us any idea of the time after the shooting?

A—I spent an hour with Mr. Hall, Ray Hall. And I was very much, I was very much broken up emotionally, and I constantly repeated that I didn't want Mrs. Kennedy to come back to trial, and those were my words, constantly repeated to Mr. Hall.

And I heard there was a statement made—now I am skipping —and then I gave Mr. Hall my complete background about things he wanted to know, my earlier background going back from the years, and I guess there was nothing else to say to Hall because as long as I stated why I did it—it is not like planning a crime and you are confessing something. I already confessed, and all it took is one sentence why I did it.

Now what else could I have said that you think I could have said? Refresh my memory a little bit.

Mr. Rankin. There was a conversation with Mr. Sorrels in which you told him about the matter. Do you remember that?

A—The only thing I ever recall I said to Mr. Ray Hall and Sorrels was, I said, "Being of Jewish faith, I wanted to show my love for my President and his lovely wife."

After I said whatever I said, then a statement came out that someone introduced Mr. Sorrels to me and I said, "What are you, a newsman?" Or something to that effect. Which is really —what I am trying to say is, the way it sounded is like I was looking for publicity and inquiring if you are a newsman, I wanted to see you.

But I am certain—I don't recall definitely, but I know in my right mind, because I know my motive for doing it, and certainly to gain publicity to take a chance of being mortally wounded, as I said before, and who else could have timed it so perfectly by seconds.

If it were timed that way, then someone in the police department is guilty of giving the information as to when Lee Harvey Oswald was coming down.

I never made a statement. I never inquired from the television man what time is Lee Harvey Oswald coming down. Because really, a man in his right mind would never ask that question. I never made the statement "I wanted to get three more off. Someone had to do it. You wouldn't do it." I never made those statements.

I never called the man by any obscene name, because as I stated earlier, there was no malice in me. He was insignificant, to my feelings for my love for Mrs. Kennedy and our beloved President. He was nothing comparable to them, so I can't explain it.

I never used any words—as a matter of fact, there were questions at the hearing with Roy Pryor and a few others—I may have used one word "a little weasel" or something, but I didn't use it, I don't remember, because Roy said it. If he said I did, I may have said it.

I never made the statement to anyone that I intended to get him. I never used the obscene words that were stated.

Anthing I said was with emotional feeling of I didn't want Mrs. Kennedy to come back to trial.

Representative Ford. It has been alleged that you went out to Parkland Hospital.

A—No; I didn't go there. They tried to ask me. My sisters asked me. Some people told my sister that you were there. I am of sound mind. I never went there. Everything that transpired during the tragedy, I was at the Morning News Building.

Congressman Ford. You didn't go out there subsequent to the assassination?

A—No; in other words, like somebody is trying to make me something of a martyr in that case. No; I never did.

Does this conflict with my story and yours in great length?

Mr. Moore. Substantially the same, Jack, as well as I remember.

Mr. Rankin. Did you say anything about people of your religion have guts, or something like that?

A—I said it. I never said it up there. I said, I could have said, "Weren't you afraid of getting your head blown off?" I said, "Well, to be truthful, I have a little nerve." I could have said that.

Now I could have said to the doctor that was sent to me, Bromberg, because there is a certain familiarity you have, because it is like you have an attorney representing you, it is there. I mean, it is there.

But I did say this. McWillie made a statement about me, something to the effect that "he is considered a pretty rough guy," this McWillie. He said, "One thing about Jack Ruby, he runs this club and no one runs over him."

419

And you have a different type of entertainment here than any other part of the country, our type of entertainment.

But I don't recall that. I could have said the sentimental feeling that I may have used.

Representative Ford. When you flew to Cuba, where did you go from Dallas en route? What was the step-by-step process by which you arrived at Havana?

A—I think I told Mr. Moore I stopped in New Orleans. Sometime I stopped in New Orleans, and I don't remember if I stopped in Florida or New Orleans, but I know I did stop in New Orleans, because I bought some Carioca rum coming back.

I know I was to Miami on a stopover. It could have been on the way back. I only went to Cuba once, so naturally, when I bought the Carioca rum, there was a couple of fellows that sell tickets for Delta Airlines, and they know me like I know you, and I am sure you gentlemen have spoken to them, and they were to tell me where to go in Havana, and have a ball, and I told them why I was going there, and who I was going to look up, and everything else.

Representative Ford. They were Delta Airlines employees in New Orleans or Dallas?

A—No; in New Orleans. Evidentally I went out to the Delta Airlines at Love Field and caught the plane. I may have taken the flight—here is what could have happened. I could have made a double stop from Havana on the way back in taking in Miami, and then taking another plane to New Orleans, I am not certain.

But I only made one trip to Havana. Yet I know I was in Miami, Fla. and I was in New Orleans.

And the next time I went to New Orleans, when I tried to look up some showgirl by the name of Jada, I stopped in to see the same fellows at Delta Airlines.

Mr. Rankin. Do you recall going up the elevator after the shooting of Oswald?

A—That is so small to remember, I guess it is automatic, you know.

Mr. Rankin. Did you have this gun a long while that you did the shooting with?

A—Yes.

Mr. Rankin. You didn't carry it all the time?

A—I did. I had it in a little bag with money constantly. I carry my money.

Chief Justice Warren. Congressman, do you have anything further?

A—You can get more out of me. Let's not break up too soon. . . .

Chief Justice Warren. Now you said there were some other things. Would you mind telling us anything you have on your mind?

A—No; because as I said earlier, you seem to have gotten the juicy part of the story up to now in the various spasmodic way of my telling it.

How valuable am I to you to give you all this information?

Chief Justice Warren. Well, how valuable is rather an indefinite term, but I think it is very helpful to our Commission report. I think the report would have been deficient if it had not been for this interview we have had with you.

So we are interested in anything that you would like to tell us, in your own language.

A—The only thing is this. If I cannot get these tests you give, it is pretty haphazard to tell you the things I should tell you.

Mr. Moore, you seem to have known more about my interrogation than anybody else, right?

Mr. Moore. I think you have told us about everything you told me.

Mr. Rankin. It isn't entirely clear how you feel that your family and you yourself are threatened by your telling what you have to the Commission.

How do you come to the conclusion that they might be killed? Will you tell us a little bit more about that, if you can?

A—Well, assuming that, as I stated before, some persons are accusing me falsely of being part of the plot—naturally, in all the time from over 6 months ago, my family has been so interested in helping me.

Mr. Rankin. By that, you mean a party to the plot of Oswald?

A—That I was party to a plot to silence Oswald.

All right now, when your family believes you and knows your mannerisms and your thoughts, and knows your sincerity, they have lived with you all your life and know your emotional feelings and your patriotism—on the surface, they see me only as the guilty assailant of Oswald, and by helping me like they have, going all out.

My brother who has a successful business, I know he is going to be killed. And I haven't seen him in years. And suddenly he feels that he wants to help me, because he believes that I couldn't be any further involved than the actual——

When I told him I did it because of Mrs. Kennedy, that is all he had to hear, because I would never involve my family or involve him in a conspiracy.

Everyone haven't let me down. Because they read the newspapers away from Dallas that stated certain facts about me, but they are untrue, because they wouldn't come out and put those things in the newspapers that they should be putting in; and people outside of Dallas read the Dallas newspapers and are all in sympathy with me, as far as the country itself.

421

That they felt, well, Jack did it. They probably felt they would do the same thing.

That sympathy isn't going to help me, because the people that have the power here, they have a different verdict. They already have me as the accused assassin of our beloved President.

Now if I sound screwy telling you this, then I must be screwy.

Chief Justice Warren. Mr. Ruby, I think you are entitled to a statement to this effect, because you have been frank with us and have told us your story.

I think I can say to you that there has been no witness before this Commission out of the hundreds we have questioned who has claimed to have any personal knowledge that you were a party to any conspiracy to kill our President.

A—Yes; but you don't know this area here.

Chief Justice Warren. No; I don't vouch for anything except that I think I am correct in that, am I not?

Mr. Rankin. That is correct.

Chief Justice Warren. I just wanted to tell you before our own Commission, and I might say to you also that we have explored the situation.

A—I know, but I want to say this to you. If certain people have the means and want to gain something by propagandizing something to their own use, they will make ways to present certain things that I do look guilty.

Chief Justice Warren. Well, I will make this additional statement to you, that if any witness should testify before the Commission that you were, to their knowledge, a party to any conspiracy to assassinate the President, I assure you that we will give you the opportunity to deny it and to take any tests that you may desire to so disprove it.

I don't anticipate that there will be any such testimony, but should there be, we will give you that opportunity.

Does that seem fair?

A—No; that isn't going to save my family.

Chief Justice Warren. Well, we can't do everything at once.

A—I am in a tough spot, and I don't know what the solution can be to save me.

And I know our wonderful President, Lyndon Johnson, as soon as he was the President of his country, he appointed you as head of this group. But through certain falsehoods that have been said about me to other people, the John Birch Society, I am as good as guilty as the accused assassin of President Kennedy.

How can you remedy that, Mr. Warren? Do any of you men have any ways of remedying that?

Mr. Bill Decker said be a man and speak up. I am making

a statement now that I may not live the next hour when I walk out of this room.

Now it is the most fantastic story you have ever heard in a lifetime. I did something out of the goodness of my heart. Unfortunately, Chief Earl Warren, had you been around 5 or 6 months ago, and I know your hands were tied, you couldn't do it, and immediately the President would have gotten ahold of my true story, or whatever would have been said about me, a certain organization wouldn't have so completely formed now, so powerfully, to use me because I am of the Jewish extraction, Jewish faith, to commit the most dastardly crime that has ever been committed.

Can you understand now in visualizing what happened, what powers, what momentum has been carried on to create this feeling of mass feeling against my people, against certain people that were against them prior to their power?

That goes over your head, doesn't it?

Chief Justice Warren. Well, I don't quite get the full significance of it, Mr. Ruby. I know what you feel about the John Birch Society.

A—Very powerful.

Chief Justice Warren. I think it is powerful, yes I do. Of course, I don't have all the information that you feel you have on that subject.

A—Unfortunately, you don't have, because it is too late. And I wish that our beloved President, Lyndon Johnson, would have delved deeper into the situation, hear me, not to accept just circumstantial facts about my guilt or innocence, and would have questioned to find out the truth about me before he relinquished certain powers to these certain people.

Chief Justice Warren. Well, I am afraid I don't know what power you believe he relinquished to them. I think that it is difficult to understand what you have to say.

A—I want to say this to you. The Jewish people are being exterminated at this moment. Consequently, a whole new form of government is going to take over our country, and I know I won't live to see you another time.

Do I sound sort of screwy in telling you these things?

Chief Justice Warren. No; I think that is what you believe, or you wouldn't tell it under your oath.

A—But it is a very serious situation. I guess it is too late to stop it, isn't it?

All right, I want to ask you this. All you men have been chosen by the President for this committee, is that correct?

Chief Justice Warren. Representative Ford and I are the only members of the Commission that are here.

Mr. Rankin of the Commission is employed as our chief counsel.

Mr. Rankin employed Mr. Specter and Mr. Ball as members of the staff.

You know who the other gentlemen here are.

You know that Mr. Moore is a member of the Secret Service, and he has been a liaison officer with our staff since the Commission was formed.

Representative Ford. Are there any questions that ought to be asked to help clarify the situation that you described?

A—There is only one thing. If you don't take me back to Washington tonight to give me a chance to prove to the President that I am not guilty, then you will see the most tragic thing that will ever happen.

And if you don't have the power to take me back, I won't be around to be able to prove my innocence or guilt.

Now up to this moment, I have been talking with you for how long?

Chief Justice Warren. I would say for the better part of 3 hours.

A—All right, wouldn't it be ridiculous for me to speak sensibly all this time and give you this climactic talk that I have?

Maybe something can be saved, something can be done.

What have you got to answer to that, Chief Justice Warren?

Chief Justice Warren. Well, I don't know what can be done, Mr. Ruby, because I don't know what you anticipate we will encounter.

Representative Ford. Is there anything more you can tell us if you went back to Washington?

A—Yes; are you sincere in wanting to take me back?

Representative Ford. We are most interested in all the information you have.

A—All I know is maybe something can be saved. Because right now, I want to tell you this, I am used as a scapegoat, and there is no greater weapon that you can use to create some falsehood about some of the Jewish faith, especially at the terrible heinous crime such as the killing of President Kennedy.

Now maybe something can be saved. It may not be too late, whatever happens, if our President, Lyndon Johnson, knew the truth from me.

But if I am eliminated, there won't be any way of knowing.

Right now, when I leave your presence now, I am the only one that can bring out the truth to our President, who believes in righteousness and justice.

But he has been told, I am certain, that I was part of a plot to assassinate the President.

I know your hands are tied; you are helpless.

Chief Justice Warren. Mr. Ruby, I think I can say this to you, that if he has been told any such thing, there is no indication of any kind that he believes it.

A—I am sorry, Chief Justice Warren, I thought I would be very effective in telling you what I have said here. But in all fairness to everyone, maybe all I want to do is beg that if they found out I was telling the truth, maybe they can succeed in what their motives are, but maybe my people won't be tortured and mutilated.

Chief Justice Warren. Well, you may be sure that the President and his whole Commission will do anything that is necessary to see that your people are not tortured.

A—No.

Chief Justice Warren. You may be sure of that.

A—No; the only way you can do it is if he knows the truth, that I am telling the truth, and why I was down in that basement Sunday morning, and maybe some sense of decency will come out and they can still fulfill their plan, as I stated before, without my people going through torture and mutilation.

Chief Justice Warren. The President will know everything that you have said, everything that you have said.

A—But I won't be around, Chief Justice. I won't be around to verify these things you are going to tell the President.

Mr. Tonahill. Who do you think is going to eliminate you, Jack?

A—I have been used for a purpose, and there will be a certain tragic occurrence happening if you don't take my testimony and somehow vindicate me so my people don't suffer because of what I have done.

Chief Justice Warren. But we have taken your testimony. We have it here. It will be in permanent form for the President of the United States and for the Congress of the United States, and for the courts of the United States, and for the people of the entire world.

It is there. It will be recorded for all to see. That is the purpose of our coming here today. We feel that you are entitled to have your story told.

A—You have lost me though. You have lost me, Chief Justice Warren.

Chief Justice Warren. Lost you in what sense?

A—I won't be around for you to come and question me again.

Chief Justice Warren. Well, it is very hard for me to believe that. I am sure that everybody would want to protect you to the very limit.

A—All I want is a lie detector test, and you refuse to give it to me.

Because as it stands now—and the truth serum, and any other—Pentothal—how do you pronounce it, whatever it is. And they will not give it to me, because I want to tell the truth.

And then I want to leave this world. But I don't want my people to be blamed for something that is untrue, that they claim has happened.

Chief Justice Warren. Mr. Ruby, I promise you that you will be able to take such a test.

A—When?

Chief Justice Warren. You will have to let me see when we can figure that out. But I assure you, it won't be delayed, because our desire is to terminate the work of the Commission and make our report to the public just as soon as possible, so there won't be any misunderstanding caused by all of these rumors or stories that have been put out that are not consistent with the evidence in the case.

But it will not be unnecessarily delayed, and we will do it on behalf of the Commission, I promise you.

A—All I want, and I beg you—when are you going to see the President?

Chief Justice Warren. Well, I have no date with the President. I don't know just when. But as soon as I do see him, I will be glad to tell him what you have said.

A—All I want is to take a polygraph to tell the truth. That is all I want to do.

Chief Justice Warren. Yes; that, I promise you you can do.

A—Because my people are going to suffer about things that will be said about me.

Chief Justice Warren. Yes; well, I promise.

A—Hold on another minute.

Chief Justice Warren. All right.

A—How do you know if the facts I stated about everything I said, statements with reference to, are the truth or not?

Chief Justice Warren. Well, if you want a test made to test those principal questions, we will work them out so they can be tested.

As I understand it, you can't use the polygraph to say now this is the story.

A—I know that.

Chief Justice Warren. To say you have the story of Jack Ruby. You can't do that.

A—I know that. You can clarify by questioning me when I conceived the idea and what my answer would naturally be that Sunday morning.

Chief Justice Warren. Maybe I can help the situation this way. Suppose you list for us, if you can, the questions that you would like to have asked of you on the polygraph to establish the truth of your testimony.

What things do you consider vital in it, and what would you like to have verified?

A—Yes; but you are telling me to do these things—these things are going to be promised, but you see they aren't going to let me do these things.

Because when you leave here, I am finished. My family is finished.

Representative Ford. Isn't it true, Mr. Chief Justice, that the same maximum protection and security Mr. Ruby has been given in the past will be continued?

A—But now that I have divulged certain information because I want to be honest, all I want to take is a polygraph test and tell the truth about things and combat the lies that have been told about me.

Now maybe certain people don't want to know the truth that may come out of me. Is that plausible?

Representative Ford. In other words, the Chief Justice has agreed, and I on the Commission wholeheartedly concur, that you will be given a polygraph test as expeditiously as possible.

And I am sure you can rely on what has been stated here by the Chairman.

A—How are we going to communicate and so on?

Chief Justice Warren. We will communicate directly with you.

A—You have a lost cause, Earl Warren. You don't stand a chance. They feel about you like they do about me, Chief Justice Warren.

I shouldn't hurt your feelings in telling you that.

Chief Justice Warren. That won't hurt my feelings, because I have had some evidence of the feeling that some people have concerning me.

A—But you are the only one that can save me. I think you can.

Chief Justice Warren. Yes?

A—But by delaying minutes, you lose the chance. And all I want to do is tell the truth, and that is all.

There was no conspiracy. But by you telling them what you are going to do and how you are going to do it is too late as of this moment.

Chief Justice Warren. You take my word for it and the word of Representative Ford, that we will do this thing at the earliest possible moment, and that it will be done in time. It will be done in time.

A—Well, you won't ever see me again, I tell you that. And I have lost my family.

Chief Justice Warren. Yes?

A—No, no; you don't believe me, do you?

Chief Justice Warren. To be frank with you, I believe that you are not stating now what is the fact.

I don't say you don't believe it, but I believe that I will be able to see you again and that we will be able to take this test that you are speaking of.

Well, I think we have tired Mr. Ruby. We have had him here for close to 4 hours now, and I am sure our reporter must be equally tired, but we appreciate your patience and your willingness to testify in this manner for us.

A—All I want to do is tell the truth, and the only way you can know it is by the polygraph, as that is the only way you can know it.

Chief Justice Warren. That we will do for you.

Ruby was first interrogated by the commission at the Dallas County Jail on June 7, 1964. On July 18, Ruby continued his testimony there and was given the lie detector test on which he had insisted the month before. Before each series of questions, Ruby was told what they would be and any misunderstanding about their meaning was cleared up:

Mr. Herndon. The test will now begin.

"Is your first name Jack?"

A—"Yes."

Mr. Herndon. "Is your last name Ruby?"

A—"Yes."

Mr. Herndon. "Did you voluntarily request this test?"

A—"Yes."

Mr. Herndon. "Did you know Oswald before November 22, 1963?"

A—"No."

Mr. Herndon. "Do you use the middle name 'Leon'?"

A—(no immediate response). How can I answer that? I don't have my driver's license, but I don't use it.

Mr. Herndon. All right, just sit still and we will discuss it. "Did you assist Oswald in the assassination?"

A—"No."

Mr. Herndon. "Have you ever been arrested?"

A—"Yes."

Mr. Herndon. "Did you take any medication this morning?"

A—"No."

Mr. Herndon. "Have you answered all my questions truthfully?"

A—"Yes."

Mr. Herndon. This first series is over. If you will just sit still for a moment, I will release the pressure on your arm, and you may now move your arm and relax and get the circulation moving.

A—I'm all right.

Mr. Herndon. That wasn't too bad, sir; was it?

A—(no response).

Mr. Herndon. Mr. Ruby, there are two questions I want to ask you about on our first series.

I know you couldn't refrain from laughing and talking about that middle name of "Leon." Do you want to further explain that?

A—Yes; I don't use it, so hence it's sort of a remembrance of a very good friend of mine. I used it on my driver's license, but since then it has become a habit of keeping it on my driver's license, but I've never been called with it and very rarely do I sign papers that way, but once I stated it on my

428

driver's license, I had to follow through with it that way, and that's the answer to it. Once you have it on your driver's license, you have to have it the same way.

Mr. Herndon. Do you like the name "Leon"?

A—Well, I did more for sentimental reasons, but as I went along later I sort of dropped it.

Mr. Herndon. Is is actually on your driver's license, though?

A—I think it's Jack L. Ruby. No—Jack Leon Ruby. It's Jack Leon Ruby on my driver's license and that's something that once you start with it, and it's been years ago, when you renew your license, it remains the same, but outside of signing papers or contracts or anything of vital importance, you only find out it's much simpler to sign "Jack Ruby."

Mr. Herndon. All right, Mr. Ruby, and one other question. I would just like to ask you what went on in your mind when you did answer the question "Yes" to "Have you ever been arrested?"

A—Well, the police had taken me—I had been arrested, because when the police officer said, "Jack, come on, we're taking you down," you're arrested.

Mr. Herndon. When was this? Are you referring to this current or some previous time?

A—Previous to that.

Mr. Herndon. What situation was that?

A—Well, it was—I was arrested for dancing after curfew. Some fellows smuggled in intoxicants after hours.

Mr. Herndon. Was this here in your own place or some other place?

A—At my own place. No felony crime, nothing serious—only misdemeanors.

Mr. Herndon. You consider that was a misdemeanor?

A—Oh, yes; in other words—a $25 fine. I never have been in any criminal activity.

Mr. Herndon. Very fine. Does your arm feel all right now?

A—Yes.

Mr. Herndon. Very good. We have finished with the first series. . . .

Mr. Herndon. I will now begin.

"Were you born in the United States?"

A—"Yes."

Mr. Herndon. "Were you born in Chicago?"

A—"Yes."

Mr. Herndon. "Are you now a member of the Communist Party?"

A—"No."

Mr. Herndon. "Have you ever been known by another name?"

Don't answer that question. I didn't review it before. Skip it. Just sit and relax.

"Have you ever been a member of the Communist Party?"

429

A—"No."

Mr. Herndon. "Did you ever make a false official statement?"

A—"No."

Mr. Herndon. "Are you now a member of any group that advocates the violent overthrow of the United States Government?"

A—"No."

Mr. Herndon. "Have you ever been a member of any group that advocates violent overthrow of the United States Government?"

A—"No."

Mr. Herndon. "Were you born in 1911?"

A—"Yes."

Mr. Herndon. That concludes that series. Just sit still for a moment, sir.

All right, you may now move your arm and relax, Mr. Ruby.

A—All right. . . .

Mr. Herndon. The test will now begin. Look straight ahead, Mr. Ruby.

"Is your last name Ruby?"

A—"Yes."

Mr. Herndon. "Do you live in Dallas?"

A—"Yes."

Mr. Herndon. "Between the assassination and the shooting, did anybody you know tell you they knew Oswald?"

A—"No."

Mr. Herndon. "Are you married?"

A—"No."

Mr. Herndon. "Aside from anything you said to George Senator on Sunday morning, did you tell anyone else that you intended to shoot Oswald?"

A—"No."

Mr. Herndon. "Were you in the military service?"

A—"Yes."

Mr. Herndon. "While in service did you receive any disciplinary action?"

A—"No."

Mr. Herndon. "Did you shoot Oswald in order to silence him?"

A—"No."

Mr. Herndon. "Have you ever served time in jail?"

A—(no response).

Mr. Herndon. The test is over. Sit still for a moment and we will release the pressure on your arm.

Do you feel a little better when I release that pressure?

A—When you elaborate on "serving time", 30 days isn't serving time.

Mr. Herndon. I was going to ask you to explain that, and you followed instructions explicitly there.

430

Then, actually in explanation to that, this 30 days to you were insignificant?

A—Well, yes, but I explained that.

Mr. Herndon. That's all right. I have to ask these questions.

A—To serve time is when you refer to a man being in the penitentiary.

Mr. Herndon. Now, there are a few questions I want to ask him with regard to that series.

Mr. Specter. Go ahead.

Mr. Herndon. Just two points I want to clarify for my own use here.

Mr. Ruby, I asked you, "Are you married?" and you replied "No." Could you tell me if anything went on in your mind at the time you responded "No"?

A—Yes; I was thinking of the young girl, that had I been married I wouldn't have been in this trouble. I guess that's what flashed back in my mind.

Mr. Herndon. Is this a former sweetheart?

A—Yes. What else?

Mr. Herndon. I just wanted to get your explanation at that particular point?

A—You noticed something there?

Mr. Herndon. Did you feel anything?

A—Yes; I knew I wasn't—something was working on me when you asked me that. I would probably have been living in another part of the city, and I wouldn't have been involved in this. . . .

Mr. Herndon. All right, that clarifies that question for me. One other area I'd like you to speak frankly and freely on, and here again it gets back to this military service. I asked you, "While in the military service, did you ever receive any disciplinary action?"

A—No.

Mr. Herndon. Did you ever get in any trouble at all while you were in the service that came to your mind during that question?

A—When you say "trouble"?

Mr. Herndon. Disciplinary action for trouble?

A—No; I have never been called down for anything. I may have had a brawl with another soldier.

Mr. Herndon. Did you while you were in the service ever have a fight?

A—Yes; but when you speak of "disciplinary" is when you go before a court-martial or the colonel calls you in or something happens.

Mr. Herndon. Were you called in before the commanding officer?

A—Sure; but it's not important enough to answer. Evidently, you're getting a pretty good reading?

Mr. Herndon. I'm having no technical difficulty with regard to giving the test. . . .

Mr. Herndon. Sit perfectly still and try to concentrate and look straight ahead and answer the questions truthfully "Yes" or "No."

I now put some pressure on that arm cuff.

The test will now begin.

Mr. Herndon. "Is your first name Jack?"

A—"Yes."

Mr. Herndon. "Is your last name Ruby?"

A—"Yes."

Mr. Herndon. "Did you first decide to shoot Oswald on Friday night?"

A—"No."

Mr. Herndon. "Did you first decide to shoot Oswald on Saturday morning?"

A—"No."

Mr. Herndon. "Did you first decide to shoot Oswald on Saturday night?"

A—"No."

Mr. Herndon. "Did you first decide to shoot Oswald on Sunday morning?"

A—"Yes."

Mr. Herndon. "Have you answered all questions truthfully?"

A—"Yes."

Mr. Herndon. The test is over. Will you sit still a moment. I will release the pressure on your arms. You may now move your hands and get the circulation back. I have no questions on that. . . .

Mr. Herndon. All right, I will now put some pressure on the arm cuff, and I will tell you when I am going to start asking you questions, Mr. Ruby.

We will now begin.

Mr. Herndon. "Do you still operate the Carousel Club?"

A—"No."

Mr. Herndon. "Were you on the sidewalk at the time Lieutenant Pierce's car stopped on the ramp exit?"

A—"Yes."

Mr. Herndon. "Did you previously live in Chicago?"

A—"Yes."

Mr. Herndon. Try to sit still, if you can.

A—All right.

Mr. Herndon. "Did you enter the jail by walking through an alleyway?"

A—"No."

Mr. Herndon. "Are your parents alive?"

A—"No."

Mr. Herndon. "Did you walk past the guard at the time Lieutenant Pierce's car was parked on the ramp exit?"

A—"Yes."

Mr. Herndon. "Did you ever make a false insurance claim?"

A—"No."

Mr. Herndon. "Did you talk with any Dallas police officers on Sunday, November 24, prior to the shooting of Oswald?"

A—"No."

Mr. Herndon. That series is over. If you will sit still for a moment, Mr. Ruby. I will now release the pressure from your arms.

A—Am I acting a little nervous?

Mr. Herndon. A little, but I think you're getting a little bit tired. That's quite all right. I notice a little motion, but I will certainly take that into consideration when I evaluate and interpret these charts.

Mr. Herndon. Is there any area of doubt at all in your mind about that question where you were on the sidewalk at the time Lieutenant Pierce's car stopped at the ramp exit?

A—I said I was on the sidewalk—I walked past.

Mr. Herndon. Yes; did that question trouble you then?

A—No.

Mr. Herndon. You were on the sidewalk?

A—Yes.

Mr. Herndon. I just wanted to clarify that. When I asked you, "Are your parents alive?", Mr. Ruby, have they been deceased for some time?

A—Yes.

Mr. Herndon. Did that question bother you or trouble you at all?

A—No; I don't know—I guess I'm nervous now—I don't know just why I said that.

Mr. Herndon. I have no further questions in that series.

A—Aren't you going to ask me whether I knew anything as to whether or not he was going to come down, or anything like that?

Mr. Herndon. We will have to prepare some more questions. . . .

Now, here's a question I want to go over with you very carefully. Did you ever hit anyone with any kind of weapon?

A—Yes.

Mr. Herndon. All right; I'll give you an opportunity now to explain that to me. This is for my purposes of the examination.

A—Well, in running a—in my business, when you get somebody with a—it's a very exciting business. One particular night a man pulled a knife on me and I took a pistol and hit him on the head in that altercation, and sometimes you get fellows with real bad reputations. They're real toughs. There's no question about it, and being in my type of business for a livelihood, the only way you can—of course, I do call the law enforcement officers. At that particular moment, it's my life or theirs, and some of these men are pretty powerful physically, and I fought in every way possible, with my fists and everything else—but

433

to minimize the various troubles I had, where there would be an altercation or something come up, I'd tell them to leave, and of course, something would happen and they would go from here—whatever it is. It happened a few times where I would pummel a few of these men.

Mr. *Herndon.* I understand, Mr. Ruby, but all of these incidents that you recall are in connection with your operating this club?

A—Yes; they are at the club. These boys are real bad boys and they all have records, and they're pretty tough guys. Will you agree with something on that?

Mr. *Alexander.* That's right.

Mr. *Herndon.* Then, on the actual test, I'm going to ask you this question: "Other than what you've told me, did you ever hit anyone with any kind of weapon?"

A—I don't follow—"Other than what you've told me?"

Mr. *Herndon.* In other words, other than your being the owner of a nightclub, which because of the type of customers you occasionally have, you would have to use some force, perhaps hit a customer or hit someone in your club?

A—Yes.

Mr. *Herndon.* Have you ever been involved in any other situation where you actually struck at somebody with a weapon? "Weapon" here I'm referring to as a gun, club, or knife or anything that would be other than just a normal fistfight.

A—Yes; that happened, but that was before I got in this trouble. This man threatened to kill me and was going to go for his gun, and I was nice enough to have him stay at my place and he was causing a nuisance in the vicinity of the club, causing brawls and all that and I tried to reprimand him, and a little boy of Italian descent and very gracious, somehow he got very belligerent with me, and I knew he had a car and he said, "I'm going to get my pistol," and there's a funny reaction about that. Once they get you cowered to that extent, then you're doomed, and there's a funny feeling, when I was with him, that you have with them. So, I got my pistol and I cornered him and I called him by his name, and I called him a name, and I said, "You're going to kill me, you so-and-so?" Finally he said, "I was only kidding, I was only kidding," and there's a certain reaction you have and I can't explain it. That's the only time any crime of that sort has ever happened outside of my business.

Mr. *Herndon.* Outside of your business?

A—Yes, sir.

Mr. *Herndon.* Then, if I asked you whether or not you told me you ever hit anyone with any kind of weapon, unless something else comes up to your mind, you would answer that "Yes"?

A—Yes, like if I was a goon or something.

Mr. Herndon. Yes, a union goon.

A—A union goon. Right. I haven't been a slugger or anything like that.

Mr. Herndon. All right, we can go along here Mr. Ruby, and I will hook up the instrument.

Mr. Herndon. Will you raise your arms, Mr. Ruby, please? Do you feel comfortable?

A—Yes.

Mr. Herndon. Now, lean back. [Attached instruments to Mr. Ruby.]

A—Have I been evading any of your questions?

Mr. Herndon. You have been most cooperative—thus far no problems.

A—But you can't tell how I stand, can you?

Mr. Herndon. Mr. Ruby, I will want to take a considerable amount of time to review these charts very thoroughly before I come to any conclusion.

A—How long would it take—how long will it take?

Mr. Herndon. Well, I can't answer that question with a definite answer. It depends on what I may run into when I study these very carefully back in Washington.

A—Bill, will I still be around when the answers come back?

Mr. Alexander. Yes.

A—Raise your right hand and give him your word.

Mr. Alexander. That's right.

A—Chief, you heard him, did you not, Chief? [Addressing the Chief Jailer Holman.] You and I should live so long. . . .

Mr. Herndon. Now, Mr. Ruby, look straight ahead. That's fine. Now, just look straight ahead and try not to move, and the test will begin.

"Is your last name Ruby?

A—"Yes."

Mr. Herndon. "Did you see the armored car before it entered the basement?"

A—"No."

Mr. Henderson. "Do you have any brothers?"

A—"Yes."

Mr. Herndon. "Did you enter the police department through a door at the rear on the east side of the jail?"

A—"No."

Mr. Herndon. "Do you have any sisters?"

A—"Yes."

Mr. Herndon. "After talking to Little Lynn did you hear any announcement that Oswald was about to be moved?"

A—"No."

Mr. Herndon. "Other than what you've told me, did you ever hit anyone with any kind of weapon?"

A—I don't know how to answer that.

Mr. Herndon. All right, just sit still and relax, sir.

435

A—Ask me that again—I got the answer.

Mr. Herndon. "Other than what you've told me, did you ever hit anyone with any kind of weapon?"

A—"No."

Mr. Herndon. "Before you left your apartment Sunday morning, did anyone tell you the armored car was on the way to the police department?"

A—"No."

Mr. Herndon. "Have you answered all questions truthfully?"

A—"Yes."

Mr. Herndon. All right, that test is over. Just sit still for a moment, and I will now release the pressure on your arm. You can move your left arm and relax. . . .

A—The most important question—you haven't asked me yet—why did I shoot Oswald?

Mr. Alexander. Jack, they can't ask that kind of question for this machine. They can only ask you—was it for a certain purpose. It has to be a "Yes" or "No" answer.

A—The point is—if I was carried away emotionally, and because I felt that, it sounds so unbelievable. Why shouldn't I be asked a question—why—what motivated me to do it?

Mr. Specter. Mr. Ruby, answer now the question, "Why did you shoot Oswald?" and then we will turn that around into a question to ask you for a "Yes" or "No" answer.

A—At the particular moment, after watching television all that——

Mr. Fowler. Jack, let me interject right now, again, as your attorney—I advise you not to answer this question.

A—Clayton, I'm sorry, I've got to answer it. I've got to, because, believe me, it means an awful lot to me. I didn't want —I felt so carried away—that at that particular time of the great tragedy, I felt somehow in my little bit of a way I could save Mrs. Kennedy the ordeal of coming back for trial here.

Mr. Specter. All right, fine, Mr. Ruby. That's the same answer to that general question that you gave when the Commission heard your testimony, and we shall phrase that in an appropriate question for the polygraph examination. Now, will you proceed, Mr. Herndon, with our next series, please? . . .

Mr. Herndon. The test will now begin.

"Is your name Jack Ruby?"

A—"Yes."

Mr. Herndon. "Did you get a Wall Street Journal at the Southwestern Drug Store during the week before the assassination?"

A—"No."

Mr. Herndon. "Are you tired?"

A—"No."

Mr. Herndon. "Do you have any knowledge of a Wall Street Journal addressed to Mr. J. E. Bradshaw?"

A—"No."

436

Mr. Herndon. "Did you previously live in San Francisco?"

A—"Yes."

Mr. Herndon. "To your knowledge, did any of your friends or did you telephone the FBI in Dallas between 2 or 3 a.m. Sunday morning?"

A—"No."

Mr. Herndon. "Did you ever overcharge a customer?"

A—"No."

Mr. Herndon. "Did you or any of your friends to your knowledge telephone the sheriff's office between 2 or 3 a.m. Sunday morning?"

A—"No."

Mr. Herndon. I think that series is over and I will release the pressure.

(Reporter's note: 7:10 p.m.)

A—Are they that important—those questions? I know more important ones than that. Of course—I'm kidding.

Mr. Herndon. We have some more coming.

Mr. Ruby, has a customer by any chance ever claimed that they were overcharged at your place? Have you ever had any problems along that line?

A—Oh, yes—we have problems with waitresses and big bills. . . .

Mr. Herndon. All right, relax. We will now begin.

"Do you intend to answer these questions truthfully?"

A—"Yes; I do."

Mr. Herndon. Just answer the questions "Yes" or "No," please.

A—OK.

Mr. Herndon. "Did you go to the Dallas police station at any time on Friday, November 22, 1963, before you went to the synagogue?"

A—"No."

Mr. Herndon. "Do you attend the synagogue regularly?"

A—How can I answer that one?

Mr. Herndon. Just relax. "Did you go to the synagogue that Friday night?"

A—"Yes."

Mr. Herndon. "Do you pray?"

A—"Yes."

Mr. Herndon. "Did you see Oswald in the Dallas jail on Friday night?"

A—"Yes."

Mr. Herndon. "Were you at one time employed by a union?"

A—"Yes."

Mr. Herndon. "Did you have a gun with you when you went to the Friday midnight press conference at the jail?"

A—"No."

Mr. Herndon. "Is everything you told the Warren Commission the entire truth?"

A—"Yes."

Mr. Herndon. That series is over. Just sit still for a moment, Mr. Ruby, and I will release the pressure on your arm, and you may now move.

Mr. Herndon. At the beginning of that series, Mr. Ruby, you displayed a little nervousness and a little tension. Perhaps it was the question I asked with regard to the synagogue. Did that upset you in any way?

A—Because—you're ashamed to admit you haven't been going regular—yet, you don't want to come out with a blunt answer "No"—it makes you sort of an atheist, and I didn't want to answer it that way, but I do go to the high holidays, but going regular and going to the high holidays are two different ways of going. People that go regular go every Friday night and pretty regular during the week, but my hours were entirely different. I mean—I'm trying to explain that to you.

Mr. Herndon. Yes; that's what I want you to do. Go ahead, sir.

A—I could say "Yes" and I would be lying to you saying "Yes." Anyway, the last couple of years—the last year and a half or 2 years have been very tough to me businesswise and I've stayed pretty close, outside the high holidays. . . .

Mr. Herndon. The test will now begin.

"Is your last name Ruby?"

A—"Yes."

Mr. Herndon. "Have you ever knowingly attended any meetings of the Communist Party or any other group that advocates violent overthrow of the Government?"

A—"No."

Mr. Herndon. "Did you legally change your last name?"

A—"Yes."

Mr. Herndon. "Is any member of your immediate family or any close friend, a member of the Communist Party?"

A—"No."

Mr. Herndon. "Were you in the Army Air Corps?"

A—"Yes."

Mr. Herndon. "Is any member of your immediate family or any close friend a member of any group that advocates the violent overthrow of the Government?"

A—"No."

Mr. Herndon. Look straight ahead, please, sir. "Did any close friend or any member of your immediate family ever attend a meeting of the Communist Party?"

A—"No."

Mr. Herndon. "Did any close friend or any member of your immediate family ever attend a meeting of any group that advocates the violent overthrow of the Government?"

A—"No."

Mr. Herndon. That series is over. . . .

We will now begin.

438

"Did you ever meet Oswald at your post office box?"

A—"No."

Mr. Herndon. "Did you use your post office mailbox to do any business with Mexico or Cuba?"

A—"No."

Mr. Herndon. "Did you do business with Castro-Cuba?"

A—"No."

Mr. Herndon. "Was your trip to Cuba solely for pleasure?"

A—"Yes."

Mr. Herndon. "Have you now told us the truth concerning why you carried $2,200 in cash on you?"

A—"Yes."

Mr. Herndon. "Did any foreign influence cause you to shoot Oswald?"

A—"No."

Mr. Herndon. "Did you shoot Oswald because of any influence of the underworld?"

A—"No."

Mr. Herndon. I'm going to stop here a moment, sir, and release the pressure on your arm and you just relax for a moment. Then I shall begin again in a moment.

A—Okay.

Mr. Herndon. Just relax, Mr. Ruby.

Does your arm feel all right?

A—Fine—I'm all right.

Mr. Herndon. I will continue this next series of questions and it will be listed as series 9a. We will begin again.

"Did you shoot Oswald because of a labor union influence?"

A—"No."

Mr. Herndon. "Did any long-distance telephone calls which you made before the assassination of the President have anything to do with the assassination?"

A—"No."

Mr. Herndon. "Did any of your long-distance telephone calls concern the shooting of Oswald?"

A—"No."

Mr. Herndon. "Did you shoot Oswald in order to save Mrs. Kennedy the ordeal of a trial?"

A—"Yes."

Mr. Herndon. "Did you know the Tippit that was killed?"

A—"No."

Mr. Herndon. "Did you tell the truth about relaying the message to Ray Brantley to get McWillie a few guns?"

A—"Yes."

Mr. Herndon. "Did you go to the assembly room on Friday night to get the telephone number of KLIF?"

A—"Yes."

Mr. Herndon. "Did you ever meet with Oswald and Officer Tippit at your club?"

A—"No."

Mr. Herndon. That completes that series. . . .

I notice during the time—all the time I ask you questions, Mr. Ruby, that you close your eyes. If that's a way that you concentrate, that's perfectly all right.

A—That's why—if I were guilty of something or if I were trying to evade something, certainly closing your eyes would be less advantageous for you to cover up something. Do you follow me? In other words, closing your eyes means that I do want to tell the truth.

Mr. Herndon. That's what I want you to do—just concentrate on the question alone and you have to make that decision whether you will answer it "Yes" or "No".

A—In other words, if I was trying to cover up anything, I wouldn't try to get more of a vision of what you're trying to refer me to.

Mr. Herndon. All right, if you will look straight ahead now, and sit perfectly still, we will begin, and I will let you know when we're going to ask the first question.

A—In other words, I'm trying to be more emphatic with the truth when I close my eyes—more than the truth.

Mr. Herndon. Would you put your complete left hand on that arm rest—that's it.

The test will now begin.

"Is your name Jack Ruby?"

A—"Yes."

Mr. Herndon. "Were you at the Parkland Hospital at any time on Friday?"

A—"No."

Mr. Herndon. "Did you say anything when you shot Oswald other than what you've testified about?"

A—"No."

Mr. Herndon. "Have members of your family been physically harmed because of what you did?"

A—"No." May I interrupt?

Mr. Herndon. Just sit perfectly still. We will discuss the questions later, Mr. Ruby.

"Do you think members of your family are now in danger because of what you did?"

A—(no response).

Mr. Herndon. "Is Mr. Fowler in danger because he is defending you?"

A—(no response).

Mr. Herndon. "Did 'Blackie' Hanson speak to you just before you shot Oswald?"

A—"No."

Mr. Herndon. That will conclude that series, and just sit still a moment, Mr. Ruby, and I will let the pressure out. Now, as soon as I shut this off, we will discuss these questions.

Mr. Herndon. On that series of questions, Mr. Ruby, you failed to respond or answer one or two of these questions, which I'll give you an opportunity now to make any comment you wish to make about them.

Question No. 5, I asked, "Do you think members of your family are now in danger because of what you did?"

A—Well, they're always exposed to it, so I don't know how to answer that.

Mr. Herndon. In other words, you felt it would be difficult for you to say either "Yes" or "No"; is that correct?

A—That's right; the same way with Fowler. I know when he's representing me, he's putting himself on the spot. . . .

Mr. Specter. Mr. Ruby, do you now have any other questions which you would like us to ask you on this polygraph examination? . . .

A— . . . They didn't ask me another question: "If I loved the President so much, why wasn't I at the parade?" Is that a very important question to ask?

Mr. Specter. We have considered those questions and that was when we reviewed the transcript of your testimony, and quite frankly, we have rejected them as being not important.

A—You have? I see. Now, isn't it strange—now, I want to tell you something that's noticeable in this part of the country about the poll tax, and there are a lot of other reasons, maybe. I'm reluctant to buy my poll tax in time, and I don't recall whether or not—is this all right to go in the record if I speak?

Mr. Specter. You may go on the record with any facet you think is important for the Commission to know about.

A—And yet, it's strange that perhaps I didn't vote for President Kennedy, or didn't vote at all, that I should build up such a great affection for him, when everything points against me. For instance, the parade issue I referred to. How can I answer that and still show my sincerity or my feelings and why I was carried away so emotionally to do something like that, that has put me in such serious trouble?

Mr. Alexander. Jack, there's no way to put that on the machine other than to ask you if you told the truth in your testimony; and that's an opinion without concrete facts.

A—But I don't remember if I got all the testimony in when Warren was here.

Mr. Specter. You testify now as to anything you want to add and we can ask you one question at the end and that will be "Have you told the truth in everything you've said here today?" That one question will cover everything you said, so that if any other phrase comes to your mind now, let us hear about it.

A—What I'm trying to bring out is this: It's—and everyone was much surprised—why should I be carried away so emotionally to commit the act, and yet knowing how I felt and knowing I know I'm telling the truth, how can we bring that point out that I am not sincere in why I did it?

Mr. Specter. We can bring that out with the one general question. Now, is there any other topic you would like to testify about and have us check you to your truthfulness?

A—Yes—whether or not I was ever mixed up with the underworld here or involved in any crime?

Mr. Specter. You've been asked that specifically, and you've testified about that.

A—Yes. You see, I've been in Dallas 17 years and yet suddenly I get involved in a very serious crime and I was very popular with the police department and a lot of other people, and the irony is—it took a complete reverse of that, because of various suspicions, nature, and so on.

I wonder if you follow what I'm trying to bring out? Maybe there's something we can cover in that area.

Mr. Alexander. Jack, let's cover it this way. "Were any of your relations with the police department improper?"

A—No—you, like doing business or something or other?

Mr. Alexander. Yes?

A—No—none whatsoever.

Mr. Alexander. Well, would that question cover what you had in mind?

A—No.

Mr. Alexander. Tell us what you had in mind and then we'll frame the question, because that's an area.

A—Whether or not I am of criminal background or whether I'm an honest and sincere person, because all those things came out and suspicions came out that Jack Ruby was involved in this and that and leaves a lot of suspicion as to my background and character. That's very vague, but that's what I'm trying to bring out.

Mr. Alexander. How would this question be? "Are you a police character?"

A—No.

Mr. Tonahill. "Are you a 100 percent patriotic American citizen?"

Mr. Alexander. "Are you a law-abiding citizen?"

A—That's better—that's the question.

Mr. Alexander. "Are you a law-abiding patriotic citizen?"

A—Yes.

Mr. Tonahill. "Are you a 100 percent American patriotic citizen?"

A—Yes.

Mr. Herndon. That can be asked.

A—That's very good, because—shall I elaborate on this?

Mr. Specter. Yes.

A—I became closely attached to our beloved President when he gave that wonderful speech when we had our problem in Cuba at that time. That was a very tremendous speech and then I followed him on television and in magazines wherever he went—to Ireland and different places.

Now, Joe asked a very good question. In other words, either you are American or you're half and half or you're

442

indifferent to the way you feel about your country and how much you love it.

When he stated to me a moment ago, "Are you 100 percent American?"—that's the way you feel about your country. I don't know how to state it but first of all, I want to make sure—I've got my flags in both colors—that doesn't show any overt—but inwardly, I'm a very unstable person. I'm very lax in certain details and things, and yet for the emotional feeling and the feeling for giving my life and for loving this country is so great, that I think when you asked me that question, "Are you 100 percent American?" and if I answered the truth, it will greater effect than any other way you can ask me.

Mr. Specter. Mr. Ruby, we can cover that one in a specific question, in another general question, on whether you have told the complete truth here today. Are there any other topics which you want to cover?

A—Oh, yes, sir. Has any of the underworld ever contributed money to me for my clubs, or was I put in here as a front for the underworld or things to that effect. I mean—this has a relationship to criminal intent.

Mr. Specter. We've asked you the question if the underworld had any connection with the shooting of Oswald.

Let me now ask you for the record while you are under oath, whether you were put in here by the underworld?

A—No.

Mr. Specter. Did the underworld contribute in any way to the financing of any of your clubs?

A—None whatsoever.

Mr. Specter. Have you had any connection or association in any way whatsoever with the underworld during the past 17 years you've been in Dallas?

A—Never have.

Mr. Specter. Now, we'll ask you in a few moments with Mr. Herndon, whether you've told the truth, and that will be covered—that will cover this underworld question.

A—Just the one question is enough to cover it?

Mr. Specter. Mr. Herndon advises that it is.

Mr. Herndon. I can ask that question and have it a matter of record.

A—You see, there are so many things that I know in the minds of the people in Dallas that you're not concerned with, that maybe I was put here as a front of the underworld and sooner or later they will get something out of me that they want done to their advantage.

Everything I have had financed, my brother Earl has contributed the money for or Ralph Paul, a friend of mine, has loaned me money.

Mr. Herndon. Mr. Spector, if I can interrupt—on some of these questions you are recently discussing here are more or less in the area of emotions and the area dealing with advance

443

psychology or of a psychiatric nature, and although I can ask them if you so wish, they are questions that don't necessarily lend themselves to the polygraph technique.

Unless you can specifically break them down to a clearcut question which could be answered truthfully "Yes or "No," that involves a specific action or emotion that he can recall in regard to a particular action, then it would not be a good question here. . . .

A—One more thing—shouldn't you ask me, or isn't it necessary, why I suddenly was so carried away to get involved in this serious crime?

Mr. Alexander. Jack, that won't work on the machine.

Mr. Specter. We have to ask you a "Yes" or "No" question, and we've already covered that by asking you the question about Mrs. Kennedy—whether you didn't shoot Oswald to avoid having her come to trial.

A—Yes; that covers that.

Mr. Specter. That covers that subject.

A—In other words, I can't answer that truthfully and have another reason for doing it; is that correct?

Mr. Specter. Correct.

A—That would answer that?

Mr. Specter. Yes. We've asked you all the reasons——

A—But you don't ask me why I did it, though? Why I was carried away so much—you don't ask me that.

Mr. Specter. We did ask you—we asked you "Why did you shoot Oswald?"

A—But you don't ask me why I got carried away so?

Mr. Specter. Well, it's the same question.

A—Oh, it's the same question.

Mr. Specter. This is the same question—in the form of: "Did you do it in order to save Mrs. Kennedy the travail of a trip to Dallas?" That subject matter has been covered as comprehensively as we can through the polygraph.

Now, will you proceed, Mr. Herndon, and ask those final questions? . . .

Mr. Herndon. I'll just ask these three questions, and once again, these are more or less summation questions here, and I want you just to relax and answer them simply, "Yes" or "No."

The series will now begin.

"Are you Jack Ruby?"

A—"Yes."

Mr. Herndon. "Do you consider yourself to be a 100 percent American patriot?"

A—"Yes."

Mr. Herndon. "Has all the testimony given by you today been the complete truth?"

A—"Yes."

Mr. Herndon. The series is over. . . .

MRS. EVA L. GRANT

The testimony of Ruby's sister:

Mr. Hubert. Could you tell us something of Jack's youth and education and his childhood—you were older than he was and, therefore, you are able to observe it, I would think.

A—I am 2 years older and how far back do you want to go—do you want me to go?

Mr. Hubert. What kind of education did he have?

A—I think he went about a year and a half to high school.

Mr. Hubert. Were your parents separated?

A—My parents were separated—yes.

Mr. Hubert. When did they separate?

A—In the spring of 1921.

Mr. Hubert. That was when Jack was about 10 years old?

A—Let's see, if he was born in 1911—yes. . . .

Mr. Hubert. Well, is it fair to state that apparently the family broke up; is that correct?

A—Yes—well, my mother had a nervous breakdown. That was the first time, because of the dissension in the home because of my father's activities of drinking.

Mr. Hubert. Is your father an alcoholic?

A—Well, he lived until 89—how can we prove it—you know, we never knew if he was drunk or sober, but he drank plenty. . . .

JESSE E. CURRY

The testimony of the chief of the Dallas Police Department:

Mr. Hubert. What is your present occupation, Chief?

A—Chief of Police, Dallas Police Department.

Mr. Hubert. And how long have you been occupying that position?

A—Since January 20, 1960.

Mr. Hubert. It appears to me from what you have said that you began at the bottom of the ranks in the police department?

A—That's right.

Mr. Hubert. And would it be fair to say that you worked your way through, as it were?

A—Yes, sir.

Mr. Hubert. Up the line?

A—Yes, sir; I worked in practically every assignment the police department has, and through civil service examinations was able to gain promotions to a detective, sergeant, lieutenant of police, captain of police, inspector of police, and inspector of police is the highest civil service rank obtainable. . . .

Mr. Hubert. When a prisoner is formally charged, as Oswald had been, what is the normal procedure to transfer the prisoner to the State prison?

A—There are two ways it is done. Sometimes the bureau

transfers the person to the sheriff's office, and sometimes the sheriff's office sends up and gets them.

Mr. Hubert. And either type is usual?

A—Either one is acceptable.

Mr. Hubert. Had Decker made any request to you to deliver what, in effect, was his prisoner?

A—Not at this time.

Mr. Hubert. So, on Saturday night, that would be the 23d, you were asked, I think, by the newsmen?

A—When we were going to transfer him and I told them I didn't know.

Mr. Hubert. All right; go on from there.

A—And some of them asked if "They were going to transfer him tonight?" And I said, "I don't think so." Then, I talked to Fritz about when he thought he would transfer the prisoner, and he didn't think it was a good idea to transfer him at night because of the fact you couldn't see, and if anybody tried to cause any trouble, they needed to see who they were and where it was coming from and so forth, and he suggested that we wait until daylight, so this was normal procedure, I mean, for Fritz to determine when he is going to transfer his prisoners, so I told him, "Okay." I asked him, I said, "What time do you think you will be ready tomorrow?" And he didn't know exactly and I said, "Do you think about 10 o'clock," and he said, "I believe so," and then is when I went out and told the newspaper people, the news media that we were not going to transfer him that night and some of them asked, "When should we be back, when are you going to transfer him?" And I said, "I don't know," because I didn't know when we were going to transfer him. Some of them said, "When should be back?" I made the remark then, "I believe if you are back here by 10 o'clock you will be back in time to observe anything you care to observe."

Mr. Hubert. Can you tell us whether on Saturday night any plans had been made for the transfer?

A—Not on Saturday night, I don't believe.

Mr. Hubert. Then, you went home?

A—Yes.

Mr. Hubert. Then, let's pick up with the 24th.

A—On Sunday morning, I came down to the office, and, as I recall, it was probably 8:30 or 8:45 when I got to the office, and as I parked my car in the basement of the city hall and started up to our office, I noticed that a large camera had been set up out in the hallway between the jail office and the end of the corridor immediately in front of the jail office, and it was in the way of traffic, and Lieutenant Wiggins came out and I told him—I told Lieutenant Wiggins, I said, "You are going to have to move this camera out of here," and then I told Wiggins, I said, "Now, if the news media come down here and want in, put them over behind the rail." There is a rail separating the ramp that comes down in the basement from the parking area. There were two cars in there, I believe a patrol wagon and a squad car and I told him to move those vehicles out and if the news media came down and wanted to observe from the basement, that they were to be placed back over in this area.

Mr. Hubert. Is it fair to state, then, that in your own mind, you had determined that the way to move him was through the basement area?

A—Yes. I believe about this—Chief Stevenson and Chief Batchelor approached me—I think they had been there earlier, and I told them I thought the best thing to do was to set up our security down there and bring Oswald down there and transfer him on to the county jail.

I went on up to the office and Chief Batchelor and Chief Stevenson, I think, remained in the basement a while and Captain Talbert was down there.

Mr. Hubert. Did you delegate to any specific person the security of Oswald?

A—No, sir; I could see that he was being taken care of by the captain on duty, Captain Talbert, and Lieutenant Wiggins was assisting in it, so I didn't see any need to particularly call some officer over there and say, "Look, you are in charge of this security in this basement." It was being taken care of, I could see.

Mr. Hubert. Well, for the record, will you tell us what you saw that satisfied you that it was being taken care of?

A—Officers were being stationed at the strategic points in the basement to screen people coming in, and they were moving out the vehicles as I asked them to, so I went upstairs and I told Chief Batchelor and Chief Stevenson that we should clean out everything in the basement and screen everything that came back in.

Mr. Hubert. When you ordered everything to be "screened" did you give any specific instructions?

A—No; I didn't.

Mr. Hubert. Or does that term have any significance in police work?

A—Well, it means to satisfy yourself that they were people who had a legitimate reason to be there when you screen them.

Mr. Hubert. In other words, within the organization of the police department, the word "screening" is understood so that you were satisfied that there would not be people there who were not supposed to be there?

A—Any unauthorized people.

Mr. Hubert. Just one more point on that—under the system, who would be considered as unauthorized persons?

A—I think I specifically stated that only newspaper reporters or police officers would be allowed in the basement.

Mr. Hubert. Only the news media?

A—Yes.

Mr. Hubert. Television people—would be included, too?

A—Yes.

Mr. Hubert. Was there any discussion of the route to be taken?

A—Not at that time.

Mr. Hubert. All right; let's go ahead.

A—Then, I went on upstairs and a little while later I went to Fritz' office and they were interrogating him—they—there were several people in there, some I recognized as FBI agents, some were Secret Service agents, some were Dallas detectives, and Captain Fritz was talking to Oswald at the time, I believe, and I stood around a few moments and when there was a lull in the interrogation, I asked Captain Fritz if he was about ready to transfer Oswald and he said, "Well, no; they were still talking to him," so I left the room.

Mr. Hubert. That was about what time?

A—As I recall, it was probably 10:30, but I didn't care when they transferred him at all. It didn't make any difference to me. The arrangements had been made to transfer him and then when it was brought to——

Mr. Hubert. What arrangements had been made?

A—That we would transfer him to the sheriff, but at that time we did not have any armored cars down there. We were just at that time, I believe it was—understood that we would just put him in the car and drive him down there.

Someone asked me if I had heard of the threats that had been made against him, and I had. They had called me at home about it, and I called Sheriff Decker, I think, from Fritz' office, and when Fritz said they were ready to transfer the man, and this is something after 11 o'clock—probably a little after 11, and Decker said, "Okay, bring him on," and at that time I said, "I thought you were coming after him."

Decker said, "Either way, I'll come after him or you can bring him to me," and I thought since we had so much involved here, we were the ones that were investigating the case and we had the officers set up downstairs to handle it, so I told Decker —I said, "Okay, we'll bring him to you."

Mr. Hubert. In other words, at first your security precaution in the basement was to take care of the situation of either your having to move him from the jail or Decker coming after him?

A—Or Decker coming after him; that's right. Then, I saw Chief Batchelor, and I believe, Chief Stevenson, and we discussed the threats that we had had.

Mr. Hubert. Now, that was, of course, after you had heard about the threats and after you had talked to Decker?

A—Yes.

Mr. Hubert. And I think you mentioned you talked to Decker a little after 11 o'clock?

A—Well, it was probably before that.

Mr. Hubert. I wanted to bring that to your attention because it seems to me it must have been earlier than that.

A—Yes; it was. Because we had to get the armored car in there after that. Anyway, after it was determined we would move him, Chief Batchelor, I believe, and Chief Stevenson and myself discussed this security and we decided it would be best to get an armored car down there in the event some one, some group tried to take our prisoner away from us, it would be better to have him in an armored car.

So. Chief Batchelor called the man, I don't recall his name now, that runs the armored motor service here in Dallas, and requested that we be furnished with an armored car, and I was told later that they had two sizes, an overland truck and a city truck and they would send them both over there when they could get the drivers and we could use whichever one we wanted.

Well, as I understand it, during this time the questioning of Oswald continued up in Captain Fritz' office, and I believe it was about a quarter to 11 or around 11 when we were told the armored cars were there and they backed them into the basement and they wouldn't go all the way down because of the height of the vehicle, and one of them was parked on the ramp and officers were placed on each side of it. In the meantime, I understand that the basement had been completely cleaned out of any unauthorized persons.

Mr. Hubert. Can you tell me why it was that the Commerce Street exit was chosen to put the armored car in and for the cars carrying Oswald to leave in, rather than the Main Street exit?

A—Because Commerce Street is one way east and all the traffic comes in on Main Street.

Mr. Hubert. Main Street is two-way traffic?

A—It is two-way traffic and the exit is one way east, so the vehicles were placed there.

Mr. Hubert. As a matter of geographical fact, except for the fact that you would have been going the wrong way, up the Main Street ramp and that you had two-way traffic on Main Street, the actual closest route would have been to go up the Main Street ramp, turn left up Main Street and go down?

A—Yes; it would. It would have been about three or four blocks closer, because when we came out of Commerce you had to go east to the second block and make a turn one block and make a turn back west.

Mr. Hubert. Chief, have you any comment to make as to why the longer route instead of the shorter route was taken?

A—Well, just because ordinarily we don't violate traffic rules and regulations in the transfer of prisoners and we thought this was the normal route that should be taken and that's the reason it was set up that way.

Mr. Hubert. The original decision, as I remember it, was to go through the Commerce Street exit and then turn left up to North Central?

A—Yes.

Mr. Hubert. And then turn left again and go to Elm and then go on down to the county jail?

A—When I went back up into the homicide office and told Fritz about our plans of transferring the prisoner, he was not particularly pleased with the idea of putting the prisoner in the armored car.

Mr. Hubert. Did he say why?

A—He said if someone tried to take our prisoner, he felt like we ought to be able to maneuver and he felt that this would be too awkward in this heavy armored car and he preferred that the prisoner be transferred in a regular police car with detectives.

Mr. Hubert. Was a policeman to drive the armored car?

A—No; not the armored car.

Mr. Hubert. Is that a factor, too—I suppose—it wouldn't be a member of the police force under your control driving that car?

A—No; but he felt like—Fritz said if anyone tried to take our prisoner we should be in a position to be able to cut out of the caravan or to take off or do whatever was necessary to protect our prisoner.

So, I didn't argue with him about it—there was some merit to his plan, so I told him, "Well, okay, but we would still use the armored car as a decoy and let it go right on down just as we had planned and if anyone planned to try to take our prisoner away from us, they would be attacking an empty armored car," and that this vehicle with the prisoner in it would have cut out of the caravan and proceeded immediately to the county jail and the prisoner would be taken into the county jail, and the way we figured it, he would be there before the other caravan got there.

Well, he asked me if everything was ready and I said, "Yes, as far as I know, everything is ready to go," and this was a little after 11 o'clock and I said, "Well, I'll go down to the basement," and was en route to the basement when I was called to the telephone and Mayor Cabell was on the telephone wanting to know something about the case, how we were progressing, what was going on, and while I was talking to him they made this transfer and Oswald was shot in the basement, and he was rushed to Parkland Hospital and I was notified that he had been shot in the basement.

Mr. Hubert. Did you know about his being shot before he moved to the hospital in the ambulance?

A—Yes, they called me from the jail office and said he had been shot and an ambulance had been ordered.

Mr. Hubert. Now, after the shooting, what action did you take—that is, the shooting of Oswald?

A—Well, I don't recall any particular action I took. I was told the man who shot him was in custody and was up in the jail. I think I notified the mayor that the man had been shot while I was still on the telephone with him and then I waited up in my office for word from Parkland Hospital, and about 1:30, or I believe about 1:30, we were informed that he had expired, and during this time I had been informed that the man who shot him was a nightclub operator named Jack Ruby, and that he was in custody up in the jail.

After I was informed that Oswald had died, I made an announcement to news media that he had expired and that we had the man who shot him in custody and as I recall, that's about the extent of my activity on that day.

Mr. Hubert. Do you remember whether on Sunday, November 24, it came to your attention that Ruby had stated that he entered the jail through the Main Street ramp?

A—I heard that, but I don't know who told it to me. I just heard a rumor that he had come in through the Main Street ramp. I understood that he told some more people that up in the jail.

After this happened, I immediately set up an investigative team to try to find out what happened.

Mr. Hubert. Now, when you say "immediately," you mean on the 24th?

A—Yes.

Mr. Hubert. And who was that?

A—Inspector Sawyer, Capt. O. A. Jones.

Mr. Hubert. What were your instructions to them?

A—To interrogate everyone that had anything to do with this and find out what they knew about it, what had happened and how and why and how it occurred.

Mr. Hubert. Is it fair to state that your instructions were then to find out exactly the truth?

A—Yes; absolutely.

Mr. Hubert. Now, you did receive a report from them ultimately?

A—Yes, I did.

Mr. Hubert. And I take it, of course, that you studied it?

A—Yes, sir.

Mr. Hubert. As I remember the report, it made certain specific findings as to how Ruby entered and so forth?"

A—Yes, according to the report he did come down the Main Street ramp.

Mr. Hubert. From your study of the report and all the statements that you got, are you satisfied with the conclusions reached in the report?

A—I believe this is the way he came in. I don't believe the officer at the top of the ramp where he came in, I don't believe that he knew that he went by, but I do state this, that I think the proper security was set up, and that had each officer carried out his assignment, I believe the transfer would have been made safely, and while I, as head of the department, have to accept responsibility for the security, I can say this, that the proper security was set up.

It was a failure of one man to carry out his assignment properly that permitted this man, apparently, to come into the basement of the city hall.

Mr. *Hubert*. And that man you mean is Roy Vaughn?

A—Vaughn—Officer Vaughn, the officer assigned to the Main Street ramp. . . .

Mr. *Hubert*. Chief, as you know, there has been some suggestion that a desire to satisfy the press dictated the time of the movement and the route. I think you ought to have an opportunity at this time to recall your own observations as to what influence, if any, considerations of pleasing the press entered into any of these plans?

A—Well, I would only say this, that we were trying in the police department to let the press have an opportunity to observe the proceedings as they were. This is an event that had not been—the like of the event had not been seen or heard, I think, in this century.

I didn't have any particular ones to come to me and insist that this be done in this manner. I saw no particular harm in allowing the media to observe the prisoner, and with no laws against it, and no policies that had ever been set up stating that the news media would not be allowed to see a prisoner.

There was no way for us to take the prisoner from the homicide office to the jail and back without the news media seeing him. I was besieged actually by the press to permit them to see Oswald. They made such remarks as, "The public has a right to see, to know," I didn't want them to think that we were mistreating Oswald; that we were carrying on this investigation in a normal manner, and that this case was handled as probably any other case would have been handled, although this had more national appeal, you might say, and had some curiosity to it. than some of the other cases we have handled.

But certainly the fact that the news media was permitted to see him and to take pictures of him was not anything unusual. This has always been done, but not to this extent because we didn't have this much press present.

Mr. *Hubert*. As I understand what you are saying, it is that had it not been for the fact that the victim was Oswald. if it was Oswald, and it was the President involved, this would have been quite normal procedure, that is to say, the press would have been allowed to see him, you would have told them when he was going to be moved?

A—That's right.

Mr. Hubert. And allowed them to take pictures?

A—That's right.

Mr. Hubert. Was any suggestion made to you by anybody that it would be best to disregard those considerations with respect to the press and use another route in making the transfer at another time?

A—No, sir: not that I recall. Fritz and I, I think, discussed this briefly, the possibility of getting that prisoner out of the city hall during the night hours and by another route and slipping him to the jail, but actually Fritz was not too much in favor of this and I more or less left this up to Fritz as to when and how this transfer would be made, because he has in the past transferred many of his prisoners to the county jail and I felt that since it was his responsibility, the prisoner was, to let him decide when and how he wanted to transfer this prisoner.

Mr. Hubert. Well, you didn't, in any case, give him instructions not to transfer the prisoner at a time when he could not be observed by the press?

A—No, sir; that's right.

Mr. Hubert. Is it fair to state that had he done so, it would have been satisfactory to you?

A—I would not have complained about it.

Mr. Hubert. Do you know whether Fritz' decision not to move him prior to the time that had been announced to the press was motivated by considerations of the press?

A—I don't know whether it was or not. I think this—that he didn't know how long he would be interrogating. I don't believe Fritz wanted to move him at night. I think he wanted to move him in the daytime so that he could see anyone that might be trying to cause him any trouble.

Mr. Hubert. Your thought is that, therefore, Fritz' decision not to move him at night was dictated by considerations of security?

A—I believe so; yes.

Mr. Hubert. Chief, I believe that I ought to offer you the opportunity to state for the record here as an overall proposition what you consider to be the cause of what was obviously a security breakdown?

A—I think the cause of the breakdown was the fact that Officer Vaughn left his post to assist this Lieutenant Pierce, and I believe Sergeant Dean, and I don't know who else was in the car, as they left the basement of the city hall going the wrong way on the ramp, and Officer Vaughn stepped across the sidewalk which he had been instructed, so I am told, to guard that ramp—to let only police officers or bona fide news media enter there. He momentarily stepped away from his assignment and while he was away from this assignment, our investigation shows that Jack Ruby went behind him and entered the ramp and went to the bottom of the ramp and stood behind some detectives and news media.

Mr. Hubert. Concerning the security at the top of the Main Street ramp where Vaughn was, what observations have you to make about that means of entry being guarded by one man only instead of, say, more?

A—Well, actually, this seemed to be the least risk in our security plan. All of the crowd and vehicles and everything was over on Commerce Street and there was very little over on Main Street, actually very little activity at all. It was only about a 12-foot ramp there that he had to guard.

Mr. Hubert. And he was standing right in the middle of it?

A—Had he stayed on his assignment, I don't see how Ruby could have gotten in.

Mr. Hubert. Of course, when the Pierce car came up, he obviously had to move away, but your thought is he moved too far away from his assignment?

A—He moved too far away from his assignment. He apparently was assisting this vehicle to get across the sidewalk, I think it was 10 or 12 feet wide, and into the street. Actually, he should have just stepped to one side and let the vehicle come by.

Now, this officer was put on a polygraph to determine whether or not he knew that Ruby went by him and according to the test, the results of the test, he did not realize that Ruby went by him. . . .

Mr. Hubert. Now, finally, is there anything at all you would like to make a matter of record concerning this whole thing? You are at liberty to say anything you want to say.

A—No; the only thing I would like to say is that I deeply regret the incidents that occurred and I feel like we did everything that could be expected of us as a police department to set up the security of the President and to cooperate with all agencies that had a responsibility in this matter, that we certainly would have liked for Oswald to have remained alive and faced trial.

According to the information that was given to me by the homicide bureau, we had developed a very good case on him and would have been able to, I'm sure, would have been able to convict him in a court of law.

Jack Ruby—I do not know, I did not know. It has been intimated that a great many of the Dallas police officers did know him, but from what I've been able to find out, there were some police officers who knew him, but most of them knew him because of the fact they had conducted police business with him at his place of business. There were a few, perhaps, that knew him and had gone to his place of business for social activities, but it was certainly not—he is not known by the majority of the police department.

Mr. Hubert. Chief, perhaps you would like to comment on

two things—one, is that, as you know, there has been some talk or rumor, of course, that the police department cooperated, or some members of it, with Ruby for an opportunity for Ruby to shoot Oswald.

Have you looked into that, and if you have, would you give us your observations about it?

A—My instructions to the investigating officers were to go into every facet of this incident and to uncover any information that might indicate that any police officer cooperated in any way with letting Ruby get in a position to where he could have an opportunity to shoot Oswald.

Mr. Hubert. Did you find any evidence that would indicate anything?

A—No evidence whatsoever were we able to find.

Mr. Hubert. You were looking for such?

A—Yes; we certainly were.

Mr. Hubert. Chief, what was your intention had you found such evidence?

A—Proper action would have been taken.

Mr. Hubert. And by that you mean what?

A—The officer, if criminal negligence had been established, he would have been filed on by us.

Mr. Hubert. Now, there has been also the rumor that while the police did not actively cooperate, that they saw Jack Ruby there, didn't pay much attention to him, were really appalled when he did what he did, and then after that, engaged in a cover-up activity to preserve the reputation of the police department. Can you tell us whether your investigative efforts were directed toward uncovering any evidence which might throw light on that matter?

A—This investigation which was conducted was a completely impartial investigation.

We in the police department for a number of years have felt like if there is anything wrong in our department, we want to know it, and if actions of the officers are improper, an examination of our records through the years will show that we have taken whatever action was indicated, whether this be filing on a man for law violations or for improper conduct or whatever it might be. The seriousness of the offense is certainly not covered up and through the years we have a reputation for a high standard of conduct and the integrity of the department has not been questioned.

Mr. Hubert. You are satisfied that from all you know that there has been no effort to cover up?

A—No, sir; not to my knowledge, and had there been and it had come to my knowledge, I certainly would have done something about it.

Mr. Hubert. You are satisfied that the evidence shows that really Ruby came through one man?

A—That's right.

Mr. Hubert. And that was Vaughn?

A—That's right.

Mr. Hubert. Have you anything else to say, chief?

A—No, sir; I believe not. . . .

Chief Curry later testified again, in part about a police showup the night of the assassination to let newsmen see Lee Harvey Oswald:

Mr. Rankin. Did you find out where Jack Ruby was during this showup?

A—I didn't know Jack Ruby. Actually the first time I saw Jack Ruby to know Jack Ruby was in a bond hearing or I believe it was a bond hearing, and I recognized him sitting at counsel's table.

The impression has been given that a great many of the Dallas Police Department knew Jack Ruby.

Mr. Rankin. What is the fact in that regard?

A—The fact of that as far as I know there are a very small percentage of the Dallas Police Department that knows Jack Ruby.

Mr. Rankin. Did you make an inquiry to find out?

A—Yes; I did, yes, sir. And so far as I know most of the men who knew Jack Ruby are men who were assigned to the vice squad of the police department or who had worked the radio patrol district where he had places and in the course——

Mr. Rankin. How many men would that be?

A—I am guessing, perhaps 25 men. This is merely a guess on my part.

Mr. Rankin. How large is your police force?

A—Approximately 1,200. I would say 1,175 people. I would say less, I believe less than 50 people knew him. From what I have found out since then that he is the type that if he saw a policeman, or he came to his place of business he would probably run up and make himself acquainted with him.

I also have learned since this time he tried to ingratiate himself with any of the news media or any of the reporters who had anything to do, he was always constantly trying to get publicity for his clubs or for himself. . . .

Mr. Dulles. Did you say Ruby was present that evening?

A—I have understood he was. But to my own knowledge, I wouldn't have known him because I didn't know him. . . .

Mr. McCloy. Did you, so far as you know, did Tippit know Ruby?

A—I don't believe he did. I am sure he didn't. . . .

Mr. Rankin. You were going to tell us about how it came to your attention about the moving of Lee Oswald to the jail from your place on Saturday?

A—To the county jail?

Mr. Rankin. Yes. . . .

A—I asked Captain Fritz a time or two when he wanted to move Oswald, because this is left up to him. Whoever will be

456

handling the case, I mean I don't enter in the transfer of prisoners, I don't ordinarily even know when they are going to be transferred.

Mr. Rankin. Why is that?

A—It is just a routine matter. . . .

Mr. Rankin. When did you talk to Officer or Captain Fritz about this?

A—I think I talked to him some on Saturday, because the newspaper people or the news media kept asking me when are going to transfer him?

Mr. Rankin. That would be November 23?

A—Yes; and I said this I don't know because that would be left up to the men doing the interrogation. . . .

Mr. Rankin. Did you have anything to do with his transfer then?

A—Other than to, I called Sheriff Decker on Sunday morning and he said, I told him and I think he had talked to Fritz prior to that time, too, and he told Fritz, he says, "Don't bring him down here until I get some security set up for him."

So, Sunday morning I talked to Sheriff Decker.

Mr. Rankin. Why didn't you do it at night? . . .

A—Well, in talking with Captain Fritz, and here again the prisoner was his, and when some of my captains, I believe it was perhaps Lieutenant Swain, it is in the record somewhere said something about, "Do you think we ought to move him at night?"

And Captain Fritz was not in favor of moving him at night because he said, "If anything does occur you can't see, anybody can immediately get out of sight, and if anything is going to happen we want to know where we can see and see what is happening."

Mr. Rankin. Were you fearful something might happen?

A—I didn't know. I thought it could happen because of a feeling of a great number of people. But I certainly didn't think anything to happen in city hall. I thought that if anything did happen to him it would probably be en route from the city jail to the county jail.

Mr. Rankin. What precautions did you take?

A—The precautions that were taken, when I came in on Sunday morning, now Captain Fritz, I had talked to him on Saturday night or Saturday evening anyway, and he said, he thought he would be ready to transfer him by 10 o'clock the next morning, that would be Sunday morning.

Mr. Rankin. Did you tell that to the media?

A—I told them at some time after that. Several of them asked me when are you going to transfer him, and I said, I don't know.

They said, "Are you going to transfer him tonight," and I said, "No we are not going to transfer him tonight." I said, "We are tired. We are going home and get some rest."

457

Something was said about well, we are tired, too. When should we come back, and I think that this is recorded in some of the tape recording, that I told them if you are back here by 10 o'clock in the morning, I don't think that you would miss anything you want to see.

Mr. *Rankin*. What did you do then about precautions?

A—The next morning when I came in, that would be about 8:30, 8:45, I think, parked in the basement of city hall, I started up to the elevator and I noticed they had moved some cameras into a hallway down in the basement and I told Lieutenant Wiggins who is in the jail office, I said, "These things will have to be moved out of here, and I also told Chief Batchelor, and Chief Stevenson, Assistant Chief Batchelor, and Assistant Chief in Charge of Investigations Stevenson who came down in the basement at the time.

Mr. *Rankin*. Those were TV cameras?

A—That was in the lobby or in near the lobby of the jail office. I told them they were—would have to move those out of there. This was also in the parking area, there was a ramp come down from Main Street and goes out on Commerce Street, and then there is a parking area east of this.

I told Lieutenant Wiggins who was there, I said, "Now, move these squad cars," there was a transfer car there and a squad car, "move these cars out of this area and if the news media wants down here put them over behind these railings, back over in the basement here."

Then that is all I did at that time. I saw that they were setting up some security. A little while later Chief Batchelor and Chief Stevenson went downstairs and found Captain Talbert who was the platoon commander, radio platoon commander had some sergeants down there and they were setting up security and were told clean everything out of the basement and not let anybody in here, I think the depositions will show that, not let anybody in except police officers and news media who had proper credentials.

Mr. *Rankin*. What about the various entrances, was anything done about that?

A—Well, the entrances to the basement, yes, and the entrances from the basement of city hall out into the basement proper where the cars come in.

Mr. *Rankin*. What was done about that?

A—Every entrance there were guards put on it with instructions not to let anyone come or go except police officers or news people that had proper credentials. . . .

Mr. *Rankin*. What other precautions were made?

A—There were a great number of police reservists and detectives and uniformed officers, I think there was a total, I believe of about 74 men in this area between the jail office and the immediate area where he would be loaded.

Mr. *Rankin*. How large an area was that?

A—Well, where he would be brought out of the jail office to put him in this car, would be, I would say, 15 or 20 feet, and then this building, this ramp runs from one street to the other, and the parking area would cover a block wide and perhaps 150 feet deep.

Mr. Rankin. Were there cars in the parking area?

A—Some cars were there. They had been searched out, all of them. All of the vehicles had been searched, and all the, where the air-conditioning ducts were, they had all been searched, every place where a person could conceal himself had been searched out.

Mr. Rankin. Was there a plan for an armored car?

A—Yes, sir; there was.

Mr. Rankin. What happened about that?

A—After they had gotten the armored car down there, in talking with Captain Fritz, and here again this prisoner was his responsibility and I don't want to be in a position of just over-riding him, and I was willing to trust his judgment, he had been doing this for, like I say, nearly 40 years, and he said, "Chief, I would prefer not to use that armored car, I don't know who the driver is. It is awkward to handle and if anybody tries to do anything to us, I am afraid we would be surrounded. I would prefer to put him in a police car with some of my men following him, and get in and just take him right down Main Street and slip him into the jail."

So I said, "It will be all right with me if you want to do it that way but let's not say anything about this."

Mr. Rankin. Now the armored car was not a Dallas police car, was it?

A—No; it was not. . . .

Mr. Rankin. How many officers would be involved in the transfer?

A—In the actual transfer, I would think perhaps 15 or 18 besides the men that were stationed at the intersections downtown.

Mr. Rankin. How far would it be from your police department to the county jail?

A—I would say 12–15 blocks.

Mr. Rankin. Were there any other precautions you haven't described?

A—No, sir; that is about all I know of, except that Captain Fritz wanted to transfer the prisoner in his car, with some of his detectives. This is not unusual. He has transferred many, many prisoners, especially where there is—it is an unusual case involving more than the ordinary routine crime, so it is not anything unusual to transfer him, for him to transfer prisoners.

But, it was then suggested or arranged that they would put his car in a position behind the armored car that we would bring the prisoner out, put him in his car, and he would have two detectives in the back seat with him, plus one driver and

459

two or three detectives following him immediately and there was supposed to be another car to pick up and go with them or get into a car van with these two.

They would follow the armored motor car and no one would know that he was not in the armored motor car except the reporters downstairs when they saw him come out. . . .

Mr. Rankin. What happened to these TV cameras that you told them to get out of there?

A—They moved them back somewhere. I don't know where they moved them but it was away from there.

Mr. Rankin. Weren't their cameras right there at the time of the shooting?

A—There were some cameras immediately over, TV cameras, I think over where I had told them to place them earlier that morning. I understood when Chief Batchelor went downstairs and I think Captain Jones of the forgery bureau, immediately prior to the transfer, they found there were some reporters and cameramen in the jail office, and Captain Jones, I believe, asked Chief Batchelor if these should not be removed and he was told yes, they should be removed out into the basement. When they were removed out into the basement instead of them being placed outside of the railing—now this is a decision made by Chief Batchelor, I suppose, because he said put them in the driveway up to the north. Now this is from where Ruby came. So apparently this afforded him an opportunity, from our investigation it was determined that he came down this Main Street ramp.

Mr. Rankin. How did you determine that?

A—We interrogated every man that was assigned in the basement. Also every witness who was around there that we could find that knew anything about it.

Mr. Rankin. Did anyone else see him come in on that ramp?

A—There was a former police officer who told us he saw him go down that ramp, a Negro former police officer.

Mr. Rankin. Who was that?

A—I believe his name was Daniels, I think perhaps you have a statement from him, don't you?

Mr. Rankin. Is he the only one who saw him come in down there?

A—I believe so.

Mr. Rankin. Now with these TV cameras down there how would your ruse work about having the armored car go ahead and Oswald climb into Captain Fritz' car? Wouldn't that all be shown on TV?

A—If it was. We didn't think there would be anybody downtown to be in a position to watching TV that quickly to do anything about it if they wanted to.

Mr. Rankin. You thought about it though?

A—Yes.

Mr. Rankin. What happened? Were you down there at the time?

A—No, sir; I would have been but I received a call from my mayor and as I was fixing to go downstairs and I wish that I had been downstairs because I don't know that I could have done anything but you always have this feeling if you were there maybe you could have done something.

But I was called to the telephone and while I was talking to the mayor, why I heard some noises from downstairs and I was up on the third floor, and I heard some shouting, and someone came in and told me that Oswald had been shot.

Mr. Rankin. Did you learn how the shooting occurred?

A—Yes.

Mr. Rankin. Will you tell us?

A—I was told that someone sprang from the crowd and pushed a gun into his stomach and fired a shot.

Mr. Rankin. Do you know who that was?

A—I was told that the man was named Jack Ruby.

Mr. Rankin. What else did you learn about it?

A—Further investigation revealed, and some of my officers who talked to Ruby and talked to his attorney, I believe, were told that he came down that north ramp, and an investigation revealed that one of our officers, who was assigned there, Officer Vaughn, who was assigned to this location just prior to this transfer.

Mr. Rankin. That is out on the street?

A—Main Street side.

Mr. Rankin. At the entrance?

A—At the entrance to the basement ramp. He had been assigned there and had been told not to let anybody come in except newspaper reporters or news media or police officers.

Mr. Rankin. Did you find out what he did?

A—We discovered or found out subsequently that he, just prior to this transfer, that when we found out we were going to transfer him and not use an armored car that Chief Stevenson had told Lieutenant Pierce "to get a couple of sergeants or a sergeant, get somebody and go around and get in front of the armored car and when we tell you to why you lead off and lead this armored car over here and just over the route we have discussed, and take it to the county jail."

Well, Lieutenant Pierce went downstairs and got a car and he got Sergeant Putnam and I don't recall the other sergeant, and because the ramp that ordinarily we would use for exit ramp to Commerce Street, it was blocked with this armored car and another vehicle, he went out in the wrong direction, that is he went north, up to north, he went north on the ramp to Main Street which ordinarily would not be done, but since he could not get out, why he did, and as he approached the ramp, our investigation showed that Officer Vaughn stepped

461

from his assignment in the entrance to this ramp, and the walk is about 10 or 12 feet wide there, stepped across and just more or less assisted the car to get into the Main Street flow of traffic.

Now he wasn't asked to do this by the lieutenant, but he just did it and according to what Ruby told some of my officers, I believe, whether you have it on the record who he told this to, that he came down that north ramp.

Mr. Rankin. At that time?

A—At that time.

Now this would only have been, it couldn't have possibly been over 2 or 3 minutes prior to the shooting, so apparently he went right down that ramp and he got in behind some of these newspaper reporters or news media and detectives, and as Oswald was brought out he sprang from behind one of my detectives and took about two steps and shoved a gun in Oswald's side and pulled the trigger.

This officer, in talking to him, he made a report, he swears that he didn't see anybody go in there.

Mr. Rankin. By this officer, you mean Vaughn?

A—Officer Vaughn. He did, I asked him myself or asked the investigating officers to see if he wouldn't take a polygraph test concerning this, just to verify his position in it, and he agreed to take the polygraph test and did take the polygraph test and the polygraph test revealed that he was not aware that Ruby came in while he stepped, when he stepped away from the entrance of that door.

Now I am not here to place the blame on anybody because, as I have said previously, as head of the department, I have got to accept the responsibility for what goes on there.

But if Officer Vaughn had properly carried out his assignment, I don't believe that Ruby could have gotten into the basement of the city hall.

Mr. McCloy. Unless he had credentials, media credentials?

A—That is correct.

Mr. McCloy. We haven't verified whether or not he did have anything?

A—We haven't been able to verify that. There were none found on his person.

Mr. Rankin. Did you make any inquiry as to whether or not any of the police force were involved with Ruby in this shooting?

A—We got reports and interrogated every officer who was there.

Mr. Rankin. What did you find out?

A—We didn't find any officer who knew he was down there or that had in any way assisted him in getting there. No one.

Mr. Rankin. You are satisfied that none of them were involved in trying to have Oswald shot?

A—Yes, sir; I certainly am.

Mr. Rankin. Did you make inquiry to determine whether

462

there was any evidence that anyone else was involved with Ruby in trying to shoot Oswald?

A—We made every effort we could in our investigation. We were not able to determine any tieup between any other individual and Ruby or Oswald.

Mr. Rankin. Did you make any inquiry to determine whether or not anyone else was involved with Oswald in the assassination of the President?

A—We attempted to. Every lead we came upon we followed it out to see whether or not we could make any connection between Ruby, Oswald, or any other group.

Mr. Rankin. Did you discover any evidence that would tend to show that Oswald had any support in the assassination?

A—No; we did not.

Mr. Rankin. Did you discover any evidence that would prove Ruby was involved with any other person in the killing of Oswald?

A—We were not able to determine any connection.

Mr. Dulles. I will just ask one question, if I may, here.

It was Officer Vaughn, I understand, who had the direct responsibility for checking the credentials.

A—Of that door, of that particular door.

Mr. Dulles. That door. Is there any evidence that Officer Vaughn knew of Ruby?

A—I don't believe he did.

Mr. Dulles. Has that been looked into?

A—He was asked that, and if I remember correctly in his deposition he didn't know him.

Mr. Dulles. He testified he didn't know him?

A—I believe so, I am not confident of that, but they have had his deposition here, which I am sure would reveal that.

Mr. Dulles. Do you know——

(Discussion off the record.)

Mr. McCloy. Do you know, chief, anybody on the staff, on your staff, on the police staff, that was particularly close to Ruby?

A—No, sir; I do not. . . .

Mr. McCloy. I guess that is all, except the general question I have of Chief Curry. Do you know anything else with respect to this whole matter that you think would be of any help to this Commission in getting at the facts?

A—Not that I know of, except to say we were extremely sorry that, of course, this thing happened in Dallas. We thought we were taking every normal precaution that we could take to insure the safety of the President in cooperating with the Secret Service and all other agencies and we felt like we had done a good job.

After the assassination and the murder of our officer, that our officers had done a good job in making a quick apprehension of the alleged person guilty of this, and that we will have

463

to admit that although we thought that adequate precautions had been taken for the transfer of this prisoner, that one of our officers momentarily stepped away from his post of duty, and that during this moment of negligence on his part, as far as we could determine Ruby went down the ramp, the Main Street ramp, and concealed himself behind some news media and detectives and as Oswald was brought out he stepped forward and shot him.

And if we had it to do over again, and I think this, that some policy should be set up for the news media, whereby if anything of this magnitude ever occurs again, that we would not be plagued by the confusion present that was present at that time, and that the news media should accept some of the responsibility for these things and agree among themselves to have representatives that can report back to them.

Mr. Rankin. Chief Curry, I am not quite clear about the situation with regard to your practices in the police force, and the news media. I understand what happened, as you described it at the time of the episodes that we have been going into, and I understand that you would, if there was a matter of this magnitude again—you would expect and want a very different change?

A—Yes.

Mr. Rankin. And eliminate the interference by the news media?

A—That is right.

Mr. Rankin. But what do you do now about the ordinary case? Have you changed your practices about the media at all?

A—Not the ordinary cases; no.

Mr. Rankin. And do they use the radio and TV in the police headquarters?

A—Yes, sir; they do.

Mr. Rankin. And they, the reporters, come in, and it is just the difference between a great many?

A—And a few is what made the difference in this.

Mr. McCloy. Do you permit reporters now to come in and interrogate prisoners as they did in this case by holding a microphone up to their mouth and saying, "How did you do it?"

A—They do the same as they do here; on the way from the interrogation room to the jail elevator as they pass by they might run along and ask him questions and try to get him to answer.

Mr. Rankin. That could be done today just the same?

A—Yes, sir. Because we have no way of keeping them out of the public halls.

Mr. Rankin. Don't you have jurisdiction as chief of police to exclude them if you thought it was the wise thing to do?

A—Yes. Now if I had it to do over again, of course, I would exclude it.

Mr. Rankin. And you could do it today in the ordinary case if you wanted to?

A—I would probably have my hide taken off by the news media, but I could do it.

Mr. Rankin. So, it is really a problem of weighing what the media will do to you against other considerations?

A—And this, too; it seemed like there was a great demand by the general public to know what was going on.

Mr. Rankin. Yes. And that is what you were trying to satisfy?

A—That is what I was trying to do.

CHARLES BATCHELOR

The testimony of the assistant chief of police of Dallas:

Mr. Griffin. . . . I believe you told me that sometime on Saturday night you were confronted by some newspaper reporters with respect to the movement of Lee Harvey Oswald?

A—Yes, sir.

Mr. Griffin. Would you tell us, Chief Batchelor, about what time of the night these reporters approached you?

A—This must have been somewhere around 7:30 or 8 o'clock at night. . . .

Mr. Griffin. Do you recall how many reporters confronted you?

A—There were two of them.

Mr. Griffin. Do you recall who they were?

A—No; I don't recall who they were now. It was a rather casual request. They asked, or they said, rather, that they were hungry and hadn't had anything to eat and they wanted to go out to dinner, and they didn't want to miss anything if we were going to move the prisoner. And I told them I had no idea when they were going to move the prisoner.

About that time Chief Curry came up and he told them, he said, "Oh, I think if you fellows are back here by 10 o'clock in the morning you won't miss anything."

So they left with that and went to eat.

Mr. Griffin. Were there any other reporters around at that time?

A—No, sir. Then later, just a very few minutes later, Chief Curry decided, well, he might tell the rest of the people out in the hall so they won't be hanging around, because they were apparently doing nothing, just waiting. So he went out and told them that if they would come back by 10 o'clock in the morning, they were not going to move the prisoner in the meantime. . . .

Mr. Griffin. What was the next thing you learned about the proposed movement of Oswald?

A—I just assumed that we would move him the next morning sometime after 10 o'clock. I didn't know exactly when, and I came down the next morning around 8 o'clock. . . .

Mr. Griffin. . . . You received a telephone call at your home about 6:30 in the morning from Captain Talbert. Can you tell us what that call was about?

A—Yes, sir. He called and informed me that he had gotten a call, and he didn't tell me at the time where he got it; he said an anonymous call.

Later I learned it came from the FBI, and they in turn had called him. That about a hundred men were going to take the prisoner Oswald and they didn't want to get any policeman hurt. So I told him to send a squad by Chief Curry's house and inform him about it. And at that moment we weren't concerned about him in the jail. We were concerned about him in the transfer.

Mr. Griffin. Why did Talbert call you rather than some other member of the police department?

A—He tried to call Chief Curry and he couldn't get him to answer his phone. I guess he was dog-tired and he couldn't get him up. And I told him to send a squad car by and tell him.

Mr. Griffin. I see. Did you have any discussion with him at that point who had responsibility to make this decision? Did you feel you had the responsibility to give instructions on the basis of having received this report that some men were going to try to go after Oswald? Did you feel you had any responsibility to take any protective action?

A—At that moment?

Mr. Griffin. Yes.

A—No. The way it came to me, it was my feeling that this was to happen when we attempted to transfer him, not to come up to the jail and get him. . . .

Mr. Griffin. Up to the time that you had this second conversation with Fleming, had you discussed with anybody the route by which you would take Oswald to the county jail?

A—Nobody but Chief Curry, that I recall, and probably Chief Stevenson. As a matter of fact, this route that they were to take was worked out more between Stevenson and Curry and Fritz than it was with me. My primary job here was to get the truck and get the cars placed, and it was decided that Chief Curry would lead the car down there, followed by a car of detectives, and then the armored car, and then followed by another car of detectives, and then followed by Stevenson and I in a rear car.

Mr. Griffin. This planned route of the movement was to go from Commerce to Central Expressway, left to Elm Street, then down Elm Street?

A—To Houston; yes, sir. . . .

Mr. Griffin. Who participated in that decision?

A—Chief Curry, Chief Stevenson, Captain Fritz, I believe —I was not in there when it was discussed. . . .

466

Mr. Griffin. Where were you standing when the armored cars arrived?

A—I was in the basement, but somebody told me down there, shouted that these armored cars had arrived, so I came up again out of the ramp to look at the two cars to see which one we wanted. I looked in the inside of the larger armored car and decided that this one is the one we would have to use because it had room not only for the prisoner, but two guards to be placed in there with him.

And this one—Mr. Hall, I believe is his name—I think it is Mr. Hall that drove the truck up there. And this truck was too large or too tall to drive clear to the foot of the basement ramp. It wouldn't clear this ceiling at that point, so I asked Mr. Hall to back it in, and he started backing it in, and he got the truck inside of the ramp with all of the body inside and the cab on the outside, on the sidewalk. He stopped and suggested that he not go to the bottom of the ramp with it because of its weight. He was afraid that in trying to pull out, he might kill the motor and stall it on the ramp, and suggested that since it blocked the entrance, if we could use it from that point, he would rather it go from that point.

Mr. Griffin. At the point this conversation took place, had you or anyone else to your knowledge told Hall what route would be taken?

A—No; we told him he would follow a lead car, and pointed out the car that he would follow. . . . In a few minutes shortly after the arrival of the truck, Chief Stevenson came down, and this was, oh, nearly 11:30. It was just a matter of minutes before—and told me of the change of plans, and that they were going to send the truck in convoy down through Elm Street, and that the car carrying——

Mr. Griffin. You mean Main Street?

A—No; Elm Street, and that the truck carrying Oswald and a car of detectives would drop out of the convoy, out on Main Street and drive down Main Street by themselves. In other words, the truck was to be a decoy, and the lead car and all the other cars would follow it on down Elm Street, while the car carrying the prisoner would go down Main Street.

Mr. Griffin. What security was there going to be?

A—We had moved the officers over from Elm Street to Main Street on the corner. The only security would have been a car carrying detectives, following the car carrying the prisoner and detectives. . . .

Mr. Griffin. Now, did you discuss with him the reasoning behind this decoy?

A—I merely asked him why the change, and he said they decided to change it up in the Homicide Bureau in a discussion with Chief Curry, because if anyone attacked, they would have the prisoner in a car separate from the convoy and the public would not know this, and they thought this would be a wise move.

Mr. Griffin. Now you all were aware that the TV cameras were going to be focusing on the car or the vehicle that Oswald was placed in, didn't you? The people in the downtown streets wouldn't be able to see that, but there were also newsmen down there who were broadcasting and they would be able to tell people listening in on the radio what car?

A—You are arguing with me. I had nothing to do with moving the prisoner.

Mr. Griffin. I didn't mean to argue with you, chief.

A—I didn't make the decision and I don't know whether it was wise or not. It is a moot question now.

Mr. Griffin. Well, now, what next happened after you talked with Chief Stevenson about this change in plan?

A—This happened when he told me about it, just moments before they actually brought him down, and he told me they were bringing a car up on the ramp, two cars up on the ramp, one to carry the prisoner and one to carry the detectives. . . .

Mr. Griffin. Now looking toward the Main Street ramp, how many rows deep, if there was more than one row at all, were the policemen who were blocking the Main Street ramp?

A—How many rows deep were the policemen?

Mr. Griffin. I'm sorry, the news people, if you understand what I mean?

A—There was about, as I remember it, about two deep along there. Some places there might have been a third man behind, but most about two deep.

Mr. Griffin. Would you come here and mark along the Main Street ramp about how deep these people were?

A—[Marking.] There weren't many along there because there were cameras there.

Mr. Griffin. How many people would you estimate were in that area there?

A—Oh, there couldn't have been too many in that particular area there. It is only 15 feet wide, maybe 20 or 25 in there, maybe 30.

Mr. Griffin. Now, just before Oswald was brought down, where were the rest of the news people placed?

A—They were along here.

Mr. Griffin. That is blocking the garage entrance?

A—Yes.

Mr. Griffin. About how many people would you say were in that area?

A—I don't know. Altogether there must have been, gee, we had around 70 policemen in that basement altogether, and there must have been 60 or 70 reporters and photographers and press people. They were fairly deep across here. . . .

Mr. Griffin. Had you given any instructions to the police

officers up to this point as to how they should stand in relationship, where they should be facing?

A—No, sir.

Mr. Griffin. Now after talking with Chief Stevenson, what next happened?

A—Almost immediately the car containing Lieutenant Pierce and I believe Sergeant Maxey pulled out of here, and these people had to step back, and they pulled out, and the detective cars were pulled here in on the ramp and backed into position.... I remember backing these or pulling up these two detective cars that were to carry Oswald, and one detective pulled up here a little ways, and he had to pull up a little further so this one could get up, and they then backed up. And this one had hardly gotten in place, barely had stopped, when somebody shouted, "Here he comes." . . .

Mr. Griffin. What happened when you heard the shot fired? What did you do?

A—Well, actually before the shot was fired, when I was standing along here, and when somebody shouted, "Here he comes." I started to go to that truck, that armored truck and close the doors on it, the back doors so it could take off. And I turned to do that when I heard the shot. I hadn't taken over a step or two over to the door when he was shot.

Mr. Griffin. Then what did you do?

A—I turned around and looked back and came over there. There was a whole group of people had him down. It was a big——

Mr. Griffin. Had Ruby down?

A—Had Ruby down. They had pulled Oswald into the jail office, and then pulled Ruby in behind him.

I went into the jail office to look at them, and they had Ruby down on the floor on his back and was trying to handcuff him.

Mr. Griffin. Let's focus on the time when they had Ruby down on the ground out there on the ramp, the ramp area. Where did you stand at that point?

A—I stood off in the crowd. I didn't even see what was going on. There was such a crowd.

Mr. Griffin. Did you hear Ruby say anything at that point?

A—No, sir.

Mr. Griffin. Did you hear any of the police officers say anything?

A—No, sir; not when I walked right up there to it. But I did hear someone shout, "Jack, don't you so-and-so," but this was before they got him down. I mean, this was almost simultaneous with the shot.

Mr. Griffin. Did you follow Ruby and Oswald into the jail office then?

A—After a little bit, a minute or two after, I remained in the jail office and asked Lieutenant Wiggins if they had called an ambulance, and he said they had.

469

I walked over and looked at Oswald, and this intern had come in and was giving him some pressure on his lower rib section.

Mr. Griffin. Where did you see Ruby at that time?

A—I saw him on the floor. I couldn't see him too well. There was several men on top. He was still struggling in the jail office, but they had already gotten the gun away from him and they were trying to get him handcuffed and get him down and laying still, but he was fighting them.

Mr. Griffin. Did you hear him say anything?

A—No; I don't recall anything he said.

Mr. Griffin. Did you hear the officers say anything to him?

A—No.

Mr. Griffin. How long did you remain there?

A—Just a few minutes. The ambulance came almost immediately. It was just—I walked out of there before the ambulance came and walked back. Someone shouted right after this happened, and there was a lot of confusion, and someone shouted, "Don't let anybody out."

There were a bunch of reporters that started running like they were frightened. I suppose they were running to telephones, but they tried to run up the Main Street ramp, and I remember very clearly the officer at the top of the ramp pulling his gun and said, "Get back down."

They turned around and walked back down, but most of them escaped through the corridor. Not out the ramp, but went out through the corridor. . . . I went as soon as the ambulance came and got him, I ran up the ramp and told him to get that truck out of there, that it was blocking the entrance to the ramp, and then I left and went upstairs and told Chief Curry what happened. By the time I got up there, somebody called him and he knew what happened.

Mr. Griffin. What did you do next?

A—Lord, I don't remember what I did next. We sat there kind of dumbfounded for a while. . . .

Batchelor was first questioned Mar. 23. He appeared again before the commission July 13 to give the following testimony:

Mr. Hubert. What is your estimate of what the number of press people and the general condition created by their presence, contributed to the failure of security? Of what the presence of the news media and the number of them contributed to the failure of security?

A—Of course if we had taken him out in secret without anyone knowing about it, including the press, it is possible that this might not have happened. But I can't say that the press caused any breakdown in security. From what we know now, believing that Oswald came in the Main Street entrance——

Mr. Hubert. You mean Ruby?

A—I mean Ruby came in the Main Street entrance, our

weakness in security lay in allowing him to come down that ramp in the first place.

Had the press not been in the basement at all, and assuming that Ruby slipped into the basement, then he might have been detected more readily.

If people had not been standing across the Main Street ramp, there would have been no place for him to screen himself. But the actual fact of the press being there is hard to say that this caused the breakdown in the security, in my opinion.

Mr. Hubert. As I understand it, you were—when I say you, I mean the police department and of course including you— you were aware of threats being made or having been made toward Oswald, isn't that correct?

A—Yes; I was aware of it. . . .

Mr. Hubert. Was that considered at all, taking him out in secret?

A—I don't recall a discussion of it myself. I am sure that Chief Curry and the rest of us possibly felt that the press had been allowed in the quarters and they got in there quite by, or were in there long before we got back from the President's assassination. They were there when we got there, when we returned to the office.

Mr. Hubert. That is on November 22?

A—Yes; and we had gone that far with them, and I suppose it was a matter of tacit understanding that they had been allowed to report the news as it developed, and in keeping the public aware, perhaps it was felt that they should be allowed to complete, if that is the word to use, their reporting on the actual transfer. This, however, was never discussed. This is just a little mental browsing on my own. I don't know that that is the way everybody felt, but it is the way it was done at any rate. . . .

Mr. Hubert. It is your thought then that the mass confusion which has been described, which existed in the hallway of the third floor at least, did not actually interfere with Captain Fritz' investigative steps excepting insofar as it made it difficult to move Oswald?

A—Well, it increased the difficulties; yes, but it didn't actually interfere with the investigation. It added to the confusion, but as far as the press, some of the things that added to the confusion were all of the various agencies that had an interest and all trying to carry on a simultaneous investigation. This within itself added to the confusion.

This was a highly unusual type of crime and we are really not set up for procedures whereby you allow every other agency to come in and go through all of your evidence in the fashion that it was here, because of the press of time and so on.

It was a most difficult investigation, but I don't think the press materially interfered with the investigation itself. They made things difficult by asking a lot of questions and taking

471

up a lot of people's time and this sort of thing, but they were not allowed in the homicide bureau. . . .

J. W. FRITZ

The testimony of the captain of the Homicide and Robbery Bureau of the Dallas Police Department on the abortive attempt to transfer Oswald to the county jail:

Mr. Hubert. Do you know Jack Ruby at all, or did you know?

A—Did I know him before; no, sir, I did not. I never knew him before, to the best of my knowledge. That is the first time I ever saw him, when he was arrested. In fact, when the shooting happened, I thought some officer had lost his reasoning and shot that man, because of so many officers being down there.

And I asked one of the officers quickly if that was an officer that shot him, and he said it was "Jack Ruby." And I said, "Who is Jack Ruby?" And he said, "He owns a club downtown."

Mr. Hubert. What officer was that?

A—I don't know, some of my officers.

Mr. Hubert. Of course you have seen pictures?

A—Several of the officers knew him, but I didn't know him.

Mr. Hubert. You have seen pictures of Ruby and perhaps you have seen him in person since?

A—Oh, yes; I have questioned him since then.

Mr. Hubert. Can you search your memory and tell us whether you saw that same person in and about the police department, particularly the third floor, on the 22d and 23d?

A—No, sir; I did not. I was very busy at that time. It is possible I could have seen him. If I did, I wouldn't have known him, because there was 200 or 300 people I didn't know.

There was a mob scene, a terrible thing, and I would have uniformed officers help me to get from my office to the chief's office, to the elevator, and back, to get through the crowd, so he could have been in that crowd and I wouldn't know it. I have heard since, he was in the crowd, and he probably was. I wouldn't have known. I would have thought he was another one of those men from the same crowd.

Mr. Hubert. Did you have anything to do with the planning of the exact transfer of Oswald to the county jail?

A—I can't say that there was a meeting of any kind planning the transfer, but if there was, I wasn't there. At the time of the transfer, when the chief told me that an armored money truck had been provided to transfer him, I know it was a surprise to me, because I had never heard of that. I had never heard of that before, and I told the chief I didn't think it was a good thing to try to move him in a money wagon, because we don't know the driver or anything about the wagon, and it would be clumsy and awkward, and I didn't think it was a good idea at all.

I had nothing to do with the setting up of the plan, until my talk with the chief just before the transfer, nor with the setting up of the security in the basement. None of that comes under my heading.

Mr. Hubert. When did you become aware that it would be the responsibility of the Dallas Police Department rather than the sheriff's office to transfer Oswald?

A—The day before the transfer.

Mr. Hubert. You mean on Saturday?

A—That would have been on Saturday, I believe. I don't want to be too positive about an hour or time, but in one of my conversations with the chief, I asked him if the sheriff intended to transfer him or if we would transfer him, and he told me that he had been talking to the sheriff and we would transfer him.

Mr. Hubert. You are pretty sure that would have been on Saturday and not Sunday morning?

A—No, sir; it wouldn't have been on Sunday morning. It would have been before Sunday morning, because some reference was made about the time of transfer.

Mr. Hubert. What reference was made about the time of transfer?

A—Well, in one of my conversations with the chief, you will see from my testimony, the chief asked me about transferring him at 4 o'clock the day before, and I told him I didn't think we could be through with our questioning at that time.

At that time he asked me about 10 o'clock the next morning, and I told him we thought we could be ready by 10 o'clock the next morning. We went, I believe, an hour overtime with the interrogation, but we tried to finish up by 10 o'clock the next morning.

Mr. Hubert. Is there anything that makes you certain that the decision that the Dallas Police Department would be responsible for the transfer rather than the sheriff's office, was made on Saturday rather than Sunday?

A—On Saturday rather than Sunday, I am sure that it was, because I had talked to the sheriff one time myself during one of those previous days, and I made some remark to him, something about the transfer, and he told me to bring him on when we were ready; so I can't tell you exactly what conversation that was, but it was pretty well understood we were to do the transferring. . . .

Mr. Hubert. Would it have been possible for you to have made the investigation and the interrogation of Oswald that was made on Saturday and Sunday morning at the county jail rather than in the homicide office?

A—No, sir; that wouldn't have been good at all.

Mr. Hubert. Can you tell us why?

A—Well, there are many reasons. First our records wouldn't

473

be there, would be one thing, and we wouldn't have the witnesses at the county jail for the lineups and would be out of contact with the office for incoming information. The city hall would be quite a distance from us. There are certain other things that might interfere with questioning at the county jail. It was bad enough where we were.

Mr. Hubert. As a matter of fact, where you were was a pretty bad situation for it?

A—Ordinarily it wouldn't be such a bad situation. It was a bad situation because of all that news media that had turned into a mob. . . .

Mr. Hubert. Were you aware on Sunday the 24th that there was quite a crowd of people in the basement, which was a part of the transfer route that was being planned?

A—I hadn't been down there in the basement. I had been, as I told you before, real busy in my office, and we had been continuing our questioning in company with some Federal officers from the Secret Service, and FBI, and at one time the marshal was over there, and some of the postal authorities, trying to finish up our investigation as fast as we could, and I hadn't been down in the basement. But I had been down there either the early morning or the night before, and I had seen all the big lights set up in the basement and in the basement door, so when the chief told me about the transfer, I told him we ought to get rid of the lights and get the people out of the door that would interfere with our getting to the car for the transfer. After I was late getting started the chief came back to my office and asked if we were ready to transfer him, I told him "When the security downstairs was ready, we were ready." And he said, "The lights have been moved back and the people have been moved back in the basement, back of the rail, and the other people have been moved across the street." Which would have given us ample room to get into the car and get rolling with him. Once we had gotten into the car, we would have been all right. . . .

Mr. Hubert. Did you ever make a suggestion that the people, the news media in the basement just be removed altogether so that there would be nobody there?

A—I didn't handle that. I had nothing to do with the arrangement in the basement. I did ask that they be moved out of our way, and I believe there was a number of officers down there to do that.

I want to say this in fairness to the chief. As we started to leave, he told me that the people were moved across the street, and the other people were back of the railing, and I think he thought they were. I think someone must have changed his order down there. We first called down and they told us everything was all right. One of my officers called on the telephone, before we went down to the jail. I kept my officers back in the jail until I asked two officers outside the jail if the security was good, and they said it was all right. But when we walked out, they climbed over my car and we met the crowd and the officers coming forward.

Mr. Hubert. Was that before the shooting?

A—Almost simultaneous. We had already gotten out of the jail door when the shooting happened. We were only a few feet out into the basement.

Mr. Hubert. As I understand it then, after you came out of the jail door and walked down the corridor to the car, there was a general surge?

A—Yes.

Mr. Hubert. Six or five feet?

A—Probably as far as from here to that door.

Mr. Hubert. That was about 8 or 9 feet?

A—Well, I don't think, any more than that, probably. We probably have the measurements.

Mr. Hubert. The fact is that as soon as you began to come out, the whole crowd surged forward?

A—I had turned toward my car to reach for the door to open the rear door, and I just told the two officers to put him right here in the rear of the car when I heard the shot. Mr. Dhority was sitting at the wheel. He was backing my car back, and he was being hindered in backing the car by people getting around and behind it—both officers and other people. And as I started to reach for the door, the shot was fired.

Mr. Hubert. As I understand it then, when you came down there, you met a condition which you had not anticipated in this sense. That it was your impression that although the news media would be down there, they would be back of that rail?

A—Had they been back there, everything would have been all right. . . .

Mr. Hubert. Now you say that when you came outside you caused Oswald and the two guards with him, Mr. Leavelle and Mr. Graves, to halt in the jail office and you went out and called out as to whether it was clear?

A—A lieutenant was standing there in uniform, and I asked him, and he told me that the security was OK. A detective also gave the same answer. . . .

Mr. Hubert. Did you have a conversation just prior to the move about the security?

A—With the chief; yes, sir.

Mr. Hubert. Do you remember what he said and what you said about it?

A—Yes. As I told you, I told him—he asked me were we ready for the transfer. . . .

And I told him we were ready to transfer him any time the security was ready in the basement, and he said everything is all right.

Mr. Hubert. Did he say he would check further, or he just told you?

A—He just told me. He didn't tell me how he checked.

Mr. Hubert. But he didn't go and check again?

A—I don't know. I can't answer that because he left my office. He told me that he and Chief Stevenson would meet me at the county jail.

Mr. Hubert. Who made the decision as to the actual moment of moving?

A—Of course, the chief asked me if we were ready. We got ready, because I had told him the night before we would try to be ready at 10 o'clock.

Mr. Hubert. So you gave the signal to go?

A—To these officers; yes. . . .

Mr. Hubert. What was your concern about the news media being on the main ramp and not behind the rail?

A—Well, they interfered with our movement upstairs each time we took Oswald to and from the jail, they would holler at him and ask questions and say things to him that would have a tendency to, I thought, aggravate him. I think part of it he seemed to enjoy, and part of it he seemed to be irritated about.

Mr. Hubert. Was your concern about the news media?

A—My concern was to do all I could to prevent a killing or an escape.

Mr. Hubert. Was your concern about the news media not being on the outside of the rail, or was it concerned with fear of Oswald's safety, or simply that these people were in the way?

A—Both. They were in the way, and anyone that hindered us or held us up could cause something to happen there.

We wouldn't have been taking all those precautions if we hadn't been afraid something might happen.

I had even thought of the possibility of someone trying to take the prisoner. That was the reason we handcuffed him to an officer.

In a case as serious as that, we certainly didn't want to lose him after a thing as serious as having had the President shot.

Mr. Hubert. What I had in mind was, whether your concern was that the position and closeness and mass of the news media there presented a threat insofar as single-man action was concerned?

A—We didn't know many of those people. We knew very few. We knew the local people. Many people were there from foreign countries, and some of them looked unkempt. We didn't know anything about who they were.

For that reason, we wouldn't want them up there with us at all if we could avoid it, plus the fact that the camera lights were blinding, and if you couldn't see where you were going or what you were doing, anything could happen.

We didn't think we would have lights in our eyes, but we were blinded by lights. Just about the time we left the jail office, the lights came on, and were blinding.

We got along all right with the press here in Dallas. They do what we ask. These people didn't act that way. These people were excited and acted more like a mob. . . .

Mr. Ball. Had you been requested by Sheriff Decker to transfer him [Oswald] there before?

A—No, sir. I had talked to the chief about transferring him down there. The chief had called me on the 23d, on the 23d, I can't give you the exact minute, probably a little after noon, he had called me and asked me when we would be ready to transfer him and I told him we were still questioning him. We didn't want to transfer him yet. He said, "Can he be ready by about 4 o'clock? Can he be transferred by 4 o'clock?" I told him I didn't think we could.

Mr. Ball. That would be Saturday afternoon?

A—That would be the 23d, would be Saturday, yes, sir. Then he asked me could he be ready by 10 o'clock in the morning, so I could tell these people something definitely, and I felt sure we would be ready by then. However, we didn't, we ran overtime as you can see by this report, an hour and a half over, when they come over to transfer him.

Mr. Ball. Why did you say you would not be ready by 4 o'clock on Saturday?

A—We wanted to ask him some more questions, to get more information.

Mr. Ball. Did you consider transferring him at night?

A—At night?

Mr. Ball. Yes.

A—During the night on Saturday night, I had a call at my home from uniformed captain, Captain Frazier, I believe is his name, he called me out at home and told me they had had some threats and he had to transfer Oswald.

And I said, well, I don't know. I said there has been no security setup, and the chief having something to do with this transfer and you had better call him, because—so he told me he would.

Mr. Ball. Did you think——

A—He called me back then in a few minutes and he told me he couldn't get the chief and told me to leave him where he was. I don' think that transferring him at night would have been any safer than transferring, may I say this?

Mr. Ball. Yes.

A—Any safer than transferring him during the day. I have always felt that that was Ruby who made that call, I may be wrong, but he was out late that night and I have always felt he might have made that call, if two or three of those officers had started out with him they may have had the same trouble they had the next morning.

I don't know whether we had been transferring him ourselves, I don't know that we would have used this same method but we certainly would have used security of some kind.

Mr. Ball. Now weren't you transferring him?

477

A—Sir, yes, sir.

Mr. Ball. What do you mean if we were transferring him ourselves?

A—I mean transferring like I was told to transfer him.

Mr. Ball. I beg your pardon?

A—I was transferring him like the chief told me to transfer him.

Mr. Ball. How would you have transferred him?

A—I did do one thing here, I should tell you about. When the chief came back and asked me if I was ready to transfer him, I told him I had already complained to the chief about the big cameras set up in the jail office and I was afraid we couldn't get out of the jail with him with all those cameras and all those people in the jail office.

So when the chief came back he asked if we were ready to transfer and I said, "We are ready if the security is ready," and he said, "It is all set up." He said, "The people are across the street, and the newsmen are all well back in the garage," and he said "It is all set."

And at that time he told me, he said, "We have got the money wagon up there to transfer him in," and I said, "Well, I don't like the idea, chief, of transferring him in a money wagon." We, of course, didn't know the driver, nor who he was, nor anything about the money wagon, and he said, "Well, that is all right. Transfer him in your car like you want to, and we will use the money wagon for a decoy, and I will have a squad to lead it up to the central expressway and across to the left on Elm Street and the money wagon can turn down Elm Street and you can turn down Main Street, when you get to Main Street, going to the county jail," and he told me he and Chief Stevenson would meet me at the county jail, that is when we started out.

Mr. Ball. How would you have done it if you were going to do it?

A—Well, I hesitate to say because it didn't work good this way. If I had done it like I would do it or usually do it or something and it hadn't worked I would be just in the same shape you know, and it would be just as bad, so I don't like to be critical of something because it turned out real bad.

You can kind of understand my—I know that our chief didn't know anything was going to happen or he surely wouldn't have told me to transfer it that way.

Mr. Ball. How would you have done it?

A—Well, we transferred Ruby the next day at about the same time, and I had two of the officers from my office to pick me up away from the office. We drove by the county jail, saw that the driveway was open. We had about the same threats on him that we did with Oswald. We saw that the driveway was open. I went back to the bus station and I called one of my officers upstairs, gave him the names of two other officers, told him to get those two officers and not tell anyone even in the office where they were going, mark Ruby transferred temporarily, which means coming to the office or going for some fingerprints or anything, mark him transferred temporarily, bring him down to the jail elevator at the bottom of the jail, put two of them to stay in the jail elevator with him. For the other one to come to the outside door and when he saw our car flush with the door, bring that man right through those cameras and put him in the back seat, and they did, they shot him right through those people and they didn't even get pictures and we had him lie down on the back seat and two officers lean back over him and we drove him straight up that same street, turned to the left down Main Street, ran him into the jail entrance, didn't even tell the jailer we were coming and put him in the jail. It worked all right.

But now if it hadn't worked, you know, I don't want to be saying that I know more about transferring than someone else, because this could happen to me. I could see if it happened to Ruby, I would have had all the blame.

Mr. Ball. Now, if on that morning at 11:15 you planned to transfer him, didn't you, according to the chief's orders?

A—Yes, sir; I did.

Mr. Ball. And you were through questioning him, weren't you?

A—Sir?

Mr. Ball. You were all through questioning him?

A—Yes, sir; we had everything that we could do at that time. I would have talked to him later in the county jail but we didn't need to hold the man any longer.

Mr. Ball. Had he been handcuffed?

A—Yes, sir; and I told—he was already handcuffed, and I told one of the officers to handcuff his left hand to Oswald's right hand, and to keep him right with him.

Mr. Ball. That was Leavelle?

A—Leavelle, yes, sir. He first started the other hand on the other side, and I told Officer Graves to get on the other side and Montgomery to follow him, and I would go down and an officer by the name of Swain who works across the hall from us came over and offered to help us, he went down the jail elevator and he went out ahead of me and I went out in back of him and I was approaching our car to open the back door to put him in, they were having a terrible time to get the car in through the people—they were crowding all over the car—and I heard the shot and I turned just in time to see the officers push Ruby to the pavement.

Mr. Ball. When you came out of the jail door were the lights on?

A—Yes, sir; the lights were on. I don't believe they were on as we came to the door, but they came out immediately as we were coming out of the door, and I asked one of the officers, two of them answered me if everything was secure and they said everything was all right. So we came out.

Mr. Ball. What about the lights?

A—The lights were almost blinding.

Mr. Ball. Did you see the people in the crowd?

A—I could see the people but I could hardly tell who they were, because of the lights. I have been wearing glasses this year and with glasses those lights don't help you facing a bright light like that, the lights were glaring.

Mr. Ball. How far ahead of Ruby were you?

A—Well. I thought they were right behind me almost but I noticed from the picture they were a little further back than I actually thought they were, probably where Mr. Baker is to this gentleman. I believe maybe a little bit farther than that, maybe about——

Mr. Ball. How far behind Oswald were you, how far behind Oswald. Oswald was behind you?

A—Behind me.

Mr. Ball. How many feet would you say?

A—In feet I would say probably 8 feet.

Mr. Ball. Did you ever know of Jack Ruby.

A—No, sir; I never did know him. I never knew him at all. Some of the officers knew him. But I never knew him.

Mr. Ball. Were there any flashbulbs or were they just steady beams of light?

A—I didn't see any flashing lights. These were steady blinding lights that I saw. That I couldn't see, you might say. . . .

Mr. Dulles. Have you discovered any connection between any of your officers and Ruby?

A—Well, I think a lot of the officers knew Ruby. I think about two or three officers in my office knew him, and I think practically all of the special service officers who handle the vice and the clubs and the liquor violations, I think nearly all of them knew him and, of course, the officer knew him who had arrested him carrying pistols a time or two, two or three times, uniformed officer mostly. He seemed to be well known. It seems a lot of people in town knew him. But I never was in his place and I didn't know him. Twenty years ago I might have been in his place. . . .

Mr. Ball. The first day that you had Oswald in custody, did you get a notice from the FBI, any of the FBI officers that there had been a communication from Washington suggesting that you take extra precautions for the safety of Oswald?

A—No. sir; there was not.

Mr. Ball. Do you recall whether or not on Friday——

The Chairman. What was your answer to that?

A—I did not, I got no such instructions. In fact, we couldn't —we would have taken the precautions without the notice but we did not get the notice. I never heard of that.

Mr. Ball. Do you recall that on Friday, November 22, Wade

asked you or did he or didn't District Attorney Wade ask you to transfer Oswald to the county jail for security?

A—That would be on the night of the 22d?

Mr. Ball. On the night of the 22d.

A—Yes, sir; he asked me if I would transfer him that night.

Mr. Ball. What did you tell him?

A—I told him we didn't want to transfer him yet. We wanted to talk to him some more. We talked a little bit. He didn't actually want him transferred. He just was more or less talking about whether or not we wanted to transfer him.

Mr. Ball. Now on Saturday Decker called you and asked you to transfer him?

A—On Saturday did he call me and ask me to transfer him?

Mr. Ball. Yes, that would be the 23d.

A—No, sir; he did not.

Mr. Ball. Did Chief Curry tell you that Decker had called or anything of that sort?

A—Yes, sir; when I was talking to Chief Curry on one of those conversations, I don't think it is the conversation now when he told me about the hours, I think it is another conversation, I told him, I said, "I don't know whether we were going to transfer him or Decker was going to transfer him," and Chief Curry said, "We are going to transfer him, I have talked to Decker, we are going to transfer him."

Mr. Ball. When were the plans for the transfer made?

A—When were the plans made?

Mr. Ball. Yes; do you know?

A—I don't know about that. The only thing I know is what I told you about when the chief told me about would he be ready by 10 o'clock that morning, and I told him I thought we could.

Mr. Ball. You didn't make the plans yourself?

A—No, sir.

Mr. Ball. They were made by the chief?

A—Yes, sir; they were made by the chief.

Mr. Ball. When did the chief first tell you what the plans were?

A—That was on the 23d. He didn't tell me about all the plans, of course, at that time because I told you when he came up to tell us about that, when he asked when we were ready to go he told me about the armored car, that is the first I had ever heard of that.

Mr. Ball. Did you ever tell any of the press the time that Oswald would be moved?

A—No, sir; I don't believe I did. I was interrogated by a bunch of them as I started to leave the office on the night of the 23d. As we started to the elevator, a group of us from my office, and some of the FBI officers, we started to the elevator some 10 or 20 reporters came up and said the chief said we were going to transfer him at 10 o'clock the next morning and if we were and I didn't talk to them so I don't think I ever said much if anything to them because I know one of them followed me almost 'to my parking lot, I know, asking me questions about the transfer.

Mr. Ball. At 11:15 when they left your office, do you know whether or not there was any broadcast over your radio as to your movements?

A—On our radio?

Mr. Ball. Yes.

A—I wouldn't know.

Mr. Ball. Or on any radio, were there any radio broadcasters on your floor at that time?

A—Any of those newsmen?

Mr. Ball. Newsmen?

A—Oh, yes; they might not have been on the floor but they were all down in the basement. You are talking about the morning of the 24th?

Mr. Ball. On the morning of the 24th when you were moving?

A—Any number of them downstairs. I don't remember whether there were any upstairs or not. There probably was maybe a few of them because I don't think there was any time when there wasn't a few of them up there, but we didn't leave through that hall and go through the elevator. We went through the mail elevator.

Mr. Ball. On the 22d and 23d, the third floor was full of newspapermen and photographers?

A—Yes, sir; all the time, completely full.

Mr. Ball. Had they left the third floor on the 24th?

A—A lot of them had; yes, sir. A lot of them had, and were downstairs in the basement.

Mr. Ball. How about the television cameras?

A—I noticed—television cameras, they were downstairs too.

Mr. Ball. They weren't up on the third floor?

A—I don't believe—there could have been one or two of them left up there, I don't think many of them were still up there.

Mr. Ball. Most of them were downstairs?

A—Most of them were downstairs. I wouldn't say there weren't any up there because I don't think there was any time when there wasn't at least a few of them up there.

Mr. Ball. Now, when you went down the jail elevator and you said you got out and went forward to see if everything was secure. What did you mean by that?

A—Well, I meant if everything, it was all right for us to go to our car with him. We didn't want to leave the jail office with him unless everything was all right because as long as we were in the jail office we could put him back in the elevator and if everything wasn't all right, I didn't want to come out with him.

Mr. Ball. And you went ahead, didn't you?

A—Yes, sir; first Lieutenant Swain and then I went out and then the other officers followed me with the prisoner.

Mr. Ball. Was the car there you were going to get in?

A—Yes, sir.

Mr. Ball. Had you reached the car yet?

A—I was just in the act of reaching for the door to open the back door, I looked at that picture, and it doesn't show the exact distance I was from the car but I couldn't have been any further than reaching distance.

Mr. Ball. When you left, or after Ruby shot Oswald, he was taken upstairs, wasn't he?

A—Yes, sir; he was. He was first carried into the jail office, you mean Ruby?

Mr. Ball. Ruby, when Ruby shot Oswald?

A—Oswald was carried into the jail office and put on the floor there. Ruby was brought into the jail office. Now I believe that Ruby was brought into the jail office after Oswald, I believe Oswald was already on the floor or behind there because I know the officers had taken Ruby upstairs went behind me and I saw them pass behind me with him to the jail.

Mr. Ball. Did you talk to Ruby?

A—Did I talk to him; no, sir; I talked to him later.

Mr. McCloy. I wonder if at this time you would want a little recess?

A—No, sir; I am comfortable.

Mr. McCloy. I think we kept the chief on a little bit too long this morning.

A—If it is all right with you.

Mr. Ball. Did you talk to Ruby at that time?

A—No, sir; not at that time.

Mr. Ball. Later?

A—I talked to him later, probably an hour later. I guess I have the exact time here if you need it.

Mr. Ball. What did Ruby say to you, do you have the exact time?

A—Well, he told me, I told him, I, of course, wanted to know something about premeditation because I was thinking about the trial too and I told him I wanted to ask him some questions and he said, well, he first said, "I don't want to talk to you. I want to talk to my lawyers," and he said, I believe he told me too that he had been advised by a lawyer, and I asked him some other question and he said, "Now if you will level with me and you won't make me look like a fool in front of my lawyers I will talk to you."

I didn't ask him one way or the other, but I did ask him some questions and he told me that he shot him, told me that he was all torn up about the Presidential killing, that he felt terribly sorry for Mrs. Kennedy. He didn't want to see her have to come back to Dallas for a trial, and a lot of other things like that.

Mr. Ball. Did you ask him how he got down to the jail?

A—Yes; I did.

Mr. Ball. What did he say?

A—He told me he came down that ramp from the outside. So I told him, I said, "No, you couldn't have come down that ramp because there would be an officer at the top and an officer at the bottom and you couldn't come down that ramp." He said, "I am not going to talk to you any more, I am not going to get into trouble," and he never talked to me any more about it.

Mr. Ball. Did you ever talk to him again?

A—I don't think I ever talked to him after that. I talked to him a little while then and I don't believe I ever talked to him after that. I asked him when he first decided to kill Oswald, and he didn't tell me that. He told me something else, talked about something else. . . .

GEORGE SENATOR

The testimony of the man who shared an apartment with Ruby:

Mr. Hubert. What happened next?

A—The next thing I know somebody was hollering at me and shaking me up. This was around 3 o'clock in the morning. [The day after the assassination.]

Mr. Hubert. That was who?

A—Jack Ruby.

Mr. Hubert. Now describe him to us at that time. What was his condition?

A—He was excited. He was moody; and the first thing come out of his mouth is the incident. Of course, the incident what happened to President Kennedy, and he said, "Gee, his poor children and Mrs. Kennedy, what a terrible thing to happen."

Mr. Hubert. Had he been drinking?

A—Jack don't drink. . . .

Mr. Hubert. And his remarks were concerning the children?

A—The children and Mrs. Kennedy and how sorry he felt for them.

Mr. Hubert. What other comments did he make?

A—Then he brought up the situation where he saw this poster of Justice of the Peace Earl Warren, impeach him, Earl Warren. . . .

Mr. Hubert. What did he tell you when he made you get dressed?

A—He was telling me about this sign here.

Mr. Hubert. Why did he want you to get dressed?

A—He wanted me to go down to see the sign, and meanwhile he had called. He had a kid sleeping in the club who helps around, and he has got a Polaroid camera. So he calls the kid up, wakes him up.

Mr. Hubert. Did you hear that call?

A—What.

Mr. Hubert. Did you hear that call?

A—Yeah, he calls him up and says, "Larry, get up, get dressed," something of that nature, "and get that Polaroid with the flashbulbs and meet me downstairs. I'll be right downtown. . . ."

I got dressed. We went downtown. We picked up Larry. He drove over to where this billboard was . . . and he had the kid take three Polaroid shots of this billboard. Now, what his intentions were with these I don't know.

Mr. Hubert. He didn't express any?

A—No; he didn't say what he was going to do with them but he wanted three shots.

Mr. Hubert. Did you ask him or did anyone else ask him why he wanted to take pictures of this?

A—No; all he said to me, "I can't understand why they want to impeach Earl Warren." He said, "This must be the work of the John Birch Society or the Communist Party." And he wanted to know why.

Mr. Hubert. Did he say how taking a picture would help him to find out?

A—No; he didn't. He didn't say how that would help him to find out. . . .

Mr. Hubert. Did he seem to be concerned about the President's death . . . ?

A—To me, I would probably say it must have been a combination of the entire thing. I know he was deeply hurt about the President, terribly.

Mr. Hubert. You say you know that. How do you know that?

A—What? By his feelings; by the way he talked about the family and the children; by tears in his eyes, which I have seen, and I am not the only one who has seen it.

Mr. Hubert. Do you think that he was more disturbed than the average person that you know was disturbed about the President's death?

A—All I know, while I can't say about the average because all I know, he was really deeply disturbed, but I can't describe an average because there might be another individual of his nature, too, who knows. Who knows the affections of each and every individual . . . ?

Mr. Hubert. What time did you awaken on Sunday morning?

A—Sunday morning I assume it was somewhere around between 8 or 9, somewheres in that time. Just something in that time. . . .

Mr. Hubert. Again I want to ask you, can you give us a comparison between the look that he had that morning, which you just described, as opposed to what it was on other occasions in the sense of whether it was growing worse or not?

A—He looked a little worse this day here. But if you ask

485

me how to break it down, how he looks worse, how can I express it? The look in his eyes?

Mr. Hubert. Well, is that one of the things?

A—Yes; that is the way it seems.

Mr. Hubert. The way he talked or what he said?

A—The way he talked. He was even mumbling, which I didn't understand. And right after breakfast he got dressed. Then after he got dressed he was pacing the floor from the living room to the bedroom, from the bedroom to the living room, and his lips were going. What he was jabbering I don't know. But he was really pacing. What he was thinking about——. . .

Mr. Hubert. How long did this pacing go on after he got dressed? It may have been a matter of only a couple of minutes, but if it was more than that, I think you would know it. I think if it was a half hour you would know it.

A—I would say that he paced back and forth 5 or 10 minutes. I don't know.

Mr. Hubert. All right. Was it at that point that he left?

A—Yes.

Mr. Hubert. Did he say anything upon leaving?

A—Yes.

Mr. Hubert. What did he say?

A—He said, "George, I am taking the dog down to the club."

Mr. Hubert. Anything else?

A—That was it, and out he went. . . .

MRS. ELNORA PITTS

The testimony of Ruby's cleaning lady who telephoned him a few hours before he shot Oswald to ask if he wanted her to come tidy up his apartment:

Mr. Hubert. Did you recognize his voice?

A—Well, I'll tell you how he talked to me, then I said, "What do I want?" I says, "This is Elnora." He says, "Yes, well, what—you need some money?" And I says, "No; I was coming to clean today."

"Coming to clean?" Like you know, like he just——

Mr. Hubert. In other words, when you told him that you were coming to clean he seemed to express some surprise, is that it?

A—Yes, sir; like he didn't know that I was going to come and clean.

Mr. Hubert. Did he recognize you?

A—I don't know if he did or not. And I says to him again, I says, "This is Elnora." And he says, "Well, what do you want?" And I said, "Well, I was coming to clean today."

"You coming now?" And I says, "No."

Mr. Hubert. He asked you then, "Are you coming now?"

A—Yes, sir; and then I says, "No." And he says, "Well, what you got to do?" And I says, "I have got to go to the store for the children." I always goes to the store for the children before I come to work whenever I come. He says, "Well," —I says, "You seem so funny to me." And I says, "Do you want me to come today?" And he says, "Well, yes; you can come, but you call me." And I says, "That's what I'm doing now, calling you so I won't have to call you again." And he says, "And you coming to clean today?" And I said, "Yes." Well, he sounded so strange to me but I still wouldn't say nothing to him. I just stopped another few minutes, and I said, "Who am I talking to? Is this Mr. Jack Ruby?" And he said, "Yes. Why?" And I said, "Oh, nothing." But he just sounded terrible strange to me, so, I said, "Well, I'll call you." And he says, "But, I don't see why I called you." And he said, "Yes, so I can tell you where the key will be and the money." And I said, "Okay." So, I hung up. . . .

Mr. Hubert. Did he ask you to call him at 2 or what?

A—No; he says, "You call me before 2," that is what he says. He says, "Be sure you call me." To call before 2, "Before you come." He says, "You call me before 2, before you start," and I says, "Well, what I have to call you again for?" And he says, "Well, so I can tell you where the key is and the money." And I said, "Uh-huh."

So, before I could, you know, hang up, he says, "Be sure and call me." "Did you say you was coming in today?" And I said, "Yes." And when he said that, that's when it kind of scared me, so, I just hung—I say, "okay," and I hung up.

Mr. Hubert. What were you scared about?

A—The way he talked. He didn't talk like—he never did sound like hisself to me. . . .

MRS. KAREN LYNN CARLIN

The testimony of "Little Lynn," a stripper who worked at Ruby's Carousel Club, who telephoned Ruby from Fort Worth to ask him for a salary advance the morning that Ruby killed Oswald:

Mr. Hubert. Do you remember what time you called him?

A—It was 10. I think it was around 10 or 10:05 or 10:15, something like that. It was between that time. . . . Jack answered the telephone. And I told him who it was, and he said, "Yes, well," and I said, "I have called, Jack, to try to get some money, because the rent is due and I need some money for groceries, and you told me to call."

And he said, "How much will you need?" And I said—I'll ask my husband, and then I said about "$25."

Mr. Hubert. Your husband was in the room with you?

A—Yes. He was in the part of the front part of the house. And he said, "Well, I have to go downtown anyway, so I will send it to you by Western Union." . . . He said, "Well," he did say it would take a little while to get dressed and something about the dog, I don't remember what it was. And he said, "I'll go on down and send it to you." And I said, "I sure would appreciate it." And that is about all there was. . . .

Mr. Hubert. Then do you know—and I don't mean from your knowledge at all, but from what you might have heard, what Jack's relationship in general with people of the opposite sex was? What his relationship with girls was?

A—No; I would rather not answer it.

Mr. Hubert. That is all right. Mind you, I want it clear I was not asking in relation to anything with respect to you yourself, but as to what you have heard? . . .

Mr. Jackson. In other words, he did do that with the girls occasionally—make advances toward them?

A—Yes.

Mr. Jackson. Proposition them?

A—Yes; I knew of them going with him.

Mr. Jackson. Dating them?

A—Yes.

Mr. Jackson. He did date them some?

A—Yes.

Mr. Jackson. Did you know or had you heard anything concerning the possibility of any kind of homosexuality on the part of Jack?

A—Yes.

Mr. Jackson. Is that just a rumor running out there, or what?

A—That was from his mouth. He was always asking the question, "Do you think I am a queer? Do you think I look like a queer? Or have you ever known a queer to look like me?" Everytime I saw him he would ask it.

Mr. Jackson. Do you mean he would bring up the subject himself?

A—Yes; he would say, "Do you think I look like one or act like one?"

Mr. Jackson. Did he say he was?

A—No; he just asked me, "Do I look like one."

Mr. Jackson. But he never admitted to you of being one?

A—No.

Mr. Jackson. Or ever made any statements that indicated that he was a homosexual?

A—Not to my knowledge.

Mr. Jackson. What you have told us here is all that you know about his abnormality, if any?

A—Yes.

Mr. Hubert. Can you throw any light upon his character with respect to whether he had a good temper or easygoing temper or quick temper?

A—He was very quick tempered. . . .

488

DOYLE E. LANE

The testimony of the clerk at the Western Union office near Dallas police headquarters who sold Ruby a money order minutes before he entered the police building and shot Oswald:

A—This is a money order application filed to send money. $25. Karen Bennett, Fort Worth, Tex., from Jack Ruby.

Mr. Hubert. I notice that there are several handwritings on that, and, of course, you will identify your own in a moment. Can you state for the record what handwriting was on that, or what was on that document at the time it was handed to you by Ruby?

A—"25.00 Karen Bennett. Will call. Fort Worth. Jack Ruby."

JIMMY TURNER

The testimony of a television director with WBAP-TV, Fort Worth, who apparently saw Ruby enter the basement of the Dallas police headquarters by the Main St. ramp seconds before Ruby shot Oswald:

Mr. Hubert. Now, did you have access during that period to the jail building on Harwood, between Commerce and Main Street?

A—Yes, sir.

Mr. Hubert. Was a particular sort of pass or identification given to you?

A—No; it was not a pass given to us. No identification was ever required. The identification I used was a press card from a Sheraton Hotel, and I was never checked about the authenticity of it or anything.

Mr. Hubert. But you were asked, in any case, to show that press pass that you have just described?

A—Yes; we were. We were wearing it on our coat.

Mr. Hubert. Would you describe that again?

A—It was a press pass that the Sheraton Dallas Hotel had when they opened the new hotel here in Dallas. It had "Press" on it, the seal of the Sheraton Hotel and my name after it. It was very vague but the only thing we had at the time.

Mr. Hubert. Were you ever accosted by anyone with respect to checking as to whether you——

A—No, sir.

Mr. Hubert. Were connected with news media?

A—No, sir.

Mr. Hubert. You felt that simply wearing this on your coat with the word, "Press," was sufficient to get around as you wanted to?

A—Correct.

Mr. Hubert. Did you see them checking any other people?

A—To my knowledge, up until the following morning after

the shooting of Oswald, there was no checking of passes that we ran into. Now, there was a checking after the shooting when we left the building, but I left the building with the pass, and came back in the building with the pass.

Mr. Hubert. I am sure that during the 48 hours, approximately, between the President's death and the shooting of Oswald, that you must have had occasion to go in and out of that building a number of times.

A—I used it at Parkland Hospital. I used it at the city hall also without being stopped, or asked what kind of pass it was.

Mr. Hubert. Prior to November 24, did you know that man now known as Jack Ruby?

A—No; I didn't, sir.

Mr. Hubert. You had never seen him before?

A—I had never seen him.

Mr. Hubert. Had you ever heard of him?

A—I had never heard of him.

Mr. Hubert. Now, of course, since November 24, you have heard of Jack Ruby. You have seen his picture, I take it?

A—Yes, sir.

Mr. Hubert. Have you ever seen him in person?

A—Yes, sir; I saw him at the trial. At various times when they took him in the courtroom, except the morning of the shooting I saw him.

Mr. Hubert. You saw him then, too? What I wanted to get at was whether you ever saw the man now known as Jack Ruby, in the police building prior to the time that you saw him immediately before the shooting?

A—To my knowledge, I had never seen him until then. . . .

Mr. Hubert. Let's go back to the police car going up the Main Street ramp towards Main Street, did you follow it with your eyes?

A—I followed it not only to about a point to where the drive had started up, because it was impossible——

Mr. Hubert. To the point where the ramp starts to go up?

A—Uphill, the slope up, which was this column here had sort of blocked our view. . . . I happened to glance up and this was at the same time the car drove out of the—I'm not sure. I couldn't—that right down where the ramp it hit—the——

Mr. Hubert. Level part?

A—Level part. I saw Mr. Ruby coming in.

Mr. Hubert. Now, had you ever seen him before?

A—No, sir; I certainly hadn't. . . .

Mr. Hubert. Now, you say you saw Jack Ruby. You had not known him to be Jack Ruby at that time?

A—No; what set him off from other men was the hat he was wearing.

Mr. Hubert. What sort of hat was it?

A—I don't know the technical name. Could you help me out? It was a felt hat, had a pretty large brim on it, and it was a—round on top, which you seldom see.

Mr. Hubert. Snap brim?

A—No; it wasn't snap brim. It was just a wide brim, and like you say, I didn't go that far.

Mr. Hubert. Do you know what color it was?

A—It seemed to be grey.

Mr. Hubert. Could you describe any other clothing?

A—Yes; he was, to my knowledge he was dressed in an overcoat, or long—it could have been a suit coat, but I didn't notice.

Mr. Hubert. Did you have a fair look at his face?

A—At an angle that I do not recognize him now. He seemed to be much heavier then than when I saw him in the Ruby trial. . . .

Mr. Hubert. Do you think that that man that you saw . . . was Jack Ruby?

A—I certainly do.

Mr. Hubert. He was coming down the Main Street ramp at that time?

A—That's right. . . .

Mr. Hubert. Did you see a man come out from the crowd and shoot Oswald?

A—Yes, sir.

Mr. Hubert. Was that man the same man that you have——

A—It was this same man.

Mr. Hubert. That you have marked as "10"?

A—As "10." It was the same man, and came out and shot him from "10."

Mr. Hubert. So, that if it were Jack Ruby who shot Oswald, it was Jack Ruby at place number "10"?

A—That's right. Right. Right.

Mr. Hubert. How long before the shooting was it that you saw a man in position number "10" there in a circle on the ramp?

A—It was not more than 15 to 30 seconds. It was——

Mr. Hubert. Did you keep your eye on the man, this man?

A—No; I had just glanced up there, and I had come back— my eye on our reporter, Tom Pettit, and also the door, which is behind Tom Pettit, which I will mark right now as "11," where Oswald made his exit.

Mr. Hubert. Now, when was the next time you saw the man whom you have previously identified as number "10" and at what position was he then?

A—The next time I saw him he walked up to Position "12," which was almost in line with our man, Pettit, which is number "8," here.

Mr. Hubert. Now, you saw him then?

A—Yes, sir.

Mr. Hubert. Was he at the front row of those people?

A—Let me mark two more positions here, sir. A policeman was over here to his right, I think, which we'll mark, "13," and then there was a reporter, or a man dressed in a suit, I'll call him the reporter at "14".

Mr. Hubert. All right, and my point is, that when you next saw the man who is now identified as Jack Ruby, and therefore I shall refer to him as Jack Ruby from now on out, he was at a position marked as number "12"?

A—Right.

Mr. Hubert. Was he standing still there, or moving?

A—There was only a matter of 4 seconds, or 5 seconds, when he arrived there that—until Oswald reached the point where he was assassinated.

Mr. Hubert. You saw Ruby arrive at the front?

A—That's right. He walked up to—see, this is all in line, from our camera position to our—there were—they were just a little back of the side light from our camera to our newscaster——

Mr. Hubert. That's number "8"?

A—That's right.

Mr. Hubert. But you are willing to say that he was standing at the front row of the group of people congregated there for possibly 5 seconds before he moved forward to shoot Oswald?

A—That's right, that's right.

Mr. Hubert. And you judge that the time that you saw him standing still, 5 seconds before this shooting of Oswald, was approximately 15 to 20 seconds after you first saw him in that position "10"?

A—I am vague about that time. Ten seconds or 20 seconds. I am very vague. I mean, but I know he was only there a short time, because I saw—we were on guard to try to move the newsmen out of our way, push them out of the way in front of the camera, and you kind of thrash around at the movement of them to keep on your shot, and that is how I come to notice another man up there. These three men are the only ones that I remember on that side except our man Pettit. There could have been more. There was some CBS cameramen over in this locality, but they had already been there, and that wasn't in my mind at all, the ones that were actually stationed there. It was the movement of people at that time that made you look at it.

Mr. Hubert. All right, let's get a little bit more about this period for Jack Ruby to move from the position you have marked "10", to the position you have marked "12", when he was standing in the front line. Did he have to go through any great mass of people?

A—No, not to my knowledge, because I didn't see a great number of men up in there.

Mr. Hubert. Did he have to push, or shoulder his way up there?

A—No.

Mr. Hubert. He could just walk up and get into that position?

A—That's right. There was some more men out there in this area, but I can't connect it at this point.

Mr. Hubert. What I want to get at, from what you tell me the group was not such that he would have to bulldoze his way through?

A—No; he just flat walked up.

Mr. Hubert. Just once again for the record. There can be no doubt in your mind but the man now identified as Jack Ruby is the man you saw at position "10"?

A—Correct. . . .

RIO S. PIERCE

The testimony of the Dallas police lieutenant who drove a police car out the Main Street ramp of police headquarters at about the time Ruby apparently walked down it:

Mr. Hubert. Were you aware of any planned route from the basement area to the county jail?

A—My instructions were that I would escort the armored car, which would be a decoy, from Commerce Street ramp to Central northbound. To Elm Street onto Houston Street, which would be the entrance to the county jail.

Mr. Hubert. Who did you receive those orders from?

A—From Chief Curry and Chief Stevenson.

Mr. Hubert. About what time did you get those orders?

A—I would assume it was about 11:15.

Mr. Hubert. What did you do then?

A—I immediately left. I received these instructions in the homicide office, which is on the third floor of the city hall. Immediately left there and rode the elevator down to the basement where I secured a car and I found that the normal exit, which is the exit on Commerce Street from the basement of the city hall, was blocked by an armored car. It was necessary for me to use the Main Street exit. I mean—actually, the Main Street entrance, because we don't exit——

Mr. Hubert. But you used it as an exit?

A—I used it as an exit.

Mr. Hubert. Who was with you?

A—Sergeant Putnam was in the front seat with me and Sergeant Maxey was in the back seat.

Mr. Hubert. Well, tell us what happened along the route then?

A—Well, we pulled out of the basement, and I would judge from the time, from the length of time, probably a length it would take it to circle city hall.

Mr. Hubert. When you got to the top of the basement, were there any guards there on the Main Street entrance?

A—Patrolman Vaughn was stationed at the top of the ramp.

Mr. Hubert. You knew him prior to that time?

A—Yes, sir.

Mr. Hubert. What happened then?

A—Well, actually, nothing happened outside of the fact that he had to move out of the way to let us out.

Mr. Hubert. Which way did he move?

A—He moved toward the street.

Mr. Hubert. I mean on which side of you?

A—He moved to my right.

Mr. Hubert. And toward the street?

A—And towards the street; yes, sir.

Mr. Hubert. What way was he facing then during the period that you were moving by him?

A—He was facing me, as well as I remember.

Mr. Hubert. That is——

A—Momentarily, anyway.

Mr. Hubert. In fact, he would have been looking from where he was standing toward the Main Street entrance?

A—Yes, sir.

Mr. Hubert. Did you see him turn his head any at all?

A—No, sir; I couldn't see him for just a matter of a second there when I pulled out. That ramp is steep and a little bit difficult to get out there.

Mr. Hubert. Did he step out in the street at all?

A—Not to my knowledge.

Mr. Hubert. Now, did you turn, immediately outside the Main Street entry or exit, to your right?

A—I was aware that people were pressed, not a large number of them, but I would say maybe four or five.

Mr. Hubert. On your right?

A—No, well, probably might have been a—I don't know. Just a guess. I don't recall the number of people now, what it would be.

Mr. Hubert. Do you recall whether there were some people on your right?

A—I was aware that people were on both sides of the car when I pulled across the sidewalk.

Mr. Hubert. And how far from the entrance?

A—Well, probably 6 or 7 feet.

Mr. Hubert. Did you recognize anybody at all?

A—Nobody except one by the name of Vaughn.

Mr. Hubert. Now, subsequently, of course, it turned out that Ruby shot Oswald. Did you know him prior to that time?

A—No.

Mr. Hubert. Ruby?

494

A—Yes, sir; I have known him 12 or 13 years, I guess.

Mr. Hubert. So, you would recognize him without any difficulty whether he had a hat on or not?

A—I don't think I would have any trouble recognizing him if I saw him.

Mr. Hubert. You did not, see him in that crowd to your right?

A—No; I didn't see him that day at all.

ROY EUGENE VAUGHN

The testimony of the Dallas patrolman who was guarding the entrance to Dallas police headquarters through which Ruby apparently entered to shoot Oswald:

Mr. Hubert. When you stated you were posted at the Main Street ramp, by that I take it you mean the exit of the Main Street ramp, that is to say, where it comes out?

A—Yes; out onto the street—onto the sidewalk.

Mr. Hubert. Now, physically where did you maintain your post?

A—I maintained it inside—actually, I would say 2 or 3 feet inside—actually—of the ramp.

Mr. Hubert. In other words, you weren't on the sidewalk?

A—Oh, no; I was inside—standing inside the ramp.

Mr. Hubert. The ramp is about how many feet wide?

A—I would just have to estimate it—I would say it was 12 to 15 feet.

Mr. Hubert. And you were standing more or less in the middle?

A—In the middle.

Mr. Hubert. And that was about from 9:30 on?

A—Yes.

Mr. Hubert. Did you ever leave that post?

A—The only time when I ever moved out of my position there was when this car which was driven by Lieutenant Pierce exited by that ramp.

Mr. Hubert. Before we get to that, let me ask you this— you mentioned that on several occasions people came in, identified themselves and you let them through, or you turned away other people?

A—Yes.

Mr. Hubert. What steps did you take to maintain the security of your post while you were talking to such people so that other people wouldn't sneak through?

A—I was still standing in the middle of the ramp.

Mr. Hubert. It would be impossible, you think, for anybody to pass on either side of you?

A—That's right—without seeing them. . . .

Mr. Hubert. . . . How long before you heard the shot did that car driven by Rio Pierce pass by you?

A—I would say not over 3 minutes.

Mr. Hubert. Now, did you recognize anybody in the car?

A—Yes, sir.

Mr. Hubert. What did you do when the car came up?

A—The first thing I noticed the car—still standing inside the ramp—and I heard someone at the bottom of the ramp holler, "Watch the car," and when I looked down you could just get a view of the front end of the car coming up the ramp. It had its red lights on, which were in the grill. As it come on up the ramp, I stepped to my right, and it come up the ramp——

Mr. Hubert. You stepped towards Pearl Street?

A—Yes—towards Pearl Street, and I stepped to my right in order to get out of the car's way, and I stepped out on the sidewalk somewhere between the sidewalk and the curb, I believe it was right around the curb, and I glanced—it would be toward the eastbound traffic, which would be traffic towards Pearl Street to see that traffic was clear, and then motioned them on and I turned around and walked back.

Mr. Hubert. You did not go into the street at all?

A—No, sir.

Mr. Hubert. You did not pass the curb?

A—No, sir; not that I recall—I don't believe I did at all. . . .

Mr. Hubert. Is it fair to say, then, that after you got back to your post, following the exit of Rio Pierce's car, that nobody passed you?

A—Nobody passed me.

Mr. Hubert. Specifically, did Jack Ruby pass you?

A—No, sir.

Mr. Hubert. Now, when the Rio Pierce car was coming out, what steps or action did you take to maintain the security of your post while that car was passing through?

A—The only steps, like I said, Mr. Hubert, on that—is when I stepped out onto the sidewalks—why—I made sure that my view of the entrance of the city hall was not completely blocked, that I could still see the entrance to the right.

Mr. Hubert. You use the words "completely blocked," do you mean to infer by that it could have been partially blocked?

A—No, sir; the only thing—when I stepped out, as the car came out, I still had a view of the actual entrance to the ramp.

Mr. Hubert. Would it have been possible that part of your view was blocked by the automobile itself?

A—It possibly—for an instant while the car was coming out—actually out of the entrance—but after it cleared the ramp—no, sir.

Mr. Hubert. After it cleared the entrance you returned your view to your post, even though you weren't at it?

A—Yes.

Mr. Hubert. And nobody entered it at that time?

496

A—No, sir; they did not.

Mr. Hubert. Did you ever see Jack Ruby standing by that concrete or marble—what do you call it?

A—Slab there.

Mr. Hubert. Standing by that slab there where Daniels was?

A—No, sir. . . .

Mr. Hubert. Now, you know, of course, that Ruby says that's the way he got in?

A—Yes, I realize that.

Mr. Hubert. What is your opinion about that statement?

A—I don't believe he did.

Mr. Hubert. You think he got in some other way?

A—I don't know definitely, but I'll say he didn't come in at the ramp. How he got in—that, I don't know, but I know—I don't believe that he came in the ramp.

Mr. Hubert. Is it your opinion beyond any reasonable doubt, and I think you are familiar with that phrase as an officer, aren't you?

A—Yes.

Mr. Hubert. That Ruby did not enter the basement through the ramp while you were there?

A—Yes, sir. . . .

C. N. DHORITY

The testimony of a Dallas Police Department detective who was assigned to drive the car in which Oswald was to be moved from police headquarters to the county jail:

Mr. Ball. Fritz gave you instructions to do what?

A—He gave me the keys to his car and told me to go down and get his car and back it up front of the jail door to put Oswald in.

Mr. Ball. Is that what you did?

A—I went downstairs and got his car, unlocked his car, and was in the process of backing it up there—in fact—I was just about ready to stop, when Captain Fritz came out and Leavelle and Oswald and Graves and Johnson and Montgomery came out the jail door.

Captain Fritz reached over to the door of the car and I was turned around to see—backing it up—still had the car moving it along and I saw someone run across the end of the car real rapid like. At first, I thought it was somebody going to take a picture and then I saw a hand come out and I heard the shot. . . .

JAMES ROBERT LEAVELLE

The testimony of the Dallas policeman to whom Oswald was handcuffed when Ruby shot Oswald:

Mr. Hubert. Just describe in your own words how the whole

497

thing happened, what you saw from the time you left the jail door?

A—From the time we left the jail door?

Mr. Hubert. Yes; push it back a little further. From the time you left the jail cell.

A—All right, when we left the jail cell, we proceeded down to the booking desk there, up to the door leading out into the basement, and I purposely told Mr. Graves to hold it a minute while Captain Fritz checked the area outside. I don't know why I did that, because we had not made any plans to do so, but I said, "Let's hold it a minute and let him see if everything is in order." Because we had been given to understand that the car would be across the passageway.

Mr. Hubert. Of the jail corridor?

A—And that—and we would have nothing to do but walk straight from the door, approximately 13 or 14 feet to the car and then Captain Fritz—when we asked him to give us the high sign on it he said, "Everything is all set."

Mr. Hubert. Did you notice what time it was?

A—No; I did not. That is the only error that I can see. The captain should have known that the car was not in the position it should be, and I was surprised when I walked to the door and the car was not in the spot it should have been, but I could see it was in back, and backing into position, but had it been in position where we were told it would be, that would have eliminated a lot of the area in which anyone would have access to him, because it would have been blocked by the car. In fact, if the car had been sitting where we were told it was going to be, see—it would have been sitting directly upon the spot where Ruby was standing when he fired the shot.

Mr. Hubert. Of course, in that case the television cameras would have been blocked out?

A—That's true.

Mr. Hubert. The car was not pulled back because pulling it back would block the——

A—That, I don't know. Of course, you are—according to one of my previous reports I earlier suggested to Captain Fritz that we make the suggestion to the chief that we take him out to the first floor and put him out at Main Street to a car and proceed to the county jail that way and leave them waiting in the basement and on Commerce Street, and we could be to the county jail before anyone knew what was taking place.

Mr. Hubert. What time did you make that suggestion, sir?

A—That was either just before or just after—probably just after I had gone there and got Oswald and we were talking about the transfer.

Mr. Hubert. Who did you make that suggestion to?

A—I made it to Captain Fritz.

Mr. Hubert. What answer did you receive from him?

A—Said he didn't think the chief would go for it.

498

Mr. Hubert. Did he say why?

A—Because, he said, the chief had given his word to the press that they would transfer him at a time when they could make pictures. . . .

My reasons for wanting to handle it the other way, I thought it would be done quicker and easier and I was fed up to my chin, in a way, with these news people, and they—as soon as we could get rid of them the better, was my sentiments, and I didn't have any desire to parade through them with the prisoner in tow. However, I can understand why the chief wanted to let them take the pictures.

Mr. Hubert. Had it been your decision you wouldn't have done it that way, is that it?

A—Either as I suggested, or at a different hour.

Mr. Hubert. Say move him in the morning early?

A—Yes, I brought Ruby down in safety and I don't think there was any—as long as it was successful, I don't think you can argue with success.

Mr. Hubert. Did you transfer Ruby?

A—Yes, I did.

Mr. Hubert. It was done at an unannounced hour?

A—Well, sir; it was so unannounced that the chief didn't know about it and neither did Sheriff Decker. I don't know whether they will admit that or not, but no one knew it but Captain Fritz and myself and three or four officers directly involved.

Mr. Hubert. You all just decided to do it, and that was it?

A—Well, the captain called me and asked me about it and told me what he was thinking about doing and he wanted to know if I thought it would work and I said, "Yes, I think it will the way it has been set up," and he said, "I haven't asked the chief about it," and I said, "All you can do is get a bawling out, but a bawling out is better than losing a prisoner."

Mr. Hubert. Did you get bawled out about it?

A—I didn't. I did not know whether he did or not. I doubt it. Because I am sure the chief was relieved to be rid of the responsibility.

Mr. Hubert. How was Ruby removed, then, just for the record?

A—Well, this would be on Monday morning, I guess, the next Monday morning around 11, around the same hour that Oswald was transferred. The captain had not showed up and I—he called on the telephone and asked for me and his secretary called me to the phone, and I was in the squad room where several officers were, and asked me if I was in a position where I could talk, and I said, "No, not really," and he said, "Well—" told me to go into his office and take the phone in there, which I did, and he said, "I am down at the Greyhound Bus Station, and I have Officers Graves and Montgomery with me."

He had run into them on the street. Said, "We have cased

the jail and it looks clear. I am going to make a suggestion to you, and if you don't think it will work I want you to tell me."

Said—he said, "We'll pull through the basement of the city hall," said, "You go get Ruby out of the jail anyway you want to, on a "tempo" or whatever you think best, and bring him down to me, down in the elevator and we'll pull through the basement at some given time, and we'll load him up and whisk him right on down and let another squad follow us and we will take him right on down to the county jail."

Said, "The sheriff—I haven't called Decker or the chief about it, either." Said, "Do you think it will work?"

I said, "Yes." Said, "How many men—got enough there to help you with him?"

I said, "Yes, there is three or four here I can get."

"Don't tell anybody where you are going. Just get them like you are going after coffee and get downstairs or somewhere and tell them what you are going to do."

So, I went into the squad room (Captain Fritz had called) Lieutenant Wells, and told him not to let the officers out of the office because he wanted us when he got in there so I just walked out and motioned to Mr. Brown and Dhority and Mr. Beck and told them to follow me, and didn't say a word to anyone, and walked downstairs, and, of course, they are curious, and when I got downstairs I outlined the deal to them and told Beck and Brown to get the car—get the other car in the basement and have it in position to go out, and Dhority and I went up and got the prisoner and brought him down.

Mr. Hubert. Brought him down the jail elevator?

A—Down the jail elevator.

Mr. Hubert. Were any newsmen down in the station?

A—Beg your pardon?

Mr. Hubert. Were there any newsmen down in the basement?

A—In fact, when I walked out one of the newspapermen asked me when we were going to transfer Ruby and I said, "Oh, I don't know." And just like that, and walked on.

Mr. Hubert. You had Ruby with you?

A—You mean—oh, no; the officers and I walking down. When we brought Ruby down in the jail elevator, that elevator is never in view of the public. It is an inside elevator. Never in view of the public, so, anyway, after talking to the captain, I set my watch with his and said, "Be there at exactly 11:15."

So, he set his watch with mine and we brought Ruby down. That is the reason—I got down there about a minute and a half, 2 minutes early to the basement and told the lieutenant on duty, told everybody not to ring for the elevator that we would have it tied up, just held him in the elevator.

Mr. Hubert. Kept Ruby in the elevator?

A—Kept Ruby in the elevator. Mr. Brown standing outside of the jail office, Mr. Beck had his car, his motor running in the parking basement, and Mr. Brown was standing there talking to one of the men in the jail office just as though he was passing the time of day, and he was to give me the nod as soon as the captain's car pulled in on the ramp, which he did.

Mr. Hubert. Which side did he pull in on?

A—Just came off the Main Street ramp and parked across the opening and when he saw him pull in, gave me the high sign and we took Ruby and told him, I said "I don't want to have to push you or shove you. I want you to move." Of course, Ruby was scared, so, he almost outran me to the car. He ran and got in the back seat of the car with Graves, who was already in the back seat, and Montgomery was driving and Mr. Beck, Dhority, and Brown got to the other car and followed us. We proceeded directly to the county jail. . . .

PATRICK T. DEAN

The testimony of the Dallas police sergeant who helped arrange security in the police building basement when Ruby killed Oswald there:

Mr. Griffin. How many newspapermen did you have to clear out of the basement at 9:15, approximately?

A—Oh, approximately 15 or 20, maybe 25.

Mr. Griffin. Now, when you went down into the basement, before the search, were there any TV cameras down there?

A—Yes, sir; I believe there was.

Mr. Griffin. Do you want to indicate on the map here where it is that you think the TV cameras, or camera was placed?

A—[Indicating.]

Mr. Griffin. Do you recall if there was a TV camera at this location [indicating]?

A—I believe there was.

Mr. Griffin. Now, I am referring, so that the record will reflect this, to a TV camera that's in the entranceway from the ramp, towards the jail office, and it's on the Commerce Street wall, along the Commerce Street wall. Did you move that TV camera at that time?

A—No, sir. Moved the operators away from it.

Mr. Griffin. Now, what did you do after that, after you completed the search and let the people back into the basement?

A—Let me think. I believe I stayed in the basement area.

Mr. Griffin. At the time that you completed the search, had you heard anything about the time that Oswald would be moved?

A—No, sir.

Mr. Griffin. Had you heard anything about the route that he would be moved by?

A—At the time——

Mr. Griffin. That you completed the search?

A—Yes. About, somewhere around 9:45, Captain Talbert

sent me a group of regular officers that had been called in off of patrol district. [Indicating.]

Mr. Griffin. Now, can I help you?

A—My report [indicating]?

Mr. Griffin. Yes [indicating].

A—I didn't have in my original report, I do have in my original notes in my locker, as to some traffic assignments that I made. This was about 9:45. These men were sent to me by Captain Talbert. I briefed them about here in the basement, away from everyone, to let no one know the route. This is when Captain Talbert advised me that the route would be to leave the Commerce Street side, go to the expressway, north to Main [indicating].

Mr. Griffin. Is that Pearl Expressway or Central Expressway?

A—Central Expressway. And then west on Main to the county courthouse, or the sheriff's office.

Mr. Griffin. Let me try to refresh your recollection a little bit here. Up to this point had you heard anything about a proposed route that would have gone from Central Expressway and turned at Elm Street, rather than Main Street?

A—I was thinking it was—I knew that they changed it, after I made my assignment I had to change them again, because they said they wasn't going to use it. It was either Main Street that they weren't going to use, they were going to Commerce—however, I think you are right. I think originally my assignments were made at the intersections—not Commerce, but Elm, and then they changed the—they being Captain Talbert, and told me that they would not use Elm, that they would use Main Street.

Mr. Griffin. Would you draw a big circle in this area where you instructed these men, to show roughly what area the men covered, and would you put an appropriate note on there as to what happened and what time?

A—[Indicating.]

Mr. Griffin. About how many men did you give instructions to?

A—13, 15.

Mr. Griffin. Why don't you just put that number there?

A—[Indicating.]

Mr. Griffin. Now, did those men then take police vehicles and go to their appointed spots?

Mr. Griffin. . . . I understand about the time that the armored car arrived, or was it shortly after the armored car arrived, you had a conversation with Lieutenant Pierce?

A—Yes, sir.

Mr. Griffin. How much after the armored car arrived would you say that conversation occurred?

A—Five minutes after the armored car arrived. . . .

Mr. Griffin. All right. What did Pierce tell you?

502

A—He said for me to go to the armored car, to the rear of the armored car, and to get him two men to go with him, and he said, "Now," Sergeant Putnam was maybe 15 or 20 feet from me, and I instructed him to get an unassigned man immediately and to go with Lieutenant Pierce, and Lieutenant Pierce, by this time, of course, he was going to get his car, or walking over to his car. Sergeant Putnam got—told Sergeant Maxey to go with him, and those three got into Lieutenant Pierce's car with Lieutenant Pierce driving, and I went to the rear of the armored car that had backed in, which was some, I guess 30 feet, 30 to 35 feet from where the shooting was. This armored car backed down, and I imagine it would probably be around 30 to 35 feet. As soon as I got to the armored car I turned around and looked back, and this is when I saw Lieutenant Pierce in this plain black car trying to get past the newsmen and to go out the wrong way.

Mr. Griffin. Up the Main Street ramp?

A—Right.

Mr. Griffin. Now, is my understanding correct that from the time that you placed your guards in the basement and then began the search, until Pierce's car drove up the ramp, you did not leave the basement area?

A—That's right.

Mr. Griffin. Yes. Now, of course, you have known Jack Ruby for 4 or 5 years?

A—I have known Jack Ruby since, I believe 19— the early part of 1960 or the early part of 1961. It was the time that I came downtown from Oak Cliff, as a sergeant. I met him. Now, the record, or your report from the FBI says that I had known him since 1959, which is erroneous.

Mr. Griffin. Okay. We will do that at the end of the deposition, because I want to get that straightened out.

A—Yes. sir.

Mr. Griffin. But you knew Ruby well enough so that you would recognize him on sight?

A—Yes, sir.

Mr. Griffin. And did you see Ruby in that area there?

A—No, sir.

Mr. Griffin. Now, after you lost sight of Pierce's car going up the ramp, what did you do?

A—Well, my attention was focused to this point, because this was a tense time, and I was, of course, watching the exit here from the jail office [indicating].

Mr. Griffin. Now, did you watch how the security developed along here; what the officers did to maintain security along here [indicating]?

A—I knew that they had just lined up. However, I didn't pay any attention particularly to this at the time. I knew that Oswald was in all probability, going to be brought out pretty soon.

Mr. Griffin. As you looked toward the Main Street ramp and

503

saw the newsmen re-form along there, can you recall how deep this line of newsmen was? Do you understand what I mean by how deep?

A—You mean lengthwise?

Mr. Griffin. Yes.

A—It was probably going to about somewhere along here. They were all trying to be within view of the——[indicating].

Mr. Griffin. Was there just a single line along there or were there four or five or six different lines; you know, four or five behind each other, or how many?

A—I know there was a double line and possibly some were standing behind them.

Mr. Griffin. Now, had you given any instructions prior to the time that Rio Pierce's car went up the ramp, to any men as to how to maintain security along this line of newsmen?

A—No, sir; I hadn't. The majority of those, I think, were detectives or plainclothesmen.

Mr. Griffin. Do you know if anybody had responsibility for giving instructions to that group?

A—To my knowledge, I don't know of anyone. I am sure that they did, but I don't know who did.

Mr. Griffin. Did you receive instructions from anybody concerning how to maintain security along the path from the jail office door to the car that Oswald would be loaded into?

A—No, sir; at one time I know that there were several cameras set up in this area, and Chief Batchelor told them that they would have to leave this area and move to the basement area. I was present during Chief Batchelor's—or when he told these TV men to move out of that area, inside the jail office, that——

Mr. Griffin. TV cameras inside the jail office?

A—Yes, sir; and lights set up. This was, I believe, before the search or shortly after the search. I am thinking it was shortly after the search, that these men were told to move out of this area and move their cameras and equipment out into the garage portion of the basement.

Mr. Griffin. Now, sergeant, did there come a time when you learned that the route was being changed?

A—The route to the sheriff's office?

Mr. Griffin. Yes.

A—This was—I believe I received both of those instructions when I assigned those men. I had already assigned—well, I do know that I had already assigned all these men along this traffic route, and then it had been changed. Captain Talbert said, "No; they are not going to use Main Street—or Elm Street. They are going to use Main," I believe. . . .

Mr. Griffin. All right. Now, what did you do after you saw Pierce's car go up the ramp?

A—I stood at the rear of the armored car and watched—my attention was focused to this point here, to the exit from the jail office, or the corridor here. I noticed that these two plain cars had pulled up behind, or in my same direction, and I assumed that these two cars would be loaded with officers that would follow the armored car. However, they hadn't loaded. They were pulling into position here and had gotten into position when all the confusion started [indicating]. . . .

Mr. Griffin. All right. Now, as the two police cars moved into position on the Commerce Street ramp behind the armored car, what happened, what did you see happen and what did you do?

A—I heard someone say, "Here he comes, they are bringing him out." Of course, you could hear voices, loud voices, or excitement, and then I saw a man just dart in—this was during all the confusion, before the shooting, but I do recall seeing a man dart out. I couldn't tell who he was. It was that fast [witness snaps fingers].

Mr. Griffin. Where did he seem to dart from?

A—From the rail over here. The side—just dart out from a group of people that were standing against the rail facing the exit [indicating]. . . .

Mr. Griffin. Now, as I understand from your statement, and interrupt me if I am incorrect, when you saw Ruby shoot Oswald, you moved toward the struggle and then Ruby was taken into the jail office, and did you follow them on in?

A—Yes, sir. I ran immediately, jumped over these cars, or one of them, jumped over the hood of it, over the top of it, and they were dragging—Ruby and several detectives that were subduing him were about at the door, or [indicating]—— . . .

Mr. Griffin. I understand why you want to, but——

A—All right.

Mr. Griffin. Did you hear, between the time that you saw Ruby move toward Oswald and the time that you reached him, did you hear anything said?

A—No, sir.

Mr. Griffin. Now, what did you do when you reached Ruby?

A—Well, I ran to assist, whatever I could do, or assist the officers, not knowing exactly what had happened—or I knew that there had been a shooting. However, they had enough men that were subduing him, and I asked the question, when they had him on the floor inside the jail office, "Who in the world is it?" And——

Mr. Griffin. Couldn't you tell by looking at him?

A—No; at the time I couldn't see him because there were so many over him. And they were—well, his face was hidden from me by the amount of officers that were around him. I said, "Who in the world is it?" And evidently I was talking loud over all the other voices, and evidently Ruby heard me and said, "I am Jack Ruby. You all know me."

Mr. Griffin. And how long did you remain with Jack Ruby there in the jail office?

505

A—I immediately walked around to where Oswald was laying.

Mr. Griffin. And how long did you remain there where Oswald was?

A—Oh, maybe—less than a minute. I saw that the doctor—there was an emergency doctor working on him.

Mr. Griffin. Where did you go from there?

A—I went back out to the basement, out to where the shooting happened.

Mr. Griffin. What did you do out there?

A—I was trying to keep all the people in. I heard Captain Talbert say, "Don't let anyone out." And I was echoing his instructions to the men on the ramp, to not let anyone in or out, no one.

Mr. Griffin. Now, did there come a time while you were down there in the basement that you were interviewed by TV men?

A—Yes, sir; that was after I had—just some few minutes, I don't know, that several newsmen had—or did interview me, yes. . . .

Mr. Griffin. Now, after you had this TV interview, what did you do?

A—I went to the third floor.

Mr. Griffin. And where did you go on the third floor?

A—Just as I got off of the elevator Chief Curry approached me, along with another man. He introduced him very quickly as Forrest V. Sorrels, with the Secret Service, or head of the Secret Service here in Dallas, gave me his keys to the outer door that has—or access to the jail elevator, told me to take Mr. Sorrels to the fifth floor to talk to Ruby. . . .

Mr. Griffin. You got up to the fifth floor, who was with Ruby?

A—Detective Archer, D. R. Archer, Detective T. D. McMillon and Detective B. S. Clardy is the three, and that's the only three I can recall standing there. I think that was all that was with him. . . .

Mr. Griffin. What state of dress or undress was Ruby in at that time?

A—He was stripped to his shorts. . . .

Mr. Griffin. Now, do you remember anything that Sorrels learned from Ruby?

A—Yes, sir.

Mr. Griffin. Can you tell us what that was?

A—Yes. He asked him what possessed him to do it. Of course, I have testified to all this in court. And he said that he was—had been despondent over the assassination of the President, also Officer Tippit, and that he was a very emotional man, and that out of grief for both these people, was one of the motivations, and that he couldn't see any reason for a long and lengthy trial, even though he believed in due process of law.

506

Mr. Griffin. Did he talk with Sorrels at all at that time about how he got into the basement?

A—No, sir. I asked him—Sorrels didn't ask any questions relative to that. I did.

Mr. Griffin. How long after Sorrels finished talking with Ruby did you ask that question?

A—Immediately. After Mr. Sorrels said, "Okay. Thank you." And I don't recall whether Mr. Sorrels stayed there or whether he walked off.

Mr. Griffin. Who else was present when you asked Ruby that question?

A—I think McMillon and them were still there. I just really didn't—I knew that I wasn't by myself with him. I knew that there was someone there and I believe it was McMillon and Archer that had stayed there. I am not sure.

Mr. Griffin. What else did you talk with Ruby about, after Sorrels finished talking to him?

A—After Sorrels finished, I said, "Ruby, I want to ask you a couple of questions myself." And he said, "All right." I said, "How did you get in the basement?" And he said, "I walked in the Main Street ramp." And he told me, he said, "I have just been to the Western Union to mail a money order to Fort Worth." And he said, "I walked from the Western Union to the ramp." And he said, "I saw Sam Pierce—" and he referred to him as Sam Pierce—"drive out of the basement. At that time, at the time the car drove out is when I walked in."

Mr. Griffin. Is there a Sam Pierce on the force?

A—Yes, sir. He is a lieutenant. He is here tonight.

Mr. Griffin. His name is also Rio Pierce?

A—Lt. Rio S. Pierce, yes sir. . . .

Mr. Griffin. All right. Now, what else did he talk to you about at that particular time?

A—After he answered that question, I said, "How long had you been in the basement when Oswald came into your view?" And he said, "I just walked in. I just walked to the bottom of the ramp when he came out."

Mr. Griffin. What else did you talk to him about at that time?

A—That's all. I heard all of Sorrels' questions and I heard all of Ruby's answers. . . .

Mr. Griffin. Now, after you finished this conversation with Ruby about how he got down into the basement, what did you do?

A—Caught the elevator back down to the basement and got my gun that had been taken there by a patrolman. If I am not mistaken, I rode down on the same elevator with Mr. Sorrels, and then I went back up to the third floor to Chief Curry's office and took him his keys that he had given me. . . .

Mr. Griffin. Let me hand you, then, what I have marked for identification as Exhibit 5010. It's a copy of a letter signed by

507

you, dated February 18, 1964, addressed to Mr. J. E. Curry, chief of police. Did you prepare that letter?

A—Yes; I did [indicating]. . . .

Mr. Griffin. . . . Now, how did you come to write this letter of February 18, 1964?

A—Chief Stevenson called me, while I was in the office on that date, and asked me to come up to see him, and I did. And he asked me was I present during the entire interview with Ruby and Mr. Sorrels. I told him I was. And he asked me did I remember most of the interview; could I recollect most of the interview and the answers that Ruby had given and I said, "Yes, sir." Then he advised me to make a report of it, asked me would I make a report of it, recalling everything that I could of that interview. To the best of my knowledge, that's all I could remember. And I did testify to all this stuff in the trial.

Mr. Griffin. Is this the first time that you told anyone that Ruby had told Sorrels that he thought about killing Oswald two nights prior when he saw him in the showup room?

A—Well, I don't recall telling it to any particular person. I knew that this would probably be later used as testimony, I felt, since it was—did make an impression on me, that I could remember it, and it's written as I do remember, just about as it happened, it correlates pretty well, even though we didn't get together with Mr. Sorrels' report. . . .

Dean first testified Mar. 24, 1964, then was recalled June 7 at his own request:

Mr. Rankin. You have given us your deposition, have you not, Sergeant?

A—Yes, sir.

Mr. Rankin. And is that correct and true as far as anything you know?

A—Yes, sir.

Mr. Rankin. Is there any part of it that you want to change or correct or modify?

A—No, sir; I feel the main reason I wanted to appear before the Commission was about the 20 or 25 minutes that was off the record that I feel I would like the Commission to have on the record, and this is between Mr. Griffin and I. He was the original one who started my deposition.

Mr. Rankin. Well, do you want to tell that at this time?

First, is there anything about what you said on the record that was not correct?

A—No, sir.

Mr. Rankin. And the truth?

A—No, sir.

Well, Mr. Griffin had questioned me about 2 hours, or maybe a little longer. There was no problems at all, no difficulties. And after that length of time, a little over 2 hours, Mr.

508

Griffin desired to get off the record, and he advised the court reporter that he would be off the record and he could go smoke a cigarette or get a Coke, and he would let him know when he wanted him to get back on the record.

Well, after the court reporter left, Mr. Griffin started talking to me in a manner of gaining my confidence in that he would help me and that he felt I would probably need some help in the future.

My not knowing what he was building up to, I asked Mr. Griffin to go ahead and ask me what he was going to ask me. He continued to advise me that he wanted me to listen to what he had to say before he asked me whatever question he was going to ask me. I finally told him that whatever he wanted to ask me he could just ask me, and if I knew I would tell him the truth or if I didn't know, I would tell him I didn't know.

Mr. Griffin took my reports, one dated February 18, the subject of it was an interview with Jack Ruby, and one dated November 26, which was my assignment in the basement.

He said there were things in these statements which were not true and, in fact, he said both these statements, he said there were particular things in there that were not true, and I asked him what portions did he consider not true, and then very dogmatically he said that, "Jack Ruby didn't tell you that he entered the basement via the Main Street ramp."

And, of course, I was shocked at this. This is what I testified to, in fact, I was cross-examined on this, and he, Mr. Griffin, further said, "Jack Ruby did not tell you that he had thought or planned to kill Oswald two nights prior."

And he said, "Your testimony was false, and these reports to your chief of police are false."

So this, of course, all this was off the record. I told Mr. Griffin then this shocked me, and I told him it shocked me; that I couldn't imagine what he was getting at or why he would accuse me of this, and I asked him, and Mr. Griffin replied he didn't or he wasn't at liberty to discuss that particular part of it with me, and that he wasn't trying to cross-examine me here, but that under cross-examination he could prove that my testimony was false, and that is when I told Mr. Griffin that these are the facts and I can't change them. This is what I know about it.

I quoted Ruby just about verbatim, and since he didn't believe me, and I was saying they were true, we might as well terminate the interview.

Mr. Griffin then got back on the record, or before he did get back on the record, he said, "Well now, Sergeant Dean, I respect you as a witness, I respect you in your profession, but I have offered my help and assistance, and I again will offer you my assistance, and that I don't feel you will be subjecting yourself to loss of your job," or some words to that effect, "If you will go ahead and tell me the truth about it."

I again told Mr. Griffin that these were the facts and I couldn't change them, so with that we got back on the record. . . .

Mr. Rankin. Now, the differences in your testimony that Mr. Griffin was discussing with you off the record, you have gone into that in detail on the record, haven't you, in your deposition?

A—Yes; I believe I have, about how Ruby entered the basement or how he told me how he entered the basement. Also that he had thought two nights prior when he saw Lee Oswald on a showup stand with a sarcastic sneer on his face is when he decided if he got the chance he would kill him. This was the thing that I testified in court about. I was cross-examined in court.

Mr. Rankin. And you have explained all that in your deposition, haven't you?

A—I believe so; I am not certain.

Mr. Rankin. And did he ask you about why you didn't have your—this information about his planning to shoot Oswald the night before, or on the Friday——

A—Now, are you asking did Mr. Griffin ask me why I didn't——

Mr. Rankin. Why you didn't put it in your February—in your statement before the February 18 one?

A—Yes, sir; I believe he did, and I explained to him this wasn't the subject—the subject of that November 26 report was my assignment. I didn't put any of the conversation as to what Mr. Sorrels and I talked to Mr. Ruby about. I did put at the closing paragraph, I think, and I have a copy of it here, that my main concern was how he got into the basement and how long he had been there because I was in charge of the security of the basement.

Mr. Rankin. So you didn't put it in your prior reports?

A—No, sir; this was later on. Chief Curry—I think probably it was February 18—and I think I probably wrote it that day, called me to his office and asked me had I heard all the interview of Ruby and Sorrels, and I told him that I did, and he asked me could I remember it pretty well, and I said, "Yes, I believe I can remember most all of it," and that is when Chief Curry told me that, he said, "Well, you are going to have to testify to it because Mr. Sorrels can't because he says he didn't warn Mr. Ruby when he was questioning him."

Well, this was fine with me. I wrote the report. This was February 18. . . .

FORREST V. SORRELS

The testimony of the special agent in charge of the Dallas district of the United States Secret Service:

Mr. Stern. Mr. Sorrels had you discussed with any official

510

of the Dallas Police the plans to move Oswald during a scheduled daylight hour, before the move was made?

A—When I heard that he was supposed to be moved at 10 o'clock in the morning, I said to Captain Fritz—and as I recall this conversation—I said to him, "Captain, I wouldn't move that man at an announced time. I would take him out at 3 or 4 o'clock in the morning, when there is nobody around."

And Captain Fritz said, "Well, the chief has gone along with these people," talking about the press and television people, and said that he wanted to continue going along with them and cooperating with them all he can. And that was all that was said about that.

I did not make that suggestion, or have a conversation like that with Chief Curry, as I recall, because I did not want to appear that I was trying to tell them how to run their business.

Mr. Stern. What were conditions like in the third floor corridor of police headquarters from Friday through Sunday?

A—Mr. Stern, you would almost have to be there to see it, to actually realize the conditions. The press and the television people just, as the expression goes, took over. I would almost every time I went up there, definitely after the 22d, I would have to identify myself to get in past the entrance of the elevator on the third floor, if I was going to the chief's office or the deputy chief's office or Captain Fritz' office. You would have to elbow your way through, and step over tripods and cables and wires, and every time almost that I would come out of Captain Fritz's office, the minute the door opened, they would flash on those bright lights, and I got where I just shadowed my eyes when I walked down there to keep the light from shining in my eyes. They had cables run through one of the deputy chief's office, right through the windows from the street up the side of the building, across the floor, out to the boxes where they could get power—they had wires running out of that, had the wires taped down to keep people from actually falling or stumbling over the wires. And it was just a condition that you can hardly explain. It was just almost indescribable. . . .

Mr. Stern. Can you estimate how many press representatives there were in that corridor?

A—I am not too good in estimating anything like that, but there were dozens of them.

Mr. Stern. Was any effort made to restrict them to a far part of the corridor, or to remove them from the floor entirely that you know of?

A—Not that I know of.

Mr. Stern. Did you ever learn why this was not done—did you ever ask?

A—No, I did not. I just thought to myself—well, if this was being handled in a Federal building, this situation would not exist. That is what I thought.

But, of course, that is a public building. I thought to myself —well, they are in here, and the chief would have a heck of a time getting them out. That is just my own thoughts about the thing, because I do know that the Dallas Police Department, the Dallas Sheriff's Office, they do try to go along with the press and everything like that.

After this thing happened, Mr. Felix McKnight, who I mentioned before, who is a personal friend of mine, executive editor of the Dallas Times Herald, he said to me, "Forrest, those people should have been out of there, and that includes us."

Of course the thing was all over then. I would imagine that Chief Curry or anybody else that would have tried to have gotten them out of there would have really had a tough time and they probably would have really blasted them in the press.

[*Sorrels also told the commission of his interrogation of Ruby minutes after he killed Oswald.*]

Mr. Hubert. Did he at that time, the first interview, indicate anything, or say anything which would indicate what his motive or reason for his act was?

A—Yes; and I might say that it was at that time that I found out his name was Ruby in place of Rubin, and he informed me his name had formerly been Rubinstein, and that he had had his name changed in Dallas.

I asked him—after I identified myself, I told him I would like to ask him some questions.

He said, "For newspapers or magazines?"

I said, "No; for myself."

He appeared to be considering whether or not he was going to answer my questions, and I told him that I had just come from the third floor, and had been looking out of the window, and that I had seen Honest Joe, who is a Jewish merchant there, who operates a second-hand loan pawn shop, so to speak, specializing in tools, on Elm Street, and who is more or less known in the area because of the fact that he takes advantage of any opportunity to get free advertising. He at that time had an Edsel car, which is somewhat a rarity now, all painted up with "Honest Joe" on there. He wears jackets with "Honest Joe" on the back. He gets writeups in the paper, free advertising about different things he loans money on, like artificial limbs and things like that. And I had noticed Honest Joe across the street when I was looking out of Chief Batchelor's office.

So I remarked to Jack Ruby, I said, "I just saw Honest Joe across the street over there, and I know a number of Jewish merchants here that you know."

And Ruby said, "That is good enough for me. What is it you want to know?"

And I said these two words, "Jack—why?"

He said, "When this thing happened"—referring to the assassination, that he was in a newspaper office placing an ad for his business. That when he heard about the assassination, he had canceled his ad and had closed his business, and he had not done any business for 3 days. That he had been grieving about this thing. That on the Friday night he had gone to the synagogue and had heard a eulogy on the President. That his sister had recently been operated on, and that she has been hysterical. That when he saw that Mrs. Kennedy was going to have to appear for the trial, he thought to himself, why should she have to go through this ordeal for this no-good so-and-so.

Mr. Hubert. Did he use any words or did he say "no-good so-and-so"?

A—He used the words "son-of-a-bitch," as I recall.

Mr. Hubert. All right.

A—That he had heard about the letter to little Caroline, as I recall he mentioned. That he had been to the Western Union office to send a telegram, and that he guessed he had worked himself into a state of insanity to where he had to do it. And to use his words after that, "I guess I just had to show the world that a Jew has guts." . . .

Mr. Hubert. Do you remember him saying then anything about that he had intended to shoot Oswald and had formed that intent as early as Friday?

A—No; I did not.

Mr. Hubert. He did not comment at all about his intent?

A—No; nothing except his response to my question as to "Jack, why?", and then his relating as I have told you there a moment ago.

In other words, after I got——

Mr. Hubert. Did he mention anything about he intended to shoot him three times?

A—No; I did not hear that statement.

Mr. Hubert. In other words, the only comments that you heard him state which bear upon intent are those you have already made—that is to say, somebody had to do it, and also that he wanted to show the world that a Jew had guts?

A—No; I did not hear him say that somebody had to do it. I heard him say that he guessed he had worked himself into a state of insanity to where he had to do it, felt he had to do it.

Mr. Hubert. But he did make the report saying he felt he had to show the world that a Jew had guts?

A—Yes; that was very plain. . . .

Mr. Hubert. Wade asked you did you hear Ruby say, "I intended to kill him since Friday night," and your answer was "No; I didn't."

A—No; I didn't hear it.

Mr. Hubert. Did Mr. Griffin mention in the telephone conversation he had with your statements allegedly made, or knowledge allegedly in the possession of Dean in regard to what Ruby had said?

A—I remember specifically there was a statement about him coming down the ramp. I remember that. And it seems that—I wouldn't be positive about that, but it seemed like there was something else that Dean was supposed to have said in my presence, and I told him no I didn't hear anything like that. . . .

Mr. Hubert. In regard to the conversation with Mr. Griffin in Dallas, do you recall a conversation which I think I can specifically state would have been on the morning of Wednesday, March 25—that is to say the morning after Dean had been deposed. And let it be noted that Dean was deposed on the night of March 24. Do you remember a conversation with Mr. Griffin about what Dean had said then, and that you then told Mr. Griffin what your version of it was, and had in fact— he asked you to prepare a memorandum or something for him, so that there would be a record of what he had told him?

A—Along about this same thing?

Mr. Hubert. Yes, about this same matter, revolving around Dean and Dean's testimony about what Ruby had said.

A—I remember that there was a conversation. It seems like I do have a recollection. It slipped my mind. But since you mention something about a memo—and you left rather suddenly, Mr. Griffin, as I recall it, right after that. . . .

Mr. Hubert. Do you remember any comment that Dean made in Wade's office?

A—The only comment that I can remember that he made is when Mr. Wade asked me if certain things were said by Ruby when I was talking to him in the jail on the morning of November 24, when Dean was there, and I told him no, that that statement was not made in my presence, I did not recall any statement like that. And Dean said, "Well, maybe it was after you left." And I said, "Well, if it was—if the statement was made, it would have had to be after I left, because I don't recall any statement like that."

Mr. Hubert. Did you ever find out how Wade or Curry or the police found out about what Dean ultimately said?

A—Will you read that question again?

Mr. Hubert. I said, did you ever find out how Wade and/or the police found out themselves what Dean ultimately testified to?

A—No, I don't know anything about that—unless it is in the court records down there in his testimony at the trial. Now, whether or not they had talked to him before what his testimony would be, I could not say about that, I don't know. . . .

514

HENRY WADE

The testimony of the District Attorney of Dallas:

Mr. Rankin. Do you remember where you were at the time you learned of the assassination of President Kennedy?

A—Well, they were having a party for President Kennedy at Market Hall and I was out at Market Hall waiting for the President to arrive. . . .

Mr. Rankin. What did you do after you heard of the assassination?

A—Well, the first thing, we were set up in a bus to go from there to Austin to another party that night for President Kennedy, a group of us, 30 or 40. We got on a bus and went. I went back to the office and sent my wife home, my wife was with me.

And the first thing that I did was go check the law to see whether it was a Federal offense or mine. I thought it was a Federal offense when I first heard about it. We checked the law, and were satisfied that was no serious Federal offense, or not a capital case, anyhow.

There might be some lesser offense. I talked to the U.S. attorney.

Mr. Rankin. Who was that?

A—Barefoot Sanders and he was in agreement it was going to be our case rather than his and he had been doing the same thing. . . .

Senator Cooper. Is your recollection, was the memorandum that was shown to you by—first, who did show you the memorandum on the 22d?

A—Chief Curry of the Dallas police. . . .

Mr. Rankin. You can tell us the rest that you said to Chief Curry and he said to you at that time, first.

A—I asked him how the case was coming along and as a practical matter he didn't know. You probably have run into this, but there is really a lack of communication between the chief's office and the captain of detective's office there in Dallas.

Mr. Rankin. You found that to be true.

A—For every year I have been in office down there. And I assume you have taken their depositions. I don't know what the relations—the relations are better between Curry and Fritz than between Hanson and Fritz, who was his predecessor. But Fritz runs a kind of a one-man operation there where nobody else knows what he is doing. Even me, for instance, he is reluctant to tell me, either, but I don't mean that disparagingly. I will say Captain Fritz is about as good a man at solving a crime as I ever saw, to find out who did it but he is poorest in the getting evidence that I know, and I am more interested in getting evidence, and there is where our major conflict comes in. . . .

Mr. Rankin. All right.

515

What happened next, as you recall?

A—I was going home. I went by the police station to talk to Chief Curry.

Mr. Rankin. Did you discuss the evidence then?

A—Well, at that time—you see, Chief Curry knew very little of the evidence at that stage. He should have known, but he didn't. But I discussed the thing with him and I told him there was too much evidence being put out in the case from his department, that I wish he would talk to Fritz and have no further statements on it.

Mr. Rankin. What did he say about that?

A—He said, "That is fine. I think that is so." . . .

Mr. Dulles. That day is Saturday?

A—Saturday; yes, sir.

Mr. Rankin. About what time? Do you recall?

A—I guess I got home 2:30 probably. I must have eaten on the way home or somewhere.

Mr. Rankin. In the afternoon?

A—Yes, sir; and I know I was amazed as I walked through the television room there and saw Chief Curry with that gun. You see, at that time they had not identified the gun as his gun, but he was telling about the FBI report on it.

Mr. Rankin. Will you just describe what you saw there at that time?

A—Well, I know he was in a crowd, and it seems to me like he had the gun, but on second thought I am not even sure whether he had the gun, but he was tracing the history of how that gun was bought under the name, under an assumed name from a mail-order house in Chicago and mailed there to Dallas, and that the serial number and everything that had been identified, that the FBI had done that, something else.

I believe they said they had a post office box here, a blind post office box that the recipients of that had identified as Oswald as the guy or something that received it.

In other words, he went directly over the evidence connecting him with the gun.

Mr. Rankin. You say there was a crowd there. Who was the crowd around him?

A—Newsmen. You see, I was at home. I was watching it on television.

Mr. Rankin. I see. Did you do anything about that, then? Did you call him and ask him to quit that?

A—No; I felt like nearly it was a hopeless case. I know now why it happened. That was the first piece of evidence he got his hands on before Fritz did.

Mr. Rankin. Will you explain what you mean by that?

A—Well, this went to the FBI and came to him rather than to Captain Fritz, and I feel in my own mind that this was something new, that he really had been receiving none of the original evidence, that it was coming through Fritz to him and so this went from him to Fritz, you know, and I think that is the reason he did it.

So I stayed home that afternoon. I was trying to think, it seems like I went back by the police station some time that night, late at night.

Mr. Rankin. This way of getting evidence to the press and all of the news media, is that standard practice in your area?

A—Yes; it is, unfortunately. I don't think it is good. We have just, even since this happened we have had a similar incident with the police giving all the evidence out or giving out an oral confession of a defendant that is not admissible in court. You know, oral admissions are not generally admissible in Texas. And they gave all the evidence out in it.

Mr. Rankin. Have you done anything about it, tried to stop it in any way?

A—Well, in this actually, in the same story they quoted me as saying, I mean the news quoted me as saying they shouldn't give the information out, that is the evidence, we have got to try the case, we will get a jury, it is improper to do this, or something to that effect. So far as taking it up with—I have mentioned many times that they shouldn't give out evidence, in talking to the police officers, I mean in there in training things, but it is something I have no control over whatever. It is a separate entity, the city of Dallas is, and I do a little fussing with the police, but by the same token it is not a situation where—I think it is one of your major problems that are going to have to be looked into not only here but it is a sidelight, I think, to your investigation to some extent, but I think you prejudice us, the state, more than you do the defense by giving out our testimony.

You may think that giving out will help you to convict him. I think it works the other way, your jurors that read, the good type of jurors, get an opinion one way or another from what they read, and you end up with poor jurors. If they haven't read or heard anything of the case—well, not generally the same type of juror.

The only thing I make a practice of saying is that I reviewed the evidence in this case in which the State will ask the death penalty, which may be going too far, but I tell them we plan to ask the death penalty or plan to ask life or plan to ask maximum jail sentence or something of that kind.

Mr. Rankin. Did you say that at any time about the Oswald case?

A—Oh, yes, sir; I have said that about both Oswald and Ruby.

Mr. Rankin. When did you say it about the Oswald case?

A—I guess it was Friday night probably. I was asked what penalty we would ask for.

Mr. Rankin. When the police made these releases about the evidence, did they ever ask you whether they should make them?

A—No, sir; like I told you, I talked Saturday morning around between 11 and 12, some time, I told him there was entirely too much publicity on this thing, that with the pressure going to be on us to try it and there may not be a place in the United States you can try it with all the publicity you are getting. Chief Curry said he agreed with me, but, like I said about 2 hours later, I saw him releasing this testimony. . . .

Mr. Rankin. Which route did you follow in regard to the Oswald case?

A—The same route. I accepted the complaint on him in the homicide department, and gave it to David Johnston, the justice of the peace who was there incidentally, or there in the homicide department.

But I didn't actually type it up. I don't know who actually typed it up, somebody typed it up, but we file about a 100 a year, murders "did with malice aforethought."

It was a straight murder indictment, murder with malice charge, and that was the procedure we followed in the Oswald case.

Mr. Rankin. Why did you not include in that complaint a charge of an international conspiracy?

A—Well, it is just like I said, it is surplusage to begin with. You don't need it. If you allege it you have to prove it. The U.S. attorney and the attorney general had called me and said that if it wasn't absolutely necessary they thought it shouldn't be done, and——

Mr. Rankin. By the "attorney general" who do you mean?

A—Mr. Carr. And actually it is never done. I mean, you see that got clear, apparently you had the press writing that up, radio or whoever was saying that was—had no idea about what murder was.

Now, to write in there, assume he was, assume we could prove he was, a Communist, which I wasn't able to prove because all I heard was he had some literature there on him and had been in Russia, but assume I knew he was a Communist, can I prove it, I still wouldn't have alleged it because it is subject actually to be removed from the indictment because it is surplusage, you know, and all a murder indictment, the only thing that a murder indictment varies on is the method of what they used, did kill John Doe by shooting him with a gun or by stabbing him or by drowning him in water or how, the manner and means is the only thing that varies in a murder indictment, all other wordage is the same. Does that clear that up?

(Discussion off the record.)

Senator Cooper. As I understand it, under Texas law there is no crime which is denominated under the term "international conspiracy."

A—No, sir. . . .

Senator Cooper. Now the last question, was there any evidence brought to you or any evidence of which you had knowledge upon which you could base an indictment or a warrant for conspiracy to commit murder in this case?

A—No, sir; you mean parties other than Oswald?

Senator Cooper. Yes.

A—No. I might say on that score, to clear that up, I haven't seen any evidence along that line. I haven't even seen any of the correspondence that they had, allegedly had with the Communist Party here in New York or the Fair Play for Cuba, I haven't seen his little black book where he is supposed to have had the Russian Embassy's telephone numbers in it which I am sure you all have gone into it.

I never did see the book, none of that.

Of course, I have been told by a lot of people and undoubtedly a lot of it was exaggerated that he was a Communist, and you have had people say he was a Communist who might say I was a Communist, you know, if they didn't agree with me on something, so I have absolutely no evidence that he was a Communist of my own knowledge, I have heard a lot, of course.

Mr. Dulles. What you are saying in this last answer relates to the present time, not only the way your knowledge has——

A—At that time and up to the present.

Mr. Dulles. Rather than the day of assassination.

A—I have no evidence myself now that he was a Communist, or ever was a Communist, and I never did see what evidence that they had on him there gathered on him. I never saw any of the physical evidence in the Oswald case other than one or two statements, and I think I saw the gun while they were taking it out of there bringing it to Washington, because I told them at that stage, they didn't want to take it out, didn't want to let the FBI have it and I told them I thought they ought to let them bring it on up here that night and get it back the next night.

There was arguing over that. I am getting off, rambling around, but their argument over that was they were still trying to identify the gun through a pawn broker or something like that and the police wanted to keep it but I said, "Let it go up there and they said they would have it back the next afternoon."

Mr. Rankin. Have you ever had any evidence that Oswald was involved with anyone else in actually shooting the President?

A—Well, I will answer that the same way, I have absolutely no evidence myself.

Now, of course, I might have some type of opinion or some connection with reference to the Fair Play for Cuba and these letters that they told me about. If that was so there may have been some connection or may not, but I have no evidence myself on it.

Mr. Rankin. Do you have any evidence as to whether Jack Ruby was involved with anyone else in the killing of Oswald?

A—No, sir; I have no evidence on that. We have some and I think you have them all, some 8 or 10 witnesses who have said they had seen Ruby and Oswald together at various times.

Some of them were, I know one of them during the trial was a lawyer there in Dallas, which I presume you all got his four-page statement, said he heard them discussing killing Connally a week before then, came out to my house and that had been sent to the FBI, and that was during the trial, and I gave him a lie detector which showed that he didn't have, this was a fanciful thing.

That, I can't think of his name, some of you all may know it, but he is a lawyer there in Dallas.

Mr. Rankin. You found that was not anything you could rely on.

A—I didn't use him as a witness and after giving him the polygraph I was satisfied that he was imagining it. I think he was sincere, I don't think he was trying—I don't think he was trying to be a hero or anything. I think he really thought about it so much I think he thought that it happened, but the polygraph indicated otherwise.

Mr. Dulles. Did you have any other evidence than the polygraph on this point that he was not telling the truth or that this was a fiction?

A—No, but I didn't—but I did see a report where the FBI interviewed the girl that was allegedly with him in Ruby's place in October, and she didn't corroborate all of it. I think she did say he was in there but I am not even sure of that. I didn't interview her but I just read a report on it.

I read where they checked with the Department of Public Safety and they did not, were not able to—he said he reported all this to the Department of Public Safety, and I don't think they found any record of him reporting it. It is very difficult to get him to come in to see me. He didn't just walk in, this went on for a month, I kept hearing that there was a certain person knew about it and I kept telling him to come on and talk to me and he finally came out to my house late one night.

The reason I think he actually must have thought it was so, but—I wasn't too interested in that theory of the case on this thing because I had a theory on this Ruby case from the start because I, even before you are going to get into some of these officers' testimony in a minute, but when this happened I was going home from church, and my own mind I said I believe that was Jack Ruby who shot him because from that Friday night, and from my theory has been from that Friday night, when he saw him there he made up his mind to kill him if he got a chance . . .

Mr. Rankin. I understood you to say when you came home

from church, after the killing of Oswald that you thought it was Ruby before you had heard that it was Ruby.

A—. . . I said that must be Jack Ruby the way he looked. He looked kind of wild to me down there Friday night the way he was running everywhere, you know, and I said to myself that must be him. I didn't tell my wife. You can't prove that. It is one of those things, that was my theory that he was likely the one. I couldn't, you know, out of a million people I couldn't say he was the one but when they announced his name I will say it didn't surprise me. . . .

Senator Cooper. Mr. Wade, can you name to the Commission the names of the persons who told you or who stated in your presence that they had seen Lee Oswald and Jack Ruby together? . . .

A—A lawyer in Dallas . . . handed me a written statement. He said, "The day after this happened I made this," it was a copy of a written statement, he said, "I sent this to J. Edgar Hoover in Washington." . . . I read that statement over. It is a rather startling thing. It didn't ring true to me. It all deals with a conversation between Oswald and Ruby about killing John Connally, the Governor of Texas, over, he says, they can't get syndicated crime in Texas without they kill the Governor.

I know enough about the situation, the Governor has practically nothing to do with syndicated crime. It has to be on a local, your district attorney and your police are the ones on the firing line on that, and they discussed at length killing him, how much they are going to pay him, "He wants five thousand, I believe or half of it now, and half of it when it is done." . . . He took a lie detector. There was no truth in it. . . .

Senator Cooper. Of course, once Oswald was killed, then your duties were connected with the prosecution of Ruby.

A—Yes, sir. . . . From what I picked up it appeared to me there was no question that he received his inspiration on this and maybe other help from somewhere.

Senator Cooper. That is what I am driving at here. You know there have been statements made that other persons could have been connected with Oswald in the assassination of President Kennedy.

Do you have any facts to give the Commission which would bear upon that question that any person other than Oswald was in any way connected with the assassination of President Kennedy?

A—I have no facts that I can give you on it. It is one of these things, and the reason I gave you what my opinion on the thing was, I have read what the U.S. World News and Report said the Commission is going to say, and also this deal out in Japan, you know, where they said that he was not instantaneous, impulsive, I believe, killer of the President, which sounded silly to me.

I mean he planned the thing. He practiced shooting, and he had his inspiration from somebody else. Whether he had a —was working with someone, I don't know. I never did know, it was rumored all over town that they had an airplane there to carry him out of town. I am sure you all have checked into that but I never know whether they did or not.

There seemed to have been something misfired in the thing if there was anybody tried to get it. I don't think there was anybody with him in the shooting but what you are getting at is if there was anyone back of him.

I always felt that the minimum was an inspiration from some cause, and the maximum was actual pay, but like you asked for evidence, I don't have any.

Senator Cooper. Did you ever hear about any evidence that there was an airplane stationed any place there?

A—They ran it in the newspapers that an airplane was supposedly to pick him up but nobody ever found the airplane, so far as I know. You have had every kind of rumor, this has been a thing that has been, that the press has been most inaccurate in a lot of things they have reported, and it is because of the pressure from their offices to get a Ruby story.

We have reporters down there coming down and said, "My office said to write something on Ruby today, what are we going to write."

And it has been so very irresponsible.

Like I said, I have no evidence and the only thing where I get my impression is reading and hearing people talking but I haven't actually figured it wasn't any of my business on Oswald, that I had a problem, a big one of trying Ruby and I have concentrated all of my efforts on that and when we had anybody of this nature we would refer them to the FBI or some other agency.

Senator Cooper. Thank you.

Mr. Dulles. You referred, Mr. Wade, to some testimony or some evidence that Oswald was at one time in the Carousel when Ruby was there.

Was that solely from this lawyer whose testimony you have mentioned?

A—The only one of my personal knowledge that I talked with was from the lawyer. He told me he was there with a certain girl, a stripper, and Ruby and Oswald were in an adjoining booth. There is lots of other people, I think your master of ceremonies, they had him on television and said he had seen them there but later on said he hadn't when they got to interviewing him. But my own personal knowledge that you are all interested in was that one man who told me that. . . .

. . . I thought you needed some type of, somebody—and your whole thing was wrong with this whole deal, you had no one in charge of the thing. You had the police, the FBI, the Secret Service, the Department of Justice, my Department, Waggoner Carr's department, but no one had any say to offer the rest of them.

Mr. Rankin. Tell us how that affected it. You had the jurisdiction of the crime itself.

A—Of the trial of the case.

Mr. Rankin. And the police department, what jurisdiction did they have?

A—They had the jurisdiction, the primary responsibility for the investigation of the assassination, and—they had the primary job of finding out who did it and getting the evidence. They were assisted, the Secret Service, of course, had the job of protecting the President. The FBI, they have criminal, pretty general, investigation, I am not sure, but they were in on it, they were all there, and assisting. It was a deal where nobody had any actual control over another person.

Mr. Rankin. Had the State authorities any jurisdiction or effect on the operation?

A—You mean the State?

Mr. Rankin. Of Texas.

A—They actually had none. They had no authority. The Governor has no authority in a situation like this nor the attorney general other than in a vague sort of way, as the police, I guess they had the police powers to some extent of maintaining order but you didn't need the National Guard or anything. I mean this was more dealing with a situation of information. I think this situation is true in many States, practically all of them.

Mr. Rankin. Was that confusing, did that make it harder to try to solve the crime and handle the problems?

A—It did; very much so. Your press was the most confusing thing. I mean you couldn't get in the police station. I mean I just barely could get into the police station myself for stomping over the press and you had a lot of reporters, not like the reporters we usually deal with down there. I mean we don't have trouble usually with the local press, people we pretty well know.

We would tell them what is going on, and they will go on, but these people just followed everybody everywhere they went, and they were throwing policemen on the corner, if he made a statement about he saw someone running that way dressed maybe like the killer—they ran all that on. They were just running everybody. There was no control over your public media. It made it worse since all television networks were on the assassination all—24 hours, I mean all day. And there was no central thing from—there was no central person who had any control of handling the thing that information was given out. You see they interviewed some of your patrolmen who were giving out evidence, you know, some of your foot patrolmen on the corner, they were interviewing anybody.

Mr. Rankin. Would it help or hinder the handling of such

a crime of the killing of the President if it was a Federal crime, in your opinion?

A—Well, offhand, I think probably it would, but——

Mr. Rankin. It would help?

A—I think it would help, but you are going to have the same situation. I am thinking if you had, if it is a Federal crime, for instance, it is still murder in Texas. If Captain Fritz and the Dallas police had arrested this man, the FBI wouldn't have had him. I don't care if it was a Federal crime. We have bank robberies where there is joint jurisdiction. The one that gets him, if it is the State police or the city police gets them, they file with me and if the FBI gets them they file with the Federal.

Mr. Rankin. You need more control over the police investigation in order to carry out your duties, is that——

A—Of course; my idea if you had it to do over, it is easy to do that, but I think you need someone where all the information is channeled through one person. If anything is given out and getting an intelligent person, not just a police officer, you know. . . . Saturday, most of my day was spent in talking to Dean R. G. Storey, and the dean of the Harvard Law School, raising, wondering what the situation was with reference to attorneys for Oswald. . . . They had started a Tippit fund in the meantime, and practically every lawyer was scared they were going to be appointed, you know, and they had gone and subscribed to that fund so they were having much trouble getting a lawyer appointed. . . .

Senator Cooper. Did anyone ever say to you in the event there was a charge of conspiracy who would be named other than Oswald?

A—No; there is no other names, there is no other name that I know of that has ever been mentioned to me as being part of the conspiracy.

The question we are talking about here, if I understand it, being that Oswald, as a part of an international conspiracy, did murder John Fitzgerald Kennedy. And there is no other names of co-conspirators, we have had lots of leads run down upon it. Somebody at the penitentiary down there, a colored person, at least the word to us, that he had told the guard he had hauled Oswald away from there, you all probably got this, but we interviewed him down there.

He was just talking and waiting to come back to Dallas. But there had been lots of things of that kind but to my knowledge none of them have actually been proven out. . . .

Mr. Rankin. Did you have anything to do with the preparation of the [Ruby] case for trial?

A—Yes; to some extent. You see, I had four assistants to assist me in the trial. . . . Alexander spent the 2 weeks we were picking a jury in viewing the witnesses. I never talked to any of the witnesses. After the first half a day of testimony,

I was very disappointed in the way the witnesses were being put on the stand; if this is of interest to you.

Mr. Rankin. Tell us what happened.

A—I told him, I said, on this case we are going on this theory, I want everybody who saw Ruby from the time of the assassination of President Kennedy down to the time he killed Oswald, I want to prove where he was every minute of the time that I can, and then we will take it from there and put the films on there and show what happened there and then afterward. We are going on the theory that he is a glory seeker and a hero because I was convinced that was the motive of the killing.

I put on seven witnesses, and about six of them testified against us, I think, or made poor witnesses saying if, they saw him down in the Dallas News where he was 2 minutes in a stare, that never made any sense.

Some of them said they thought there was something wrong with him and none of them were the type of witnesses that I wanted testifying for the State. . . . I put all the witnesses on the next morning. I talked to all of the officers, I talked to Officers Dean, McMillon, Archer, King, never had talked with them about the case before and I talked with them then and I put all of them on next morning.

Mr. Rankin. Tell us what, starting with—which one did you talk to first, Archer, Dean, or McMillon.

A—I think I talked to all of them at first in a body. I talked to——

Mr. Rankin. I see.

A—I had them all in there and said, "Now what do you know about the case?" because a lot of them I didn't know what they knew.

Mr. Rankin. What did they say?

A—As a matter of fact, I wasn't familiar with Dean's testimony until he told me right there a day before he testified. Then he showed me the memorandum that he had made on the thing. I talked with him there and I put Archer on the next morning and McMillon on, who stayed all day. They cross-examined him from 11:30 until 5:30. Then I put King on, and then Dean, I believe the next morning, and we rested. But they told me just what they testified to in the trial which I don't know whether I can give all of it but I can tell you roughly that McMillon and Archer were partners and heard Ruby say some things, "I hope I killed the sonofabitch."

Mr. Rankin. When?

A—Within about a few seconds after the killing and then upstairs then, "I meant to shoot three times but you all got me before I did."

Incidentally, you may not know it but their psychiatrist corroborated that statement.

Mr. Rankin. Who was that?

A—Dr. Guttmacher on cross-examination. We asked Dr. Guttmacher, "Well, didn't Ruby tell you that he meant to shoot three times?"

He said, "Yes; and he told me that."

He said, "One time he told me that." He also said at one time he told him otherwise but he corroborated that portion of it. Then it seemed like there was something else said. Archer said to him as he got up in the jail, "I believe he is going to die, Jack," I may be getting these wrong, but they are roughly —he said something about, "You fellows couldn't do it," or talking about the police, and I believe that was Archer and McMillon. . . .

They had heard previous to this coming up there the conversation about Jack, "I think he is going to die," and Jack answered some question, I believe he said, "You couldn't do it, somebody had to," or something like that. Jack Ruby, I am referring to. . . .

ALAN H. BELMONT

Testimony of the assistant to the Director of the Federal Bureau of Investigation:

Mr. McCloy. In your investigation of the President's assassination, did you have occasion, after the event, to make an investigation of Ruby's background or Ruby's relationship to Oswald?

A—Yes, sir; we went into that very thoroughly. . . .

Mr. McCloy. Have you come to any conclusions or opinions in regard to Ruby and his connection with Oswald, if any?

A—The reports, of course, speak for themselves. But in summation, we did not come up with anything of a solid nature, that is anything that would stand up to indicate that there was any association between Ruby and Oswald. We had numerous allegations which we ran out extensively and carefully, but there is nothing, no information, that would stand up to show there was an association between them. . . .

Representative Ford. Was there any evidence that the FBI found to the effect that Ruby was a Communist?

A—No, sir.

Representative Ford. None whatsoever?

A—No, sir.

Representative Ford. Was there any evidence found by the FBI to the effect that Ruby was connected with in any way whatsoever so-called rightist groups?

A—No, sir; I do not recall anything of that nature.

Mr. McCloy. No association that you know of as a result of the investigation of Ruby with any foreign government or agency of a foreign government?

A—No, sir. . . .

V. The President's Safety

JAMES J. ROWLEY

The testimony of the Chief of the United States Secret Service:

The Chairman. Chief Rowley will be asked to testify with respect to the protective measures taken by the secret service in Dallas, changes in such measures made as a result of the Dallas experience, and with regard to the investigation of the assassination and any information he may have respecting the assassination of the President. . . .

Mr. Rankin. I have suggested to Chief Rowley that as he moves along in his testimony he might have various matters that he would think should not be on the record because of the security of the country, and if he would just suggest that, when he came to that point, and say specifically that it did involve the security of the country, then we would proceed to go off the record, if it was satisfactory to the Commission, and consider those questions off the record. And then return to the record as soon as we had completed those security matters.

Would that be satisfactory?

The Chairman. I think that is an appropriate way to proceed. . . .

Mr. Rankin. Did you become familiar with what did happen on that trip, in your position as chief?

A—I was first informed while addressing a graduating class of our Secret Service school on that day. I was summoned by Mr. Behn to the White House, at which time he told me that the President had been shot. He was then at the hospital, and subsequently we were notified that the President had died; that the Vice President would take the oath of office in the airplane at Love Field.

In the meantime, I asked my deputy, who was in his office while I was at the White House, to arrange with the Immigration Service to close the border, Texas being in close proximity to the border. There might have been a conspiracy or something, we didn't want to take any chances. And then I immediately dispatched an inspector from my staff to the Capitol to protect the Speaker, and directed the other activities as we got the information from Dallas.

Mr. Rankin. Did you learn in connection with the trip when the assassination occurred that certain of the Secret Service agents had been in the press club and what is called the Cellar, at Fort Worth, the night before?

A—Well, that came to my attention through a broadcast

. . . that the agents were inebriated the night before at the Fort Worth Press Club. I immediately dispatched Inspector McCann to Fort Worth to investigate the report, and to interview the agents.

Mr. Rankin. What did you learn?

A—I learned that there were nine agents involved at the Press Club. And I might say this—the agents on duty throughout that day had no opportunity to eat. When they arrived at Fort Worth, they were informed that there was a buffet to be served at the Fort Worth Club. This is what I ascertained in personal interviews. Upon going over there, they learned there was no buffet, and some of them stayed for a drink. Three, I think, had one scotch, and others had two or three beers. They were in and out—from the time they arrived, I would say roughly around 12:30, until the place closed at 2 o'clock.

Now, after that some of them went to the Cellar. This is a place that does not serve alcoholic beverages. They went there primarily, I think, out of curiosity, because this was some kind of a beatnik place where someone gets up and recites, or plays the guitar.

Mr. Rankin. Did you learn whether or not there were any violations of the regulations of the Secret Service by these men?

A—Yes; there was a violation. At that time there was a section in our manual in effect that said that during——

Mr. Rankin. Now, will you tell the Commission about what the regulation was?

A—"The use of liquor. Employees are strictly enjoined to refrain from the use of intoxicating liquor during the hours they are officially employed at their post of duty or when they may reasonably expect that they may be called upon to perform an official duty."

The one that applies here—"However, all members of the White House detail and special agents cooperating with them on presidential and similar protective assignments are considered to be subject to call for official duty at any time while in travel status. Therefore, the use of intoxicating liquor of any kind, including beer and wine, by members of the White House detail and special agents cooperating with them or by special agents on similar assignments, while they are in a travel status, is prohibited."

Mr. Rankin. Can you tell the Commission how many men were involved in these trips to the Press Club and the Cellar, where these things were done?

A—There were 9 men involved at the Press Club, and there were 10 men involved at the Cellar.

Mr. Rankin. Now, how many men, of those 10 men, were in the Presidential motorcade on the day of the assassination?

A—Four—four men were in the followup car.

The Chairman. Who were they?

Mr. Rankin. Do you know their names?

A—Yes; Landis, Hill, Ready, and Bennett.

Mr. Rankin. Did you make any investigation to determine whether or not their violation of the Secret Service regulations had anything to do with the assassination of the President?

A—Yes. They performed their duties from the time they departed in the followup car from Love Field until the point of the tragedy in a most satisfactory manner. There was nothing deficient in their actions or their alertness. They went through the heaviest part of downtown Dallas, through the crowds, and performed in an exemplary manner.

Mr. Rankin. How do you know that?

A—From the reports that I got from their superiors.

Mr. Rankin. In the work that you did with the White House detail before you became Chief of the Secret Service, did you know the various responsibilities of the members of the White House detail?

A—Yes, sir.

Mr. Rankin. Did you ever participate in such motorcades yourself?

A—I have; yes, sir.

Mr. Rankin. How much?

A—Well, I have participated, in rough numbers, over a period of 22 years—roughly, maybe a thousand or more.

Mr. Rankin. Will you briefly describe the functions of the Secret Service agents in connection with the President's car?

A—When the President's car leaves the airport or a railroad station or any other location, the agents accompany him to the car and stand to the right and left, in the same order as their designated positions on the followup car, and screen him. And then the car moves out, slowly, because the rest of the cars have to have an opportunity to follow in the motorcade, so that none lingers behind, or is left behind. And when the agent in the lead car determines that the motorcade is intact and is moving, then he steps up his speed, which is a cue to the Presidential driver to step up his speed, and then they go at a speed consistent with the crowd that is there, and so forth.

Now, upon leaving the airport, if there is a huge crowd there, the men are still on the ground running on the right and left side of the President, both rear and front of the vehicle. After they get out of the crowd, then the men in the front beside the Presidential vehicle drop back and take their positions in the followup car.

This is so that they are not in the way of the men running on the right and left rear. They move back last and have a clear opportunity to jump onboard the followup car in the event the speed of the motorcade is stepped up.

When the motorcade comes to intersections or turns which

are always vulnerable points, in that if you make a right turn, that is the closest point for someone to come out, the agents on the right side before reaching that point, will jump off, to be available alongside the President's car in the event someone darts out with some malicious plan.

There have also been times when, innocently, ladies and young people will come out to throw a bouquet of flowers. And then if there is a crowd that is sparse, they return to their position in the followup car.

Now, when they come into a big crowd, they take it on foot, and at a little jog, if necessary.

In some instances, if the crowd continues for a prolonged distance, the agents work together. In other words, there are rear steps on the right and left rear of the Presidential car with handrails. These have two purposes. One, for agents to ride on and to screen the President from anything from above; the second, in a situation like this, to keep an additional man available in case of trouble, and also to alternate with the men to the right rear of the President, who are jogging along warding off the crowd.

Mr. Rankin. Now, what positions did the four men that you referred to that were involved in the press club and the Cellar matter occupy on the day of the assassination?

A—Well, Mr. Ready occupied the right front, Mr. Landis to his rear——

Mr. Rankin. What do you mean by right front?

A—Right front running board position of the followup car. It was his responsibility or duty to jump off in crowds and to take the position at the right rear of the President's car.

Mr. Landis, if necessary, to jump off if the occasion demanded and take the right front of the President's car.

Mr. Hill was on the left front running board of the followup car, and his responsibility was at the rear of the President's car. His position was assigned there because he was in charge of the First Lady's detail, and she was seated on the left side.

And Mr. McIntyre was to his rear on the left running board. So his assignment would have been up to the left front of the President's car. Mr. Bennett was in the rear seat of the followup car.

Mr. Rankin. Now, how can you tell that the fact that they were out as they were the night before and violated the regulations, had nothing to do with the assassination?

A—Well, based on the reports of my investigating agents and the facts as to how they performed at the time of the tragedy. Mr. Hill, who was on the left side, responded immediately—as he looked toward the Presidential car, being on the left side, he scanned from left to right, and when he saw there was something happening to the President following a noise, he immediately jumped from his position to get aboard from his side.

Mr. Ready scanned to the right so he was looking away from the President, because he was looking around from the right side. As a consequence, he wasn't aware of what was happening in the front. The car was also going on a turn at that time.

Mr. Rankin. What about the other two?

A—The other two were watching—they reacted normally —the man on the left side looked to his left rear, and the man, Landis, looked to his right rear.

Mr. Rankin. Have you done anything to discipline these men for violation of the regulations of the Secret Service?

A—Well, I did consider what type of punishment would be provided.

Then I also considered the fact that these men in no way had—their conduct had no bearing on the assassination. And, therefore, I thought that in the light of history, to place a stigma on them by punishing them at that time, from which inevitably the public would conclude that they were responsible for the assassination of the President—I didn't think this was fair, and that they did not deserve that, with their family and children.

Mr. Dulles. You described the assignment of the four men with respect to the followup car and the President's car. Do they have different assignments with regard to watching what is happening around them, or does that depend on the circumstances in which they are?

A—Both. When they start off they have a certain area that they have to watch. Like the man in the right front would naturally watch slightly to the right and in front of him. The fellow on the side, behind him, will watch to the right and rear. In other words, as they are going by a building, he should scan the building. In the meantime, he picks up where the man in the front has finished. In other words, the scan of the man in the front will cover the building to his front and side; the fellow behind will scan alongside from rear to forward. Their scanning joins. This is the way they are accustomed to doing it.

Mr. Dulles. Who would cover straight ahead?

A—The man in the front seat has that responsibility.

Mr. Rankin. Chief Rowley, how do you construe subparagraph (c) of your regulation 10 regarding the use of alcoholic liquors?

The Chairman. Will you read it for the record?

Mr. Rankin. Will you kindly read it?

A—"Violation or slight disregard of the above paragraphs or the excessive or improper use of intoxicating liquor at any time will be cause for removal from the service. In interpreting the words 'excessive' and 'improper,' slight evidence tending to indicate unusual or questionable conduct will be considered proof that the use of liquor has been improper or excessive.

531

Association with others who drink to excess will be considered as an indication of using more than a moderate amount of liquor. The excuse that liquor was used for medicinal purposes will not be accepted."

Mr. Rankin. How do you construe and apply that?

A—Well, in this instance, it was wrong.

Mr. Rankin. Now, were these men under this regulation considered to be on travel status, so that they should not be using intoxicating liquor?

A—Yes, sir.

Mr. Rankin. And there is no question about that in your mind?

A—No, sir.

Mr. Rankin. Has anything been done to reprimand and cause them to realize that this is a violation of your regulations?

A—They were interviewed by the inspector at the time. The seriousness of the matter was impressed upon them. And I think they recognize the seriousness of their acts.

The men we recruit are men that are college graduates and mature, and we screen them very carefully, particularly before we assign them to the White House detail. They know and we know that they are in a fishbowl 24 hours a day, and that, therefore, their conduct is always subject to scrutiny, and so forth, and that they are responsible individuals. Their records have indicated that they have been performing in a high degree. They have worked endless hours of overtime. They are dedicated. And if they were not, they would not be on the detail.

They realize the seriousness of the violation, and I went over it with my special agent in charge. He understands it. And I am quite sure that they all understand it at this time. . . .

Representative Ford. Mr. Rankin, I don't recall Chief Rowley saying precisely what the reprimands were specifically for these violations of the regulations in this one instance.

You spoke highly of their background, and you spoke very high in their praise. But I did not hear what reprimand, if any, had actually been lodged against them.

A—There was no reprimand. You are talking about the current thing?

Representative Ford. I am talking about the Dallas trip.

A—I stated in considering what would be an appropriate punishment at the time, I felt that these men, by their conduct, had no bearing on the assassination of the President in Dallas. That to institute formal punishment or disciplinary action would inevitably lead the public to conclude that they were responsible for the assassination of President Kennedy. I did not think in the light of history that they should be stigmatized with something like that, or their families or children. And, for that reason, I took the position that I did.

Representative Ford. So there was no official reprimand or disciplinary action?

A—No, sir.

Mr. Rankin. Did you talk to the agents, to indicate and make it plain to them that this was a violation of the regulations?

A—I talked to some of the agents, as did my inspector at the time, who interviewed each and every one of them.

Mr. Rankin. And I think the Commission would be interested in whether you can be assured, or assure them that the action you took was sufficient so that this would not happen again.

A—Well, I am confident that it would not happen again, Mr. Rankin.

Mr. Rankin. Can you tell us why you think so?

A—Because they realize the seriousness of their action.

Initially I can understand the situation—they thought they were going for a dinner, buffet, and they got into the place and it wasn't there.

I talked personally with the agents there, and they just thought while they were there they would have a drink. It was one of those situations.

The important thing was that it was pointed out to them this was wrong, this was a violation. These men are young men with futures, they realize the true situation, innocent as they may have seemed to think it was.

But I am quite confident that we will not have a repetition of that.

And in talking to Mr. Behn—I am confident, too, in him— I know that he will see to it that they are well supervised.

Mr. Rankin. When they are out on a trip of this kind, Chief Rowley, as I understand your regulations, it is understood by the regulations and by the Secret Service that they are on duty all the time—that is, subject to call?

A—Yes, sir.

Mr. Rankin. And even though it is late in the evening or they had gone to bed in the early hours of the morning, they could be called to go on duty and perform their responsibility of taking care of the President or the Vice President, or whoever they are charged with; is that right?

A—That is right.

Mr. Rankin. So that do they understand that when they are out on that kind of duty, they are subject to call at all times, and anything they do contrary to regulations is a violation, because they are subject to the call and must be ready at any moment to perform their duties.

A—They certainly do, because there have been situations, whether or not they have had it with the Kennedy administration I don't know—but I know there have been situations where we have moved fast, all hours of the night. I remember one instance, that has never been disclosed—as Mr. Dulles knows, you never advertise your successes, you just get the other things—that I would like to give you as an example off the record, to answer your question, if I may.

(Discussion off the record.)

The Chairman. Back on the record.

Chief, it seems to me that on an assignment of that kind, to be alert at all times is one of the necessities of the situation. And I just wonder if you believe that men who did what these men did, being out until early morning hours, doing a little— even a small amount of drinking—would be as alert the next day as men should be when they are charged with the tremendous responsibility of protecting the President.

A—Well, we checked on that, Mr. Chief Justice, and the agent in charge reported that they were in good physical condition. I don't condone these late hours; no. This is not a rule. This case is an exception. However, because of the activities of any travel such as the Presidents today make from one place to another, to maybe seven States in a weekend, there is constant going.

I don't condone this at all. But these men are young. They are of such age that I think that they responded in this instance adequately and sufficiently as anyone could under the circumstances.

The Chairman. Well, I am thinking of this. As you go along in the motorcade, you have men who are scanning the buildings along the way, don't you?

A—Yes, sir.

The Chairman. And they have submachineguns in one of the cars.

A—No; for security reasons, I would like to—we don't have machineguns now, sir.

The Chairman. I just thought I heard that from the record here, that they had some kind of guns.

A—They had a weapon, a new weapon; yes, sir.

Mr. Chairman. Well, whatever it is.

Now, other people, as they went along there, even some people in the crowds, saw a man with a rifle up in this building from which the President was shot. Now, don't you think that if a man went to bed reasonably early, and hadn't been drinking the night before, would be more alert to see those things as a Secret Service agent, than if they stayed up until 3, 4, or 5 o'clock in the morning, going to beatnik joints and doing some drinking along the way?

A—If I remember that witness' testimony—and that was one of the first statements that he made—that witness was with his wife, and he happened to look up there, and I think he said, "There is a man with a rifle, it is a Secret Service man," and let it go at that. He didn't inform any of the authorities.

The Chairman. No; nobody did. But I say wouldn't an alert

534

Secret Service man in this motorcade, who is supposed to observe such things, be more likely to observe something of that kind if he was free from any of the results of liquor or lack of sleep than he would otherwise?

A—Well, yes; he would be. But then, on the other hand, Mr. Chief Justice, in some instances the men come in from a trip at 1:30 in the morning, which there have been cases on travels that I have made, and have to be up at 3:30 or 4 o'clock, and out in time for a 5 o'clock departure. Then you go all that day until 1 or 2 o'clock the next morning. This is what has happened in the past.

The Chairman. I am not talking about the past. We are talking about nine men here who were out until rather unusual hours of the morning.

A—Yes, sir.

The Chairman. They were to be on duty the next day.

The next day—or if not sooner.

The next day they were supposed to be alert to anything that might occur along the line of march. Don't you think that they would have been much more alert, sharper, had they not been doing these things?

A—Yes, sir; but I don't believe they could have prevented the assassination.

The Chairman. Isn't it a substantial violation of these rules to do a thing of that kind?

A—Yes, sir—on the basis of this section here.

The Chairman. Yes. Now, Chief I noticed, also, in reading some of the reports that three of these men whom you speak of, were actually on night duty, protecting the life of the President. And around 4 o'clock in the morning, when they were protecting him at the Texas Hotel, they said that they had a coffee break, and they went from the hotel over to the beatnik joint. Now, is that consistent with your regulations?

A—In this case, I talked to these three agents. They were relieved at different times—because their posts are in the corridor of a stuffy hotel——

The Chairman. Of the what?

A—The corridor that they were on post outside the President's suite was a stuffy one, and they went downstairs to get a breath of fresh air. And they walked—it was a block—and out of curiosity they went into this place. One fellow looked in and left, he didn't buy any coffee. Another fellow went in and felt, I suppose, when he went in that he would buy a cup of coffee. But they were on what we call reliefs, the same as we relieve them around the White House. There are only so many posts, but you have a group of men in one of the rooms of the hotel where they are available, like an alert squad, and they relieve everyone on post every half hour. It is a part of the rotation of positions we have.

535

The Chairman. Do you have any regulations concerning where they shall remain when they are relieved for this short period of time?

A—No, sir.

The Chairman. They can go any place they want?

A—No; not any place. They usually stay within the immediate confines. That is understood. The hotel or the residence.

The Chairman. Well, they didn't do that here, did they?

A—No, sir.

The Chairman. They went to the beatnik joint.

A—Yes, sir.

The Chairman. Now, is that consistent with their duty?

A—No; it is not consistent or inconsistent with their duty. But as they explained to me, they wanted to get a breath of fresh air. If they are at a residence in a remote place, and they want to walk around the area, they might walk maybe a city block or so, which is what they do on a lot of these assignments—particularly in hotels. This was not an air-conditioned hotel.

The Chairman. It would seem to me that a beatnik joint is a place where queer people of all kinds gather anyway, and that the mere fact that these men did leave their post of duty might be an indication to someone that the President was not being protected, and might leave an opening for them to go there and try to do something.

A—They were relieved, Mr. Chief Justice. They didn't leave their post of duty. They would not leave their post of duty until they were relieved by someone. . . .

Mr. Rankin. Did you have enough agents at that time to perform the required duties in connection with this trip for both Dallas and the other cities in Texas to be visited?

A—Well, we never have enough agents for the activities that the President today is engaged in. We draw from the field to supplement or augment the agents from the White House detail. We move the agents from one point to another where we can —particularly in the area of the advance men.

But in Dallas we had sufficient agents with prior experience in Presidential protection who assisted Mr. Lawson in the advance preparations. . . .

The Chairman. Chief, I have wondered about this question. Some months before Ambassador Adlai Stevenson had been handled very roughly in Dallas. Did you make—did your people make any investigation as to that group that caused that disturbance for him, to see if there might be some possibilty of the same thing happening to the President?

A—Not immediately at the time of the incident that occurred to Mr. Stevenson, but when the advance man came down, that was one of the things that we assigned a local agent to inquire into, to ascertain the hard core of that group, if you will, that were responsible for stimulating that activity. And he contacted an informant, and with the local police, who are members of a special squad that are involved in this kind of activity, they went and identified through pictures, which they saw in the newsreel, the principal members. They had photographs made, and they issued them to the agents on their visit there, to be on the lookout for these men as potential troublemakers.

The Chairman. Did they do the same thing concerning the incident that Vice President Johnson had a year or so before that?

A—No, sir; not at that time. That was more or less in the heat of a political campaign. I don't think it was a similar type of activity.

The Chairman. I see.

But you did do it with the Stevenson matter?

A—That is right.

Mr. Rankin. Chief Rowley, could you inform the Commission about the advance publicity concerning trips of the President to various parts of the country? There has been the question raised as to whether that is a threat to the President, and might make the work of the Secret Service and others who are doing protective work more difficult.

A—Well, we have found that it is. And we always consider it as a potential threat in that it might give someone the opportunity who had any plans, whether it be an individual as in this case, or a group, to select an area, if they knew what the route was, or conduct a reconnaissance, if you will. I have always been opposed to it, and I have always tried to prevail upon the staff of the various Presidents who might be responsible for the release, not to release it too far in advance.

Mr. Rankin. Could you tell the Commission what the problem is in that regard?

A—Well, in this regard, it is a political thing, and the President cannot be contained in a vacuum. If he wants to go out and meet the people under our form of government, he will in his own way. Each and every President has his own thoughts and methods as it pertains to these visits, and the need for publicity. This trip in Dallas was an opportunity for the people to see the President, as are the trips of any President. I remember well when President Truman started this trip across the country in June 1948, the purpose being to get the feel of the people and let the people see him at the time.

And it was then, as a result of that trip, that he determined he would run for reelection. That I know of my own personal knowledge.

But these are the things that are hard on security, as far as developing a close screen on the President. . . .

Mr. Rankin. Would you tell us the gist of the new information criteria, and what the difference is as you conceive it from the old standard?

A—Well, if I may do this. We have sent this criteria to the intelligence agencies that we think would be of help to us, with a covering letter in which we say that studies are now underway, "by which we hope to develop more detailed criteria. Our experience with the attached guidelines will also be carefully evaluated with a view towards amendments if required. We will appreciate your cooperation and suggestions concerning these guidelines, so that the person of the President will be protected to the best of our combined abilities and resources."
. . . We have gotten some 9,000 reports on the members of the Communist Party from the FBI. At this time we have read and evaluated and catalogued them and indexed them. There has been a small percentage that have been to date of interest to us. But this is the beginning. And except for the indexes, we are more or less current as a result of that. . . .

Mr. Rankin. Now, how is the new standard different from the prior standard?

A—Well, we have always had the basic standard. The other standard was the threat to harm or embarrass the President, however, this time we added three factors.

Mr. Rankin. And these are in addition to the threat of harm to the President?

A—That is correct. . . . The interest of the individual or the organization, capabilities of the individual or the organization, and the activities of the individual or organization. The interests of the individual or organization is the prime factor to be considered in the criteria, but must be coupled with the capability and activity of the individual or organization in any determination for referral to the Secret Service.

"The interest must be towards the President, or others named, or other high Government official in the nature of a complaint, coupled with an expressed or implied determination to use a means other than legal or peaceful to satisfy any grievance, real or imagined. After the interest phase of the criteria is met, then the activity which encompass previous history, that is, mental instability, history of violence and the capability of the individual or organization for furthering this interest will dictate whether the case should be referred to the Secret Service. In making referrals to the Secret Service, it is requested that the agency furnish all pertinent background information relating to each of the three factor criteria."

Mr. Rankin. And when did that become effective?

A—That became effective in the last 3 weeks as we developed and explored and examined the many reports that we were receiving.

Mr. Rankin. Now, the language that you read into the record, where you invited comment and suggestions from the various other agencies to whom you sent communication, what did you mean by that? Is that asking them for their ideas so that you may further change the criteria?

A—Where we may get in a position later on to break it down into categories. In other words, if every agency forwards and inundates us with many reports—say we expand to 3 million, obviously, the whole intelligence family could not cope with that. You have to get it down to a workable number. On the other hand, if you try to restrict the categories too much, then you find yourself in a position that you may miss another Oswald, and then the utilities of your file are of no consequence. So you have to try to reach the level in between there where it is going to be practical for us to react or develop the type of risks that we think should be covered by our organization in the protection of the President of the United States.

Mr. Rankin. Are you doing anything about the use of equipment that might help you to secure information about any particular locality the President was going to travel to more readily?

A—In connection with the PRS?

Mr. Rankin. Yes.

A—Well, we have conferred with the IBM. Can I go off the record on this?

(Discussion off the record.)

The Chairman. Back on the record.

Mr. Rankin. Chief Rowley, you have described off the record certain matters that involve the security of the country and cannot be made public. But can you tell us whether you have done anything in the past to try to improve your methods in testimony that can be made public?

A—Well, I have tried to secure in the appropriations funds to enable us to procure the equipment and personnel that we thought would be necessary.

With the approval of the Congress, we were able 2 years ago to secure funds to enable us, in our check forgeries program, to try to adapt the characteristics of handwriting to an ADP processing program. We are hopeful this will work out. And we have used the Bureau of Standards to assist us in this program. We have prints out and have programmed part of the operation.

Now, it was my thought that if we succeeded in that area, we could also apply it to PRS. So we are working quite hard on this other area. And I knew the need would be eventually for us to get into the PRS stage on the electronic machine situation.

Mr. Rankin. Now, did you know that we had asked Mr. Bouck when he testified if he could inform us at a later date about people who were in institutions or otherwise might be dangerous, and with regard to whom you asked that the Secret Service be notified, so that they could make adequate protection for the President?

A—Yes, sir.

Mr. Rankin. Do you know how many such cases you now have?

A—Approximately a thousand.

Mr. Rankin. Would you tell the Commission what your practice was for the Secret Service concerning the route of the motorcade at the time of the assassination—that is, whether you made inspection of adjacent buildings?

A—At that time, and prior to that time, except for the inaugurations in Washington, and other parades, involving the visit of foreign dignitaries in Washington, in which the President would ride in the motorcade with the head of state, where we had ample time to make these surveys, we had never conducted on trips out of Washington surveys of this nature. I have here a statement of the conditions that prevailed in Dallas as well as other areas—if I may read this.

Mr. Rankin. Yes.

A—"Except for inauguration or other parades involving foreign dignitaries accompanied by the President in Washington, it has not been the practice of the Secret Service to make surveys or checks of buildings along the route of a Presidential motorcade. For the inauguration and certain other parades in Washington where the traditional route is known to the public long in advance of the event, buildings along the route can be checked by teams of law enforcement officers, and armed guards are posted along the route as appropriate. But on out-of-town trips where the route is decided on and made public only a few days in advance, buildings are not checked either by Secret Service agents or by any other law enforcement officers at the request of the Secret Service. With the number of men available to the Secret Service and the time available, surveys of hundreds of buildings and thousands of windows is not practical.

"In Dallas the route selected necessarily involved passing through the principal downtown section between tall buildings. While certain streets thought to be too narrow could be avoided and other choices made, it was not practical to select a route where the President could not be seen from roofs or windows of buildings. At the two places in Dallas where the President would remain for a period of time, Love Field and the Trade Mart, arrangements were made for building and roof security by posting police officers where appropriate. Similar arrangements for a motorcade of 10 miles, including many blocks of tall commercial buildings, is not practical. Nor is it practical to prevent people from entering such buildings or to limit access in every building to those employed or having business there. Even if it were possible with a vastly larger force of security officers to do so, many observers have felt that such a procedure would not be consistent with the nature and purpose of the motorcade to let the people see their President and to welcome him to their city.

"In accordance with its regular procedures, no survey or

540

other check was made by the Secret Service, or by any other law enforcement agency at its request, of the Texas School Book Depository Building or those employed there prior to the time the President was shot." . . .

Mr. Dulles. I wonder if you could explain that (new information criteria) a little more? I ask this question because I have been studying the previous assassinations a good deal. And in many of these cases, it seems to me this definition would not have covered the assassin. That is, there has been in some cases opposition to government, opposition to people in authority, but there has been no expressed hatred toward or animus against a particular President. And I was wondering whether this went too far on a definition to meet your purposes.

A—This is a beginning, as I indicated to you here. We hope to improve it. But this is one of the things where we want to include the Oswald-type individual.

Now, Oswald wrote to the Governor intimating that he would use whatever means was necessary to obtain the change of his undesirable, or as he called it, dishonorable discharge. All legal means had been used in his case, where the Navy Review Board had examined it and came to a decision.

And this is an example of what we were trying to include in the area of this type of individual. Now, the other people——

Mr. Dulles. But that was not a threat directed against the President. That was directed against the Secretary of the Navy.

A—That is right; but then, on the other hand, they transfer the threats. I am quite sure that the Congressmen here get many threats, and that sometimes they may not come off. But these people are obsessed.

You take the individual that attempted the assassination of the late President Roosevelt in Miami that time. His original purpose was to shoot President Hoover. But then when he heard Roosevelt was there, he transferred.

Now, I remember a situation involving a member of Truman's staff, where a fellow stalked this man at his home. And finally we got into the case on his request. We satisfied ourselves that he wasn't a real threat to him—but we picked up the paper a year later and found out he shot at an assemblyman in Staten Island. So if they make a threat or something like this, even though it is against the Government as a group, or have some grievance, they transfer it—particularly, to the President. They use that father complex, as indicated in the research work that these different agencies have submitted to us.

Representative Ford. Under these criteria, which you are now following, Oswald would have been designated? Is that your judgment?

A—That is correct; yes, sir.

Mr. Dulles. I had some questions about that in reading it.

That did not occur to me, because Oswald had never expressed any antagonism toward the President, as far as I know, up to this time—the President personally, or even afterward.

A—That is right; but under this criteria he would. Namely, he had the interest because of the letter he wrote to Governor Connally. The activity, because he was a defector, and he demonstrated for the Fair Play for Cuba Committee. The capability, because he traveled, and he had knowledge of firearms.

Mr. Dulles. Yes; but those do not come, it seems to me, within this definition. Maybe I interpret it differently than you. The last interest Oswald showed was directed toward General Walker. It wasn't against—of course, that wasn't known.

A—No; it wasn't known but the first interest of this type was the letter to Governor Connally as Secretary of the Navy, in which he said he would use whatever means he could to correct that discharge, inferring, of course, that he would apply illegal means if he could.

Representative Ford. If we only had the letter that he wrote to Governor Connally, and no other information, how would that threat, or that course of action, become known to the Secret Service?

A—It would not, unless it was furnished by the Navy Department or Secretary of the Navy's office.

Just like you gentlemen get letters that never come to our attention. But you might pick up a paper some day and read that this fellow hit somebody, and he was in to see you or wrote you letters.

Representative Ford. Would this criteria be circulated among the 50 Governors, for example, or their staffs, so that if threats are received against a Governor, then the Governor's staff in that particular State would so notify the Secret Service?

A—It could. In this case it would be a help. But they refer all their complaints to the FBI. Threats of this kind.

Representative Ford. The State?

A—The Governors do in most cases. So that the FBI under this system would bring it to our attention.

Mr. Dulles. I would think, Mr. Rowley, this might be subject to misinterpretation as being rather narrower than you suggest.

A—Well, this is something—actually, we have to develop something, and we have to, if you will, have a crash program; we are working constantly to develop the categories and breakdowns as I indicated earlier.

(At this point, Senator Cooper entered the hearing room.)

Mr. Rankin. Chief Rowley, did you supply to us the statements of the Secret Service agents who were informed about the assassination in Dallas? You gave us written statements, did you?

A—Yes.

542

Mr. Rankin. I hand you Commission Exhibit No. 1024, and ask you if that is the letter of transmittal, together with the attached statements that you have just described from the various agents about the events at Dallas.

A—Yes, sir.

(The document referred to was marked Commission Exhibit No. 1024 for identification.)

(At this point, Mr. Dulles withdrew from the hearing room.)

Mr. Rankin. Mr. Chairman, I offer in evidence Commission Exhibit No. 1024.

The Chairman. It may be admitted.

(The document heretofore marked for identification as Commission Exhibit No. 1024, was received in evidence.)

Mr. Rankin. I would like to inform the Commission that these are copies of the statements you already have in connection with the Secret Service report, but we wanted to make it part of the record.

The Chairman. Very well.

Mr. Rankin. Chief, did you write me a letter for the Commission on April 22, in which you enclosed the statements of five of your agents in regard to President Kennedy's views about agents riding on the back of the car?

A—Yes, sir. . . .

Mr. Rankin. Chief Rowley, I should like to have you state for the record, for the Commission, whether the action of President Kennedy in making these statements was understood by you or properly could have been understood by the agents as relieving them of any responsibility about the protection of the President.

A—No; I would not so construe that, Mr. Rankin. The agents would respond regardless of what the President said if the situation indicated a potential danger. The facilities were available to them. They had the rear steps, they would be there as a part of the screen. And immediately in the event of any emergency they would have used them.

Mr. Rankin. Do you know why there was no one riding on the rear step at the time of the assassination?

A—From normal practice, based on my own experience over the years, I know that the agent in charge in the front or any experienced agent, who is either on the right front or the left front of the followup car, without being told, will react immediately. If he determines there is a situation here, there is a big crowd, and so forth, he will immediately leave that followup car.

Now, the running board on the followup car has an important place in the setup. It is a much better place to be than on the rear step if you see a situation, and you want to move fast. Suppose someone is coming toward the President's car—you would be surprised how fast you are propelled by jumping off that car, and you are in motion fast, where you can either tackle somebody, or block him or anything like that. So this is an important part. You cannot do that from the rear step of the President's car.

Now, when the agents are in a heavy crowd, as we have been abroad, in places where we had to run, say, for 10 miles alongside the car, agents could stand on the rear steps and screen the President. In addition, there would be agents on the side, protecting him on his right side. The crowd is surging close to him, you are bouncing off the car, and the people, trying to ward them off from touching the President.

After a period of time you are weary. But with the aid of this step, you can be replaced by the agent there, and he takes your place until you revive yourself, and you are acting as a screen.

Now, if the thing gets too sticky, you put the agent right in the back seat, which I have done many times with past Presidents.

When you come out of a big crowd like that, and the crowd is sparse, and it doesn't look like there is a potential danger, you return to the followup car to be ready for any emergency in the event somebody darts across.

In this instance, when the Presidential car was coming toward the freeway and the people were sparse, the men at some point came back to this car. This is one of the automatic operations, if you will, that the agents respond to. So it wasn't until the first shot was fired that, as I said earlier, Hill had the opportunity to scan from his left to his right, that he saw the President—the action of the President. Then he responded immediately. That is why he got up to the President's car.

Mr. Rankin. Has it ever been the practice of the Secret Service to have an agent ride all of the time on the back step?

A—No; it hasn't. Because there are times when you pick up your speed, for instance on a freeway. And when you pick up your speed, it is the most difficult thing on a step maybe 10 to 12 inches wide, and a grip, to stand up. And you would not be a very good screen going that fast, because you would have to bend down. That has happened to me, because I have been caught on it.

Now, I was in Costa Rica and worked the followup car. Whenever I was on a trip abroad, I would work the followup car to see how the agents work, and work myself, because it wasn't what you might refer to as a routine trip.

But the followup car conked out. The crowds were surging around the President's car. We had two men next to the President's car. I left the followup car immediately, from my experience, and jumped on the step, to the right rear of the President, and held onto the handgrip, and was there. And then when the man came back, I relieved him and took my position on the side—until, for a distance of a mile or two, until such time as the followup car got underway, and the other people came up. But you had to stay with the President under those circumstances.

So those are the different things that occur in a given situation.

The Chairman. Chief, as I understand this, President Kennedy did not give any general instructions to the agents never to ride on his car. It was only in specific circumstances where for one reason or another he did not want them on there at that particular time.

A—No President will tell the Secret Service what they can or cannot do. Sometimes it might be as a political man or individual he might think this might not look good in a given situation. But that does not mean per se that he doesn't want you on there. And I don't think anyone with commonsense interprets it as such.

The Chairman. Yes.

A—I think there are certain things that you have to allow the man who is operating as a politician, and not as head of state. I mean this makes a difference in your operation.

Representative Boggs. Would you have any notion as to why names of defectors were not provided to you prior to November 22?

A—Yes; under the broad picture, Mr. Congressman, there was no indication that they had made any threat toward the President or members of his family. Whenever there was a threat made, we were furnished promptly by the different agencies the information on the individual's name. And this was done in voluminous reports by the FBI, and the other agencies. When they got any information, they would notify the local office, notify their liaison, who notified us by telephone, and confirmed by memorandum. The same obtained with respect to the CIA.

Representative Boggs. This fellow was interviewed by the FBI several times—he was interviewed in New Orleans when he allegedly had his Fair Play Committee. If my memory serves me correctly, Mrs. Paine was interviewed about him shortly before the visit of the President, after he had gone to work at the Texas School Book Depository. I agree that there had been no indication of a threat on the President's life. But, obviously he was a person in the FBI files who was under some degree of surveillance. It would seem to me strange that the FBI did not transmit this information to the Secret Service.

A—The FBI, Mr. Congressman, are concerned with internal security. And I think their approach was internal security as it related to this individual, whether or not he was a potential recruit for espionage, intelligence, or something like that. . . . And then you get in the area of civil rights and all, if you start going into individuals——

Representative Boggs. And if I remember correctly, there

has never been—we have had no testimony from anyone that Oswald ever threatened the President of the United States. Is that correct?

Mr. Rankin. That is correct.

Representative Boggs. Is it not a fact that probably the greatest deterrent that you have is the very fact that the public knows that there is a Secret Service?

A—Yes, sir.

Representative Boggs. That you do guard the life of the President. And that the chances of an assassin escaping with his own life are pretty remote. So this psychological weapon is one of the things you rely on?

A—That is correct.

Representative Boggs. And you must necessarily keep a degree of secrecy about the methods you employ.

A—Yes, sir; otherwise they could develop countermethods, to thwart anything we might set up. . . .

Representative Ford. In listening to the testimony, Chief Rowley, sometime ago, I was a little concerned—more than a little, I should say—with the process by which the man in charge of a Presidential trip undertakes his relationship with the local law enforcement agencies.

As I recall the testimony, the man in charge has contact with the local police and the sheriff's department and any other local law enforcement agency. But the impression that I gained was that there was no clear delineation of responsibility. They sat around, they talked about what this local law enforcement agency would do and what another one would do.

But it seems to me that a more precise checklist, a clear understanding, would be wholesome and better.

What is your reaction on that?

A—Well, No. 1, in our revised Manual on Presidential Protection, this is part of the thing.

Now, I would hesitate to prepare a checklist for everybody, because you may be embarrassed to find it in the press some day, because of the activity of reporters around the police.

I do not want to downgrade any police department, but this is what happens through no fault of theirs. There are variations in different cities.

Now, I think what you are referring to, Mr. Congressman, is that they complained they did not have a sufficient notice of the route and so forth, so they could make the proper preparations. That is true. Neither did we have sufficient notice. Because they were going back and forth trying to establish—until they were told they had 45 minutes alloted to them for this route, and first our man had to go, which is a natural operation, to look over the route to see whether or not it could be negotiated within that particular period of time.

Once establishing that it could, and the thing looked safe, then they notified the police and went over it with the police.

546

And then with the police they indicated what they would like done here at intersections and so forth, and other features.

Now, it is true in most cases we ourselves like to get sufficient advance information, we like to send our men out in advance so they do not have to cope with these fast operations, because when a police department has sufficient notice of the route and so forth, then they have adequate time to get out instructions to their own police department—whether by precinct or by group commanders, and so forth. And this is what I think in this instance they are complaining about.

Representative Ford. As I understand it, however, at the present time, and for the future, there will be a more precise procedure for the relationships of the Secret Service on the one hand and local law enforcement agencies on the other.

A—Yes, sir.

Representative Ford. That is set forth in your manual as presently revised?

A—In our present revised manual.

Representative Ford. So that when your agent-in-charge goes to city X, he now has the procedures set forth for many to follow on, so there are no uncertainties, if that is possible?

A—That is right. . . .

Mr. Rankin. Chief Rowley, would you tell us the salary scale for your agents for the first 2 years?

A—Yes; we recruit an agent at grade GS-7, at $5,795.

Mr. Rankin. How does that compare with the starting salary for the FBI?

A—I think it is a difference of three grades. As I understand, the lowest FBI grade is GS-10.

Mr. Rankin. $10,000.

A—Grade 10.

Mr. Rankin. What salary would that be?

A—It might be—for example, GS-11 is $8,410. Now, it could be somewhere between $7,500 and $8,000.

Mr. Rankin. Are you able to get at that salary the quality of men that you should for this kind of work?

A—Yes; we have found to date that we have been able— we have been selective. And, of course, the fact that we have only appropriations for a limited number of men.

For example, today we have well over 40 men waiting to be accepted, with completed investigations, some a year or more. Sometimes when we put in requests for a given number of men, we want to put those men on at the beginning of the fiscal year, so we undertake to recruit them and complete their investigation, so that everything—the character and the physical is up to date—and we can put them on, if we get the funds precisely at the beginning of the fiscal year.

Mr. Rankin. You recognize that your starting salary is not favorable in comparison with some police forces, do you not?

A—I recognize that. But at the same time, we are guided by

547

the Treasury law enforcement examinations, and the other Treasury investigative standards. But we are below some of the west coast police organizations, for example. They are well-paid and great organizations.

Mr. Rankin. Now, what kind of a workload do your agents have on an average?

A—Well, at the present time we have a caseload of 110.1 cases per man.

Mr. Rankin. How does that compare with other intelligence agencies?

A—Well, I think—a satisfactory caseload per man per month is from 14 to 15 cases.

Now, I am quite certain that in other agencies it is a little more than that. But whether or not it is as high as ours at the present time, I have no way of knowing at this time.

Mr. Rankin. Do you think that is a handicap to your operation?

A—Well, it is a handicap. But I think it is testimony to the dedication and the industry of our men, that we are not complaining. We are conducting ourselves and performing our services for the Government to the point that even though we are understaffed, nevertheless we are not quitters, and we are carrying on the work within the responsibility entrusted to us.

Mr. Rankin. Now, do you have any information of a credible nature that would suggest to you that Oswald was or could have been an agent or informant of any Federal agency?

A—I have no credible information of that kind; no, sir.

Mr. Rankin. Was he an agent or informant or directly or indirectly connected with the Secret Service in any way?

A—Not in any way. We did not know of him until the event.

Mr. Rankin. From the way that the Secret Service employment is arranged, and the records are kept, and the payments are made, if he had ever been placed in any such capacity with the Secret Service, would it have come to your attention?

A—It would; yes, sir.

Mr. Rankin. And you are certain that he never was hired directly or indirectly or acted in that capacity.

A—He was never hired directly or indirectly in any capacity.

Mr. Rankin. Do you have any credible information that would cause you to believe that Lee Harvey Oswald was an agent of any foreign country?

A—I have no such credible information.

Mr. Rankin. Do you have any credible information to cause you to believe that he was involved in any conspiracy in connection with the assassination, either domestic or foreign?

A—I have no credible information on any of those. . . .

Mr. Dulles. I have one general question.

From the testimony, and from my own study, it would seem to me that it was likely that there would be parallel, somewhat parallel structures to develop the investigative capabilities with regard to possible suspects in the area of Presidential protection. And my question is as to whether, in order to avoid that undue expense, you think there would be any advantage in putting the responsibility of that within the FBI, who would then be responsible for advising you as to potential suspects and possibly following up on that, rather than putting that responsibility now to a certain extent on the Secret Service—whether there is not a division of responsibility in this field which is unfortunate and may possibly lead to greater expense, personnel doing somewhat duplicative work?

A—As it applies to this law now?

Mr. Dulles. As it applies to the situation today, without the law which is recommended in your memorandum, and might apply also after that, because the investigation would be required in either casein either case to turn up possible suspects.

My question is, where should that responsibility be primarily centered in order to avoid undue duplication and expense, and yet accomplish our objective? . . .

A—Well, I think you want to keep the concept of Presidential protection by a small, closely knit group, because of the intimate relationship. But if you want to expand it and give it to another group, to take the long-range view, you do not know what may develop from something like that—whether a police organization could lead to a police state or a military state—if you want to delegate it to some organization like that.

The Chairman. I suppose also, Chief Rowley, that if your people were not doing the spadework on this thing, and keeping their minds steeped in this protection matter, but were obliged to rely on the written records of someone else presented to you, that they would not be in the proper state of mind, would they, to be alert to it?

A—That is right. There would be a tendency to relax and say John Jones is taking care of it. This is always the possibility that you might encounter something like that.

The Chairman. And in law enforcement, you have to have the feel of the situation, do you not?

You have to do the spadework in order to be aware of every possibility that might develop?

A—That is true. Because you see in this, Mr. Dulles, on the Presidential detail, it is a unique detail. This is something that they think 24 hours a day. They do it 24 hours a day. They are not otherwise involved. For example, they have the principle of screening the President and being always ready to make a quick exit. They do not have to stop to investigate or identify any person, whoever the assailant might be. Their responsibility is only to protect the President at all times.

Mr. Dulles. But they have to know against whom to protect him.

A—That is right. But they are ready for anything under the present close screening.

But if I understand your question, Mr. Dulles, you also want to know whether or not in the screening or the investigation of certain groups, like the Communist group, and so forth, since it is their responsibility and not ours, because they have the internal security of the United States, this is something that we have to develop.

Mr. Dulles. Is "they" the FBI?

A—The FBI.

That is something that we have to have a formal arrangement about, because it enters the realm of internal security. We do not want to conflict with them, if that is what is uppermost in your mind. We have to be most correct about that, in any of the agencies, as you know.

Mr. Dulles. How much larger staff do you think you are going to have to have to cover that situation in the future?

A—Well, I would not know until we see the volume of reports that we get that we have to refer to the field for investigation. Since we are processing them now, we have to wait to make that determination.

Mr. Dulles. Should you do field investigations as contrasted with the FBI—the FBI have a large number of people in a large number of cities throughout the United States. You do not have that?

A—No; but on the basis of the criteria we discussed earlier, the FBI would give us the information, and if in our evaluation we determined that it should be referred to the field for investigation, particularly in the case of individuals, we would conduct our investigation, to determine whether this individual is a high risk to the President.

Now, where it comes to the group, this is something for the FBI to do, because it ties in with their responsibility for internal security.

Now, if there is a close connection between the two, then we would have to have a formal agreement. But because of our responsibility, and the fact that this is part of the work that we have to undertake, then we would conduct our own investigation, because we know what we are looking for.

Mr. Dulles. If the name of Lee Harvey Oswald had been submitted to you by the FBI, what would you, in the normal course, have done?

Would you have referred that back to them for investigation, or would you have carried on an independent investigation?

I am talking now if that name had been referred to you when you knew you were going to go to Dallas.

A—If we knew we were going to Dallas and we had this present criteria, then we would investigate him.

Mr. Dulles. You would carry on the investigation?

A—Yes, sir. . . .

ROBERT INMAN BOUCK

The testimony of Special Agent in Charge, Protective Research Section, Secret Service:

Mr. Dulles. Did the name of Lee Harvey Oswald appear in your files at any time prior to the 22d of November 1963?

A—No, sir; we had never heard of him in any context.

Mr. Dulles. His name doesn't appear at all?

A—Not as of that time. Prior to Dallas, it did not appear in any fashion. We had no knowledge of the name.

Mr. Dulles. You had no report from the State Department or the FBI that covered his trip to Russia or anything of that kind?

A—No, sir.

Mr. McCloy. Or of the CIA?

A—No, sir.

Mr. Stern. Mr. Bouck, what kind of information do you look for, what are the criteria you apply, in determining whether someone is a potential danger to the President? What do you ask other agencies, Federal, State, and local to be on the lookout for?

A—Our criteria is broad in general. It consists of desiring any information that would indicate any degree of harm or potential harm to the President, either at the present time or in the future.

Mr. Stern. Had you ever prior to Dallas had occasion to— for any part of your activities—list criteria that you would apply in trying to determine whether someone is a potential danger?

A—We had not had a formal written listing of criteria as such except in this general form of desiring everything that might indicate a possible source of harm to the safety of the President. We had some internal breakdown of information for the processing of certain kinds of material where the criteria were involved.

Mr. Stern. I didn't mean to restrict my question to criteria for external sources, but those you used internally as well.

A—We had some internal, as well. . . .

Mr. Stern. What instructions does the White House mailroom have as to mail that is to be sent to you?

A—The White House mail has two general instructions: One, we supply them with identification information on all existing cases in which mail is concerned: that any further mail in those cases is automatically referred to us.

Their criteria are the same as our other general criteria— that in addition to these known cases we desire letters, telegrams, or any other document they receive that in any way indicates any one may have possible intention of harming the President. . . .

Mr. Dulles. I note that this list does not include membership in various types of organizations, such as the, for example, the organizations that are on the Attorney General's list. Have you ever considered that?

A—Yes; if I might explain, sir; the letters we are talking about are letters that are written by people, and they rarely include that kind of information, but we do in other categories, this is for a special purpose. This is letters only that are sent to the President which is all this is applied to. This does not apply to other sources of information, only the one source of letters. . . .

Mr. Stern. What requests do you make to other Federal agencies?

A—We make this same request—that we desire any and all information that they may come in contact with that would indicate danger to the President.

Mr. Stern. How are these requests communicated?

A—They are fundamentally communicated by personal contact of varying degrees with the FBI. We have a personal liaison contact in which an individual, a liaison officer actually makes daily contact.

With the other agencies, other security agencies and enforcement agencies, we are—people on my staff have personal relationships where we can call on the telephone and do call on the telephone very frequently, sometimes some agencies every day, and they in turn call us.

Mr. Stern. What agencies do you have these liaison relationships with—Federal agencies?

A—We have on a commonly used basis, we have some liaison with almost all of them but on a common using basis we have these relationships with CIA, with the several military services, with the Department of State. I have mentioned the FBI.

Mr. Stern. Central Intelligence Agency?

A—Oh, yes; very much so. They are, especially on trips very, very helpful.

Mr. Dulles. Foreign trips?

A—Foreign trips, yes.

Representative Ford. How often do your people check to see procedures which are used by these various agencies for the determination of whether an individual is a dangerous person?

A—We don't do that systematically. We frequently have such discussions but they are usually on a specific basis. Our representative will call up and say, "We just received this information. Would this be of interest to you.". . .

Mr. Dulles. Have you made any study going back in history of the various attempts that have been made, and successful and unsuccessful attempts, that have been made against Presidents or——

A—Rulers.

Mr. Dulles. Or people about to be President, or who have been President?

A—Yes, yes. We have not only studied all of our own but we have studied all of the assassinations that we could find any record of for 2,000 years back. And strangely enough some of the thinking that went on 2,000 years ago seems to show up in thinking of assassinations today.

Mr. Stern. Do you increase protection on the Ides of March?

Mr. Dulles. Is that available? Is that—I don't know.

A—It is available in a rather crude form. It has not been boiled down to a concise report.

Mr. Dulles. How voluminous is this? I should be very much interested in thumbing through it because I have been trying to study the past history.

A—The rough notes on this are this high.

Mr. Dulles. A few thousand pages?

A—The studies didn't go beyond that.

Mr. Dulles. By cases?

A—Yes. Of course, in many of these cases it is very spotty and these are handwritten notes. We never, outside of extracting in this in training material and what not, we have never systematized it down to where it is a readable document as such.

Mr. Dulles. Have you tried to draw any conclusion out of this study as to the type of people, the types of causes, the types of incentives?

A—Yes; we have.

Mr. Dulles. That is in your department, is it, to do this?

A—Yes; it is. We have arrived at some conclusions from it.

(Discussion off the record.)

Mr. McCloy. On the record. Your study of the prior assassinations would take into account Czolgosz, Guiteau, what type of persons they were?

A—Yes, sir.

Mr. McCloy. The thing to me that seems very worthy of research is the plotter, I mean the political plotter as against, for want of a better word, the loner, the man who is self-motivated against the man who has to have a group around him. How do you tell one from the other? I just was reading last night in Loomis about Madame Corday. She was just as much of a loner as apparently Mr. Oswald was.

Mr. Dulles. So was Czolgosz so far as I can make out, and so was Zangara. Zangara, I was told, planned to shoot Hoover and then he decided that the climate of Washington wasn't very healthy in February and March for him because he had stomach trouble, so he decided that F.D.R. was coming to Miami and it was just as good to shoot him. You have situations of that kind that defy it.

A—I believe he intended to shoot the King of Italy before

553

that but he got a chance to migrate before he got an opportunity.

Mr. Dulles. Zangara?

A—Yes.

Mr. McCloy. Do you have any lookout for defectors as such?

A—As such we have never been quite able to determine that that is a valid criterion. We do not as such.

Mr. McCloy. You have some suspicions, now, don't you?

A—Yes; we have some suspicions now; yes, sir.

Mr. Dulles. I wonder whether it would not be useful for this Commission to have, if it could be reduced to readable form and to assist, the conclusions of your study if you have such conclusions?

A—We will do that, sir.

Mr. Dulles. What do you think, do the rest of you agree to that?

Mr. McCloy. I think it is part of our mission to try to make recommendations in regard to the future protection of the Presidents. Actually, we don't want to go into anything which is going to compromise the future security of Presidents. We simply want to augment. What we are concerned about is how well equipped we are to do the job in the light of all the circumstances and I would think that any conclusions that you have in this regard, if you—the Secret Service, Treasury— could convey them to us in a form that perhaps we might endorse, it might be helpful from your point of view and our point of view.

Representative Ford. I would agree with that observation.

Mr. Dulles. You can possibly define categories. You may find the loner, you may find a fellow engaged in a plot with others for political reasons and that would help us very much because we find that particularly the case we are investigating falls into one of these classes. . . .

Mr. Stern. Fine, Mr. Chairman. I would like to turn now to the actual processing by PRS of the information they receive and have Mr. Bouck tell us what happens to an item of information when it is received, how it is processed, how the references to field offices are made, and perhaps you might illustrate . . .

A—When a document is received by the Secret Service, it is first searched against our files to see if we have any previous experience with this individual or with this threat. If it is found that we do have previous material there is an analysis made, and then a determination is made at that point as to what the apparent degree of threat would be on this.

If it appears that on the surface there is a threat, lookouts will immediately be issued to the White House detail, the White House police and various other security details, in order that they may be alerted to any danger that happens.

If the danger seems quite strong, a telephone call will be made to the field office in order to begin the investigation without even waiting for the mail. The threat is then processed and sent through the mail with the documents to the office concerned.

If it is determined that it is a possible danger, a card is put in a particular file which would alert us in case the President went to that area that an investigation of a dangerous person were underway. After the field office has investigated they would attempt to take corrective action if a law has been violated, the individual will be prosecuted, if practical, and if the individual is determined to be mentally ill, attempts will be made to get commitment into a mental institution.

When the report is submitted back, if the individual is not confined or is not evaluated as being no danger, then we would put cards in several control devices, one being a trip index file to make sure that we alerted the field office when the President went to that area; another being a control checkup device which means that if this individual is regarded as dangerous we will keep checking up on him every few months to see if he is getting worse or see what he is doing. . . .

Mr. Dulles. May I ask a question here? When you refer to the field offices, this is the field office of the Secret Service?

A—Field offices of the Secret Service.

Mr. Dulles. How many do you have?

A—Sixty.

Mr. Dulles. Sixty?

A—In the United States, and I believe one of those is in Puerto Rico and one is in Paris, of the 60. . . .

Mr. Stern. You might mention, perhaps, Mr. Bouck, the cases under the last tab of your exhibit which were cases that were not investigated, just as a contrast.

A—That is right. These referrals from the FBI are all through here. Page 8 is another one where they picked up information and gave it to us. The first four sections relate to the cases in the four offices of Texas during a 2-year period. The very final one illustrates just a little sample of the kind of cases we received in Texas which we did not think warranted investigation. That will give you an idea of what those cases amounted to. Why we didn't go into them.

Mr. McCloy. Let me ask you this: Are your records and equipment modern in the sense that you have got punchcards on all these, have you got the type of equipment that you would think that extensive files and extensive information and quick access to them might be very important. Do you have IBM machines and do you have punchcards, for example, so that you can have quick cross references?

A—No, sir. Our files are conventional, card indexes, conventional folders. We do not have machine operation in that sense.

Mr. McCloy. Don't you think that with all this mass of information that comes in that that would be an asset to you?

555

A—If I might defer to Mr. Carswell again, I believe that is in the document you are handling, discussion of that, am I right. Mr. Carswell, or in the studies that are going on?

Mr. Carswell. Yes.

A—This is part of this big overall consideration again.

Mr. McCloy. It just seems to me this is almost a typical case of where that type of thing can do you a great deal of good. You have it in industry to a very marked degree. I wonder whether it could be—I don't know enough about the flow of these things.

A—This is under a great deal of consideration as a part of this post-Dallas study that Mr. Carswell referred to and I am quite sure that it will be contained in the final results. . . .

Mr. Dulles. You say at the bottom of the page, this introductory table page, that the total exceeded 32,000 items.

A—Yes.

Mr. Dulles. Does that mean now you have cards on 32,000 people?

A—Oh, no; we have cards on close to a million people.

Mr. Dulles. A million people?

A—Yes.

Mr. Dulles. This total then is 1-year total?

A—This is a 2-year total—no, wait a minute. I beg your pardon.

Mr. McCloy. 1963.

A—This is a 1 year total for 1943, 1-year total for 1953, and 1-year total for 1963.

Mr. Dulles. That is just the number, and these figures are cumulative that you have here?

A—No; everyone is a year.

Mr. Dulles. That is what I mean, you have the total you have to add this up for previous years, but you don't keep them forever, you take some of these out.

A—These are not all cards, but these are items of information. In 1-year cases we might get 40, 50 items in a particular case, and these items would go in the case files.

Mr. Dulles. Do you know how many names you have carded now, approximately?

A—We have not counted them but we think in the vicinity of a million but they are not all active, you see. We have no way of knowing when people die in some cases and things like that. So we don't know just how many of these million are now active. Certainly very much less than a million.

Mr. Dulles. But you have a million names carded?

A—Yes. In the indexes.

Mr. Stern. In the files which you describe as basic files, I believe, how many cases are current, either in your office or within easy access?

A—About 50,000.

Mr. Stern. About 50,000. So that 950,000 are in some other storage?

A—Not all of these cards, you see, will represent cases because we have some cases in which many people are involved. There would be considerably less cases than there would be card indexes, but we do have a very sizable storage of cases under National Archives, some of the older ones having gone to places like the Roosevelt Library.

Mr. Stern. These are your basic files which now have something in the order of 50,000 active cases?

A—Yes.

Mr. Stern. And some of these involve more than one individual?

A—Yes.

Mr. Stern. In these cases?

A—Yes.

Mr. Stern. A case might be an organization, as I understand it, rather than an individual?

A—That is right.

Mr. Stern. And the members of that organization would be collected under that one case?

A—Yes.

Mr. Stern. Would they also be listed individually?

A—They would be listed individually if they were of interest to us as individuals. Sometimes we would get the membership of a group of people that attended a lecture, let's say, where very derogatory information was given out about the President, but most of these people seem like ordinary citizens and it doesn't seem like worth investigating. We might have 200 people listed in that, this would not be normal, but it would be a few cases like that.

Mr. Stern. Now, as I understand it you by no means investigate every individual who is in one of these 50,000 cases?

A—That is correct.

Mr. Stern. And what are the criteria that you use?

A—The criteria for investigation are feelings that there is indeed an indication that there may be a danger to the President.

Mr. Stern. But there has to be some indication of a potential danger to the President to get that individual into a case to begin with, I take it. If it were clear he was not?

A—Yes; but not necessarily a current indication. We take many of these where we think an individual is becoming hostile and a little bit disgusted with the President, we take many of those cases to watch these people. We keep getting information here and there along, and frequently after we get the second or third piece of information, we decide indeed this individual is perhaps—does perhaps constitute a menace, and at that point we would investigate it.

557

Mr. Stern. As I understand it, one of the main purposes of your investigation is to attempt to deal with the dangerous individual at that time?

A—Yes, sir.

Mr. Stern. How would you deal with these people whom we are speaking about?

A—We deal with them primarily in three ways. First, if a law violation is involved an attempt will be made to see if a prosecution is in order. . . .

If the investigation indicates that the individual is mentally unbalanced, which a high percentage are, then attempt will be made to persuade local authorities to get hospitalization, confinement in an institution.

If neither of those are possible, attempts will be made to get local officers and family, if they will cooperate, to help us keep track of him, and we will institute checkups from time to time when we are investigating. Those are basically the control measures that we are able to use. In some cases we may conduct surveillance, by the way, if we can't do any of those, and we regard the man as very dangerous. . . .

Mr. Stern. When an individual is determined after investigation to present some level of danger but not sufficient to warrant prosecution or not to be a mentally disturbed person warranting commitment, how do you control that individual, keep track of him?

A—If we think he is in fact dangerous, he would be in our checkup file which is really a control device by which at least every 6 months we re-investigate and in between times we try to have arrangements with the family and local officers to let us know if he leaves town or buys a gun or anything.

The other device is a geographical card file in which we would put a card to let us know about this individual in case the President went to that geographical area so that the office might take a further look and see if he was a menace. . . .

Mr. Stern. How many at the time of Dallas would be in your checkup control file system with this periodic review?

A—About 400.

Mr. Stern. 400 individuals?

A—That is nationwide.

Mr. Stern. Again, at the time of Dallas, how many individuals would have been listed in the trip-index file which you have described?

A—About a hundred.

Mr. Stern. One hundred in the Nation?

A—Yes.

Mr. Stern. What are the criteria for putting someone's name in the trip-index file?

A—The belief on the part of the local field office, with confirmation from the Protective Research Section that this individual would indeed constitute a risk to the President's safety, if he went to that area.

Mr. Stern. This is done, this is organized, on a geographic basis?

A—Yes.

Mr. Stern. By Secret Service field offices?

A—Yes.

Mr. Stern. Is there any other control device that you employed at the time of Dallas?

A—We had at the time a very small device that we call an album which has a few, perhaps 12 or 15 people that we consider very dangerous or at least dangerous and so mobile that we can't be sure where they might be. This is a constant thing. Copies of these are kept before the protective personnel at the White House all the time. This resides in their office.

Senator Cooper. On that point, if this last category represents a group that is so highly dangerous, have any individuals in that group reached the place where they have made such statements as would bring them under the Federal act which would require prosecution?

A—No, sir; if they were prosecutable we would seek that solution immediately, and many of them have been taken to the district attorney and it has just been determined they do not quite meet the requirements for prosecution.

Some have been prosecuted, and have served sentences and are out at the end of sentences but still thought to be dangerous. . . . Some have been in mental institutions and discharged, and there isn't ground to put them back but we are still afraid of them.

Mr. Stern. Are the individuals who are listed in the trip-index file, which numbered at the time of Dallas about 100, also listed in the checkup control files?

A—Yes. Yes; they would, primarily that 100 would to a large degree be in both places. . . .

Mr. Stern. In point of fact, Mr. Bouck, when you looked at the checkup control file and the trip-index file before the Dallas trip how many names were reported for the areas in the Dallas field office territory where the President was to visit?

A—We found no uncontrolled people in the trip file for Dallas. All of the cases in Dallas were controlled to our satisfaction. We found also in the checkup file no uncontrolled individuals that we thought warranted an alert for Dallas.

Mr. Dulles. Did you ask the FBI or any other local agency for any cases they might have?

A—Yes, sir.

Mr. Dulles. In connection with the trip?

A—In fact, they referred several cases to us in connection with the trip, right prior to the trip on the local level.

Mr. Dulles. On the local level?

A—On the local level.

Mr. McCloy. Being as objective as you can be under the circumstances, what would you have done if the FBI had told you there was a man named Oswald in Dallas, who was a defector, had been a defector?

A—I think if they had told us only that, we probably would not have taken action. If I might qualify it further, if we had known what all of the Government agencies knew together, and knew that he had that vantage point on the route, then we certainly would have taken very drastic action.

Mr. McCloy. If they had told you that there was a man named Oswald in Dallas, who had been a defector, who was employed at the Texas School Book Depository?

A—Yes, sir; we would have looked at that.

Mr. McCloy. You would have looked at that?

A—Yes, sir.

Mr. McCloy. Knowing that the Texas School Book Depository was on the President's route?

A—On the President's route.

Mr. Stern. Would it have made a difference to you if he was a legitimate employee of that institution?

A—Well, not from our standpoint of having us look at it. I can't predict too well what the field office would have done after they looked. It would depend on what they found out, but the field office would have checked that. We would have asked them to check it and they would in fact have checked it not knowing what conclusions they would have arrived at, I don't quite—I am not quite able to predict just what measures they would have taken. . . .

Mr. Stern. Were there any other characteristics of Oswald that you believe to have been known to other Federal agencies before November 22 that would have been important to you in deciding whether or not he was a potential threat?

A—Yes. I think I have supplied you with a list of about 18 things that were known to the Federal agencies, but these, I believe, were spread from Moscow to Mexico City in at least four agencies, so I am not aware of how much any one agency or any one person might have known.

But there was quite a little bit of derogatory information known about Oswald in this broad expanse of agencies.

Mr. Stern. Without respect to any such list, what other characteristics, trying as much as possible to avoid hindsight, do you think were germane to determine his potential danger?

A—I would think his continued association with the Russian Embassy after his return, his association with the Castro groups would have been of concern to us, a knowledge that he had, I believe, been court-martialed for illegal possession of a gun, of a hand gun in the Marines, that he had owned a weapon and did a good deal of hunting or use of it, perhaps in Russia, plus a number of items about his disposition and unreliability of

560

character, I think all of those, if we had had them altogether, would have added up to pointing out a pretty bad individual, and I think that, together, had we known that he had a vantage point would have seemed somewhat serious to us, even though I must admit that none of these in themselves would be—would meet our specific criteria, none of them alone.

But it is when you begin adding them up to some degree that you begin to get criteria that are meaningful.

Senator Cooper. I am sure you have answered what I am going to ask but I will ask it anyway. Then it is correct prior to the assassination the Secret Service had no information from any agency or any source——

A—That is correct.

Senator Cooper. Relating to Lee Oswald?

A—That is correct.

Mr. Stern. I believe you said earlier, Mr. Bouck, that before Dallas you thought the liaison arrangements were satisfactory and that other Federal agencies, in particular, had full awareness of the kind of information that the Secret Service was looking for under the general criteria that you articulated?

A—Yes, sir.

Mr. Stern. Why then, do you think you were not notified of Oswald? Was there perhaps something wrong with the system?

A—This, of course, is opinion. In my opinion, there was no lack of knowledge of what we should have. Insofar as I know no individual knew enough about Oswald to judge him to meet our criteria of presenting a danger to the President. I know of no individual who knew all about Oswald, including the fact that he had a vantage point on the route.

If that is so, I don't know. I didn't know.

Mr. McCloy. Somebody in the FBI knew it, didn't they?

A—I have no record to know that. They knew certain information. I have no record that would indicate they knew all of the degoratory information.

Mr. McCloy. I don't know I would say they knew all the derogatory information but they certainly knew the vantage point and they certainly knew the defection elements.

A—I know they knew he was in Dallas. Whether they recognized that as being on the route, I don't know that. . . .

Mr. Stern. We will move very quickly to questions concerning Oswald and I would like to go back now and cover the details of your file search and other PRS activity for the Texas trip, the total Texas trip. If you would start with the first date you heard that the President was preparing to travel to Texas and tell us what your Section did and what you found.

A—Our first knowledge of the Texas trip was on November 8 when the advance agent, Agent Lawson, reported to the Protective Research Section that the President was going to Texas, and that Dallas was one of the stops. A check at that time was made of our trip index, and no cards were found on Dallas to indicate that there was an uncontrolled dangerous person in Dallas.

Two such people were found at the Houston stop. This information was imparted to Mr. Lawson at that time.

Mr. Stern. Excuse me, could you identify the two Houston cases? . . .

A—Yes; they are in here. Case No. 21 is one. This individual is a local law-enforcement officer that was not considered awfully dangerous but again because he might have an unusual vantage point we made arrangements each time to see that he was not used in any way that he might have a vantage point. Case 26 is the other one, which is a case that goes back many, many years of an individual who has been repeatedly threatening but we have been unable to do much about. She has been in and out of mental hospitals. . . .

These were the two cases. The one we had alerted on a previous trip, the deputy sheriff one, had not been, that had occurred since a previous trip and so this was the first time that we had told the detail an the field office that this individual should be looked at. Making a total of two.

Mr. Stern. Were there entries in the trip-index file then for the other cities that the President was planning to visit or the other field office areas, Dallas, San Antonio, and El Paso?

A—No; there were no cards on any of the other three cities, indicating uncontrolled people. . . .

Mr. McCloy. I have one more question I would like to ask you. In the light of what you know now about the whole episode, have you come to any conclusions as to how you ought to operate in the future other than you did in the Dallas situation? . . .

A—A great deal of study is being conducted. I think there are a number of other things that can be done. Great problems arise as to human rights and constitutional rights and costs and resources and just sheer—dealing with just sheer volumes of millions of people, and I do not feel I would want to give final judgment as to whether we should do these things until we have completed all of these studies, but perhaps there will be some that will——

Mr. McCloy. Do you at this stage have any definite ideas about any steps that ought to be taken for the added protection of the President?

A—Well, I have quite a lot of them which are incorporated in this study. I have been, and as I understand it, the Commission perhaps will have the benefit of that but I have been very heavily involved in many, many ways in this study, and as to the final conclusions, of course, I think maybe it goes all the way to the Congress to decide the practicality of some of this.

Mr. McCloy. I am sure it does.

A—I just don't quite feel in a position to say that I would want to recommend most of these things without reservation at this time. If I might, without presuming to evade your question, if we could delay that a little bit until we have completed this rather massive look that we are now taking.

Mr. McCloy. Very well. Thank you very much for your cooperation, and very much obliged to you and the Treasury Department for helping us. . . .

C. DOUGLAS DILLON

The testimony of the Secretary of the Treasury, who has jurisdiction over the Secret Service:

Senator Russell. Has there been any increase, Mr. Secretary, in the number of agents assigned to guard the President. I thought there had been some increase in recent years?

A—There has been some increase, and we have tried very hard to increase the Secret Service in the last 3 or 4 years. We have asked for more people every year, and while we never got the amount we asked for, we did get increases. I have the figures here. In 1961, the entire Secret Service amounted to 454 individuals, of whom 305 were classified as agents. In 1964, that is the fiscal year just finished, the figure was 571, of which 167 were clerks and 404 were agents. So we had achieved an increase of about 100 agents, a little over a third.

Mr. Dulles. That included both the counterfeiting responsibilities of the Secret Service as well as the Presidential protection?

A—That is right. . . .

Representative Ford. Wasn't the specific request for an increase in the White House detail—I use this in a broad sense for both the President and Vice President—primarily aimed at the increase of personnel for the Vice President?

A—That was in one year.

Representative Ford. 1962? . . . But there had been no reduction in the funds for the protection of the President?

A—For the White House detail; no.

Representative Ford. It was a reduction for the protection of the Vice President.

A—That is correct. But the thing that I think we are coming to is, it is perfectly obvious that we have to do a great deal more in this advance work, field work, in interviewing people who are dangers to the President or could be classified as such. We need more people in the field on account of this. That is what I say was not probably fully realized, although Rowley specifically, when he first went up in 1962 asking for an increase, pitched it on that basis, but he did not have a very good reception from the Appropriations Committee at that time because they felt that the White House detail was the White House detail, right around the President. I don't think anyone fully understood the connection with people in the field. I am not sure that Secret Service made as good a case as they should, to be really understood on this. It has become clear now.

Representative Ford. Mr. Rowley in that presentation asked for additional funds for and personnel for the Protective Research Service?

A—I don't think it was specifically for that. It was for protection of the President, and he was the first person that made this type of request. Baughman had always said that people in the field were counterfeiting and just worked a little bit for the President, and Rowley when he came in was the first one that made this claim that they were needed to actually protect the President. He wanted more people in the field to do these things, and that was the thing that did not go over right away. . . .

I have one thing I would like to say about that, and I think it should go into the record. What this is is our report as to how many personnel are needed and what has to be done and what they should do. We have transmitted that with a covering letter to the Bureau of the Budget. The final decision on what will be done on many of these things is taken in the light of recommendations of the Bureau of the Budget to the President and what he finally decides for budgetary reasons. So ordinarily budgetary matters are not published prior to the time the President has approved them. He hasn't approved this. He hasn't seen it, but I think under the circumstances I see no reason under this special circumstance, why this report should not go into the record, and I think it is perfectly all right. . . .

Representative Ford. This would be the recommendation of the Treasury Department to the Bureau of the Budget for the personnel and the funds for the Secret Service in fiscal year 1966?

A—No. This is a recommendation to the Bureau of the Budget for the personnel and equipment that would be needed to put the Secret Service in what they consider adquate position to fully handle this problem. They feel that it would take about 20 months to get all the necessary people on board and trained. If this were started right away, as we think it could be if a reapportionment on a deficiency basis were approved, this could start in fiscal year 1965 and depending on whether such is approved, the fiscal year 1966 final recommendation would be affected. But this is the total picture, and it is assuming our recommendation that they start in the next couple of months.

Representative Ford. In other words, this is the plan that you would like instituted immediately regardless of budget considerations.

A—That is right. . . .

Mr. Rankin. Now, Mr. Secretary, will you very briefly describe the general plan of your planning document. We have that so we can use it in considerable detail, but if you can just summarize briefly.

A—Well, in brief, this asks for a total of 205 additional agents, which is about—not quite but nearly—a 50 percent increase from the 415 agents they now have. It asks also for 50 clerks to add to the 171 that are presently there. Those are stenographers, typists and other clerical workers. And for five technicians. Of this the idea is to put 17 agents and the 5 technicians in the PRS. Five would be used to maintain 24-hour coverage in the PRS which is not presently in force because of lack of personnel. One would add to the Research and Countermeasures Unit to fill out three full units that could be operating all the time. Six of them would do advance work for PRS with local agencies and institutions. One of the new things we have instituted is that each time they do an advance, someone from the PRS goes out and works with the local law enforcement agencies. I think that is obviously a very important thing. They need more people in view of the volume of traveling. Then they also need five more employees to expand our liaison with the other law enforcement and intelligence agencies. We now have one man assigned really full time to that. We found even in the period that we have been doing this that while that is a great help, much the best way would be to have individuals assigned to each agency that work full time with the agency, know the people in the agency, and that is the only way we can be sure we have adequate liaison. . . .

Representative Ford. Could you specify those agencies. I was interested in what agencies you were referring to.

A—Well, I would think certainly it would be the military, the FBI, the security services of the State Department, and the CIA.

Now, there may be additional ones. There are additional ones within the Treasury Department. I think we probably have one, for instance, with the intelligence section of the Internal Revenue Service. Alcohol and Tobacco Tax Unit, and so forth, which a good deal can come out of.

In addition we recommend here five technical specialists, two of which would be highly trained computer technicians, programmers, and three less well trained to work with these others. The purpose of this is to automate the whole PRS operation. We have been thinking of that for some time. It was something that obviously needed to be done.

Mr. Rankin. Excuse me, Mr. Secretary. Will you describe a little more what you mean by automate.

A—I mean using electronic processing, punchcard systems, so that they would be able to pull out of their files for any locality, various different types of people that might be a danger or might have made threats to the President or to other high officials, so that they would be able to function rapidly and well in planning protection as the President travels to these various cities.

Mr. Rankin. Does that include computer systems? . . .

One of the things we recommend here is appropriation of $100,000 to get consultants from IBM Co., Honeywell or other companies, and get pilot machines to try to work out the details of this system.

Mr. McCloy. For the record, Mr. Secretary, you had no electronic system of this character operating before the assassination?

A—No. Now, the total of that is 17 agents and 5 specialists for the PRS.

In addition, for a long time, Mr. Rowley has believed that it would be preferable to improve the capacity of the White House detail if we could establish a headquarters pool of 18 men where new individuals who are going into the White House detail would be fully trained first—before, they had to be trained sort of partially on the job—and also through which you could rotate people from the field from time to time, bringing them up to date on Presidential protection.

So we would ask for 18 people, 18 spaces for that.

We have asked for 25 spaces to provide adequate protection for the Vice President in addition to the 10 that are already on board.

Mr. Rankin. Mr. Secretary, excuse me. I think spaces may not be clear to all our readers. Will you explain what that means?

A—Twenty-five job positions. I think the thing that is very important here is to keep in mind that to keep one man on the job around the clock covering a post, which is the way the Secret Service works—one man that would be always with the President or the Vice President, that would be always watching his house—to get one man requires five job positions. In the first place, the coverage required is for 24 hours a day.

In the second place, there are holidays, there are weekends off. On a full-time basis, the Secret Service works a 40-hour week, 5-day week, as the rest of the Government does, and there are provisions for sickness and leave, and so forth. When the number of hours that a man can work a year full time is figured out, it requires 5 men to fill one spot.

So that is one reason why these protective numbers may seem rather high to the uninitiated.

When you are talking about the Vice President, and 10 people are required to produce two posts, coverage of two posts, it is obviously not adequate because you have to cover his house, whether he is there or not, so that someone can't come in and put a destructive device in it.

This simply can't be done with the present numbers that are assigned.

566

Then, going beyond this to complete this list, there is a request for 145 agents in the field offices who would handle the substantially increased volume of security investigations. We are now getting about twice as many referrals already as we did before. Instead of something *like 25,000, we are up to something over 50,000, and they expect it will go over 60,000 next year.*

To really run these down out in the districts, they need, obviously, more men than they have had.

Now, one thing that they also need these fellows for, which I think is important, is keeping track of more dangerous individuals. They have tried to keep track of a few of them. But I think that probably a good many more should be put on that list. It requires more people, so they can periodically check up, and particularly before a visit, that all of these people are looked at to see where they are and what they have been doing recently before the President visits a particular place. . . .

Mr. McCloy. May I just ask you about the armored car, Mr. Secretary. Is that to transport the President?

A—Yes; that is right. A protected car, a second one. One was fixed for the Government free by the Ford Motor Co., but our guess is that it cost the Ford Motor Co. somewhere between $175,000 and $200,000 to do this, and it didn't cost the Secret Service anything, although there was some research work done on the glass and armor by the Defense Department. This was combined with research work they needed for their own use, to develop protective glass and armor to use in helicopters in Vietnam. They split the cost. It cost about $30,000. So I think they assigned $15,000 of it to this project. But it was paid by the Defense Department. That is the only cost on that one. But I think the companies think that the Government should buy the new car.

Mr. McCloy. We had some testimony here in connection with the assassination where it was developed that the access within the car to the body of the President became very important. In the car in which the President was assassinated there was a bar behind the front seat making it very difficult if not impossible for the Secret Service man who was operating from the front seat to get to the body of the President, and we were strongly of the view that cars that should be hereafter designed should have freedom of access. Either the man should be in the jump seat or there should be means by which you could get, the Secret Service man could get to the body of the President in case of a threat of an attack, and I think it is likely we will mention that in the report. But it seemed to me this is something to bear in mind in connection with the design of a new armored car.

A—That would apply to an open car.

Mr. McCloy—Yes.

A—It wouldn't apply I think to a fully——

Mr. McCloy. Fully armored; no. That is right.

A—Closed car.

Mr. McCloy. Usually on those motorcades you like to be seen.

A—Yes. . . .

Mr. McCloy. You testified, Mr. Secretary, you felt with these additions that the Secret Service would be competent to cope with the added requirements for the protection of the President which have occurred.

In testifying to that effect, do you include—you include the investigative services of your own which are quite apart, as I understand it, from the information that you may gather from other agencies?

A—That is correct; yes.

Mr. McCloy. We have had the thought that perhaps the Protective Research Section or Division of your organization wasn't as well equipped as it should have been nor as it might have been presumably for the purely preventive investigative work.

Do you feel that with this new plan of yours, that that would be adequately taken care of?

A—Yes; I do. It was not equipped, I think, adequately in two ways. First, it did not, as is clearly shown by the events in Dallas, receive information on enough dangerous people. At least they didn't receive the information on Lee Oswald.

So that what is required is the development of criteria, better criteria, that can be circulated to law enforcement agencies generally, and which will insure that adequate information comes in. We are making progress there.

I think you have already seen a document with some criteria that were developed, which has been circulated in Washington. A similar document has now been circulated by the Secret Service Chief to all special agents asking them to write a briefer but somewhat similar letter to all chiefs of police, sheriffs, and State police in their localities which asks them to furnish any such information to the local Secret Service agent. That is being disseminated now throughout the country. It will be completed within the next 6 weeks or so.

In addition, we have established an interagency committee which has as one of its jobs the development of better criteria that will really result in getting the kind of information we want without swamping us. If we are too broad in our criteria and we get a million names, obviously nothing can work.

This committee is holding its first formal meeting next week. It has representatives of the President's Office of Science and Technology, of the Department of Defense, which is the Advanced Research Projects outfit, of the CIA, an individual who is highly competent in their file section and who understands the setting up of complex files and retrieval, that sort of business, and four people from PRS, the PRS head inspector, Mr. Thacker, the head of the research and development, Mr.

Bouck, the head of the files section, Mr. Young, and Mr. Stoner, who is now handling the liaison job.

There will also be, although the individual has not yet been named, a representative of the FBI, and with that I think that we will be able to develop criteria that will both be useful to us and be an improvement on criteria that was so far developed with the help of outside consultants.

Mr. McCloy. Mr. Secretary, the impression has been gained, I think, by the Commission that perhaps too great emphasis has been directed to the mere investigation of the threat, of the particular individual, the crank, or the fellow that sends the poison food or the threatening letter, and perhaps not enough in a broader scope, recognizing, of course, that you can't be too broad without defeating your own purpose, but that there are perhaps groups or other areas of ferment that could provoke an attack quite without the threat. Would you comment on that?

A—Yes; one of the criteria that is presently out is meant to cover individuals who have threatened bodily harm to any high Government official, with the idea that the threat might be switched and visited upon the President.

That would have worked in this particular case in Dallas if that had been a specific criterion on at that time, which it wasn't. We are just talking about threats to the President. So I think that was one obvious case.

We hope that this committee would be able to possibly come up with other groups that can be identified that would fit into this without bringing in too many names.

There is one that may or may not work out. I just cite this as an example. People with bad conduct records in the Marine Corps for some reason have had a very bad record thereafter and there is quite a connection of crime with that class of individual.

It may be that it would even be worthwhile, if it is not too large, to cover this. Why that is so, nobody has quite figured out. I think the eye was focused on them because of this event in Dallas, but then it was discovered that this group has been involved in an awful lot of other crimes of violence. . . .

Mr. Rankin. Mr. Secretary, it has been suggested to the Commission that it might be of assistance to you and other Secretaries of the Treasury and the Secret Service to have someone acting as Special Assistant to the Secretary of the Treasury, having supervision, under your direction, of the Secret Service in its various activities, both protection of the President and otherwise. Do you think that that would be of help or would it not?

A—Well, I am not sure. You see, we have an Assistant Secretary, and I should think he probably would be able to do it as adequately as having another special assistant. . . .

One aspect of this matter, I think, is the advent of computers,

569

of course, which is very recent and has changed what can be done effectively in this PRS. I think that should be done anyway. One aspect of this matter that probably hasn't had as close and detailed supervision as we may feel appropriate now is the White House detail. It has always operated over the years in very close contact with the President and has operated in a slightly different manner with different Presidents, depending on their wishes.

And it has been felt that as long as they were doing an adequate job, that it was pretty hard to come in and tell them exactly what they should do on a day-by-day basis because the President might not want them to do that sort of thing. . . .

Mr. Dulles. Doug, in the field that in the Commission here we have described as the preventive intelligence field; that is, trying to identify beforehand the individuals or the type of individuals who might be a danger to the President, have you ever thought of any possible division of responsibility and of work between the Secret Service and the FBI to define more clearly which each should do in that field?

A—Well, my own feeling is that the agency that handles the actual work of deciding who the individuals are that the Secret Service should watch out for, which is the PRS, would function much better and would strengthen the Service if it works as it does now as part of the whole Secret Service operation, and working very closely with the people who are on the White House detail and not having to be involved in a liaison operation somewhere else.

So I think our problem is to strengthen this PRS, and I think that this long-range plan is a good beginning.

I don't think it is necessarily an end because as soon as we develop the automated machinery that we need, then we will know a little better, and we may need some people to make full use of that. . . .

WINSTON G. LAWSON

The testimony of the Secret Service Agent in charge of advance preparations for President Kennedy's visit to Dallas, Texas:

Mr. McCloy. In your presence, in the instructions to the police in Dallas, did you tell the police to keep their eye on windows as you went along?

A—I cannot say definitely that I told the police to watch windows. I usually do. On this particular case I cannot say whether I definitely said that. I believe I did, but I would not swear to the fact that I said watch all the windows. . . .

Mr. McCloy. I have heard it rumored that there was a general routine in the Secret Service that when you were going through in a motorcade or by car, that the problem of watching windows was so great that you didn't do it. It was only as you came to a stop that it was the standing instructions that then roofs should be watched and places of advantage would be inspected or looked at. Is that true?

A—No, sir; the agents in the motorcade are to watch the route and the rooftops and the windows as they can. Of course there were thousands of windows there, over 20,000 I believe on that motorcade. But agents are supposed to watch as they go along.

Representative Ford. An advance agent such as yourself goes to talk with local police officials?

A—Yes, sir.

Representative Ford. Do you have a checklist? Do you have a procedure in writing that you hand to a local law enforcement agent so that he is clear as to the responsibilities of himself and his people?

A—No, sir; I have no checklist, although myself I have a number of things that I have marked down from past advances and seeing what other individuals do that I usually try to follow.

However, every situation is so different. Sometimes there are motorcades and sometimes there are not, and it just wouldn't fit every situation.

Representative Ford. But there is no specific list of instructions that the Secret Service gives to a local law enforcement agency?

A—No. . . .

Mr. McCloy. Did you see anybody in the School Book Depository?

A—No, sir; at this point just as we started around the corner I asked Chief Curry if it was not true that we were probably 5 minutes from the Trade Mart, and it is quite usual to make a radio call to your next point of stop that you are 5 minutes away. Therefore right about the time we turned that corner and were a little ways past it, I am sure I was speaking on the radio, because the White House Communications Agency has about the time I gave the 5 minutes away warning signal, and within seconds after that the shots were fired.

Representative Ford. As you came or as the lead car came down Houston Street——

A—Yes, sir.

Representative Ford. You were facing the Texas School Depository?

A—Right.

Representative Ford. Did you look at or scan that building?

A—I did not, no, because part of my job is to look backwards at the President's car. The speed of the motorcade is controlled by the President's car, unless it is an emergency situation. If he stands up and is waving at the crowd and there are quite a few crowds then, of course, the car goes slower. If the density of the crowd is quite scarce or there is a

571

time factor why you are going faster. So the person in the lead car in this rolling command car usually keeps turning around and watching the President's car. If his car comes up on our bumper that means we are not going fast enough and we should go faster, and you tell the command officer to call the motorcycles, the pilot car, et cetera, to move out faster. If you notice that his car is dropping back from you, that means their car wants to go slower and you do the same thing in reverse. So I was watching the crowds along the sides, requesting Chief Curry to move motorcycles up or back, depending on the crowd, move them up toward the President's car because at certain times people were almost out to the car, and to use them as kind of a wedge. Other times they were able to drop back or go forward, so that I was looking back a good deal of the time, watching his car, watching the sides, watching the crowds, giving advice or asking advice from the Chief and also looking ahead to the known hazards like overpasses, underpasses, railroads, et cetera.

Representative Ford. But as the lead car turned from Main onto Houston and proceeded toward Elm, you were more preoccupied with looking at the President?

A—I don't know whether I was looking sideways or backwards then, but I do recall noticing the Book Depository Building and that corner and then deciding that we must be about 5 minutes away, and asking Chief Curry if this was not so and then making a radio broadcast.

Representative Ford. So as you drove down Houston Street, you didn't have an opportunity to look at the Texas School Depository?

A—I may have, but I don't remember if I saw this. I was doing so many things all at once. . . .

Mr. Stern. Have you ever had occasion to provide for building checks along a motorcade route when you were doing an advance, or is it just never done? This is as of the time of Dallas.

A—I have never had an advance where I had buildings checked on our route. . . .

Mr. Stern. It is not a question of your instructions? You could if you wanted to, I take it? It is just a matter of your discretion and your training, is that correct?

A—I don't believe it is discretion. It is just that to my knowledge only inaugurations or when a foreign president or king comes to Washington, like that where it is a motorcade route known practically for years in advance of how you are going to do we check, start out with enough men, enough time ahead of time to check the whole route up to that time.

Mr. Dulles. Is there any practice of going to the superintendent of a building and putting any responsibility on him to see that strangers don't come into the building at that time, or assuming any responsibility at all with respect to the inmates of the building? I don't know what the practices are.

A—As I stated, sir, there was for inaugurations here in Washington—we have done building surveys of buildings that overlook the White House, that overlook the grounds, that overlook areas where the President goes quite often or where he might be out or something like that. Yes, sir; we keep those quite up to date. Out on a trip away from Washington, I have never requested building superintendents to do this. This was not the usual practice. . . .

Mr. Dulles. What would have been your normal practice so far as you can judge if you had been informed that a man, an American had defected to the Soviet Union and had returned to the United States and was living in Dallas and was working in the Texas School Book Depository, would that have been sufficient cause alone to cause you to make an investigation or report it to the Dallas police?

A—If I had had that information—again this is supposition.

Mr. Dulles. I realize that.

A—But I probably would have asked advice on it from either the PRS section or the White House detail ahead of it; yes, sir. . . .

Mr. Stern. Turning to your memorandum of December 1, it mentions on page 1 discussion of weather conditions and the decision whether or not to use the bubble-top on the Presidential automobile. Could you expand on that for us and tell us what happened?

A—Yes, sir; it was quite rainy early in the morning of the 22d in Dallas, and I received a phone call from the Assistant Agent in Charge Mr. Kellerman, who was in Fort Worth with the President, asking about weather conditions in Dallas, and what they probably would be, and discussing whether to use the bubble-top on the President's car or not. I was told the bubble-top was to be on if it was raining, and it was to be off if it was not raining.

Mr. Stern. And then what happened? Did the weather clear?

A—The weather cleared quite fast. I can't recall now. It was approximately an hour or 45 minutes before the President was scheduled to arrive, and we had purposely put off changing the top until the last minute when we could find out what the weather was going to be.

But it cleared and the weather became quite sunny all of a sudden. Also I received a phone call from Fort Worth from Agent Hill, who was assigned to Mrs. Kennedy, asking what the weather was and whether the top would be on or not. I suppose that was so he could let her know whether she had to wear a hat or something because of the weather.

I told him that it looked like it was starting to clear, but we still had not made up our minds whether to have the bubble-top on or off at the point of his call. But I told him if it was raining it would be on, and if it was clear it would be off.

Mr. Stern. Were you involved in the final decision respecting the bubble-top?

A—Yes, sir; the weather was clear so I told them to have it off. . . .

Mr. Stern. I think perhaps now you could tell us what you observed and what transpired from the time your car turned into Houston Street off to Main.

A—As I have said previously today, right around that corner I gave this radio broadcast that we were 5 minutes away.

Mr. Stern. Was this while you were on Houston or had you turned?

A—We had turned the corner. We were either at the corner, I believe we were just about at the corner when I asked the question if I shouldn't give about a 5-minute signal now so we must have been around the corner then when I actually finished broadcasting. It doesn't take long.

Mr. Stern. Around the Houston-Elm corner?

A—Yes, sir; right in front of the Book Depository Building, and then a little ways away from that probably by the time I had finished broadcasting.

I noticed a few people along the right-hand side I can recall now, and more people on the right-hand side than out in the center strip median which is there, a grassy center strip. There weren't many people on the left at all.

I recall thinking we are coming to an overpass now, so I glanced up to see if it was clear, the way most of them had been, the way all of them had been up until that time on the way downtown, and it was not. There was a small group, between 5 and 10 that looked like workmen. I got the impression, whether it was wrong or not I don't know, that they were railroad workers. They had that type of dress on.

And I was looking for the officer who should have been there, had been requested to be there, and I noticed him just a little bit later, that he was there, and I made a kind of motion through the windshield trying to get his attention to move the people from over our path the way it should have been.

But to my knowledge I never got his attention, and I have said in one of these statements that we were under the bridge, and I have said in another one that we were just approaching this overpass when I heard the shot. I really do not know which one is so, because it was so close, but we were about at the bridge when I heard the first report.

Mr. Stern. Now just to finish up with the people on the overpass, were they in a crowd together, or spread out?

A—They were spread out 1 or 2 deep, and as I say, between 5 and 10 of them to my knowledge, and I noticed the police officer standing behind them about in the middle of the group.

Mr. Stern. And as far as you can remember now, in a position to observe all of them. Were they in close enough a group?

A—Oh, yes; observed them from the back.

Mr. Stern. Observed them from the back. Did you notice any unusual movement?

A—I did not.

Mr. Stern. Did you know whether the policeman saw your signal or acknowledge it?

A—I didn't have any acknowledgment of it, and I don't know if he saw the signal or not. At least the people didn't move. They still stayed there in the middle.

Mr. Stern. Were you able to see the sides of the overpass, apart from the area directly over the lane you were traveling in? Could you observe more?

A—I am sure I could have, but I can only recall the people. My immediate problem was right up there on the bridge, and I was concentrating right there. I don't recall anything on either side of the embankments.

Mr. Stern. Or any people?

A—No, sir; I do not recall any.

Mr. Stern. Just this group?

A—This group up on the bridge.

Mr. Dulles. Could I ask one question there. I think you testified just now that your car was very close to the overpass.

A—I believe it was.

Mr. Dulles. And yet your car was only—well, how many feet ahead of the President's car was your car at that time, roughly?

A—I am not sure because I wasn't looking back right at that time at the President's car. I was looking at the bridge because of the people up on the bridge.

Mr. Dulles. What was the normal distance?

A—I think it was a little further ahead than it had been in the motorcade, because when I looked back we were further ahead.

(Discussion off the record.)

Mr. Stern. Then what happened?

A—I heard this very loud report which at first flashing through my mind did not say rifle shot to me. It sounded different than a rifle shot. It sounded louder and more of a bang rather than a crack.

My first impression was firecracker or bomb or something like that. I can recall spinning around and looking back, and seeing people over on the grassy median area kind of running around and dropping down, which would be this area in here.

Mr. Dulles. I might just add the witness is now referring to an aerial photograph.

Mr. Stern. Indicating the area between Elm Street and Main Street, the grassy area between the two streets.

Did you observe anything on the grass strip to the right of Elm Street?

A—No; I didn't, and it is my impression that my car was in this direction, so that when I looked back, that is why I saw this particular area here and not things over here that we had actually, see, started this curve so that when I looked back I was looking this way.

Mr. Stern. You were looking to the grass strip?

A—Yes, sir.

Mr. Stern. In between Elm and Main and not to the grass strip across Elm Street?

A—That is correct.

Mr. Stern. North of Elm Street.

Mr. Dulles. The curve you referred to is the curve to the right.

A—It curves to the right just as it starts at the underpass, and continues to the right.

Representative Ford. Why did you look back? Is that the direction of sound?

A—The direction of the sound and the direction of the President.

Representative Ford. Are you sure that the sound you heard came from the rear and not from the front?

A—I am positive that it came from the rear, and then I spun back that way to see what had occurred back there.

Mr. Dulles. Could you tell at all whether the sound came from above you?

A—No; I could not. It was quite a general loud bang, an echoing-type bang.

Representative Ford. At the time of the sound you were within 15 or 20 feet of the overpass approximately?

A—I was quite close to the overpass, yes, sir; but I don't know exactly how close.

Representative Ford. You are sure that the sound didn't come from the overpass?

A—I am in my own mind that it didn't. It came from behind me. Then I heard two more sharp reports, the second two were closer together than the first. There was one report, and a pause, then two more reports closer together, two and three were closer together than one and two.

Mr. Stern. What else did you observe when you looked back?

Representative Ford. May I ask a question here. Had you turned around by the time the second and third shots had been fired?

A—Yes; I had.

Representative Ford. Did you get an impression from where they came?

A—Again just behind me is the only impression I got, but in relation to behind me, where I do not know.

Representative Ford. Certainly not in front of you?

A—No.

Mr. Stern. You were in a closed car?

A—Yes; I was. The windows were open.

Mr. Stern. And you were on the right-hand side in the front?

A—The right-hand side; yes, sir.

Mr. Dulles. Could you see the President's car when you looked back?

A—Not that first time. As I looked back I looked right straight and saw the grassy median. Then the second and third shots, reports, I noticed the President's car back there, but I also noticed right after the reports an agent standing up with an automatic weapon in his hand, and the first thing that flashed through my mind, this was the only weapon I had seen, was that he had fired because this was the only weapon I had seen up to that time.

The events after that are a little bit jumbled, but I recall seeing Agent Hill on the rear of the President's car receiving a radio message that we should proceed to the nearest hospital. The nearest hospital was a continuation of our route.

Mr. Stern. Did you know that or were you told that?

A—I knew that. Let me make a correction. I don't know if it was the nearest hospital, but I knew that it would be the fastest one that we could get to under the circumstances of where we were going under this freeway.

Mr. Stern. Did you know as part of your preparation or did you merely observe it in the arrangements you were making?

A—I had observed this from all the times I had passed the hospital going over the route; yes, sir.

Mr. Stern. But it is not ordinarily a part of your advance work, or is it, to locate hospitals?

A—This is not a part of our report, but quite often in my own report in other times I have listed hospitals and so forth, bed facilities in some of my other reports. I did not in this case, but I had noted this hospital.

Mr. Stern. But it is something you pay attention to yourself?

A—Yes, sir; it is. Again we depend upon the police knowing the city even better naturally than the advance agent to get us to a hospital depending where we are or anything like that, that would occur.

Mr. Dulles. What was the lead car doing at this time?

A—The car that I was in, sir?

Mr. Dulles. I thought you were in the second car.

Mr. Stern. The pilot car.

Mr. Dulles. The pilot car, not the lead car.

A—The pilot car was up ahead of us, so appeared other things I recall noting a police officer pulled up in a motorcycle alongside of us, and mentioned that the President had been hit.

When the Presidential car leaped ahead, although there was quite a distance, not quite a distance but there was some distance between the two cars, they came up on us quite fast before we were actually able to get in motion. They seemed to have a more rapid acceleration than we did.

Mr. Dulles. Did they actually pass you?

A—No, sir; they never did. We stayed ahead of them. The route was clear to the Trade Mart anyway, which was part of the route that we used to get to the hospital.

And then from the Trade Mart on, the route was going to be policed after we arrived at the Trade Mart, so that on the route from the Trade Mart to the Parkland Hospital, which isn't very far, we had to do some stopping of cars and holding our hands out the windows and blowing the sirens and the horns to get through, but we made it in pretty good time.

I also asked Chief Curry to notify, to have the hospital notified that we were on the way. I heard Chief Curry broadcast to some units to converge on the area of the incident down by where it happened. I don't recall how he phrased it, so that they would know to go to the Texas Book Depository area. He told them to converge on a certain area, and that is what it turned out to be.

When we arrived at the hospital, as our car pulled up and was still moving, I jumped out and a couple of the motorcycle policemen that had arrived there ahead of us, I asked them to keep any crowd back, any press people back, etc. as I went running for the building.

I was looking for the stretchers that might be coming our way, and didn't notice any at first until I looked quite a ways down the corridor and saw two stretchers being pushed my way, and I ran down, turned around, put one hand on each one and then as they pushed and I pulled, we ran outside.

The stretchers had to be placed in tandem because of the ambulance area and Governor Connally being ahead of President Kennedy was placed on the first one and taken immediately away. President Kennedy was placed on the second one by myself and some other individuals, and we went into the emergency room area and were shown into a particular emergency room.

(Discussion off the record.)

Mr. Stern. Mr. Lawson, your memorandum is quite complete on the events from arrival at the hospital to your return to Love Field. If there is anything you would like to add to that, please do so, or to anything you have told us from the departure from Love Field to the arrival at Parkland Hospital.

A—I can't recall anything.

Mr. Stern. I would like then to cover with you just a few points on your opportunities to observe Lee Harvey Oswald following his arrest. As I understand it, you returned to the Dallas Police Headquarters with Chief Curry and other police officials after he was informed that a suspect has been arrested,

578

and arrived at the police headquarters somewhere between 3:30 and 3:45; is that correct. . . .

A—Quite a bit was happening. I got the impression they had squads of detectives doing all kinds of things, people working on the Presidential assassination, people working on the Tippit killing. I know that they had squads of men going out doing various things and coming back, and it was quite hard just to keep abreast of things that were breaking as to what each group was finding out as it was happening, and quite often we were way behind.

Mr. Stern. What about the appearance of the press and television reporters and cameramen at that time?

A—At least by 6 or 7 o'clock they were quite in evidence up and down the corridors, cameras on the tripods, the sound equipment, people with still cameras, motion picture-type hand cameras, all kinds of people with tape recorders, and they were trying to interview people, anybody that belonged in police headquarters that might know anything about Oswald——

Mr. Stern. Can you estimate how many reporters?

A—There were quite a few. The corridors, up and down the corridors towards the chief's office to the right of the elevator, around the elevator landing and down the corridors to the left of the elevator towards the homicide area were quite packed. You had to literally fight your way through the people to get up and down the corridor.

Representative Ford. Did you stay with Chief Curry most of the time?

A—No, sir; I was in various rooms and with various people for the rest of the evening. I saw Chief Curry quite often that evening.

Mr. Dulles. Who was in command at that time of the Secret Service detachment in giving the orders and coordinating the Secret Service men?

A—Sorrels. My advance as such, was over, and I was just another Secret Service agent. . . .

Mr. Stern. When did you first observe Lee Harvey Oswald, Mr. Lawson?

A—It was early in the evening of November 22. He had been in police headquarters for a little while at least before I first saw him, and they had already interrogated him as I understand it, and various detectives, police officials, and Mr. Sorrels and a couple other agents and myself saw Lee Harvey Oswald when he was brought in for Mr. Sorrels to talk to at Mr. Sorrels' request.

Mr. Stern. Did you interrogate him?

A—No, sir; I did not.

Mr. Stern. Did Mr. Sorrels handle the interrogation alone?

A—Yes, sir. . . .

579

Representative Ford. What was his attitude? What was the attitude of Oswald during this period?

A—Oswald just answered the questions as asked to him. He didn't volunteer any information. He sat there quite stoically, not much of an expression on his face.

Mr. Dulles. Quite what?

A—Stoically.

Mr. Dulles. Stoical?

A—Yes, sir.

Representative Ford. Was he belligerent?

A—No, sir; he didn't seem to be belligerent at all.

Representative Ford. Did he resent the interrogation?

A—I didn't get the impression that it was a great resentment. He just answered the questions as they were asked of him.

Mr. Dulles. Did he answer all the questions?

A—I believe he did. . . .

Mr. Stern. What was his physical condition?

Mr. Dulles. Could I ask one question there? The question wasn't asked him at this time, at least while you were present, whether he was or was not guilty of the attack on the President?

A—This I do not recall. . . .

Mr. Stern. What was his physical condition?

A—He was quite, well, unkempt looking, and I recall that he had a few bruises on his face.

Mr. Stern. A few bruises?

A—I believe over an eye, a bruise or two. I can recall that he had a bruise over an eye or on a cheekbone, or someplace on his face, in looking back. And had a shirt and a pair of pants on. He wasn't very tidy looking, a little unkempt in his appearance.

Mr. Stern. Was he handcuffed, do you recall?

A—I don't recall. I know I saw him handcuffed around police headquarters quite a bit, but during this interrogation I don't remember if he was handcuffed or not.

Representative Ford. How long did this interrogation go on?

A—This was not long.

Representative Ford. Five minutes?

A—Five to ten minutes at the most; yes, sir.

PERDUE WILLIAM LAWRENCE

Testimony of a captain in the Dallas Police force who was in charge of traffic control for the presidential motorcade:

Mr. Griffin. Did you ever receive any instructions as to what the men were to do whom you stationed at the various intersections and elsewhere along the route?

A—Yes; I discussed this with Chief Lunday two or three times and Chief Batchelor two or three times before this meeting ever took place and we discussed the fact that maybe some demonstrators with placards might show up and that the officers stationed along the route should be instructed to be on the alert for any persons that might throw anything or make any movement that might endanger the President at all, and if there were any incident of that nature, that the person would be arrested immediately.

Mr. Griffin. Was there any discussion between you and your superior officers about watching the buildings and windows in the buildings or the tops of the buildings?

A—No, no instructions were given to me about my men watching the buildings—no, so, mine were more crowd control instructions—to watch the crowds, to keep them back, and to block off the traffic and to block off the streets on the approach of the motorcade and not to let them by—and to keep the crowds back.

Mr. Griffin. Were there other men who were going to have other responsibilities?

A—Yes, it was my understanding that the other responsibilities in regard to security were to be handled by the special service bureau and the members of the criminal investigation division.

Mr. Griffin. And were they going to be stationed along the routes?

A—It was my understanding that they would be.

Mr. Griffin. Were you ever informed as to how many men would be in each particular location?

A—I was not. . . .

Mr. Griffin. I take it from what you said, that your principal concern then was keeping the motorcade moving smoothly?

A—That's right.

Mr. Griffin. And there was no special attention brought on your part to the question of actually protecting the President other than from some impediment to the actual movement of the automobile.

A—Mainly—my understanding was mainly that my assignment was for crowd control and, of course, security would be involved in it, as far as anyone making any movements in the crowd. . . .

JACK REVILL

The testimony of the chief of Criminal Intelligence Section, Dallas Police Department, charging that a Dallas agent of F.B.I. knew of Oswald's job in the building along the route of the Kennedy motorcade as well as his "capability" to become an assassin but did not inform the Dallas Police:

Mr. Rankin. Do you know James P. Hosty, Jr.?

A—Yes, sir; I do.

Mr. Rankin. How long have you known him?

A—I have known Jim, Mr. Hosty, since 1959, when I took over the intelligence section.

Mr. Rankin. Did you see him on November 22?

A—Yes, sir; I did.

Mr. Rankin. Where?

A—In the basement of the city hall.

Mr. Rankin. Just before you saw Special Agent Hosty, where had you been?

A—I had been at the Texas School Book Depository.

Mr. Rankin. What did you do there?

A—We conducted a systematic search of the building, evacuated the people working in the building, and took names, addresses and phone numbers of all of these people before they were permitted to leave.

Mr. Rankin. Was anyone working with you there?

A—Yes, sir.

Mr. Rankin. Who?

A—Numerous people.

Mr. Rankin. I see. Was Detective Brian with you there?

A—Yes, sir. I had taken Detective Brian with me from the Trade Mart, Dallas Trade Mart, upon hearing of the shots being fired at Mr. Kennedy. I took Detective Brian and two other officers assigned to my unit, Detective R. W. Westphal and Detective Tarver, O. J. Tarver.

Mr. Rankin. How did you come back to the police department?

A—By automobile.

Mr. Rankin. By car?

A—Yes, sir.

Mr. Rankin. Was anyone with you?

A—Yes, sir, I had Detectives Brian, Tarver, and Westphal.

Mr. Rankin. They were all in the car with you?

A—Yes, sir.

Mr. Rankin. And which way did you enter the building?

A—The Main Street ramp into the basement of the city hall.

Mr. Rankin. About what time of the day?

A—It must have been about 2:45, 2:50.

Mr. Rankin. All of these officers were with you?

A—Yes, sir.

Mr. Rankin. Where did you see Special Agent Hosty?

A—If I might explain that, I followed Mr. Hosty into the basement of the city hall. He drove into the basement, parked his car. I did the same, and Mr. Hosty departed from his car, ran over to where I was standing, Detective Brian and I.

The other two officers, Westphal and Tarver, as well as I recall, had remained in the rear talking to some other officers. I don't know who they were. At that time everything was mass confusion, and we were all upset.

Mr. Rankin. Will you explain to the Commission where you parked the car with reference to the point where you saw Agent Hosty?

A—I got out of my car, and we have two attendants

assigned to the basement, two Negro attendants, and one of these individuals parked my vehicle for me, I don't know where he parked it. But as I got out of the car, Mr. Hosty ran toward me—— . . .

Mr. Rankin. Is that a part of the basement area of the police department?

A—Yes, sir; it is.

Mr. Rankin. All right; proceed.

A—And Mr. Hosty ran over to me and he says, "Jack"—now as I recall these words—"a Communist killed President Kennedy."

I said, "What?"

He said, "Lee Oswald killed President Kennedy."

I said, "Who is Lee Oswald?"

He said, "He is in our Communist file. We knew he was here in Dallas." At that time Hosty and I started walking off, and Brian, as well as I recall, sort of stayed back, and as we got onto the elevator or just prior to getting on the elevator Mr. Hosty related that they had information that this man was capable of this, and at this I blew up at him, and I said, "Jim"——

Mr. Rankin. What did he say in regard to his being capable?

A—This was it. They had—"We had information that this man was capable"——

Mr. Rankin. Of what?

A—Of committing this assassination. This is what I understood him to say.

Mr. Rankin. Are those his exact words?

A—As well as I recall. Give him the benefit of the doubt; I might have misunderstood him. But I don't believe I did, because the part about him being in Dallas, and the fact that he was a suspected Communist, I understand by the rules of the Attorney General they cannot tell us this, but the information about him being capable, I felt that we had taken a part in the security measures for Mr. Kennedy, and if such, if such information was available to another law enforcement agency, I felt they should have made it known to all of us, and I asked Hosty where he was going at that time. By this time we were on the elevator and he said he was going up to homicide and robbery to tell Captain Fritz the same thing. I said, "Do you know Captain Fritz?" and he said he had never met him. I said, "All right, I will take you up and introduce you to Captain Fritz." So Detective Brian and I and Hosty went to the third floor of the city hall and went to Captain Fritz' office, the homicide and robbery bureau. We didn't see Captain Fritz, he may or may not have been there. His office door was closed.

Mr. Dulles. What time of the day, could you give me the approximate time?

A—Between 2:30 and 3 o'clock, and I have the reason for

583

saying this because of the typing of this report here. Our secretary got off at 4 o'clock.

Mr. Dulles. And Chief Curry had not yet returned, had he?

A—I don't know where he was.

Mr. Dulles. You didn't know about that?

A—No, sir.

Mr. Rankin. Did you say anything about this to Captain Fritz?

A—I did not talk to Captain Fritz, as I said, I didn't see him. I introduced Mr. Hosty to Lieutenant Ted Wells, who is one of the lieutenants assigned to the homicide and robbery bureau and also present at that time was another special agent, Mr. Bookhout, and Hosty, there was confusion within this office, so Brian and I, after introducing Mr. Hosty to Wells, left and went back to the special service bureau office.

Mr. Rankin. And you didn't say anything to the inspector about it?

A—The inspector?

Mr. Rankin. Lieutenant Wells.

A—No, sir; I did not.

Mr. Rankin. You didn't tell him this important information?

A—Hosty was going up to tell him the same thing.

Mr. Rankin. Did he tell you that?

A—Yes, sir; he told me that.

Mr. Rankin. And Hosty told you then that he was going up to tell him that they knew he was capable of being the assassin?

A—Yes, sir; being at that time I was out of touch with everything, being in the building, I had put no connection between the shooting of Tippit and the President.

Mr. Rankin. Did you know that Oswald had been arrested?

A—No, sir; at that time I did not.

Mr. Rankin. You just knew about the someone by the name of Lee, didn't you?

A—Yes, sir; Lee. . . .

Mr. Rankin. When did you learn that Oswald had been arrested?

A—I really don't know, sir. Because time, we were all shocked that this thing had happened in our city and I personally felt that maybe a sense of responsibility, maybe we could have done more to prevent this thing. I just don't know when I heard that he had been arrested.

Mr. Rankin. Did you know it by the time you went to Lieutenant Wells' office?

A—No, sir; I did not. He may have been in the office at that time.

Mr. Rankin. You didn't know that Oswald was already in the police department?

A—No, sir; I did not. I had been in this building since word came of the shots being fired until about 2:30, 2:35, and at that time I decided that my unit could possibly do more at our

584

office where we kept all of our files, cataloging these people, the suspects that were running through my mind at that time. . . . And as I pulled into the basement this conversation took place with Mr. Hosty.

Mr. Rankin. And the particular words about Oswald being capable of being an assassin those were told you by Agent Hosty in the elevator?

A—No, sir; either just outside the elevator and as we got on. He never mentioned this again because I guess I lost my temper at him for withholding this type of information.

Mr. Rankin. I see. Did you do anything about losing your temper, did you say anything?

A—No; Jim Hosty and I are friends, and this has hurt me that I have involved Hosty into this thing, because he is a good agent, he is one of the agents there that we can work with; that has been most cooperative in the past, and I worked with him just like he is one of us.

Mr. Rankin. You went to the third floor on the elevator?

A—Yes, sir.

Mr. Rankin. Who else went with you?

A—Detective Brian and Hosty, the elevator was—had several people on it. I don't recall who they were. . . .

Mr. Rankin. Now, will you tell us exactly what you said to Hosty and also what he said to you?

A—After hearing about the information that they were purported to have had——

Mr. Rankin. Have you told us all the information that Hosty told you?

A—As well as I recall; yes, sir.

Mr. Rankin. Now, did you say anything to him about it?

A—Yes, sir.

Mr. Rankin. What?

A—i asked him why he had not told us this, and the best, my recollection is that he said he couldn't. Now, what he meant by that I don't know. Because in the past our relations had been such that this type of information, it surprised me they had not, if they had such information he had not brought it or hadn't made it available to us.

Mr. Rankin. And you are certain you went up there on the elevator together?

A—Yes, sir; took him to the third floor and introduced him to Lieutenant Wells.

Mr. Rankin. Are you sure you didn't go up the stairs together.

A—No, sir; we went to the third floor on the elevator.

Mr. Rankin. You are positive?

A—Yes, sir; because we caught the elevator in the basement, and there would have been no reason to walk up the stairs.

Mr. Rankin. If Agent Hosty said you went up the stairs rapidly together, that would be untrue?

A—Yes, sir; this would be untrue. . . .

Representative Ford. Your first contact with Mr. Hosty was in the basement there?

A—Yes, sir.

Representative Ford. What did he say there?

A—He come running up to me, and he said, "Jack, a Communist killed President Kennedy." I said, "What? What are you talking about?" He said, "Lee Harvey Oswald killed President Kennedy," and at that I said, "Who is Lee Harvey Oswald?" And then he told me about him having him in their security files, and then that, "We had information that he was capable of this." By "we" I assumed he meant the Federal Bureau of Investigation. . . .

Representative Ford. At what point in the sequence did you blow up, as you say?

A—When he told me about the capability. By blowing up——

Representative Ford. Was that standing in the basement near the car or was it over toward the elevator?

A—We were walking over toward the elevator during this conversation and as far as blowing up, this is semantics. I wanted to know why they had not given us this information.

Representative Ford. What is his reaction to that?

A—"We couldn't." I do not know what he meant by that.

Representative Ford. When you use words like "We couldn't" that "Oswald was a Communist" this is what I am trying to find out. You mean these are the precise words he said or are these your interpretations of what he said?

A—The time involved it could be my interpretation, to give him the benefit of the doubt, because as I said Hosty is a friend of mine, and the last thing I wanted to do was to cause this man any trouble, because of our relations in the past.

Representative Ford. Have you ever had any doubt in the interval between that time and now that what your recollection is is accurate or inaccurate, fair or unfair?

A—As far as I am concerned I have; this report is honest, and it was made within an hour after he made the thing. And since this assassination I have gone over in my mind could I have misunderstood him. I sometimes wish or hoped that I have. But this is in essence what he said to me. It might not be exactly the "we's" the "I's" but in essence it is what Mr. Hosty said.

Representative Ford. At one point as I recall your testimony, you said Hosty said that Oswald was a Communist. A few minutes after that testimony I think you said that Hosty suspected he was a Communist. Now, did you say that deliberately or did you just——

A—No sir; if I said that I was wrong.

Representative Ford. Was that just confusion?

A—As I mentioned earlier he come hurrying up to me and he said. "Jack. a Communist killed the President." I said, "What?" He said, "Lee Harvey Oswald, a Communist, killed the President," and then he went into the fact that they had known he was there, and then at the conclusion of our, not the conclusion because we continued to discuss this thing going up on the elevator, he made the statement that they had information that he was capable of this. He might have said probably or possibly capable of it, I don't recall, because in Dallas that day, the town died, and I know I was sick that this thing happened in my city, and I felt that maybe we could have done something else to prevent it.

Mr. Dulles. You stress the word "capable", that sticks in your mind, does it?

A—Yes, sir.

Mr. Dulles. He didn't say might have done it?

A—No, sir; capable.

V. J. BRIAN

The testimony of a detective in the criminal intelligence division of the Dallas Police Department who supported the testimony of detective Revill:

Mr. Rankin. Did you have anything to do with the Lee Harvey Oswald case?

A—Yes, sir.

Mr. Rankin. When was the first time that you had anything to do with that matter?

A—Well, we started interrogating people and talking to people immediately after the assassination.

Mr. Rankin. About what time of the day?

A—In the middle of the afternoon, probably——

Mr. Rankin. November 22, 1963?

A—Yes, sir. The first thing that we done, I was, I personally that day was, assigned at the Dallas Trade Mart where the President was to speak, I was on the side of the speaker stand when he was to come in, and they came in and got us and told us that he had been shot, and the President of the United States had been shot, and that a man in the Book Depository down there and told us to go down there and see if we could get him out, and four of us detectives down there got in a car and we went to the Book Depository and we arrived there a short time, I don't know what time it was, a short time after the shooting occurred.

Mr. Rankin. Who were the four you are describing now?

A—Lieutenant Revill, myself, a detective, O. J. Tarver, and a detective, Roy W. Westphal.

Mr. Rankin. What did you do there?

A—We searched the Book Depository for a couple of hours.

We spent about 2 hours, I would guess, approximately 2 hours down there searching the Depository. . . .

Mr. Rankin. You were making a complete search of each floor, were you?

A—Yes, sir; I was with, I mean there were a number of officers there, I didn't do it by myself, there were a number of us there and we were searching it.

Mr. Rankin. Then you left the building?

A—Yes, sir.

Mr. Rankin. Did you leave with some other officers?

A—Yes, sir; Lieutenant Revill, myself, and Tarver and Westphal all went back to the car and left to go to city hall.

Mr. Rankin. Then you got back to the city hall. What did you do?

A—We drove into the basement and parked.

Mr. Rankin. What time of the day was that, can you tell us?

A—Probably around 2 o'clock or somewhere in that. I don't really know to be truthful because I didn't pay any attention to the time but it was around 2 o'clock, I would guess. . . . We came around the ramp and we parked in the basement. We were parked in the basement, and we got out, and started around, there is a railing there, we started around the railing and at that time Jim Hosty was coming across the basement, at a fast trot, or moving fairly fast——

Mr. Rankin. Special Agent Hosty of the Bureau?

A—Yes, sir.

And he came across there and I know him, and I had known him for a good while to speak to him.

Mr. Rankin. Where were you with reference to Lieutenant Revill at that point?

A—I think I was on his, probably his right-hand side.

Mr. Rankin. Close to him?

A—Fairly close; yes, sir.

And so we walked over to meet, kind of cornered, you cross paths and we walked up there to meet Jim, and he said, he came up there and he said, that Lee Oswald, a Communist, killed the President, and then Revill said, "What?" He said, Lee Oswald, a Communist, killed the President.

He was in—nervous—in a hurry, and was just talking.

And then he said, he said that he knew that he was a Communist and he knew he worked in the Book Depository, and then Lieutenant Revill said something else to him, I am not— I don't know what he said, and they walked off in front of me going in around and in through the door over to the elevator to go up, and then we accompanied Agent Hosty up to Captain Fritz' office which is on the——

Mr. Dulles. Was the elevator there at the basement floor when you took it or did you have to wait?

A—We had to wait just a very short time on it. It wasn't standing open waiting; no, sir.

We had to wait on it just a very short time, I believe, and we went up to the third floor, and Hosty and Lieutenant Revill went in there and talked. I went to the door and just stepped inside and waited and then we went back downstairs to our office which is on two, right underneath Captain Fritz' office.

Mr. Dulles. You accompanied them to the third floor and then you came down?

A—Yes, sir.

Mr. Dulles. In the elevator?

A—That I am not sure.

Mr. Dulles. Or did you get out and come down the stairs?

A—I am not sure.

Mr. Dulles. But you weren't with Lieutenant Revill any further?

A—When we came back down to our office, we came back down, I am not sure whether we rode the elevator or not. It is a short trip down and I am—I would be afraid to say whether we walked, rode, or how we got down, but we went into Captain Gannaway's office and Revill told, Lieutenant Revill told the Captain what Hosty had said, so he said, "Write a report."

Mr. Rankin. What did he say at that time? What did he tell the Captain that Agent Hosty had said?

A—He told him, short and very quick, that they knew that Oswald was a Communist and that he was in the Book Depository, and he said, "Write a report and get it back to me right now."

And he went right back and wrote a report.

JAMES PATRICK HOSTY, JR.

The testimony of the F.B.I. special agent assigned to investigate Oswald in Dallas before the assassination:

Mr. Stern. I think we can turn to the events of November 22, and have you tell us what transpired that day, beginning with the morning.

A—All right. The first order of business from 8:15 to 9 o'clock the special agent in charge held the regular biweekly conference. Now we held a conference in our office every other Friday morning. It so happened that this was the Friday morning which we would hold this conference, at which time the agent in charge would bring various items to our attention. Among the items he brought to our attention was the fact that President Kennedy would be in Dallas on that date.

Mr. Dulles. Who was the special agent in charge?

A—Gordon Shanklin. Gordon L. Shanklin.

Representative Ford. How many others besides yourself were under his jurisdiction?

A—About 75 agents.

Representative Ford. Seventy-five?

A—Yes. Now only the ones at headquarters city in Dallas were present. That would be about 40 of the agents were present at this conference.

Mr. Shanklin advised us, among other things, that in view of the President's visit to Dallas, that if anyone had any indication of any possibility of any acts of violence or any demonstrations against the President, or Vice President, to immediately notify the Secret Service and confirm it in writing. He had made the same statement about a week prior at another special conference which we had held. I don't recall the exact date. It was about a week prior.

Mr. Stern. Did you know that there was going to be a motorcade on November 22?

A—I found out about 9 p.m. the night before that there was to be a motorcade in downtown Dallas. I read it in the newspaper. That was the first time I knew of it.

Mr. Stern. Did you know that the motorcade would pass the School Book Depository Building?

A—No, sir.

Mr. Stern. Did you know the route of the motorcade?

A—No, sir.

Mr. Dulles. Had there been any contact between you or the Dallas office with the Secret Service on this point?

A—On the motorcade route, sir?

Mr. Dulles. Yes.

A—No.

Mr. Dulles. Had not been?

A—No.

Mr. Stern. The newspaper stories did not as far as you can recall tell what the motorcade route would be?

A—Yes; they did. There was a description of the motorcade route, but as I say, I didn't bother to read it in detail. I noticed that it was coming up Main Street. That was the only thing I was interested in, where maybe I could watch it if I had a chance.

Mr. Stern. So that the fact that Lee Harvey Oswald was working in the Texas School Book Depository meant nothing——

A—No.

Mr. Stern. In connection with the motorcade route?

A—No.

Mr. Stern. Did you think of him at all in connection with the President's trip?

A—No, sir. . . .

The motorcade was scheduled to pass down Main Street near our office at approximately noon. I was now on my lunch hour, so I stood and watched the motorcade go by at the corner of Field and Main Street in Dallas.

After the President passed by, I then went across the street, started eating lunch. While I was eating my lunch, the waitress came up and told me she had just heard a radio report that the President and the Vice President had both been shot. I immediately stopped my lunch.

Mr. Stern. The President and the Vice President?

A—That was the earliest report, that the Vice President had been shot too. These were the rumors. I then of course left the lunchroom immediately and headed back for the office, which is only a block away. I got back to the office.

One of the supervisors told me to get a radio car and get out on the street right away and I would get further instructions. I did that. I got in the car and started out. I gave the signal that I was on the air and I was told to proceed towards Parkland Hospital. Just as I got to Parkland Hospital I got a call to return to the office immediately.

Mr. Stern. Do you know why you were sent to Parkland Hospital?

A—No. We were just told they wanted four cars to proceed to Parkland Hospital to stand by for further orders.

Mr. Stern. Were you told why you were ordered to return to the office?

A—When I got back they told me they wanted me to start reviewing our files to see if I could develop any information, any leads at all on the possible assassin, to help out administratively in the office.

Mr. Stern. Did the case of Oswald come to your mind at that time?

A—No, sir.

Mr. Stern. As a possible——

A—No, sir; it was approximately 1:30 that we got the report that a police officer had been killed in the Oak Cliff area of Dallas, and that the police were surrounding a movie theatre where the suspect was allegedly located.

Shortly after 2 o'clock, we received information that this man had been captured and taken to the Dallas Police Department. One of our agents called from the Dallas Police Department and identified this man as Lee Harvey Oswald. I immediately recognized the name.

Mr. Stern. What was your reaction?

A—Shock, complete surprise.

Mr. Stern. Because?

A—I had no reason prior to this time to believe that he was capable or potentially an assassin of the President of the United States. . . . The agent in charge instructed me to proceed to the Dallas Police Department and to sit in on the interview of Lee Oswald, which was apparently in progress at this time. Just prior to my leaving, I was told that a communication had just come in that day from the Washington field office advising that Lee Oswald had been in contact with the Soviet Embassy in Washington, D.C.

Mr. Stern. Were you told anything more about that?

A—No; I mean this is the point I was given this information. I then went and got a car and drove to the Dallas Police Department, pulled my car into the basement garage of the Dallas Police Department, parked my car.

Mr. Stern. What were conditions like?

A—Very chaotic. The press was swarming all over the police station. There were television cameras being brought into the building. Many people were running, coming and going. The place was a beehive of activity.

I parked the car, got out, and started in the door of the basement, at which time I observed a Dallas police car, an unmarked car, drive in, in which there were four detectives. The man sitting on the right-hand side of the front seat next to the driver was a man I recognized as Lieutenant Revill. He signaled me that he wanted to talk to me, at which time he jumped out of the car at the head of the ramp and came over towards me. The rest of the detectives in the car continued down the ramp to be parked.

We then proceeded in, Lieutenant Revill and I proceeded into the police department and started up the stairs. Lieutenant Revill advised me that—I might add he was in a very excited state—he advised me that he had a hot lead, that he had just determined that the only employee from the Texas School Book Depository who could not be accounted for was a man named Lee.

Now this conversation took place at approximately 3 p.m., about an hour after Lee Harvey Oswald had been arrested by the Dallas Police Department. I told Lieutenant Revill that Lee Harvey Oswald had been arrested about an hour ago, that he was an employee of the Texas School Book Depository, and that he was the man who had defected to Russia and had returned to the United States in 1962.

Now either Lieutenant Revill—I don't recall if he made a statement doubting that Oswald was the one who assassinated the President, or whether it was just a look of doubt on his face, but there was doubt came into Lieutenant Revill's—at this time I stated to him that Lee Oswald was the main suspect in this case.

Now this conversation took place running up the stairs from the basement to the third floor. At this time the level of noise was very high. As I said, there were many press representatives, TV representatives, curious bystanders, police officers, everybody running all over the place.

It was not too much unlike Grand Central Station at rush hour, maybe like the Yankee Stadium during the world series games, quite noisy. We got to the head of the stairs and I left Lieutenant Revill and went into Captain Fritz' office.

Mr. Stern. Was anyone else with you and Lieutenant Revill as you came up the stairs, as you recall?

A—As I say, the place was swarming with people. Just the two of us were going up the stairs together. My conversation was with Lieutenant Revill only.

Mr. Stern. I now show you a document marked for identification Commission 831, a letter dated April 27, 1964, from Director Hoover to Mr. Rankin, the General Counsel of this Commission, having attached a one-page copy of a newspaper article and an affidavit. Do you recognize this letter?

A—Yes, sir; I do.

Mr. Stern. Where have you seen it?

A—I have seen the file copy of this letter in the FBI files.

Mr. Stern. Do you recognize the newspaper article which is the first attachment to this letter?

A—Yes, sir. It appeared in the Dallas Morning News on April 24, 1964, I believe.

Mr. Stern. And the attachment after this is?

A—My affidavit.

Mr. Stern. Your affidavit of five pages?

A—Of five pages, bearing my signature.

Mr. Stern. Now tell us what the reason for your making this affidavit was.

A—It was to refute the story that appeared in the Dallas Morning News on April 24, 1964, to set the record straight as to what actually did take place in my conversation with Lieutenant Revill.

Mr. Stern. What did that story state?

A—It stated in substance, alleged that I was aware that Lee Harvey Oswald was capable of assassinating the President of the United States, but did not dream he would do it.

Mr. Stern. Did you say that?

A—No, sir. I want to state for the record at this time that I unequivocally deny ever having made the statement to Lieutenant Revill or to anyone else that, "We knew Lee Harvey Oswald was capable of assassinating the President of the United States, we didn't dream he would do it."

I also want to state at this time that I made no statement to Lieutenant Revill or to any other individual at any time that I or anyone else in the FBI knew that Lee Harvey Oswald was capable of assassinating the President of the United States or possessed any potential for violence.

Prior to the assassination of the President of the United States, I had no information indicating violence on the part of Lee Harvey Oswald. I wish the record to so read.

J. EDGAR HOOVER

The testimony of the Director of the Federal Bureau of Investigation:

Mr. Rankin. You have furnished us a considerable amount of information, Mr. Hoover, about whether or not Lee Harvey Oswald was ever an agent or acting for the Bureau in any capacity as informer or otherwise at any time. Are those statements correct?

A—They are correct. I can most emphatically say that at no time was he ever an employee of the Bureau in any capacity, either as an agent or as a special employee, or as an informant. . . . When President Johnson returned to Washington he communicated with me within the first 24 hours, and asked the Bureau to pick up the investigation of the assassination because as you are aware, there is no Federal jurisdiction for such an investigation. It is not a Federal crime to kill or attack the President or the Vice President or any of the continuity of officers who would succeed to the Presidency.

However, the President has a right to request the Bureau to make special investigations, and in this instance he asked that this investigation be made. I immediately assigned a special force headed by the special agent in charge at Dallas, Tex., to initiate the investigation, and to get all details and facts concerning it, which we obtained, and then prepared a report which we submitted to the Attorney General for transmission to the President.

Mr. Rankin. From your study of this entire matter of the assassination and work in connection with it, do you know of any credible evidence that has ever come to your attention that there was a conspiracy either foreign or domestic involved in the assassination?

A—I know of no substantial evidence of any type that would support any contention of that character. I have read all of the requests that have come to the Bureau from this Commission, and I have read and signed all the replies that have come to the Commission.

In addition, I have read many of the reports that our agents have made and I have been unable to find any scintilla of evidence showing any foreign conspiracy or any domestic conspiracy that culminated in the assassination of President Kennedy.

Representative Ford. May I ask this, Mr. Hoover. As I understand your testimony, it is based on the evidence that has been accumulated thus far?

A—That is correct, sir.

Representative Ford. Is the Federal Bureau of Investigation continuing its investigation of all possible ramifications of this assassination?

A—That is correct. We are receiving and we, I expect, will

continue to receive for days or weeks to come, letters from individuals that normally would probably be in the category of what we would call crank letters in which various weird allegations are made or in which people have reported psychic vibrations. We are still running out letters of that character and in turn making a report to this Commission upon it, notwithstanding the fact that on the face of it the allegation is without any foundation. Individuals who could not have known any of the facts have made some very strange statements. There have been publications and books written, the contents of which have been absurd and without a scintilla of foundation of fact. I feel, from my experience in the Bureau, where we are in constant receipt over the years of these so-called crank letters, that such allegations will be going on possibly for some years to come.

I, personally, feel that any finding of the Commission will not be accepted by everybody, because there are bound to be some extremists who have very pronounced views, without any foundation for them, who will disagree violently with whatever findings the Commission makes. But I think it is essential that the FBI investigate the allegations that are received in the future so it can't be said that we had ignored them or that the case is closed and forgotten. . . .

Representative Ford. Under your authority from the President, the authority which gave you, the FBI, the responsibility to conduct this investigation it is not an authority with a terminal point. It is an authority that goes on indefinitely?

A—Very definitely so. The President wanted a full and thorough investigation made of this matter, and we have tried to do so. As I have stated, I think we will continue to receive allegations. I think this will be a matter of controversy for years to come, just like the Lincoln assassination. There will be questions raised by individuals, either for publicity purposes or otherwise, that will raise some new angle or new aspect of it. I think we must, and certainly we intend in the FBI to continue to run down any such allegations or reports of that kind. . . .

I think the extreme right is just as much a danger to the freedom of this country as the extreme left. There are groups, organizations, and individuals on the extreme right who make these very violent statements, allegations that General Eisenhower was a Communist, disparaging references to the Chief Justice and at the other end of the spectrum you have these leftists who make wild statements charging almost anybody with being a Fascist or belonging to some of these so-called extreme right societies. Now, I have felt, and I have said publicly in speeches, that they are just as much a danger, at either end of the spectrum. They don't deal with facts. Anybody who will allege that General Eisenhower was a Communist agent, has something wrong with him.

A lot of people read such allegations because I get some of the weirdest letters wanting to know whether we have inquired to find out whether that is true. I have known General Eisenhower quite well myself and I have found him to be a sound, level-headed man.

In New York City there is a woman by the name of Kraus who must be mentally deranged as she stands on a Broadway corner there handing out leaflets in which she charges me with being in the conspiracy with the Communists to overthrow this Government and so forth.

Well now, if any person has fought communism, I certainly have fought it. We have tried to fight it and expose it in democratic ways. I think that is the thing we have to very definitely keep in mind in this whole problem in the security of the President and the successor to office.

Just how far you are going to go for his protection and his security. I don't think you can get absolute security without almost establishing a police state, and we don't want that. You can't put security in a black groove or a white groove. It is in a gray groove, and certain chances have to be taken. You are dealing with a human being when you are dealing with the President of the United States. President Johnson is a very down to earth human being, and it makes the security problem all the more difficult, but you can't bar him from the people.

There are certain things that can be done, and I submitted a memorandum to the Secret Service, and to the White House on certain security steps that might be taken and tightened up. But you are dealing with the general public and that is what has given me great concern in the recent expansion, of the criteria for dissemination that we adopted after the assassination.

Prior to that time we reported to the Secret Service all information that dealt with individuals who were potential killers or by whom acts of violence might be anticipated. The Secret Service would take that information and would do with it as they saw fit. I gave great consideration to it because I am not very happy with the criteria expansion, but I felt we had to include subversives of various character, and extremists. We have, in turn, furnished their names to the Secret Service. I think 5,000 names up to the present time already have been submitted and there are at least three or four thousand more that will be submitted within the next few months.

Then you come to the problem of what you are going to do when the Secret Service gets those names. They have to call upon the local authorities. Just recently, in the city of Chicago, when the President was there, the local authorities were asked to give assistance as they usually do to the Secret Service and they went to the homes of some of these people, and it resulted really almost in a house arrest.

Now, I don't think there is any place in this country for

that kind of thing, but these people who belonged to extreme subversive organizations or organizations that advocated the overthrow of government by force and violence were told that they couldn't leave their house or if they did they would be accompanied by a police officer. That gives me great concern because in New York City alone, you run into maybe three or four thousand such individuals who would be members of subversive organizations, and then you get into the twilight zone of subversive fronts. . . .

Some ministers get drawn into organizations, some of which are under the domination of the Communist Party. Now, those ministers don't know that. They are just as loyal and patriotic as you and I are, but they happen to belong. Now, that is where the question of human judgment has to be used. We try to use it in selecting these names. But I was startled when I learned of the incident in Chicago because there you come pretty close to a house arrest and we don't want that. We don't want a gestapo. We have to, I think, maintain an even balance.

Mr. Dulles. May I ask you, Mr. Hoover, was this house arrest based on names you had furnished the Secret Service and they furnished the local authorities?

A—Yes, sir.

Representative Boggs. I read the FBI report very carefully and the whole implication of the report is that, number one, Oswald shot the President; number two, that he was not connected with any conspiracy of any kind, nature or description.

A—Correct.

Representative Boggs. Do you still subscribe to that?

A—I subscribe to it even more strongly today than I did at the time that the report was written. You see, the original idea was that there would be an investigation by the FBI and a report would be prepared in such form that it could be released to the public.

Representative Boggs. Surely.

A—Then a few days later, after further consideration, the President decided to form a commission, which I think was very wise, because I feel that the report of any agency of Government investigating what might be some short-comings on the part of other agencies of Government ought to be reviewed by an impartial group such as this Commission. And the more I have read these reports, the more I am convinced that Oswald was the man who fired the gun; and he fired three times, killed the President, and wounded Governor Connally.

And I also am further convinced that there is absolutely no association between Oswald or Ruby. There was no such evidence ever established.

Mr. Dulles. Or Oswald and anybody else? Would you go that far?

A—Anybody else who might be——

Mr. Dulles. In connection with the assassination?

A—Yes; I would certainly go that far. There was suspicion at first this might be a Castro act. . . .

Representative Boggs. The FBI interviewed practically everybody who ever associated with Oswald?

A—It did.

Representative Boggs. You didn't find any indication of why anyone should even suspect that Oswald would do this, did you?

A—We found no indication at all that Oswald was a man addicted to violence. The first indication of an act of violence came after he, Oswald, had been killed, and Mrs. Oswald told us about the attempt on General Walker's life by Oswald. No one had known a thing about that. . . .

Representative Boggs. You have spent your life studying criminology and violence and subversion. Would you care to speculate on what may have motivated the man? I know it would be just speculation.

A—My speculation, Mr. Boggs, is that this man was no doubt a dedicated Communist. He prefers to call himself a Marxist, but there you get into the field of semantics. He was a Communist, he sympathized thoroughly with the Communist cause.

I don't believe now, as I look back on it, that he ever changed his views when he asked to come back to this country. I personally feel that when he went to the American Embassy in Moscow originally to renounce his citizenship he should have been able right then and there to sign the renouncement. He never could have gotten back here. I think that should apply to almost all defectors who want to defect and become a part of a system of government that is entirely foreign to ours. If they have that desire, they have that right, but if they indicate a desire for it, let them renounce their citizenship at once.

That was not done. He stayed in Moscow awhile and he went to Minsk where he worked. There was no indication of any difficulty, personally on his part there, but I haven't the slightest doubt that he was a dedicated Communist. . . .

But just the day before yesterday information came to me indicating that there is an espionage training school outside of Minsk—I don't know whether it is true—and that he was trained at that school to come back to this country to become what they call a "sleeper," that is a man who will remain dormant for 3 or 4 years and in case of international hostilities rise up and be used.

I don't know of any espionage school at Minsk or near Minsk, and I don't know how you could find out if there ever was one because the Russians won't tell you if you asked them.

They do have espionage and satotage schools in Russia and they do have an assassination squad that is used by them but there is no indication he had any association with anything of that kind. . . .

Mr. Rankin. Now, in light of what happened, Mr. Hoover, I think the Commission would desire to have your comments or whatever you care to tell them, concerning the reasons why you did not furnish the information you had concerning Lee Harvey Oswald to the Secret Service prior to the time of the President's assassination.

A—In going back over the record, and I have read each one of the reports dealing with that and the reports of Mr. Hosty who had dealt with the Oswald situation largely in Dallas, we had the matter that I have previously referred to, the report of the State Department that indicated this man was a thoroughly safe risk, he had changed his views, he was a loyal man now and had seen the light of day, so to speak.

How intensive or how extensive that interview in Moscow was, I don't know. But, nevertheless, it was in a State Department document that was furnished to us.

Now, we interviewed Oswald a few days after he arrived. . . . We interviewed him twice in regard to that angle that we were looking for. We had no indication at this time of anything other than his so-called Marxist leanings, Marxist beliefs.

We wanted to know whether he had been recruited by the Soviet government as an intelligence agent, which is a frequent and constant practice. There is not a year goes by but that individuals and groups of individuals, sometimes on these cultural exchanges, go through Russia and recruits are enlisted by the Russian intelligence, usually through blackmail. The individual is threatened that if he doesn't come back to this country and work for them they will expose the fact that he is a homesexual or a degenerate or has been indiscrete.

Pictures are usually taken of individuals who become implicated in that sort of thing, so the individual is really desperate. Such blackmail has occurred year after year for some time.

In Oswald's case we had no suspicion that any pressure like that had been brought to bear on him because he had gone voluntarily and had obviously wanted to live in Russia and had married a Russian woman. . . .

There was nothing up to the time of the assassination that gave any indication that this man was a dangerous character who might do harm to the President or to the Vice President. . . .

Mr. Dulles. How many names, Mr. Director, in general, could the Secret Service process? Aren't their facilities limited as to dealing with vast numbers of names because of their limited personnel?

A—I think they are extremely limited. The Secret Service

is a very small organization and that is why we are fortifying them, so to speak, or supplementing them by assigning agents of our Bureau which is, of course, quite a burden on us. Our agents are assigned about 24 to 25 cases per agent and cover such involved matters as bankruptcy and antitrust cases.

Now, the Secret Service has a very small group and I would estimate that the names we have sent over number some 5,000. I would guess there are about another 4,000 that will go over in the next month to them. Frankly, I don't see how they can go out and recheck those names. We keep the records up to date; if additional information comes in on these names we furnish it to the Secret Service. They will have to call upon the local authorities, unless the Secret Service force is enlarged considerably so that they can handle it entirely on their own. I think the Secret Service is entirely too small a force today to handle the duties that they are handling. . . .

We are giving to Secret Service more and more names. The total, in addition to the names they already had, will reach 10,000. I don't see how they are going to be able to handle the situation as they would want to handle it. They have to depend upon local police organizations. Many local police departments are capable and efficient; some are not. . . .

Mr. Rankin. Mr. Hoover, do you have any suggestions that you would like to tell the Commission about of your ideas that might improve the security of the President, and you might comment upon information the Commission has received.

A—Regarding travel, first, advise the Secret Service as far in advance as possible of the President's travel plans and proposed itinerary. The reason for that is there have been Presidents who suddenly decide they are going somewhere and the Secret Service does not have the chance always to cover the area and check the neighborhood and check the hotel or place where it may be.

Representative Boggs. You have one like that right now, Mr. Director.

A—I know from experience.

Second, avoid publicizing exact routes of travel as long as possible. Again, it has been the practice in the past to announce the President is going along a certain route and, therefore, great crowds will gather along that route. And, therefore, I thought that was something that should not be given out and the President should be taken along some routes which are not announced. At the present time, he goes to cities and he wants to see people and the crowd wants to see him. In Dallas, the route was publicized at least 24 hours before so everybody knew where he would be driving.

Third, use a specially armored car with bulletproof glass and have such cars readily available in locations frequently visited. The President, as I observed earlier in my testimony, had no armored car. He has one now which I supplied to Secret Service and they will have one made no doubt in due time for the President's use. But if it had been armored, I believe President Kennedy would be alive today.

Fourth, avoid setting a specific pattern of travel or other activity such as visiting the same church at the same time each Sunday.

Regarding public appearances. First, use maximum feasible screening of persons in attendance including use of detection devices sensitive to the amount of metal required in a firearm or grenade.

Second, use a bulletproof shield in front of the entire rostrum in public appearances such as the swearing in ceremony at the Capitol on inauguration day, the presidential reviewing stand in front of the White House on the same day and on the rear of trains.

Third, keep to a minimum the President's movements within crowds, remain on the rostrum after the public addresses rather than mingling with the audience. Again, there is great difficulty in that field.

Fourth, in appearances at public sporting events such as football games, remain in one place rather than changing sides during half-time ceremonies.

(Discussion off the record.)

Mr. Dulles. About the armored car you said if Kennedy had an armored car that might have saved him. Would the back of the armored car have some protection to protect his head?

A—Oh, yes.

Mr. Dulles. Because if the armored car had been open——

A—He must never ride in an open car; that has been my recommendation.

Mr. Dulles. The back never comes down?

A—The back never comes down, and it is bulletproof. The top, sides, and underpart are all of bulletproof construction. So that except by opening a window and waving through the window the occupant is safe. A person can shoot through the window if the glass window is lowered.

Fifth, limit public appearances by use of television whenever possible.

Sixth, avoid walking in public except when absolutely necessary.

Now, on legislation. First, I recommended that the President and the Vice President be added to the list of Federal officers set out in section 1114, title 18 of the U.S. Code which deals with assaults which are punishable under Federal law.

Mr. Rankin. You would add to that I understood from your prior remarks, the Speaker and the President pro tempore?

A—In view of the situation which prevails at the present

601

time the Speaker and President pro tempore, in other words, the line of succession under the Constitution but not below that.

(Discussion off the record.)

A—Second, furnish the Secret Service authority to request assistance and cooperation from other U.S. agencies including the military, particularly in connection with foreign travel.

Now, my reason for that is that sometimes requests for assistance have to clear through red-tape channels here at Washington through some high official of Government. If an emergency arises abroad, or even in this country, it may be of such character that you do not have time to telephone back to Washington or to telephone back to the Pentagon. Aid ought to be immediately available by calling on the local authorities and the nearest military authority.

Third, improve control of the sale of firearms requiring as a minimum registration of every firearm sold together with adequate identification of the purchaser. . . .

Fourth, a ban on picketing within the vicinity of the White House as is now done at the U.S. Capitol and Supreme Court. Some of these pickets are well-meaning and law-abiding individuals, some are for peace and some are more or less dedicated Communists. . . .

I think such picketing at the White House, of large or small groups, should be forbidden. I think at the White House they tried to get the pickets to walk across the street along Lafayette Park. That at least takes them away from being close to the gates at the White House. I think there ought to be some control. Picketing, of course, is legitimate if it is orderly. Many times it doesn't continue to be orderly, and sometimes pickets, as in this city, have thrown themselves on the pavement and the police have to come and pick them up or drag them away. Then, of course, the charge is made of brutality right away.

Delegations of colored groups have visited me and asked why I don't arrest a police officer for hitting some Negro whom he is arresting in a sit-in strike, lay-in strike or demonstration in some southern cities.

We have no authority to make an arrest of that kind. Under the authority the Bureau has we have to submit those complaints to the Department of Justice and if they authorize us to make an arrest we will do it.

Those in general are the recommendations I made and I will furnish the committee with a copy of this memorandum.

Mr. Rankin. Mr. Hoover, I would like to ask you in regard to your recommendations, do you think you have adequately taken into account that the President is not only the Chief Executive but also necessarily a politician under our system?

A—I have taken that into account, and I would like to say this off the record.

(Discussion off the record.)

Mr. Rankin. That is all I have, Mr. Chairman.

The Chairman. Any other questions, gentlemen?

Representative Boggs. I would just like to thank the Director again for all the help he has given us.

A—I am happy to.

ALAN H. BELMONT

The testimony of the Assistant to the Director of the Federal Bureau of Investigation:

Mr. Stern. Did you have any particular involvement that you can recall in the investigation of his case before November 22—personally?

A—No; this case was not of the importance or urgency that it was considered necessary to call to my personal attention for personal direction. You must bear in mind that during the fiscal year 1963 the FBI handled something in the nature of 636,000 investigative matters. Necessarily, then, those matters which would be called to my personal attention for personal handling would have to be on a selective basis.

Mr. Stern. Have you been personally involved in the investigation since the assassination?

A—I have indeed.

Mr. McCloy. Before we get to this, how many cases of defections to the Soviet Union would you be investigating in the course of a fiscal year?

A—I couldn't give you an exact figure on that. It is our system to investigate any individual where there is information or evidence that indicates a necessity for investigation within our jurisdiction. I do know that we have investigated, and currently are investigating, defectors not only to the Soviet Union but in other areas of the world.

Mr. McCloy. They also would not come per se to your attention, your personal attention?

A—Depending on the case. If there is a matter which has some urgency or there is a question of policy, it would and does come to my attention, and indeed comes to the attention of Mr. Hoover. . . .

Mr. McCloy. Is the matter of defection just out of its own character of such significance that it becomes a matter of out of the ordinary importance to the Bureau when you learn of it.

A—Again, Mr. McCloy, I have no way of knowing the extent to which those particular cases would be called to my attention.

As shown in the Oswald case itself, we do take cognizance of these. Immediately upon the publicity on Oswald, there was a case opened. I do know that I see many such cases and where there is an indication of possible damage to the country through the leak of information, classified or in some other instance where there is a question of policy or urgency it is

603

immediately called to my attention. I can only say in general I do see many such cases.

Mr. McCloy. Well, we had testimony here yesterday that in a preassassination investigation of Oswald that they learned he was a defector, they had interviews with him, and then they marked the case closed.

At one stage it was reopened and then it was closed again because, as I gather it, there was no indication other than his defection that would lead to their, to the agents, feeling that this man was capable of violence or that he was a dangerous character in any sense.

I gather that whether or not he was thought to be a dangerous character or whether he was capable of violence would be settled by the man in the field office, in the office that had charge, the man who was in charge of the office that was dealing with that case locally, is that right?

A—That is a judgment that he would render, but that judgment would be passed on by our headquarters staff.

Mr. McCloy. Passed on by Washington?

A—Yes, indeed. In this instance by the domestic intelligence division. . . .

Mr. Dulles. Do I correctly read your report and those of your agents to the general effect that you had no evidence that there was any attempt (by the Soviet Union) to recruit Oswald in the United States?

A—No evidence whatsoever. . . .

Mr. Stern. What were the criteria you employed and instructed your agents to employ before the assassination in determining what information should be reported to the Secret Service regarding threats against the President, members of his family, the President-elect, and the Vice President?

A—These are contained in detail in the attachments which represent sections of our manual of instructions which are available to all of our personnel in the field as well as the seat of Government, and also in the FBI handbook which is in possession of the individual agent in the field. These instructions require that any information indicating the possibility of an attempt against the person or safety of the persons mentioned by you must be referred immediately by the most expeditious means of communications to the nearest office of the Secret Service. Further, that our headquarters in Washington must be advised by teletype of the information and the fact that it has been furnished to Secret Service.

Mr. Stern. Have you broadened——

A—I may say, sir that this practice was assiduously followed, and you will find that the files of the Secret Service are loaded with information over the years that we have furnished them. That was a practice religiously followed and a practice voluntarily followed without request. In other words, we do not have a written request for this type of information but rather considered it our responsibility and duty to furnish this information.

Mr. Stern. Did you ever participate in or do you know of any discussion with the Secret Service before the assassination regarding the kind of information they were interested in?

A—We had close liaison with Secret Service, and I have no doubt that in oral discussions that the question came up. I wasn't present but I would assume it has come up, particularly as we were constantly furnishing information. We have no written criteria, you might say, as to what should be furnished.

Mr. Stern. That is, established by the Secret Service.

A—That is correct.

Mr. Stern. And you yourself never participated in any discussion of——

A—No; I did not.

Mr. Stern. This liaison function.

A—This is something we have done for years on the basis that we consider it our responsibility not only as far as the President goes. As you know, Mr. Chairman, we have also followed the same policy relative to other high officials when it appears desirable.

Mr. Stern. Have you subsequent to the assassination augmented your instructions to special agents in this respect?

A—Yes. On December 26, 1963, we prepared additional instructions reiterating those already in effect, and adding other dissemination to Secret Service concerning the security of the President. . . .

It extends the dissemination to "subversives, ultrarightists, racists, and fascists, (a) possessing emotional instability or irrational behavior, (b) who have made threats of bodily harm against officials or employees of Federal, State or local government or officials of a foreign government, (c) who express or have expressed strong or violent anti-U.S. sentiments and who have been involved in bombing or bomb-making or whose past conduct indicates tendencies toward violence, and (d) whose prior acts or statements depict propensity for violence and hatred against organized government." That was prepared in an effort to provide additional, and a voluntary effort, without request, to provide additional information that might be helpful to avoid such an incident as happened November 22, 1963.

Mr. Stern. This did not come about, this change did not come about, through any request from the Secret Service or discussion with the Secret Service?

A—No. We made these changes, as I say, in an effort to provide any additional information in the light of what happened that might be of assistance to Secret Service and might assist in protecting the President. . . .

Mr. Stern. Has the expansion of your criteria led to any problem or difficulty for you or for individuals or do you anticipate any problem or difficulty under the expanded criteria?

A—It seems to me that there is a necessity to balance security against freedom of the individual. This is a country of laws and a government of law, and not a government of men. Inevitably the increase in security means an increase in the control of the individual and a diminishment, therefore, of his individual liberties. It is a simple matter to increase security. But every time you increase security you diminish the area of the rights of the individual. In some countries the problem of a visiting dignitary is met without much difficulty. Persons who are suspect or may be considered dangerous are immediately rounded up and detained while the individual is in the country. The authorities have no problem because in those countries there is not a free society such as we enjoy, and the people who are detained have no redress. The FBI approaches this whole field of security—I am not boring you with this, am I?

The Chairman. No, indeed. This is tremendously important.

A—The FBI approaches this whole field of security and its tremendous responsibilities to protect the internal security of the country as a sacred trust. In carrying out our investigations and our work in the security field, we do it in such a manner under the law that we strengthen rather than weaken the free society that we enjoy. It is for that reason that our men are trained carefully, thoroughly, and supervised carefully, to insure that their approach to the entire security field, which inevitably touches on control of thought, is handled with extreme care. Our activities are directed to meet the terrific responsibility we have for the internal security of the country, but to meet it under the law. We feel that to place security as such above the rights of the individual or to increase these controls beyond what is absolutely essential is the first step toward the destruction of this free society that we enjoy.

We have been asked many times why we don't pick up and jail all Communists. The very people who ask those questions don't realize that if action, unrestrained action, is taken against a particular group of people, a precedent is set which can be seized on in the future by power-hungry or unscrupulous authorities as a precedent, and which inevitably will gnaw away at this free society we have, and sooner or later will be applied to the very individuals who are seeking this action. Up until the time of the assassination we religiously and carefully and expeditiously furnished to Secret Service immediately on a local basis as well as on a national basis, headquarters basis, any and all information that in any way was indicated to be a possible threat against the President. This permitted Secret Service to take such action as was required against these individuals who had by their action set the stage for appropriate restraint or observation based on something they did. Therefore, they were not in a position to complain legitimately because they had by some word or deed set in motion a threat against the President of the United States. Since the assassination, as I have testified, we have broadened the area of dissemination in an effort to be helpful. It stands without question that we could have said, "No; we won't go any further." But we felt that it was our responsibility to do whatever we could do and, hence, we have broadened these criteria, and we have distributed thousands of pieces of information on individuals to Secret Service.

(At this point in the proceedings, Representative Ford enters the hearing room.)

We are not entirely comfortable about this, because under these broadened criteria after all we are furnishing names of people who have not made a threat against the President, people who have expressed beliefs, who have belonged or do belong to organizations which believe in violent revolution or taking things into their own hands. Unless such information is handled with judgment and care, it can be dangerous.

For example, we know that in one city when the President recently visited, the police went to these people and told them, "You stay in the house while the President is here or if you go out, we will go with you." We know that these people have threatened to consult attorneys, have threatened to make a public issue of the matter on the theory that this is restraint that is not justified as they have made no threats against the President. Now, when you examine this a bit further, we give these names to Secret Service. Secret Service must do something with those names, and Secret Service solicits the assistance of the police, quite properly. But I don't need, I think, to paint this picture any further, that when you get away from a specific act or deed of threats against the President, and you go into the broader area of what, perhaps, a man is thinking and, therefore, he may be a threat, and you take action against the man on the basis of that, there is a danger.

That is why, despite the fact that we have given this additional information and will continue to do so, we are uneasy. Again, if I may be permitted to continue, this is inherent in the entire approach of the FBI to the security field. We go as far in our investigations as is necessary. But we go no further. We do not harass people. We do not conduct an investigation of a man for what he may be thinking. We attempt to the very best of our ability to carry out this responsibility for internal security without adopting tactics of harassment or unwarranted investigation, and we will not pursue a security matter beyond that which is essential to carry out our responsibilities. Now, I say that because that is the broad field of our policy, and I say it with complete sincerity, because I know. I have been in this work with the FBI both in the actual investigative field and in the policymaking and supervisory field for 27 years, and I know the policies and the procedures that are followed, and the care with which this problem is approached, and I agree with it fully.

Mr. McCloy. You are going to impose a pretty heavy burden on the Secret Service when you dump them with the 5,000 more names than they have been used to having.

A—It will be more than 5,000, sir. This will continue.

Mr. McCloy. From your knowledge of the situation, do you feel that the Secret Service is equipped to cope with this added burden? Is it something that you feel——

A—The Secret Service, as it has in the past, is required to call on the police for assistance in this field when the President visits a city. I do not know the exact complement of personnel of Secret Service, but they are a relatively small organization.

Mr. McCloy. It may be they will have to reorganize some of their procedures to cope with this, won't they?

A—I do not know.

Mr. McCloy. You have got a pretty broad classification here. "All investigative personnel should be alert for the identification of subversives, ultrarightists, racists, and Fascists (*a*) possessing emotional instability or irrational behavior." That may include a good many people in the United States and maybe some members of this Commission—I am speaking for myself. There is irrational behavior that I have been guilty of many times. [Laughter.] This doesn't mean you are going to send everybody over there, but the names that—all those under your classification, all of those in your opinion come under that classification unless you feel they have some, there is some, reason behind it. In other words, you are selective in this list. You purport to be selective in the numbers that you are going to convey to, the names you are going to convey to, the Secret Service.

A—We endeavor to use good judgment, sir. Now, as you indicate there are what, 190 million people in this country, and who knows when someone may adopt abnormal behavior.

You cannot tell tomorrow who will pose a risk. This is an effort to be as helpful as possible and, as we have in the past, we will use our best judgment. But this will broaden considerably the type of people and the number of people who go to the Secret Service.

Mr. McCloy. That is what I am getting at really, Mr. Belmont. You are not saying that all those people that you characterize here under this paragraph 2 will ipso facto be sent over to the Secret Service every time the President makes a move. This simply says that all investigative personnel should be alert in that situation; am I right in that?

A—No, sir. If you will follow in the next paragraph, we say, "If cases are developed falling within the above categories, promptly furnish Secret Service locally a letterhead memorandum" with the information.

Mr. McCloy. So without any further ado all the people in your list who are in that category will be transferred over to the Secret Service when there is an occasion, when the President travels?

A—No. This is a continuing procedure. In other words, during our investigations we come across someone who is in this area or category, and this is a requirement that that man's name go to Secret Service with a brief description of him, and Secret Service then has that filed and is in a position to know that that individual has been referred to them.

Mr. McCloy. Well, that brings up again the comment that I originally made. This does put a big burden of investigation and judgment on the Secret Service, one which they have not heretofore presumably had placed on their shoulders.

A—I think you are correct.

Mr. McCloy. The reason I am asking these questions is bceause by implication, at least, one of our directives is to look into this situation for the future protection of the President, and we want to see that we have got something that is practical as well as cautious. . . .

Representative Ford. Under the new criteria would Oswald's name have gone to the Secret Service automatically?

A—Well, Congressman, right now we are including all defectors automatically.

Now, the question whether Oswald meets these criteria here as set forth is a question of judgment. As I say, right now we do furnish all defectors.

Representative Ford. Defectors are for the time being at least a special category other than what is set forth here unless for some other reason they would fall into one of these categories.

A—Yes.

Mr. McCloy. Do you under that category send forward all Communists?

A—Yes.

Mr. McCloy. All Communists, yes.

Mr. Dulles. Mr. Chairman, I wonder whether or not it would be wise for the record at this point to read into the record, in view of the importance of this, this paragraph which we are now discussing and which, as I understand it, contains the new definition of investigative cases?

The Chairman. Yes; we can put it into the record. . . .

(Paragraph 2 reads as follows:)

"Other dissemination to Secret Service concerning security of the President. All investigative personnel should be alert for the identification of subversives, ultrarightists, racists, and Fascists (*a*) possessing emotional instability or irrational behavior, (b) who have made threats of bodily harm against officials or employees of Federal, State, or local government or officials of a foreign government, (c) who express or have expressed strong or violent anti-U.S. sentiments and who have been involved in bombing or bomb making or whose past conduct indicates tendencies toward violence, and (d) whose prior acts or statements depict propensity for violence and hatred against organized government."

Mr. Dulles. Do I understand you, Mr. Belmont, to say, as drafted you would not consider that defectors automatically fell under this paragraph 2, but it is your practice to notify the Secret Service about defectors?

A—We do notify Secret Service of any defectors coming to our attention.

Mr. Dulles. And by defectors, I guess we mean here maybe a redefector, meaning those who have gone to Russia and have come back or maybe those who have gone and not come back.

A—If they haven't come back——

Mr. Dulles. They are not a danger.

A—They are not within our cognizance and we don't notify Secret Service.

Mr. Dulles. These would be defectors who have gone to the Soviet Union and who then come back to the United States and tried to defect while they are over there.

Mr. McCloy. Not necessarily, not exclusively the Soviet Union, of course.

Mr. Dulles. Communist countries, I would say.

Representative Ford. Just to get an order of magnitude, how many are there? Is this a sizable number?

A—I don't have a figure, Mr. Ford. You have had defectors in Korea from the military. You have had defectors——

Mr. McCloy. Germany.

A—Berlin. When these are military personnel they are within the cognizance of the military, so that it is very difficult for me to give you a figure.

When we become interested is when they return to this country and warrant action by us from an internal security standpoint.

As in the Oswald case, we started our action based on newspaper publicity that he had attempted to or indicated his intention to, renounce his citizenship in Moscow. But I do not have a figure because many of these people are members of the armed services and I would hesitate to give you an estimate.

Mr. Stern. Mr. Belmont, do these terms "subversives, ultra-rightists, racists, and Fascists" have a particular meaning of art in FBI parlance? Can you tell us how you use these terms in this regulation or what these mean to you and your agents?

A—I will have to refer you to the dictionary, I think, Mr. Stern. A subversive is an individual who is active in the Com-

610

munist Party or front groups associated with it or one of the other groups that we term subversive, such as the Socialist Workers Party.

The ultrarightists——

Mr. Dulles. Socialist Workers Party is a Trotskyite Party, is it not?

A—Yes, sir.

The ultrarightists, I believe here we attempt to spell out those people who are so far to the right that they do not consider themselves subject to the law and the proper procedures, and take things into their own hands.

The racists, I think, are—that speaks for itself, individuals who will go beyond the bounds of propriety in seeking their goals, and who adopt violence.

The Fascists——

Mr. McCloy. I was wondering how you were going to define that one.

A—Is to give you the opposite end of the spectrum of subversives.

Mr. Dulles. Do we have anarchists in this country at the present time? There used to be an old anarchist society in the old days.

A—That used to be, but it is dissolved. There is no organization. I venture to say we have individual anarchists at this time.

Mr. Dulles. No organized anarchist organization.

A—No. . . .

Mr. Rankin. About subversives, including persons who are members of Communist front groups. You mean to say that that includes any person who is a member of a Communist front group because, as you know, many leading citizens have been members of such groups.

A—Now, Mr. Rankin, I wouldn't carry it by any means that far. It would be dependent upon the front group, the extent of activity in it, and the activities of the individual. By no means would we classify someone as a subversive who was connected with a front group by name or——

Mr. Dulles. By front groups you mean those on the Attorney General's list; you are taking that as a criterion of a front group?

A—No, sir; not necessarily that, sir. There are other groups that we consider front groups.

Mr. Dulles. I see.

A—I am glad you raised that because each case would have to be considered on its own individual merits as to what is the extent of the activity and the purpose and intent of the activity.

Mr. Rankin. You recognize in the work in this field that there are many Americans who are interested in certain causes and purposes and front groups in connection with them who are loyal Americans, don't you?

A—I have no doubt of that whatsoever.

Mr. Rankin. I just wanted to get that in the record.

A—I also know many loyal Americans, unfortunately, who don't look behind some of these groups to determine their intents and purposes, and allow their names to be used where they would not otherwise do so if they took the time and trouble to check into what the organization was.

Mr. Rankin. So you don't lump them all under the term "subversive," that is what I was trying to get at.

A—Right.

The Chairman. I suppose some join before an organization is infiltrated, too.

A—That is correct, sir.

The Chairman. They find themselves in a mousetrap then.

A—That is correct, sir; that is right.

Mr. McCloy. In other words, you would expect your agents to exert some selection before they would send these names over to the Secret Service.

A—Our agents use judgment in the pursuance of this work, and they would continue to use judgment in the selection of people who meet this criterion. Otherwise if you carried this to the extreme you would get out of hand completely. So that there is judgment applied here and our agents are capable of applying the judgment.

Representative Ford. What has been the reaction of the Secret Service to this greater flow of information that they have received?

A—They have taken it. There has been no official reaction, to my knowledge.

Representative Ford. Have they objected to the greater burden?

A—No, sir; I would like to say, I don't know whether you are going to cover this, Mr. Stern, that our relations with the Secret Service are excellent. We work closely together. . . .

Mr. McCloy. I have one or two questions. Mr. Belmont, you do know the charge has been made by some that Oswald was what is called a secret agent. Do you have any information whatever that would cause you to believe that Oswald was or could have been an agent or an informant of the FBI?

A—I have covered that in some considerable detail, Mr. McCloy, and I will make a positive statement that Oswald was not, never was, an agent or an informant of the FBI.

Mr. McCloy. In the course of your investigation do you have any reason to make you believe that he was an agent of any other country?

A—No, sir; we have no reason to believe that he was an agent of any other country.

Mr. McCloy. Or any other agency of the United States?

A—Or any other agency of the United States.

Mr. McCloy. Do you feel there are any areas as of the present time that you feel at the present time require or justify further investigation other than routine checkups that have not already been undertaken?

A—No, sir; frankly, I don't. I will say that from the requests we have received from the Commission, you have explored this most thoroughly. We do not have any unexplored areas in this investigation that should be explored. There are some pending requests that you have made, and we are running them out as rapidly as we can.

Mr. McCloy. Maybe this isn't a fair question to ask you, but, after all, you have had a long record of criminal investigation, and you have had a long exposure to investigation in this case.

As a result of your investigation do you feel that there is any credible evidence thus far which would support a conclusion or an opinion that the death of the President was the result of a conspiracy or anything other than the act of a single individual?

A—No, sir; we have no evidence, and I could support no conclusion that this was other than an act of Oswald.

Mr. McCloy. Now, the investigation does lead you to the conclusion that he was the President's assassin?

A—Yes, sir. . . .

Mr. McCloy. Do you feel that in view of the evidence that Oswald was a defector, that he engaged in this Fair Play for Cuba business, that he lied in his communications with the FBI, that Mr. Hosty should have been alerted by locating Oswald in the School Book Depository early in November, that he should have been alerted to informing the Secret Service of that?

A—No, sir; I do not. You must take this matter in its proper context. I pointed out to you previously that this man came back from Russia; he indicated that he had learned his lesson, was disenchanted with Russia, and had a renewed concept—I am paraphrasing, a renewed concept—of the American free society.

We talked to him twice. He likewise indicated he was disenchanted with Russia. We satisfied ourselves that we had met our requirement, namely to find out whether he had been recruited by Soviet intelligence. The case was closed.

We again exhibited interest on the basis of these contacts with The Worker, Fair Play for Cuba Committee, which are relatively inconsequential.

His activities for the Fair Play for Cuba Committee in New Orleans, we knew, were not of real consequence as he was not connected with any organized activity there. . . .

He gave evidence of settling down. Nowhere during the course of this investigation or the information that came to us from other agencies was there any indication of a potential for violence on his part.

Consequently, there was no basis for Hosty to go to Secret Service and advise them of Oswald's presence. Hosty was alert, as was the Dallas office, to furnish information to Secret Service on the occasion of the President's visit.

It is my recollection that Hosty actually participated in delivering some material to Secret Service himself, and helped prepare a memorandum on another matter that was sent over there. So that most certainly the office was alert. The agent in charge had alerted his agents, even on the morning of the visit, as he had previously done a week or 10 days before the visit.

So that, in answer to your question, I cannot even through the process of going back and seeking to apply this against what happened, justifiably say that Hosty should have given this information under the existing conditions and with the history of this matter, that he was in a position to give it to the Secret Service. Now, most certainly——

Mr. McCloy. We wish he had.

A—Of course.

Representative Ford. Mr. Chairman, I have a call from the floor of the House. I wonder if I could ask Mr. Belmont a question.

The Chairman. Yes, indeed.

Representative Ford. In response to a question by Mr. McCloy, you categorically said that Federal Bureau of Investigation under no circumstances had employed Oswald as an informant, as an agent or in any other way whatsoever.

A—Yes, sir.

Representative Ford. You would be in a position to know specifically that information?

A—Yes, sir.

Representative Ford. You also said, as I recall, that you had found no credible information or evidence thus far that Oswald was connected in any way whatsoever with another country as an agent. Is that about what you said or do you wish to reaffirm it in another way?

A—I will affirm what you said.

Representative Ford. There is a difference, however, between your knowledge as to whether the FBI had hired Oswald, you can be very categorical about that.

A—That is correct.

Representative Ford. You can only——

A—Say based on the evidence that we have or which developed or all information that we received, there was no indication that Oswald was in any way connected or within the service of a foreign government.

Representative Ford. But there is a difference in the way you can answer those two questions.

A—There is a difference, yes; there is a difference because in the one case we know, in the other case we rely on all the information and evidence available.

Representative Ford. But as far as a foreign government is concerned, you only know what you have been able to find out?

A—That is correct, sir.

Representative Ford. There is always the possibility in the second case, involving a foreign government, that something might come up at some other time.

A—There is always the possibility. We have no indication of it. There is always the possibility; yes, sir.

Representative Ford. But you cannot be as categorical about the future in the second case as you were in the first case.

A—Yes, sir; you are right.

FORREST V. SORRELS

The testimony of the special agent in charge of the Dallas district of the United States Secret Service:

Mr. Stern. Can you estimate the overall time from the first shot to the third shot?

A—Yes. I have called it out to myself, I have timed it, and I would say it was very, very close to 6 seconds.

Mr. Stern. It sounds like you can still hear the shots.

A—I will hear them forever—it is something I cannot wipe from my mind ever.

List of Witnesses

The following are the original Prefaces as published in HEARINGS BEFORE THE PRESIDENT'S COMMISSION ON THE ASSASSINATION OF PRESIDENT KENNEDY, Vols. I-XV:

VOLUME I—Mrs. Marina Oswald, the widow of Lee Harvey Oswald; Mrs. Marguerite Oswald, Oswald's mother; Robert Edward Lee Oswald, Oswald's brother; and James Herbert Martin, who acted for a brief period as Mrs. Marina Oswald's business manager.

VOLUME II—James Herbert Martin, who acted for a brief period as the business manager of Mrs. Marina Oswald; Mark Lane, a New York attorney; William Robert Greer, who was driving the President's car at the time of the assassination; Roy H. Kellerman, a Secret Service agent who sat to the right of Greer; Clinton J. Hill, a Secret Service agent who was in the car behind the President's car; Rufus Wayne Youngblood, a Secret Service agent who rode in the car with then Vice President Johnson; Robert Hill Jackson, a newspaper photographer who rode in a car at the end of the motorcade; Arnold Louis Rowland, James Richard Worrell, Jr., and Amos Lee Euins, who were present at the assassination scene; Buell Wesley Frazier, who drove Lee Harvey Oswald home on the evening of November 21, and back to work on the morning of November 22; Linnie Mae Randle, Buell Wesley Frazier's sister; Cortlandt Cunningham, a firearms identification expert with the Federal Bureau of Investigation; William Wayne Whaley, a taxicab driver, and Cecil J. McWatters, a busdriver, who testified concerning Oswald's movements following the assassination; Mrs. Katherine Ford, Declan P. Ford, and Peter Paul Gregory, acquaintances of Lee Harvey Oswald and his wife; Comdr. James J. Humes, Comdr. J. Thornton Boswell, and Lt. Col. Pierre A. Finck, who performed the autopsy on the President at Bethesda Naval Hospital; and Michael R. Paine and Ruth Hyde Paine, acquaintances of Lee Harvey Oswald and his wife.

VOLUME III—Ruth Hyde Paine, an acquaintance of Lee Harvey Oswald and his wife; Howard Leslie Brennan, who was present at the assassination scene; Bonnie May Williams, Harold Norman, James Jarman, Jr., and Roy Sansom Truly, Texas School Book Depository employees; Marrion L. Baker, a Dallas motorcycle officer who was present at the assassination scene; Mrs. Robert A. Reid, who was in the Texas School Book

Depository Building at the time of the assassination; Luke Mooney and Eugene Boone, Dallas law enforcement officers who took part in the investigative effort in the Texas School Book Depository Building immediately following the assassination; Patrolman M. N. McDonald, who apprehended Lee Harvey Oswald in the Texas Theatre; Helen Markham, William W. Scoggins, Barbara Jeanette Davis, and Ted Callaway, who were in the vicinity of the Tippit crime scene; Drs. Charles James Carrico and Malcolm Perry, who attended President Kennedy at Parkland Hospital; Robert A. Frazier, a firearms identification expert with the Federal Bureau of Investigation; Ronald Simmons, an expert in weapons evaluation with the U.S. Army Weapons Systems Division; Cortlandt Cunningham, a firearms identification expert with the Federal Bureau of Investigation; and Joseph D. Nicol, a firearms identification expert with the Bureau of Criminal Identification and Investigation of the Illinois Department of Public Safety.

VOLUME IV—Sebastian F. Latona, a fingerprint expert with the Federal Bureau of Investigation; Arthur Mandella, a fingerprint expert with the New York City Police Department; Paul Morgan Stombaugh, a hair and fiber expert with the Federal Bureau of Investigation; James C. Cadigan, a questioned document examiner with the Federal Bureau of Investigation; Drs. Robert Roeder Shaw and Charles Francis Gregory, who attended Governor Connally at Parkland Hospital; Governor and Mrs. John Bowden Connally, Jr.; Jesse Edward Curry, chief, Dallas Police Department; Capt. J. W. Fritz and Lts. T. L. Baker and J. C. Day of the Dallas Police Department, who participated in the investigation of the assassination; Lyndal L. Shaneyfelt, a photography expert with the Federal Bureau of Investigation; Robert Inman Bouck, special agent in charge of the Protective Research Section of the Secret Service; Robert Carswell, Special Assistant to the Secretary of the Treasury; Winston G. Lawson, a Secret Service agent who worked on advance preparations for the President's trip to Dallas; Alwyn Cole, a questioned document examiner with the Treasury Department; and John W. Fain, John Lester Quigley, and James Patrick Hosty, Jr., agents of the Federal Bureau of Investigation who interviewed Oswald, or people connected with him, at various times during the period between Oswald's return from Russia in 1962 and the assassination.

VOLUME V—Alan H. Belmont, assistant to the Director of the Federal Bureau of Investigation; Jack Revill and V. J. Brian of the Dallas police, who testified concerning conversations Revill had with James Patrick Hosty, Jr., a special agent of the FBI; Robert A. Frazier, a firearms expert with the FBI; Drs. Alfred Olivier, Arthur Dziemian, and Frederick W. Light, Jr., wound ballistics experts with the U.S. Army laboratories at Edgewood Arsenal, Md.; J. Edgar Hoover, Director of the Federal Bureau of Investigation; John A. McCone, Director of the Central Intelligence Agency; Richard M. Helms, Deputy Director for Plans of the Central Intelligence Agency; Thomas J. Kelley, Leo J. Gauthier, and Lyndal L. Shaneyfelt, who testified concerning efforts to reconstruct the facts of the assassination; Mrs. John F. Kennedy; Jack Ruby; Henry Wade, district attorney of Dallas; Sgt. Patrick T. Dean, of the Dallas police, who testified concerning a conversation with Ruby; Waggoner Carr, attorney general of Texas; Richard Edward Snyder, John A. McVickar, Abram Chayes, Bernice Waterman, and Frances G. Knight, of the U.S. Department of State; Secretary of State Dean Rusk; Mrs. Lee Harvey Oswald; Harris Coulter, an interpreter with the Department of State; Robert Alan Surrey, a Dallas citizen who testified regarding his relationship with General Walker; James J. Rowley, Chief of the U.S. Secret Service; Robert Carswell, special assistant to the Secretary of the Treasury; Bernard William Weissman, who testified concerning an advertisement signed by him which appeared in the Dallas Morning News on November 22, 1963; Robert G. Klause, a Dallas citizen who testified regarding a "Wanted For Treason" handbill; Mark Lane, a New York attorney; President Lyndon B. Johnson and Mrs. Lyndon B. Johnson; Llewellyn E. Thompson, former U.S. Ambassador to the Soviet Union, and Secretary of the Treasury C. Douglas Dillon.

VOLUME VI—Drs. Charles J. Carrico, Malcolm Oliver Perry, William Kemp Clark, Robert Nelson McClelland, Charles Rufus Baxter, Marion Thomas Jenkins, Ronald Coy Jones, Don Teel Curtis, Fouad A. Bashour, Gene Coleman Akin, Paul Conrad Peters, Adolph Hartung Giesecke, Jr., Jackie Hansen Hunt, Kenneth Everett Salyer, and Martin G. White, who attended President Kennedy at Parkland Hospital; Drs. Robert Roeder Shaw, Charles Francis Gregory, George T. Shires, and Richard Brooks Dulany, who attended Governor Connally at Parkland Hospital; Ruth Jeanette Standridge, Jane Carolyn Wester, Henrietta M. Ross, R. J. Jimison, and Darrell C. Tomlinson, who testified concerning Governor Connally's stretcher; Diana Hamilton Bowron, Margaret M. Henchcliffe, and Doris Mae Nelson, who testified concerning President Kennedy's stretcher; Charles Jack Price, the Administrator of Parkland Hospital; Malcolm O. Couch, Tom C. Dillard, James Robert Underwood, James N. Crawford, Mary Ann Mitchell, Barbara Rowland, Ronald B. Fischer, Robert Edwin Edwards, Jean Lollis Hill, Austin L. Miller, Frank E. Reilly, Earle V. Brown, Royce G. Skelton, S. M. Holland, J. W. Foster, J. C. White, Joe E. Murphy, Roger D. Craig, George W. Rackley, Sr., James Elbert Romack, Lee E. Bowers, Jr.,

B. J. Martin, Bobby W. Hargis, Clyde A. Haygood, E. D. Brewer, D. V. Harkness, J. Herbert Sawyer, and Gerald Dalton Henslee, who were present at the assassination scene; William H. Shelley, Nat A. Pinkston, Billy Nolan Lovelady, Frankie Kaiser, Charles Douglas Givens, Troy Eugene West, Danny G. Arce, Joe R. Molina, Jack Edwin Dougherty, Eddie Piper, Victoria Elizabeth Adams, Geneva L. Hine, and Doris Burns, employees of the Texas School Book Depository; Mary E. Bledsoe, William W. Whaley, and Mrs. Earlene Roberts, who gave testimony concerning Oswald's movements following the assassination; and Domingo Benavides, and Mrs. Charles Davis, who were present in the vicinity of the Tippit crime scene.

VOLUME VII—Johnny Calvin Brewer, Julia Postal, Warren H. Burroughs, Bob K. Carroll, Thomas Alexander Hutson, C. T. Walker, Gerald Lynn Hill, J. M. Poe, John Gibson, James Putnam, Rio S. Pierce, Calvin Bud Owens, William Arthur Smith, George Jefferson Applin, Jr., Ray Hawkins, Sam Guinyard, and Helen Markham, who were present either in the vicinity of the Tippit crime scene or at the Texas Theatre, where Lee Harvey Oswald was arrested; L. D. Montgomery, Marvin Johnson, Seymour Weitzman, W. R. Westbrook, Elmer L. Boyd, Robert Lee Studebaker, C. N. Dhority, Richard M. Sims, Richard A. Stovall, Walter Eugene Potts, John P. Adamcik, Henry M. Moore, F. M. Turner, Guy F. Rose, W. E. Perry, Richard L. Clark, Don R. Ables, Daniel Gutierrez Lujan, C. W. Brown, L. C. Graves, James R. Leavelle, W. E. Barnes, J. B. Hicks, Harry D. Holmes, James W. Bookhout, Manning C. Clements, Gregory Lee Olds, H. Louis Nichols, and Forrest V. Sorrels, who participated in or observed various aspects of the investigation into the assassination; William J. Waldman and Mitchell J. Scibor, who testified concerning the purchase of the rifle used in the assassination; Heinz W. Michaelis, who testified concerning the purchase of the revolver used to kill Officer Tippit; J. C. Cason, Roy S. Truly, Warren Caster, Eddie Piper, William H. Shelly, and Mrs. Donald Baker, employees at the Texas School Book Depository Building; Edward Shields, an attendant at a parking lot near the TSBD; Thomas J. Kelley and John Joe Howlett of the Secret Service and J. C. Day, J. W. Fritz, and Marrion L. Baker of the Dallas police, all of whom participated in the investigation into the assassination; Mary Jane Robertson, a secretary with the Dallas police; Lyndal L. Shaneyfelt, a photography expert with the Federal Bureau of Investigation; James C. Cadigan, a questioned document expert with the Federal Bureau of Investigation; Earlene Roberts, housekeeper in the roominghouse occupied by Lee Harvey Oswald at the time of the assassination; Senator Ralph W. Yarborough, who was riding in the motorcade; Kenneth O'Donnell, Lawrence F. O'Brien, and David F. Powers, assistants to President Kennedy, who were riding in the motorcade and testified concerning the planning of the Dallas trip and the motorcade; Clifton C. Carter, assistant to President Johnson, Earle Cabell, former Mayor of Dallas, and Mrs. Earle Cabell, all of whom were riding in the motorcade; Philip L. Willis, James W. Altgens, and Abraham Zapruder, who took pictures of the motorcade during the assassination, and Linda K. Willis, Philip L. Willis' daughter; Buell Wesley Frazier, who drove Oswald home on the evening of November 21, and back to work on the morning of November 22; Joe Marshall Smith, Welcome Eugene Barnett, Eddy Raymond Walthers, James Thomas Tague, Emmett J. Hudson, and Edgar Leon Smith, Jr., who were present at the assassination scene; Perdue William Lawrence, a Dallas police captain who testified concerning the positioning of policemen along the motorcade route; Ronald G. Wittmus, a fingerprint expert with the Federal Bureau of Investigation; Robert A. Frazier, Cortlandt Cunningham, and Charles L. Killion, firearms identification experts with the Federal Bureau of Investigation; Robert Brock, Mary Brock, and Harold Russell, who were present in the vicinity of the Tippit crime scene; and David Goldstein, the owner of a firearms store in Dallas.

VOLUME VIII—Edward Voebel, William E. Wulf, Bennierita Smith, Frederick S. O'Sullivan, Mildred Sawyer, Anne Boudreaux, Viola Peterman, Myrtle Evans, Julian Evans, Philip Eugene Vinson, and Hiram Conway, who were associated with Lee Harvey Oswald in his youth; Lillian Murret, Marilyn Dorothea Murret, Charles Murret, John M. Murret, and Edward John Pic, Jr., who were related to Oswald; John Carro, Dr. Renatus Hartogs, and Evelyn Grace Strickman Siegel, who came into contact with Oswald while he was in New York during his youth; Nelson Delgado, Daniel Patrick Powers, John E. Donovan, Lt. Col. A. G. Folsom, Jr., Capt. George Donabedian, James Anthony Botelho, Donald Peter Camarata, Peter Francis Connor, Allen D. Graf, John Rene Heindel, David Christie Murray, Jr., Paul Edward Murphy, Henry J. Roussel, Jr., Mack Osborne, Richard Dennis Call, and Erwin Donald Lewis, who testified regarding Oswald's service in the Marine Corps; Martin Isaacs and Pauline Virginia Bates, who saw Oswald when he returned from Russia; and Max E. Clark, George A. Bouhe, Anna N. Meller, Elena A. Hall, John Raymond Hall, Mrs. Frank H. Ray (Valentina); and Mr. and Mrs. Igor Vladimir Voshinin, who became acquainted with Oswald and/or his wife after their return to Texas in 1962.

VOLUME IX—Paul M. Raigorodsky, Natalie Ray, Thomas M. Ray, Samuel B. Ballen, Lydia Dymitruk, Gary E. Taylor,

Ilya A. Mamantov, Dorothy Gravitis, Paul Roderick Gregory, Helen Leslie, George S. De Mohrenschildt, Jeanne De Mohrenschildt and Ruth Hyde Paine, all of whom became acquainted with Lee Harvey Oswald and/or his wife after their return to Texas in 1962; John Joe Howlett, a special agent of the U.S. Secret Service; Michael R. Paine, and Raymond Franklin Krystinik, who became acquainted with Lee Harvey Oswald and/or his wife after their return to Texas in 1962.

VOLUME X—Everett D. Glover, who became acquainted with Lee Harvey Oswald following his return to Texas in 1962; Carlos Bringuier, Francis L. Martello, Charles Hall Steele, Jr., Charles Hall Steele, Sr., Philip Geraci III, Vance Blalock, Vincent T. Lee, Arnold Samuel Johnson, James J. Tormey, Farrell Dobbs, and John J. Abt, who testified concerning Oswald's political activities and associations; Helen P. Cunningham, R. L. Adams, Donald E. Brooks, Irving Statman, Tommy Bargas, Robert L. Stovall, John G. Graef, Dennis Hyman Ofstein, and Charles Joseph Le Blanc, who testified concerning Oswald's employment history; Adrian Thomas Alba, who was acquainted with Oswald in New Orleans in 1963; Chester Allen Riggs, Jr., Mr. and Mrs. Mahlon F. Tobias, Sr., Mr. and Mrs. Jesse J. Garner, Richard Leroy Hulen, Colin Barnhorst, and Mr. and Mrs. Arthur Carl Johnson, who testified concerning Oswald's various residences; and Clifton M. Shasteen, Leonard Edwin Hutchison, Frank Pizzo, Albert Guy Bogard, Floyd Guy Davis, Virginia Louise Davis, Malcolm Howard Price, Jr., Garland Glenwill Slack, Dr. Homer Wood, Sterling Charles Wood, Theresa Wood, Glenn Emmett Smith, W. W. Semingsen, and Laurance R. Wilcox, who testified concerning contacts they believed they had with Oswald under varying circumstances.

VOLUME XI—John Edward Pic, Lee Harvey Oswald's half-brother; Edward John Pic, Jr., John Edward Pic's father; Kerry Wendell Thornley, a Marine Corps acquaintance of Oswald; George B. Church, Jr., Mrs. George B. Church, Jr., and Billy Joe Lord, who were on the boat Oswald took when he left the United States for Russia; Alexander Kleinlerer, Mrs. Donald Gibson, Ruth Hyde Paine, Michael Ralph Paine, and Gary Taylor, who became acquainted with Oswald and his wife after their return to Texas in 1962; M. Waldo George, the Oswald's landlord at Neely Street in Dallas; William Kirk Stuckey, who gave testimony relating to Oswald's political views; Horace Elroy Twiford and Estelle Twiford, who gave testimony relating to the date and route of Oswald's trip to Mexico in 1963; Virginia H. James, James D. Crowley, James L. Ritchie, and Carroll Hamilton Seeley, Jr., of the U.S. State Department; Louis Feldsott, who gave testimony relating to the purchase of the C2766 rifle; J. Philip Lux and Albert C. Yeargan, Jr., employees of sporting-goods stores in Dallas; Howard Leslie Brennan, who was present at the assassination scene; Louis Weinstock, an official of the Communist Party, Vincent T. Lee, an official of the Fair Play for Cuba Committee, and Farrell Dobbs, an official of the Socialist Workers Party, who testified concerning contacts Oswald had with their groups; Virginia Gray, who gave testimony concerning a letter written by Oswald; Albert F. Staples, who gave testimony concerning records relating to Marina Oswald; Katherine Mallory, Monica Kramer, and Rita Naman, who encountered Oswald while touring Russia in 1961; John Bryan McFarland, Meryl McFarland, and Pamela Mumford, who were on the bus Oswald took to Mexico in the fall of 1963; Dial Duwayne Ryder, Hunter Schmidt, Jr., Charles W. Greener, Gertrude Hunter, Edith Whitworth, James Lehrer, and Mrs. Lee Harvey Oswald, who gave testimony concerning an allegation that Oswald had taken a rifle to a gun-repair shop in Dallas; Eugene D. Anderson and James A. Zahm, of the U.S. Marine Corps, experts on the subject of marksmanship; C. A. Hamblen, Robert Gene Fenley, and Aubrey Lee Lewis, who gave testimony concerning an allegation that Oswald was sending and receiving telegrams through a Dallas Western Union office; Dean Adams Andrews, Jr., Evaristo Rodriguez, Orest Pena, Ruperto Pena, and Sylvia Odio, who testified concerning contacts they believed they had with Oswald in New Orleans and Dallas under various circumstances; Edwin A. Walker, who testified concerning an attempt on his life on April 10, 1963, and his attorney, Clyde J. Watts; Ivan D. Lee, an agent of the FBI, who gave testimony regarding photographs which he took of General Walker's residence; Bernard Weissman, who paid for an advertisement concerning President Kennedy which appeared in a Dallas newspaper on November 22, 1963; Warren Allen Reynolds, who was present in the vicinity of the Tippit crime scene; Priscilla Mary Post Johnson, who interviewed Oswald in Moscow; Eric Rogers, who lived in the same building as Oswald and his wife in New Orleans in 1963; Bardwell D. Odum, James R. Malley, and Richard Helms, who testified concerning a photograph which was shown to Marguerite Oswald for purposes of identification; Peter Megargee Brown, who testified concerning records relating to Oswald when he lived in New York during his youth; Francis J. Martello of the New Orleans Police Department, who interrogated Oswald in August 1963; John Corporon, an official of a New Orleans broadcasting station; Mrs. J. V. Allen, who testified concerning the schooling of Oswald's brothers; Lillian Murret, Oswald's aunt; and John W. Burcham, Emmett Charles Barbe, Jr., Hilda L. Smith, J. Rachal, Bobb Hunley, Robert J. Creel, Helen P. Cunningham,

Theodore Frank Gangl, Gene Graves, and Robert L. Adams, who testified concerning Oswald's employment history.

VOLUME XII—Charles Batchelor, Jesse E. Curry, J. E. Decker, W. B. Frazier, O. A. Jones, Jack Revill, James Maurice Solomon, M. W. Stevenson, and Cecil E. Talbert, Charles Oliver Arnett, Buford Lee Beaty, Alvin R. Brock, B. H. Combest, Kenneth Hudson Croy, Wilbur Jay Cutchshaw, Napoleon J. Daniels, William J. Harrison, Harold B. Holly, Jr., Harry M. Kriss, Roy Lee Lowery, Frank M. Martin, Billy Joe Maxey, Logan W. Mayo, Louis D. Miller, William J. Newman, Bobby G. Patterson, Rio S. Pierce, James A. Putnam, Willie B. Slack, Don Francis Steele, Roy Eugene Vaughn, James C. Watson, G. E. Worley, and Woodrow Wiggins, Dallas law enforcement officers who were responsible for planning and executing the transfer of Lee Harvey Oswald from the Dallas City Jail to the Dallas County Jail; and Don Ray Archer, Barnard S. Clardy, and Patrick Trevore Dean, who participated in the arrest and questioning of Jack L. Ruby.

VOLUME XIII—The testimony of the following witnesses is contained in volume XIII: L. C. Graves, James Robert Leavelle, L. D. Montgomery, Thomas Donald McMillon, and Forrest V. Sorrels, who participated in the arrest and questioning of Jack L. Ruby; Dr. Fred A. Bieberdorf, Frances Cason, Michael Hardin, and C. E. Hulse, who testified concerning the time at which Lee Harvey Oswald was shot; Ira Jefferson Beers, Jr., Robert Leonard Hankal, Robert S. Huffaker, Jr., George R. Phenix, and Jim Turner, news media personnel who observed the shooting of Oswald; Harold R. Fuqua, Edward Kelly, Louis McKinzie, Edward E. Pierce, Alfreadia Riggs, and John Olridge Servance, janitorial employees of the Dallas Municipal Building who gave testimony relating to the manner in which Ruby may have entered the building; A. M. Eberhardt, Sidney Evans, Jr., Bruce Ray Carlin, Karen Bennett Carlin, Doyle E. Lane, Elnora Pitts, Hal Priddy, Jr., Huey Reeves, Warren E. Richey, Malcolm R. Slaughter, Vernon S. Smart, John Allison Smith, Jesse M. Strong, and Ira N. Walker, Jr., all of whom saw Ruby for brief times during the period November 22–24, 1963, prior to the shooting of Oswald; John L. Daniels and Theodore Jackson, attendants at parking lots near the point at which Ruby's car was parked on November 24, 1963; and Andrew Armstrong, Jr., Bertha Cheek, and Curtis LaVerne Crafard, who were acquainted with Ruby prior to November 22, 1963.

VOLUME XIV—Curtis LaVerne Crafard, Wilbyrn Waldon (Robert) Litchfield II, Robert Carl Patterson, Alice Reaves Nichols, Ralph Paul, George Senator, Nancy Perrin Rich,

Breck Wall (Billy Ray Wilson), Joseph Alexander Peterson, Harry N. Olsen, and Kay Helen Olsen, all of whom were friends, acquaintances, employees, or business associates of Jack L. Ruby; Earl Ruby and Sam Ruby, two of Ruby's brothers, and Mrs. Eva Grant, one of his sisters; Jack L. Ruby; Dr. William Robert Beavers, a psychiatrist who examined Ruby; and Bell P. Herndon, an FBI polygraph expert who administered a polygraph test to Ruby.

VOLUME XV—Hyman Rubenstein, a brother of Jack L. Ruby; Glen D. King, administrative assistant to the chief of the Dallas police; C. Ray Hall, an FBI agent who interviewed Ruby; Charles Batchelor, assistant chief of the Dallas police; Jesse E. Curry, chief of the Dallas police; M. W. Stevenson, deputy chief of the Dallas police; Elgin English Crull, city manager of Dallas; J. W. Fritz, captain in charge of the Dallas Homicide Bureau; Roland A. Cox, a Dallas policeman; Harold J. Fleming, vice president of the Armored Motor Car Service of Dallas, and Don Edward Goin, Marvin E. Hall and Edward C. Dietrich, employees of the Armored Motor Car Service; Capt. Cecil E. Talbert of the Dallas Police Department, who was in charge of the patrol division on November 26, 1963; Marjorie R. Richey, James Thomas Aycox, Thomas Stewart Palmer, Joseph Weldon Johnson, Jr., Edward J. Pullman, Herbert B. Kravitz, Joseph Rossi, Norman Earl Wright, Lawrence V. Meyers, William D. Crowe, Jr., Nancy Mennell Powell, Dave L. Miller and Russell Lee Moore (Knight), former employees, business associates, friends, or acquaintances of Ruby; Eileen Kaminsky and Eva L. Grant, sisters of Ruby; George William Fehrenbach, a purported acquaintance of Ruby; Abraham Kleinman, Ruby's accountant; Wanda Yvonne Helmick, an employee of a business associate of Ruby; Kenneth Lawry Dowe, who talked to Ruby over the telephone on November 23, 1963; T. M. Hansen, Jr., a Dallas police officer; Nelson Benton, a Dallas news reporter who spoke with Chief Curry on the morning of November 26; Frank Bellocchio, an acquaintance of Ruby, who spoke with him on November 23, 1963; Alfred Douglas Hodge, an acquaintance of Ruby; David L. Johnston, the justice of the peace who arraigned Oswald for the murder of President Kennedy and Officer Tippit, and who also gave testimony concerning Ruby's whereabouts on November 22, 1963; Stanley M. Kaufman, Ruby's attorney, who spoke to him on November 23; William S. Biggio and Clyde Franklin Goodson, Dallas police officers; Roger C. Warner, a Secret Service agent who participated in the investigation of the killing of Lee Harvey Oswald; Seth Kantor, Danny Patrick McCurdy, Victor F. Robertson, Jr., Frederic Rheinstein, Icarus M. Pappas, John G. McCullough, Wilma May Tice, John Henry Branch, William Glenn Duncan, Jr., Garnett Claud Hallmark, John Wilkins

Newman, Robert L. Norton, Roy A. Pryor, Arthur William Watherwax, Billy A. Rea, Richard L. Saunders, Thayer Waldo, Ronald Lee Jenkins, Speedy Johnson, and Roy E. Standifer, all of whom gave testimony concerning Ruby's whereabouts on November 22 and/or November 23, 1963; William Kline and Oran Pugh, U.S. Customs officials who gave testimony regarding their knowledge of Oswald's trip to Mexico; Lyndal L. Shaneyfelt, a photography expert with the FBI; and Bruce Ray Carlin, Mrs. Bruce Carlin, and Ralph Paul, acquaintances of Jack Ruby; Harry Tasker, taxicab driver in Dallas; Paul Morgan Stombaugh, hair and fiber expert, FBI; Alwyn Cole, questioned document examiner, Treasury Department; B. M. Patterson and L. J. Lewis, witnesses in the vicinity of the Tippit crime scene; Arthur Mandella, fingerprint expert, New York City Police Department; John F. Gallagher, FBI agent; and Revilo Pendleton Oliver, member of the council of the John Birch Society.

List of Exhibits

INDEX

Ables, Don R., 619
Abt, John J., 130-131, 287-288, 322, 325-326, 621
Adamcik, John P., 132, 619
Adams, R. L., 621, 623
Adams, Victoria Elizabeth, 619
Akin, Gene Coleman, 618
Alba, Adrian Thomas, 621
Allen, Mrs. J. U., 622
Altgens, James W., 620
Anderson, Eugene D., 134, 136, 622
Andrews, Dean Adams, Jr., 622
Applin, George Jefferson, Jr., 619
Arce, Danny G., 619
Archer, Don Ray, 506, 507, 525-526, 623
Armstrong, Andrew, Jr., 393, 623
Arnett, Charles Oliver, 623
Aycox, James Thomas, 624

Baker, Marrion L., 101, 616, 619
Baker, Mrs. (Rachley) Donald, 619
Baker, T. L., 480, 617
Ballen, Samuel B., 620
Barbe, Emmett Charles, Jr., 622
Bargas, Tommy, 621
Barnes, W. E., 619
Barnett, W. E., 620
Barnhorst, Colin, 621
Bashour, Fouad A., 87, 618
Batchelor, Charles, 447, 449, 458, 460, 465, 504, 512, 580, 623-624
Bates, Pauline Virginia, 620
Baxter, Charles Rufus, 90-91, 618
Beaty, Buford Lee, 623

Beavers, William Robert, 624
Beers, Ira J. "Jack," Jr., 623
Bellocchio, Frank, 415, 416, 624
Belmont, Alan H., 526, 603, 608, 610, 612, 614, 617
Benavides, Domingo, 619
Benton, Nelson, 624
Bieberdorf, Fred A., 623
Biggio, William S., 624
Blalock, Vance, 621
Bledsoe, Mary E., 105, 619
Bogard, Albert Guy, 621
Bookhout, James W., 584, 619
Boone, Eugene, 617
Boswell, J. Thornton, 93, 616
Botelho, James Anthony, 620
Bouck, Robert Inman, 539, 551, 555, 559, 561, 569, 617
Boudreaux, Anne, 620
Bouhe, George A., 150-151, 155, 620
Bowers, Lee E., Jr., 618
Bowron, Diana Hamilton, 84, 618
Boyd, Elmer L., 619
Branch, John Henry, 624
Brennan, Howard Leslie, 98, 100, 616
Brewer, E. D., 619
Brewer, Johnny Calvin, 110, 619
Brian, V. J., 583, 585, 587, 617
Bringuier, Carlos, 621
Brock, Alvin R., 623
Brock, Mary, 620
Brock, Robert, 620
Brooks, Donald E., 621
Brown, C. W., 500, 619
Brown, Earle V., 501, 618
Brown, Peter Megargee, 622
Burcham, John W., 622
Burns, Doris, 619
Burroughs, Warren H., 111, 619

627

629

631

632